Teacher's Edition

CENTER STAGE 2
Express Yourself in English

Lynn Bonesteel
Samuela Eckstut-Didier

Teacher's Edition by Wendy Long

PEARSON
Longman

Center Stage 2: Express Yourself in English
Teacher's Edition

Copyright © 2007 by Pearson Education, Inc.
All rights reserved.
No part of this publication may be reproduced, stored in a retrieval system, or transmitted in any form or by any means, electronic, mechanical, photocopying, recording, or otherwise, without the prior permission of the publisher.

Pearson Education, 10 Bank Street, White Plains, NY 10606

Staff credits: The people who made up the **Center Stage 2 Teacher's Edition** team, representing editorial, production, design, and manufacturing, are Elizabeth Carlson, Dave Dickey, Christine Edmonds, Gosia Jaros-White, Laura Le Dréan, Julie Schmidt, and Jennifer Stem.

Special thanks for the writing of the Multilevel Strategies goes to Daniel S. Pittaway, North Orange County Community College District, Anaheim, CA; Rancho Santiago Community College District, Santa Ana, CA; Mt. San Antonio College, Walnut, CA.

Text composition: ElectraGraphics, Inc.

Text font: 9.5/11 Minion Pro

Photo Credits: **p. 5** (top left) Leland Bobbe/Corbis; (top right) LWA-Dann Tardif/zefa/Corbis; (bottom left) Medio Images/Getty Images; (bottom right) Royalty-Free/Corbis; **p. 7** Royalty-Free/Corbis; **p. 10** Royalty-Free/Corbis; **p.11** Masterfile/Digital Vision/Fotosearch; **p. 12** Alamy Limited; **p. 17** (left) Anwar Hussein/Contributor/Getty Images; (middle) Lynn Goldsmith/Corbis; (right) 2000 Twentieth Century Fox Film Corporation-All Rights Reserved © 2000 Fox Broadcasting/FotofestNYC; **p. 21** Michael Prince/Corbis; **p. 22** Rufus F. Folkks/Corbis; **p. 33** Stone/David Sacks/Getty Images; **p. 35** Will & Deni McIntyre/Corbis; **p. 36** Royalty-Free/Corbis; **p. 42** (left) Alaska Stock LLC/Alamy; (middle) Free Agents Limited/Corbis; (right) Sylvain Grandadam/Getty Images; **p. 43** Ed Kashi/Corbis; **p. 44** (top left) Royalty-Free/Corbis/Fotosearch; (top right) Royalty-Free/Corbis; (bottom left) Kelly-Mooney Photography/Corbis; (bottom right) Macduff Everton/Corbis; **p. 45** Design Pics Royalty Free/Fotosearch; **p. 46** Royalty-Free/Corbis; **p. 47** (left) Chad Slattery/Getty Images; (right) image 100/Alamy; **p. 54** Royalty-Free/Corbis; **p. 57** Index Stock Imagery, Inc.; **p. 61** Photodisc Red/Ryan McVay/Getty Images; **p. 62** (top) Robert Holmes/Corbis; (bottom) Richard Cummins/Corbis; **p. 71** Getty Images-Stockbyte; **p. 72** Grace/zefa/Corbis; **p. 73** (top left) AFP/Staff/Getty Images; (top middle) Nicklaham/Staff/Getty Images; (top right) AFP/Staff/Getty Images; (bottom left) Chris Trotman/NewSport/Corbis; (bottom middle) Paul Hanna/Reuters/Corbis; (bottom right) Alessandro Bianchi/Reuters/Corbis; **p. 83** Tom Stewart/Corbis; **p. 86** (first) Sean Justice/Getty Images; (second) Stock Image Pixland/Alamy; (third) Comstock Images/Alamy; (fourth) Ron Chapple/Getty Images; **p. 87** bildagentur-online.com/th-foto/Alamy; **p. 91** Royalty-Free/Corbis; **p. 96** Artiga Photo/Corbis; **p. 97** (top left) Penny Tweedie/Getty Images; (top right) Jeff Greenberg/Alamy; (bottom left) Sylvain Grandadam/Getty Images; (bottom right) Ryan McVay/Getty Images; **p. 104** Photo Edit, Inc.; **p. 105** Digital Vision/Getty Images; **p. 107** Stephanie Maze/Corbis; **p. 109** Andersen Ross/Photodisc Red/Getty Images; **p. 111** Jim Arbogast/Getty Images; **p. 117** Royalty-Free Corbis; **p. 121** Thomas Northcut/Getty Images; **p. 123** (top left) Royalty-Free/Corbis; (top right) Creatas ESD/Fotosearch; (bottom left) Randy Faris/Corbis; (bottom right) Getty Images-Stockbyte; **p. 124** David Young Wolff/Photo Edit; **p. 128** Ray Kachatorian/Getty Images; **p. 129** Royalty-Free/Corbis; **p. 130** Mitch Hrdlicka/Getty Images; **p. 131** (left) Albeiro Lopera Reuters/Corbis; (right) Royalty-Free/Corbis; **p. 132** Peter Dazeley/The Image Bank/Getty Images; **p. 133** Royalty-Free/Corbis; **p. 134** Zubin Shroff/Stone/Getty Images; **p. 136** Stephen Oliver/Dorling Kindersley Media Library; **p. 140** Adam Crowley/Getty Images; **p. 146** ColorBlind Images/Getty Images; **p. 147** Dynamic Graphics Group/Alamy; **p. 148** Reed Kaestner/Corbis; **p. 155** (first) George Doyle/Getty Images; (second) Royalty-Free/Corbis; **p. 160** Royalty-Free/Corbis; **p. 171** Robert Harding Picture Library Ltd./Alamy; **p. 179** Digital Vision/Getty Images; **p. 181** Holly Harris/Getty Images; **p. 182** Steve Klaver/Star Ledger/Corbis; **p. 183** Brooks/Kraft Corbis; **p. 184** (top) Robert Landau/Corbis; (bottom) Bettmann/Corbis; **p. 185** San Francisco Museum of Modern Art/Pearson Asset Library; **p. 186** Courtesy of Lynn Bonesteel; **p. 192** Ariel Skelley/Corbis; **p. 194** Don Mason/Corbis; **p. 195** (top) Royalty-Free Corbis; (bottom) Royalty-Free/Corbis; **p. 196** Charles & Josette Lenars/Corbis; **p. 197** BrandX Pictures/Alamy; **p. 198** (second) George Hall/Corbis; (fourth) Jennie Woodcock/Reflections Photolibrary/Corbis; **p. 199** Catherine Karnow/Corbis; **p. 210** Royalty Free/Corbis; **p.220** Stuart Dee/Getty Images; **p. 221** Anthony Bolante/Reuters/Corbis; **p. 222** (top) Sam Sargent/Getty Images; (bottom) Bob Rowan/Progressive Image/Corbis; **p. 223** Annie Belt/Corbis; **p. 229** (top) David Vintiner/zefa/Corbis; (bottom) LWA Stephen Welstead/Corbis; **p. 233** Denis Scott/Corbis; **p. 235** Kevin Cooley/Getty Images; **p. 236** Fabio Cardoso/zefa/Corbis; **p. 240** Royalty-Free/Corbis; **p. 247** Royalty-Free/Corbis.

Illustration credits: A Corazón Abierto (Marcela Gómez), Steve Attoe, Keith Batcheller, Kenneth Batelman, Marty Harris, Alan King, Luis Montiel, Francisco Morales, Precision Graphics, Mari Rodríguez, Roberto Sadí, John Schreiner, Gary Torrisi, Cam Wilson

13-Digit ISBN: 978-0-13-187492-3
10-Digit ISBN: 0-13-187492-6

Printed in the United States of America

1 2 3 4 5 6 7 8 9 10—VHG—11 10 09 08 07

Contents

Scope and Sequence .... T-iv
To the Teacher .... T-xiv

- Unit 1: People T-2
- Unit 2: Families T-14
- Unit 3: Jobs T-26
- Unit 4: Places T-38
- Unit 5: Food and Drink T-52
- Unit 6: Physical Exercise T-64
- Unit 7: Do's and Don'ts T-76
- Unit 8: Possessions T-88
- Unit 9: Routines T-102
- Unit 10: Shopping T-114
- Unit 11: Holidays and Special Occasions T-126
- Unit 12: At Work T-138
- Unit 13: Feelings and Opinions T-152
- Unit 14: Fact or Fiction T-164
- Unit 15: Life Stages T-176
- Unit 16: Looking Ahead T-188
- Unit 17: Health T-202
- Unit 18: A Place to Live T-214
- Unit 19: Future Changes T-226
- Unit 20: Transportation T-238

Grammar Summaries T-252
Charts T-262
Partner Activities T-266
Audioscript T-276
Index T-294
Unit Tests T-298
Unit Test Answer Key and Audioscript T-358
Multilevel FAQs T-368

Center Stage 2

Scope and Sequence

Unit	Grammar	Listening	Speaking	Reading
1 People Page 2	*Be:* Affirmative and Negative Statements *Be: Yes / No* Questions Regular Count Nouns and Irregular Nouns	Listen to a description of someone's appearance Listen to a TV report about quality of life Identify a person from a description Listen for numbers and percentages Distinguish final –s	Introduce yourself Interview your classmates Ask and answer personal information questions Describe people's appearances Describe people's personalities Use *be* to describe people Pronounce final –s	Read a school registration form Read for details
2 Families Page 14	Possessive Adjectives Possessive Nouns *Be:* Information Questions	Listen to descriptions of families around the world Identify people from descriptions Listen for details	Talk about family relationships Describe family members Ask and answer personal information questions	Read a personal information form Understand government forms Understand the American system of measuring dimensions Read for details Guess meaning from context
3 Jobs Page 26	*A* and *An* Adjective and Noun Word Order *A / An / Ø* and *The*	Listen to a conversation about jobs Listen to a conversation between an employer and a job applicant Understand how to communicate in the workplace Listen for the main idea Listen for details	Ask and answer questions about jobs Talk about workplaces Discuss job qualifications Describe people	Read business cards Read and evaluate a resume Read classified ads Understand how to find and apply for a job Read for main ideas Guess meaning from context
4 Places Page 38	*There is / There are:* Statements *Some / A lot of / Any* *Is there / Are there*	Listen to a comparison of neighborhoods Listen to a comparison of shopping in different countries Listen for details Listen for the main idea	Compare neighborhoods Describe geographical features Describe photographs Ask about and describe hometown / country of origin	Read postcards Read a map Read about U.S. states, cities, geographical features and points of interest Read about world geograph... Draw conclusions from a ch... Read for the main idea

Center Stage 2

CORRELATIONS TO STANDARDS

Writing	CASAS	LAUSD	FL. Adult ESOL High Beginning	Life Skills and Test Prep 2
Solve simple math problems Prewriting: Complete a school registration form Write a paragraph about yourself Writing Tip: Use capital letters for nationalities	0.2.1, 0.2.2, 0.2.3, 0.2.4 0.1.2, 0.2.2	Competencies: 1, 3, 4, 5 Grammar: 1a, 16a, 16b, 16d, 20a, 27, 28a Competencies: 3, 6, 63	3.05.01, 3.14.02, 3.15.11, 3.16.01, 3.16.02, 3.16.03, 3.16.05, 3.16.09, 3.17.01, 3.17.02, 3.17.03, 3.17.05 3.05.01, 3.16.01, 3.16.03	**Unit 1, Lesson 1** • Fill out a registration form **Unit 2, Lesson 3** • Describe physical characteristics of family and friends; use pronouns
Complete a family tree Prewriting: Write personal information questions Write a paragraph about a classmate Writing Tip: Use full forms in formal writing	0.2.1, 0.2.2, 0.2.3, 0.2.4, 4.1.6 0.1.2, 0.1.4, 0.2.1, 0.2.2, 1.1.4, 4.1.2, 6.6.4	Competencies: 3, 4, 6, 63 Grammar: 1a, 16b, 16c, 17c, 27, 28a, 28c Competencies: 1, 3, 4, 5, 10, 31, 52	3.14.01, 3.15.01, 3.15.02, 3.15.05, 3.16.01, 3.16.02, 3.16.03, 3.16.07 3.01.03, 3.05.01, 3.05.03, 3.14.01, 3.16.03	**Unit 1, Lesson 2** • Ask and answer questions about personal information **Unit 2, Lessons 1-4** • Learn words for family relationships; give basic information about family members; describe physical characteristics; give and receive compliments **Unit 7, Lesson 2** • Understand the American system of measuring dimensions **Unit 11, Lesson 2** • Fill out a simple job application
Prewriting: Read an employee evaluation form Complete an evaluation form Summarize an employee's job performance Understand the qualities needed to be a good worker Writing Tip: Write the main ideas in a summary	0.2.3, 0.2.4, 4.1.1, 4.1.7, 4.1.8, 4.4.1, 4.4.2, 4.4.4 0.1.2, 0.2.1, 4.1.3, 4.1.5, 4.1.6, 4.1.7	Competencies: 51, 52, 54 Grammar: 1a, 17c, 20a, 20b, 27, 28a, 28c Competencies: 3, 12, 51, 53, 54	3.01.01, 3.01.02, 3.03.01, 3.15.01, 3.15.02, 3.15.04, 3.15.05, 3.15.06, 3.16.01, 3.16.02, 3.16.03, 3.16.05 3.01.01, 3.01.06, 3.05.01, 3.16.03	**Unit 1, Lesson 4** • Learn names for school employees **Unit 2, Lesson 3** • Describe physical characteristics **Unit 11, Lessons 1-4** • Read help wanted ads that include common abbreviations; respond appropriately to job interview questions; practice appropriate job interview behavior
Draw a map Prewriting: Complete a chart Write a postcard Writing Tip: Begin letters with *Dear* Address letters	2.2.1, 2.2.5, 2.3.3, 2.6.1 2.2.1, 2.5.4	Competencies: 23a, 23b, 23c Grammar: 17e, 18, 21b, 27, 28a, 28c Competencies: 23	3.09.03, 3.15.01, 3.15.06, 3.15.08, 3.16.01 3.09.03	**Unit 4, Lesson 3** • Locate places on a map

All information printed in blue pertains to *Life Skills and Test Prep 2*

Scope and Sequence

LIFE SKILLS

Unit	Grammar	Listening	Speaking	Reading
5 Food and Drink Page 52	Count and Noncount Nouns; Quantifiers: *Some / A little / A lot of / A few / Any*; Count and Noncount Nouns: Questions	Listen to supermarket staff assisting customers; Listen to a comparison of supermarkets; Listen for main topics; Listen for details	Identify common foods and their containers; Ask about and compare prices; Compare quantities of foods; Describe favorite dishes; Ask about availability of food / drinks; Evaluate quality of products and stores	Read a recipe; Read a receipt; Read an ad; Read a menu; Read a newsletter about U.S. food / culture; Understand how to prepare meals; Understand measurements; Read for details; Guess meaning from context
6 Physical Exercise Page 64	Present Progressive: Statements; Present Progressive: *Yes / No* Questions; Present Progressive: Information Questions	Listen to a telephone conversation about peoples' activities; Listen to a news report about sports events; Listen for main topics; Listen for details	Ask about and describe people's activities; Ask about and describe people appearance/ clothing; Talk about sports	Read descriptions of sports events; Draw conclusions; Read for the main idea; Guess meaning from context
7 Do's and Don'ts Page 76	Imperatives; Prepositions; Object Pronouns	Listen to a mother giving instructions to her son; Listen to instructions and warnings; Understand requests from a police officer; Understand child rearing practices and parenting skills; Make inferences; Identify speakers and locations	Give orders; Give instructions; Give warnings; Explain where objects are located; Talk about appropriate classroom behavior; Talk about rules in the community; Talk about safety and emergency procedures	Read about safety procedures; Read instructions for hospital patients; Read about evacuation plans in case of fire; Draw conclusions; Understand common signs
8 Possessions Page 88	*This / That / These / Those*; Possessive Adjectives and Possessive Pronouns; Simple Present: *Have*	Listen to a salesperson assisting customers; Listen to a customer ordering food in a restaurant; Listen to a conversation between a police officer and a driver; Understand ways to thank and apologize; Understand requests for clarification; Identify locations; Draw conclusions	Identify and describe objects; Compliment people; Talk about possessions; Talk about things you want to buy; Translate words for everyday objects from English to other languages; Request clarification	Read a home insurance form; Read for details; Guess meaning from context; Understand how to insure property; Understand parts of electronic goods

Center Stage 2

CORRELATIONS TO STANDARDS

Writing	CASAS	LAUSD	FL. Adult ESOL High Beginning	*Life Skills and Test Prep 2*
Prewriting: Make a list of traditional food Write a paragraph about a traditional dish Writing Tip: Use *for example*	0.2.3, 1.1.7, 1.2.1, 1.2.2, 1.2.5, 1.3.8, 1.6.1, 3.5.1, 3.5.2, 3.5.9, 7.2.1, 7.2.4 0.1.2, 0.1.3, 0.1.6, 1.1.7, 1.2.1, 1.2.2, 1.3.8, 1.3.9, 2.6.4, 8.1.4	Competencies: 27, 31a, 32, 34, 35, 36 Grammar: 16d, 16e, 17a, 17e, 18, 27, 28a, 28c Competencies: 11, 27, 30, 32, 34, 36	3.07.05, 3.11.01, 3.11.03, 3.15.05, 3.15.08, 3.16.01, 3.16.02, 3.16.03, 3.16.04, 3.16.07 3.05.03, 3.07.05, 3.08.01, 3.11.01, 3.11.03, 3.12.03	**Unit 5, Lessons 1-2, 4-6** • Identify common foods and their containers; identify and ask for common quantities of food; read and compare information in advertisements; read and order from a simple menu; ask for clarification using different strategies **Unit 6, Lessons 2, 4** • Read and compute a receipt; make a simple request about availability of items in a store
Prewriting: Make a list of action verbs to describe an event Write about an event in progress Writing Tip: Use *and* with verbs in a series	0.1.3, 0.2.3, 3.5.5, 3.5.8, 3.5.9, 7.2.1, 7.2.2, 7.2.4 0.1.4, 2.1.8	Competencies: 62, 63 Grammar: 2a, 27, 28a, 28c Competencies: 17	3.05.03, 3.15.01, 3.15.02, 3.15.03, 3.16.01, 3.16.02, 3.16.03, 3.16.07 3.06.02	**Unit 3, Lesson 1** • Begin and end telephone conversations
Prewriting: Read advice from a travel guide Write advice for a travel guide Writing Tip: Use adjectives in a series	0.1.3, 3.4.1, 3.5.5, 3.5.7, 3.5.8, 4.3.1, 4.6.1, 4.8.1, 4.8.3 5.5.6	Competencies: 8a, 15, 48 Grammar: 8, 19a, 27a, 27b Competencies: 42	3.09.01, 3.09.03, 3.09.04, 3.15.01, 3.15.02, 3.15.03, 3.16.01, 3.16.02, 3.16.03, 3.16.04, 3.16.07	**Unit 10, Lesson 3** • Learn how to respond to requests from a police officer
Prewriting: Complete a form Write a paragraph about your property Writing Tip: Use pronouns	0.2.3, 1.2.5, 1.3.4, 7.2.1, 7.2.2, 7.2.4 0.1.4, 0.1.6	Competencies: 62, 63 Grammar: 17a, 17b, 17c, 19b, 20a, 20b Competencies: 10, 11	3.05.03, 3.15.01, 3.15.02, 3.15.03, 3.16.01, 3.16.02, 3.16.03 3.05.03	**Unit 2, Lesson 4** • Give and receive compliments **Unit 5, Lesson 6** • Ask for clarification using different strategies

All information printed in blue pertains to *Life Skills and Test Prep 2*

Scope and Sequence

LIFE SKILLS

Unit	Grammar	Listening	Speaking	Reading
9 Routines Page 102	Simple Present: Affirmative Statements; Simple Present: Spelling Rules; Simple Present: Negative Statements	Listen to conversations about daily routines in different countries; Listen for details; Listen for numbers and percentages; Understand simple statistical information; Distinguish final –s	Talk about daily routines; Talk about cultural norms; Talk about people in pictures; Pronounce final –s	Read a survey for a study on daily routines; Read a daily planner; Understand schedules; Understand clock time; Understand the months of the year and the days of the week; Read for main ideas; Read for details
10 Shopping Page 114	Frequency Adverbs; Simple Present: Yes / No Questions; Simple Present: Information Questions	Listen to a couple talk about shopping; Listen to salespeople assisting customers; Understand shopping with credit cards and cash; Understand prices and sales; Make inferences; Identify shopping locations; Listen for details	Talk about shopping habits and stores; Talk about wants and needs; Talk about opening and closing times; Ask about availability of items in stores; Talk about computers; Ask for assistance in a store	Read a mall directory; Read a newsletter; Read about yard sales; Read about using credit cards and checks; Understand different ways to buy goods and services; Read for details
11 Holidays and Special Occasions Page 126	Direct and Indirect Objects; Simple Present: Information Questions; Who as Subject and Object	Listen to information about gift-giving around the world; Understand information about different ethnic and cultural groups; Listen for details	Talk about gift-giving; Talk about holiday traditions; Talk about celebrations	Read a newsletter about a popular American holiday; Understand details
12 At Work Page 138	Simple Present and Present Progressive; Stative Verbs; Like / Need / Want + Infinitive	Listen to workplace discussions; Listen to an interview with a career counselor; Understand work schedules; Understand clock time; Understand the months of the year and the days of the week; Understand how to communicate at work; Make inferences	Describe jobs; Talk about current activities; Talk about goals; Make inferences about people's lives, daily routines, and current activities; Ask and answer questions for a job interview	Read a description of a person's educational background, work experience, and goals; Understand paychecks; Understand basic job interview etiquette; Understand a job application form; Read for the main idea; Read for details

CORRELATIONS TO STANDARDS

Writing	CASAS	LAUSD	FL. Adult ESOL High Beginning	*Life Skills and Test Prep 2*
Prewriting: Complete a daily planner Write an answer to a survey question about daily routines Writing Tip: Use *or*	0.1.2, 0.2.1, 0.2.2, 0.2.3, 0.2.4 0.1.2, 4.4.1, 4.4.3, 4.6.5	Competencies: 7a, 59, 62, 63 Grammar: 1c, 27, 30a Competencies: 4, 55	3.15.01, 3.15.02, 3.15.03, 3.15.04, 3.15.05, 3.15.06, 3.16.01, 3.16.02, 3.17.01, 3.17.02 3.05.01, 3.14.01	**Unit 2, Lesson 2** • Give basic information about family members **Unit 12, Lesson 3** • Read and talk about a work schedule
Prewriting: Read a paragraph about outdoor markets Write a paragraph about shopping customs Writing Tip: Use *because*	0.2.3, 1.2.1, 1.2.2, 1.2.3, 1.2.5, 1.3.1, 1.6.4, 7.2.1, 7.2.2, 7.2.3, 7.2.4 0.1.3, 1.3.3, 1.3.9, 1.6.3, 1.8.1, 1.8.2, 8.1.4	Competencies: 27, 32 Grammar: 1c, 23f, 24, 28a, 28c, 30a Competencies: 28, 29, 30, 33, 59	3.05.03, 3.11.03, 3.15.01, 3.15.02, 3.15.03, 3.15.04, 3.16.01, 3.16.02, 3.16.03, 3.16.04, 3.16.05, 3.16.07, 3.16.08 3.08.06	**Unit 6, Lessons 1, 3, 4-5** • Use an ATM; read and fill out a check; make a simple request about availability of items in a store; give reasons for returning or exchanging an item
Prewriting: Answer questions about a holiday in your country Write a newsletter paragraph about a holiday Writing Tip: Place adverbs correctly in sentences	0.2.3, 2.7.1, 2.7.2 0.1.4	Competencies: 5, 7, 62 Grammar: 1a, 1c, 19a, 28c Competencies: 9 Grammar: 28c	3.15.01, 3.15.02, 3.15.05, 3.16.01, 3.16.02, 3.16.03, 3.16.07, 3.16.08 3.05.03, 3.16.02, 3.16.07	**Unit 1, Lesson 3** • Ask questions with *When* and *Where* **Unit 4, Lesson 2** • Make and respond to invitations
Prewriting: Complete a career counseling form Write about educational and career goals Writing Tip: Use paragraphs	2.7.3, 4.1.2, 4.1.3, 4.1.5, 4.1.6, 4.1.7, 4.1.8, 4.2.1, 4.4.1, 4.4.4, 4.4.5 0.2.1, 0.2.2, 4.1.2, 4.1.5, 4.1.6, 4.1.7, 4.2.1, 4.4.1, 4.4.3, 4.6.5	Competencies: 52, 54, 55, 59, 62, 63 Grammar: 1a, 1b, 1c, 2a, 3, 27, 28a, 28b, 28c Competencies: 52, 53, 54, 55, 56, 59	3.01.02, 3.01.06, 3.02.03, 3.05.03, 3.15.01, 3.15.02, 3.15.03, 3.15.06, 3.16.01, 3.16.02, 3.16.03, 3.16.07 3.01.03, 3.01.06, 3.02.04, 3.15.07	**Unit 11, Lessons 2-4** • Fill out a simple job application; put events in chronological order; respond appropriately to job interview questions; practice appropriate job interview behavior **Unit 12, Lessons 1, 3** • Read a simple paycheck stub; read and talk about a work schedule

All information printed in blue pertains to *Life Skills and Test Prep 2*

Scope and Sequence

LIFE SKILLS

Unit	Grammar	Listening	Speaking	Reading
13 **Feelings and Opinions** Page 152	Simple Past of *Be*: Statements Simple Past of *Be*: *Yes / No* Questions Simple Past of *Be*: Information Questions	Listen to descriptions of past events / experiences Listen for details Listen for topics	Describe a memorable event Describe recent travels Make inferences Complain	Read a letter of complaint Read an ad Understand a calendar Understand dates and times Read for the main idea Recognize tone Understand details
14 **Fact or Fiction** Page 164	Simple Past: Regular Verbs Simple Past: Irregular Verbs Simple Past: Negative Statements	Listen to descriptions of unusual events Listen for the main topic Listen for gist Make inferences Distinguish *–ed* endings	Talk about recent activities Tell a story Pronounce final *–ed*	Read a police report Read newspaper headlines Understand the order of events in a narrative Understand U.S. laws Understand the American system of measuring dimensions Understand how to report a crime Understand how to interact with law enforcement
15 **Life Stages** Page 176	Simple Past: *Yes / No* Questions Simple Past: Information Questions Information Questions with *Who* and *What* as Subject *How long ago* and *How long*	Listen to a conversation about life experiences Listen to a report about the life of an artist Listen for details Listen for main ideas	Talk about childhood experiences Talk about first-time experiences Talk about important life events Understand how to become a U.S. resident or citizen Talk about the life stories of famous people	Read timelines Read about a café worker's daily routine Read a biography Read for the main idea Identify topics
16 **Looking Ahead** Page 188	*Be going to*: Statements *Be going to*: *Yes / No* Questions *Be going to*: Information Questions	Listen to a conversation about short-term plans Listen to a weather report Listen for the main idea Listen for details	Talk about the weather Talk about everyday activities Talk about home-care skills Talk about long-term and short-term goals Talk about travel plans	Read a community calendar Read a personal note Read for details Make inferences Understand a weather chart Understand temperatures

CORRELATIONS TO STANDARDS

Writing	CASAS	LAUSD	FL. Adult ESOL High Beginning	*Life Skills and Test Prep 2*
Write a formal letter of complaint Writing Tip: Use business letter format Address letters	0.2.3, 1.6.3, 2.3.2, 2.3.3, 2.7.1 1.2.1, 1.2.2, 2.3.2	Competencies: 5, 7, 30 Grammar: 5a, 20a, 20b, 21a, 22c, 27 Competencies: 25, 32	3.15.01, 3.15.02, 3.15.03, 3.15.04, 3.15.05, 3.15.06, 3.15.12, 3.16.01, 3.16.02, 3.16.03, 3.16.07 3.08.03, 3.11.03	Unit 4, Lesson 1 • Read calendars Unit 5, Lesson 4 • Read and compare basic information in simple advertisements
Prewriting: Discuss and take notes on crimes Complete a police report Write a paragraph about a crime Describe a person Writing Tip: Use *when*	0.1.2, 0.1.4, 0.2.3, 0.2.4, 7.2.1, 7.2.2, 8.2.2 1.1.4, 2.1.2, 6.6.4	Competencies: 7, 64 Grammar: 5b, 5c, 24, 27, 28a, 28b, 28c Competencies: 20, 31	3.10.01, 3.15.01, 3.15.02, 3.15.03, 3.15.04, 3.15.05, 3.15.06, 3.16.01, 3.16.02, 3.16.03, 3.16.07, 3.17.01, 3.17.02 3.06.01, 3.10.01	Unit 7, Lesson 2 • Understand the American system of measuring dimensions Unit 10, Lesson 2 • Learn how to call 911 to report an emergency
Draw timelines Prewriting: Write interview questions Organize information into paragraphs Write a short biography Writing Tip: Use time expressions	0.1.2, 0.2.1, 0.2.3, 0.2.4, 2.7.6 0.1.4	Competencies: 4, 5, 7, 59 Grammar: 28a, 28b, 28c, 29 Competencies: 10	3.15.01, 3.15.02, 3.15.03, 3.15.04, 3.15.05, 3.15.06, 3.16.01, 3.16.02, 3.16.03, 3.16.07 3.05.03	Unit 2, Lesson 5 • Give and receive sympathy and congratulations
Prewriting: Make weekend plans Write a note about weekend plans Writing Tip: Use contractions	0.1.2, 0.1.6, 0.2.1, 0.2.2, 0.2.3, 2.3.2, 2.3.3, 5.2.4, 5.2.5 1.1.5, 2.3.2	Competencies: 3, 5, 7, 59 Grammar: 3, 28a, 28b, 28c Competencies: 25, 26	3.09.01, 3.13.01, 3.15.01, 3.15.02, 3.15.03, 3.15.07, 3.16.01, 3.16.02, 3.16.03, 3.16.04, 3.16.07, 3.16.08 3.08.03	Unit 4, Lesson 1 • Read calendars Unit 7, Lesson 1 • Understand temperatures in Celsius and Fahrenheit

All information printed in blue pertains to *Life Skills and Test Prep 2*

Scope and Sequence

LIFE SKILLS

Unit	Grammar	Listening	Speaking	Reading
17 **Health** Page 202	*Should*: Affirmative and Negative Statements *Should*: Yes / No Questions *Should*: Information Questions	Listen to a conversation about a health problem Listen to a radio report about a healthy diet Identify food groups Understand U.S. weights and measurements Make inferences Listen for details Listen for numbers and amounts	Talk about illnesses Talk about injuries Talk about common symptoms Give advice on staying healthy Talk about unhealthy behavior Discuss medical treatments	Read medicine labels Read an email Understand common dosages Read for details
18 **A Place to Live** Page 214	Comparative of Adjectives Superlative of Adjectives Comparative and Superlative	Listen to a comparison of apartments Listen to a report about quality of life in different cities Understand housing costs Listen for main topics Listen for details	Describe different types of housing Describe housing problems Compare neighborhoods and housing Compare ads Compare the quality of life in different cities Talk about living standards	Read apartment listings Read a web page Understand how to look for housing Understand the American system of measuring distances Understand how to use the Internet and e-mail Read for the main idea Read for details
19 **Future Changes** Page 226	*Will*: Affirmative and Negative Statements *Will*: Yes / No Questions *Will*: Information Questions	Listen to a fortune teller's predictions Listen to a report about future developments in technology Listen for gist Listen for reasons	Make predictions about future events Ask about future changes Make predictions about changing technology Set goals for the future	Read a horoscope Read new year resolutions Read for the main topic Read for details Make inferences
20 **Transportation** Page 238	Have to Would like Can / Could / Would	Listen to a passenger making reservations Listen to a conversation between passengers on a plane Listen for gist Listen for details	Talk about travel requirements and restrictions Describe public transportation Make travel arrangements Request information Offer help	Read a letter of complaint Read for the main idea Read for details Make inferences

| Grammar Summaries page 252 | Charts page 262 | Partner Activities page 266 | Audioscript page 276 | Index page 294 |

Center Stage 2

CORRELATIONS TO STANDARDS

Writing	CASAS	LAUSD	FL. Adult ESOL High Beginning	*Life Skills and Test Prep 2*
Write an email to a medical professional Writing Tip: Use *Sincerely* in formal letters / e-mails	0.2.1, 0.2.3, 0.2.4, 3.1.1, 3.3.2, 3.3.3, 3.4.1, 3.5.4, 3.5.7, 3.5.8, 3.5.9 0.1.2, 1.1.7, 1.2.1, 1.3.8, 1.6.1, 2.5.5, 3.1.1, 3.1.2, 3.2.1, 3.3.1, 3.3.2, 3.3.3, 3.5.1	Competencies: 5, 45, 46, 47 Grammar: 15, 28a, 28b, 28c Competencies: 16, 34, 35, 43, 44, 45, 46, 47	3.07.02, 3.07.03, 3.15.01, 3.15.02, 3.15.03, 3.15.05, 3.15.06, 3.16.01, 3.16.02, 3.16.03 3.07.01, 3.07.03, 3.07.04, 3.07.05, 3.08.01, 3.11.01, 3.14.04	**Unit 1, Lesson 6** • Write an absence note to your child's teacher **Unit 5, Lessons 1-3** • Identify common foods and their containers; identify common quantities of food; read information on food packaging and labels **Unit 9, Lessons 1-7** • Identify parts of the body and face; talk about injuries; identify common symptoms; make a doctor's appointment; identify common diseases and conditions; identify common medicines; read medicine labels
Prewriting: Find the main idea in an e-mail Write an e-mail Writing Tip: Use expressions of opinion	0.2.3, 1.4.1, 1.4.2, 5.2.4, 5.2.5 0.1.2, 1.1.4, 1.2.1, 1.2.2, 1.4.2, 1.4.7, 4.5.1, 6.6.4	Competencies: 37, 38 Grammar: 20c, 20d, 28a, 28b, 28c Competencies: 31, 32, 37, 38, 39, 60	3.11.04, 3.11.05, 3.15.01, 3.15.02, 3.15.03, 3.15.05, 3.15.06, 3.16.01, 3.16.02, 3.16.03 3.04.01, 3.11.03, 3.11.04	**Unit 5, Lesson 4** • Read and compare information in advertisements **Unit 7, Lesson 3** • Understand the American system of measuring distance **Unit 8, Lessons 1-3** • Read ads for apartments; ask about an apartment for rent; describe common problems in an apartment **Unit 12, Lesson 4** • Identify the parts of a computer
Prewriting: Make a list of new year resolutions Write a paragraph about future goals Writing Tip: Use *instead*	0.2.1, 0.2.3, 2.7.3, 3.5.7, 3.5.9, 4.4.1, 7.2.3 0.1.4	Competencies: 7, 59, 63 Grammar: 4, 28a, 28b, 28c Competencies: 10	3.15.01, 3.15.02, 3.15.03, 3.15.05, 3.15.06, 3.16.01, 3.16.02, 3.16.03 3.05.03	**Unit 2, Lesson 5** • Give and receive sympathy and congratulations
Prewriting: Make a list of problems in your town Write a letter of complaint Identify community needs Understand social issues Writing Tip: Indent paragraphs Address letters	0.1.2, 0.1.3, 0.1.4, 0.2.3, 2.2.3, 2.2.4, 7.2.1, 7.2.2, 7.2.4 0.1.2, 0.1.3, 0.1.4, 1.3.8, 2.1.1, 2.2.1, 2.5.4, 7.4.5	Competencies: 8, 9 Grammar: 9, 11a, 12, 14, 28a, 28b, 28c Competencies: 8, 9, 19, 23, 36, 58	3.09.01, 3.09.02, 3.15.01, 3.15.02, 3.15.03, 3.15.05, 3.15.06, 3.16.01, 3.16.02, 3.16.03 3.05.03, 3.06.05, 3.09.03, 3.11.01, 3.12.03	**Unit 1, Lesson 7** • Use *Could I* and *Could you* to make requests and ask for permission **Unit 3, Lessons 4-5** • Use the yellow, blue, and white pages of a phone directory **Unit 4, Lessons 2-3** • Make and respond to invitations; ask for and give directions **Unit 5, Lesson 5** • Read a menu

All information printed in blue pertains to *Life Skills and Test Prep 2*

Scope and Sequence T-xiii

To the Teacher

The Center Stage Program

Center Stage is a four-level, four-skills course that supports student learning and achievement in everyday work and life situations. Practical language and timely topics motivate adult students to master grammar along with speaking, listening, reading, and writing skills. The *Center Stage* program includes the following components:

- The **Student Book** features twenty units that explore relevant themes for the adult learner, integrating grammar practice with speaking, listening, reading, and writing activities.
- **Life Skills and Test Prep 2**, the companion student text, provides thorough practice of life skills and is linked to the unit themes and vocabulary of *Center Stage*.
- The **Teacher's Edition** includes step-by-step teaching notes as well as multilevel strategies, learner persistence tips, expansion activities, culture notes, and grammar notes.
- A **Teacher's Resource Disk** in the back of the Teacher's Edition offers worksheets for supplementary grammar exercises, supplementary vocabulary exercises, and learner persistence.
- The **ExamView® Assessment Suite** includes hundreds of test items, providing flexible, comprehensive assessment of the skills taught in *Center Stage*.
- **Color transparencies** and **worksheets** offer teachers a flexible way to introduce, practice, and review vocabulary.
- The **Audio Program** contains recordings for all listening activities in the Student Book.

The Student Book

Each unit in the Student Book is divided into six lessons. Each lesson is presented on two facing pages and provides clear, self-contained instruction taking approximately 45 to 60 minutes of class time. The lessons include:

- **Vocabulary and Listening:** The unit opens with a vivid illustration that sets the context and presents high-frequency, leveled vocabulary that is recycled in the unit and throughout the course. After practicing the new words, students listen to a conversation related to the unit theme.
- **Grammar to Communicate:** The three *Grammar to Communicate* lessons present target structures in easy-to-read charts. Students practice each language point by completing a variety of exercises that progress from controlled to open-ended. Every *Grammar to Communicate* lesson ends with a speaking activity, *Time to Talk*. This communicative activity promotes fluency and self-expression by giving students additional practice with the language in speaking contexts.
- **Review and Challenge:** This section helps students review the unit material, consolidate their knowledge, and extend their learning with more challenging grammar, dictation, speaking, and listening activities.
- **Reading and Writing:** The reading lesson recycles the grammar and vocabulary that have been taught in the unit. In the reading section, students practice essential reading skills, such as understanding main ideas, reading for details, and recognizing topics. Students also encounter a wide variety of reading genres, including e-mail, formal letters, administrative forms, and medical instructions.

    In the writing section, students take their first steps to writing a paragraph and practice writing tasks, such as completing forms, writing e-mails, and writing letters. In addition, students engage in prewriting activities such as listing, interviewing, and using graphic organizers to write a paragraph.
- **Games:** After every four units these colorfully illustrated activities review the language presented in the units in a light and communicative context.

Standards

The *Center Stage 2 Student Book,* together with the companion text, *Life Skills and Test Prep 2,* is a comprehensive course, ensuring student success on key grammar and life skills standards. The scope and sequence on pages iv–xiii links the two books with CASAS, LAUSD, and Florida Adult ESOL standards.

Assessment

Center Stage includes the following assessment tools:

- *Time to Talk* activities and the *Review and Challenge* sections provide teachers with multiple opportunities to gauge student performance in class.
- The review *Games* help students assess their understanding of the material.
- The printed unit tests found in the *Teacher's Edition* allow teachers to assess students' mastery at the end of each unit.
- The *ExamView® Assessment Suite,* sold separately, offers teachers additional ready-made unit tests and allows them to create new tests by mixing and matching items from different units or skills areas. ExamView tests can be administered as pre-tests before the print tests, or as achievement tests at any time during the course.
- *Life Skills and Test Prep 2* includes 12 listening and reading tests that specifically assess life skill competencies.

The Teacher's Edition

The *Teacher's Edition* includes:

- Step-by-step unit notes as well as learning goals, suggested teaching times, learner persistence tips, multilevel strategies, expansion activities, culture notes, and grammar notes
- References to lessons in *Life Skills and Test Prep 2*
- Unit tests with answer key and audioscripts
- A *Teacher's Resource Disk* with reproducible supplementary Grammar and Vocabulary Exercises worksheets and Learner Persistence tips worksheets.
- Audioscript, grammar summaries, grammar charts, and index from the *Student Book* for easy reference

Classroom Management

Teachers of adult students face a number of specific challenges. *Center Stage* offers a wealth of specific strategies on how to address these challenges.

Multilevel Strategies

Many adult classes have students of widely differing English proficiencies. In these "multilevel" classes, teachers are asked to serve the needs of pre-level, at-level, and above-level students, all at the same time. Further, almost no student in any given class will be completely at any one level. Individual learners have different strengths—a student may be pre-level in one skill, at-level in another skill, and above-level in another. Some students, for example, are quite proficient in reading but have more trouble when it comes to speaking activities.

Center Stage provides ample support for teachers of multilevel classes. Multilevel strategies are offered for many of the student book activities. These strategies are designed to help teachers tailor the activities to the needs of students at different levels of proficiency. In this way, students all work on a task that is appropriate for them while staying focused on the objectives of the lesson. In addition, the supplementary Grammar and Vocabulary

Exercises worksheets on the *Teacher's Resource Disk* can serve as useful tools in multilevel classes. The teacher can assign these exercises as homework or independent study, giving individual students tasks that are appropriate to their level.

Learner Persistence

Learner persistence is often defined as *adults staying in programs for as long as they can, engaging in self-directed study when they must drop out of their programs, and returning to a program as soon as the demand of their lives allow.* This is something unique to adult learners because, unlike children, adults make a conscious decision to participate in educational programs. Also unlike children, most adult students have many "positive and negative forces" outside of their control that impact their ability to attend class, including caring for children or other relatives and working full-time. Should a "negative force" arise, students may have to "stop out" for a period of time. Teachers can address these concerns in a variety of ways:

- First, be sensitive to the positive and negative forces that help and hinder persistence.
- Second, help adult students build self-confidence about reaching their goals.
- Third, have students establish unique goals for themselves.
- Finally, provide services and systems toward achieving these goals.

Every unit of the *Teacher's Edition* opens with a Learner Persistence tip—a concrete, easy-to-implement strategy for dealing with learner persistence issues. These tips can also help teachers to foster a sense of classroom community and to encourage good study practices which can be used during a "stop out" period. The Learner Persistence worksheets found on the *Teacher's Resource Disk* offer yet more practical strategies for keeping students engaged and motivated.

Creating a Dynamic Learning Environment

Research has shown that dynamic learning environments foster student engagement and learning. Here are some easy, tried and true "best practices" to help you create an active classroom.

1. Make sure that all students participate in lessons by teaching to the three learning styles (audio, visual, tactile/kinesthetic) and by providing a variety of expansion tasks to reinforce the learning.
2. Make sure that students personalize activities as much as possible so that they can easily make the connection between what they learn in class and what they experience in their lives outside the classroom.
3. Make sure that students have opportunities to work with a variety of partners for pair and group activities so that they get used to working with different people and help to build a sense of classroom community.
4. Always review the directions with the class before beginning any activity. Be sure that all students completely understand the task and what they must do to complete it.
5. Give students opportunities to guess the meanings of words from both pictures and text.
6. Before presenting a new point, remind students of what they already know and build upon it. This will increase students' understanding and confidence.
7. Always tell students how many times they will hear a recording. This will help reassure them and reduce their stress if they do not understand what they hear the first time. If students have difficulty, replay the corresponding track as many times as necessary.
8. Do not correct every error. Focus your feedback on the point(s) presented and practiced in that specific lesson.
9. Once you have corrected students' writing, have them revise their writing so that they can focus on correcting their errors.

10. Have students role-play conversations to give them useful practice in pronunciation and fluency.
11. Use graphic organizers (charts, mind maps, and Venn diagrams) to help students learn new words and ideas.
12. Show students how they can use classroom materials to study on their own outside of the classroom.

About the Authors

Lynn Bonesteel has been teaching ESL since 1988. She is currently a full-time senior lecturer at the Center for English Language and Orientation Programs at Boston University, Center for English Language and Orientation Programs (CELOP). Ms. Bonesteel is also the author of *Password 3: A Reading and Vocabulary Text*.

Samuela Eckstut-Didier has taught ESL and EFL for over twenty-five years in the United States, Greece, Italy, and England. She currently teaches at Boston University, Center for English Language and Orientation Programs (CELOP). She has authored and co-authored numerous texts for the teaching of English, notably *Strategic Reading 1, 2, and 3; What's in a Word? Reading and Vocabulary Building; Focus on Grammar Workbook; In the Real World; First Impressions; Beneath the Surface; Widely Read;* and *Finishing Touches*.

About the Series Consultants

MaryAnn Florez is the lead ESL Specialist for the Arlington Education and Employment Program (REEP) in Arlington, Virginia, where she has program management, curriculum development, and teacher training responsibilities. She has worked with Fairfax County (VA) Adult ESOL and the National Center for ESL Literacy Education (NCLE), and has coordinated a volunteer adult ESL program in Northern Virginia. Ms. Florez has offered workshops throughout the United States in areas such as teaching beginning level English language learners, incorporating technology in instruction, strategies for a multilevel classroom, and assessment. Her publications include a variety of research-to-practice briefs and articles on adult ESL education. Ms. Florez holds an M.Ed. in Adult Education from George Mason University.

Sharon Seymour is an ESL instructor at City College of San Francisco, where she has extensive experience teaching both noncredit adult ESL and credit ESL. She recently completed ten years as chair of the ESL Department at CCSF. She is also currently a co-researcher at the Center for Advancement of Adult Literacy Project on Exemplary Noncredit Community College ESL Programs. Ms. Seymour has been president of CATESOL and a member of the TESOL board of directors and has served both organizations in a variety of capacities. She has served on California Community College Chancellor's Office and California State Department of Education committees relating to ESL curriculum and assessment. Ms. Seymour holds an M.A. in TESOL from San Francisco State University.

Unit 1
People

Learning Goals

- Learn words to describe people
- Learn about *Be*: affirmative and negative statements; *Be*: yes / no questions and short answers; and regular count nouns and irregular nouns
- Listen to a conversation and a TV report
- Read a form and write a paragraph about yourself
- Talk about people

Learner Persistence

Students who set real goals for their learning are more likely to persist in order to reach those goals. At the beginning of the course, help students set specific goals for their language learning. Have students revisit their goals periodically to help them keep track of whether or not they are achieving them.

Warm-up

Teaching Time: 3–5 min.

- Have students look at the picture.
- Say the number of each person and ask students to say whether the person is a man or a woman.

Vocabulary

Teaching Time: 15–20 min.

- Have students look at the picture and describe the people before looking at the words.
- 🎧 Play Track 2 while students read, and listen.
- Read each word aloud and have students repeat chorally.
- Have students complete the task.
- PAIRS. Have students compare answers.
- **LIFE SKILLS TEST PREP** 2 Go to Unit 2, Lesson 3 for more practice in describing physical characteristics of family and friends.

Unit 1
People

Grammar
- *Be*: Affirmative and Negative Statements
- *Be*: Yes / No Questions and Short Answers
- Regular Count Nouns and Irregular Nouns

Vocabulary

🎧 **2** Read and listen. Then circle the words that describe you. *Answers will vary.*

1. beautiful
2. average height
3. tall
4. short
5. heavy
6. serious
7. talkative
8. quiet
9. good-looking
10. young
11. thin
12. average weight
13. funny
14. middle-aged
15. old

2 Unit 1

Expansion

- Draw the following graphic organizer on the board.
- Explain each category. For example, say: *General appearance means the way a person looks.*
- Call on students to come to the board and complete the graphic organizer with other words in the list.

Height	Weight	Age	Personality	General appearance
tall	average weight	middle-aged	serious	beautiful

Culture Note

Vocabulary. Explain that the word *beautiful* is usually used to describe women. *Good-looking* is used for men and women.

T-2 Center Stage 2

Listening

A 🎧 3 **Listen. Two women talk about Patty and Alvaro. Complete the sentences. Write P (Patty) or A (Alvaro).**

1. _Alvaro_ is not American.
2. _Alvaro_ isn't heavy.
3. _Patty_ is a student.
4. _Alvaro_ is a doctor.
5. _Patty_ is 35.
6. _Alvaro_ is 22.

B 🎧 4 **Read and listen again. Write the missing words. Use the words in the box.**

| Are | ~~he's~~ | isn't | not | They're |

Ava: Alvaro? Is he American?

Mia: No, __he's__ not. He's Mexican.
         1.

Ava: Is he good-looking?

Mia: He's OK. He's tall. He __isn't__ thin, but
                               2.
he isn't heavy. He's average weight.

Ava: __Are__ he and Patty students in the same
     3.
class?

Mia: No, they're not. __They're__ neighbors. And
                      4.
he's a doctor, not a student.

Ava: A doctor? Is he old?

Mia: No, he's __not__ old. He's about 35.
              5.

Ava: 35? But Patty's only 22.

Mia: So? 35 isn't old!

People 3

Listening

A Teaching Time: 10–15 min.

- **Warm-up:** Write *Patty* and *Alvaro* on the board. Ask students which name is a woman's name and which is a man's name.
- Ask students to read through the sentences before they listen.
- 🎧 Play Track 3 while students listen.
- 🎧 Play Track 3 again while students complete the task.
- PAIRS. Have students compare their answers.
- Call on students to say answers. Correct as needed.

B Teaching Time: 15–20 min.

- Have students read through the answer choices before they listen.
- 🎧 Play Track 4 while students listen and write the words they hear.
- 🎧 Play Track 4 again while students check their answers.
- Call on students to say answers. Correct as needed.
- Read the conversation aloud. Pause after each few words and have students repeat chorally.
- PAIRS. Have students role-play the conversation.

Multilevel Strategy

- **Pre-level:** Have students role-play the completed conversation.
- **At-level, Above-level:** Write the conversation on the board without the answers. Have students recall the answers as they role-play.

Option

Assign Unit 1 Supplementary Vocabulary Exercise on the Teacher's Resource Disk as homework or on the Student Persistence CD-ROM as self-access practice.

Unit 1   T-3

Grammar to Communicate 1

Be: Affirmative Statements

Teaching Time: 5–10 min.

- Write *I, you, he, she, is, we, you, they* on the board. Explain the meanings of the words. For example, point to yourself and say *I*.
- Write *be* on the board. Say: *Be has different forms for different subjects.* Add to the board the present tense forms of *be* next to the subject pronouns (*I am, You are*, etc.).
- Say: *We can make contractions from the subject pronouns and forms of* be. Add contractions to the board next to the subject pronouns and forms of *be*.
- Have students study the chart and the Look Box.
- Read the sentences and contractions in the chart and have students repeat chorally.

A   **Teaching Time:** 5–10 min.

- Read the example with the class.
- Have students complete the task.
- Call on students to say answers. Correct as needed.

Multilevel Strategy

- **Pre-level:** Have students work in pairs or small groups. Help students identify the subject of each sentence before they complete the task. Knowing the subject will help them write the correct form of *be*.
- **At-level, Above-level:** Have above-level students write one additional item for each picture on the board. (e.g., *Martha ____ happy.*) Have at-level students come to the board and write the answers.

B   **Teaching Time:** 10–15 min.

- Read the example with the class.
- Have students complete the task.
- Tell students to first choose the correct subject pronoun to replace the subject in Exercise A, and then to make the contraction with that pronoun and the form of *be*.

Grammar to Communicate 1

BE: AFFIRMATIVE STATEMENTS

Subject	Be	Adjective
I	am	
He / She / It	is	quiet.
We / You / They	are	

Contractions
I + am → I'm
He + is → He's
She + is → She's
It + is → It's
We + are → We're
You + are → You're
They + are → They're

Look
You are quiet, John.
(*You* = 1 person)
You are quiet, John and Anna.
(*You* = 2 or more people)

A   Complete the sentences. Use *is* or *are*.

1. Martha __is__ smart.
2. The dog __is__ friendly.
3. David and Laura __are__ married. 
4. Jack __is__ single.
5. Jen and Ed __are__ noisy. 
6. Sam __is__ hardworking.

B   Rewrite the sentences in Exercise A. Use *He's, She's, It's,* or *They're*.

1. She's smart.
2. It's / He's / She's friendly.
3. They're married.
4. He's single.
5. They're noisy.
6. He's hardworking.

PAIRS. Write three sentences about yourself on a piece of paper. Use *I'm* and the adjectives above. Tell your sentences to your partner. Answers will vary.

4   Unit 1

- Call on students to say answers. Correct as needed.
- PAIRS. Have students write three sentences about themselves.
- Have students take turns reading their sentences to a partner.
- **LIFE SKILLS TEST PREP 2** Go to Unit 2, Lesson 3 for more practice in using pronouns.

Multilevel Strategy

- **Pre-level:** Have students write one sentence about themselves.
- **Above-level:** Have students report to the class what they have learned about their partner.

Grammar Notes

1. The subject of a sentence tells who or what the sentence is about. The subject is a noun or subject pronoun.
2. The forms of *be* change depending on the subject.
3. Use full forms or contractions with subject pronouns and forms of *be*.
4. For more information on this grammar topic, see page 252.

Watch Out!

Exercise C. In some languages, the verb *have* is used to talk about a person's age. Listen for and correct errors such as *I have 25 years.*

T-4   Center Stage 2

BE: NEGATIVE STATEMENTS

Subject	Be	Not	Adjective	Contractions		
I	am			I'm		
He She It	is	not	quiet.	He's She's It's	not	quiet.
We You They	are			We're You're They're		

Look
We also say:
Isn't and aren't

C Write sentences about the ages of the people. Use contractions.

1.  (25, 65) — They're not 25. They're 65.
2.  (18, 8) — She's not 18. / She isn't 18. She's 8.
3.  (45, 22) — They're not 45. / They aren't 45. They're 22.
4.  (30, 55) — He's not 30. / He isn't 30. He's 55.

TIME to TALK

PAIRS. Tell your partner about yourself. Make six statements. Use the words in the box.
Answers will vary. Accept all answers which are complete sentences with correct verb forms.

Example:
A: I'm not tall. I'm average height.

| average height | married | old | serious | single | tall |
| funny | middle-aged | quiet | short | talkative | young |

WRAP-UP. Now describe your partner to the class.

Example:
B: Maria isn't tall. She's average height.

People 5

Be: Negative Statements
Teaching Time: 5–10 min.

- Write on the board as you say: *I am [age]. I am not [incorrect age].*
- Say: *Use the word* not *to make a sentence negative.*
- Call on volunteers to make sentences about their own age.
- Have students study the chart and the Look Box. Tell students that there are two ways to make contractions with *is not* and *are not*. (*Isn't = He's not. Aren't = We're not.*)
- Read the sentences in the chart and have students repeat chorally.

C   Teaching Time: 5–10 min.

- Read the example with the class. Remind students that there are two ways of making contractions with *is / are + not*.
- Have students complete the task.
- Call on students to write answers on the board. Write corrections on the board as needed.

Grammar Notes
1. The word *not* makes a sentence negative.
2. *Not* goes after a form of *be*.
3. There are two ways to make contractions with *is not* and *are not*. *He's not = He isn't. We're not = We aren't.*
4. For more information on this grammar topic, see page 252.

Option
Assign Unit 1 Supplementary Grammar to Communicate 1 Exercises on the Teacher's Resource Disk as homework or on the Student Persistence CD-ROM as self-access practice.

TIME to TALK

Teaching Time: 10–15 min.

- Have two students read the example.
- PAIRS. Have students complete the task.
- Walk around and help as needed.
- Have each student tell the class three things about his or her partner.

Multilevel Strategy
- **Pre-level:** Have students write down their sentences before they talk with their partner.

Unit 1   T-5

Grammar to Communicate 2

Be: Yes / No Questions and Short Answers

Teaching Time: 5–10 min.

- Draw the following graphic organizer on the board.

Sentence	Question
I am talkative.	
You are single.	
Carla is thin.	

Yes short answer	*No* short answer

- Read the first sentence. Say: *To make a question, put* be *before the subject.* Write: *Am I talkative?* in the second column. Have students say questions for the other sentences.
- Say: *When you answer with* yes, *use the subject and the form of* be. *When you answer with* no, *use the subject and the form of* be + not *or use a contraction.* Complete the remaining rows with the students.
- Read the questions and answers in the graphic organizer and have students repeat chorally.

A Teaching Time: 5–10 min.

- Read the example with the class.
- Have students complete the task.
- Call on students to say answers. Correct as needed.

B Teaching Time: 10–15 min.

- Have students study the Look Box. Remind them to put *be* before the subject in questions.
- Read the example with the class.
- Have students complete the task.
- Call on students to say answers. Correct as needed.

Multilevel Strategy

- **Pre-level, At-level:** Pair pre-level students with at-level students to complete the task. Have at-level students form the correct questions and dictate them to their partner. Have pre-level students form the answers. After checking the answers, have pairs take turns asking and answering the questions.
- **Above-level:** Pair students and have them practice asking and answering the questions after they have completed the task. Have students ask three new questions in addition to the questions in Exercise B. Walk around and prompt students with suggestions. Tell students they can ask about their partner's age, job, or where they are from.

Grammar to Communicate 2

BE: YES/NO QUESTIONS AND SHORT ANSWERS

Be	Subject	Adjective		Affirmative			Negative	
Am	I			I	am.		I'm	
Is	he / she / it	quiet?	Yes,	he / she / it	is.	No,	he's / she's / it's	not.
Are	we / you / they			we / you / they	are.		we're / you're / they're	

A Answer the questions about you and people you know. Use short answers.

1. Is your class quiet? — Yes, it is. OR No, it's not.
2. Are you friendly? — Yes, I am. OR No, I'm not.
3. Are your classmates hardworking? — Yes, they are. OR No, they're not. OR No, they aren't.
4. Is your best friend married? — Yes, he / she is. OR No, he's / she's not. OR No, he / she isn't.
5. Are you and the people in your family tall? — Yes, we are. OR No, we're not. OR No, we aren't.
6. Are your neighbors noisy? — Yes, they are. OR No, they're not. OR No, they aren't.

Look
Statements: You are old. ✗ She is old. ✗
Questions: Are you old? ✓ Is she old? ✓

B Write questions. Put the words in the correct order. Then complete the answers.

1. Is Carla from Canada? (Carla / from / Canada / is) — Yes, she is.
2. Are Ken and Lori married? (are / married / Ken and Lori) — Yes, they are.
3. Is the teacher friendly? (the teacher / is / friendly) — Yes, she / he is.
4. Are you and your friend hardworking? (are / hardworking / you and your friend) — Yes, we are.
5. Is Tom 20? (20 / is / Tom) — No, he's not. OR No, he isn't.
6. Are you late? (you / late / are) — No, I'm not.
7. Is she Brazilian? (Brazilian / she / is) — No, She's not. OR No, she isn't.
8. Are they here? (are / here / they) — No, they're not. OR No, they aren't.

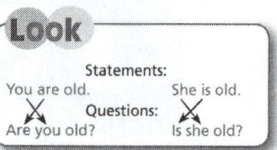

Unit 1

Grammar Notes

1. The form of *be* goes before the subject in a *yes / no* question.
2. To make affirmative short answers, use *Yes* + the subject + a form of *be*. Do not use contractions in affirmative short answers.
3. To make negative short answers, use *No* + the subject + a form of *be + not*. Use full forms or contractions in negative short answers. (*No, you are not. No, you're not. No, you aren't.*)
4. For more information on this grammar topic, see page 252.

T-6 Center Stage 2

C **5** Complete the conversation. Use *am* or *are*. Then listen and check your answers.

Lara: <u>Are you</u> a student in this class?
   1. (you)

Bob: No, <u>I'm</u> the teacher.
   2. (I)

Lara: Oh, <u>are you</u> Professor Michaelson?
   3. (you)

Bob: Yes, <u>I am</u>. <u>Are you</u> in English 101?
   4. (I)   5. (you)

Lara: Yes, <u>I am</u>.
   6. (I)

Bob: Then <u>you're</u> in my class. Welcome.
   7. (you)

D Write questions. Use *am*, *is*, or *are*. Then answer the questions about you and people you know. Use short answers.

1. <u>Are you tall?</u> — No, I'm not. OR Yes, I am.
   (you / tall)

2. <u>Are you 35?</u> — No, I'm not. OR Yes, I am.
   (you / 35)

3. <u>Are you and your family from New York?</u> — No, we're not. OR No, we aren't. OR Yes, we are.
   (you and your family / from New York)

4. <u>Are your classmates friendly?</u> — No, they're not. OR No, they aren't. OR Yes, they are.
   (your classmates / friendly)

5. <u>Is your best friend talkative?</u> — No, he's / she's not. OR No, he / she isn't. OR Yes, he / she is.
   (your best friend / talkative)

6. <u>Are your neighbors noisy?</u> — No, they're not. OR No, they aren't. OR Yes, they are.
   (your neighbors / noisy)

PAIRS. Ask and answer the questions above.

TIME to TALK

ON YOUR OWN. Write the names of four classmates on a piece of paper. Answers will vary.

PAIRS. Try to guess the names of the classmates on your partner's list. Ask questions. Then change roles and answer your partner's questions.

Example:
A: *Is this classmate tall?*
B: *No, he isn't.*
A: *Is he friendly?*
B: *Yes, he is.*
A: *Is the classmate Marco?*
B: *Yes!*

People 7

C Teaching Time: 5–10 min.

- Read the example with the class.
- Have students complete the activity.
- Play Track 5 and have students check their answers.
- PAIRS. Ask students to role-play the completed conversation with a partner.

D Teaching Time: 5–10 min.

- Read the example with the class.
- Have students complete the task.
- Call on students to read the questions and answers to the class. Correct as needed.
- PAIRS. Have students take turns asking and answering each question.

Multilevel Strategy

- **Pre-level:** Give students the *be* form for each question in addition to the words in parentheses. They can produce the *be* forms in their responses to the questions.

Language Note

Exercises A and B. When a noun is the subject of a question, we often use a subject pronoun in the short answer. For example: *Is Bob married? Yes, he is.*

Option

Assign Unit 1 Supplementary Grammar to Communicate 2 Exercises on the Teacher's Resource Disk as homework or on the Student Persistence CD-ROM as self-access practice.

TIME to TALK

Teaching Time: 10–15 min.

- Have two students read the example conversation.
- PAIRS. Have students complete the task.
- Walk around and help as needed.

Expansion Have students play the game again with names of celebrities instead of classmates. Walk around and help as needed.

Unit 1   T-7

Grammar to Communicate 3

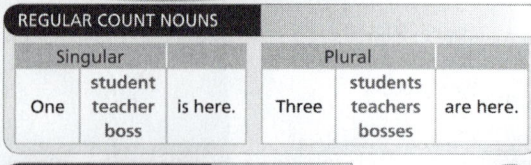

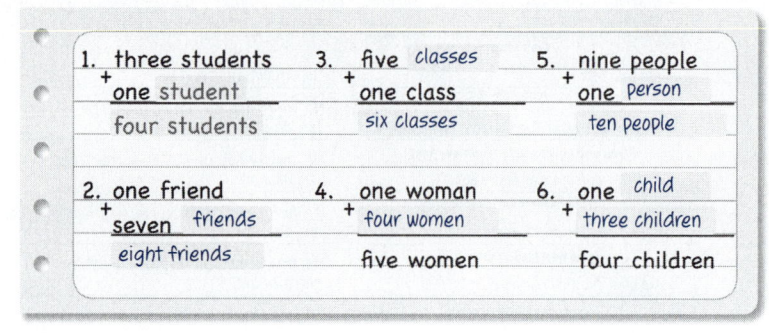

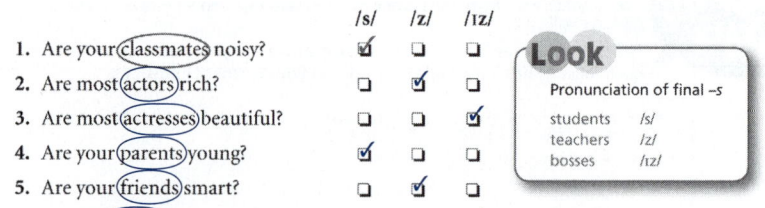

Regular Count Nouns; Irregular Nouns

Teaching Time: 5–10 min.

- Have students study the charts and the Look Box.
- Make two columns on the board, and label them *singular (1)* and *plural (2, 3, 4 . . .)*. Say: *The word* singular *means one person or thing. The word* plural *means more than one.*
- Under the singular column, write *one friend*.
- Say: *For most words, add the letter* s *to make the word plural.* Add *two friends* to the plural column.
- Add to the singular column *one class*. Say: *If a word ends in the letter* s, *add* –es *to make it plural.* Under the plural column, write *three classes*.
- Explain that some nouns have irregular plurals. We don't add –s or –es to these words. Under *singular* write: *one man, one woman, one child*. Under *plural*, write: *four men, five women, seven children*.
- Read the sentences and phrases in the chart and have students repeat chorally.

A Teaching Time: 5–10 min.

- Read the example with the class.
- Call on volunteers to come to the board and complete each item. Write corrections on the board as needed.

B Teaching Time: 10–15 min.

- Have students study the Look Box. Tell students that the plural *s* can be pronounced three different ways. Point to the symbols and say: /s/ *is for the sound* /s/, /z/ *is for the sound* /z/, *and* /ɪz/ *is for the sound* /ɪz/.
- Read the example with the class.
- Have students circle the plural nouns.
- Call on students to say answers. Correct as needed.
- 🎧 Play Track 6 while students listen and complete the task.
- 🎧 Play Track 6 again while students check their answers.
- Call on students to say answers. Correct as needed.

- PAIRS. Have students take turns asking and answering each question. Walk around and assist students with correct pronunciation of the plural forms.

Grammar Notes

1. A noun is a person, place, thing, or idea.
2. Most nouns can be singular and plural. When a noun is singular, there is only one. When a noun is plural, there is more than one.
3. Add –s (or –es if the word ends in s) to most nouns to make them plural.
4. Some nouns have irregular plural forms.
5. For more information on this grammar topic, see page 252.

T-8 Center Stage 2

C Rewrite the sentences. Make the nouns plural.

1. My friend is smart.   My friends are smart.
2. My classmate is talkative.   My classmates are talkative.
3. My neighbor is middle-aged.   My neighbors are middle-aged.
4. My boss is hardworking.   My bosses are hardworking.
5. My child is quiet.   My children are quiet.

D Look at the pictures. Write sentences about the people. Use *is*, *isn't*, *are*, or *aren't*.

1. The men are tall.
   (The men / tall)
2. The women aren't tall.
   (The women / tall)
3. The men aren't short.
   (The men / short)
4. The girl is thin.
   (The girl / thin)
5. The boys aren't thin.
   (The boys / thin)
6. The children are young.
   (The children / young)

TIME to TALK

PAIRS. Make six sentences with the nouns and adjectives in the boxes.
Answers will vary. Accept all answers which are complete sentences with correct plural forms.

Nouns		
actor	doctor	student
boss	man	teacher
child	person	woman

Adjectives		
beautiful	good-looking	quiet
friendly	hardworking	smart
funny	noisy	talkative

Example:
A: Many actors are good-looking.
B: And some actors are funny.

People 9

C Teaching Time: 5–10 min.
- Read the example with the class.
- Have students complete the task.
- Call on students to write sentences on the board. Write corrections on the board as needed.

D Teaching Time: 5–10 mins
- Read the example with the class.
- Have students complete the task.
- Call on students to write sentences on the board. Write corrections on the board as needed.

Language Notes
- **Exercises A and B.** Tell students that a noun is a person, place, thing, or idea.
- Explain that count nouns are nouns we can count. They have singular and plural forms.

Option
Assign Unit 1 Supplementary Grammar to Communicate 3 Exercises on the Teacher's Resource Disk as homework or on the Student Persistence CD-ROM as self-access practice.

TIME to TALK

Teaching Time: 10–15 min.
- Have two students read the example. If necessary, explain that *many* means a large number of people or things, and *some* refers to a number of people or things, but not all of them.
- PAIRS. Have students complete the task.
- Walk around and help as needed.
- Call on volunteers to present their sentences to the class.

Multilevel Strategy
- **Pre-level:** Have students write three sentences. Walk around and help students form the correct plural forms.
- **At-level, Above-level:** Challenge students to talk to their partner without writing down the sentences.

Unit 1   T-9

Review and Challenge

Grammar

Teaching Time: 5–10 min.

- Read the example with the class.
- Have students complete the task.
- 🎧 Play Track 7 while students check their answers.
- PAIRS. Ask students to role-play the corrected conversation with a partner.

Dictation

Teaching Time: 5–10 min.

- 🎧 Play Track 8 while students listen and write what they hear.
- 🎧 Play Track 8 again while students check their answers.
- Call on students to write answers on the board.
- 🎧 Play Track 8 again and correct the sentences on the board.

Multilevel Strategy

- **Pre-level:** Give students a worksheet with some of the words from the dictation already provided.

Speaking

Teaching Time: 5–10 min.

- Have two students read the example.
- If necessary, explain that *perfect* means *good, without any problems.*
- PAIRS. Have students complete the task.
- Walk around and help as needed.
- Call on volunteers to tell the class one of their sentences. Conduct informal surveys about students' opinions of each sentence.

Review and Challenge

Grammar

🎧 **7** Correct the conversation. There are seven mistakes. The first mistake is corrected for you. Then listen and check your answers.

Juan: Hello. ~~I~~ I'm Juan Montero.

Nicole: Hi. My name is Nicole Summers.

Juan: Are you from Miami?

Nicole: Yes, ~~I'm~~ I am. My boyfriend ~~he~~ is from here, too.

Juan: My girlfriend and I are ~~no~~ not from here. ~~They're~~ We're from Caracas, Venezuela.

Nicole: ~~Caracas is~~ Is Caracas nice?

Juan: Very nice. The ~~persons~~ people are friendly.

Dictation

🎧 **8** Listen. You will hear five sentences. Write them on a piece of paper. *See the audioscript on page 276 for the sentences.*

Speaking

PAIRS. Make sentences with the words in the boxes and your own ideas. *Answers will vary. Accept all answers which are complete sentences with correct verb forms.*

The perfect ...
boss
boyfriend
friend
girlfriend
student
teacher

beautiful	honest	smart
cute	nice	strict
funny	patient	strong
good-looking	quiet	sweet
hardworking	serious	talkative

Example:
A: The perfect teacher is patient and hardworking.
B: Yes, and the perfect teacher isn't strict.

10 Unit 1

Option

Before class, make a copy of the grammar exercise as a transparency to use with an overhead projector. Have students make corrections to the conversation on the transparency.

T-10 Center Stage 2

Listening

A 🎧 9 Listen. A TV reporter talks about the secrets to a happy life. Write the percentages (%).

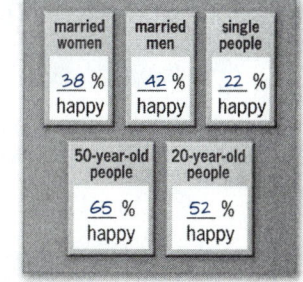

married women	married men	single people
_38_ % happy	_42_ % happy	_22_ % happy

50-year-old people	20-year-old people
_65_ % happy	_52_ % happy

B 🎧 10 Listen again. Circle the correct answers. There may be more than one correct answer.

1. The first man thinks that the secrets to a happy life are
   a. good health. ✓
   b. marriage.
   c. love. ✓
   d. fun.

2. The second man thinks the secret to a happy life is
   a. good health.
   b. marriage.
   c. love.
   d. fun. ✓

3. The woman is
   a. happy.
   b. late. ✓
   c. at work.
   d. married.

TIME to TALK

ON YOUR OWN. In your opinion, what are the secrets to a happy life? Write *1* for very important, *2* for important, and *3* for not important. *Answers will vary.*

____ a big family   ____ fun   ____ hard work   ____ money
____ children   ____ good food   ____ love   ____ music
____ education   ____ good health ____ luck   ____ a nice car
____ friends   ____ a good job   ____ marriage   ____ a nice house

GROUPS. Compare your answers.

Example:
A: *A big family is very important.*
B: *A big family is not important for me. Education is very important.*

People 11

Listening

A Teaching Time: 5–10 min.

- **Warm-up:** Write on the board and say: *People are happy when they have ___.* Call on volunteers to complete the sentence in their own way. Record students' answers on the board.
- Tell students they will write percentages or numbers.
- 🎧 Play Track 9 while students listen.
- 🎧 Play Track 9 again while students listen again and complete the task.
- Call on students to say answers. Correct as needed.

B Teaching Time: 5–10 min.

- Ask students to read through the sentences and answer choices before they listen.
- 🎧 Play Track 10 while students listen and complete the task.
- 🎧 Play Track 10 again while students check their answers. Pause the recording each time an answer is given.

Option

Assign Unit 1 Supplementary Review and Challenge Exercises on the Teacher's Resource Disk as homework or on the Student Persistence CD-ROM as self-access practice.

TIME to TALK Teaching Time: 10–15 min.

- Have students complete the first part of the task.
- Have two students read the example.
- GROUPS. Have students compare their answers.
- Walk around and help as needed.
- Call on volunteers to tell the class one of their sentences. Conduct informal surveys about students' opinions of each sentence.

Unit 1   T-11

Reading and Writing

Reading

Teaching Time: 10–15 min.

- Hold up the student book page and point to the form (or point to the form on a transparency). Explain that people give information about themselves on a registration form.
- Ask students when they have to fill out this kind of form (e.g., when they want to register for school).
- Have students read the paragraph and the form silently. Then read them aloud. Pause after each few words and have students repeat chorally.
- Have students circle the correct answers.
- PAIRS. Have students compare answers.
- Call on students to say answers. Correct as needed.
- **LIFE SKILLS TEST PREP 2** Go to Unit 1, Lesson 1 for more practice in filling out a registration form.

Reading and Writing

Reading

Jacques Chaumin wants to study at Centerville Community College. Read the paragraph and the registration form. Then read the questions. Circle the correct answers.

My name is Jacques Georges Chaumin. I am married. My birthday is in December. I am 25 and my wife, Jeanette, is 22. We are from Port au Prince, Haiti. We are Haitian.

Centerville Community College
Jacques Chaumin
10 Monitor Street
Centerville, NY
11111

CENTERVILLE COMMUNITY COLLEGE REGISTRATION FORM

PLEASE PRINT. DATE __May 25, 2007__
NAME __Chaumin__ __Jacques__ __G.__
         LAST   FIRST   MIDDLE INITIAL
ADDRESS __10 Monitor Street__ __Centerville,__ __NY__ __11111__
              STREET   CITY   STATE   ZIP CODE
TELEPHONE NUMBER __(917) 111-4570__
SEX (MALE) FEMALE   DATE OF BIRTH __December 15, 1980__
                          NATIONALITY __Haitian__

1. What is Jacques Georges Chaumin's last name?
   a. Jacques
   b. Georges
   (c.) Chaumin

2. What is Jacques's middle initial?
   a. Georges
   (b.) G.
   c. C.

3. What is Jacques's street address?
   (a.) 10 Monitor Street
   b. Centerville, NY
   c. 11111

4. Where is Centerville?
   (a.) New York
   b. New Mexico
   c. New Jersey

5. What is Jacques's nationality?
   a. New York
   (b.) Haitian
   c. Haiti

12 Unit 1

Culture Notes

- **Reading.** Explain to students that in the United States, dates are written with the month first, then the day, then the year, for example, March 18, 2007. When spoken, the day is expressed as an ordinal number (first, second, tenth, eighteenth).
- Have students practice reading and writing random dates. Write five dates on the board, and ask volunteers to read them aloud. Then say five dates and have students write them down. Have volunteers write the correct dates on the board.

T-12 Center Stage 2

Prewriting

You want to study at the college, too. Fill in the form with information about yourself. *Answers will vary.*

CENTERVILLE COMMUNITY COLLEGE REGISTRATION FORM

PLEASE PRINT.   DATE _____

NAME _____
            LAST   FIRST   MIDDLE INITIAL

ADDRESS _____
            STREET   CITY   STATE   ZIP CODE

TELEPHONE NUMBER _____

SEX   MALE   FEMALE   DATE OF BIRTH _____
                             NATIONALITY _____

Writing

Now write several sentences about yourself. Use the paragraph on page 12 as a model. *Answers will vary.*

Writing Tip
Use a capital letter for nationalities.
Example: I am **D**ominican.

People 13

Prewriting

Teaching Time: 10–15 min.

- Have students find the directions on the form. If necessary, explain that when you print, you don't join together the letters. When you print, you write neatly.
- Have students complete the task.
- Walk around and help as needed.

Writing

Teaching Time: 20–30 min.

- Have students reread Jacques Chaumin's paragraph on page 12. Point out that each sentence begins with a capital letter and ends with a period.
- Have students complete the task.
- Walk around and help as needed.
- Call on volunteers to read their paragraphs. You can also have students write their paragraphs on a separate piece of paper. Collect students' work and provide individual feedback.

Multilevel Strategy

- **Pre-level:** While students are completing the prewriting task, copy the paragraph from page 12 on the board. Underline the information that students should substitute in their paragraphs. Have students copy the paragraph and substitute the underlined parts with true information.
- **Above-level:** Challenge students with the task by having them add more information to their paragraphs. Prompt them with suggestions (e.g., *Write where you live now. Write what you want to study.*).

Culture Note

Reading. Tell students that each state in the United States can be written with two letters. Write some state names and their abbreviations on the board, for example, *California / CA*. Ask students where they see these abbreviations (e.g., on forms and mail).

Watch Out!

- **Writing.** In some languages, it's not necessary to capitalize nationalities. Look for and correct errors such as *I am dominican*.
- Have students study the Writing Tip. If necessary, write on the board a few small and capital letters to show the difference between the two.

Expansion

- Before class, make copies of the blank form on page 13. Draw on the board part of the form, such as the section for the student's name.
- Model asking for and recording a student's information. Point to a student and ask, *Last name?* After he or she responds, write the student's last name in the appropriate place on the board. Continue with first name and middle initial.
- Say *Excuse me?* and *Repeat, please.* Tell students to use these phrases when they're not sure what the other person has said.

Unit 1   T-13

Unit 2
Families

Learning Goals
- Learn family words
- Learn about possessive adjectives; possessive nouns; and *Be*: information questions
- Listen to a conversation and TV report
- Read a form and write a paragraph about a classmate
- Talk about family and friends

Learner Persistence
Create a sense of community and belonging in the classroom. Whenever possible, give students the opportunity to learn more about one another in order to create more personal relationships.

Warm-up
Teaching Time: 3–5 min.
- Draw the following graphic organizer on the board.

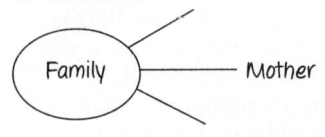

  Family —— Mother

- Explain that this is a family and that a mother is in the family. Have students say as many family words as they can. Write these words in the graphic organizer.
- Say each word and have students repeat chorally.

Vocabulary
Teaching Time: 15–20 min.
- 🎧 Play Track 11 while students read and listen.
- Read each word aloud and have students repeat chorally.
- Write the following graphic organizer on the board.

Men	Women	Both

- Have students complete the task.
- Call on students to say answers. Fill in the graphic organizer on the board.

T-14   Center Stage 2

Unit 2
Families

Grammar
- Possessive Adjectives
- Possessive Nouns
- *Be*: Information Questions

Vocabulary

🎧 **11** Read and listen. Look at the two families. Which words are used for men? For women? For both? Tell your partner.

Men: father, brother, grandfather, husband, son, father-in-law, brother-in-law, nephew, uncle

Women: mother, sister, grandmother, wife, daughter, mother-in-law, sister-in-law, niece, aunt

Both: parents, grandparents, cousin

Antonio Rivera's Family
1. grandparents
2. grandfather
3. grandmother
4. parents
5. father
6. mother
7. sister
8. brother — Antonio
9. wife

Shelly Novak's Family
13. mother-in-law
14. father-in-law
15. sister-in-law
16. brother-in-law
17. niece
18. nephew

14   Unit 2

Expansion
- Point to the grandfather on the family tree and say *grandfather*. Point to the grandmother and say *grandmother*.
- Then point to Antonio and his brother and say *grandson*. Write *grandson* on the board. Point to Antonio's sister and say *granddaughter*. Write *granddaughter* on the board.
- Have a volunteer add the words *granddaughter* and *grandson* to the correct columns in the graphic organizer on the board.

Culture Note
Vocabulary. Tell students that family trees show family relationships. Hold up the student book and point to the vertical (|) lines. Explain that these lines show parents and children. Point to horizontal (—) lines. Explain that these lines show married people.

Language Note
Vocabulary. Write on the board: *mother, father, grandfather, grandmother*. Then tell students that *mom* is an informal way to say mother. Ask students to say the informal words for the other family members (*dad, daddy, grandpa, grandma*, etc.). Have them write the words underneath the pictures on the page.

Listening

A 🎧 **12** Listen. A woman talks about pictures of her family. Who are the people in the pictures? Check (✓) the correct answers.

- ☑ her mother
- ☐ her sister
- ☐ her aunt
- ☐ her father
- ☐ her brothers
- ☑ her uncles

B 🎧 **13** Read and listen again. Write the missing words. Use the words in the box.

father's	my	Who	your

Mark: Is this ___your___ family?
1.

Elena: Yes, it is.

Mark: Wow, your family is big! Is she your mother?

Elena: Yeah. She's ___my___ mom.
2.

Mark: She's beautiful—like you!

Elena: Thank you!

Mark: ___Who___ are they? Are they your brothers?
3.

Elena: No, they're my ___father's___ brothers—my uncles.
4.

Mark: Really? How old are they?

Elena: Eduardo is 10, and Felipe is 12.

Mark: Wow . . . Your uncles are children!

Families 15

Listening

A Teaching Time: 10–15 min.

- **Warm-up:** Point to the pictures on pages 14 and 15. Ask students what the pictures show (a family). Tell them that they are going to listen to a woman talk about pictures of her family.
- Ask students to read the words in the box. Explain that the words in the box are key words. Ask students to listen for the key words and to make a check [✓] next to each one they hear when the audio plays.
- 🎧 Play Track 12 while students listen.
- 🎧 Play Track 12 again while students complete the task.
- PAIRS. Have students compare answers.
- Call on students to say answers. Correct as needed.

B Teaching Time: 15–20 min.

- 🎧 Play Track 13 while students listen and complete the task.
- Call on students to say answers. Correct as needed.
- Read the conversation aloud. Pause after each few words and have students repeat chorally.
- PAIRS. Have students role-play the conversation.
- **LIFE SKILLS TEST PREP 2** Go to Unit 2, Lesson 4 for more practice in giving and receiving compliments.

Language Note

Exercise B. Write *Wow!* and *Really!* on the board. Tell students that these words show that you are very surprised or very interested. Say each word and have students repeat chorally. Then say various sentences and ask students to respond with *Wow* or *Really*. For example, say: *My aunts are 10 years old!*

Option

Assign Unit 2 Supplementary Vocabulary Exercise on the Teacher's Resource Disk as homework or on the Student Persistence CD-ROM as self-access practice.

Multilevel Strategy

- **Pre-level:** Write a few lines of the conversation on the board but leave a blank where the family information is:

  A: *Is this your family?*
  B: *Yes, it is.*
  A: *Wow, your family is big! Who is that?*
  B: *It's my _____.*

  Have students role-play the conversation substituting new information in the blank. Have students practice with different family words.

- **At-level:** Have students role-play the completed conversation. Challenge them to use different family words and substitute some phrases (e.g., A: *It's my sister.* B: *She's a pretty girl.*).

- **Above-level:** Have students create a new conversation about family members using the conversation in the book as a model. Call on pairs to role-play in front of the class.

Unit 2 T-15

Grammar to Communicate 1

Possessive Adjectives

Teaching Time: 5–10 min.

- Introduce possessive adjectives by writing on the board: *I am a teacher. My book is blue.*
- Say: *I is a subject pronoun. It tells us who the sentence is about.*
- Say: *My is a possessive adjective. It shows belonging. The possessive adjective tells us who the book belongs to.*
- Have students study the chart. Say each example in the chart and have students repeat chorally.
- Explain that in the United States, people often call their pets *he* or *she* instead of *it*.
- Have students study the Look Box. Say sentences with *your* and singular and plural nouns about students and their belongings. For example: *Oliva, your book is green.*

A Teaching Time: 10–15 min.

- Read the example with the class.
- Have students complete the task.
- Call on students to say answers. Correct as needed.

Multilevel Strategy

- **Pre-level:** Review vocabulary for family relationships with the students. Read each sentence and have students say the correct word from the box. Then have them complete the task.
- **At-level, Above-level:** Pair students and have them take turns quizzing each other on the subject pronouns and possessive adjectives. One student says the subject pronoun and the other student says its corresponding possessive adjective and an example sentence.

B Teaching Time: 5–10 min.

- Read the example with the class. Tell students that the example can help them guess the missing words in the paragraph. Explain that "*My* name is Shelly" shows that Shelly is the person speaking in the paragraph. So, the answer to item 2 must also be *my*.
- Have students complete the task.
- Call on students to say answers. Correct as needed.

Grammar to Communicate 1

POSSESSIVE ADJECTIVES

Subject Pronoun	Possessive Adjective	Example Sentence
I	my	My husband is from Colombia.
you	your	Your cousin is tall.
he	his	His wife is friendly.
she	her	Her brother is good-looking.
it	its	Its name is Spot.
we	our	Our children are young.
they	their	Their grandmother is 90.

A Complete the sentences. Use the words in the box.

> **Look**
> Lucy, your mother is tall. (*Your* = 1 person)
> Ken and Lucy, your mother is tall. (*Your* = 2 or more people)

| ~~children~~ | daughter | grandson |
| cousin | grandfather | parents |

1. I'm their mother.
   They are my ___children.___
2. We're her parents.
   She is our ___daughter.___
3. He's our son.
   We are his ___parents.___
4. She is my grandmother.
   I'm her ___grandson.___
5. They are your cousins.
   You are their ___cousin.___
6. She is my granddaughter.
   I'm her ___grandfather.___

B Complete the sentences. Use *my, his, her, its, our,* or *their*.

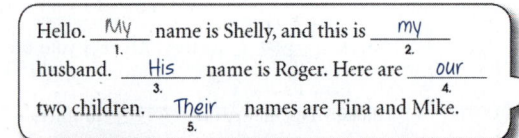

Hello. __My__(1) name is Shelly, and this is __my__(2) husband. __His__(3) name is Roger. Here are __our__(4) two children. __Their__(5) names are Tina and Mike.

Hi. I'm Antonio. I'm married to Marisol. __Our__(6) home is here in St. Paul, but Marisol isn't from here. __Her__(7) family is in Lima, Peru. It's just Marisol and me here in St. Paul — oh, yeah, and __our__(8) dog. __Its / His__(9) name is Oscar.

16 Unit 2

Grammar Notes

1. Possessive adjectives are used to show ownership or relationships.
2. Possessive adjectives come before nouns.
3. Possessive adjectives do not change forms (e.g., *my dog; my dogs*).
4. For more information on this grammar topic, see page 252.

Watch Out!

Exercise B. Students might confuse *its* and *it's*. To explain the difference between them, write on the board: ___ name is Spot. ___ a big dog. Ask: *Which sentence takes it's? Which sentence takes its?* If students don't know, complete the sentences. Then explain that *its* is a possessive adjective, and *it's = it is*.

T-16 Center Stage 2

C **14** Complete the conversation. Then listen and check your answers.

Stan: Hi. I'm _your_ new neighbor. _My_ name is Stan Sims.
　　　　　　 1. (you / your)　　　　　2. (I / My)

Betty: It's nice to meet you, Stan. _I'm_ Betty.
　　　　　　　　　　　　　　　　3. (I'm / My)

Stan: Nice to meet you, too. Um . . . are _you_ Josh's mother?
　　　　　　　　　　　　　　　　　　　 4. (you / your)

Betty: No, Ann and Jim Parr are _his_ parents. _Their_ apartment is next door.
　　　　　　　　　　　　　　　　 5. (he / his)　　　　 6. (They / Their)

Stan: Oh. Well, _he's_ very noisy! _His_ music is always so loud.
　　　　　　　　 7. (he's / his)　　　　　 8. (He / His)

Betty: Um . . . that's _our_ daughter's music. Is _it_ loud? Sorry!
　　　　　　　　　　 9. (we / our)　　　　　　　　　10. (it / Its)

Stan: Oh! Um . . . that's OK . . . It *is* nice music. Is _she_ a music student?
　　　　　　　　　　　　　　　　　　　　　　　　　 11. (she / her)

Betty: Yes, she is. _We're_ very proud of her.
　　　　　　　　 12. (We're / Our)

TIME to TALK

PAIRS. Look at the pictures of three famous families. Point ☞ at the people and make sentences about the family relationships. Answers will vary but the correct family relationships should be expressed.
Example:
A: Queen Elizabeth is his mother. Prince Charles is her son.

a. Prince Charles, Prince William, Queen Elizabeth

b. Ellis Marsalis, Wynton Marsalis

c. Homer, Marge, Lisa, Bart, Maggie

Families 17

C Teaching Time: 10–15 min.

- Explain what the words *next door*, *noisy*, and *proud* mean. For example, draw three houses on the board. Point to the first house. Then point to the second house, and explain that it is *next door* to the first house.
- Read the example with the class.
- Have students complete the task.
- 🎧 Play Track 14 while students check their answers. Pause the recording each time the answer is given.
- PAIRS. Have students role-play the completed conversation.

Watch Out!

Exercise C. Students may have trouble distinguishing between the similar sounds of *he's* and *his*. To help them, write on the board: *He's my friend.* = /i/ and *I'm his friend.* = /ɪ/

Say the sounds. Exaggerate the difference between the vowels. Have the class repeat chorally.

Option

Assign Unit 2 Supplementary Grammar to Communicate 1 Exercises on the Teacher's Resource Disk as homework or on the Student Persistence CD-ROM as self-access practice.

TIME to TALK

Teaching Time: 10–15 min.

- Have students turn back to page 14 OR quickly draw Antonio's and Shelly's family trees on the board. Point to Antonio and his wife and say: *Antonio is her husband. She is his wife.* Then ask students to tell their partner the relationships between the people in the family. Ask Student A to describe Antonio's family. Ask Student B to describe Shelly's family.
- Read the example with the class.
- Explain family relationships for the people in the pictures if students are not familiar with them. For example, *Homer is the father. Marge is the wife.*
- PAIRS. Have students write their sentences in their notebooks.
- Walk around and help as needed.
- Have pairs compare their sentences. Then call on a few pairs to read their sentences out loud. Write corrected sentences on the board and have the class repeat chorally.

Unit 2　T-17

Grammar to Communicate 2

Possessive Nouns

Teaching Time: 5–10 min.

- Have students study the chart.
- Introduce possessive nouns by writing on the board: *My brother's school. My brothers' school.*
- Circle *'s* in the first sentence. Say: *We use an apostrophe before the s for one person or thing.*
- Circle *s'* in the second sentence. Say: *We usually use an apostrophe after the s for many people or things.*
- Write *child's room* and *children's room* on the board. Circle the *'s* in both words. Say: *Children has no s at the end, so the apostrophe goes before the s in children's.*
- Say each example in the chart and have students repeat chorally.

A Teaching Time: 5–10 min.

- Read the example with the class. Remind students that vertical lines on a family tree show parents and children and horizontal lines show married people.
- Have students complete the task.
- Call on students to say answers. Correct as needed.
- **LIFE SKILLS TEST PREP 2** Go to Unit 2, Lesson 1 for more practice in identifying family members and family relationships.

B Teaching Time: 5–10 min.

- Have students write their sentences.
- Call on a few students to write their sentences on the board. Write corrections on the board as needed.
- GROUPS. Ask groups to read their lists of names for the class. Write the most common names on the board.

Multilevel Strategy

- **Pre-level:** Write the following on the board: *My father's name is ___. My children's names are ___. My cousin's name is ___. My sister's (brother's) name is ___.* Have students choose two of the sentences on the board, fill in the blanks, and use them to talk about their family.

T-18 Center Stage 2

Grammar to Communicate 2

POSSESSIVE NOUNS

Singular		Plural	
My brother's	school is across the street.	My brothers'	school is in the next town.
Angelica's	parents are in Mexico.	Her parents'	names are César and Inez.
The child's	room is clean.	The children's	room is clean.

A Look at Vera's family tree. Then complete the sentences with the names of her relatives.

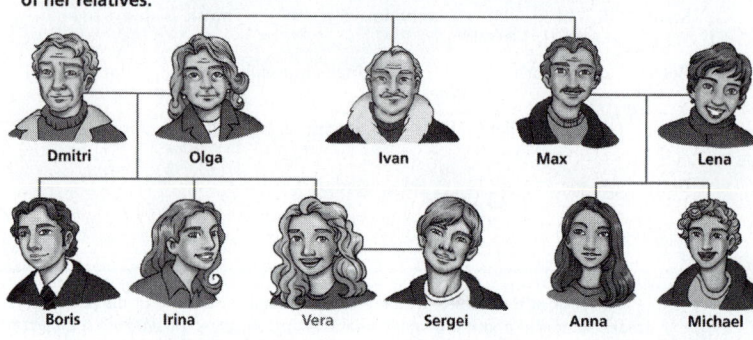

Dmitri — Olga — Ivan — Max — Lena

Boris — Irina — Vera — Sergei — Anna — Michael

1. Vera's parents' names are __Olga__ and __Dmitri__.
2. Her husband's name is __Sergei__.
3. Her sister's name is __Irina__.
4. Her uncles' names are __Ivan__ and __Max__.
5. Her cousins' names are __Anna__ and __Michael__.

B Write sentences about your family on a piece of paper. *Answers will vary.*

Example:
My mother's name is Celia.

GROUPS. Read your sentences to the other people in your group. Are any of the names in your families the same? Make a list.

C Complete the sentences with *'s* or *'*.

1. My cousins__'__ last names are Yu and Li.
2. My cousin__'s__ last name is Pang.
3. The children__'s__ aunt and uncle are old.
4. My sister__s'__ husbands are nice.
5. Uncle John__'s__ father-in-law isn't talkative.

18 Unit 2

C Teaching Time: 5–10 min.

- Read the examples with the class.
- Have students identify the subject of each sentence. Then have them indicate whether the subject is singular, plural or irregular. Remind students that for singular and irregular nouns *s* goes after the apostrophe and in plural nouns *s* goes before the apostrophe.
- Have students complete the task.
- Call on students to say answers. Correct as needed.

Grammar Notes

1. Possessive nouns (ending in *'s*, *'*, or *s'*) are used to show belonging.
2. Possessive nouns come before nouns.
3. Possessive nouns have different forms for singular and plural nouns.
4. For more information on this grammar topic, see page 252.

Teaching Tip

To avoid overlooking errors in the use of the possessive *'s*, ask students to write their answers on the board or collect their notebooks to check answers.

D Rewrite the sentences. Change the underlined words to a possessive adjective or pronoun.

1. My sister-in-law's name is Fay.
   Her name is Fay.
2. My sister-in-law is from Taiwan.
   She is from Taiwan.
3. My nephew is a teacher.
   He is a teacher.
4. My nephew's job is good.
   His job is good.
5. His children's school is small.
   Their school is small.
6. His children are students.
   They are students.
7. Their dog is very big.
   It / He / She is very big.
8. Their dog's name is Bingo.
   Its / His / Her name is Bingo.

TIME to TALK

ON YOUR OWN. Draw your family tree on a separate piece of paper. Write your name on the tree, but do not write the names of your family members. Then give your family tree to your partner. Answers will vary.

PAIRS. Tell your partner the names of your family members. Then listen and write the names of your partner's family members in the correct places on the tree.

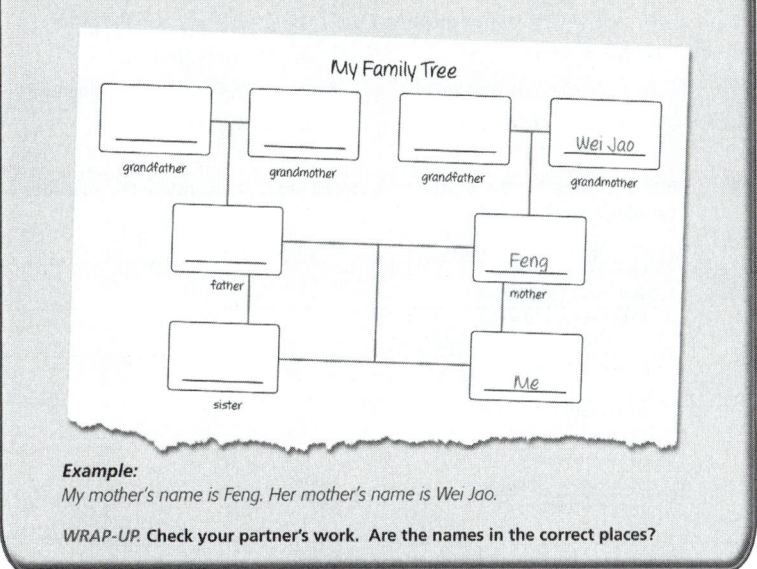

My Family Tree

- grandfather — grandmother | grandfather — Wei Jao (grandmother)
- father — Feng (mother)
- sister | Me

Example:
My mother's name is Feng. Her mother's name is Wei Jao.

WRAP-UP. Check your partner's work. Are the names in the correct places?

Families 19

D Teaching Time: 5–10 min.
- Read the examples with the class.
- Call on students to come to the board and write the sentences. Correct as needed.

Multilevel Strategy
- **At-level, Above-level:** Call on only at-level and above-level students to write the sentences on the board.
- **Pre-level:** Have students copy the sentences from the board.

Watch Out!

Exercise D. Many students need practice in the different pronunciations of the final –s. Have students look at the pronunciation chart on page 263. Say the sounds and have students repeat chorally. Then ask students for more examples (such as the names of students in the class) for each sound.

Option

Assign Unit 2 Supplementary Grammar to Communicate 2 Exercises on the Teacher's Resource Disk as homework or on the Student Persistence CD-ROM as self-access practice.

TIME to TALK

Teaching Time: 15–20 min.
- Review family trees by looking at the example.
- PAIRS. Have students complete the task on pieces of paper.
- Walk around and help as needed.
- Display the students' family trees on the wall of the classroom. Encourage students to walk around and look at each other's family trees.

Unit 2 T-19

Grammar to Communicate 3

Be: Information Questions

Teaching Time: 5–10 min.

- Have students study the chart.
- Say each example in the chart and have students repeat chorally.
- Tell students that in information questions, *be* goes after the *wh*-word.
- Explain that *where* asks about a place, *who* asks about a person, *when* asks about time, *what* asks about things. You say *How are you?* to ask people how they feel.
- For each *wh*-word, ask additional questions with different verbs/subjects and have students answer. For example: *[Student's name], where are you?* (in English class).
- Have students study the Look Box. Explain that *How old* and *How tall* ask for information about a person's age and height.
- Start a chain game. Ask Student A: *How old are you?* Student A answers and asks Student B another *wh*-question. Student B continues the chain.

A Teaching Time: 10–15 min.

- Read the example. Ask students to look at the response in each item and say whether it is about a location, person, thing, etc.
- Have students complete the task.
- Call on students to say answers. Correct as needed.

B Teaching Time: 10–15 min.

- Read the example with the class.
- Have students complete the task.
- PAIRS. Have students take turns asking and answering the questions.
- Call on pairs to role-play their conversations for the class. Correct as needed.
- **LIFE SKILLS TEST PREP 2** Go to Unit 2, Lesson 2 for more practice in giving basic information about family members.

Grammar to Communicate 3

BE: INFORMATION QUESTIONS

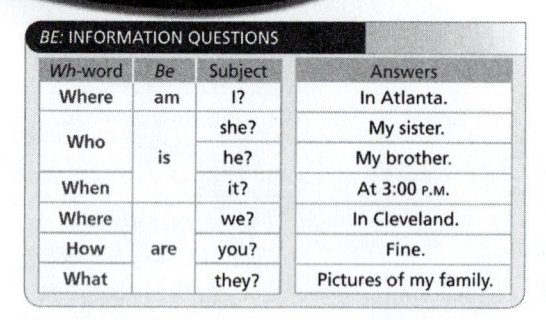

Wh-word	Be	Subject	Answers
Where	am	I?	In Atlanta.
Who	is	she?	My sister.
		he?	My brother.
When		it?	At 3:00 P.M.
Where		we?	In Cleveland.
How	are	you?	Fine.
What		they?	Pictures of my family.

Look
Use *how* + adjective to ask questions:
How old are you? 18.
How tall are you? 5 feet, 3 inches.

A Complete the questions. Use *Who, What, Where, How, How old,* or *How tall*.

1. A: __What__ is your name?
   B: It's Chris.
2. A: __How old__ are your children?
   B: Six and ten.
3. A: __Where__ is your wife from?
   B: South Africa.
4. A: __How tall__ is your son?
   B: He's 4 feet 6 inches tall.
5. A: __How__ is your family?
   B: Fine, thanks.
6. A: __What__ is your telephone number?
   B: 555-3639.
7. A: __Who__ is in the picture?
   B: My wife's brother.
8. A: __Where__ is your daughter?
   B: She's at school.

B Write questions. Put the words in the correct order. Then answer the questions with true information.

1. __What is your last name?__ __Answers will vary.__
   (last / is / your / what / name)
2. __How old is your friend?__ _____
   (friend / old / your / how / is)
3. __Where is your teacher from?__ _____
   (is / your / from / teacher / where)
4. __Where is your family's home?__ _____
   (where / family's / is / your / home)
5. __How tall are you?__ _____
   (tall / you / are / how)
6. __When is your birthday?__ _____
   (your / when / birthday / is)

PAIRS. Ask and answer the questions above.

Unit 2

Multilevel Strategy

- **Pre-level:** Group all pre-level students to complete the task. Dictate complete questions to students and have them write the answers. After checking answers, have pairs take turns asking and answering the questions.
- **Above-level:** For the pair activity, have students ask three additional questions about their partner's family or friends.

Grammar Notes

1. In information questions, *is* or *are* comes after the *wh*-word.
2. In conversations, the contracted form of *is* (*'s*) is common after *wh*-words. For example, *What's your name?*
3. For more information on this grammar topic, see page 252.

Language Note

Exercises A and B. *Where* questions with *be* often end in *from*. Write: *Where are you from? —The United States* on the board. Underline *Where* and *from*. Have students ask and answer the question with true information about themselves.

T-20 Center Stage 2

C 🎧 15 Read the answers. Then write questions. Use *Who, What, Where, How, How old,* or *How tall.* Then listen and check your answers.

1. **A:** Where are your parents from?
   B: My parents are from South Korea.
2. **A:** How is your family?
   B: My family's fine, thanks.
3. **A:** How old are you?
   B: I'm 19.
4. **A:** Who's Nina?
   B: Nina is my aunt—my mother's sister.
5. **A:** Where are the children?
   B: The children are at my mother's house.
6. **A:** How tall is your brother?
   B: My brother is 6 feet tall.
7. **A:** What are your uncles' names?
   B: My uncles' names are Greg and Norman.

TIME to TALK

GROUPS. Bring photographs of your family and friends to class. Ask and answer questions about the pictures.
Answers will vary.
Example:
A: Who is she?
B: She's my sister.
A: What's her name?
B: Lisa.
A: Is she married?
B: No, she's single.

Families 21

C Teaching Time: 10–15 min.

- Read the example with the class. Point out that when you answer a *Where . . . from* question with a complete sentence, you must say *from* in the answer.
- Have students complete the task.
- 🎧 Play Track 15 while students check their answers.
- Call on students to say answers. Correct as needed.
- PAIRS. Have students practice asking and answering the questions.

Multilevel Strategy

- **Pre-level:** Provide students with the appropriate *wh*-word for each item: (2) *How*; (3) *How old*; (4) *Who*; (5) *Where*; (6) *How tall*; and (7) *What.*
- **Above-level:** Have students ask and answer the questions with true information about themselves. Tell them they can make up answers if they can't answer with true information. Call on a few pairs to role-play their conversations for the class.

Culture Notes

- **Exercise B.** In the United States, it is usually not polite to ask middle-aged or elderly people how old they are.
- In the United States, height is measured in feet and inches. 3.28 feet = 1 meter.
- **LIFE SKILLS TEST PREP** 2 Go to Unit 7, Lesson 2 for more practice in understanding the American system of measuring dimensions.

Option

Assign Unit 2 Supplementary Grammar to Communicate 3 Exercises on the Teacher's Resource Disk as homework or on the Student Persistence CD-ROM as self-access practice.

TIME to TALK

Teaching Time: 10–15 min.

- The class before you assign this task, ask students to bring photos of family and friends to class. Bring in photos of your own family and/or pictures from magazines that students can use to "create" a family or friends.
- Ask two students to role-play the example.
- To model the activity further, ask a student to show you his or her photo. Ask and answer questions about the photo.
- GROUPS. Have students complete the task.
- Walk around and help as needed.

Expansion Have each student borrow a photo they have learned about in their group. Then have them ask and answer questions about the photo with a new group. To model the activity, hold up a photo belonging to one of your students. Encourage the class to ask you *wh-* questions about the photo.

Unit 2

Review and Challenge

Grammar

Teaching Time: 5–10 min.

- Read the example with the class.
- Have students complete the task.
- 🎧 Play Track 16 while students check their answers. Pause the recording each time an answer is given.
- **LIFE SKILLS TEST PREP 2** Go to Unit 2, Lesson 3 for more practice in describing physical characteristics of family and friends.

Dictation

Teaching Time: 5–10 min.

- 🎧 Play Track 17 while students listen and write what they hear.
- 🎧 Play Track 17 again while students check their answers.
- Call on students to write answers on the board.
- 🎧 Play Track 17 again and correct the sentences on the board.

Multilevel Strategy

- **Pre-level:** Give students a worksheet with some of the words from the dictation already provided.

Speaking

Teaching Time: 10–15 min.

- In the class session before you assign this task, ask each student to bring a photo of a famous person to the next class. Have students write the names of the people on the back of the photos. Bring in photos of famous people yourself to distribute if necessary.
- Role-play the example conversation with a student.
- Tell students that if they do not know an answer they can say: *I don't know.* If they are not sure, they can say: *I think so* or *I don't think so.*
- GROUPS. Have students complete the task.
- Walk around and help as needed.
- Ask students to present the famous people they learned about to the class.

Review and Challenge

Grammar

🎧 **16** Complete the conversation. Use the words in the box. Then listen and check your answers. (Be careful! There are two extra words.)

boy's	her	she's	their
boys'	~~his~~	sister's	they're

Andrea: This is a nice picture. Who's in it?

Leona: Oh, that's my son, Paul. And here's a picture of ___his___ children—my two grandsons and my granddaughter.
                                                    1.

Andrea: What are ___their___ names?
                      2.

Leona: The ___boys'___ names are Bill and Tommy. Their ___sister's___ name is Alicia.
                3.   4.

Andrea: They're cute! How old is Alicia?

Leona: Oh, ___she's___ seven years old. And here she is in a picture with ___her___ mother.
              5.   6.

Andrea: Oh, so that's your daughter-in-law. She's pretty.

Leona: Yes, she is.

Dictation

🎧 **17** Listen. You will hear five sentences. Write them on a piece of paper. *See the audioscript on page 277 for the sentences.*

Speaking

GROUPS. Bring in magazines or newspapers with photos of famous people. Ask your classmates questions about the people.
Answers will vary.
Example:
A: Who is he?
B: He's Will Smith. He's an American actor.
A: He's handsome! Is he married?
B: I think so.

22 Unit 2

Option

Have students bring photos of famous people from their native countries. Put them in groups with people from other countries to make the discussion more interesting.

Language Note

Exercise B. Write on the board: *1. mother-in-law; mothers-in-law 2. daughter-in-law; daughters-in-law.* Point out that to form the plural, add –s to the family word.

Center Stage 2

Listening

A 🎧 **18** Listen. A TV reporter talks about families in Italy and Saudi Arabia. For each sentence, write *T* (true) or *F* (false).

__F__ 1. Silvia's parents are the same age.
__F__ 2. The age of marriage for most Italian women is 20.
__T__ 3. Silvia's family is small.
__F__ 4. Saleh's family is very different from other Saudi families.
__T__ 5. There are many people in Saleh's house.
__F__ 6. All of Saleh's sisters are married.

B 🎧 **19** Listen again. Check (✓) all of the people that live in Saleh's house.

- ☑ his mother and father
- ☑ his married brothers
- ☐ his married sisters
- ☑ his grandparents
- ☑ his sisters-in-law
- ☐ his brothers-in-law
- ☑ his single sisters
- ☑ his brothers' children
- ☐ his sisters' children

TIME to TALK

ON YOUR OWN. In your opinion, are the sentences true or false? Write *T* (true) or *F* (false). *Answers will vary.*

____ 1. Small families are very common.
____ 2. Girls are close to their mothers.
____ 3. Boys are close to their fathers.
____ 4. Good friends are the same as family.
____ 5. For women, it is good to get married at 35.
____ 6. For men, it is good to get married at 35.
____ 7. Mothers-in-law and daughters-in-law are usually not friends.

GROUPS. Talk about the sentences. Explain your answers to the people in your group.

Families 23

Option

Assign Unit 2 Supplementary Review and Challenge Exercises on the Teacher's Resource Disk as homework or on the Student Persistence CD-ROM as self-access practice.

Listening

A Teaching Time: 5–10 min.

- **Warm-up:** Tell students that they are going to listen to a program called "World Beat." Ask students what they think the program will be about (People around the world).
- Have students read through the True / False statements before they listen.
- 🎧 Play Track 18 while students listen.
- 🎧 Play Track 18 again while students listen and write their answers.
- 🎧 Play Track 18 again while students check their answers.
- Read each statement and call on students to say whether it is true or false.

Multilevel Strategy

- **At-level, Above-level:** When checking answers, challenge students to correct the false sentences about Silvia and Saleh.

B Teaching Time: 5–10 min.

- Ask students to read through the answer choices before they listen.
- 🎧 Play Track 19 while students listen and complete the task.
- Call on a student to list all the choices he or she checked. Ask other students if they agree. Correct as needed.

Expansion Start a discussion about the information in the listening. Ask students if they can think of any similarities and differences between families in Italy, Saudi Arabia, and the United States.

TIME to TALK

Teaching Time: 5–10 min.

- GROUPS. Have students read the sentences. Have them discuss any new words and look them up in their dictionaries. Walk around and help as needed.
- Have groups complete the task. Walk around and help as needed. Encourage students to discuss each sentence before marking *T* or *F*.
- Ask a student from each group to tell their group's opinion about one of the sentences. Ask the other groups if they agree.

Unit 2 T-23

Reading and Writing

Reading

Teaching Time: 10–15 min.

- Hold up the student book page and point to the form (or point to the form on a transparency). Tell students that this is a form people write on to give information about themselves. Ask what people use forms like this for (the government, taxes, a job, etc.).
- Have students read the form. Ask them questions about the different parts of the form and the more difficult vocabulary. For example, ask: *Where do you write your name? What does* employment *mean?*
- Have students complete the task.
- Call on students to say answers. Correct as needed.
- Read the form out loud. Stop to define any words students still don't understand.
- **LIFE SKILLS TEST PREP 2** Go to Unit 11, Lesson 2 for more practice in filling out a simple job application form.

Reading and Writing

Reading

Look at the form. Then answer the questions.

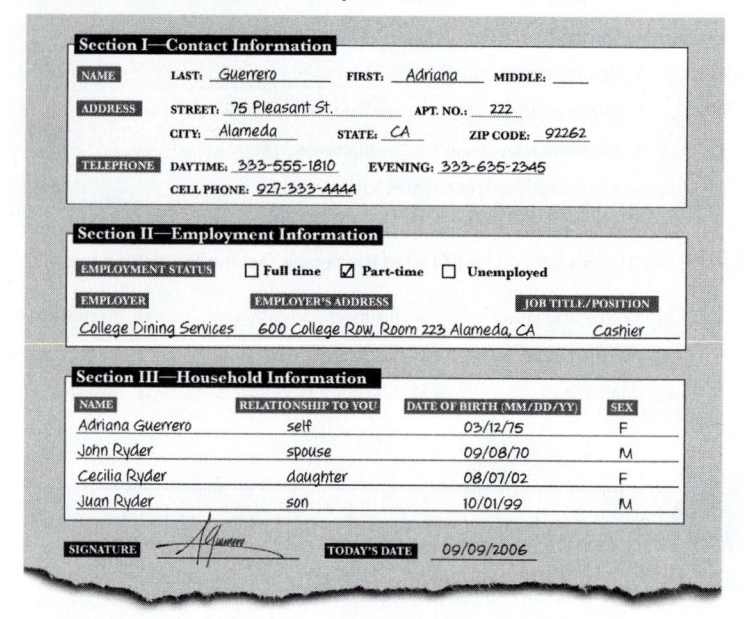

Section I—Contact Information
- NAME: LAST: Guerrero FIRST: Adriana MIDDLE: ___
- ADDRESS: STREET: 75 Pleasant St. APT. NO.: 222
  CITY: Alameda STATE: CA ZIP CODE: 92262
- TELEPHONE: DAYTIME: 333-555-1810 EVENING: 333-635-2345
  CELL PHONE: 927-333-4444

Section II—Employment Information
- EMPLOYMENT STATUS: ☐ Full time ☑ Part-time ☐ Unemployed
- EMPLOYER: College Dining Services
- EMPLOYER'S ADDRESS: 600 College Row, Room 223 Alameda, CA
- JOB TITLE/POSITION: Cashier

Section III—Household Information

NAME	RELATIONSHIP TO YOU	DATE OF BIRTH (MM/DD/YY)	SEX
Adriana Guerrero	self	03/12/75	F
John Ryder	spouse	09/08/70	M
Cecilia Ryder	daughter	08/07/02	F
Juan Ryder	son	10/01/99	M

SIGNATURE: *A. Guerrero* TODAY'S DATE: 09/09/2006

1. You need to talk to Adriana. It's 7:00 P.M. What number do you call?
   a. 333-555-1810 b. 333-927-4444 **(c.)** 333-635-2345
2. What does *unemployed* mean?
   (a.) not working b. working full time c. working part-time
3. What is Adriana's position?
   a. College Dining Services b. part-time **(c.)** cashier
4. In this form, who is *self*?
   (a.) Adriana b. Adriana's son c. Adriana's brother
5. What does *spouse* mean?
   a. man or woman b. brother or sister **(c.)** husband or wife
6. What is Adriana's son's date of birth?
   a. January 10, 1999 b. August 7, 2002 **(c.)** October 1, 1999

Unit 2

Option

Before class, make a copy of page 24 as a transparency to use with an overhead projector.

Language Note

Exercise A. Tell students that some of the words in this reading are mainly used in official forms. We do not usually use them when we talk. Examples include *employment status, job title / position, household information, spouse,* and *sex* (male or female).

Center Stage 2

Prewriting

Make a list of questions to ask a classmate. Use the words in the box.

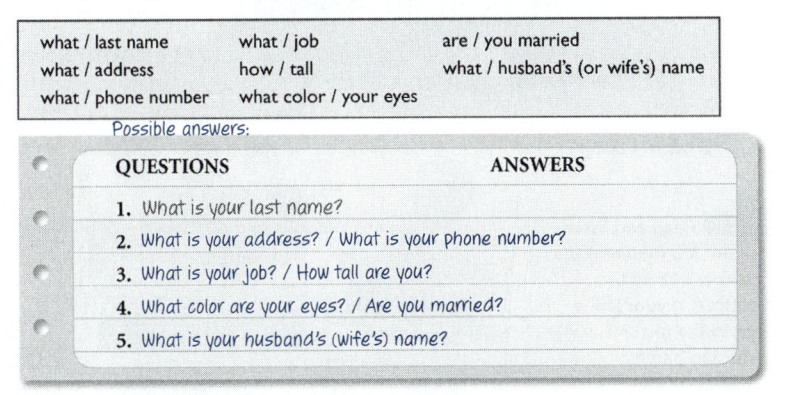

what / last name	what / job	are / you married
what / address	how / tall	what / husband's (or wife's) name
what / phone number	what color / your eyes	

Possible answers:

QUESTIONS	ANSWERS
1. What is your last name?	
2. What is your address? / What is your phone number?	
3. What is your job? / How tall are you?	
4. What color are your eyes? / Are you married?	
5. What is your husband's (wife's) name?	

PAIRS. Ask and answer the questions above. Write your classmate's answers.

Writing

Read the paragraph. Then write about your classmate. Use the information from your list above. Answers will vary.

> My classmate's name is Adriana Guerrero. Her address is 75 Pleasant Street. Her phone number is 333-327-1810. Adriana is a part-time cashier at College Dining Services on College Row. She is 5 feet 4 inches tall. Her eyes are green. She is married, and she is a mother. Her husband's name is John Ryder. Their children's names are Cecilia and Juan.

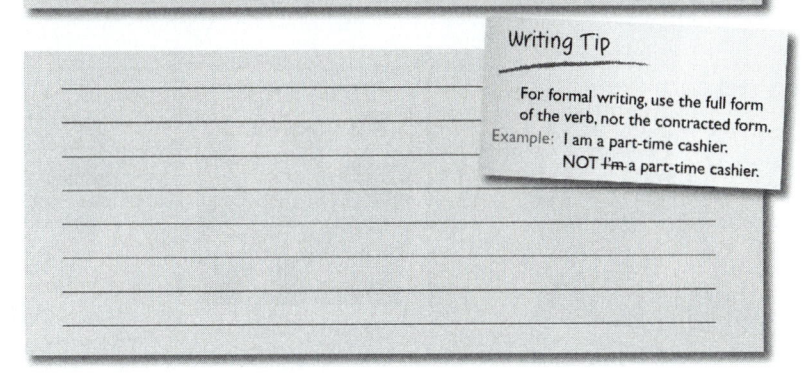

Writing Tip
For formal writing, use the full form of the verb, not the contracted form.
Example: I am a part-time cashier.
NOT I'm a part-time cashier.

Families 25

Culture Note

Exercise A. Write today's date on the board. For example: *12/12/07*. Explain that in the United States, people write dates in the order of month, day, year, usually with only the last two numbers of the year.

Prewriting

Teaching Time: 15–20 min.

- To review information questions with *be*, write a few examples of *wh-*questions on the board. Have students repeat chorally.
- Read the example with the class.
- Have students complete the task.
- PAIRS. Have students practice asking and answering questions. Walk around and help as needed.
- **LIFE SKILLS TEST PREP 2** Go to Unit 1, Lesson 2 for more practice in asking and answering questions about personal information.

Writing

Teaching Time: 20–30 min.

- Read the Writing Tip out loud. Ask students for more examples of full forms of verbs and write them on the board.
- Have students complete the task. Walk around and help as needed. Encourage students to refer to the model as they work.
- Call on volunteers to read their paragraphs. Correct as needed.

Multilevel Strategy

- **Pre-level:** While students are completing the prewriting task, copy the paragraph on the board. Underline the information that students should substitute in their paragraphs. Have students copy the paragraph and substitute the underlined parts with information they recorded in Prewriting.
- **Above-level:** Challenge students with the task by having them write additional information about their classmate. Prompt them with suggestions if necessary (e.g., *What is her husband's job? How old are his children?*).

Unit 2 T-25

Unit 3
Jobs

Learning Goals
- Learn job words
- Learn about *a* and *an* with singular count nouns; adjectives and noun word order; and *a / an / ø* and *the*
- Listen to conversations about jobs
- Read an employee evaluation form and write an employee evaluation
- Talk about jobs

Learner Persistence

Create a location where students can find assignments and homework if they are absent. This will help students not to fall behind when they miss class, and encourage them to return to class up-to-date with the rest of the group.

Warm-up

Teaching Time: 3–5 min.

Tell students that a job is work that someone does for money. Ask students to name some jobs. Record their answers on the board.

Vocabulary

Teaching Time: 15–20 min.

- Have students study the pictures and captions. Explain unfamiliar vocabulary. For example, an *interpreter* is a person who listens to words in one language and then says the words in a different language. An *engineer* plans or builds things like roads and machines.
- 🎧 Play Track 20 while students read and listen.
- Read each word aloud and have students repeat chorally.
- Have students complete the activity. Provide unfamiliar job vocabulary if necessary.

Expansion Have volunteers act out jobs, including the ones in the pictures, their own jobs, or other jobs they know. For example, for a mechanic, students might act out driving, getting out of a car, and looking under the hood.

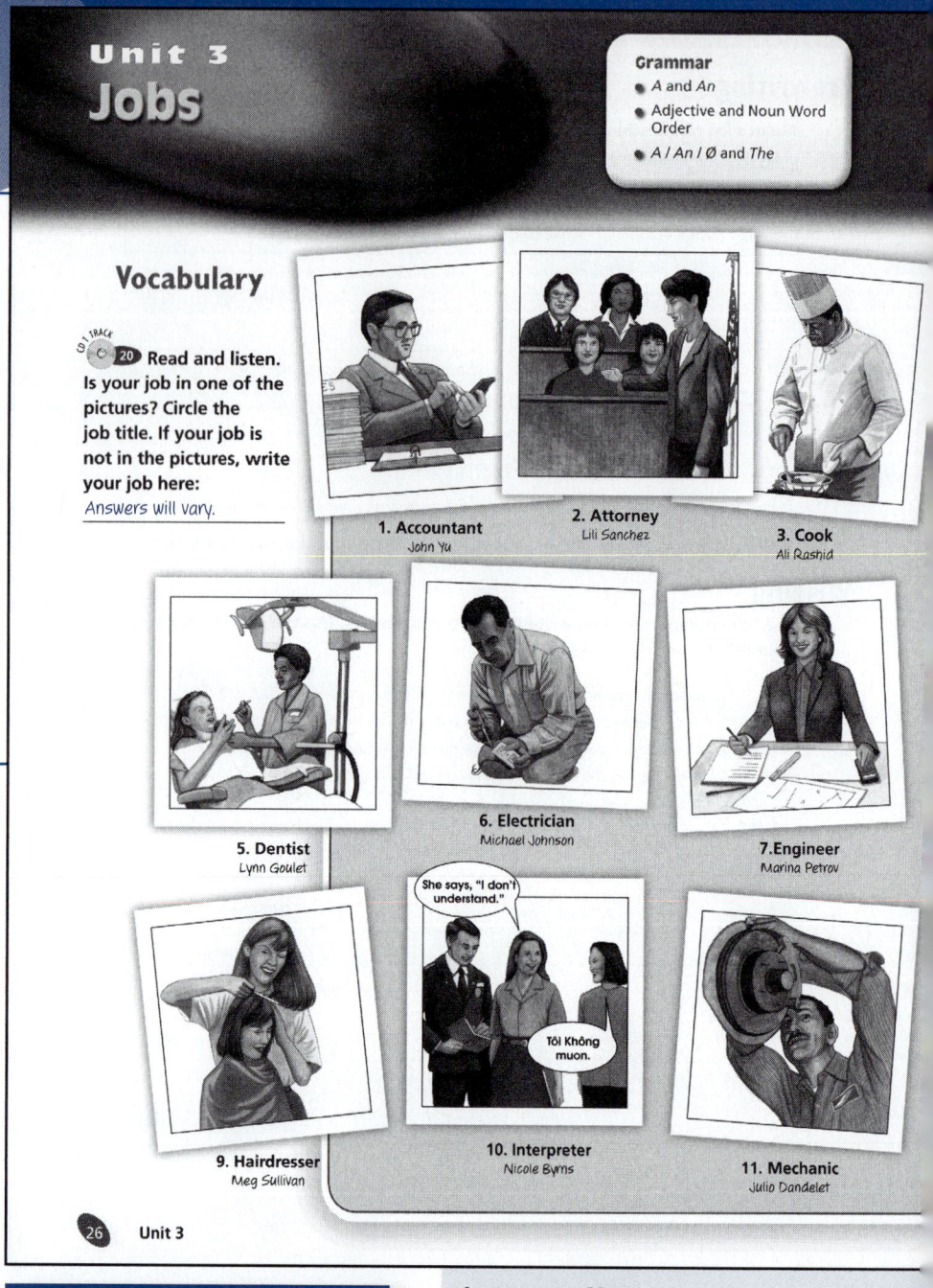

Unit 3
Jobs

Grammar
- *A* and *An*
- Adjective and Noun Word Order
- *A / An / Ø* and *The*

Vocabulary

🎧 **20** Read and listen. Is your job in one of the pictures? Circle the job title. If your job is not in the pictures, write your job here:
Answers will vary.

1. Accountant — John Yu
2. Attorney — Lili Sanchez
3. Cook — Ali Rashid
5. Dentist — Lynn Goulet
6. Electrician — Michael Johnson
7. Engineer — Marina Petrov
9. Hairdresser — Meg Sullivan
10. Interpreter — Nicole Byrns
11. Mechanic — Julio Dandelet

26 Unit 3

Multilevel Strategy

- **All-levels:** Have pre-level students take turns acting out words shown in the pictures. Have at-level and above-level students guess the words being acted out by the pre-level students.

Language Note

- **Vocabulary.** Tell students that most jobs in English are the same word for men and women.
- Point to the pictures of the waiter and waitress. Explain that this job has different words for a man and a woman.
- Write on the board *actor* and *actress*. Tell students that this is another job with different words for a man and a woman. Explain that an actor is a man on television or in a movie or play and an actress is a woman on television or in a movie or play.

T-26 Center Stage 2

Listening

A 🎧 **21** Listen. Bill and Nick are talking about their jobs. Write their jobs.

Nick is a ___cook___.   Bill is an ___electrician___.

B 🎧 **22** Read and listen again. Write the missing words. Use the words in the box.

| a | nice | an | ~~new~~ | the |

Bill: Hey, Nick, what's up? How are you?

Nick: I'm great. I have a ___new___ job.
                        1.

Bill: Really?

Nick: Yeah, I'm ___a___ cook at Rico's on First
                 2.
Street.

Bill: Oh, my friend Andy is a cook there too.

Nick: Oh yeah, Andy... he's ___the___ breakfast
                                3.
cook. I'm the lunch cook.

Bill: So, how is it?

Nick: Well, it isn't ___an___ easy job, but it's
                      4.
interesting. The restaurant is always busy.

Bill: Is the pay good?

Nick: It's not bad. And the boss is a ___nice___ guy.
                                        5.

Jobs 27

Listening

A   **Teaching Time: 5–10 min.**

- **Warm-up:** Have students look at the pictures on pages 26 and 27. Say people's names and have students say each person's job.
- Ask students to read through the statements before they listen.
- 🎧 Play Track 21 while students listen.
- 🎧 Play Track 21 again while students complete the task.
- 🎧 Play Track 21 again while students check their answers. Pause the recording each time an answer is given.

B   **Teaching Time: 15–20 min.**

- Have students read through the answer choices before they listen.
- 🎧 Play Track 22 while students listen and write the words they hear.
- 🎧 Play Track 22 again while students check their answers.
- Call on students to say answers. Correct as needed.
- Read the conversation aloud. Pause after each few words and have students repeat chorally.
- PAIRS. Ask students to role-play the conversation.

Language Notes

- **Exercise B.** Tell students that *What's up?* is an informal way to ask a person what is happening.
- Explain that *yeah* is an informal way to say *yes*.

Option

Assign Unit 3 Supplementary Vocabulary Exercise on the Teacher's Resource Disk as homework or on the Student Persistence CD-ROM as self-access practice.

Multilevel Strategy

- **Pre-level:** Write a few lines of the conversation on the board but leave blanks where the name and job information is:
  A: Hey, __, what's up? How are you?
  B: I'm great. I have a new job.
  A: Really?
  B: Yeah, I'm a ___ at ___.
  Have students role-play the conversation substituting new information in the blanks. Have students switch roles and practice with different job words.
- **At level:** Have students role-play the completed conversation. Challenge them to use different job words and substitute some phrases.
- **Above-level:** Have students create a new conversation about real or imaginary jobs using the conversation in the book as a model. Call on pairs to role-play in front of the class.

Unit 3   T-27

Grammar to Communicate 1

A and An with Singular Count Nouns

Teaching Time: 5–10 min.

- Remind students that a singular noun is one of something.
- Write on the board *a* and *an*. Tell students that *a* and *an* go before singular nouns.
- Have students study the chart and the Look Box.
- Say: *An* goes before a noun that starts with a vowel. The vowels in English are a, e, i, o, and u. Write these vowels on the board.
- Say: *A* goes before a noun that starts with a consonant. Consonants are letters that aren't vowels.
- Say: Use *a* and *an* to talk about one person or thing in general, not a specific person or thing.
- Read the phrases in the chart and have students repeat chorally.

A Teaching Time: 5–10 min.

- Have students identify the jobs shown in the pictures.
- Read the first example with the class.
- Have students complete the first task.
- Call on students to say answers. Correct as needed.
- Read the second example with the class.
- Have students identify the people on pages 26–27 and complete the task.
- Call on students to say answers. Correct as needed.

B Teaching Time: 5–10 min.

- Have students study the Look Box. Tell students that *a* and *an* can't be used with plural nouns.
- Explain that *unscramble* means to put in the correct order. Tell students to organize the letters to make words.
- Read the example with the class.
- Have students complete the task.
- Call on students to write answers on the board. Write corrections on the board as needed.
- **LIFE SKILLS TEST PREP 2** Go to Unit 1, Lesson 4 for more practice in learning names for school employees.

T-28 Center Stage 2

Grammar to Communicate 1

A AND AN WITH SINGULAR COUNT NOUNS

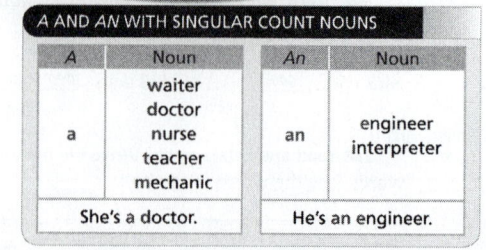

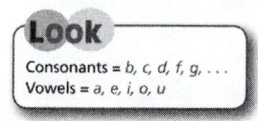

A	Noun	An	Noun
a	waiter doctor nurse teacher mechanic	an	engineer interpreter
She's a doctor.		He's an engineer.	

Look
Consonants = b, c, d, f, g, ...
Vowels = a, e, i, o, u

A Look at the pictures. Complete the sentences with *a* or *an*.

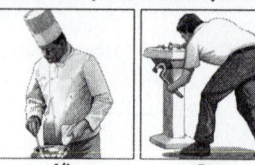

Ali   Pete   Maria   Meg   Marina

1. Ali Rashid is __a__ cook.
2. Pete Murphy is __a__ plumber.
3. Maria Recine is __a__ waitress.
4. Meg Sullivan is __a__ hairdresser.
5. Marina Petrov is __an__ engineer.

Now make sentences about the people's jobs on pages 26–27.

6. Lynn Goulet __is a dentist.__
7. John Yu __is an accountant.__
8. Nicole Byrns __is an interpreter.__
9. Michael Johnson __is an electrician.__
10. Mónica Gómez __is a nurse.__
11. Mario Tecce __is a waiter.__

B Unscramble the words. Then write sentences with the words.

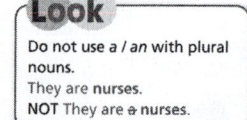

Look
Do not use *a / an* with plural nouns.
They are nurses.
NOT They are a nurses.

1. ratheec __teacher__   You __are a teacher.__
2. nudetts __student__   I __am a student.__
3. suern __nurse__   She __is a nurse.__
4. yettrano __attorney__   He __is an attorney.__
5. oock __cook__   You __are a cook.__

Unit 3

Grammar Notes

1. *A* and *an* go before singular nouns.
2. Use *a* and *an* to talk about one person or thing in general, but not a specific person or thing.
3. Use *a* before singular count nouns that begin with a consonant.
4. Use *an* if the first letter of a singular count noun is a vowel.
5. For more information on this grammar topic, see page 253.

C Make the sentences in Exercise B plural.

1. You are teachers.
2. We are students.
3. They are nurses.
4. They are attorneys.
5. You are cooks.

D Write sentences about the jobs of people you know. *Answers will vary.*

1. My friend Danny is an accountant.
2. My brothers are mechanics.
3. _____
4. _____
5. _____
6. _____
7. _____
8. _____

TIME to TALK

ON YOUR OWN. Find out the jobs of 10 classmates. Ask "What do you do?"
Answers will vary.

Example:
Carlos: Mariela, what do you do?
Mariela: I'm a homemaker. What do you do?

GROUPS. Now play a memory game. Say the jobs of your classmates.

Example:
I'm a cab driver. Mariela is a homemaker. Carlos and Yong are cooks.

Jobs 29

C Teaching Time: 5–10 min.

- Remind students not to use *a* and *an* with plural nouns.
- Read the example with the class.
- Have students complete the task.
- PAIRS. Have students compare answers.
- Call on students to write answers on the board. Write corrections on the board as needed.

D Teaching Time: 10–15 min.

- Read the examples with the class.
- Have students complete the task.
- Walk around and help as needed.
- PAIRS. Have students take turns reading their sentences to each other.
- Call on volunteers to say a sentence about the job of someone they know.

Multilevel Strategy

- **Pre-level.** Ask all students what jobs they have and make a list on the board with names connected to jobs (e.g., *Juan—mechanic*). Have pre-level students make sentences from the information on the board (e.g., *Juan is a mechanic.*).

Language Note

Time to Talk. Write the word *homemaker* on the board. Tell students that a person who works at home cleaning the house, cooking, and taking care of the children is a homemaker.

Option

Assign Unit 3 Supplementary Grammar to Communicate 1 Exercises on the Teacher's Resource Disk as homework or on the Student Persistence CD-ROM as self-access practice.

TIME to TALK

Teaching Time: 10–15 min.

- Explain that *What do you do?* means *What is your job?*
- Have two students read the first example.
- Explain that if students only go to school and don't have another job, they can answer the question with *I am a student.*
- Have students complete the first part of the task.
- Walk around and help as needed.
- Read the second example with the class.
- GROUPS: Have students play a memory game.

Unit 3 T-29

Grammar to Communicate 2

Adjectives and Noun Word Order

Teaching Time: 5–10 min.

- Have students study the chart.
- Say: *A noun is a person, place, thing, or idea. Nouns can be singular or plural.*
- Say: *Adjectives describe nouns.* Write on the board a few nouns and adjectives, such as *waiter, good, teacher, interesting*. Have students say which are nouns and which are adjectives.
- Say: *Adjectives can go after be.* Write on the board a few examples such as: *The electrician is smart.*
- Say: *Adjectives can go before a noun.* Write on the board a few examples such as: *a beautiful person.*
- Point to the words *a* and *an*. Say: *Use* a *or* an *before an adjective and a singular noun. Don't use* a *or* an *before an adjective alone.*
- Read the sentences in the chart and on the board and have students repeat chorally.

A   Teaching Time: 5–10 min.

- Have students complete the first part of the task.
- PAIRS. Have partners compare answers.
- Call on students to say answers. Correct as needed.
- Have students study the Look Box. Explain that adjectives don't change forms for plural nouns.
- PAIRS. Have students make the plurals.
- Walk around and help as needed.

Grammar to Communicate 2

ADJECTIVES AND NOUN WORD ORDER

	Adjective	Singular Noun		Adjective	Plural Noun
He is a	good	engineer.	They are	good	engineers.

A Underline the adjectives in the sentences. Circle the nouns.

1. His (taxi cab) is neat.
2. Her (taxi cab) is messy.
3. Her (job) is difficult. *Their jobs are difficult.* 
4. His (job) is easy. *Their jobs are easy.*
5. He is a careful (hairdresser). *They are careful hairdressers.* 
6. She is careless. *They are careless.*
7. Her (job) is boring. *Their jobs are boring.* 
8. His (job) is interesting. *Their jobs are interesting.*

PAIRS. Make the sentences above plural. Take turns.

Example:
A: *Their taxi cabs are neat.*
B: *Their taxi cabs are messy.*

Look
Nouns have singular and plural forms.
Adjectives do not have plural forms.

His **job** is easy.
Their **jobs** are easy.
NOT Their **jobs** are easys.

Unit 3

Grammar Notes

1. Adjectives describe nouns.
2. Adjectives go before a noun or after a form of *be*.
3. Adjectives never change form.
4. Use *a* or *an* before an adjective and a noun. Do not use *a* or *an* before an adjective alone.
5. For more information on this grammar topic, see page 253.

Option

- Have students guess the meanings of the adjectives *neat, messy, careful, careless, boring,* and *interesting* from the pictures.
- If necessary, give students options. For example, have students look at the first

Center Stage 2

B Read the questions. Write *a*, *an*, or leave the sentence blank.

1. Are you __a__ neat worker?
2. Are you _____ messy?
3. Is your job _____ boring?
4. Is your boss __an__ interesting person?
5. Are you _____ happy at your job?
6. Are you __a__ fast worker?

Look

Use *a* / *an* + adjective + singular count noun.
You are a good worker.

Do not use *a* / *an* when there is no noun after the adjective.
You are good.
NOT You are a good.

Find classmates with jobs. Ask and answer the questions above.

C Write sentences. Put the words in the correct order.

1. My job is interesting.
   (job / interesting / my / is)
2. I am a good student.
   (am / student / a / good / I)
3. Our teacher's job is difficult.
   (teacher's / our / is / job / difficult)
4. My classmates are serious students.
   (classmates / my / are / students / serious)
5. My friends are hardworking.
   (hardworking / my / friends / are)
6. I am not a slow worker.
   (I / slow / worker / am / a / not)

PAIRS. Which sentences are true about you and people you know? Tell your partner.
Answers will vary.

TIME to TALK

ON YOUR OWN. Which qualities are important for the jobs below? Check (✓) the boxes. Answers will vary.

	CAREFUL	FAST	FRIENDLY	HONEST	KIND	PATIENT	SMART	STRONG
accountant	✓							
attorney								
dentist								
interpreter								
mechanic								

GROUPS. Now talk about your opinions.

Example:
A: In my opinion, good accountants are careful and neat.
B: In my opinion, good accountants are honest.

Jobs 31

---

picture and ask: *Which word means clean and organized?* For the third picture, ask: *Is careful good or is careless good?* For the fourth picture, ask: *Is it fun to do something boring or something interesting?*

Option

Assign Unit 3 Supplementary Grammar to Communicate 2 Exercises on the Teacher's Resource Disk as homework or on the Student Persistence CD-ROM as self-access practice.

B Teaching Time: 10–15 min.

- Have students study the Look Box. Remind students not to use *a* or *an* before an adjective alone.
- Have students complete the first part of the task.
- Call on students to say answers. Correct as needed.
- PAIRS. Have students ask and answer the questions.
- Ask volunteers to tell the class something they learned about their partner's job.

C Teaching Time: 5–10 min.

- Read the example with the class.
- Have students complete the task.
- Call on students to say answers. Correct as needed.
- PAIRS. Have students put a check next to sentences that are true for them or people they know.
- Have students read the sentences that are true for them to their partners.

Multilevel Strategy

- **Pre-level, At-level:** Pair pre-level students with at-level students to complete the task. Have at-level students form each correct sentence and dictate it to pre-level students. Then have pairs take turns reading the true sentences to each other.
- **Above-level:** For the pair activity, challenge students to correct the sentences that are not true about them (e.g., *My job isn't interesting. My job is boring.*).

TIME to TALK Teaching Time: 15–20 min.

- Have students complete their charts.
- Have two students read the example.
- GROUPS. Have students complete the task.
- Walk around and help as needed.

Unit 3   T-31

Grammar to Communicate 3

A / An / Ø and The

Teaching Time: 5–10 min.

- Have students study the first chart.
- Say: *Use* a *and* an *to talk about one person or thing in general, not a specific person or thing*. Write on the board a few examples, such as: *I'm a teacher.*
- Say: *Do not use* a *and* an *for plural nouns.*
- Have students study the second chart.
- Write *the* on the board. Say: *Use* the *when you want to identify someone or something or to talk about someone or something specific*. Write on the board a few examples, such as: *Lisa is the tall girl in my class.* (There are more girls in my class, but only Lisa is tall.). Tell students they can use *the* with singular and plural nouns.
- Say: *Use* a *or* an *the first time you talk about something. Use* the *for the second time you talk about it*. Write on the board a few examples, such as: *She works in a restaurant. The restaurant is very good.*
- Point to the Ø symbol. Explain that it means that no word is necessary. Have students study the Look Box.
- Read the sentences in the chart and on the board and have students repeat chorally.

A Teaching Time: 5–10 min.

- Call on volunteers to read each sentence out loud.
- Have the class identify the correct person and write the number of the sentence.
- Call on a student to say the correct order. Correct as needed.
- **LIFE SKILLS TEST PREP 2** Go to Unit 2, Lesson 3 for more practice describing physical characteristics of family and friends.

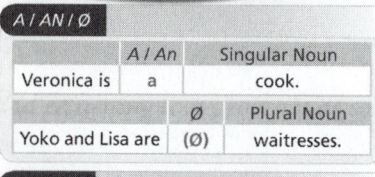

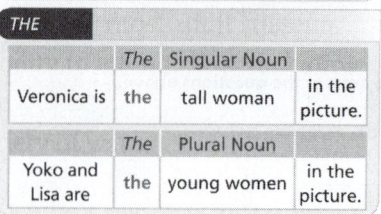

Grammar to Communicate 3

A / AN / Ø

	A / An	Singular Noun
Veronica is	a	cook.
	Ø	Plural Noun
Yoko and Lisa are	(Ø)	waitresses.

THE

	The	Singular Noun	
Veronica is	the	tall woman	in the picture.
	The	Plural Noun	
Yoko and Lisa are	the	young women	in the picture.

Look

Use *a*, *an*, or Ø to make a general statement about someone or something.

Use *the* to identify someone or something.

A Look at the picture and read the sentences. Then label the people in the picture.

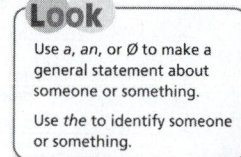

1. Keith is the little boy in the picture.
2. The short guy is Tom.
3. Joe is the heavy guy.
4. Mary is the woman with long hair.
5. The woman with black hair is Lucy.
6. Jim is the tall, thin guy.

Unit 3

Grammar Notes

1. *The* never changes form. It goes before singular and plural nouns. It goes before nouns that begin with consonants and vowels.
2. Use *the* to talk about a specific person / people or thing(s). Use *the* before a noun that is the only one in a situation.
3. Use *the* for the second time you talk about something.
4. Do not use *a*, *an*, or *the* with a plural noun that is two (or more) of many.
5. For more information on this grammar topic, see page 253.

T-32 Center Stage 2

B Look again at the picture in Exercise A. Sam is showing it to his friend. Read what he says and fill in the blanks with *a*, *the*, or Ø.

Tom and Jim are __Ø__ cooks. They are __Ø__ funny guys. Joe's our boss. He's __a__
          1.   2.   3.
nice guy, and he's __a__ good cook. Mary is __a__ waitress. Lucy is __a__ cook.
                    4.   5.   6.
__The__ little boy is Mary's son, Keith. He's __a__ good kid. Mary's husband is not in
  7.   8.
__the__ picture, but he's __a__ waiter.
  9.   10.

C Look at the business cards. Write sentences. Put the words in the correct order.

1. The attorney's first name is Lili.
   (is / Lili / attorney's first name / the)

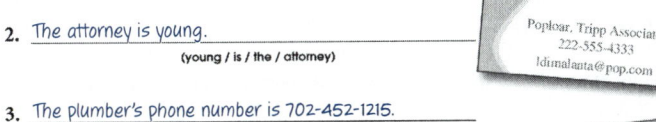

2. The attorney is young.
   (young / is / the / attorney)

3. The plumber's phone number is 702-452-1215.
   (the / 702-452-1215 / is / plumber's phone number)

4. The plumber's e-mail address is atorres@yoohoo.com.
   (the / plumber's email address / atorres@yoohoo.com / is)

Lili Dimalanta
Attorney

Poploar, Tripp Associates
222-555-4333
ldimalanta@pop.com

Alonzo Torres
Plumbers, Inc
1 Lamb Avenue
Las Vegas, NV 89104
702-452-1215
atorres@yoohoo.com

Now write sentences in your notebook about other information in the business cards.

TIME to TALK

PAIRS. Student A: Look at the pictures on page 266.
Student B: Look at the pictures on page 275.
Ask your partner questions about the missing information in your picture. Talk about the missing names or jobs. Use *a*, *an*, or *the*. Answers will vary.

Example:
A: Who is the waiter in Picture 1?
B: His name is Martin. In picture 10, what is Lili's job?
A: She's an attorney.

Jobs 33

B Teaching Time: 5–10 min.
- Read the example with the class.
- Have students complete the task.
- PAIRS. Have students compare answers.
- Call on students to say answers. Correct as needed.

C Teaching Time: 5–10 min.
- Read the example with the class.
- Have students complete the first part of the task.
- Call on students to write sentences on the board. Write corrections on the board as needed.
- Have students complete the second part of the task.
- Walk around and help as needed.
- Call on volunteers to write some of their sentences on the board.

Multilevel Stratetgy
- **Pre-level:** Allow students to copy other students' additional sentences instead of writing their own if the task is too challenging.

Culture Note
- **Exercise C.** Tell students that a business card usually shows a person's name, job, company, address, phone number, fax number, and e-mail address.
- People in the United States usually exchange business cards at meetings.

Option
Assign Unit 3 Supplementary Grammar to Communicate 3 Exercises on the Teacher's Resource Disk as homework or on the Student Persistence CD-ROM as self-access practice.

TIME to TALK
Teaching Time: 15–20 min.
- Have two students read the example conversations.
- PAIRS. Have students complete the task.
- Walk around and help as needed.
- Have students compare their answers to check their work.

Unit 3   T-33

Review and Challenge

Grammar

Teaching Time: 5–10 min.

- Have students complete the task.
- PAIRS. Have students compare answers.
- Call on students to write sentences on the board. Write corrections on the board as needed.

Multilevel Strategy

- **Pre-level:** Tell students what the mistakes are and have them rewrite the sentences.

Dictation

Teaching Time: 5–10 min.

- 🎧 Play Track 23 while students listen and write what they hear.
- 🎧 Play Track 23 again while students check their answers.
- PAIRS. Have students compare their answers.
- Call on students to write answers on the board.
- 🎧 Play Track 23 again and correct the sentences on the board.

Multilevel Strategy

- **Pre-level:** Give students a worksheet with some of the words from the dictation already provided.

Speaking

Teaching Time: 5–10 min.

- Have students study the Look Box.
- Have students study Minh Tran's information. Ask questions such as: *What is Minh's e-mail?*
- Have students turn to page 267. Read each ad and explain unfamiliar vocabulary.
- PAIRS. Have students complete the task.

T-34 Center Stage 2

Review and Challenge

Grammar

Find the mistake in each sentence. Circle the letter and correct the mistake.

1. She is a hairdresser careful.   Correct: She is a careful hairdresser.
     A   B   (C)
2. Waiter's name is Henry.   Correct: The waiter's name is Henry.
   (A)   B   C
3. The attorneys are youngs.   Correct: The attorneys are young.
    A   B   (C)
4. My neighbor is a accountant.   Correct: My neighbor is an accountant.
   A   B   (C)
5. It isn't interesting job.   Correct: It isn't an interesting job.
   A (B)   C
6. The waiters are people nice.   Correct: The waiters are nice people.
    A   B   (C)

Dictation

🎧 **23** Listen. You will hear five sentences. Write them on a piece of paper. *See the audioscript on page 277 for the sentences.*

Speaking

PAIRS. Read the information about Minh Tran. Look at page 267. Which job is good for him? Explain your choice to the class. *Answers will vary.*

> **Look**
> Experience = the kind of work you have done and the amount of time you have done it

```
MINH TRAN
Wilson Avenue
Bronx NY 10469
(718) 898-3075
email: Mtran@yoo.com

Work experience:
Eric's Auto Shop, Bronx, NY 2005–2006

Education:
Automotive Career and Technical Education High School
Brooklyn, NY, diploma 2006
```

34 Unit 3

- Call on students to explain their choices to the class.
- **LIFE SKILLS TEST PREP 2** Go to Unit 11, Lesson 1 for more practice in reading help wanted ads that include common abbreviations.

Expansion

- Have students write their own information. Tell them to include their own contact information as well as their work experience and education. Encourage them to use Minh Tran's information as an example.
- Walk around and help as needed.

Culture Note

Speaking. Point to the abbreviations in the job ads on page 267. Tell students that newspapers often use abbreviations to save space on the page. Tell students it is important to know what they mean to understand the job requirements.

Listening

A 🎧 24 Listen. Who is Gabriella talking to? Check (✓) the correct answer.

- ❏ a customer
- ❏ a waiter at Stage Restaurant
- ☑ the manager at Stage Restaurant

B 🎧 25 Listen again. Check (✓) the sentences that are true about Gabriella.

- ❏ 1. She's the morning waitress at the Stage Restaurant
- ☑ 2. She's an experienced waitress.
- ☑ 3. She's fast.
- ❏ 4. She's a messy worker.
- ❏ 5. She's available on Sundays.

TIME to TALK

ON YOUR OWN. In your opinion, what is important in a job? Write *1* for very important, *2* for important, and *3* for not important. *Answers will vary.*

- ____ a lot of money
- ____ nice people to work with
- ____ interesting work
- ____ a nice manager
- ____ an organized workplace
- ____ easy work
- ____ a hardworking manager
- ____ a clean workplace
- ____ no work on weekends
- ____ benefits (health insurance, vacation, etc.)

GROUPS. Compare your answers.

Example:
A: *A lot of money is important in a job.*
B: *A lot of money isn't important. I think interesting work is more important.*

Jobs 35

Listening

A **Teaching Time: 5–10 min.**

- **Warm-up:** Have students look at the picture and read the answer choices. If necessary, explain that customers are people who buy things. Ask where the people are (a restaurant). Ask what the woman's job is (a waitress).
- 🎧 Play Track 24 while students listen.
- 🎧 Play Track 24 again while students listen and choose the correct answer.
- Call on a student to say the answer. Correct as needed.

B **Teaching Time: 5–10 min.**

- Ask students to read through the sentences before they listen.
- 🎧 Play Track 25 while students listen and complete the task.
- **PAIRS.** Have students compare answers.
- Read each statement and call on students to say whether it is true or false.
- **LIFE SKILLS TEST PREP 2** Go to Unit 11, Lesson 4 for more practice in responding appropriately to job interview questions and practicing appropriate job interview behavior.

Multilevel Strategy

- **At-level, Above-level:** When checking answers, challenge students to correct the statements that are not true about Gabriela.

Culture Note

Speaking. Explain to students that part-time means about twenty hours of work a week and full-time means forty hours of work a week.

Option

Assign Unit 3 Supplementary Review and Challenge Exercises on the Teacher's Resource Disk as homework or on the Student Persistence CD-ROM as self-access practice.

TIME to TALK

Teaching Time: 10–15 min.

- Ask students to read through the words before they begin. Explain unfamiliar vocabulary. For example, explain that Saturday and Sunday are a *weekend* and that *benefits* are extra things you get from a job besides money, such as health insurance.
- Give students a few minutes to complete the first part of the task.
- Have two students read the example.
- **GROUPS.** Have students compare their answers.
- Walk around and help as needed.
- Conduct an informal survey. Ask students what the most important thing in a job is for them. Invite volunteers to share their answers.

Unit 3   T-35

Reading and Writing

Reading

A   Teaching Time: 10–15 min.

- Point to the words *Employee Evaluation*. Tell students that an employee is a worker and that an employee evaluation form tells if a person is good at his or her job.
- Have students read the form. Ask them comprehension questions about the different parts of the form. For example, ask *What is Maria's job? What does the word* manager *mean?* Explain unfamiliar vocabulary as needed.
- Call on a student to say whether Maria is a good worker. Ask other students if they agree.

B   Teaching Time: 10–15 min.

- Tell students to use the other words in the evaluation form to help them guess the meanings of the italicized words.
- Have students complete the task.
- PAIRS. Have students compare answers.
- Call on students to say the answers. Correct as needed.

Expansion

- Conduct an informal survey. Say: *Raise your hand if there are employee evaluation forms at your job.*
- Start a discussion on employee evaluation forms. Prompt students with questions such as: *Are employee evaluation forms a good idea? Why or why not? What if you don't agree with your evaluation?*

Reading and Writing

Reading

A Read the evaluation form. Is Maria a good waitress? Write *yes* or *no*. __Yes__

EMPLOYEE EVALUATION

Name: Maria Recine   Position: Waitress
Date of Hire: 1/15/05   Date of Review: 1/15/06

Please evaluate the employee. Circle one number for each item.

Rating System: 1 = poor   2 = fair   3 = good

Relationship with kitchen staff	1	2	③
Relationship with customers	1	2	③
Organization	1	2	③

Summary

Maria is an excellent waitress. She is hardworking and serious. She is friendly and kind to the customers. The cooks and other kitchen staff are happy with her work. They say that she is an organized worker. She is never late. Her work area is always neat. She is never careless.

Manager (please sign): *Lisa Shvinheite*

B Find the italic words in the form. Circle the correct answers.

1. An *employee* is
   - **a.** a worker.
   - b. a job.
2. *Position* is the same thing as
   - a. name.
   - **b.** job.
3. On a job evaluation, *poor* is
   - a. very good.
   - **b.** bad.
4. *Fair* is
   - **a.** okay.
   - b. very bad.
5. The *staff* are
   - a. customers.
   - **b.** workers.
6. A *manager* is
   - a. a customer.
   - **b.** a boss.

36   Unit 3

T-36   Center Stage 2

Prewriting

Look at the picture of Doug Malone and read his evaluation form.

EMPLOYEE EVALUATION

Name: Doug Malone   Position: Waiter
Date of Hire: 12/10/05   Date of Review: 1/10/07

Please evaluate the employee. Circle one number for each item.

Rating System: 1 = poor 2 = fair 3 = good

Relationship with kitchen staff	①	2	3
Relationship with customers	①	2	3
Organization	①	2	3

Writing

Complete the summary part of the form for Doug Malone. Use the summary on page 36 as a model.

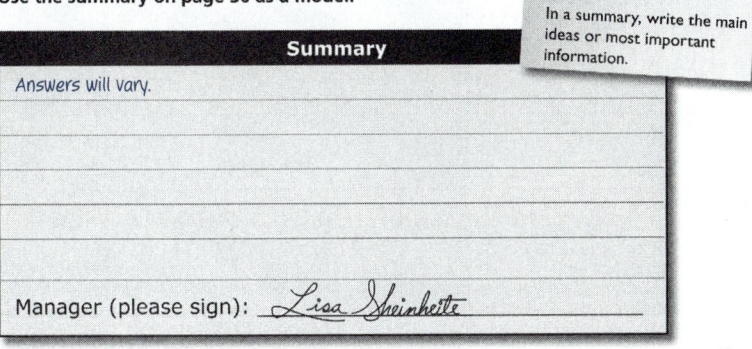

Writing Tip
In a summary, write the main ideas or most important information.

Summary
Answers will vary.

Manager (please sign): Lisa Sheinheite

Jobs 37

Prewriting

Teaching Time: 5–10 min.

- Have students look at the picture and read Doug's evaluation form.
- Ask questions such as: *What is Doug's job?* (a waiter) and *Is the kitchen staff happy with Doug?* (no).

Writing

Teaching Time: 15–20 min.

- Have students reread the summary on Maria's evaluation form on page 36.
- Have students complete the task.
- Walk around and help as needed.
- Call on volunteers to read their summaries. Correct as needed.

Multilevel Strategy

- **Pre-level:** Write the following on the board: *Doug is not a __ waiter. He is ___. The cooks and customers are not ___ with his work. He is always ___.* Group pre-level students and work with them to brainstorm possible answers. Then have them complete the paragraph.
- **Above-level:** Challenge students with the task by having them write additional sentences about Doug.

Language Notes

- **Writing.** Have students study the Writing Tip.
- Tell students that a paragraph is about one specific idea. Explain that we indent at the beginning of paragraphs to show the reader that a new idea begins.

Unit 3   T-37

Unit 4
Places

Learning Goals
- Learn words to describe places in the neighborhood
- Learn about *There is / There are*: statements; *Some / A lot of / Any*; and *Is there / Are there*
- Listen to conversations about places
- Read and write a postcard
- Talk about places

Learner Persistence
Help students stay connected to the class. Set up a partner or "buddy" system to make sure that students stay connected to the class even when they are absent.

Warm-up
Teaching Time: 3–5 min.

- Write the word *neighborhood* on the board. Explain that a neighborhood is one part of a city or town.
- Tell students that a school is in the neighborhood on the picture. Ask: *What other places are in a neighborhood?* (supermarket, restaurant). Record students' answers on the board.

Vocabulary
Teaching Time: 15–20 min.

- Have students look at the vocabulary list. Explain any unfamiliar vocabulary. For example, say: *An outdoor market is a place to buy things. It's not inside a building.*
- 🎧 Play Track 26 while students read and listen.
- Read each word aloud and have students repeat chorally.
- Have students complete the task.
- PAIRS. Have students compare answers.

Expansion
- Have students read the words again.
- Pair same-level students and have them practice the vocabulary.

T-38 Center Stage 2

Unit 4
Places

Grammar
- *There is / There are*: Statements
- *Some / A lot of / Any*
- *Is there / Are there*

Vocabulary

🎧 **26** Read and listen. Then circle the places in your neighborhood.
Answers will vary.

1. airport
2. office building
3. café
4. supermarket
5. apartment building
6. buildings
7. outdoor market
8. hotel
9. movie theater
10. hospital
11. restaurant
12. museum
13. store
14. shopping mall

38 Unit 4

Multilevel Strategy

- **Pre-level:** Have one student point to the picture and the other student say the word. Then have them switch roles.
- **At-level:** Have students cover the vocabulary list. Have one student say the number and the other student say the correct word. Then have them switch roles.
- **Above-level:** Have students cover the vocabulary list and take turns dictating the words to each other from memory.

Listening

A 🎵 27 Listen. Check (✓) the places in the woman's neighborhood.

- ☐ a shopping mall
- ☐ an old movie theater
- ☐ a supermarket
- ✓ an expensive restaurant
- ✓ some cheap restaurants
- ✓ some stores
- ✓ some cafés
- ☐ a park
- ✓ a beach

B 🎵 28 Read and listen again. Write the missing words. Use the words in the box.

| ~~any~~ | aren't | isn't | some | There's |

Natasha: There are some nice stores and cafés, and there's a new movie theater on the next street.

Pedro: It sounds nice. Are there __any__ good restaurants?
                                              1.

Natasha: Yes. __There's__ a good restaurant near my apartment building. It's expensive, but the food is excellent. There are also __some__ cheap restaurants in the neighborhood.
                    2.   3.

Pedro: Is there a supermarket near your apartment?

Natasha: No, there __isn't__ a supermarket, but there's a big outdoor market.
                          4.

Pedro: And is there a nice park?

Natasha: There __aren't__ any parks, but there's a beautiful beach.
                      5.

Places 39

Listening

A Teaching Time: 10–15 min.

- **Warm-up:** With books closed, ask students to try to remember and say as many neighborhood places as they can. Record students' answers on the board.
- Tell students that they are going to listen to a woman talk about places in her neighborhood.
- 🎧 Play Track 27 while students listen.
- 🎧 Play Track 27 again while students complete the task.
- 🎧 Play Track 27 again while students check their answers. Pause the recording each time an answer is given.

B Teaching Time: 15–20 min.

- Have students read through the answer choices before they listen.
- 🎧 Play Track 28 while students listen and write the words they hear.
- 🎧 Play Track 28 again while students check their answers.
- Call on students to say answers. Correct as needed.
- Read the conversation aloud. Pause after each few words and have students repeat chorally.
- PAIRS. Ask students to role-play the conversation.

Multilevel Strategy

- **Pre-level:** Have students copy the conversation in their notebooks to reinforce the language before they role-play.
- **At-level:** Have students continue the conversation as they role-play. Prompt them with suggestions (e.g., *Talk about a shopping mall.*).
- **Above-level:** Have students role-play a new conversation and talk about their neighborhoods using the conversation in the book as a model. Call on pairs to role-play in front of the class.

Language Note

Exercise B. Point out the word *near* in the conversation. Point to two students sitting next to each other. Say: [Student A] is near [Student B]. Point to two students sitting at opposite ends of the room. Say: [Student A] is not near [Student B].

Option

Assign Unit 4 Supplementary Vocabulary Exercise on the Teacher's Resource Disk as homework or on the Student Persistence CD-ROM as self-access practice.

Unit 4 T-39

Grammar to Communicate 1

There is / There are: Statements

Teaching Time: 5–10 min.

- Have students study the chart.
- Say: *We use* there is *and* there are *to say that something exists.*
- Place a book on your desk and say: *There is a book on my desk.* Write the sentence on the board.
- Remove the book and say: *There isn't a book on my desk.* Write the sentence on the board.
- Place two books on your desk and say: *There are two books on my desk.* Write the sentence on the board.
- Remove the books and say: *There aren't books on my desk.* Write the sentence on the board.
- Read the sentences in the chart and have students repeat chorally.
- Have students study the Look Box. Tell students that a subject needs to follow *there is* and *there are*.

A Teaching Time: 5–10 min.

- Have students say places on the map.
- Read the example with the class. Remind students to use *there is / isn't* with a singular subject and *there are / aren't* with a plural subject.
- Have students complete the task.
- Call on students to say answers. Correct as needed.

Multilevel Strategy

- **Pre-level:** Help students identify the nouns following each blank as either singular or plural. Remind them to use *is* with singular nouns and *are* with plural nouns.
- **At-level, Above-level:** Have students rewrite singular items as plural and plural items as singular (e.g., *1. There are outdoor markets.*) after they have completed the task.

Grammar to Communicate 1

THERE IS / THERE ARE: STATEMENTS

There	Be	Subject		There	Be + Not	Subject	
There	is	a restaurant / an airport	here.	There	isn't	a restaurant / an airport	here.
There	are	restaurants / big airports		There	aren't	restaurants / big airports	

Contractions
there + is → there's

A Look at the map of River City. Complete the sentences with *is, isn't, are,* or *aren't*.

Look
The subject comes after *There is* or *There are*. *There* is not the subject.
There is a restaurant. (Singular subject)
There are restaurants. (Plural subject)

1. There ___is___ an outdoor market.
2. There ___are___ two supermarkets on River Street.
3. There ___is___ a movie theater.
4. There ___is___ a bank on Center Street.
5. There ___aren't___ any restaurants on Center Street.
6. There ___is___ a big park on Center Street.
7. There ___is___ a dog in the park.
8. There ___are___ students at the college.
9. There ___isn't___ a hotel on Center Street.

40 Unit 4

Grammar Notes

1. Use *there is / there are* to say that something exists.
2. Use contractions or full forms: *there is = there's, there is not = there isn't, there are not = there aren't*. *There are* doesn't have a contracted form.
3. Use *there is / isn't* with singular nouns. Use *there are / aren't* with plural nouns.
4. For more information on this grammar topic, see page 253.

Watch Out!

Exercise B. In some languages, only one word is used for *in* and *on*. Listen for and correct errors like *There's an apartment building in Oak Street.*

T-40   Center Stage 2

B Look at the pictures. Then look back at the map of River City in Exercise A. Complete the sentences. Use *There is* or *There are* and the places in the box.

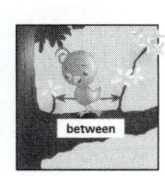

| ~~bank~~ | buildings | movie theater | outdoor market | shopping mall |

1. __There is__ a hospital between the __bank__ and the park.
2. __There is__ an __outdoor market__ in the park.
3. __There are__ some __buildings__ on River Street.
4. __There is__ a __shopping mall__ across from the supermarket.
5. __There is__ a __movie theater__ next to the shopping mall.

C Complete the sentences. Use *There's* or *There are*.

1. __There are restaurants__ next to the shopping mall.
   (restaurants)
2. __There's an old museum__ across from the college.
   (an old museum)
3. __There's a movie theater__ between the shopping mall and the hotel.
   (a movie theater)
4. __There are stores__ in the shopping mall.
   (stores)
5. __There's an apartment building__ on Elm Street.
   (an apartment building)

PAIRS. Talk about the map in Exercise A. Where are the places in the box? Tell a partner.
Answers will vary.

| apartment building | movie theater | museum | restaurants | stores |

TIME to TALK

ON YOUR OWN. Draw a map of your neighborhood on a separate piece of paper. Write in the street names, but do not write the names of the buildings.
Answers will vary.
PAIRS. Give your map to your partner. Tell your partner the names and locations of the places in your neighborhood. Use *in, on, next to, between,* and *across from*. Your partner will write the places on your map. Then change roles and write the places on your partner's map.

WRAP-UP. Check your partner's map. Is everything in the correct place?

Places 41

B Teaching Time: 5–10 min.
- Have students study the pictures. Explain the meaning of each preposition.
- Read the example with the class.
- Have students complete the task.
- Call on students to say answers. Correct as needed.

C Teaching Time: 10–15 min.
- Read the example with the class.
- Have students complete the activity.
- Call on students to write answers on the board. Check for correct use of the apostrophe in *There's*. Write corrections on the board as needed.
- PAIRS. Have students complete the task. Walk around and help as needed.
- **LIFE SKILLS TEST PREP 2** Go to Unit 4, Lesson 3 for more practice in locating places on a map.

Multilevel Strategy
- **Pre-level, At-level:** Pair pre-level students with at-level students for the partner activity. Have at-level students tell the location of the places in the box and pre-level students confirm their statements. For example:
  A: *There's a movie theater next to the hotel.*
  B: *Yes, there is.*
- **Above-level:** Have students exchange false statements about the places in the box. Have students correct each other's statements. For example:
  A: *There's a movie theater next to the hospital.*
  B: *No, there's a movie theater next to the hotel.*

Teaching Tip
Exercise B. Use objects and people in the classroom to demonstrate the meanings of prepositions of place. For example, put a pencil inside a paper bag to show *in*. Point to two students sitting next to each other. Say: *[Student A] is next to [Student B]*.

Option
Assign Unit 4 Supplementary Grammar to Communicate 1 Exercises on the Teacher's Resource Disk as homework or on the Student Persistence CD-ROM as self-access practice.

TIME to TALK

Teaching Time: 15–20 min.
- Have students draw a map of their own neighborhood. Tell students to label a few places on the map (to be used as references for identifying other locations).
- Have students complete the activity.
- Walk around and help as needed.

Unit 4 T-41

Grammar to Communicate 2

Some / A lot of / Any

Teaching Time: 5–10 min.

- Place three or four pencils on your desk and say: *There are some pencils on my desk.* Write the sentence on the board.
- Add about ten more pencils and say: *There are a lot of pencils on my desk.* Write the sentence on the board.
- Remove all but two pencils and say: *There aren't a lot of pencils on my desk.* Write the sentence on the board.
- Remove all the pencils and say: *There aren't any pencils on my desk.* Write the sentence on the board.
- Have students study the chart and the Look Box. Tell students that *any* is used only with negative sentences and means zero.
- Read each example in the chart and have students repeat chorally.

A Teaching Time: 3–5 min.

- Read the example with the class.
- Have students complete the task.
- Call on students to say answers. Correct as needed.

B Teaching Time: 5–10 min.

- Read the picture captions and the example with the class.
- Have students complete the task.
- Call on students to say answers. Correct as needed.

Grammar to Communicate 2

SOME / A LOT OF / ANY

There	Be	Some / A lot of	Subject		There	Be + Not	Any	Subject
There	are	some / a lot of	stores here.		There	aren't	any	stores here.

A Look at the picture on pages 38–39. Check (✓) the sentences that are true about the city.

☑ 1. There is a park.
☑ 2. There aren't any colleges.
☐ 3. There are a lot of banks.
☐ 4. There isn't an airport.
☐ 5. There are some restaurants.
☑ 6. There is a hospital.
☑ 7. There are some stores.
☑ 8. There aren't a lot of big hotels.

Look
A lot of = large numbers
Some = small numbers
Any = 0

There are **a lot of** people here. (50 people)
There are **some** people here. (5 people)
There aren't **any** people here. (0 people)

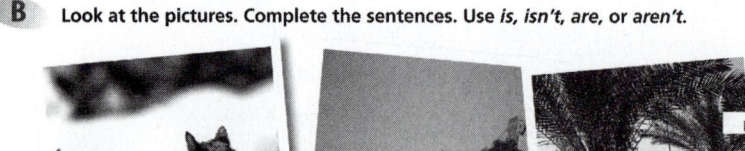

B Look at the pictures. Complete the sentences. Use *is, isn't, are,* or *aren't*.

sled dogs in Alaska   *The Great Wall of China*   *The Nile River, Egypt / palm tree*

1. There __isn't__ a very big city in Alaska.
2. There __are__ sled dogs in Alaska.
3. There __aren't__ palm trees in Alaska.
4. There __is__ a famous wall in China.
5. There __are__ a lot of mountains in China.
6. There __are__ some palm trees in Egypt.
7. There __aren't__ any sled dogs in Egypt.
8. There __is__ a famous river in Egypt.

Unit 4

Grammar Notes

1. Use *some, a lot of,* and *any* with plural nouns. *Some* means a small number. *A lot of* means a large number. *Any* means zero when it's in a negative sentence.

2. Use *some* in affirmative sentences. (*There are some restaurants.*) Use *any* in negative sentences. (*There aren't any restaurants.*) Use *a lot of* in affirmative and negative sentences. (*There are a lot of restaurants. There aren't a lot of restaurants.*)

3. For more information on this grammar topic, see page 253.

Center Stage 2

C PAIRS. Look at pages 38–39. Use the vocabulary to tell your partner about your hometown. Answers will vary.

Example:
A: There's a shopping mall in Lahore.
B: There isn't a shopping mall in Cap Haïtien.

shopping mall in Lahore, Pakistan

D Write sentences about good and bad things in your hometown. Use the words in the box and *There is / are / isn't / aren't*, and *a, an, some, any,* or *a lot of.* Answers will vary.

beautiful parks	expensive supermarkets	good schools
beautiful rivers	famous museums	interesting stores
big shopping malls	good hospitals	movie theaters
cheap apartments	good jobs	nice people
excellent colleges	good restaurants	young people

Good Things
1. There are some good schools.
2. _____
3. _____
4. _____
5. _____
6. _____

Bad Things
1. There aren't a lot of cheap apartments.
2. _____
3. _____
4. _____
5. _____
6. _____

TIME TO TALK

GROUPS. Talk about five good and bad things in the city or town you are in now. Answers will vary.

Example:
A: There are some famous museums in this city. That's a good thing.
B: But there aren't a lot of cheap apartments. That's a bad thing.

Places 43

Option

Assign Unit 4 Supplementary Grammar to Communicate 2 Exercises on the Teacher's Resource Disk as homework or on the Student Persistence CD-ROM as self-access practice.

C Teaching Time: 5–10 min.
- Have two students read the example.
- Have students complete the task.
- Walk around and help as needed.
- Call on volunteers to say one sentence about their partner's hometown.

D Teaching Time: 10–15 min.
- Read the examples with the class.
- Have students complete the task.
- Walk around and help as needed.
- Call on volunteers to read their sentences. You can also collect students' work and provide individual feedback.

TIME TO TALK

Teaching Time: 10–15 min.
- Have two students read the example conversation.
- GROUPS. Have students complete the activity.
- Walk around and help as needed.
- Have groups say sentences about good and bad things. Conduct an informal survey with the class for each one. Say: *Raise your hand if you think that's a good / bad thing.*

Multilevel Strategy
- **All-levels:** Place students in mixed-level groups. Allow pre-level students to use the sentences from Exercise D to talk about their hometown. Challenge above-level students to work with their books closed and recall the vocabulary from memory as they talk with other classmates.

Unit 4 T-43

Grammar to Communicate 3

Is there / Are there

Teaching Time: 5–10 min.

- Place a book on your desk. Ask: *Is there a book on my desk?* Write the question on the board. Write: *Yes, there is. It is [green].*
- Add another book. Ask: *Are there any books on my desk?* Write the question on the board. Write: *Yes, there are. They are [green].*
- Ask: *Are there a lot of books on my desk?* Write the question on the board. Write: *No, there aren't.*
- Have students study the chart.
- Say: *Put* is *and* are *before* there *to ask questions.*
- Read each example and have students repeat chorally.
- Ask a few questions about objects in the classroom and have students answer with positive or negative short answers.

A Teaching Time: 5–10 min.

- Have students look at the postcards. Read aloud the captions and explain each picture. Point to objects in the pictures and name them. For example: *lake, mountains,* etc.
- Read the example with the class.
- Have students complete the task.
- Call on students to say answers. Correct as needed. If students answer a question with *yes*, ask: *Where?*

Grammar to Communicate 3

IS THERE / ARE THERE

Be	There	Quantifier	Subject		Short Answers
Is	there	a / an	college art museum	here?	Yes, there is. / No, there isn't.
Are		any / a lot of	schools museums		Yes, there are. / No, there aren't.

A Look at the postcards. Circle the correct answers.

Québec City, Québec — Canada
The Rocky Mountains, Alberta — Canada
Niagara Falls, Ontario — Canada
Lake Huron, British Columbia — Canada

1. Is there a beach in the postcards?
   a. No, there isn't.   b. Yes, there is.
2. Are there any buildings?
   a. Yes, there is.   **b.** Yes, there are.
3. Are there any mountains?
   a. Yes, there is.   **b.** Yes, there are.
4. Is there a waterfall?
   a. No, there isn't.   **b.** Yes, there is.
5. Are there a lot of people?
   a. No, there isn't.   **b.** No, there aren't.
6. Is there a lake?
   a. Yes, there is.   b. No, there isn't.

Unit 4

Grammar Notes

1. Use *Is there* and *Are there* to ask questions.
2. Use *Is there a / an* with singular subjects. (*Is there a hotel?*) Use *Are there any / a lot of* with plural subjects. (*Are there any good restaurants?*)
3. Don't use contractions in short answers with *yes.* (*Yes, there is / there are.*) Use contractions or full forms in short answers with *no.* (*No, there is not / there are not. No there isn't / there aren't.*)
4. For more information on this grammar topic, see page 253.

Center Stage 2

B
Write questions about the pictures in Exercise A. Put the words in the correct order.

1. Are there any tall mountains in Canada?
   (any / Canada/ are / there / tall / in / mountains)
2. Is there a nice lake in Canada?
   (there / is / nice / a / in / Canada / lake)
3. Is there a beautiful waterfall in Canada?
   (beautiful / is / waterfall / a / in / there / Canada)
4. Are there old cities in Canada?
   (Canada / there/ old / in / cities / are)
5. Are there any beautiful buildings in Canada?
   (beautiful / there / buildings / are / in / Canada /any)

PAIRS. Ask and answer the questions above.

Example:
A: Are there any tall mountains in Canada?
B: Yes, there are. They're in Alberta.

Look
Use *There is* or *There are* to talk about something the first time. Use *It* or *They* the second time.
There is a famous waterfall in Canada. **It's** in Ontario.
There are some old cities in Canada. **They're** in Quebec.

C
Write questions about your country with *Is there* or *Are there*. Use *a*, *an*, or *any*.

1. Is there a desert in your country?
   (desert)
2. Is there a famous waterfall in your country?
   (famous waterfall)
3. Are there any beautiful lakes in your country?
   (beautiful lakes)
4. Are there any tall mountains in your country?
   (tall mountains)
5. Is there an island in your country?
   (island)

desert

TIME to TALK
PAIRS. Ask and answer five questions about your country. Use the questions in Exercise C and your own ideas. Answers will vary.

Example:
A: Are there any nice beaches in your country?
B: Yes, there are. Copacabana and Ipanema Beaches are beautiful. They're in Rio de Janeiro.

Places 45

B Teaching Time: 10–15 min.
- Read the example with the class.
- Remind students that questions start with a capital letter and end with a question mark.
- Have students complete the task.
- Call on students to write questions on the board. Write corrections on the board as needed.
- Have students study the Look Box.
- Have two students read the example.
- PAIRS. Have students take turns asking and answering questions with short answers. Remind them to look at the pictures on page 44 for the answers.
- Walk around and help as needed.

Multilevel Strategy
- **Pre-level, At-level:** Pair pre-level students with at-level students for the partner activity. Have pre-level students read the questions and at-level students form the answers.

C Teaching Time: 10–15 min.
- Read the example with the class.
- Have students complete the task.
- Call on students to read their questions. Correct as needed.

Option
Assign Unit 4 Supplementary Grammar to Communicate 3 Exercises on the Teacher's Resource Disk as homework or on the Student Persistence CD-ROM as self-access practice.

TIME to TALK
Teaching Time: 10–15 min.
- Have two students read the example.
- PAIRS. Have partners take turns asking and answering questions about their countries. Remind students to give information about each place when they answer questions, such as where something is or its name.
- Walk around and help as needed.
- Ask volunteers to present their interviews to the class.

Multilevel Strategy
- **Pre-level:** Have students only use the questions from Exercise C to talk about their country.
- **Above-level:** Challenge students with the task by having them ask three original questions. Prompt students with suggestions if necessary.

Unit 4   T-45

Review and Challenge

Grammar

Teaching Time: 5–10 min.

- Read the example with the class.
- Have students complete the task.
- PAIRS. Have students compare answers.
- 🎧 Play Track 29 while students check their answers.
- Have two students role-play the corrected conversation in front of the class.

Dictation

Teaching Time: 5–10 min.

- 🎧 Play Track 30 while students listen and write what they hear.
- 🎧 Play Track 30 again while students check their answers.
- Call on students to write answers on the board.
- 🎧 Play Track 30 again and correct the sentences on the board.

> **Multilevel Strategy**
>
> - **Pre-level:** Give students a worksheet with some of the words from the dictation already provided.

Speaking

Teaching Time: 5–10 min.

- Have two volunteers read the example conversation.
- PAIRS. Have students complete the task.
- Walk around and help as needed.

> **Multilevel Strategy**
>
> - **Pre-level:** Copy the example on the board. Tell students to use it as a model to talk about the places on the map. Underline the information that students should substitute in their conversations.

T-46 Center Stage 2

Review and Challenge

Grammar

🎧 **29** Correct the conversation. There are seven mistakes. The first one is corrected for you. Then listen and check your answers.

A: I'm from Pittsburgh. It's ~~great~~ *a great* city. There are a lot of stores and beautiful houses.

B: Are there any ~~goods~~ *good* restaurants?

A: Oh, yes. There are ~~any~~ *some* Italian and Chinese restaurants in my neighborhood. And they're cheap, too.

B: ~~Is~~ *there* an art museum in Pittsburgh?

A: Yes. ~~They~~ *There* are three.

B: Is there a new airport?

A: No, ~~it~~ *there* isn't. But our airport is nice.

B: So Pittsburgh is *a* small city.

A: Yes, it is. But it's really nice.

Dictation

🎧 **30** Listen. You will hear five sentences. Write them on a piece of paper. *See the audioscript on page 278 for the sentences.*

Speaking

PAIRS. Look at the map on page 268. Ask and answer questions about places in the U.S. Use the words in the box. Make the words plural where necessary. *Answers will vary.*

| big city | desert | island | old building |
| big lake | famous waterfall | nice beach | tall mountain |

Example:
A: Are there any tall mountains in the U.S.?
B: Yes, there are.
A: Where are they?
B: There are some tall mountains in Arizona, California, and Colorado. And there's also a tall mountain in Alaska. It's Mount McKinley.

46 Unit 4

Option

Before class, make a copy of the grammar exercise on page 46 as a transparency to use with an overhead projector. Ask a volunteer to make corrections to the conversation on the transparency. Correct as needed. Have students check their work with the transparency.

Option

- Divide the class into two groups. One student from each group plays at a time.
- Ask pairs of students (one from each group) questions with *Is there / Are there* as students look at their maps. For example: *Is there an island in Colorado?*
- Students answer as quickly as possible.

Listening

A 🎧 31 Listen. Two women talk about food shopping in their countries. Check (✓) the correct sentence.

- ☐ 1. Food shopping is expensive in the two countries.
- ☑ 2. Food shopping is different in the two countries.
- ☐ 3. Food shopping is the same in the two countries.

B 🎧 32 Listen again. Read the sentences below. Write *C* (Colombia), *U.S.* (the United States), or *B* (both Colombia and the United States).

bakery   supermarket

- _B_ 1. There are big supermarkets.
- _C_ 2. There are a lot of small food stores.
- _C_ 3. Small stores and outdoor markets are popular.
- _U.S._ 4. Small food stores are expensive.
- _C_ 5. Supermarkets are expensive.

TIME to TALK

GROUPS. Compare neighborhoods in the U.S. and neighborhoods in your home country. Make five sentences. Use the words from page 38 and your own ideas. Answers will vary.

Example:
A: *In Los Angeles, there are a lot of big supermarkets. In my city, Dalian, China, there are a lot of outdoor markets.*
B: *I'm from Berlin, Germany. There are a lot of big supermarkets in Berlin.*

Places   47

Listening

A   Teaching Time: 5–10 min.

- **Warm-up:** Point out, or have students identify, Colombia and the United States on a world map. Then ask students to say some places in their city where people buy food.
- Have students read through the answer choices before they listen.
- 🎧 Play Track 31 while students listen.
- 🎧 Play Track 31 again while students listen and complete the task.
- Call on a student to say the answer. Correct as needed.
- Ask students comprehension questions about the conversation. Modify the questions to the level of the students.

Multilevel Strategy

- **Pre-level:** Ask students *yes / no* questions (e.g., *Is shopping in the United States different than in Colombia?*).
- **At-level:** Ask students information questions (e.g., *Where do you buy fresh bread in Colombia?*).
- **Above-level:** Ask students open-ended or critical thinking questions (e.g., *Do you think it is better to shop in a supermarket or a small shop?*).

B   Teaching Time: 5–10 min.

- Ask students to read through the sentences before they listen.
- 🎧 Play Track 32 while students listen and complete the task.
- PAIRS. Have students compare answers.
- 🎧 Play Track 32 again while students check answers. Pause the recording each time an answer is given.

TIME to TALK   Teaching Time: 10–15 min.

- Ask two volunteers to read the example.
- Before dividing into groups, have students suggest topics they might discuss, such as *supermarkets, buildings,* and *stores.* Record these on the board.
- GROUPS. Have students complete the task.
- Walk around and help as needed.
- Have students take turns telling the class facts they learned about neighborhoods in their group members' home countries.

The first to answer the question correctly gets one point for his or her group. You may award additional points for correct answers to further questions such as: *What are the names of the cities?*
- After each student has had a turn, the group with the most points wins.

Option

Assign Unit 4 Supplementary Review and Challenge Exercises on the Teacher's Resource Disk as homework or on the Student Persistence CD-ROM as self-access practice.

Unit 4   T-47

Reading and Writing

Reading

Teaching Time: 15–20 min.

- Have students look at the chart. Point out the key and explain that it shows the meaning of the pictures.
- Ask questions about the chart. For example, point to the third column and ask: *What information is here?* (cold days).
- Have students read the postcards silently.
- Read each postcard aloud. Pause after each few words and have students repeat chorally.
- Have students label each postcard.
- Call on students to say answers. Correct as needed.

Expansion Review information about names and addresses. Have students look at the address section of each postcard and ask questions such as the following: *What is Tommy's last name?* (Grant). *What is Mr. and Mrs. Grant's zip code?* (77009).

Reading and Writing

Reading

Look at the chart. Then read the postcards. Where is each postcard from? Write the correct city below each postcard.

CITY	👥	❄	☀	🏛	📖
Boston	590,192	* * *	*	* *	* * *
Orlando	201,389	*	* * *	*	*
Chicago	2,898,025	* * *	*	* * *	* * *

KEY: 👥 = population ❄ = cold days ☀ = warm days 🏛 = museums 📖 = libraries
* = not many   * * = some   * * * = a lot of / many

Dear Mom and Dad:

How are you? My new neighborhood is great. There are museums and libraries everywhere! There are a lot of people too—more than 2 million! But there is one big problem. It's very cold! Take care. I'll call you soon.

Love,
Tommy

Mr. and Mrs. Grant
105 Hogan St.
Houston, TX 77009

1. _Chicago_

Dear Susie:

I'm here in my hotel. The city is small, and there aren't many museums, but that's OK. The weather is beautiful, and the lakes are wonderful. The shopping is great, too. There are a lot of nice stores. Is there anything you want? Call me at the hotel.

See you soon,
Jimmy

Susie Tan
207 7th Ave.
San Diego, CA 92103

2. _Orlando_

Unit 4

Culture Note

- **Reading.** Point out the stamps on the postcards. Explain that in the United States you can use a special stamp for postcards. It costs less than the stamp for a letter.
- Explain that a regular stamp for a letter can also be used.

Center Stage 2

Prewriting

Complete the chart with information about a city you know. Answers will vary.

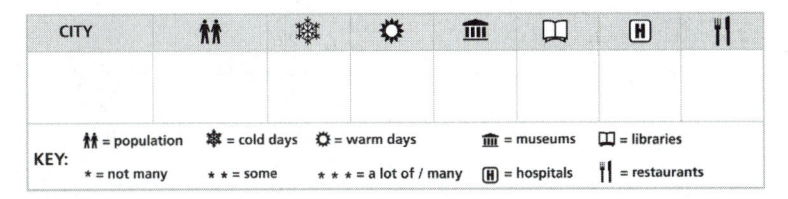

CITY	👫	❄	☀	🏛	📖	H	🍴

KEY:
- 👫 = population
- ❄ = cold days
- ☀ = warm days
- 🏛 = museums
- 📖 = libraries
- H = hospitals
- 🍴 = restaurants
- * = not many
- ** = some
- *** = a lot of / many

Writing

Write a postcard to a friend about the city in your chart above. Use the postcards on page 48 as a model. Answers will vary.

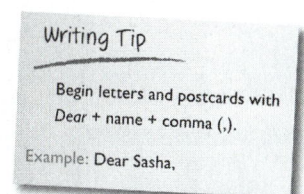

Writing Tip

Begin letters and postcards with *Dear* + name + comma (,).

Example: Dear Sasha,

Places 49

Prewriting

Teaching Time: 15–20 min.

- Have students look at the key. Encourage them to consider the information they know about different cities.
- Have students complete the task.
- Allow students to look for information in books or on the Internet if necessary.

Expansion Have the class use the information in the chart on page 48 to write a paragraph about Boston. Call on students to contribute individual sentences about each piece of information. Record the paragraph on the board.

Writing

Teaching Time: 15–20 min.

- Have students study the Writing Tip.
- Tell students to decide who they want to write a postcard to. Have them address the postcard.
- Point out the words *Love* and *See you soon* at the end of the postcards on page 48. Say: *Use* Love *when you write to someone in your family. Use* See you soon *with friends. You can also use* Sincerely *when you write to friends.*
- Have students complete the task.
- Walk around and help as needed.
- Call on volunteers to read their postcards to the class. Correct as needed. You can also have students write their postcards on a separate piece of paper. Collect their work and provide individual feedback.

Multilevel Strategy

- **Pre-level:** While students are completing the prewriting task, copy one of the postcards from page 48 on the board. Underline the information that students should substitute in their postcards. Have students copy the postcard and substitute the underlined parts with the information from Prewriting.
- **Above-level:** Challenge students with the task by having them add more information about the city they have chosen. Prompt them with suggestions if necessary.

Unit 4 T-49

Game 1
Units 1–4

Answers will vary. Possible answers:

1. **A:** Is she an engineer?
   B: Yes, she is.

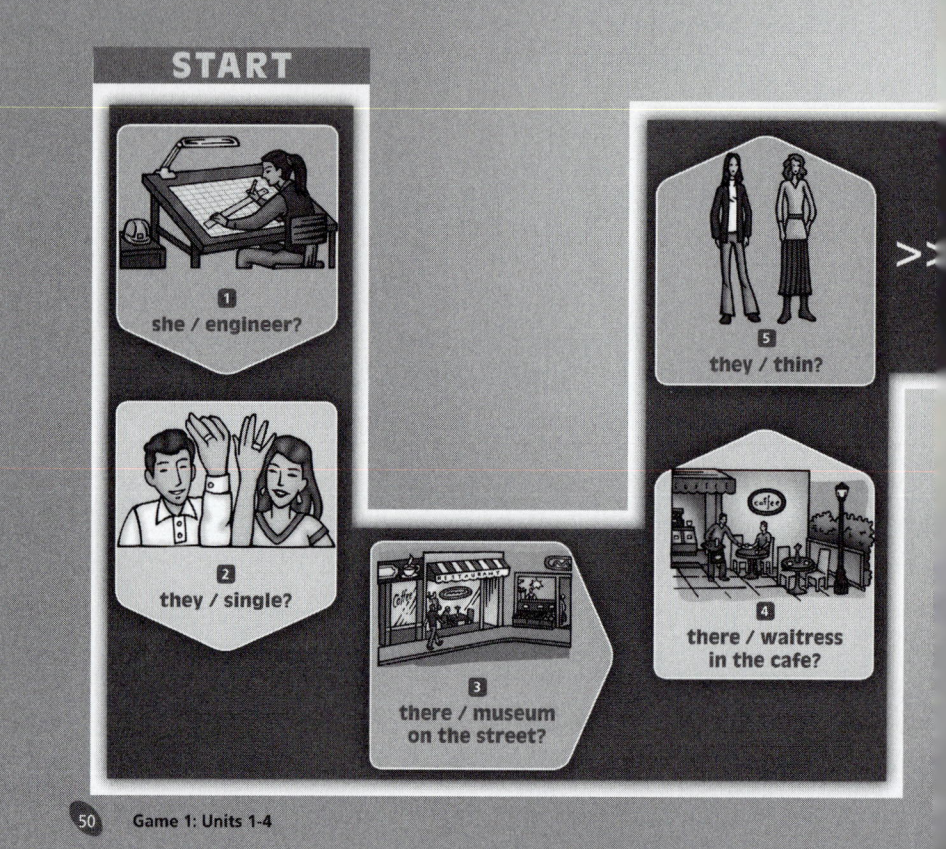

2. **A:** Are they single?
   B: No, they aren't. / No, they're not.

3. **A:** Is there a museum on the street?
   B: No, there isn't.

4. **A:** Is there a waitress in the cafe?
   B: No, there isn't.

5. **A:** Are they thin?
   B: Yes, they are.

T-50   Center Stage 2

6. **A:** Is Pablo's aunt a dentist?
   B: No, she isn't. / No, she's not.
7. **A:** Is there an outdoor market in the park?
   B: Yes, there is.
8. **A:** How old are they?
   B: They're 80.
9. **A:** How tall is Arthur's mother?
   B: She's 5 feet 1 inch tall.
10. **A:** Is there a waterfall?
    B: Yes, there is.
11. **A:** Is Molly's job interesting?
    B: No, it isn't. / No, it's not.
12. **A:** Are Jeff's children quiet?
    B: No, they aren't. / No, they're not.
13. **A:** Where is the beach?
    B: It's in Mexico.
14. **A:** Are they hardworking mechanics?
    B: Yes, they are.
15. **A:** Are there buildings on the island?
    B: No, there aren't.
16. **A:** What's Li's last name? / What's her last name?
    B: It's Pang. / Her last name is Pang.

Unit 5
Food and Drink

Learning Goals
- Learn words for food and drink
- Learn about count and noncount nouns; quantifiers: *Some / A little / A lot of / A few / Any*; and count and noncount nouns: *yes / no* questions and information questions
- Listen to conversations about food shopping
- Read and write a newsletter
- Talk about food and drink

Learner Persistence
Using incentives can help increase attendance. Create a system to reward good attendance.

Warm-up
Teaching Time: 5–10 min.

- GROUPS. Pass out a supermarket ad to each group. Give students a few minutes to look through it. Have students tell their group some things that they usually buy.
- Ask students to name some items that most people in the group usually buy.

Vocabulary
Teaching Time: 10–15 min.

- Ask students to point to and name any of the foods they know in the pictures.
- Explain unfamiliar vocabulary. For example, say: *Beef is food that comes from a cow. A carton is a small box made of thick paper.*
- Tell students that *healthy* means *good for your body.*
- 🎧 Play Track 33 while students read and listen.
- Read each word aloud and have students repeat chorally.
- Have students complete the task.
- PAIRS. Have students compare their answers.
- Call on volunteers to read the words they have circled. Ask other students if they agree with their classmates' choices.

Unit 5
Food and Drink

Grammar
- Count and Noncount Nouns
- Quantifiers: *Some / A little / A lot of / A few / Any*
- Count and Noncount Nouns: Questions

Vocabulary

🎧 **33** Read and listen. Then circle the things that are good for you.
Answers will vary.

1. fruit
2. apples
3. bananas
4. oranges
5. vegetables
6. carrots
7. tomatoes
8. spinach
9. ice cream
10. mayonnaise
11. eggs
12. bread
13. meat
14. beef
15. chicken
16. fish
17. a box of rice
18. a carton of juice
19. a can of soup
20. a box of tea
21. a carton of milk
22. a bag of candy
23. a package of cookies

52   Unit 5

Expansion
- Draw the following graphic organizer on the board.

Good for you to eat every day	Good for you to eat every week	Good for you to eat once a month

- GROUPS. Have students write each item from the list in one of the categories.
- Have groups say their answers. Invite groups to disagree and explain their reasons.

Culture Notes
- **Exercise B.** Remind students that weight in the United States is measured in pounds and that 1 pound = .45 kilograms.
- **LIFE SKILLS TEST PREP 2** Go to Unit 5, Lesson 2 for more practice in identifying common quantities of foods.
- Point out Lynn's line: *Wow, these tomatoes are expensive—$5.00 a pound!* Tell students that *$5.00 a pound* means that one pound (of tomatoes) costs $5.00.
- **LIFE SKILLS TEST PREP 2** Go to Unit 5, Lesson 4 for more practice in reading and comparing basic information in simple advertisements.

T-52   Center Stage 2

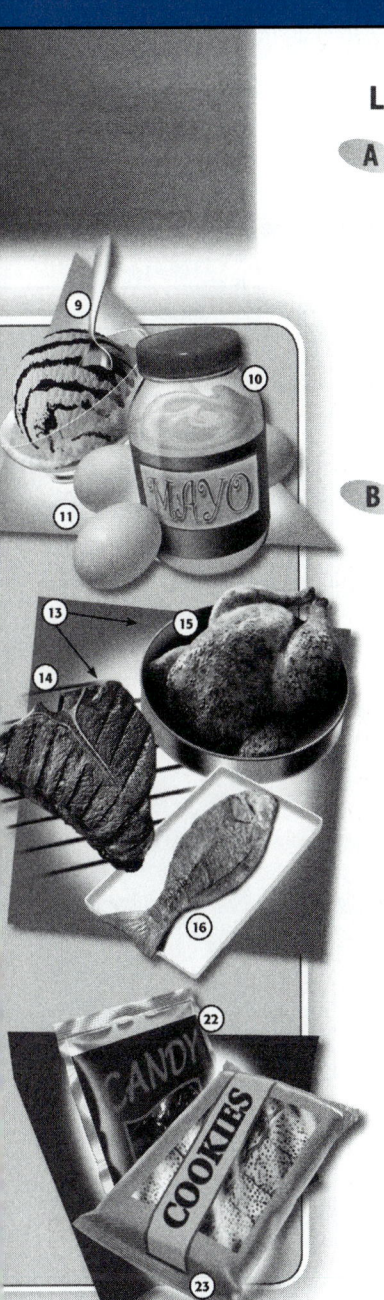

Listening

A 🎧 34 Listen. A man and a woman talk about food shopping. Check (✓) the statements that the man agrees with.

☐ 1. The oranges in the store are cheap.
☑ 2. Fruit is expensive in the U.S.
☐ 3. Vegetables are cheap in the U.S.
☑ 4. Rice is cheap in Haiti.
☐ 5. Meat isn't expensive in Haiti.
☑ 6. Tomatoes are cheap in Haiti.

B 🎧 35 Read and listen again. Write the missing words. Use the words in the box.

| A few | a little | How many | ~~How much~~ |

René: And fruit is really cheap. Hmm... There aren't any tomatoes.

Worker: There are a few tomatoes over there, next to the bananas.

René: Oh, great. Thanks. Hmm, is there any spinach?

Worker: It's right here. _How much_ do you need?
                                    1.

René: Just _a little_. One package is fine.
              2.

Lynn: Wow, these tomatoes are expensive—$5.00 a pound!

René: $5.00 a pound? _How many_ are there in a pound?
                              3.

Worker: _A few_ —about 3 or 4.
          4.

Food and Drink 53

Listening

A Teaching Time: 10–15 min.

- **Warm-up:** Point out or have students locate Haiti on a world map. Ask a few questions about the country, such as: *Is Haiti an island? What are some cities in Haiti? What are some countries near Haiti?*
- Ask students to read through the statements before they listen.
- 🎧 Play Track 34 while students listen.
- 🎧 Play Track 34 again while students listen and complete the task.
- PAIRS. Have students compare their answers.
- 🎧 Play Track 34 again while students check their answers. Pause the recording each time an answer is given.

B Teaching Time: 15–20 min.

- Have students read through the answer choices before they listen.
- 🎧 Play Track 35 while students complete the task.
- 🎧 Play Track 35 again while students check their answers.
- Call on students to say answers. Correct as needed.
- Read the conversation aloud. Pause after each few words and have students repeat chorally.
- GROUPS. Ask students to role-play the conversation.

Multilevel Strategy

- **Pre-level:** Have students role-play the completed conversation.
- **At-level, Above-level:** Have students continue the conversation while they role-play. Prompt them with suggestions (e.g., *Ask about more fruit.*). Ask them to role-play in front of the class.

Option

Assign Unit 5 Supplementary Vocabulary Exercise on the Teacher's Resource Disk as homework or on the Student Persistence CD-ROM as self-access practice.

Unit 5 T-53

Grammar to Communicate 1

Count and Noncount Nouns

Teaching Time: 5–10 min.

- Say: *Count nouns are things you can count. They have singular and plural forms. To find out if a thing is a count noun, try to count it. For example, one apple, two apples, three apples.*
- Say: *Noncount nouns are things you can't count. They don't have plural forms. For example,* water *is a noncount noun.*
- Name a few nouns such as *tomato* and *juice* and ask about each one: *Is it a count noun or a noncount noun?*
- Have students study the chart and the Look Box.
- Read the sentences in the chart and have students repeat chorally.

A Teaching Time: 5–10 min.

- Read the examples with the class.
- Tell students to try to count the noun if they are unsure whether the noun is count or noncount.
- Have students complete the task.
- Call on students to say answers. Correct as needed.

Multilevel Strategy

- **Pre-level:** Group all pre-level students to complete the task. Help students with the task by having them try to count each noun. Tell students that if they can't count the noun it is noncount.
- **Above-level:** Challenge students with the task by having them add words not included on pages 52–53 and write them in the correct column. Call on students to read the additional words to the class.

B Teaching Time: 5–10 min.

- Read the examples with the class.
- Remind students that if a noun is noncount, they can't make it plural.

- Have students complete the task.
- Call on students to say answers. Correct as needed.

C Teaching Time: 5–10 min.

- PAIRS. Have students complete the task.
- Walk around and help as needed.
- Call on volunteers to say one of their sentences. Conduct an informal survey after each sentence. Ask students to raise their hands if they agree.

Grammar to Communicate 1

COUNT AND NONCOUNT NOUNS

	Count Noun	Be			Noncount Noun	Be	
The	banana	is	50¢.	The	meat	is	$3.00 a pound.
	bananas	are	69¢ a pound.		fruit		inexpensive.
			inexpensive.		candy		

A Look at pages 52–53. Write the food and drinks in the correct column.

COUNT NOUNS	NONCOUNT NOUNS
vegetables	fruit
apples	rice
bananas	spinach, ice cream,
oranges	mayonnaise, bread,
carrots	meat, beef, chicken,
tomatoes	fish, juice, soup, tea,
eggs	milk, candy
cookies	

Look
Count nouns:
1 sandwich, 2 sandwiches
Noncount nouns:
rice NOT ~~rices~~

B If the sentence has a count noun, make the noun plural. Then rewrite the sentence. If the sentence has a noncount noun, write *noncount*.

1. The tea is hot. — noncount
2. The sandwich is in the bag. — The sandwiches are in the bag.
3. The tea isn't in the kitchen. — noncount
4. The cookie is delicious. — The cookies are delicious.
5. The fruit isn't fresh. — noncount
6. The orange is big. — The oranges are big.
7. The apple is bad. — The apples are bad.
8. The lettuce isn't very good. — noncount

C PAIRS. Which things on pages 52–53 are good for you? Make five sentences with *is, isn't, are,* or *aren't*. Answers will vary.

Example:
A: Fish is good for you.
B: Candy isn't good for you.

Unit 5

Grammar Notes

1. Count nouns are things that you can count. They have singular and plural forms.
2. Noncount nouns are things that you can't count. They do not have plural forms.
3. Use *How much* to ask about the price of something. Use *How much is* with a singular or a noncount noun. Use *How much are* with plural nouns.
4. For more information on this grammar topic, see page 254.

T-54 Center Stage 2

D 🎧 36 Look at the supermarket receipt. Ask and answer questions. Use *How much*. Then listen and check your answers.

```
ACE 🛒 SUPERMARKET
BANANAS      $  1.79
MILK         $  1.89
JUICE        $  3.06
RICE         $  2.89
POTATOES     $  1.99
EGGS         $  1.79
CANDY        $  2.50
COFFEE       $  3.49
ORANGES      $  2.00
```

Look
There are two ways to say prices:
$1.79 = one seventy nine OR
one dollar and seventy nine cents

1. (bananas)   How much are the bananas?   They're $1.79.
2. (milk)   How much is the milk?   It's $1.89.
3. (juice)   How much is the juice?   It's $3.06.
4. (rice)   How much is the rice?   It's $2.89.
5. (potatoes) How much are the potatoes?   They're $1.99.
6. (eggs)   How much are the eggs?   They're $1.79.
7. (candy)   How much is the candy?   It's $2.50.
8. (coffee)   How much is the coffee?   It's $3.49.
9. (oranges)   How much are the oranges?   They're $2.00.

TIME to TALK

PAIRS. Student A: Look at the supermarket ad on page 267.
Student B: Look at the supermarket ad on page 269.
Ask and answer questions about the prices in your partner's store. Which store has better prices? *Answers will vary.*

Example:
A: How much are potatoes in your store?
B: They're 69 cents a pound. How much are they in your store?
A: They're 59 cents a pound.

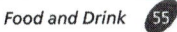

Food and Drink 55

D Teaching Time: 10–15 min.
- Have two students read the example.
- Tell students to use *How much is* with singular and noncount nouns and *How much are* with plural nouns.
- Have students complete the task.
- 🎧 Play Track 36 while students check their answers.
- **LIFE SKILLS TEST PREP 2** Go to Unit 5, Lesson 6 for more practice in asking for clarification using different strategies.

Multilevel Strategy
- **Pre-level, At-level:** Pair pre-level students with at-level students to complete the task. For each item, have at-level students form the question and dictate it to their partner. Then have pre-level students form the answer and dictate it to at-level students.
- **Above-level:** Have students role-play as customer and clerk as they take turns asking and answering questions about prices. Encourage students to comment on whether the prices are reasonable or not (e.g., *Juice is $3.06? So expensive!*).

Expansion
- Have students study the Look Box.
- Have students practice saying each price on the receipt both ways.
- **LIFE SKILLS TEST PREP 2** Go to Unit 6, Lesson 2 for more practice in reading and computing receipts.

Language Note

Grammar chart. Point out the ¢ sign. Explain that this sign means *cents* and it is used with amounts of less than one dollar. For example: 75¢ = $0.75 = seventy-five cents.

Option

Assign Unit 5 Supplementary Grammar to Communicate 1 Exercises on the Teacher's Resource Disk as homework or on the Student Persistence CD-ROM as self-access practice.

TIME to TALK

Teaching Time: 10–15 min.
- Have two students read the example conversation.
- PAIRS. Have students complete the task.
- Walk around and help as needed.

Expansion
- Ask students to bring in weekly supermarket ads.
- PAIRS. Have partners ask and answer questions similar to the ones in *Time to Talk* about the prices of sale items.
- Walk around and help as needed.
- Ask volunteers to tell the class about any good prices they found.

Unit 5   T-55

Grammar to Communicate 2

Quantifiers: *Some / A little / A lot of / A few / Any*

Teaching Time: 5–10 min.

- Draw the following graphic organizer on the board.

count
  nouns   any / no   a few   some   a lot of
    0- →
noncount
  nouns   any / no   a little   some   a lot of

- Say: *Any* and *no* mean zero. *A few* and *a little* mean very small amounts. Use *some* to talk about small or medium amounts. Use *a lot of* to talk about large amounts.
- Say: Use *any / no, some,* and *a lot of* with count and noncount nouns. Use *a few* with count nouns. Use *a little* with noncount nouns.
- Say: *Only use any in negative sentences, such as There isn't any tea.*
- Have students study the chart.
- Read the sentences in the chart and have students repeat chorally.

A   Teaching Time: 3–5 min.

- Have students study the pictures and read the examples.
- Have students complete the task.
- Call on students to say answers. Correct as needed.

B   Teaching Time: 5–10 min.

- Read the example with the class.
- Call on volunteers to come to the board and write the complete sentences. Correct as needed.

Multilevel Strategy

- **At-level, Above-level:** Call on only at-level and above-level students to write the sentences on the board.
- **Pre-level:** Have students copy the sentences from the board.

Grammar to Communicate 2

QUANTIFIERS: *SOME / A LITTLE / A LOT OF / A FEW / ANY*

		Quantifier	Noncount Noun				Any	Noncount Noun
There	is	some a little a lot of	rice fruit sugar	on the counter.	There	isn't	any	rice. fruit. sugar.

		Quantifier	Count Noun				Any	Count Noun
There	are	some a few a lot of	eggs bananas vegetables	on the counter.	There	aren't	any	eggs.

A   Look at the pictures. Write *a, an, some, a few, a little,* or *a lot of*.

NONCOUNT NOUNS
(butter, pepper, salt, sugar, cheese, FLOUR)

1. _some_ butter   3. _some_ salt   5. _some_ cheese
2. _a little_ pepper   4. _some_ sugar   6. _a lot of_ flour

COUNT NOUNS
(mushroom, nuts, onion, peppers, oranges)

7. _a_ mushroom   9. _an_ onion   11. _a lot of_ oranges
8. _a lot of_ nuts 10. _a few_ peppers

B   Write sentences. Put the words in the correct order. Add *some* or *any*.

1. There is some cheese on a pizza.
   (pizza / is / a / cheese / there / on / some)
2. There aren't any apples in a hamburger.
   (aren't / hamburger / a / there / apples / in)
3. There is some milk in ice cream.
   (ice cream / milk / is / in / there)
4. There is some sugar in cookies.
   (cookies / there / in / sugar / is)
5. There aren't any nuts on a pizza.
   (a / on / there / pizza / nuts / aren't)

Unit 5

Grammar Notes

1. A quantifier tells about the quantity or amount of something.
2. Use *some, a little,* and *a lot of* with noncount nouns in affirmative sentences.
3. Use *some, a few,* and *a lot of* with count nouns in affirmative sentences.
4. *A little* and *a few* mean a very small amount. *Some* means a small or medium amount. *A lot of* means a large amount.
5. Use *any* with count and noncount nouns in negative sentences. Use *no* with count and noncount nouns in affirmative sentences. *Not any* and *no* mean zero.
6. For more information on this grammar topic, see page 254.

Center Stage 2

C Read the ingredients in the recipe. Then complete the sentences. Use *some* or *any*.

1. There __are some__ tomatoes in the soup.
2. There __isn't any__ milk.
3. There __is some__ water.
4. There __aren't any__ eggs.
5. There __is some__ butter.
6. There __isn't any__ flour.
7. There __is some__ pepper.
8. There __are some__ onions.

TOMATO-SPINACH SOUP

Ingredients:
6 tomatoes
2 cups water
2 onions
3 cups spinach
1 teaspoon salt
1 teaspoon sugar
1 teaspoon pepper
1 tablespoon butter

Instructions on the back

D Look at the picture. Complete the sentences. Use the words in the box and *a little* or *a few*.

Look
a few eggs = 3 to 5
a little water = a small amount

1. There's a little butter.
2. There's a little cheese.
3. There's a little pepper.
4. There are a few oranges.
5. There are a few peppers.
6. There's a little sugar.

TIME to TALK

GROUPS. Talk about typical dishes in your country. What are your favorite dishes? What are the ingredients?
Answers will vary.
Example:
My favorite dish is shish kebab. There is a lot of meat in shish kebab, and there are some onions and peppers in it, too.

WRAP-UP. Now tell the class about the most interesting dish in your group.

shish kebab

Unit 5 Food and Drink 57

C Teaching Time: 5–10 min.
- Read the examples with the class.
- Tell students a recipe gives instructions for making food. Ingredients are the foods that you put together to make something. Ask students to name some ingredients in common foods such as cookies (*flour, sugar, eggs, butter,* etc.).
- Tell students to use contractions in their answers.
- Have students complete the task.
- Call on students to say answers. Correct as needed.

Expansion
- Bring to class a set of measuring cups and a set of measuring spoons. Tell students that people in the United States usually use these measurements for recipes.
- Hold up each cup and spoon. Say and write on the board its size. Also write abbreviations. For example: ½ cup = ½ C = half a cup.

D Teaching Time: 5–10 min.
- Have students study the Look box. Remind them to use *a few* with count nouns and *a little* with noncount nouns.
- Tell students to write one sentence for each picture.
- Have students complete the task.
- Call on students to write answers on the board. Write corrections on the board as needed.

Option
Assign Unit 5 Supplementary Grammar to Communicate 2 Exercises on the Teacher's Resource Disk as homework or on the Student Persistence CD-ROM as self-access practice.

TIME to TALK Teaching Time: 15–20 min.
- Read the example with the class.
- GROUPS. Have students complete the task. Encourage them to use a dictionary or ask someone to find unknown vocabulary.
- Walk around and help as needed.
- Ask volunteers to tell the class about their group's most interesting dish.

Multilevel Strategy
- **Pre-level:** Copy the example on the board. Tell students to use it as a model to talk about their favorite dish. Underline the information that students should substitute in their examples. If necessary, have students write their examples before talking with their classmates.

Unit 5

Grammar to Communicate 3

Count and Noncount Nouns: *Yes / No* Questions

Teaching Time: 3–5 min.

- Write on the board: *Is there a ___ ?* Say: *Use this with singular count nouns.*
- Write: *Are there any ___ ?* Say: *Use this with plural count nouns.*
- Write: *Is there any ___ ?* Say: *Use this with noncount nouns.*
- Tell students to answer these questions with *Yes, there is. / Yes, there are.* or *No, there isn't. / No, there aren't.*
- Have students study the chart and the Look Box.
- Read the sentences in the chart and have students repeat chorally.

A Teaching Time: 5–10 min.

- Read the example with the class.
- Have students complete the task.
- 🎧 Play Track 37 while students check their answers.
- Call on students to say answers. Correct as needed.
- Have students take turns asking and answering the questions.

B Teaching Time: 5–10 min.

- Have two students read the examples.
- Have students complete the task.
- Call on pairs of students to say questions and answers. Correct as needed.

Multilevel Strategy

- **Pre-level:** Group all pre-level students. Dictate complete questions to students and have them form answers. After checking answers, have pairs take turns asking and answering the questions.
- **At-level, Above-level:** After checking answers, pair students and have them take turns asking and answering the questions. Encourage them to add more information to their answers (e.g., A: *Are there any potatoes?* B: *Yes, there are. There are some potatoes.*).

Grammar to Communicate 3

COUNT AND NONCOUNT NOUNS: YES / NO QUESTIONS

Be	There	Any	Noun		Yes	There	Be		No	There	Be + Not
Is	there	any	rice	in the box?	Yes,	there	is.		No,	there	isn't.
Are			cookies				are.				aren't.

A 🎧 37

Look at the supermarket sign. Answer the questions about Aisle 4. Then listen and check your answers.

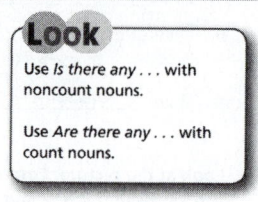

Look
Use *Is there any . . .* with noncount nouns.
Use *Are there any . . .* with count nouns.

AISLE 4
Coffee
Tea
Sugar
Flour
Cookies

1. Is there any coffee? <u>Yes, there is.</u>
2. Are there any eggs? <u>No, there aren't.</u>
3. Is there any tea? <u>Yes, there is.</u>
4. Are there any cookies? <u>Yes, there are.</u>
5. Are there any nuts? <u>No, there aren't.</u>
6. Is there any sugar? <u>Yes, there is.</u>
7. Is there any candy? <u>No, there isn't.</u>
8. Is there any juice? <u>No, there isn't.</u>

B

Write questions about the food in your home today. Then answer the questions.

1. (potatoes) <u>Are there any potatoes?</u> Yes, there are. OR No, there aren't.
2. (rice) <u>Is there any rice?</u> Yes, there is. OR No, there isn't.
3. (fruit) <u>Is there any fruit?</u> Yes, there is. OR No, there isn't.
4. (carrots) <u>Are there any carrots?</u> Yes, there are. OR No, there aren't.
5. (milk) <u>Is there any milk?</u> Yes, there is. OR No, there isn't.
6. (vegetables) <u>Are there any vegetables?</u> Yes, there are. OR No, there aren't.
7. (beef) <u>Is there any beef?</u> Yes, there is. OR No, there isn't.
8. (apples) <u>Are there any apples?</u> Yes, there are. OR No, there aren't.

Unit 5

Grammar Notes

1. To ask about singular count nouns, use *Is there a / an.* (*Is there an egg?*)
2. To ask about plural count nouns use *Are there any.* (*Are there any apples?*)
3. To ask about noncount nouns, use *Is there any.* (*Is there any sugar?*)
4. Use short answer for *yes / no* questions.
5. For more information on this grammar topic, see page 254.

Teaching Tip

Teach students to use the sentence *I'm not sure* when they don't know or don't remember the answer to a question.

Center Stage 2

INFORMATION QUESTIONS: HOW MUCH / HOW MANY					
How	Much / Many	Noun	Be		Answers
How	much	rice	is	there?	One box.
	many	cookies	are		Two.

Look

Use *How much* with noncount nouns.
Use *How many* with count nouns.

C Write questions. Use *How much* or *How many*.

1. (water) How much water is there? — There are two bottles.
2. (rice) How much rice is there? — There's one box.
3. (milk) How much milk is there? — There's one carton.
4. (potatoes) How many potatoes are there? — There's one bag.
5. (coffee) How much coffee is there? — There are two cans.
6. (cookies) How many cookies are there? — There are two packages.

D Rewrite the questions. Use *How much* or *How many*.

1. How much water is there? (bottles) — How many bottles of water are there?
2. How much rice is there? (boxes) — How many boxes of rice are there?
3. How much candy is there? (bags) — How many bags of candy are there?
4. How much spinach is there? (packages) — How many packages of spinach are there?
5. How much milk is there? (cartons) — How many cartons of milk are there?
6. How much tea is there? (boxes) — How many boxes of tea are there?
7. How much soda is there? (bottles) — How many bottles of soda are there?
8. How much soup is there? (cans) — How many cans of soup are there?

TIME to TALK

PAIRS. Student A: Study the picture on pages 52-53. Then close your book. Student B: Ask Student A questions about the picture on pages 52-53. Use *Is there* and *Are there*. If Student A answers yes, ask a question with *How much* or *How many*. After a few minutes, change roles. Answers will vary.

Example:
A: Are there any tomatoes?
B: Yes, there are.
A: That's correct. How many tomatoes are there?
B: There are four.
A: That's wrong. There are two.

Food and Drink 59

Grammar Notes

1. To ask about the amount of a count noun, use *How many*. For example: *How many mushrooms are there?*
2. To ask about the amount of a noncount noun, use *How much*. For example: *How much salt is there?*
3. For more information on this grammar topic, see page 254.

Option

Assign Unit 5 Supplementary Grammar to Communicate 3 Exercises on the Teacher's Resource Disk as homework or on the Student Persistence CD-ROM as self-access practice.

Information Questions: How much / How many

Teaching Time: 5–10 min.

- Say: *Use* How much *and* How many *to ask about quantities or amounts of things.*
- Write on the board: *How much milk is there? How many apples are there?*
- Say: *Use* How much *with noncount nouns. Use* How many *with count nouns.*
- Tell students they can answer with a specific amount, such as *There are two cookies*. Or they can answer with a quantifier, such as *There is a lot of rice*.
- Have students study the chart and the Look Box.
- Read the sentences in the chart and have students repeat chorally.

C Teaching Time: 5–10 min.

- Read the example with the class.
- Call on volunteers to come to the board and write the questions. Correct as needed.

D Teaching Time: 5–10 min.

- Read the example with the class.
- Remind students to use *how much* with noncount nouns and *how many* with count nouns.
- Call on volunteers to come to the board and write the questions. Correct as needed.
- **LIFE SKILLS TEST PREP 2** Go to Unit 5, Lesson 1 for more practice in identifying common foods and their containers.

Multilevel Strategy

- **At-level, Above-level:** Call on only at-level and above-level students to write the questions in Exercises C and D on the board.
- **Pre-level:** Have students copy the questions in Exercises C and D from the board.

TIME to TALK

Teaching Time: 10–15 min.

- Have two students read the example conversation.
- PAIRS. Have students complete the task.
- Walk around and help as needed.
- Invite volunteers to say how many questions they answered correctly.

Unit 5 T-59

Review and Challenge

Grammar

Teaching Time: 5–10 min.

- Read the example with the class.
- Have students complete the task.
- PAIRS. Have students compare answers.
- 🎧 Play Track 38 while students check their answers. Pause the recording each time an answer is given.
- PAIRS. Have students role-play the completed conversation.
- **LIFE SKILLS TEST PREP 2** Go to Unit 6, Lesson 4 for more practice in making simple requests about availability of items in a store.

Dictation

Teaching Time: 5–10 min.

- 🎧 Play Track 39 while students listen and write what they hear.
- 🎧 Play Track 39 again while students check their answers.
- PAIRS. Have students compare their answers.
- Call on students to write answers on the board.
- 🎧 Play Track 39 again and correct the sentences on the board.

> **Multilevel Strategy**
>
> **Pre-level:** Give students a worksheet with some of the words from the dictation already provided.

Speaking

Teaching Time: 10–15 min.

- Have two students read the example conversation.
- Tell students to ask questions about the restaurants and to choose the restaurant to go to.
- PAIRS. Have students complete the task. Walk around and help as needed.
- Call on students to tell the class which restaurant they chose. Ask: *Why is Lou's good? Why is Sheila's good?*
- **LIFE SKILLS TEST PREP 2** Go to Unit 5, Lesson 5 for more practice in reading and ordering from a simple menu.

T-60 Center Stage 2

Review and Challenge

Grammar

🎧 **38** Complete the conversation. Use the words in the box. Then listen and check your answers. (Be careful! There is one extra word.)

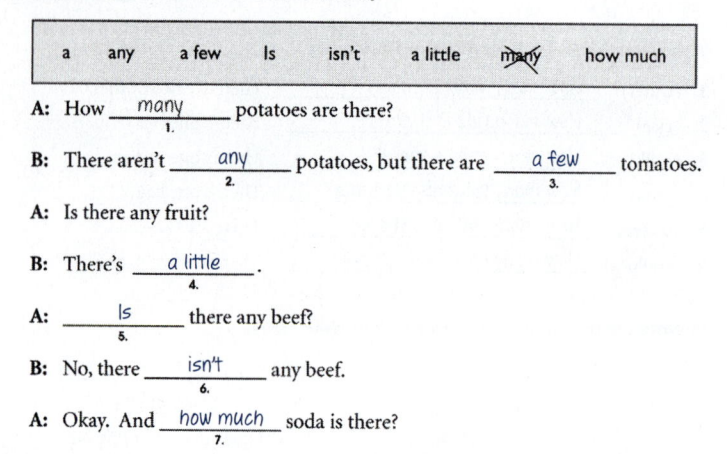

| a | any | a few | Is | isn't | a little | ~~many~~ | how much |

A: How __many__ potatoes are there?

B: There aren't __any__ potatoes, but there are __a few__ tomatoes.

A: Is there any fruit?

B: There's __a little__.

A: __Is__ there any beef?

B: No, there __isn't__ any beef.

A: Okay. And __how much__ soda is there?

Dictation

🎧 **39** Listen. You will hear five sentences. Write them on a piece of paper. *See the audioscript on page 279 for the sentences.*

Speaking

PAIRS. Student A: Look at the menu on page 269.
Student B: Look at the menu on page 274.
Ask and answer five questions about the menus. *Answers will vary.*

Example:
A: Are there any hamburgers on the menu?
B: Yes, there are hamburgers and cheeseburgers.
A: How much is a cheeseburger?
B: It's $8.00.
A: That's expensive. At my restaurant, a cheeseburger is $5.50.

WRAP-UP. Which restaurant would you like to go to? Tell the class. *Answers will vary.*

Unit 5

Option

Start a discussion on the best supermarkets in your neighborhood or city. Prompt students with questions such as: *Which supermarkets are good? What is good about that supermarket: prices, workers, locations, etc.?*

Listening

A 🎧 **40** Listen. The women talk about two supermarkets. Check (✓) the things that the women talk about.

customers in line — shopping cart

- ☐ fruit and vegetables
- ☐ meat
- ✓ shopping carts
- ✓ lines
- ✓ prices
- ☐ workers

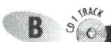

B 🎧 **41** Listen again. Read the sentences. Check (✓) the correct boxes.

	Joe's	Sam's
1. There aren't any shopping carts.	✓	☐
2. There are long lines.	✓	☐
3. The workers aren't helpful.	✓	☐
4. It's clean.	☐	✓
5. It's expensive.	✓	✓

TIME to TALK

In your opinion, what are the two most important things you find in a good supermarket? Check (✓) two. *Answers will vary.*

- ☐ The prices are good.
- ☐ There aren't any long lines.
- ☐ It's close to my home.
- ☐ There are friendly workers.
- ☐ It's open at night and on weekends.
- ☐ The food is fresh.

GROUPS. Talk about your answers. Do you agree?

Food and Drink   61

Listening

A Teaching Time: 5–10 min.

- **Warm-up:** Have students look at the picture. Ask: *Where are the people?* (in a supermarket) *What does the sign 50% mean?* (there is a sale)
- Ask students to read through the answer choices before they listen. Explain unfamiliar vocabulary. For example, say: *The people are waiting in line. Meat is food that comes from animals.*
- 🎧 Play Track 40 while students listen.
- 🎧 Play Track 40 again while students listen and choose the correct answers.
- Call on students to say answers. Correct as needed.
- Ask students comprehension questions about the conversation. Modify the questions to the level of the students.

Multilevel Strategy

- **Pre-level:** Ask students *yes / no* questions (e.g., *Are Sarah and Alice at an outdoor market?*).
- **At-level:** Ask students information questions (e.g., *Where are Sarah and Alice?*).
- **Above-level:** Ask students open-ended or critical thinking questions (e.g., *Which supermarket do you think is better, Joe's or Sam's?*).

B Teaching Time: 5–10 min.

- Ask students to read through the sentences before they listen.
- 🎧 Play Track 41 while students listen and complete the task.
- **PAIRS.** Have students compare answers.
- 🎧 Play Track 41 again while students check their answers. Pause the recording each time an answer is given.

Option

Assign Unit 5 Supplementary Review and Challenge Exercises on the Teacher's Resource Disk as homework or on the Student Persistence CD-ROM as self-access practice.

TIME to TALK

Teaching Time: 10–15 min.

- Give students a few minutes to complete the first part of the task.
- GROUPS. Have students talk about their answers.
- Walk around and help as needed.
- Call on volunteers to say which things are important for most people in their group.

Unit 5   T-61

Reading and Writing

Reading

A   Teaching Time: 10–15 min.

- Tell students that a newsletter is a short report of news or information for people with certain interests. Point to the title of the newsletter and ask: *Who is this newsletter for?* (people who are new to the U.S.). Point to the title of the article. Ask: *What is the newsletter about?* (American food).
- Ask students to read through the answer choices before they read the paragraph.
- Have students read the paragraph silently.
- Read the paragraph aloud. Pause after each few words and have students repeat chorally.
- Have students check the foods from the paragraph.
- Call on students to say the answers. Correct as needed. Show students where they can find each word in the paragraph.

B   Teaching Time: 10–15 min.

- Tell students to use the other words in the reading to help them guess the meanings of the words in italics.
- Have students complete the task.
- Call on students to say the answers. Correct as needed.

Expansion Start a discussion on the foods that are typical in students' U.S. neighborhood and / or city. Prompt students by asking: *What are some foods that a lot of people in your neighborhood eat? Think about the kinds of restaurants in your neighborhood and the kinds of foods in the supermarkets.*

Reading and Writing

Reading

A   Read the paragraph from a newsletter. Check (✓) the kinds of food in the paragraph.

- ☐ apples
- ☑ French fries
- ☐ hot dogs
- ☐ onions
- ☑ peppers
- ☐ cookies
- ☑ hamburgers
- ☑ ice cream
- ☐ oranges
- ☑ tomatoes

New to the U.S.
A NEWSLETTER FOR NEWCOMERS
Volume XXXIII

What is American food? Is it hamburgers and French fries? Is it ice cream and apple pie? In fact, there are many different kinds of American food. There are two important reasons for this. First, the United States is a big place, and the weather is different in different parts of the country. For example, in the Southeast there is a lot of sun and warm weather *year-round*. That's why there are a lot of warm-weather vegetables like tomatoes and peppers in Southern *recipes*. Second, the United States is a country of *immigrants*, and immigrants bring their *traditional* food with them. For example, the first immigrants to New Orleans, Louisiana, were from France, Spain, and Africa. Today, the recipes for many famous New Orleans foods, such as beignets and rice and beans, are a *delicious mixture* of French, Spanish, and African cooking.

B   Look at the words in italics. Find them in the newsletter. Then circle the correct meaning.

1. *Year-round* is
   a. 6 months.
   b.) 12 months.
2. *Recipes* tell us how to
   a. eat something.
   b.) cook something.
3. *Immigrants* are from
   a. New Orleans.
   b.) other countries.
4. Something that is *traditional* is
   a. new.
   b.) old.
5. Something that is *delicious* is
   a.) good to eat.
   b. easy to cook.
6. A *mixture* has
   a.) two or more things.
   b. one thing.

62   Unit 5

Option

- Tell students to make a menu for an imaginary restaurant that serves food from their country.
- Tell students to give some information about each dish. Write an example on the board, such as: *Cobb salad, lettuce, tomatoes, peppers, eggs, chicken, and cheese.*
- Teach students the words *appetizers, main dishes,* and *desserts* so they can include these categories and examples in each in their menus.
- Walk around and help as needed.
- If possible, display students' menus for others to look at.

T-62   Center Stage 2

Prewriting

Make a list of the different kinds of traditional food in your country.

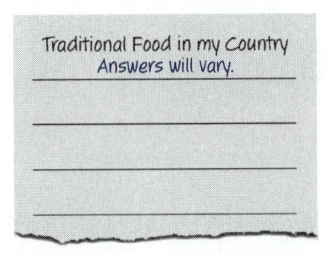

> Traditional Food in my Country
> Answers will vary.

Writing

Write about the traditional food of your country for the newsletter. Use the newsletter on page 62 as a model. Answers will vary.

New to _____
A NEWSLETTER FOR NEWCOMERS
Volume XXXIII

Writing Tip

Use *for example* to give an example of something. We usually use *For example* and a comma (,) at the beginning of a sentence.

Example: The U. S. has many different kinds of food in different parts of the country. **For example,** in the Northwest there is a lot of fish.

Food and Drink 63

Prewriting

Teaching Time: 5–10 min.

- Have students list four different kinds of food from their country.
- Walk around and help as needed.

Writing

Teaching Time: 15–20 min.

- Draw the following graphic organizer on the board.

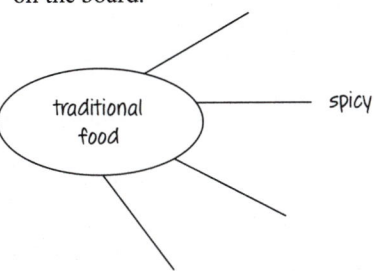

  traditional food — spicy

- Tell students to use a graphic organizer to organize their ideas before they write.
- Ask: *What are some words to describe traditional food in your country? What is important for people to know about traditional food in your country?* Have students write as many words as they can on their graphic organizers. Record some of them on the graphic organizer on the board.
- Then tell students to use some of the ideas on their graphic organizer and the information they wrote in the previous exercise to write the paragraphs.
- Have students complete the task.
- Walk around and help as needed.
- Call on volunteers to read their paragraphs to the class. Correct as needed. You can also have students write their paragraphs on a separate piece of paper. Collect their work and provide individual feedback.

Language Note

- **Writing.** Have students study the Writing Tip.
- Say: *If the second sentence shows something about the first sentence, add* For example *and a comma.*
- Write on the board: *A lot of Mexican food is spicy. For example, enchiladas, chilaquiles, and chalupas are typical spicy dishes.*

Multilevel Strategy

- **Pre-level:** While students are completing their graphic organizers, write the following on the board:

  In ___ there are many kinds of traditional food. The popular dishes are ___ . The food in ___ is ___ and ___ . People in ___ use a lot of ___ and ___ in their recipes. They also drink a lot of ___ . Their favorite dessert is ___ .

  Work with students to brainstorm possible words for each blank. Then have them complete the paragraph.

Unit 5 T-63

Unit 6
Physical Exercise

Learning Goals

- Learn words to describe sports and physical activities
- Learn about present progressive: statements, yes / no questions, and information questions
- Listen to a conversation and a sports commentary
- Read and write a report from a sports event
- Talk about sports and physical activities

Learner Persistence

Create anonymous evaluation forms to find out how students feel about your class. Incorporate students' likes and needs into your lessons. The more students like the class and feel that it is useful to them, the more likely they are to persist.

Warm-up

Teaching Time: 3–5 min.

- Explain that exercises are activities people do to stay healthy and strong. Sports are one way to exercise.
- Ask students to name some kinds of exercises, activities, and / or sports.

Vocabulary

Teaching Time: 15–20 min.

- Have students look at the pictures. Explain unfamiliar vocabulary. For example: *When you practice something, you do it a lot of times to get better at it.*
- 🎧 Play Track 42 while students read and listen.
- Read each word aloud and have students repeat chorally.
- Have students complete the activity.
- Call on students to point to the correct answers on the picture.

Expansion

- Have students read the words again.
- Pair same-level students and have them practice the vocabulary.

T-64 Center Stage 2

Unit 6
Physical Exercise

Grammar
- Present Progressive: Statements
- Present Progressive: Yes / No Questions
- Present Progressive: Information Questions

Vocabulary

🎧 **42** Read and listen. Then circle the people who are exercising.

1. take a shower
2. swim
3. run
4. go for a walk
5. sit
6. play tennis
7. practice tennis
8. play soccer
9. watch a soccer game
10. ride a bike
11. do exercises
12. go home

64 Unit 6

Multilevel Strategy

- **Pre-level:** Have one student point to the pictures and the other student say the word or phrase. Then have them switch roles.
- **At-level:** Have students cover the vocabulary list. Have one student say the number and the other student say the correct word or phrase. Then have them switch roles.
- **Above-level:** Have students cover the vocabulary list and take turns dictating the words and phrases to each other from memory.

Watch Out!

- **Vocabulary.** It's a common error to use the preposition *to* in the phrase *go home*. Listen for and correct errors such as *I'm going to home*.
- Some languages use an article when talking about sports. Listen for and correct errors such as *She's playing the soccer. They are practicing the tennis.*

Language Notes

- **Exercise B.** Point out the word *Yup* in the conversation. Tell students that it is a way to say *yes*. It is normally only used in speaking, not writing.

Listening

A 🎧 **43** Listen to Maria and Jenny's conversation. Look at the chart. Who is doing the activities? Check (✓) the correct answers.

	SWIMMING	RIDING A BIKE	RUNNING	PLAYING TENNIS
Mom is . . .	✓			
Dad is . . .		✓		
Bob is . . .				✓

B 🎧 **44** Read and listen again. Write the missing words. Use the words in the box.

| aren't watching | ~~doing~~ | he's running | is riding |

Maria: What's he ___doing___?
1.

Jenny: He's out riding his bike.

Maria: What? Dad ___is riding___ a bike!
2.

Jenny: Yup.

Maria: Amazing. . .Well, is Bob at home?

Jenny: Nope.

Maria: Wait, let me think . . . ___he's running___.
3.

Jenny: No, he's playing tennis.

Maria: Bob? Playing tennis? Are you kidding? It's Sunday afternoon, and he and Dad ___aren't watching___ a soccer game on TV?
4.

Physical Exercise 65

Listening

A Teaching Time: 10–15 min.

- **Warm-up:** Ask students: *Are some sports usually for just for boys and men or just for girls and women?* Ask students to explain their answers. Invite students to disagree and explain their ideas.
- Ask students to look at the chart before they listen.
- 🎧 Play Track 43 while students listen.
- 🎧 Play Track 43 again while students listen and complete the task.
- PAIRS. Have students compare their answers
- Call on students to say answers. Correct as needed.

B Teaching Time: 15–20 min.

- Have students read through the answer choices before they listen.
- 🎧 Play Track 44 while students listen and complete the task.
- 🎧 Play Track 44 again while students check their answers.
- Call on students to say answers. Correct as needed.
- Read the conversation aloud. Pause after each few words and have students repeat chorally.
- PAIRS. Have students role-play the conversation.

Multilevel Strategy

- **Pre-level:** Have students role-play the completed conversation.
- **At-level, Above-level:** Write the conversation on the board without the answers. Have students close their books and recall the answers as they role-play.

- Point out the question *Are you kidding?* Tell students that people sometimes ask this if they think something is hard to believe.

Option

Assign Unit 6 Supplementary Vocabulary Exercise on the Teacher's Resource Disk as homework or on the Student Persistence CD-ROM as self-access practice.

Unit 6 T-65

Grammar to Communicate 1

Present Progressive: Statements

Teaching Time: 5–10 min.

- Have students look again at the picture on pages 64 and 65. Point to the man running. Say: *He is running.* Sit down and say: *I'm sitting. I'm not standing.* Write these statements on the board and have students repeat chorally.
- Write on the board: be + verb + ing = now. Say: *We use a present form of be and a verb + ing to talk about actions that are happening now. This is called the present progressive.*
- Have students study the chart and the Look Box. Tell students to use contractions when using present progressive in conversations.
- Read the sentences in the chart and have students repeat chorally.
- Say a few sentences with the present progressive about the actions of students in the classroom.

A Teaching Time: 3–5 min.

- Have students look at the pictures. Explain unfamiliar vocabulary. For example: *A track suit is pants and a jacket that people wear to exercise.*
- Read the example with the class.
- Have students complete the task.
- Call on students to say answers. Correct as needed.

B Teaching Time: 5–10 min.

- Have students study the Look box.
- Write a few verbs on the board and have students spell the correct –ing forms. For example: *make, making; stop, stopping.*
- Read the examples with the class.
- Have students complete the task.
- Call on students to write answers on the board. Write corrections on the board as needed.

Expansion

- Before class, make two sets of flashcards, one set with a different subject pronoun on each card and one set of about twenty cards, each with a different action verb or phrase. Make some verbs affirmative and some negative (for example, *do exercises* and *not take a shower*).
- Keep the two piles separate. Take one card from each pile and show them to the class. Students make present progressive sentences with the words from the two cards.

Grammar Notes

1. Use the present progressive to talk about things that are happening now.
2. Form the present progressive with a present form of *be* and a verb + *ing*.
3. Make negative present progressive sentences with a present form of *be* + *not* and a verb + *ing*.
4. Use full forms or contractions. Contractions are more common in speaking. Two negative contractions are possible with *is* and *are*: *he's not* = *he isn't*; *you're not* = *you aren't*.
5. For more information on this grammar topic, see page 254.

Grammar to Communicate 1

PRESENT PROGRESSIVE: STATEMENTS

Subject	Be	Verb + –ing	Subject	Be	Not	Verb + –ing
I	am		I	am		
He / She / It	is	working.	He / She / It	is	not	working.
We / You / They	are		We / You / They	are		

Look

Use the present progressive to talk about things happening now.

We use contractions in conversation:
I'm working, he's working, we're working.

A Look at the pictures. What are the people wearing? Complete the sentences with the correct form of *wear*.

1. The man ___is wearing___ white sneakers.
2. The women ___are wearing___ tennis whites.
3. The man ___is wearing___ a blue helmet.
4. The girls ___are wearing___ black shorts.
5. The women ___are wearing___ blue track suits.

Look

If a verb ends in –e, drop the –e and add –ing:
  exercise   exercising

If a verb ends in 1 vowel + 1 consonant, double the consonant and add –ing:
  run   running

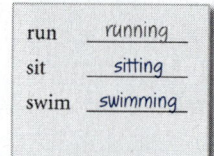

B Write the –ing forms of the verbs. Follow the patterns of the verbs in each column.

go	going	exercise	exercising	run	running
eat	eating	practice	practicing	sit	sitting
play	playing	ride	riding	swim	swimming
walk	walking	take	taking		

Unit 6

Center Stage 2

C Complete the sentences with the correct form of the verbs. Use contractions with pronouns.

1. The woman <u>is doing</u> exercises.
   (do)
   She <u>'s not taking</u> a shower.
   (not / take)
2. The women <u>aren't eating</u>. They <u>'re walking</u>.
   (not / eat) (walk)
3. The old man <u>is running</u>. He <u>'s not walking</u>.
   (run) (not / walk)
4. The young man <u>isn't sitting</u>. He <u>'s riding</u>
   (not / sit) (ride)
   a bicycle.

PAIRS. Write seven sentences about other people in the picture on pages 64–65. Take turns.
Answers will vary.

TIME TO TALK

PAIRS. Look at the pictures. Talk about what the people are doing. What is wrong with the pictures? Make three affirmative and three negative sentences.
Answers will vary.

Example:
A: *The woman is running. She is not wearing sneakers.*

Physical Exercise 67

C Teaching Time: 10–15 min.

- Read the example with the class.
- Remind students to pay attention to verb endings in order to spell the correct *-ing* forms.
- Have students complete the task.
- Call on students to say answers. Correct as needed.
- PAIRS. Have students make present progressive sentences about the pictures on pages 64 and 65.
- Walk around and help as needed.

Option
Assign Unit 6 Supplementary Grammar to Communicate 1 Exercises on the Teacher's Resource Disk as homework or on the Student Persistence CD-ROM as self-access practice.

TIME TO TALK

Teaching Time: 15–20 min.

- Have a student read the example.
- PAIRS. Have students complete the task.
- Walk around and help as needed.
- Call on volunteers to say some of their sentences, including what is wrong with each picture.

Multilevel Strategy

- **Pre-level:** Group all pre-level students and work with them to brainstorm possible sentences. Then pair students, have them choose two sentences and take turns reading them with a partner. Have students switch partners twice.
- **Above-level:** Challenge students with the task by having them write three sentences about each person in the pictures. Call on students to read their sentences to the class.

Unit 6 T-67

Grammar to Communicate 2

Present Progressive: *Yes / No* Questions and Short Answers

Teaching Time: 5–10 min.

- Say: *To ask yes / no questions about things that are happening now, put* be *before the subject.*
- Write on the board a few sentences such as: *We are practicing.* Have volunteers change each sentence into a question.
- Ask a few *yes / no* questions and have students answer.
- Have students study the grammar chart. Read each question and short answer and have students repeat chorally.

A Teaching Time: 5–10 min.

- Read the examples with the class.
- Have students complete the task.
- Call on pairs of students to read questions and answers. Correct as needed.

B Teaching Time: 10–15 min.

- Have students study the Look Box. Remind them to put *be* before the subject to ask questions.
- Read the example with the class.
- Have students complete the task.
- Call on students to write answers on the board. Write corrections on the board as needed.

Grammar to Communicate 2

PRESENT PROGRESSIVE: YES / NO QUESTIONS AND SHORT ANSWERS

Be	Subject	Verb + -ing		Affirmative			Negative	
Am	I			I	am.		I	am not.
Is	he / she / it	working?	Yes,	he / she / it	is.	No,	he / she / it	isn't.
Are	we / you / they			we / you / they	are.		we / you / they	aren't.

A Answer the questions with true information. Write short answers.

1. Are you swimming right now? — No, I'm not.
2. Is your teacher talking to your family? — No, she's not. OR No, he's not.
3. Are you exercising right now? — No, I'm not.
4. Are you learning English now? — Yes, I am.
5. Are you and a friend talking right now? — No, we aren't. OR No, we're not.
6. Is a friend sitting near you? — Yes, he / she is.
7. Are your classmates taking a shower? — No, they aren't. OR No, they're not.
8. Is your best friend working today? — Yes, he / she is. OR No, he's / she's not. OR No, he / she isn't.

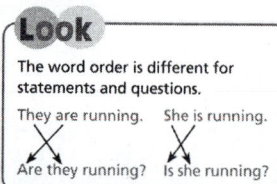

B Read the sentences. Write questions.

1. A: I'm not running.
   B: Are you walking? (walk)

2. A: They're not playing tennis.
   B: Are they playing soccer? (play soccer)

3. A: She's not eating ice cream.
   B: Is she eating cookies? (eat cookies)

4. A: I'm not talking to my friend.
   B: Are you talking to your neighbor? (talk to your neighbor)

5. A: He's not practicing tennis.
   B: Is he practicing baseball? (practice baseball)

6. A: We're not exercising at home.
   B: Are you exercising in a park? (exercise in a park)

Look
The word order is different for statements and questions.
They are running.   She is running.
Are they running?   Is she running?

Unit 6

Multilevel Strategy

- **Pre-level:** Pair students and have them take turns reading the sentences and questions.
- **At-level:** Pair students and have them take turns forming new answers using different verbs (e.g., *I'm not running. Are you standing?*).
- **Above-level:** Pair students and have them role-play and continue the conversations for at least two more exchanges. For example:
  A: *I'm not running.*
  B: *Are you walking?*
  A: *No, I'm not.*
  B: *Are you sitting?*
  A: *Yes, I am.*

Grammar Notes

1. To make *yes / no* questions in the present progressive, change the order of the form of *be* and the subject.
2. Do not use contractions in affirmative short answers. Use full forms or contractions in negative short answers.
3. For more information on this grammar topic, see page 254.

Option

- Before class, make two sets of flashcards, one set with a different subject pronoun on each card and one set of about twenty cards, each with a different action verb or phrase.

T-68 Center Stage 2

C Look at the pictures. Write questions. Put the words in the correct order.

1. Are the man and the woman running?
   (the man / running / the woman / are / and)
2. Is the woman wearing sneakers?
   (sneakers / is / the woman / wearing)
3. Are the people wearing track suits?
   (wearing / track suits / are / the people)
4. Are the children watching TV? 
   (TV / the children / are / watching)
5. Is the man swimming?
   (is / the man / swimming)
6. Is the man watching TV?
   (watching / is / the man / TV)

PAIRS. Ask and answer the questions above.
Example:
A: Are the man and woman running?
B: Yes, they are.

2. No, she's not. OR No, she isn't.
3. Yes, they are.
4. No, they're not. OR No, they aren't.
5. No, he's not. OR No, he isn't.
6. Yes, he is.

TIME to TALK

GROUPS. Student A: Choose a verb from page 64. Act it out for the other students. Can they guess the verb? Answer their questions with "Yes, I am" or "No, I'm not."
GROUP: Try to guess Student A's verb. Ask questions. Now another student acts out a verb. Continue until every student in the group has acted out two verbs. Answers will vary.

Example:
Group: Are you playing tennis?
A: No, I'm not.
Group: Are you swimming?
A: Yes, I am.

Physical Exercise 69

C Teaching Time: 10–15 min.
- Read the example with the class.
- Remind students that questions start with a capital letter and end with a question mark.
- Have students complete the task.
- Call on students to say answers. Correct as needed.
- Have two students read the example.
- PAIRS. Have students take turns asking and answering the questions.

Multilevel Strategy
- **Pre-level, At-level:** Pair pre-level students with at-level students for the partner activity. Have pre-level students read the questions and at-level students say the answers.

- Take one card from each pile and show them to the class. Have students make questions with each subject and verb. For example: If you draw *I* and *do sit-ups*, students say: *Am I doing sit-ups?*

Option

Assign Unit 6 Supplementary Grammar to Communicate 2 Exercises on the Teacher's Resource Disk as homework or on the Student Persistence CD-ROM as self-access practice.

TIME to TALK
Teaching Time: 10–15 min.
- Divide the class into groups.
- Have two students act out the example.
- GROUPS. Have students complete the task.
- Walk around and help as needed.

Unit 6   T-69

Grammar to Communicate 3

Present Progressive: Information Questions

Teaching Time: 5–10 min.

- Review *yes / no* questions by having students change a few present progressive statements into questions.
- Say: *To ask information questions, use a question word before the form of* be. Give a few examples, such as: *What is she doing?* Have students answer.
- Review the meaning of each of the *wh*-words if necessary.
- Have students study the chart.
- Read the sentences in the chart and have students repeat chorally.

A **Teaching Time: 5–10 min.**

- Have two students read the example.
- Have students complete the task.
- Call on students to say answers. Correct as needed.

B **Teaching Time: 10–15 min.**

- Read the example with the class.
- Have students complete the task.
- Call on students to write questions and answers on the board. Write corrections on the board as needed.

Multilevel Strategy

- **Pre-level:** Group all pre-level students and work with them to complete the questions. Help students identify what each *wh*-word refers to (person, thing, etc.). Knowing the meaning of each *wh*-word will help students choose the correct answer.
- **At-level:** Have students take turns asking and answering the questions after they have completed the task.
- **Above-level:** Have students take turns asking and answering the questions. Have them continue each exchange. For example:
  A: *What are you doing?*
  B: *I'm exercising.*
  A: *Why are you exercising?*
  B: *I want to be healthy.*

Grammar to Communicate 3

PRESENT PROGRESSIVE: INFORMATION QUESTIONS

Wh- word	Be	Subject	Verb + -ing	Answers
What	am	I	eating?	Cake.
Where	are	you / we	going?	To his office.
Why	is	he / she		Because it's late.
Who	are	they	calling?	Their friends.

A Complete the questions. Use *is* or *are* and *you, he, she, we,* or *they*.

1. A: I'm reading.
   B: What **are you** reading?
2. A: Maria's playing tennis.
   B: Who **is she** playing tennis with?
3. A: The students are talking to the teacher.
   B: Why **are they** talking to the teacher?
4. A: Tom is swimming.
   B: Where **is he** swimming?
5. A: I'm going home.
   B: Why **are you** going home?
6. A: The children and I are eating.
   B: What **are you** eating?

B Write questions. Use the present progressive. Then answer the questions with the words in the box.

A track suit	Because she's late	I'm exercising	With some friends
At the health club	Dan	~~Jeremy~~	

1. **Who is Sylvia talking to?**
   (who / Sylvia / talk to) — Jeremy. OR Dan.
2. **What are you doing?**
   (what / you / do) — I'm exercising.
3. **Where are you exercising?**
   (where / you / exercise) — At the health club.
4. **Who are Paul and Jake playing soccer with?**
   (who / Paul and Jake / play soccer with) — With some friends. OR Dan.
5. **Why is your mother running?**
   (why / your mother / run) — Because she's late.
6. **What is the boy wearing?**
   (what / the boy / wear) — A track suit.

Grammar Notes

1. To make information questions, use the same word order as *yes / no* questions, and put a question word at the beginning. For example: *Are you going? Where are you going?*
2. It's common in speaking to make contractions with question words and *is*. For example: *Why's she doing that? What's Mike doing?*
3. For more information on this grammar topic, see page 254.

C 🎵 **45** Read Jean and Alice's conversation. Then write the missing questions. Use *What*, *Where*, *Who*, and *Why*. Listen and check your answers.

Alice: Hi? Jean? This is Alice. Is Rita there?
Jean: No, she's not.
Alice: <u>What's she doing?</u>
   1. (do)
Jean: She's playing tennis with Sue.
Alice: How about Tom? Is he at home?
Jean: No, he's not.
Alice: <u>What's he doing?</u>
   2. (do)
Jean: He's playing soccer.
Alice: <u>Who's he playing with?</u>
   3. (play with)
Jean: With Phil and some other friends.
Alice: <u>Where are they playing?</u>
   4. (play)
Jean: At Sandy Field.
Alice: Sandy Field? <u>Why are they playing</u> at Sandy Field?
   5. (play)
Jean: Because another team is playing at Bradley Field today.
Alice: <u>What are you eating?</u>
   6. (eat)
Jean: Me? I'm eating an apple . . . And why are you asking so many questions today?

TIME to TALK

PAIRS. Student A: Look at the picture on page 269.
Student B: Look at the picture on page 271.
Ask and answer questions about the pictures. What is the same?
What is different? *Answers will vary.*

Example:
A: *Is there a little boy in your picture?*
B: *Yes, there is.*
A: *What is he doing?*
B: *He's swimming in a lake.*
A: *In my picture, he isn't swimming. That's one difference.*

Physical Exercise 71

C Teaching Time: 10–15 min.

- Have two students read the example.
- Tell students to use contractions where possible.
- Have students complete the task.
- 🎧 Play Track 45 while students check their answers. Pause the recording each time an answer is given.
- PAIRS. Have students role-play the completed conversation.
- **LIFE SKILLS TEST PREP 2** Go to Unit 3, Lesson 1 for more practice on how to begin and end telephone conversations.

Multilevel Strategy

Pre-level: Provide students with the appropriate *Wh*-word for each item: (2) *What*; (3) *Who*; (4) *Where*; (5) *Why*; and (6) *What*.

Language Note

Exercises A and B. Teach students the following question: *What are you doing?* Tell students they can ask this question if they want to know about a person's activity at the moment.

Option

Assign Unit 6 Supplementary Grammar to Communicate 3 Exercises on the Teacher's Resource Disk as homework or on the Student Persistence CD-ROM as self-access practice.

TIME to TALK

Teaching Time: 10–15 min.

- Have two students read the example conversation.
- PAIRS. Have students complete the task.
- Walk around and help as needed.
- After they have finished asking and answering questions, have students look at each other's pictures to see if they've found all the differences.

Unit 6 T-71

Review and Challenge

Grammar

Teaching Time: 5–10 min.

- Read the example with the class.
- Have students complete the task.
- PAIRS. Have students compare answers.
- 🎧 Play Track 46 while students check their answers.
- Call on students to say answers. Correct as needed.
- GROUPS. Have students role-play the corrected conversation two times, switching roles after the first time.

Dictation

Teaching Time: 5–10 min.

- 🎧 Play Track 47 while students listen and write what they hear.
- 🎧 Play Track 47 again while students check their answers.
- PAIRS. Have students compare their answers.
- Call on students to write answers on the board.
- 🎧 Play Track 47 again and correct the sentences on the board.

> **Multilevel Strategy**
>
> - **Pre-level:** Give students a worksheet with some of the words from the dictation already provided.

Speaking

Teaching Time: 10–15 min.

- Have two students read the example conversation.
- Tell students that before making the conversations, they should decide who is talking and where they are for each one. Tell students to give clues in the conversations to help other students guess where they are.
- PAIRS. Have students complete the task. Walk around and prompt students with suggestions as needed.
- Call on pairs of students to act out their conversations for the class. Have other students guess the situation for each conversation.

T-72 Center Stage 2

Review and Challenge

Grammar

🎧 **46** Correct the conversation. There are seven mistakes. The first mistake is corrected for you. Then listen and check your answers.

Mike: Hi, Tina. It's me, Mike. What ~~you are doing~~ *are you doing*?
Tina: I'm ~~read~~ *reading* a book.
Mike: Where are you?
Tina: At the health club.
Mike: Why ^*are* you reading a book at the health club?
Tina: I'm sitting in the café. I'm waiting for Sara.
Mike: ~~Are~~ *Is* she exercising?
Tina: No, ~~she~~ *she's* not. She's taking a shower. Oh, she's coming now.
Sara: Hi, Tina! . . . Who ~~is~~ *are* you talking to?
Tina: ~~I~~ *I'm* talking to Mike.

Dictation

🎧 **47** Listen. You will hear five sentences. Write them on a piece of paper. *See the audioscript on page 280 for the sentences.*

Speaking

PAIRS. Read the sentences. Write a conversation for each sentence. *Answers will vary.*

1. You're sitting in my seat.
2. Your dog is eating my flowers.
3. You're using my tennis ball.
4. Your daughter is swimming in the pool alone.
5. You're drinking my coffee.
6. Your telephone is ringing.

Example:
A: Excuse me. You're sitting in my seat.
B: No, I'm not.
A: Yes, you are. Here's my ticket.
B: Oh, you're right. I'm sorry.

WRAP-UP. Now perform one conversation for the class. Can they guess where you are?

72 Unit 6

> **Multilevel Strategy**
>
> - **Pre-level:** Have students choose one sentence and develop a short conversation. Have pairs practice the conversation for natural delivery before they present it to the class.

> **Option**
>
> Before class, make a copy of the grammar exercise on page 72 as a transparency to use with an overhead projector. Ask a volunteer to make corrections to the conversation on the transparency. Correct as needed. Have students check their work with the transparency.

Listening

A 🎧 **48** Listen. Reporters at the Summer Olympics are talking about three sports. Circle the pictures of the sports they talk about.

> **Look**
> win = to be first in a game or race
> athlete = a person who plays sports

- (tennis) — *circled*
- marathon — *circled*
- volleyball
- (swimming) — *circled*
- cycling
- soccer

B 🎧 **49** Listen again. Match the countries of the athletes with the sports. Use one sport two times.

- _b_ 1. Kenya
- _a_ 2. Canada
- _c_ 3. Japan
- _b_ 4. Brazil

a. tennis
b. the marathon
c. swimming

TIME TO TALK

GROUPS. Make a list of popular sports. If you don't know the name of a sport in English, ask your teacher or use a dictionary. Then answer the questions.
Answers will vary.
1. Who are some famous athletes of the sports on your list? What countries are they from?
2. Is your country famous for any sport? Which sport(s)?
3. What are your favorite sports? Why?

Physical Exercise 73

Listening

A Teaching Time: 5–10 min.

- **Warm-up:** Have students look at the pictures. Read each caption and have students repeat chorally. Tell students that they are going to listen to reporters talk about three sports at the Summer Olympics. Have students study the Look Box.
- Explain unfamiliar vocabulary as necessary. For example, say: *A marathon is a race that is 26 miles long.*
- 🎧 Play Track 48 while students listen.
- 🎧 Play Track 48 again while students listen and complete the task.
- PAIRS. Have students compare answers.
- Call on students to say answers. Correct as needed.
- Ask students comprehension questions about the conversation. Modify the questions to the level of the students.

Multilevel Strategy

- **Pre-level:** Ask students *yes / no* questions (e.g., *Is the Japanese runner winning the marathon?*).
- **At-level:** Ask students information questions (e.g., *Who is practicing tennis?*).
- **Above-level:** Ask students open-ended or critical thinking questions (e.g., *Do you think running a marathon is difficult? Why?*).

B Teaching Time: 5–10 min.

- Ask students to read through the answer choices before they listen.
- 🎧 Play Track 49 while students listen and complete the task.
- 🎧 Play Track 49 again while students check their answers. Pause the recording each time an answer is given.

Option
Point out or have students find Kenya, Canada, Japan, and Brazil on a world map.

Option
Assign Unit 6 Supplementary Review and Challenge Exercises on the Teacher's Resource Disk as homework or on the Student Persistence CD-ROM as self-access practice.

TIME TO TALK Teaching Time: 10–15 min.
- GROUPS. Have students complete the task.
- Walk around and help as needed.
- Call on volunteers to tell the class some of their answers.

Unit 6 T-73

Reading and Writing

Reading

A   **Teaching Time: 10–15 min.**

- Tell students to look for clues in the paragraphs to help them guess the sports.
- Have students read the paragraphs silently. Then read each paragraph aloud. Pause after each few words and have students repeat chorally.
- Have students name the sports.
- Call on students to say answers. Correct as needed.
- Have students point out clues about the sport in each paragraph. For example, in the first paragraph, there are twenty-two players, there are two teams, and the players are kicking the ball.

B   **Teaching Time: 5–10 min.**

- Tell students to use the other words in the reading to help them guess the meanings of the italicized words.
- Have students complete the task.
- PAIRS. Have students compare answers.
- Call on students to say answers. Correct as needed.

Reading and Writing

Reading

A   Read the reports from sports events. What are the sports? Write the sport above each paragraph.

PARAGRAPH 1   _soccer_

Twenty-two girls are playing today. The players on our team are wearing black shorts and red T-shirts. The other players are wearing black shorts and blue T-shirts. Today's game is really interesting because there's an excellent player out there—Janet Abu.... And she's *kicking* the ball right now! The girls on our team are trying to get the ball. It's not easy for them!

PARAGRAPH 2   _baseball_

There are many people here at the game today. Some people are standing. Some people are sitting. Some people are eating hot dogs. They are talking and laughing. It's very noisy. Dirk Bailey is standing and *holding* the ball. Most of his *teammates* are standing in the *field* behind him. Mickey Montoya from the other team is holding a bat. He's waiting for the ball. I am, too! It's so exciting!

B   Read the sentences. Look at the italic words. Then find them in the paragraphs. Circle the letter of the sentence that has a similar meaning.

1. You are *kicking* a ball.
   a. You are using your hands.
   (b.) You are using your feet.

2. You are playing in a *field*.
   (a.) You are playing in a large outdoor area.
   b. You are playing in a large indoor room.

3. You are *holding* a ball.
   a. The ball is near your feet.
   (b.) The ball is in your hand.

4. Your *teammates* are standing in the field.
   a. They are watching your team.
   (b.) They are playing the game with you.

Unit 6

Prewriting

Watch or go to a sporting event or a place with a lot of activity (for example, a busy shopping mall). What is happening? Make a list of action verbs. *Answers will vary.*

Writing

Write a report about what you saw. Use the reports on page 74 as a model. Do not write the place or the activity.
Answers will vary.

Writing Tip

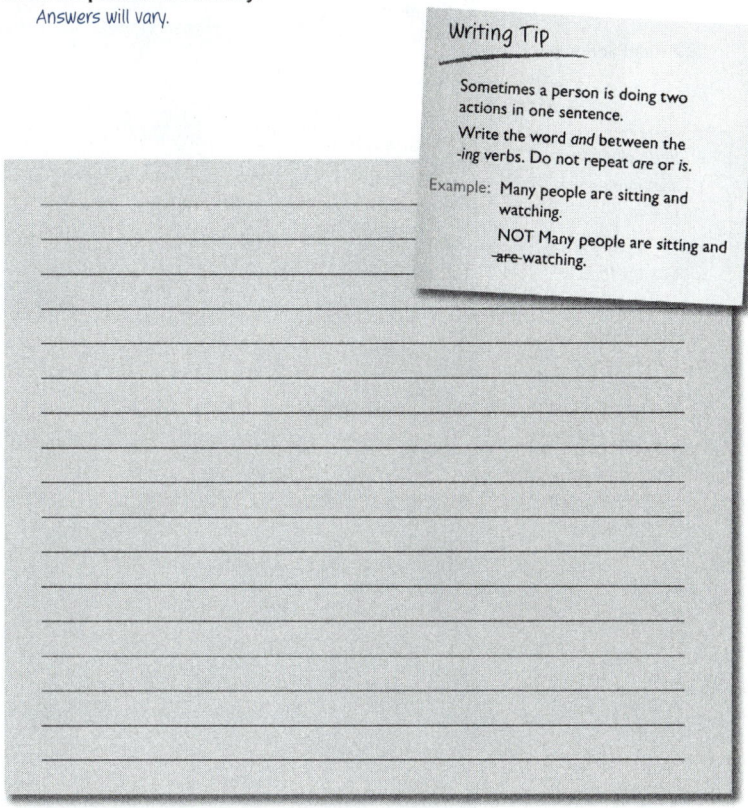

Sometimes a person is doing two actions in one sentence.
Write the word *and* between the *-ing* verbs. Do not repeat *are* or *is*.

Example: Many people are sitting and watching.
NOT Many people are sitting and ~~are~~ watching.

PAIRS. Show your report to your partner. Can he or she guess the activity?

Physical Exercise 75

Prewriting
Teaching Time: 5–10 min.

- Ask students to name some events. If necessary, prompt them to consider sporting events, celebrations, concerts, etc. Record their answers on the board.
- Have students choose one event and make a list of action verbs.
- Call on volunteers to read their lists to the class. Correct as needed.

Writing
Teaching Time: 20–25 min.

- Have students study the Writing Tip.
- Write on the board: *At a ___, people are ___ and ___.* Name different events and call on volunteers to complete the sentence in their own way. For example: *At a party, people are dancing and talking.*
- On the board, write questions such as: *What's happening? Who is there? What are people doing? What are you seeing? What are you hearing?*
- Point to the questions on the board. Tell students to write answers to the questions on the board as they write their paragraph.
- Have students complete the task.
- Walk around and help as needed.
- PAIRS. Have partners switch paragraphs and try to guess the event described.
- Call on volunteers to read their paragraphs to the class. Correct as needed. You can also have students write their paragraphs on a separate piece of paper. Collect their work and provide individual feedback.

Multilevel Strategy

- **Pre-level:** Have students write answers to the questions on the board. Walk around and help students form the answers.
- **At-level, Above-level:** Have students add details to the answers as they write about the event.

Unit 6   T-75

Unit 7
Do's and Don'ts

Learning Goals

- Learn words to describe activities
- Learn about imperatives; prepositions; and object pronouns
- Listen to conversations about activities
- Read safety instructions and write about a country
- Talk about everyday activities

Learner Persistence

Have students create portfolios for their work so they can see their progress in the class. Helping students recognize and monitor their progress is one way to increase persistence.

Warm-up

Teaching Time: 5–10 min.

- Draw the following graphic organizer on the board.

At dinner:	
Good things to do	Bad things to do

- Ask students to list some good and bad things to do at dinner.
- Record students' answers on the graphic organizer.
- Have students look at the pictures on pages 76 and 77. Invite students to add to the graphic organizer any ideas shown in the pictures that they didn't already include.

Vocabulary

Teaching Time: 15–20 min.

- 🎧 Play Track 50 while students read and listen.
- Read the words on the list aloud and have students repeat chorally.

Unit 7
Do's and Don'ts

Grammar
- Imperatives
- Prepositions
- Object Pronouns

Vocabulary

🎧 **50** Read and listen.

1. finish dinner
2. start dinner
3. turn on
4. ask for something
5. take the food
6. touch
7. move a chair
8. put the food on the table
9. turn off
10. ask someone
11. wait for the bus

76 Unit 7

Expansion

- Draw the following graphic organizer on the board.

Breakfast	Lunch	Dinner

- Ask students what they would say or do at different meal times (e.g., Breakfast: *Have some toast.*). Record students' answers on the graphic organizer.

Watch Out!

- **Exercise B.** In some languages, there is only one word for *make* and *do*. Students may confuse these words in English. Point out to students that in English we say: *do homework* and *make the bed*.
- Listen for and correct errors such as: *I'm making my homework* and *I'm doing my bed*.

T-76 Center Stage 2

Listening

A 🎧 51 **Listen. Why is Matthew's mother unhappy? Check (✓) all of the reasons.**

- ☐ 1. Matthew is listening to music.
- ☑ 2. Matthew is watching TV and doing homework.
- ☐ 3. Matthew is calling a friend.
- ☑ 4. Matthew's room is messy.
- ☑ 5. Matthew is eating in his bedroom.

B 🎧 52 **Read and listen again. Write the missing words. Use the words in the box.**

| don't | her | me | ~~Turn~~ |

Mother: You aren't doing your homework. You're watching TV! __Turn__ it off right now!
1.

Matthew: But I am doing my homework . . .

Mother: So where is it?

Matthew: Here.

Mother: OK, now listen to __me__. First,
2.
finish your homework. Do it right now, and __don't__ be careless. Then, clean
3.
your room. Make your bed and put your clothes in the closet. Don't put them under your bed, like last time.

Matthew: Yes, Mom.

Mother: Oh, and one more thing. Don't touch the telephone!

Matthew: But Sylvia is waiting for me to call!

Mother: Well, too bad. Call __her__ tomorrow.
4.

Do's and Don'ts 77

Listening

A Teaching Time: 10–15 min.

- **Warm-up:** Have students look at the pictures on pages 76 and 77. Ask them to identify the mother in each one. Have students suggest what the children are doing that might make the mothers unhappy. Have them complete the following sentence for each picture: *The mother is unhappy because. . . .*
- Ask students to read through the answer choices before they listen.
- 🎧 Play Track 51 while students listen.
- 🎧 Play Track 51 again while students listen and complete the task.
- Call on students to say answers. Correct as needed.

B Teaching Time: 15–20 min.

- Have students read through the answer choices before they listen.
- 🎧 Play Track 52 while students listen and complete the task.
- 🎧 Play Track 52 again while students check their answers.
- Call on students to say answers. Correct as needed.
- Read the conversation aloud. Pause after each few words and have students repeat chorally.
- PAIRS. Ask students to role-play the conversation with a partner.

Multilevel Strategy

- **Pre-level:** Have students role-play the completed conversation.
- **At-level:** Have students practice the completed conversation. Challenge them to use different commands and instructions.
- **Above-level:** Have students create a new conversation between a mother and a child using the conversation in the book as a model. Call on pairs to role-play in front of the class.

Language Note

- **Exercise B.** Point out the phrase *too bad* at the end of the conversation. Tell students that people often use this phrase to mean *There's nothing you can do about it.*
- Tell students that this expression is informal.

Option

Assign Unit 7 Supplementary Vocabulary Exercise on the Teacher's Resource Disk as homework or on the Student Persistence CD-ROM as self-access practice.

Unit 7   T-77

Grammar to Communicate 1

Imperatives

Teaching Time: 5–10 min.

- Tell students that we use imperatives to give instructions.
- Say: *An affirmative imperative is the base form of the verb.* Give students a few simple commands, such as: *Open your books.* Prompt them to do the actions.
- Say: *A negative imperative is* do not *or* don't *and the base form of the verb.* Give students a few simple commands, such as: *Don't touch your desk.* Prompt them to do the actions.
- Have students study the chart. Read the sentences in the chart and have students repeat chorally.
- Have students study the Look Box. Explain that *please* can be placed before or after the imperative.
- Say a few commands and have students repeat them with the word *please*.

A Teaching Time: 5–10 min.

- Have students look at the pictures. Ask them to say each person's job.
- Have students complete the task.
- Call on students to say answers. Correct as needed.

Multilevel Strategy

- **Pre-level, At-level:** Pair pre-level students with at-level students to complete the task. Have pre-level students read each sentence and at-level students point to the correct picture and name the job.
- **Above-level:** Have students write one additional sentence for each picture (e.g., a: *please write on the board*). Call on students to read their sentences to the class.

Grammar to Communicate 1

IMPERATIVES

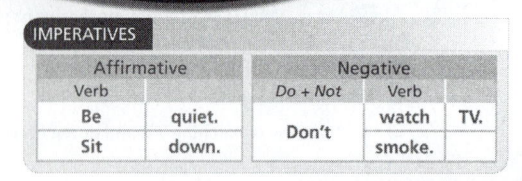

Affirmative		Negative		
Verb		Do + Not	Verb	
Be	quiet.	Don't	watch	TV.
Sit	down.		smoke.	

Look
Say *please* to be polite.
Please be quiet.
Be quiet, please.

A Match the pictures with the sentences.

_b_ 1. Be careful. The food is hot.
_c_ 2. Exercise every day.
_d_ 3. Close your mouth, please.
_a_ 4. Please open your books.
_e_ 5. Don't move your head.
_f_ 6. Don't turn on the water.

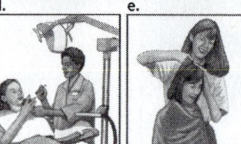

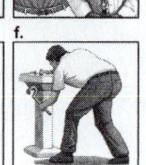

B Rewrite the sentences with *Don't*. Use the words in the box.

close	run	stand	~~talk~~

1. Be quiet.   Don't talk.
2. Sit down.   Don't stand.
3. Walk.   Don't run.
4. Open the door.   Don't close the door.

Make the sentences affirmative. Use the words in the box.

Be careful	Be early	Be neat	~~Turn off~~

5. Don't turn on the light. Turn off the light.
6. Don't be late.   Be early.
7. Don't be careless.   Be careful.
8. Don't be messy.   Be neat.

Unit 7

B Teaching Time: 10–15 min.

- Read the example with the class. Tell students to make sentences with similar meanings.
- Have students complete the task.
- Call on students to say answers. Correct as needed.

Grammar Notes

1. Imperatives give instructions.
2. The affirmative imperative is the base form of the verb.
3. Make a negative imperative with *do not* or *don't* and the base form of the verb.
4. Imperatives do not change forms.
5. For more information on this grammar topic, see page 255.

C The people in the first sentence are doing something wrong. What do the people in the second sentence say? Use the words in the box.

| be quiet | ~~drink~~ | eat | run | smoke | turn on |

1. Andy is drinking soda.
   His dentist says, "Don't drink soda."
2. The teenagers are waiting for their mother at her office. They are very noisy.
   The receptionist says, "Be quiet."
3. The children are running in the hospital.
   The doctor says, "Don't run."
4. The little boy is eating in the store.
   The salesperson says, "Don't eat."
5. Nancy is smoking in the restaurant.
   The waitress says, "Don't smoke."
6. The students are sitting in a room with no light.
   Their teacher says, "Turn on the light."

TIME to TALK

PAIRS. What do the signs below mean? Where do you usually see each sign? Who are the signs for? Use the verbs in the box. Answers will vary.

| eat | drink | smoke | use | ~~wash~~ | wear |

Example:
A: Sign 1 is in restaurant restrooms. It means "Wash your hands." It's for the cooks and waiters.
B: Sign 1 is also in hospitals. It's for the doctors and nurses.

Now compare your answers with your classmates' answers.

Do's and Don'ts 79

C Teaching Time: 10–15 min.

- Ask students to read through the answer choices before they begin. Explain unfamiliar vocabulary. For example, say: *People smoke cigarettes.*
- Have students complete the task.
- PAIRS. Have students compare answers.
- Call on students to say answers. Correct as needed.

Expansion

- Have students each write a list of three to five imperatives that they often give to someone they know.
- Walk around and help as needed.
- GROUPS. Students take turns reading their imperatives. The rest of the group guesses who the person says the things to. For example:
  A: *Please call someone. Make copies of this. Don't forget the meeting.*
  B: *Is it your husband?*
  A: *No.*
  C: *Is it your assistant?*
  A: *Yes!*

Option

Assign Unit 7 Supplementary Grammar to Communicate 1 Exercises on the Teacher's Resource Disk as homework or on the Student Persistence CD-ROM as self-access practice.

TIME to TALK

Teaching Time: 10–15 min.

- Have two students read the example conversation.
- PAIRS. Have students complete the task.
- Walk around and help as needed.
- Call on volunteers to say the meaning for each sign.

Multilevel Strategy

- **Pre-level:** Help students match the signs with the words in the box before they talk with a partner.

Unit 7 T-79

Grammar to Communicate 2

Prepositions

Teaching Time: 10–15 min.

- Write the following words on the board: *in, on, next to, across from, between*. Briefly review the meanings of the words with objects in the classroom. For example, put a piece of paper between the pages of a book and say: *The paper is in the book*. Write the sentences on the board.
- Then say: *A noun or a pronoun always goes after a preposition*. Underline the object of each preposition in the sentences on the board. For example, *the book* is the object in the sentence above.
- Have students study the chart and the picture.
- Read each sentence and have students repeat chorally.

A   **Teaching Time: 5–10 min.**

- Ask students to read through the answer choices.
- Have students study the *Before* and *After* pictures.
- Ask a few students to say some of the differences between the pictures. For example: *Before, the telephone is on the bed. After, the telephone is on the desk*.
- Have students complete the task.
- Call on students to say answers. Correct as needed.

B   **Teaching Time: 5–10 min.**

- Read the example with the class.
- Have students complete the task.
- Call on students to say answers. Correct as needed.

Expansion

Have students identify the object of each preposition in Exercise A (the desk, the bed, the shelf, the door, the desk, the closet) and Exercise B (the door, your room, the bed, the closet, the window, the table).

Grammar to Communicate 2

PREPOSITIONS

		Preposition	
	cat	on	the rug.
	shoes	under	
	picture	above	
Put the	chair	behind	the table.
	rug	in front of	
	wastebasket	near	
	paper	in	the wastebasket.

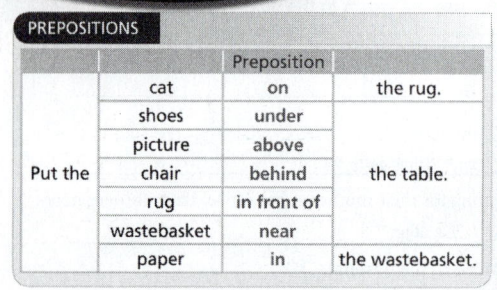

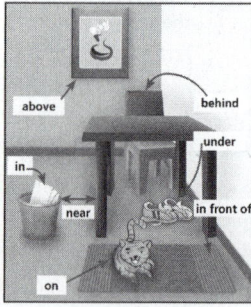

A   Look at the pictures. Frank's mother sees his room. What does she say? Complete the sentences with the words in the box.

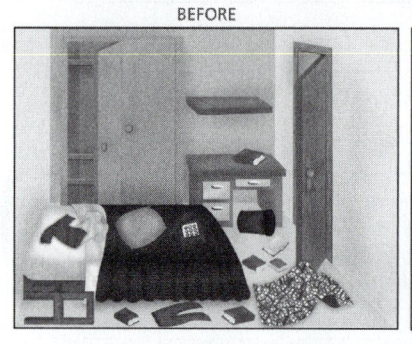

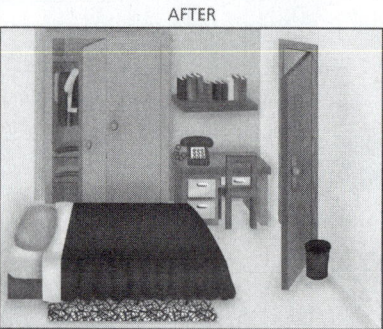

BEFORE   AFTER

books   chair   clothes   rug   ~~telephone~~   wastebasket

1. Put the ___telephone___ on the desk.
2. Put the ___rug___ under the bed.
3. Put the ___books___ on the shelf.
4. Put the ___wastebasket___ behind the door.
5. Put the ___chair___ in front of the desk.
6. Put the ___clothes___ in the closet.

B   Where do people usually put these things? Circle the correct preposition.

1. Put the wastebasket (**behind**)/ on the door.
2. Put your clothes (**in**)/ in front of your room.
3. Put the picture (**above**)/ under the bed.
4. Put your shoes (**in**)/ under the closet.
5. Put the chair above /(**in front of**) the window.
6. Put the food (**on**)/ behind the table.

80   Unit 7

Grammar Notes

1. Some prepositions tell about the locations of things.
2. A noun or a pronoun always follows a preposition. This is the object of the preposition.
3. For more information on this grammar topic, see page 255.

Language Note

Exercise C. Tell students that some verbs need a preposition to make their meaning complete. Explain that these verbs have different meanings without these words. For example, you *ask* a question to get information, but you *ask for* something you want.

T-80   Center Stage 2

C Complete the sentences. Use the prepositions *at, for,* and *to*.

1. Molly, be nice __to__ your sister.
2. Molly, wait __for__ your brother.
3. Molly, listen __to__ your teacher.
4. Molly, look __at__ the cute boy.
5. Molly, write __to__ your grandmother.
6. Molly, ask __for__ some money.
7. Molly, talk __to__ your father.

Look
Some verbs need prepositions after them.
Listen **to** him.
Write **to** me.
Talk **to** us.
Ask **for** it.
Wait **for** them.
Look **at** the board.

PAIRS. Molly is sixteen. Which sentences do you think Molly's mother says? Which sentences do you think Molly's friend says? *Answers will vary.*

TIME to TALK

ON YOUR OWN. Where are the things below in your room at home? Draw them on page 270. Do not show your drawing to your partner.
Student A: Now tell Student B where to draw the things in your room.
Student B: Listen and draw things in your classmate's room on page 272.
Student A: Check Student B's picture. Is it correct? Then change roles.
Answers will vary.
Example:
A: Put the sofa in front of the windows.

Do's and Don'ts

C Teaching Time: 5–10 min.

- Have students study the Look Box. Explain to students that some verbs need prepositions and that these prepositions don't tell about place.
- Read the example with the class.
- Have students complete the task.
- Call on students to say answers. Correct as needed.
- PAIRS. Have students decide who says each sentence.
- Call on students to say answers. Ask other students if they agree.

Option
Assign Unit 7 Supplementary Grammar to Communicate 2 Exercises on the Teacher's Resource Disk as homework or on the Student Persistence CD-ROM as self-access practice.

TIME to TALK
Teaching Time: 15–20 min.
- Read the example with the class.
- PAIRS. Have students complete the task.
- Walk around and help as needed.

Multilevel Strategies
- **Pre-level:** Provide students with the appropriate prepositions and phrases to complete the task (e.g., *on the wall, next to the table*).

Unit 7

Grammar to Communicate 3

Object Pronouns

Teaching Time: 5–10 min.

- Write on the board *I, you, he, she, it, we, they*. Remind students that these words are subject pronouns. Say: *A subject pronoun tells who or what a sentence is about.*
- Tell students that pronouns can also be objects. Object pronouns replace nouns after a verb or a preposition.
- Have students study the chart and the Look Box.
- Read the examples in the chart and the Look Box and have students repeat chorally.
- Write on the board a few sentences with object pronouns, such as: *Talk to me*. Have students identify the object in each one.

A Teaching Time: 10–15 min.

- Read the examples with the class.
- Have students complete the task.
- Call on students to say answers. Correct as needed.

B Teaching Time: 5–10 min.

- Read the example with the class.
- Have students complete the task.
- Call on students to say answers. Correct as needed.

Grammar to Communicate 3

OBJECT PRONOUNS

	Noun		Object Pronoun
Take	John.	Take	him.
	Debra.		her.
	the bus.		it.
	John and me.		us.
	Debra and John.		them.

Look

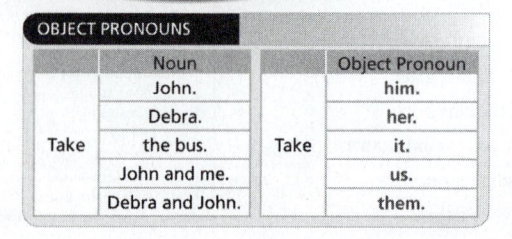

Pronouns

Subject	Object
I	me
you	you
he	him
she	her
it	it
we	us
they	them

A Rewrite the sentences. Replace the underlined words with words from the box.

Anna	David	~~the answers~~	the conversation	your classmates

1. Read them. _Read the answers._
2. Listen to it. _Listen to the conversation._
3. Wait for her. _Wait for Anna._
4. Don't ask him. _Don't ask David._
5. Don't talk to them. _Don't talk to your classmates._

Now replace the underlined words with an object pronoun.

6. Help Mrs. Wu. _Help her._
7. Play the music. _Play it._
8. Watch the children. _Watch them._
9. Don't touch the plates. _Don't touch them._
10. Go with Mr. Montero. _Go with him._

B Complete the sentences. Use an object pronoun.

1. Gabriel and I are going to a café. Come with __us__.
2. I'm talking. Listen to __me__.
3. Here are the answers. Read __them__.
4. Don't do the homework now. Do __it__ at home.
5. You're sitting next to Julia. Work with __her__.
6. Your classmates are doing the same exercise. Ask __them__ for the answers.
7. Tony isn't at work today. Call __him__ at home.

82 Unit 7

Grammar Notes

1. A pronoun takes the place of a noun.
2. Use different pronouns for subjects and objects.
3. Use an object pronoun after a verb or a preposition.
4. For more information on this grammar topic, see page 255.

Option

- Before class, find several magazine pictures (two or three for each group) that show at least two people talking.
- Divide students into groups of 4–6 students. Distribute magazine pictures to each group.

T-82 Center Stage 2

Reading and Writing

Reading

Teaching Time: 10–15 min.

- Read aloud the captions for the pictures and have students repeat chorally.
- Have students read the instructions silently. Then read them aloud. Pause after each few words and have students repeat chorally. Explain any unfamiliar vocabulary.
- Have students match the pictures with the instructions.
- Call on students to say answers. Correct as needed.

Expansion Invite students to say additional Do's and Don'ts for each list of instructions. Write them on the board and have students copy them in their notebooks.

Reading and Writing

Reading

Read the instructions. Who are they for? Match the pictures with the instructions. Write the correct letters.

1. _b_

INSTRUCTIONS
- Put on a hospital gown.
- Make a list of questions to ask the doctor.
- Keep your insurance card with you.
- Do not keep money in your room.
- Be ready to take more medical exams.

a. science laboratory

2. _a_

- Wear safety glasses at all times.
- Wear a lab coat over your clothes.
- Do not wear open-toed shoes.
- Do not wear shorts.

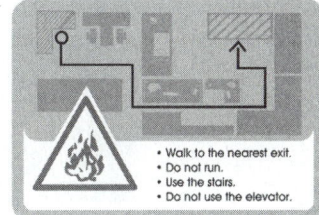

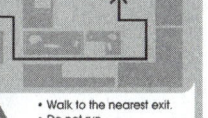

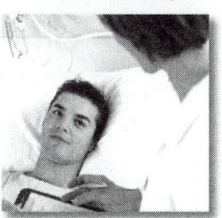

b. patient in hospital

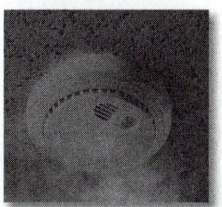

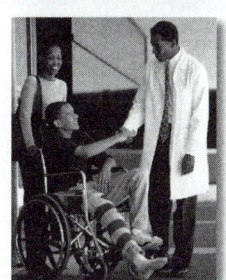

3. _d_

May 13, 2006
- Do not take a shower or go swimming for three days.
- Do not lift anything heavy.
- Call the nursing staff at 111-222-6777 with any questions.
- Come to the hospital immediately if get a fever.

Dr. _____

c. fire

4. _c_

- Walk to the nearest exit.
- Do not run.
- Use the stairs.
- Do not use the elevator.

d. patient leaving hospital

86 Unit 7

T-86 Center Stage 2

Listening

A 🎧 55 Listen. You will hear six conversations. Check (✓) the correct answers. (Be careful! There are two extra answers.)

WHO IS SPEAKING?	A DENTIST	A DOCTOR	A POLICE OFFICER	A CAB DRIVER
conversation 1			✓	
conversation 2		✓		
conversation 3	✓			

WHERE ARE THE PEOPLE?	AT THE AIRPORT	IN A CAR	ON AN AIRPLANE	ON THE STREET
conversation 4				✓
conversation 5			✓	
conversation 6	✓			

B 🎧 56 Listen again to the conversations. For each sentence, write *T* (true), or *F* (false).

F 1. The man is friendly. (Conversation 1)
F 2. The man is not listening to the woman. (Conversation 2)
T 3. The man is working. (Conversation 3)
T 4. The people are standing on the street. (Conversation 4)
F 5. The woman is a waitress. (Conversation 5)
T 6. The woman is going. The man is staying. (Conversation 6)

TIME to TALK

GROUPS. Talk about Do's and Don'ts for the places in the box. Make a list.
Answers will vary.

| at the beach | on a bus | at home | in a store | on the street |

Example:
A: *Don't walk alone on the street at night.*
B: *Yes. And watch your children on the street.*

Now compare your Do's and Don'ts with another group.

Do's and Don'ts 85

Listening

A **Teaching Time: 5–10 min.**

- **Warm-up:** Write on the board *dentist*. Ask students to list some imperatives that a dentist says (*Open your mouth. Brush your teeth.* etc.). Repeat with *doctor, cab driver,* etc. If necessary, explain that a cab driver is a person who drives a taxi.
- 🎧 Play Track 55 while students listen.
- 🎧 Play Track 55 again while students listen and complete the task.
- Call on students to say answers. Correct as needed.

B **Teaching Time: 5–10 min.**

- Ask students to read through the sentences before they listen.
- 🎧 Play Track 56. Have students listen and complete the task.
- 🎧 Play Track 56 again while students check their answers.
- Call on students to say answers. Correct as needed.

Multilevel Strategy

- **Pre-level:** Tell students there are three false statements.
- **At-level, Above-level:** When checking answers, challenge students to correct the false statements.

Option

Assign Unit 7 Supplementary Review and Challenge Exercises on the Teacher's Resource Disk as homework or on the Student Persistence CD-ROM as self-access practice.

TIME to TALK

Teaching Time: 10–15 min.

- Have two volunteers read the example.
- GROUPS. Have students complete the task.
- Walk around and help as needed.
- Call on groups to tell the class some of their ideas.

Review and Challenge

Grammar

Teaching Time: 5–10 min.

- Read the example with the class.
- Have students complete the task.
- Call on students to write sentences on the board. Write corrections on the board as needed.

> **Multilevel Strategy**
>
> - **Pre-level:** Tell students what the mistakes are and have them rewrite the sentences.

Dictation

Teaching Time: 5–10 min.

- 🎧 Play Track 54 while students listen and write what they hear.
- 🎧 Play Track 54 again while students check their answers.
- Call on students to write answers on the board.
- 🎧 Play Track 54 again and correct the sentences on the board.

> **Multilevel Strategy**
>
> - **Pre-level:** Give students a worksheet with some of the words from the dictation already provided.

Speaking

Teaching Time: 10–15 min.

- Read the situations with the class.
- Have two students read the example.
- PAIRS. Have students complete the task. Walk around and prompt students with suggestions as needed.
- Call on pairs of students to act out their conversations for the class. Have students tell the class their roles before they begin.
- Have students vote to choose the conversations that were the funniest and the most realistic.

Review and Challenge

Grammar

Find the mistake in each sentence. Circle the letter and correct the mistake.

1. Put the chair next to she.   Correct: _Put the chair next to her._
2. Children, stand in front your desks.   Correct: _Children, stand in front of your desks._
3. No listen to him.   Correct: _Don't listen to him._
4. Please wait to me.   Correct: _Please wait for me._
5. Don't talk to we.   Correct: _Don't talk to us._
6. Turning off the TV, please.   Correct: _Turn off the TV, please._

Dictation

🎧 54 Listen. You will hear five sentences. Write them on a piece of paper. _See the audioscript on page 281 for the sentences._

Speaking

PAIRS. Choose one situation and write a conversation. Then perform your conversation for the class. _Answers will vary._

> **Situation 1**
>
> *Student A:* You are a mother or father. Your son or daughter is listening to loud music and playing computer games. He or she isn't doing homework.
>
> *Student B:* You are the son or daughter.

> **Situation 2**
>
> *Student A:* You are a teacher. You are teaching an English class. One student is not listening to you. He is listening to music and drawing pictures in a notebook. His English book is not open. The student's feet are on the desk in front of him or her.
>
> *Student B:* You are the student.

Example:
A: Listen to me! Turn off that music!
B: But Mom! I'm busy! . . .

84 Unit 7

> **Multilevel Strategy**
>
> - **Pre-level:** Allow students to role-play the conversation on page 77 instead of creating a new conversation.

Option

- Write on the board: *police officer*. Ask students: *What are some imperatives that a police officer says?* (*Put your hands up. Give me your ID.*, etc.).
- PAIRS. Have pairs of students take turns role-playing a police officer and following the police officer's commands. Walk around and help as needed.
- **LIFE SKILLS TEST PREP 2** Go to Unit 10, Lesson 3 for more practice in learning how to respond to requests from a police officer.

Center Stage 2

C Complete the conversation. Then listen and check your answers.

Ana: What exercises are you doing?

Tomás: B and C.

Ana: Are __they__ difficult?
    1. (they / them)

Tomás: __I__'m not sure.
    2. (I / Me)
    __I__'m starting __them__ now. Sit down and help __me__.
    3. (I / Me)   4. (they / them)   5. (I / me)

Ana: Okay. Hmm. __They__ are difficult.
    6. (They / Them)

Tomás: David's a good student. Ask __him__ for help.
    7. (he / him)

Ana: __He__'s not in class today.
    8. (He / Him)

Tomás: Then ask __her__.
    9. (she / her)

Ana: Who?

Tomás: Safira. __She__'s your friend, right?
    10. (She / Her)

Ana: Yes, she is. Hey, Safira! Help __us__ with Exercises B and C.
    11. (we / us)

Safira: __I__'m busy.
    12. (I / Me)

TIME to TALK

GROUPS. Talk about Do's and Don'ts for the classroom. For each rule, write one sentence with a noun. Write the sentence again with a pronoun. Make a list.
Answers will vary.

Example:
A: Here's a Do rule. Listen to the teacher.
B: Yes. Listen to *her*.
C: Here's a Don't rule. Don't write in the book.
A: Yes. Don't write in *it*.

Now compare your lists to the other groups' lists. Which group has the most sentences?

Do's	Don'ts
Listen to the teacher.	Don't talk in class.

Do's and Don'ts   83

C Teaching Time: 5–10 min.
- Have students complete the task.
- PAIRS. Have students compare answers.
- 🎧 Play Track 53 while students check their answers. Pause the recording each time an answer is given.
- GROUPS. Have students role-play the completed conversation twice, having students switch roles for the second reading.

- Tell students to look at the pictures and imagine what the people are saying. Encourage students to write funny and creative imperatives.
- Ask volunteers to show the class their pictures and say the imperatives that their group imagined the people are saying.

Option
Assign Unit 7 Supplementary Grammar to Communicate 3 Exercises on the Teacher's Resource Disk as homework or on the Student Persistence CD-ROM as self-access practice.

TIME to TALK Teaching Time: 15–20 min.
- Have three students read the example conversation.
- GROUPS. Have students complete the task.
- Have groups present their rules to the class. Correct them as needed. Record them on the board.
- Ask students which rules they think are good for the class.
- After students discuss which rules are good for the class, invite volunteers to say any other rules they want to add.
- Have volunteers make posters with the rules to display in the classroom.

Multilevel Strategy
- **All-levels:** Place students in mixed-level groups. Have at-level and above-level students brainstorm ideas for the list of rules. Assign pre-level students as recorders and have them write the list of rules to present to the class.

Unit 7

Prewriting

Read the paragraph about Albania.

Albania

Here is some advice for your trip to Albania. First, go to Tirana. It's a nice city. There are many restaurants and cafés, and Albanian food is very good. Shish kebab and meatballs are two popular dishes. Try them! Then go to an outdoor café and have coffee. Second, visit Kruja. It is a beautiful old town in the mountains. But don't drive there. The mountain roads are sometimes dangerous. Take the bus. Next, visit Saranda. It is a small city near Corfu, Greece. There are beautiful beaches, and the sea is deep, clean, and blue. Finally, learn some words in Albanian. The Albanian people are kind and friendly, but many of them do not speak English.

Writing

Write a paragraph for a travel guide to your country. Write about the Do's and Don'ts. Use the paragraph above as a model.
Answers will vary.

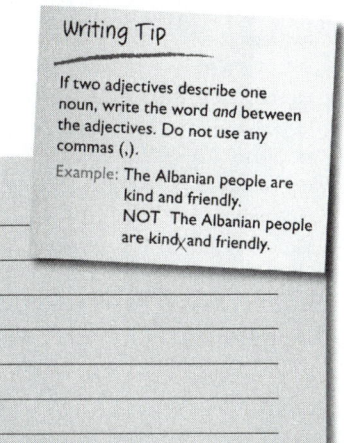

Writing Tip

If two adjectives describe one noun, write the word *and* between the adjectives. Do not use any commas (,).

Example: The Albanian people are kind and friendly.
NOT The Albanian people are kind, and friendly.

Do's and Don'ts

Prewriting
Teaching Time: 10–15 min.

- Tell students that a travel guide is a book or web site that gives information about a place to people who want to visit it. Ask students to suggest some kinds of information that travel guides often contain (*how to get there, places to see,* etc.). Record students' answers on the board.
- Have students read the example paragraph silently. Then read the paragraph out loud. Pause after each few words and have students repeat chorally.

Writing
Teaching Time: 20–25 min.

- Draw the following graphic organizer on the board.

Do's	Don'ts

- Have students copy the graphic organizer into their notebooks. Tell them to use it to organize their ideas.
- Tell students to give reasons for their Do's and Don'ts. For example: *Visit Ipanema Beach. It's beautiful and fun.*
- Have students complete the task.
- Walk around and help as needed.
- Call on volunteers to read their paragraphs to the class. Correct as needed. You can also have students write their paragraphs on a separate piece of paper. Collect their work and provide individual feedback.

Language Note

- **Writing.** Before students begin to write, have them study the Writing Tip.
- Write on the board the following nouns and adjective pairs: *the food / cheap, delicious; my country / warm, sunny place; the mountains / tall, beautiful; the beaches / clean, nice.* Tell students to use the words to make sentences. Model the first one on the board: *The food is cheap and delicious.*
- Have students complete the task.
- Call on students to write answers on the board. Write corrections on the board as needed.
- Remind students to use *and* between two adjectives that describe one noun in their paragraphs.

Unit 7

Unit 8
Possessions

Learning Goals
- Learn words to describe possessions
- Learn about *this / that / these / those*; possessive adjectives and pronouns; and simple present: *have*
- Listen to conversations about possessions
- Read and write an insurance application form
- Talk about possessions

Learner Persistence
Teach students ways to practice English outside of the class. Recommend reading materials, videos, or online activities.

Warm-up
Teaching Time: 3–5 min.

- Have students make a list of some things that are often in a bedroom. Have groups read their lists.
- Have students look at the pictures on pages 88 and 89. Have them point out objects in the pictures that are also on their lists.

Vocabulary
Teaching Time: 15–20 min.

- Have students look at the pictures. Explain unfamiliar vocabulary. For example, say: *Speakers are the parts of a radio or stereo where the sound comes out.*
- 🎧 Play Track 2 while students read and listen.
- Read the words aloud and have students repeat chorally.
- Have student complete the activity.
- PAIRS. Have students compare their answers.

Expansion PAIRS. Have students ask each other questions about the objects on the vocabulary list. For example:
A: *Do you have a radio?* B: *Yes, I do.*

Unit 8
Possessions

Grammar
- *This / That / These / Those*
- Possessive Adjectives and Pronouns
- Simple Present: *Have*

Vocabulary

🎧 **TRACK 2** Read and listen. Then circle the things you see that are in your room.
Answers will vary.

1. painting
2. calendar
3. radio
4. alarm clock
5. keys
6. glasses
7. record player
8. speakers
9. camera
10. records
11. CD player
12. CDs
13. cell phone
14. wallet
15. contact lenses
16. computer
17. credit card
18. digital camera
19. DVD player
20. DVDs

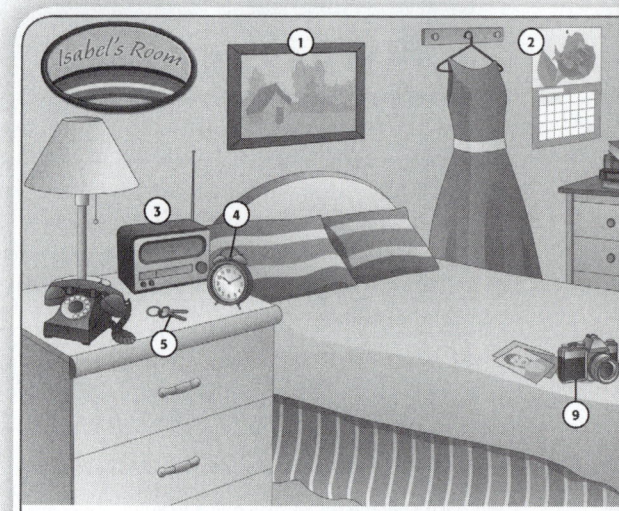

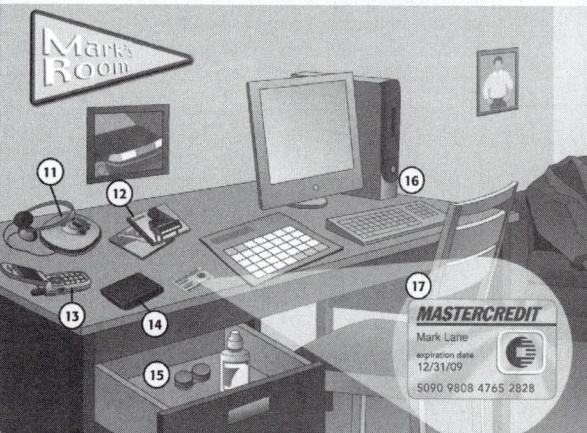

88 Unit 8

Multilevel Strategy

- **Pre-level:** Have students write down three questions to ask their partner.
- **Above-level:** Have students ask each other questions about the location of the objects in their homes. For example:
A: *Do you have a radio?*
B: *Yes, I do.*
A: *Where is the radio in your house?*
B: *It's in my bedroom.*

Language Note

- **Exercise B.** Point out the word *hey* in the conversation. Tell students that people use *hey* in different situations. For example, to get someone's attention: *Hey! Wait for me.* To show surprise, interest, or annoyance: *Hey, that's my wallet. Please don't move it.* To say hello: *Hey! What's up?*
- Tell students that *hey* is informal. They should use it with people they know well.

T-88 Center Stage 2

Listening

A 🎧 **3** Listen. Two friends are in a store. Check (✓) the things that they see.

- ✓ a camera
- ☐ a stereo
- ✓ speakers
- ☐ an alarm clock
- ☐ a credit card
- ✓ a radio
- ✓ a cell phone
- ☐ a DVD player

B 🎧 **4** Read and listen again. Write the missing words. Use the words in the box.

| mine | These | this | those | ~~yours~~ |

Saleswoman: That's mine. It's not for sale.

Bob: But what is it?

Saleswoman: It's a radio. We have other radios over there.

Sammi: Amazing... it's so thin—like a piece of paper! Is this ___yours___ too?
1.

Saleswoman: No, it isn't. Phil, is ___this___ cell phone yours?
2.

Phil: No, it's not ___mine___.
3.

Bob: Hey, that cell phone is mine. And ___those___ keys are mine too.
4.

Sammi: ___These___? Here you are. And are these your sunglasses?
5.

Possessions 89

Listening

A Teaching Time: 10–15 min.

- **Warm-up:** Have students read through the answer choices. Ask: *Which thing is something that you don't buy at a store?* (a credit card). Ask: *What do you use a credit card for?*
- 🎧 Play Track 3 while students listen.
- 🎧 Play Track 3 again while students listen and complete the task.
- PAIRS. Have students compare their answers.
- 🎧 Play Track 3 again while students check answers. Pause the recording each time an answer is given.

B Teaching Time: 15–20 min.

- Ask students to read the words in the box before they listen.
- 🎧 Play Track 4 while students listen and complete the task.
- 🎧 Play Track 4 again while students check their answers.
- Call on students to say answers. Correct as needed.
- Read the conversation aloud. Pause after each few words and have students repeat chorally.
- GROUPS. Ask students to role-play the conversation twice. Have students switch roles for the second reading.

Multilevel Strategy

- **Pre-level:** Have students role-play the completed conversation.
- **At-level, Above-level:** Write the conversation on the board without the answers. Have students recall the answers as they role-play.

Option

Assign Unit 8 Supplementary Vocabulary Exercise on the Teacher's Resource Disk as homework or on the Student Persistence CD-ROM as self-access practice.

Unit 8 T-89

Grammar to Communicate 1

This / That / These / Those

Teaching Time: 5–10 min.

- Have students study the charts and the Look Box.
- Say: *Use* this *and* these *to talk about things near you.* Point to a book near you and say: *This book is [green].* Place another book on top of the first. Point to both and say: *These books are [green].* Write the examples on the board.
- Say: This *and* these *are adjectives. They go before a noun.* This *and* these *can also be pronouns. Don't use a noun after a pronoun.* Point to just the first book again. Say: *This is [green].* Add the second book again and point. Say: *These are [green].* Write the examples on the board.
- To explain *that* and *those*, repeat the steps above, but place different books farther away from you. Give examples such as: *That book is [red]. Those are [red].*
- Read the sentences in the chart and have students repeat chorally.

A Teaching Time: 3–5 min.

- Read the example with the class.
- Have students complete the task.
- PAIRS. Have students compare answers.
- Call on students to say answers. Correct as needed.

B Teaching Time: 5–10 min.

- Read the example with the class.
- Have students complete the task.
- PAIRS. Have students compare answers.
- Call on students to say answers. Correct as needed.

Grammar to Communicate 1

THIS / THAT

Adjective	Noun		Pronoun	
This	flower	is white. →	This	is white.
That	flower	is red. →	That	is red.

THESE / THOSE

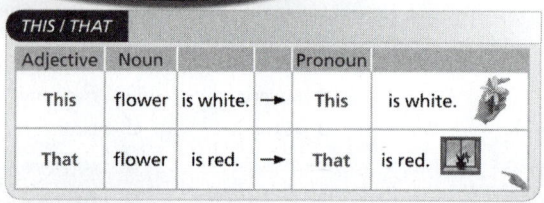

Adjective	Noun		Pronoun	
These	flowers	are pink. →	These	are pink.
Those	flowers	are purple. →	Those	are purple.

Look
Use *this* and *these* for things near you.
Use *that* and *those* for things far away from you.

A Look at the pictures. Complete the sentences. Use the adjectives *This* or *That*.

1. __This__ cell phone is modern.
2. __This__ necklace is cheap.
3. __That__ watch is plastic. 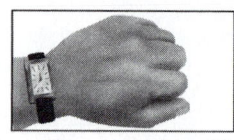
4. __That__ phone is old.
5. __That__ necklace is expensive.
6. __This__ watch is gold.

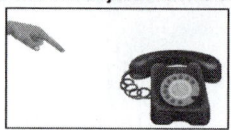

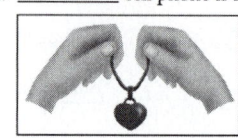

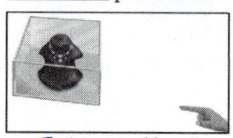

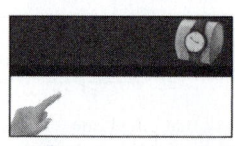

B Rewrite the sentences from Exercise A. Use the pronouns *This* or *That*.

1. This is modern.
2. This is cheap.
3. That is plastic.
4. That is old.
5. That is expensive.
6. This is gold.

Unit 8

Grammar Notes

1. *This / That / These / Those* show a specific thing or things. They can be adjectives or pronouns.
2. Adjectives go before a noun. For example: *This radio is nice. That phone is hers.*
3. Pronouns can be the subject or object of a sentence. For example: *These are great. I want those.*
4. *This* and *these* refer to things close to the speaker. *That* and *those* refer to things far away from the speaker.
5. *This* and *that* are singular. *These* and *those* are plural.
6. For more information on this grammar topic, see page 255.

Center Stage 2

C 🎵 5 Complete the questions. Use *this*, *that*, *these*, or *those* and *is* or *are*. Then listen and check your answers.

Look
Use *it* to answer questions with *this* or *that*.
A: What's this? B: It's a book.
Use *they* to answer questions with *these* or *those*.
A: What are those? B: They're books.

1. A: What's __this__?
   B: It's a wallet.
2. A: What are __these__? 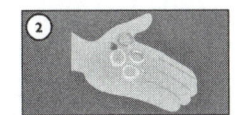
   B: They're rings.
3. A: What's __that__? 
   B: It's a backpack.
4. A: What are __those__? 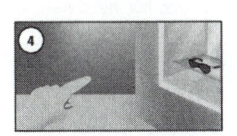
   B: They're sunglasses.
5. A: What are __these__? 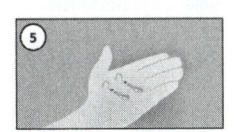
   B: They're earrings.
6. A: What's __that__? 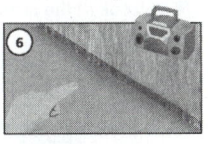
   B: It's a radio.

D 🎵 6 Complete the compliments. Use *That* or *Those*, and *is* or *are*. Use *a* if necessary. Then listen and check your answers.

1. __That is a__ nice ring.
2. __Those are__ beautiful earrings.
3. __That is a__ nice watch.
4. __Those are__ beautiful sunglasses.

Now talk to other students. Make compliments about their possessions.

TIME to TALK

ON YOUR OWN. Find pictures of five things you want to buy in a magazine, catalog, or newspaper. Bring your pictures to class.

PAIRS. Show your pictures to your classmate. Teach your classmate the words. Then learn your classmate's words. Answers will vary.

Example:
A: What are these?
B: They're headphones
A: How do you spell that?
B: h-e-a-d-p-h-o-n-e-s

Possessions 91

C Teaching Time: 5–10 min.
- Have students study the Look Box.
- Have students complete the task.
- 🎧 Play Track 5 while students check their answers.
- Call on students to say answers. Correct as needed.

Multilevel Strategy
- **Pre-level:** Have students work in pairs to complete the task. After checking answers, have students take turns asking and answering the questions.
- **At-level, Above-level:** After checking answers, pair students and have them take turns asking and answering questions about the items in the classroom using *this / that* and *these / those*.

D Teaching Time: 5–10 min.
- Explain to students that when you give someone a compliment, you say something nice about the person or something that he or she has.
- Have students complete the task.
- 🎧 Play Track 6 while students check their answers.
- Call on students to say answers. Correct as needed.
- Have students walk around the room and take turns giving and receiving compliments.
- **LIFE SKILLS TEST PREP 2** Go to Unit 2, Lesson 4 for more practice in giving and receiving compliments.

Language Note
Exercises A and B. You can make the words *that is* into a contraction: *that's*.

Option
Assign Unit 8 Supplementary Grammar to Communicate 1 Exercises on the Teacher's Resource Disk as homework or on the Student Persistence CD-ROM as self-access practice.

TIME to TALK
Teaching Time: 15–20 min.
- A few days before you assign this task, ask students to bring in pictures of five things they want to buy. Encourage them to look for pictures in newspapers, magazines, and catalogs.
- Have two volunteers read the example.
- PAIRS. Have students complete the task.
- Walk around and help as needed.
- Call on volunteers to tell the class about something that their partner wants.
- **LIFE SKILLS TEST PREP 2** Go to Unit 5, Lesson 6 for more practice in asking for clarification using different strategies.

Unit 8   T-91

Grammar to Communicate 2

Possessive Adjectives and Possessive Pronouns

Teaching Time: 5–10 min.

- Write on the board: *my, your, his, her, our, their.* Remind students that possessive adjectives show who something belongs to. They go before nouns. Say sentences such as: *My desk is big.*
- Write on the board: *mine, yours, his, hers, ours, theirs.* Say: *These are possessive pronouns. Use them instead of a possessive adjective and a noun.*
- Make sentences with a possessive adjective and a noun. Then repeat each sentence with a possessive pronoun. For example: *That's her notebook. That's hers.*
- Have students study the chart and the Look Box. Read the sentences in the chart and have students repeat chorally.

A Teaching Time: 3–5 min.

- Read the example with the class.
- Have students complete the task.
- Call on students to say answers. Correct as needed.

B Teaching Time: 5–10 min.

- Read the example with the class.
- Have students complete the task.
- Call on students to write answers on the board. Write corrections on the board as needed.

Grammar to Communicate 2

POSSESSIVE ADJECTIVES AND POSSESSIVE PRONOUNS

		Possessive Adjective	Noun				Possessive Pronoun
That	is	my	book.	→	That	is	mine.
		your					yours.
		his					his.
Those	are	her	books.	→	Those	are	hers.
		our					ours.
		their					theirs.

Look
Possessive pronouns can replace singular or plural nouns.
This is his book. Mine is over there.
Those are my books. Yours are over there.

A Look at the pictures. Complete the sentences. Use *mine, yours, his, hers, ours,* or *theirs*.

1. **Makiko:** John, is that camera __yours__?
2. **John:** Yes, the camera is __mine__.
3. **Greta:** Daddy, is the little dog __hers__?
4. **Charlene and Tom:** This car is __ours__.
5. **Ben:** Their names are Charlene and Tom. The prizes are __theirs__.

B Complete the sentences. Use possessive adjectives or possessive pronouns.

1. This isn't my digital camera. That's __mine__.
2. This isn't her cell phone. __Hers__ is in the car.
3. Those aren't __his__ shoes. These are his.
4. That's not our car. __Ours__ is over there.
5. This watch isn't mine. That's __my__ watch.
6. That's not their home. __Theirs__ is on Elm Street.

Unit 8

Grammar Notes

1. Possessive adjectives and pronouns show who something belongs to.
2. Possessive adjectives go before a noun. They do not change form.
3. Possessive pronouns replace a possessive adjective and a noun. For example: *my car = mine, your keys = yours,* etc.
4. Possessive pronouns do not change form.
5. Possessive pronouns can be subjects and objects. For example: *This jacket isn't mine. Mine is over there.*
6. For more information on this grammar topic, see page 255.

Center Stage 2

C

Complete the conversations. Use possessive adjectives or possessive pronouns. Then listen and check your answers.

1. **A:** Are these glasses ___yours?___
   B: Yes, they are.
2. **A:** Are these Nicole's glasses?
   B: No. ___Hers___ are different.
3. **A:** Hello. I'm Ming Lee and this is ___my___ wife, Chiao-lun.
   B: It's nice to meet you.
4. **A:** ___My___ name is Ed. What's ___yours___?
   B: Hi, Ed. I'm Stella.
5. **A:** Is that the children's dog?
   B: No. ___Theirs___ is black.
6. **A:** Is that a picture of you and Chris?
   B: Yes. And that's ___our___ home.
7. **A:** Who's the woman with Ari?
   B: That's ___his___ wife.
8. **A:** Is Ari's home in Boston?
   B: No. ___His___ is in Cambridge. His brother's is in Boston.

D

Rewrite Speaker B's answers. Replace the underlined words with possessive pronouns. Then listen and check your answers.

1. **A:** Here's your book.
   B: That's not <u>my book</u>.
   That's not mine.
2. **A:** Bill and Sue, your dogs are nice.
   B: Those dogs aren't <u>our dogs</u>.
   Those dogs aren't ours.
3. **A:** Are those our records?
   B: No, these are <u>your records</u>.
   No, these are yours.
4. **A:** Is Anna's cell phone black?
   B: No, <u>her cell phone</u> is blue.
   No, hers is blue.
5. **A:** They can't find their keys.
   B: Are those keys on the table <u>their keys</u>?
   Are those keys on the table theirs?
6. **A:** Is that his car in front of the house?
   B: No, <u>his car</u> is at home.
   No, his is at home.

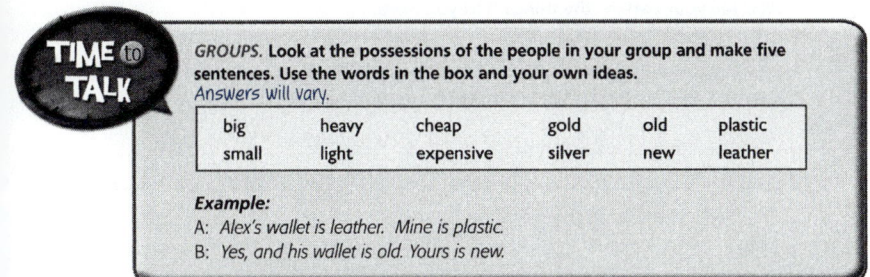

TIME to TALK

GROUPS. Look at the possessions of the people in your group and make five sentences. Use the words in the box and your own ideas.
Answers will vary.

| big | heavy | cheap | gold | old | plastic |
| small | light | expensive | silver | new | leather |

Example:
A: Alex's wallet is leather. Mine is plastic.
B: Yes, and his wallet is old. Yours is new.

Possessions 93

Watch Out!

Exercises A and B. Students might use a possessive pronoun with a noun. Listen for and correct errors such as *Mine coat is in the car.*

Option

Assign Unit 8 Supplementary Grammar to Communicate 2 Exercises on the Teacher's Resource Disk as homework or on the Student Persistence CD-ROM as self-access practice.

C Teaching Time: 10–15 min.

- Have two students read the example.
- Have students complete the task.
- 🎧 Play Track 7 while students check their answers.
- Call on students to say answers. Correct as needed.

Multilevel Strategy

- **Pre-level:** Help students identify the correct possessive adjective or pronoun for each blank. After checking answers, have students take turns asking and answering the questions.
- **At-level, Above-level:** After checking answers, pair students and have them take turns asking and answering the questions. Challenge students with the task by having them ask questions about other students' possessions.

D Teaching Time: 5–10 min.

- Have two students read the example.
- Have students complete the task.
- 🎧 Play Track 8 while students check their answers.
- PAIRS. Have students take turns asking and answering the questions.

Expansion

- GROUPS. Have students put in a pile a few objects that belong to them, such as keys, glasses, pencils, etc.
- Students take turns picking up objects and making sentences with possessive pronouns. For example: *This is mine. These keys are hers.*
- If students don't know who something belongs to, they can ask: *Is this yours?*
- Walk around and help as needed.

TIME to TALK

Teaching Time: 10–15 min.

- Have two students read the example.
- GROUPS. Have students complete the task.
- Walk around and help as needed.
- Ask volunteers to tell the class about some group members' possessions.

Unit 8   T-93

Grammar to Communicate 3

Simple Present: *Have*

Teaching Time: 10–15 min.

- Write on the board *have*. Say: *Use the verb* have *to talk about people's possessions.*
- Write on the board a few sentences, such as: *This desk is mine. I have a desk.*
- Then say: *Use* has *if the subject is* he, she, *or* it. Write a few sentences such as: *The book is his. He has the book.*
- Have students study the chart.
- Read the sentences in the chart and have students repeat chorally.
- Have students study the Look Box. Say: *Use* don't *before* have *to say negative sentences when the subject is* I, you, we, *or* they. *Use* doesn't *when the subject is* he, she, *or* it.
- Say a few sentences with *don't have* and *doesn't have* and have students repeat chorally.

A Teaching Time: 5–10 min.

- Read the example with the class.
- Have students complete the task.
- Call on students to say answers. Correct as needed.
- PAIRS. Have students tell their sentences to a partner.

Multilevel Strategy

- **Pre-level:** Give students more time to complete the task.
- **At-level:** When students tell each other their sentences, have them ask questions about their partner's belongings. For example:
  A: *I have a camera.*
  B: *Really? Is it digital?*
- **Above-level:** When students tell each other their sentences, have them ask why their partner has or does not have something. For example:
  A: *I don't have a camera.*
  B: *Really? Why not?*
  A: *Because my sister has a camera.*

T-94   Center Stage 2

Grammar to Communicate 3

SIMPLE PRESENT: HAVE

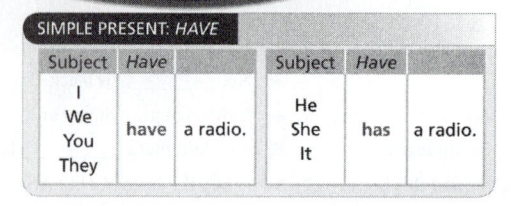

Subject	Have		Subject	Have	
I / We / You / They	have	a radio.	He / She / It	has	a radio.

Look
I **don't have** a radio.
She **doesn't have** a radio.

A Which things in the picture do you have or not have? Write sentences. *Answers will vary.*

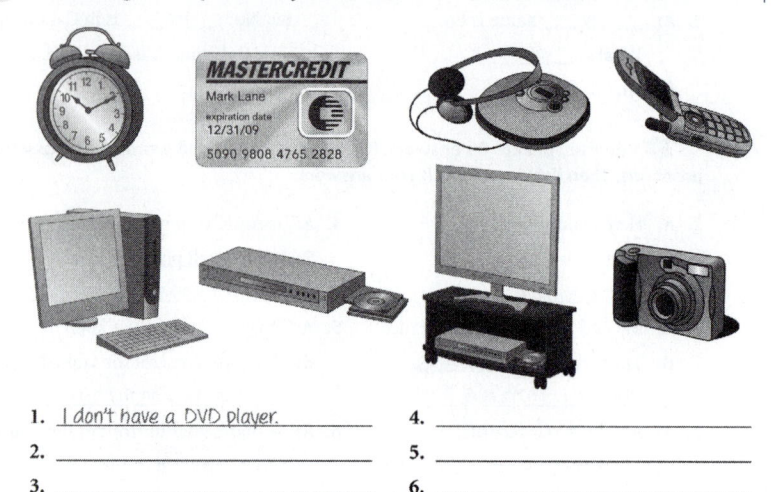

1. I don't have a DVD player.   4. _____
2. _____   5. _____
3. _____   6. _____

PAIRS. Tell your partner the things that you have.

B Look at the pictures on pages 88–89. What things do Mark and Isabel have? Complete the sentences. Use the correct names and *has* or *have*.

1. Mark and Isabel have paintings.
2. Isabel has a CD player.
3. Mark and Isabel have cameras.
4. Mark has a cell phone.
5. Mark has DVDs.
6. Mark and Isabel have calendars.
7. Isabel has a radio.
8. Isabel has glasses.

94 Unit 8

B Teaching Time: 3–5 min.

- Read the examples with the class.
- Have students complete the task.
- Call on students to say answers. Correct as needed.

Grammar Notes

1. Use the verb *have* to talk about things that belong to people.
2. Use *have* with the subjects *I, you, we,* and *they*. Use *has* with *he, she,* and *it*.
3. For more information on this grammar topic, see page 255.

Language Note

Time to Talk. Have students read the example conversation. Point out the word *too* and explain that it means *also*.

C Write sentences about your classmates. Use the words in the boxes. *Answers will vary.*

One student	has	a book	an eraser	a pen	a CD player
Some students	have	books	erasers	pens	CD players
A lot of students		a dictionary	a notebook	a pencil	an earring
All the students		dictionaries	notebooks	pencils	earrings

1. A lot of students have notebooks.
2. _____
3. _____
4. _____
5. _____
6. _____

PAIRS. Compare sentences with a classmate.

TIME to TALK

GROUPS. What possessions do you have? Find out if people in your group have the same things. Talk about the things in the box and your own ideas. *Answers will vary.*

apartment	cat	house	old car	a lot of books
bike	dog	motorcycle	piano	a lot of clothes
bird	guitar	new car	truck	a lot of shoes

Example:
A: I have a cat. Her name is Chili.
B: I have a cat, too.
C: Me, too!
D: I have a dog. His name is Max.

Now tell the class about your group.

Example:
E: Angelo, Rami, and Nellie have cats. Sal has a dog.

Possessions

C Teaching Time: 15–20 min.

- Read the example with the class. Ask students to stand up, mingle, and ask each other questions about possessions listed in the box. Tell students to record their classmates' answers on a piece of paper.
- Tell students to use one word or phrase from each box.
- Have students write their sentences.
- Walk around and help as needed.
- PAIRS. Have students compare sentences.
- Call on students to say answers. Correct as needed.

Option
Assign Unit 8 Supplementary Grammar to Communicate 3 Exercises on the Teacher's Resource Disk as homework or on the Student Persistence CD-ROM as self-access practice.

TIME to TALK

Teaching Time: 10–15 min.

- Have five students read the example conversation.
- Remind students that they can ask questions to find out about other people's possessions. For example: *Do you have a . . . ?*
- GROUPS. Have students complete the task.
- Walk around and help as needed.
- Ask students to report back to the class things they learned about people in their group.

Unit 8

Review and Challenge

Grammar

Teaching Time: 5–10 min.

- Read the example with the class.
- Ask students to read the words in the box before they complete the task.
- Have students complete the task.
- 🎧 Play Track 9 while students check their answers. Pause the recording each time an answer is given.
- PAIRS. Have students role-play the completed conversation.

Dictation

Teaching Time: 5–10 min.

- 🎧 Play Track 10 while students listen and write what they hear.
- 🎧 Play Track 10 again while students check their answers.
- Call on students to write answers on the board.
- 🎧 Play Track 10 again and correct the sentences on the board.

Multilevel Strategy

- **Pre-level:** Give students a worksheet with some of the words from the dictation already provided.

Speaking

Teaching Time: 10–15 min.

- Have four students read the example conversation.
- GROUPS. Have students complete the task. Walk around and help as needed.
- Call on volunteers to say a few new words they have learned.
- Ask students: *Are any words similar in some languages? Which words are completely different in different languages?*

Review and Challenge

Grammar

🎧 **9** Complete the conversation. Use the words in the box. Then listen and check your answers. (Be careful! There are three extra words.)

| has | have | her | hers | mine | my | that | ~~these~~ | they | this |

Carrie: Are __these__ your earrings?
1.

Nadia: Yes, __they__ are. And these are __my__ rings.
2.   3.

Carrie: They're nice. And is __that__ your cell phone over there on the table?
4.

Nadia: No, __this__ is my cell phone.
5.

Carrie: Maybe it's Ann's phone. She __has__ a red phone.
6.

Nadia: No, it's not __hers__. Her phone is in her bag.
7.

Dictation

🎧 **10** Listen. You will hear five sentences. Write them on a piece of paper. *See the audioscript on page 282 for the sentences.*

Speaking

GROUPS. Learn a few words in a new language from your classmates. Student A: point to things in the room. The group asks and answers questions about the words in other languages. Use *this, that, these,* and *those*.
Answers will vary.

Example:
A: What are these?
B: In English, these are called keys.
    In French, they're <u>clefs</u>.
C: And in Spanish, they are <u>llaves</u>.
    What is that?
D: In English, that's called an earring.
    In Russian, it's *sergá*.

earring

Unit 8

Listening

A 🎧 **11** Listen. Where are the people? Match the conversations with the places in the pictures.

_c_ 1. Conversation 1
_d_ 2. Conversation 2
_a_ 3. Conversation 3
_b_ 4. Conversation 4

B 🎧 **12** Listen again. Complete the sentences. Circle the correct answers.

Conversation 1
The woman is eating   (a.) with a male friend.   b. with a female friend.

Conversation 2
The briefcase is the   a. woman's briefcase.   (b.) man's briefcase.

Conversation 3
There are some sneakers in   a. Jamie's room.   (b.) the living room.

Conversation 4
The man's car is   (a.) on the left side of the street.   b. on the right side of the street.

TIME to TALK

Write five of your favorite possessions on a piece of paper, and give the paper to your teacher. Do not write your name on the paper.

GROUPS. Your teacher will give your group some papers. Match each paper to a student in another group. Explain your answers.
Answers will vary.
Example:
A: We think this is Ahmed's paper.
Teacher: Why?
B: Well, he has a new car and he likes computers a lot.
Ahmed: You're wrong. That's not mine.

MY FAVORITE POSSESSIONS
my record player
my computer
my computer games
my digital camera
my soccer ball

Possessions 97

Option

Assign Unit 8 Supplementary Review and Challenge Exercises on the Teacher's Resource Disk as homework or on the Student Persistence CD-ROM as self-access practice.

Listening

A Teaching Time: 5–10 min.

- **Warm-up:** Have students identify the place in each picture. Ask who is in each picture and what the person is doing. For example: _He's in a restaurant. He's a waiter. He's working._
- 🎧 Play Track 11 while students listen.
- 🎧 Play Track 11 again while students listen and complete the task.
- Call on students to say answers. Correct as needed.
- Ask students comprehension questions about the conversations. Modify the questions to the level of the students.

Multilevel Strategy

- **Pre-level:** Ask students _yes / no_ questions (e.g., _In conversation 2, is it the woman's briefcase?_).
- **At-level:** Ask students information questions (e.g., _In conversation 3, why is the mother angry?_).
- **Above-level:** Ask students open-ended or critical thinking questions (e.g., _Why do you think the man in conversation 2 thinks there is a problem?_).

B Teaching Time: 5–10 min.

- Ask students to read through the sentences before they listen.
- 🎧 Play Track 12 while students listen and complete the task.
- PAIRS. Have students compare answers.
- 🎧 Play Track 12 again while students check answers. Pause the recording each time an answer is given.

TIME to TALK

Teaching Time: 10–15 min.

- Before class, cut sheets of paper into equal-sized pieces. Cut enough for each student to have one small piece of paper.
- Read the example conversation with three students.
- Distribute the paper and have students complete the first part of the task.
- Collect and redistribute the papers.
- GROUPS. Have students complete the task.
- Walk around and help as needed.
- Ask students whose possessions surprised them.

Unit 8   T-97

Reading and Writing

Reading

A   **Teaching Time: 10–15 min.**

- Explain that when you buy insurance, you complete a form to tell the insurance company about the things you have.
- Have students read the paragraph silently. Then read the paragraph aloud. Pause after each few words and have students repeat chorally.
- Have students complete the form. Tell students to use the information in the paragraph to help them guess words they don't know, like *make* and *model*.
- Call on students to say answers. Correct as needed.

B   **Teaching Time: 5–10 min.**

- Have students complete the task. Tell students to use the answers in Exercise A to help them.
- PAIRS. Have students compare answers.
- Call on students to say answers. Correct as needed.

Expansion

- Distribute ads from electronic stores to pairs.
- PAIRS. Have students take turns asking and answering: *What is the make? What is the model? What is the value?*
- Walk around and help as needed.

Reading and Writing

Reading

A   Read the paragraph. Then complete the insurance form.

My wife and I have two cameras and a CD player. My camera is a Makki 510. Hers is a Shannon 600. I have the serial number of mine, but not hers. The serial number of my camera is 888576213. My camera is digital, and it is worth about $700. Hers is not digital. It is worth about $200. Our CD player is a Rory E50. It is worth about $500. The serial number is 765890133.

STANDARD HOME INSURANCE APPLICATION FORM

Property Description
Please include the serial number and value. If you are not sure, write *?*.

Quality	Description	Make	Model	Serial number	Value
1	digital camera	Makki	510	888576213	$700
1	camera-not digital	Shannon	600	?	$200
1	CD player	Rory	E50	765890133	$500

B   Label the drawing. Write *make*, *model*, *serial number*, and *value*.

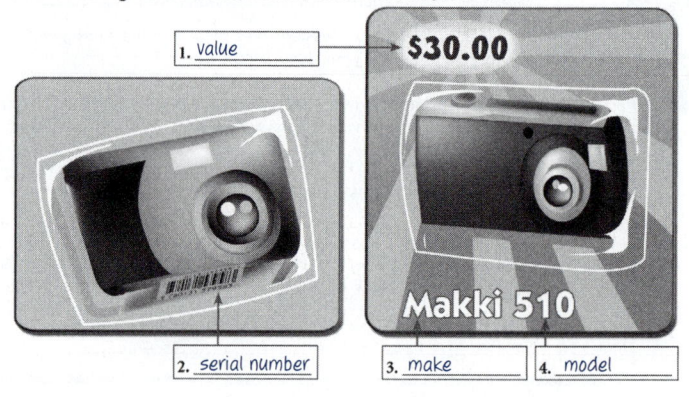

1. value
2. serial number
3. make
4. model

$30.00

Makki 510

Unit 8

Culture Note

Exercise A. Before students read, explain *insurance*. Tell students that when people buy insurance, the insurance company pays them money if something bad happens, for example if their home is damaged or if someone steals things. Ask students to list some things they can buy insurance for.

Center Stage 2

Prewriting

Complete the insurance form. Write about your family's most important possessions.
Answers will vary.

STANDARD HOME INSURANCE APPLICATION FORM

Property Description
Please include the serial number and value. If you are not sure, write ?.

Quality	Description	Make	Model	Serial number	Value
_____	_____	_____	_____	_____	_____
_____	_____	_____	_____	_____	_____
_____	_____	_____	_____	_____	_____

Writing

Now write a paragraph. Describe your property for your insurance company. Use the paragraph on page 98 as a model.
Answers will vary.

Writing Tip
After we use a noun one time, we often use a pronoun the second time.
Example: Our CD player is a Rory E50.
It is worth $200.
(It = Our CD player)

Possessions

Language Note

- **Writing.** Before class, make a copy of the paragraph on page 98 as a transparency to use with an overhead projector. Circle the following pronouns on the transparency: *Hers, hers, it, Hers, It, It*.
- Have students study the Writing Tip.
- Ask students to say the noun that each pronoun replaces (*Hers = my wife's camera, hers = my wife's camera, it = my camera, Hers = my wife's camera, It = my wife's camera, It = our CD player*). Correct as needed.

Prewriting
Teaching Time: 10–15 min.

- Ask students to suggest some things they can include on their insurance forms (*camera, DVD player, TV, stereo*, etc.). Record their ideas on the board. Tell students to write true or made-up information.
- Tell students to look at the form on page 98 to help them complete the form.
- Have students complete the task. Walk around and help as needed.

Writing
Teaching Time: 15–20 min.

- Have students reread the paragraph on page 98. Tell students to use the information in Prewriting to help them write the paragraph.
- Have students complete the task.
- Walk around and help as needed.
- Call on volunteers to read their paragraphs. Correct as needed. You can also have students write their paragraphs on a separate piece of paper. Collect their work and provide individual feedback.

Multilevel Strategy

- **Pre-level:** While students are completing the prewriting task, write the following on the board:
  I have ___ and ___. The make of ___ is ___ and the serial number is ___. It is worth ___. My ___ is ___. It is worth ___. The serial number is ___.
  Have students copy the paragraph and fill in the blanks with information from Prewriting. Walk around and help as needed.

Unit 8   T-99

Game 2
Units 5–8

1. How much is; It's
2. How many; are; There are
3. How much is; It's
4. Are there any; there is
5. Give; I'm

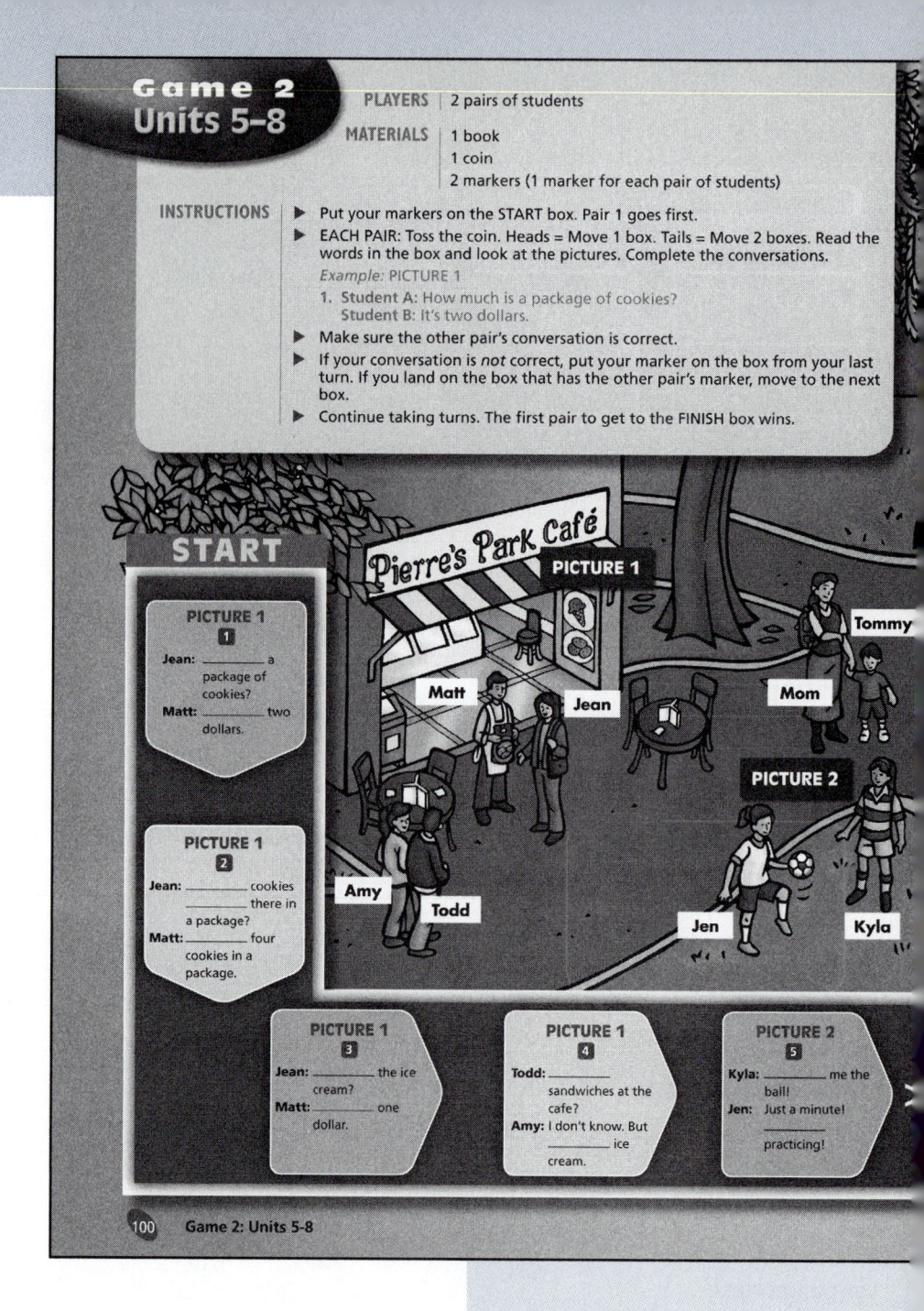

T-100   Center Stage 2

PICTURE 6 — 16
Nina: Look! I _____ a new camera.
Liz: That's great! I want one, too. _____ is old.

PICTURE 6 — 15
Omar: _____ my new cell phone!
Celia: It's cool!

PICTURE 6 — 14
Emma: _____ your bike?
Ben: No, it's _____.

PICTURE 6 — 13
Vicky: _____ nice shoes.
Pam: Thanks _____ are nice, too.

PICTURE 5 — 12
Iris: Carl, _____ that cookie.
Bill: _____ your lunch first!

PICTURE 4 — 11
Dad: (on phone) _____ he playing with?
Mom: A dog. The dog is _____ in the pool.

PICTURE 4 — 10
Dad: (on phone) _____ Neal doing?
Mom: He's _____ in the park.

PICTURE 3 — 9
Bob: Ed, we _____ to the movies now!
Ed: OK! _____ for me!

PICTURE 2 — 6
Tommy: _____ there _____ candy in the backpack?
Mom: Yes, _____.

PICTURE 2 — 7
Tommy: Mom, _____ are those girls _____?
Mom: They're _____ soccer.

PICTURE 2 — 8
Tommy: Why _____ wearing soccer uniforms?
Mom: _____ only practicing.

Game 2: Units 5–8

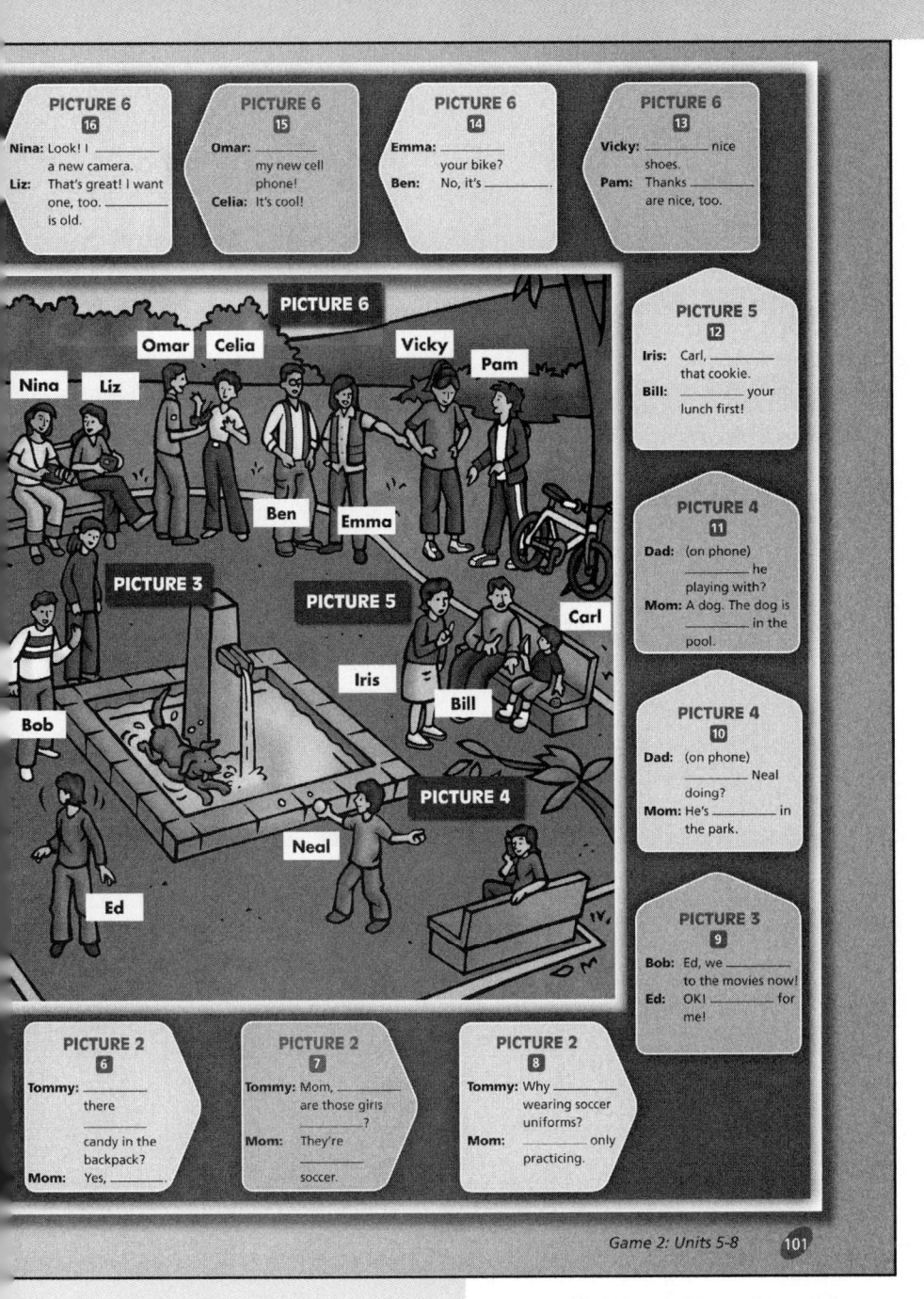

6. Is; any; there is
7. what; doing; playing
8. aren't they; They're
9. 're going; Wait
10. What is; playing
11. Who is; swimming
12. don't eat; Eat
13. These are; yours
14. Is that; hers
15. Look at
16. have; Mine

Game 2 T-101

Unit 9
Routines

Learning Goals
- Learn words to describe routines
- Learn about simple present: affirmative and negative statements; and simple present: spelling rules
- Listen to a conversation and radio report about daily routines
- Read and write about daily routines
- Talk about routines

Learner Persistence
Have the class write and send a postcard or letter to students who have been absent for a significant amount of time. It will let students know that they are missed, and that they're welcome to return as soon as possible.

Warm-up
Teaching Time: 3–5 min.

- Write on the board *routine*. Explain that a routine is the things that you usually do every day. Ask: *What are some things you do every morning? Every night? What time do you do those things?*
- Record students' answers on the board.

Vocabulary
Teaching Time: 15–20 min.

- Have students look at the pictures and captions.
- 🎧 Play Track 13 while students read and listen.
- Read the phrases and words on the list aloud and have students repeat chorally.
- Have students complete the activity.
- Call on students to say the phrases they circled.

Expansion
- Have students read the vocabulary list again.
- PAIRS. Have students tell each other their daily routines using *every day*.

Unit 9
Routines

Grammar
- Simple Present: Affirmative Statements
- Simple Present: Spelling Rules
- Simple Present: Negative Statements

Vocabulary

🎧 **13** Read and listen. Then circle the things you do every day.
Answers will vary.

1. stay up late
2. brush your teeth
3. sleep
5. have lunch
6. wash the dishes
7. take the bus
9. drink coffee
10. read a magazine
11. do the laundry

102 Unit 9

Multilevel Strategy
- **Pre-level:** Have students work with their books open.
- **At-level:** Have students work with their books closed.
- **Above-level:** Have students work with their books closed. Challenge students with the task by having them talk about routines not mentioned on the list.

Language Notes
- **Vocabulary.** Tell students to use a possessive pronoun with the phrase *brush teeth*. For example: *I brush my teeth every day. He brushes his teeth at night.*
- Point out the phrase *have lunch*. Tell students that *have lunch* is the same as *eat lunch*. Explain that they can also use *have* or *eat* with breakfast and dinner.

T-102 Center Stage 2

Listening

A 🎧 **14** Listen. Two people talk about work schedules in their countries. Which country is each sentence about? Write *F* (France), *J* (Japan) or *F, J* (both).

__F__ 1. Many people have long lunch breaks.
__F__ 2. Many people eat lunch at home.
__F, J__ 3. Most people start work at 8:00 or 8:30.
__J__ 4. Most people have an hour for lunch.
__F__ 5. Banks and shops aren't open on Mondays.

B 🎧 **15** Read and listen again. Write the missing words. Use the words in the box.

doesn't	don't	~~have~~	works

Taka: Hey, Monique, you come from France, right?

Monique: Yes, why?

Taka: It says here that in France, most workers __have__₁ a two-hour break for lunch. Is that true?

Monique: Well, it depends on the job, but in general, it's true. Many people in France have lunch at home. My mother, my sister, and I eat lunch together every day. But my father __works__₂ in another city, so he __doesn't__₃ eat with us.

Taka: Really? That's interesting. In Japan, we only have an hour for lunch, so we __don't__₄ have time to go home. I think I like the French way!

Routines

4. get up early

8. work

12. eat out

Listening

A Teaching Time: 10–15 min.

- **Warm-up:** Ask students: *What time is the beginning of this class? What time is the end?* Then say: *Our class schedule is from [8:00 to 10:45]. A schedule tells what happens at certain times.*
- Ask students to read through the sentences before they listen.
- 🎧 Play Track 14 while students listen.
- 🎧 Play Track 14 again while students listen and complete the task.
- PAIRS. Have students compare answers.
- Call on students to say answers. Correct as needed.
- **LIFE SKILLS TEST PREP 2** Go to Unit 12, Lesson 3 for more practice in reading and talking about a work schedule.

B Teaching Time: 15–20 min.

- Ask students to read through the answer choices before they listen.
- 🎧 Play Track 15 as students listen and write the words they hear.
- 🎧 Play Track 15 again while students check their answers.
- Call on students to say answers. Correct as needed.
- Read the conversation aloud. Pause after each few words and have students repeat chorally.
- PAIRS. Ask students to role-play the conversation.

Multilevel Strategy

- **Pre-level:** Have students copy the conversation in their notebooks to reinforce the language before they role-play.
- **At-level:** Write the conversation on the board and erase some words. Have students recall the conversation as they role-play.
- **Above-level:** Have students role-play the conversation using information about lunch customs in their countries. Call on students to role-play in front of the class.

Culture Note

Exercises A and B. Tell students that lunch time in the United States is usually noon. Lunch isn't the most important meal for most families. Children usually have lunch at school. Workers usually have lunch at work. A lunch break is usually between half an hour and an hour.

Option

Assign Unit 9 Supplementary Vocabulary Exercise on the Teacher's Resource Disk as homework or on the Student Persistence CD-ROM as self-access practice.

Unit 9

Grammar to Communicate 1

Simple Present: Affirmative Statements

Teaching Time: 5–10 min.

- Remind students to use the present progressive to talk about things that are happening now. Write a few examples on the board, such as: *Right now you are studying English.*
- Say: *Use the simple present to talk about things that usually or often happen.* Add to the board: *You study English [on Tuesdays and Fridays].*
- Say: *Use the base form of the verb for subjects* I, you, we, *and* they. *Add –s to most verbs for subjects* he, she, *and* it.
- Have students study the chart.
- Have students say more affirmative statements. Write them on the board and have students repeat chorally.
- Read the sentences in the chart and have students repeat chorally.

A   Teaching Time: 5–10 min.

- Have students circle all verbs that end in –s. Remind them to use singular subjects for verbs that end in –s.
- Have students complete the task.
- Call on students to say answers. Correct as needed.

B   Teaching Time: 5–10 min.

- Read the example with the class.
- Have students complete the task.
- Call on students to say answers. Correct as needed.
- PAIRS. Have partners take turns reading sentences aloud.
- **LIFE SKILLS / TEST PREP 2** Go to Unit 2, Lesson 2 for more practice in giving basic information about family members.

Grammar to Communicate 1

SIMPLE PRESENT: AFFIRMATIVE STATEMENTS

Subject	Verb		Subject	Verb	
I / We / You / They	cook	a lot.	He / She	cook<u>s</u>	a lot.
			It	work<u>s</u>	well.

A   Make sentences about the people you know. Use the words in the box. *Answers will vary but 1, 6, and 8 must have plural subjects.*

best friends	family and I	friends and I	mother
boyfriend	father	girlfriend	parents
children	friends	husband	wife

1. My _____ get up early.
2. My _____ stays up late.
3. My _____ eats out a lot.
4. My _____ sleeps late a lot.
5. My _____ works five days a week.
6. My _____ wash the dishes at night.
7. My _____ cooks in the evening.
8. My _____ go for a walk every day.

B   Complete the paragraph.

I'm from Guadalajara, Mexico. During the week I <u>get up</u> early, at about 5:00 A.M. My wife, Sandra, <u>sleeps</u> until 7:30. Then she and our children <u>get up</u>. I <u>work</u> full time from 8:00 to 2:00 and then from 4:00 to 6:00. Sandra <u>works</u> part-time, from 9:00 to 1:00. Then she <u>drives</u> home and <u>cooks</u> lunch. We <u>eat</u> lunch a little after 2:00.

1. (get up)
2. (sleep)
3. (get up)
4. (work)
5. (work)
6. (drive)
7. (cook)
8. (eat)

Unit 9

Grammar Notes

1. The simple present describes actions that generally or usually happen. Use the simple present to talk about routines and habits.
2. Use the base form of the verb with subjects *I*, *you*, *we*, and *they*.
3. Add *–s* or *–es* to verbs with subjects *he*, *she*, and *it*.
4. For more information on this grammar topic, see page 256.

Culture Note

Exercise B. In the United States a person who works forty hours or more a week is considered full-time. A part-time worker works less than forty hours a week.

Center Stage 2

C What do you think these people probably do? Write sentences. Use the verbs in the box and *a lot*.

| cook | eat out | play | sleep | ~~talk on the phone~~ | work |

1. Teresa and Angela are 16 years old.
   They probably talk on the phone a lot.
2. Billy is a three-month-old baby.
   He probably sleeps a lot.
3. Melanie is a mother of six children.
   She probably cooks a lot.
4. Annie is five years old.
   She probably plays a lot.
5. Sylvia and David Lin like good food.
   They probably eat out a lot.
6. Mark is a doctor.
   He probably works a lot.

PAIRS. Compare your answers. Do you agree? Then talk about the activities. Which activities do you do a lot?
Answers will vary.

Look
Time expressions
at night
every day
in the afternoon
in the morning
in the evening
on weekends

TIME to TALK

PAIRS. Tell your partner about the routines of five people you know. Use time expressions and the words in the boxes or your own ideas.
Answers will vary.

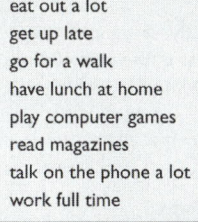

best friend	drink coffee
brother or sister	eat out a lot
children	get up late
English teacher	go for a walk
father	have lunch at home
grandparents	play computer games
mother	read magazines
neighbor	talk on the phone a lot
roommate	work full time

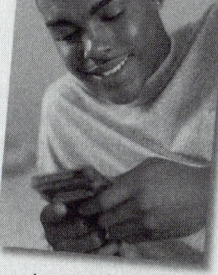

play computer games

Example:
A: My best friend plays computer games every day.

Routines 105

C Teaching Time: 10–15 min.
- Read the example with the class.
- Tell students to use *probably* when they think something is true, but they are not 100 percent sure.
- Tell them that *probably* goes after the subject and before a simple present verb.
- Have students complete the task.
- PAIRS. Have students compare answers.
- PAIRS. Have students take turns telling each other about the activities they do a lot.

Multilevel Strategy
- **Pre-level:** Group all pre-level students to complete the task. Read each sentence and have students call out the correct verb from the box for each new sentence. Then have students complete the task. Walk around and help students form sentences as needed.
- **At-level, Above-level:** For the pair activity, have students talk about other activities they do that are not listed in the exercise. Call on students to tell the class something that their partner does a lot.

Option
Assign Unit 9 Supplementary Grammar to Communicate 1 Exercises on the Teacher's Resource Disk as homework or on the Student Persistence CD-ROM as self-access practice.

TIME to TALK

Teaching Time: 10–15 min.
- Have students study the Look Box.
- Tell students to use the words in the boxes and time expressions in the Look Box to talk about people they know.
- Read the example with the class.
- PAIRS. Have students complete the task.
- Walk around and help as needed.

Multilevel Strategy
- **Pre-level:** Have students write down their sentences before they talk with their partner.

Unit 9   T-105

Grammar to Communicate 2

Simple Present Third Person Singular: Spelling Rules

Teaching Time: 5–10 min.

- Remind students that we add *-s* to verbs when the subject is the pronoun *he, she,* or *it.*
- Say: *Some verbs change their spelling when you add –s.*
- Have students study the chart.
- Say: *When the base form of a verb ends in* y, *change* y *to* i *and add* –es.
- Say: *When the base form of a verb ends in* sh, ch, ss, *or* x, *add* –es.
- Write on the board: *go / goes* and *do / does.* Tell students to add *–es* to *go* and *do* for sentences with subjects *he, she,* and *it.*
- Read the examples in the chart and the Look Box aloud and have students repeat chorally.
- Write a few different verbs on the board. Have students come up to the board and rewrite the verbs for the third person singular. Correct as needed.

A Teaching Time: 5–10 min.

- Have students complete the task.
- PAIRS. Have students compare answers.
- Call on students to write answers on the board. Write corrections on the board as needed.

B Teaching Time: 10–15 min.

- Tell students that sometimes the letter *s* sounds like *z.* Have students study the Look Box. Read the words in the Look Box, exaggerating the pronunciation of final *-s.* Have students repeat chorally.
- Say a few verbs ending in *–es,* and have students say which sound they hear. Say, for example: *misses* (/ɪz/), *studies* (/z/), *talks* (/s/).
- Have students circle the verb in each sentence.
- Call on students to read the verbs they circled. Correct as needed.
- Play Track 16 while students listen and check the sounds they hear.
- Play Track 16 again if necessary to allow students to complete the task.
- Call on students to say answers. Correct as needed.

Grammar to Communicate 2

SIMPLE PRESENT THIRD PERSON SINGULAR: SPELLING RULES

Example	Spelling Rule
study → studies He studies every day.	End of verb: consonant + *–y* Spelling: change *y* to *i*, add *–es*

Example	Spelling Rule
finish → finishes watch → watches miss → misses fix → fixes He misses his family.	End of verb: *sh, ch, ss, x* Spelling: Add *–es*

Look
We **go** to the movies a lot.
He **goes** to the movies a lot.

A Complete the sentences.

1. Ming __relaxes__ with her husband at night.
   (relax)
2. Ann __cries__ at sad movies.
   (cry)
3. Tina __finishes__ lunch at 2:00 P.M.
   (finish)
4. Al __fixes__ cars with Sal every day.
   (fix)
5. Lynn __washes__ her hair in the morning.
   (wash)

B CD 2 TRACK 16 Circle the verbs in the sentences. Then listen. What are the sounds of the verb endings? Check (✓) the correct column.

Look
Pronunciation of final *-s*
walks /s/
comes /z/
watches /ɪz/

	/s/	/z/	/ɪz/
1. My daughter (brushes) her hair all the time.	☐	☐	✓
2. My mother (reads) the newspaper.	☐	✓	☐
3. My friend Sam (drinks) coffee.	✓	☐	☐
4. My sister (takes) the bus to work.	✓	☐	☐
5. My uncle (washes) his car once a week.	☐	☐	✓

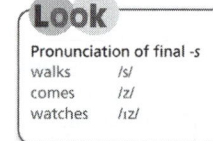

106 Unit 9

Grammar Notes

1. When the subject is *he, she,* or *it,* the verb in the simple present ends in *–s.*
2. For most verbs, add *–s* to the base form.
3. When the base form of a verb ends in *y,* change *y* to *i* and add *–es.*
4. When the base form of a verb ends in *sh, ch, ss,* or *x,* add *–es.*
5. Add *–es* to *go* and *do.*
6. For more information on this grammar topic, see page 256.

C PAIRS. Change the underlined words in Exercise B to people you know. Read your sentences to your partner. Answers will vary.

Example:
A: My best friend brushes her hair all the time.

D Look at the chart. It shows schedules in different countries. Complete the sentences with the correct words.

	COLOMBIA	SOUTH KOREA	IRAN	TAIWAN
start work	8:00 A.M.	9:00 A.M.	8:00 A.M.	9:00 A.M.
finish work	6:00 P.M.	6:00 P.M.	4:00 P.M.	5:00 P.M.
have lunch	12:00 – 2:00 P.M.	12:00 – 1:00 P.M.	12:00 – 1:00 P.M.	12:00 – 1:00 P.M.
go to school	7:00 A.M. – 3:00 P.M.	7:45 A.M. – 5:00 P.M.	8:00 A.M. – 3:30 P.M.	8:00 A.M. – 5:00 P.M.

1. Most students in South Korea __go to school__ for almost nine hours.
2. Most people in Taiwan __finish work__ at 5:00 P.M.
3. Most people in Iran __start work__ at 8:00 A.M.
4. Rosa lives in Colombia. She __has lunch__ from 12:00 to 2:00 P.M.
5. Jae lives in South Korea. He __goes to school__ from 7:45 to 5:00 P.M.
6. Chia-Pei lives in Taiwan. She __starts work__ at 9:00 A.M.

PAIRS. Talk about the schedules of people in your country. Answers will vary.

TIME to TALK

GROUPS. Make five sentences about classmates in other groups. Use the words in the box or your own ideas. Answers will vary.

| cry at sad movies | fix his friends' computers | wash her hair every day |
| exercise every day | miss his family | watch a lot of DVDs |

Example:
Aly fixes his friend's computers.

WRAP-UP. Now tell the class your sentences. For every correct sentence, your group gets a point. The group with the most points wins.

Routines 107

Language Note

Review how to read times with students. Remind them that 8:00 = eight o'clock, 7:45 = seven forty-five, and 3:30 = three thirty. Remind them that A.M. refers to times from 12:00 midnight to 11:59 in the morning. P.M. refers to times from 12:00 noon to 11:59 at night.

Option

Assign Unit 9 Supplementary Grammar to Communicate 2 Exercises on the Teacher's Resource Disk as homework or on the Student Persistence CD-ROM as self-access practice.

C Teaching Time: 5–10 min.

- Read the example with the class.
- Have students complete the task. Walk around and help as needed.
- PAIRS. Have students read their sentences aloud to each other.

D Teaching Time: 5–10 min.

- Have students study the chart. Point out the headings of the rows and columns. Demonstrate how to use the chart by asking a few questions and locating the answers. For example: *What is the time to have lunch in South Korea?* (12:00–1:00 P.M.) *What happens at 4 P.M. in Iran?* (People finish work.)
- Read the example with the class.
- Have students complete the task.
- Call on students to say answers. Correct as needed.
- PAIRS. Have students talk about the schedules of people in their countries.

Multilevel Strategy

- **Pre-level:** While students are completing the task, write the following on the board:
People in ___ start work at ___. They have lunch from ___ to ___. Most people finish work at ___. Children go to school from ___ to ___.
Tell students to fill in the blanks with true information and read the paragraph to their partner for the pair activity.
- **Above-level:** Have students report on the schedules of people in their partner's country.

TIME to TALK

Teaching Time: 10–15 min.

- Read the example with the class.
- GROUPS. Have students complete the task.
- Walk around and help as needed.
- Call on groups to take turns reading their sentences aloud.

Multilevel Strategy

- **All-levels:** Place students in mixed-level groups. Have at-level and above-level students make sentences about other classmates. Assign pre-level students as recorders and have them write down the sentences to read to the class.

Unit 9

Grammar to Communicate 3

Simple Present: Negative Statements

Teaching Time: 5–10 min.

- Say: *To make negative sentences in the simple present, use* do not *or* does not *and the base form of the verb.*
- Say: *Use* do not *if the subject is* I, you, we, *or* they. *Use* does not *if the subject is* he, she, *or* it.
- Say: *Use full forms and contractions.* Write on the board: *Do not = don't. Does not = doesn't.*
- Have students study the chart.
- Read the sentences in the chart and have students repeat chorally.
- Write a few affirmative statements on the board. Have students change them into negative statements. Correct as needed.

A Teaching Time: 15–20 min.

- Read the example with the class.
- Have students complete the task.
- Call on students to say answers. Correct as needed.
- Read the example for the second part of the task.
- PAIRS. Have students talk about things they do or don't do every day.
- Walk around and help as needed.

Multilevel Strategy

- **Pre-level:** Have students work in pairs or groups to complete the task. For the pair activity, have students write one affirmative and one negative sentence and read it to their partner.
- **At-level, Above-level:** Have students write at least five sentences about where their classmates usually sit. Prompt students with different prepositions if necessary (e.g., *Who sits next to Pavel?*). Call on students to say their sentences while one student creates a seating chart on the board based on what students say.

T-108 Center Stage 2

Grammar to Communicate 3

SIMPLE PRESENT: NEGATIVE STATEMENTS

Subject	Don't	Verb		Subject	Doesn't	Verb	
I You We They	don't	work	every day.	He She It	doesn't	work	every day.

A Read the sentences. Write the correct names on the desks in the picture.

1. Ali sits behind Maria. He doesn't sit near a window or door.
2. Jin and Ozan sit next to Maria. They don't sit next to Ali.
3. Lin sits near the door. She doesn't sit in front of Jin.
4. Pedro and Ozan sit near the window. They don't sit next to Lin.

[Seating chart: Row 1 (back): 1-Lin, 2-Ali, 3-Pedro; Row 2 (front): 4-Jin, 5-Maria, 6-Ozan]

PAIRS. Look at the pictures on page 102–103. Write sentences about the things you do and don't do every day. *Answers will vary.*

Example:
I cook every day. OR *I don't cook every day.*

B Complete the sentences. Use the negative form of the verb.

1. David goes out on Saturday night, but he ___doesn't go___ out on Sunday night.
2. Mr. and Mrs. Kim drink coffee, but they ___don't drink___ tea.
3. I do the dishes every day, but I ___don't do___ the laundry every day.
4. The children have dinner at home, but they ___don't have___ lunch at home.
5. My friends and I play tennis, but we ___don't play___ soccer.
6. Ms. Li works on Mondays, but she ___doesn't work___ on Tuesdays.
7. I get up late on weekends, but I ___don't get up___ late during the week.
8. Amy watches TV in the morning, but she ___doesn't watch___ TV in the evening.

108 Unit 9

B Teaching Time: 5–10 min.

- Read the example with the class.
- Have students complete the task.
- Call on students to say answers. Correct as needed.

Grammar Notes

1. Use *do not / does not* and the base form of a verb to make negative sentences in the simple present.
2. Use *do not* with subjects *I, you, we,* and *they.* Use *does not* with subjects *he, she,* and *it.*
3. Use full forms and contractions. *Do not = don't. Does not = doesn't.*
4. For more information on this grammar topic, see page 256.

C Look at the chart. Make sentences about the people.

WEEKEND ACTIVITIES	CARLOS	ALICIA	PAUL	OLIVA
eat out	no	yes	yes	no
go to the movies	no	yes	yes	yes
play computer games	yes	no	no	yes
watch sports on TV	yes	no	yes	no

1. Alicia and Oliva don't watch sports on TV.
   (TV / Alicia and Oliva)
2. Alicia and Paul eat out.
   (eat out / Alicia and Paul)
3. Carlos doesn't go to the movies.
   (movies / Carlos)
4. Alicia and Paul don't play computer games.
   (computer games / Alicia and Paul)
5. Alicia doesn't watch sports on TV.
   (sport on TV / Alicia)
6. Carlos and Oliva don't eat out.
   (eat out / Carlos and Oliva)

PAIRS. Talk about your friends' activities on the weekend. Say what they do and don't do.
Answers will vary.

Look
too = *also* in affirmative responses
A: Maria likes movies.
B: John does, **too**.
either = *also* in negative responses
A: Maria doesn't exercise
B: I don't **either**.

TIME to TALK

PAIRS. Look at the pictures on pages 102–103. Make a story. What are the people's names? What do they do every day? What don't they do every day?
Answers will vary.

Example:
A: Susie Li is a student. She stays up late every night.
B: She doesn't sleep much.

Routines 109

C Teaching Time: 5–10 min.
- Read the example with the class.
- Show how to locate information on the chart to determine the correct answers. Point to the row *watch sports on TV*. Point to *no* under Alicia. Say: *Alicia doesn't watch sports on TV.*
- Have students complete the task.
- Call on students to say answers. Correct as needed.
- Have students study the Look Box. Remind them that *too* means *also*. Tell students to use *either* to show that a negative statement is also true about another person or thing.
- PAIRS. Have students talk about their friends' activities. Walk around and help as needed.

Watch Out!

Exercise B. English language learners often use the third-person singular verb form with *does not* instead of the base form of the verb. Listen for and correct errors such as *He does not has . . .* and *She doesn't finishes. . . .*

Option

Assign Unit 9 Supplementary Grammar to Communicate 3 Exercises on the Teacher's Resource Disk as homework or on the Student Persistence CD-ROM as self-access practice.

TIME to TALK

Teaching Time: 10–15 min.
- Have two students read the example.
- PAIRS. Have students complete the task.
- Walk around and help as needed.
- GROUPS. Have pairs of students tell their story to another pair.
- Ask volunteers to tell the class their stories.
- Ask students to raise their hands to vote for the most interesting story.

Unit 9 T-109

Review and Challenge

Grammar

Teaching Time: 5–10 min.

- Read the example with the class.
- Have students complete the task.
- 🎧 Play Track 17 while students check their answers.
- Call on students to say each error and its correction. Correct as needed.

Dictation

Teaching Time: 5–10 min.

- 🎧 Play Track 18 while students listen and write what they hear.
- 🎧 Play Track 18 again while students check their answers.
- PAIRS. Have students compare their answers.
- Call on students to write answers on the board.
- 🎧 Play Track 18 again and correct the sentences on the board.

> **Multilevel Strategy**
>
> - **Pre-level:** Give students a worksheet with some of the words from the dictation already provided.

Speaking

Teaching Time: 10–15 min.

- Read the example with the class. If necessary, explain that *most* means *more than half*.
- GROUPS. Have students complete the task.
- Conduct informal surveys on students' beliefs about each sentence. Read each sentence aloud and have each group say whether they think it is true or false.

> **Multilevel Strategy**
>
> - **All-levels:** Place students in mixed-level groups. Have pre-level students read each statement and at-level and above-level students decide whether the statement is true or false and why. Prompt students with suggestions if necessary.

T-110 Center Stage 2

Review and Challenge

Grammar

🎧 **17** Correct the paragraph. There are seven mistakes. The first mistake is corrected for you. Then listen and check your answers.

My roommates and I ~~not have~~ *don't have* the same routines. Julia ~~get~~ *gets* up late, at around 10:00 A.M. Katie and I get up early. Katie ~~have~~ *has* class at 8:00 A.M., and I start work at 9:00 A.M. Julia ~~don't~~ *doesn't* work. She just takes two classes in the afternoon. She's lucky because she ~~finishs~~ *finishes* early. Then she goes out with friends. She doesn't ~~studies~~ *study* very much, and she doesn't cook. Katie and I study and ~~goes~~ *go* to work every day. Julia's life is pretty good!

Dictation

🎧 **18** Listen. You will hear five sentences. Write them on a piece of paper. *See the audioscript on page 283 for the sentences.*

Speaking

GROUPS. Talk about the sentences below. For each sentence, write *T* (true), *F* (false), or *?* (not sure). If the sentence is false, change it to make it true. *Answers will vary. Suggested answers:*

__F__ 1. Most people in the U.S. ~~speak~~ *don't speak* two languages.

__F__ 2. Most people in the U.S. ~~watch~~ *don't watch* soccer on TV. *Most people watch baseball.*

__F__ 3. Most people in the U.S. ~~have~~ *don't have* two hours for lunch. *Most people have one hour for lunch.*

__F__ 4. Most people in the U.S. ~~ride~~ *don't ride* a bike to work. *Most people drive cars to work.*

__F__ 5. Most women in the U.S. ~~don't~~ work outside the home. *Most women work outside the home.*

__T__ 6. Most men in the U.S. don't do housework.

__T__ 7. Most children in the U.S. don't wear uniforms to school.

__T__ 8. Most teenagers in the U.S. have a part-time job.

housework

Unit 9

Expansion

- Ask students to say true sentences about the same topics in their own countries. For example: *Most people in Argentina don't ride a bike to work.*
- Start a discussion to compare differences among students' countries and the United States. Ask questions such as: *Most people in Argentina don't ride a bike to work. Is that the same in your country?*

Option

Before class, make a copy of the grammar exercise on page 110 as a transparency to use with an overhead projector. Ask a volunteer to make corrections to the paragraph on the transparency. Correct as needed. Have students check their work with the transparency.

Listening

A 🎧 **19** Listen. A radio reporter talks about how people around the world spend their time. Match the activities with the worldwide averages.

Look
- John works 40 hours a week. Paul works 50 hours a week. Sarah works 60 hours a week. On **average**, they work 50 hours a week. (40 + 50 + 60 = 150 ÷ 3 = 50)
- % = **percent**.
- 2.5 = two **point** five

	Activities	Worldwide Averages
_e_	1. hours of sleep a night	a. 21%
_d_	2. hours of work a day	b. 79%
_c_	3. percent of men who do housework	c. 15%
_b_	4. percent of people who eat at home every day	d. 9.6
_a_	5. percent of men who cook	e. 7.4

B 🎧 **20** Listen again. Complete the sentences. Circle the correct verb.

1. People in Japan **sleep** / (**don't sleep**) a lot.
2. People in South Africa **work** / (**sleep**) 7.9 hours a day.
3. People in Argentina and Turkey **cook** / (**work**) a lot.
4. Men in Turkey and Egypt **do** / (**don't do**) a lot of housework.
5. Most women in Egypt (**cook**) / **work**.

TIME to TALK

Complete the sentences about your country. *Answers will vary.*
1. On average, I think people in my country get _____ hours of sleep a night.
2. On average, I think people in my country work _____ hours a day.
3. I think _____% of people in my country eat at home every day.
4. I think _____% of men in my country do housework every day.
5. I think _____% of men in my country cook every day.

GROUPS. Compare your answers. Discuss any differences. Then tell the class about your countries.

Routines 111

Option

Have students calculate averages of different numbers, such as grades, prices on a receipt, electric bills over several months, etc.

Option

Assign Unit 9 Supplementary Review and Challenge Exercises on the Teacher's Resource Disk as homework or on the Student Persistence CD-ROM as self-access practice.

Listening

A Teaching Time: 5–10 min.

- **Warm-up:** Have students study the Look Box. Explain that *average* is a usual amount of something. A *percentage* is a part of something. *Percent* is part of 100. For example, 50% is half of something.
- Ask students to read through the answer choices before they listen.
- 🎧 Play Track 19 while students listen.
- 🎧 Play Track 19 again while students listen and complete the task.
- 🎧 Play Track 19 again while students check their answers.
- Call on students to say answers. Correct as needed.
- Ask students comprehension questions about the report. Modify the questions to the level of the students.

Multilevel Strategy

- **Pre-level:** Ask students yes / no questions (e.g., *Do people in Japan sleep a lot?*).
- **At-level:** Ask students information questions (e.g., *What is the percentage of men who do housework in South Africa?*).
- **Above-level:** Ask students open-ended or critical thinking questions (e.g., *Are you surprised people in Japan sleep less than 7 hours? Why?*).

B Teaching Time: 5–10 min.

- Ask students to read through the sentences before they listen.
- 🎧 Play Track 20 while students listen and complete the task.
- PAIRS. Have students compare answers.
- 🎧 Play Track 20 again while students check answers. Pause the recording each time an answer is given.

TIME to TALK

Teaching Time: 10–15 min.
- Give students a few minutes to complete the sentences.
- GROUPS. Have students compare answers.
- Call on volunteers to tell the class about similarities and differences between the countries that people in their group are from.

Unit 9 T-111

Reading and Writing

Reading

A Teaching Time: 10–15 min.
- Have students read the paragraph.
- Give example sentences about differences between your day and Linda's, such as: *Linda goes to work at night. I go to work in the morning.*
- Have students read the paragraph silently. Then read the paragraph aloud. Pause after each few words and have students repeat chorally.
- Have students write two differences.
- Walk around and help as needed.
- Call on volunteers to read their sentences to the class.

B Teaching Time: 5–10 min.
- Have students complete the task.
- PAIRS. Have students compare answers.
- Call on students to say answers. Correct as needed. If necessary, refer back to the paragraph to show students where each piece of information is located.

Reading and Writing

Reading

A Linda writes about her day for a study on how people spend their time. Read about her typical day. How are you and Linda different? Write two differences. *Answers will vary.*

1. _____ 2. _____

> **Describe how you spend your time on an average day.**
>
> I work in a hospital. My hours are from 11:00 P.M. to 7:00 A.M. Monday to Friday. I get home at 7:30 A.M. and drive my children to school. Then I go home and go to bed. I sleep only about 5 hours a day, from 9:00 A.M. to 2:00 P.M. My children get home from school at 3:00 I help them with their homework. Then we eat dinner together between 5:00 and 6:00. After dinner, we watch TV. They go to bed at 7:30 P.M. Then I read a magazine or talk to my friends on the phone. At about 9:00 P.M., I get ready for work. At 9:30 my husband comes home and we talk about our day for an hour. At 10:30 I leave for work.

B Complete Linda's diary for the study. Use information from the paragraph in Exercise A.

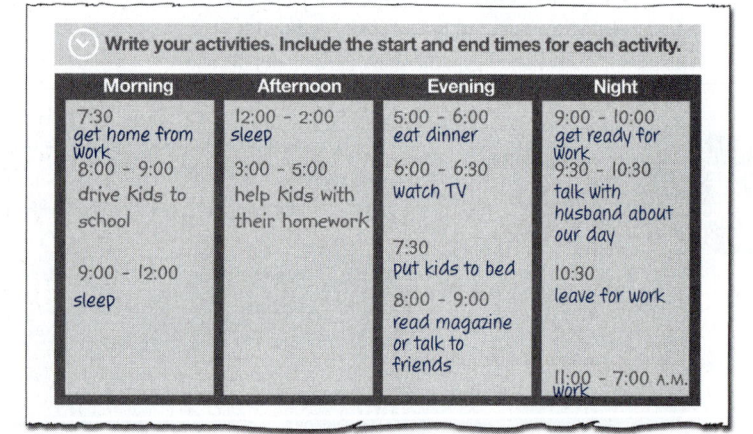

> Write your activities. Include the start and end times for each activity.

Morning	Afternoon	Evening	Night
7:30 get home from work	12:00 – 2:00 sleep	5:00 – 6:00 eat dinner	9:00 – 10:00 get ready for work
8:00 – 9:00 drive kids to school	3:00 – 5:00 help kids with their homework	6:00 – 6:30 watch TV	9:30 – 10:30 talk with husband about our day
9:00 – 12:00 sleep		7:30 put kids to bed	10:30 leave for work
		8:00 – 9:00 read magazine or talk to friends	11:00 – 7:00 A.M. work

Unit 9

Language Note
- **Exercise A.** Use the word *but* to connect two sentences when the second sentence gives information that is different.
- Write examples on the board, such as: *Linda goes to work at night, but I go to work in the morning.*
- Point out the use of the comma before *but*.

Option
- Write the word *admire* on the board. Tell students: *When you admire someone, you like the person because you think that they do something well.* Write the sentence: *I admire ___.*

Prewriting

Complete the diary with your daily activities. Answers will vary.

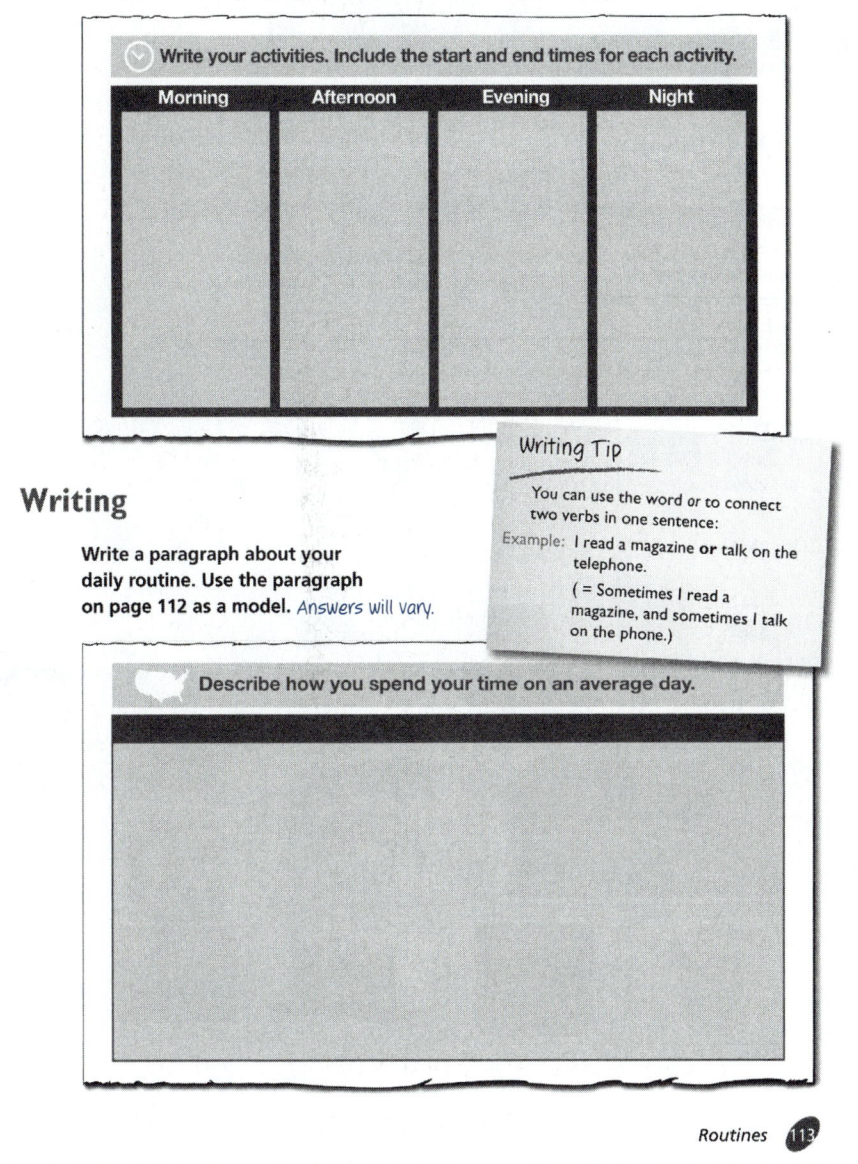

Write your activities. Include the start and end times for each activity.

Morning	Afternoon	Evening	Night

Writing

Write a paragraph about your daily routine. Use the paragraph on page 112 as a model. Answers will vary.

Writing Tip

You can use the word *or* to connect two verbs in one sentence:

Example: I read a magazine **or** talk on the telephone.

(= Sometimes I read a magazine, and sometimes I talk on the phone.)

Describe how you spend your time on an average day.

Routines 113

Prewriting

Teaching Time: 10–15 min.

- Have students complete the task.
- Walk around and help as needed.
- PAIRS. Have students compare their diaries.

Writing

Teaching Time: 15–20 min.

- Have students reread Linda's diary on page 112.
- Have students complete the activity.
- Walk around and help as needed.
- Call on volunteers to read their paragraphs. Correct as needed. You can also have students write their paragraphs on a separate piece of paper. Collect their work and provide individual feedback.

Expansion

- GROUPS. Have students within each group collect, mix up, and redistribute students' paragraphs.
- Have students read each paragraph and try to guess whose routine it describes.

- Have students copy the sentence and complete it in their own way.
- Have students then write five sentences about why they admire that person. Tell them to write sentences about what the person does and doesn't do.
- Walk around and help as needed.
- Collect students' work and provide individual feedback.

Language Note

Writing. Have students study the Writing Tip. Tell students that the word *or* shows choices. Read the example sentence aloud. The choices in this sentence are *read a magazine* and *talk on the telephone*.

Unit 9 T-113

Unit 10
Shopping

Learning Goals
- Learn words for shopping
- Learn about frequency adverbs; simple present: *yes / no* questions; and information questions
- Listen to conversations about shopping
- Read and write a newsletter
- Talk about shopping

Learner Persistence

Invite former students of your program to return to your class and speak to your students. Your students will be able to relate to people who have overcome obstacles similar to their own. People who have successfully completed the program can be a powerful motivation for students to persist, achieve their goals, and complete the program.

Warm-up

Teaching Time: 3–5 min.

Ask students to name some types of stores (an electronics store, a supermarket, a pet shop, a toy store, etc.). Record students' answers on the board.

Vocabulary

Teaching Time: 15–20 min.

- Have students look at the pictures. Explain unfamiliar vocabulary. For example, say: *When you buy something with cash, you use paper money and coins, not a check or credit card.*
- Play Track 21 while students read and listen.
- Read the words and phrases on the list aloud and have students repeat chorally.
- PAIRS. Have students tell each other names of department stores and convenience stores in their town.
- Call on students to tell the class their answers.

Expansion
- Draw the following graphic organizer on the board.

T-114   Center Stage 2

Unit 10
Shopping

Grammar
- Frequency Adverbs
- Simple Present: Yes / No Questions
- Simple Present: Information Questions

Vocabulary

21 Read and listen. What is the name of a department store or convenience store in your town? Tell a partner.
Answers will vary.

1. department store
2. on sale
3. spend money on
4. 25% off
5. sell
6. pay for
7. receipt
8. convenience store
9. open
10. close
11. cash

Unit 10

Actions	Things

- Call on students to come to the board and write the words and phrases from the vocabulary list in the correct column.

Multilevel Strategy
- **Above-level:** Encourage students to write words and phrases that are not on the list (e.g., *credit card, return things*).

Language Note

Vocabulary. Explain the difference between the phrases *for sale* and *on sale*. If something is *for sale*, then someone is selling it. If something is *on sale*, its price is lower than usual.

Listening

A 🎧 22 Listen. A husband and wife are talking. Why is the wife unhappy with her husband? Check (✓) the reasons.

___ 1. He doesn't like shopping.
✓ 2. He never has his credit card.
✓ 3. He buys a lot of things.
✓ 4. He uses her credit card.
___ 5. He goes to the movies a lot.

B 🎧 23 Read and listen again. Write the missing words. Use the words in the box.

does it	Do we	never	~~what do you~~

Veronica: You don't, but I do! So, __what do you__ want this time?
   1.

Martin: Great Buy has DVD players on sale. They're 25% off.

Veronica: __Do we__ need a DVD player?
   2.

Martin: Well, movies are all on DVD these days.

Veronica: But we __never__ watch movies.
   3.

Martin: That's because we don't have a DVD player.

Veronica: Okay, so what kind is it?

Martin: It's a Sovy.

Veronica: And how much __does it__ cost?
   4.

Shopping 115

Listening

A Teaching Time: 10–15 min.

- **Warm-up:** Start a discussion on students' shopping habits. Ask questions such as: *Do you like to shop? What kinds of things do you like to buy?*
- Ask students to read the statements before they listen.
- 🎧 Play Track 22 while students listen.
- 🎧 Play Track 22 again while students complete the task.
- Call on students to say answers. Correct as needed.

B Teaching Time: 15–20 min.

- Have students read through the answer choices before they listen.
- 🎧 Play Track 23 while students listen and complete the task.
- 🎧 Play Track 23 again while students check their answers.
- Call on students to say answers. Correct as needed.
- Read the conversation aloud. Pause after each few words and have students repeat chorally.
- PAIRS. Ask students to role-play the conversation.

Multilevel Strategy

- **Pre-level:** Have students role-play the completed conversation.
- **At-level, Above-level:** Have students continue the conversation while they role-play. Prompt them with suggestions (e.g., *Talk about buying a new radio.*). Ask pairs to role-play in front of the class.

Expansion

- Ask students to think of something they want to buy. Have them think of two reasons why it's a good thing for them to buy and one reason why it's *not* a good thing for them to buy.
- PAIRS. Have partners tell each other what they want and their reasons for and against buying it.

Option

Assign Unit 10 Supplementary Vocabulary Exercise on the Teacher's Resource Disk as homework or on the Student Persistence CD-ROM as self-access practice.

Unit 10   T-115

Grammar to Communicate 1

Frequency Adverbs with the Simple Present

Teaching Time: 5–10 min.

- Draw the following graphic organizer on the board.

0% -------------------------------- 100%
never hardly some- often usually always
       ever   times

- Say: *Use these words to talk about how often things happen. Never means that something doesn't happen. Each word moving to the right on the chart means that something happens more times. Always means* all the time *or* every time.
- Explain that adverbs of frequency go before the verb, except in sentences with a form of *be*, adverbs of frequency go *after* the verb. Write on the board examples, such as: *She always stays late at work. She is never home at 8:00.*
- Have students study the chart and the Look Box.
- Read the sentences in the chart and have students repeat chorally.

A Teaching Time: 5–10 min.

- Have students complete the task.
- GROUPS. Have students compare their answers.
- Ask volunteers to tell about similarities or differences in shopping among students' different countries.

B Teaching Time: 10–15 min.

- Read the example with the class.
- Have students complete the task.
- Call on students to say the sentences. Correct as needed.

Multilevel Strategy

- **Pre-level:** Help students form the sentences. Remind them that the adverb goes after the subject and before the verb. After students have completed the task, walk around and have them read the true sentences to you.
- **At-level:** After students have completed the task, have them change the untrue sentences into true sentences (e.g., *I never buy food at a convenience store. I always buy food at a convenience store.*). Call on students to read their sentences to the class.
- **Above-level:** After students have completed the task, have them write three additional sentences about their shopping habits using frequency adverbs. Call on students to read their sentences to the class.

Grammar to Communicate 1

FREQUENCY ADVERBS WITH THE SIMPLE PRESENT

Subject	Adverb	Verb		Subject	Be	Adverb	
I				I	am		
We	always	use	cash.	We	are	always	at the mall.
You				You			
They				They			
He	often	uses	cash.	He	is		
She				She			
It	never	costs	a lot.				

Look
100% always
90% usually
70% often
50% sometimes
10% hardly ever
0% never

A Complete the sentences about shopping in your country. Use *always, usually, often, sometimes, hardly ever,* or *never.* Answers will vary.

1. People _____ buy things from a catalog.
2. People _____ buy fruit at outdoor markets.
3. People _____ go shopping at malls.
4. People _____ buy bread at a supermarket.
5. People _____ go shopping on Sundays.
6. Stores _____ have sales.
7. Stores _____ close in the afternoon.
8. Stores _____ close for two weeks in the summer.

catalog

GROUPS. Compare your answers with students from other countries.

B Make sentences. Put the words in the correct order. Then check (✓) the sentences that are true about you.

❑ 1. I never buy food at a convenience store.
    (I / at a convenience store / buy / never / food)
❑ 2. I hardly ever buy clothes from a catalog.
    (buy / from a catalog / clothes / I / hardly ever)
❑ 3. My family and I often shop at department stores.
    (at department stores / shop / my family and I / often)
❑ 4. I usually buy things on sale.
    (on sale / I / things / usually / buy)
❑ 5. My classmate sometimes pays for my lunch.
    (sometimes / pays for / my classmate / my lunch)
❑ 6. I always ask for a receipt.
    (ask for / a / I / always / receipt)

Unit 10

Grammar Notes

1. Adverbs of frequency tell how often something happens.
2. Adverbs never change forms.
3. In sentences with the simple present, adverbs of frequency go before the verb. In sentences with a form of *be,* adverbs of frequency go after the verb.
4. The adverb *sometimes* can also go at the beginning or end of a sentence.
5. For more information on this grammar topic, see page 256.

C 🎵 24 Linda Kelly talks about her job in a department store. Listen and complete the sentences. Use the adverbs from the box. Then listen again and check your answers. Some words may be used two times.

Look
Frequency adverbs come after the verb *be*.
    Chin **is often** at the mall.
Frequency adverbs come before all other verbs.
    Chin **often goes** to the mall.

| always | often | never | sometimes | usually |

1. I ___am always___ friendly.
   (am)
2. The store ___sometimes has___ sales.
   (has)
3. I ___am never___ late for work.
   (am)
4. The store ___always opens___ at 9:00.
   (opens)
5. The customers ___are usually___ nice.
   (are)
6. I love my job. It ___is never___ boring.
   (is)
7. The customers ___often ask___ me questions.
   (ask)

TIME to TALK

ON YOUR OWN. Where do you buy the things in the chart? Write the names of the stores. *Answers will vary.*

CLOTHES	SHOES	ELECTRONICS	FRUIT AND VEGETABLES	MEAT	TOILETRIES
	Pay Little				

GROUPS. Tell your classmates about where you shop, and talk about how often you shop at the places in your classmates' charts. Use frequency adverbs.

Example:
A: *I usually buy shoes at Pay Little.*
B: *Really? I hardly ever shop at Pay Little.*

Shopping 117

C Teaching Time: 5–10 min.
- Have students study the Look Box. Remind students to put the frequency adverbs after the verb *be* and before other verbs.
- Read the example with the class.
- 🎧 Play Track 24 while students listen and complete the task.
- 🎧 Play Track 24 again while students check their answers. Pause the recording each time an answer is given.

Option
Assign Unit 10 Supplementary Grammar to Communicate 1 Exercises on the Teacher's Resource Disk as homework or on the Student Persistence CD-ROM as self-access practice.

TIME to TALK

Teaching Time: 10–15 min.
- Have two students read the example.
- Have students complete their charts.
- GROUPS. Have students complete the task.
- Walk around and help as needed.
- Encourage students to say why each store is their favorite.

Unit 10 T-117

Grammar to Communicate 2

Simple Present: Yes / No Questions and Short Answers

Teaching Time: 5–10 min.

- Have students study the chart and the Look Box.
- Write on the board: *do / does + subject + verb*. Tell students that this is the way to make questions in simple present. Say: *Use* do *for questions with* I, you, we, *or* they. *Use* does *for questions with* he, she, *or* it. Write a few examples, such as: *You buy things on sale. Do you buy things on sale?*
- Say: *Answer the questions with short answers. For example:* Yes, I do. No, she doesn't.
- Read the sentences in the chart and the Look Box. Have students repeat chorally.
- Ask students questions in simple present and have them answer with *Yes, I do* or *No, I don't*.

A   Teaching Time: 10–15 min.

- Have students study the chart.
- Read the examples with the class.
- Have students complete the task.
- Call on students to say answers. Correct as needed.

Multilevel Strategy

- **Pre-level:** Help students identify the subject of each sentence. Knowing the subject will help them write the correct form of *do*.
- **At-level:** Have students take turns asking and answering the questions after they have completed the task.
- **Above-level:** Have students work in pairs and create three new questions using the information in the box. Have students take turns asking and answering the questions.

Grammar to Communicate 2

SIMPLE PRESENT: YES / NO QUESTIONS AND SHORT ANSWERS

Do/Does	Subject	Verb	Affirmative			Negative		
Do	I / we / you / they	have	food?	Yes,	I / we / you / they	do.	No,	I / we / you / they	don't.
Does	he / she / it				he / she / it	does.		he / she / it	doesn't.

A Read the chart. Complete the questions with *do* or *does*. Then answer the questions.

Look
Statements: → Questions:
They need a car. → Do they need a car?
He needs a car. → Does he need a car?

	has:	needs:	wants:
ERIC	cell phone / computer / camera	new TV / sunglasses / new sneakers	new watch / bike / new computer games
SUSANNA	has: new car / CD player / computer	needs: cell phone / new shoes / alarm clock	wants: DVD player / camera / new CDs
SHEILA AND TONY	have: stereo / TV / old car	need: computer / radio / new phone	want: new car / DVD player / DVDs

1. __Does__ Eric have a cell phone? — Yes, he does.
2. Eric, __do__ you need a new camera? — No, I don't.
3. __Do__ Sheila and Tony want a TV? — No, they don't.
4. __Does__ Susana need a cell phone? — Yes, she does.
5. Susana, __do__ you have a new car? — Yes, I do.
6. Tony, __do__ you and Sheila have a stereo? — Yes, we do.
7. __Does__ Eric want a computer? — No, he doesn't.
8. __Do__ Sheila and Tony want a DVD player? — Yes, they do.
9. __Does__ Susana have a CD player? — Yes, she does.
10. __Does__ Eric need a camera? — No, he doesn't.

118 Unit 10

Grammar Notes

1. To make questions in the simple present, use *do / does* + subject + base form of the verb.
2. To answer with short answers, use *I, you, we, they* + *do / do not*. Use *he / she / it* + *does / doesn't*.
3. Use full forms for affirmative short answers. Use full forms or contractions for negative short answers. *Do not* = *don't*. *Does not* = *doesn't*.
4. For more information on this grammar topic, see page 256.

Watch Out!

- **Exercise A.** It is common for students to mistakenly use *–s* at the end of verbs

T-118   Center Stage 2

B Complete the questions about the pictures. Then answer the questions.

1. <u>Does Trudy need</u> a new coat?   Yes, she does.
    (Trudy / need)
2. <u>Do the sisters have on</u> the same clothes?   Yes, they do.
    (the sisters / have on)
3. <u>Does Jeff have</u> a lot of ties?   Yes, he does.
    (Jeff / have)
4. <u>Do the children want</u> the jackets?   Yes, they do.
    (the children / want)
5. <u>Does the bathing suit cost</u> a lot?   Yes, it does.
    (the bathing suit / cost)
6. <u>Does the woman like</u> her husband's new suit?   No, she doesn't.
    (the woman / like)

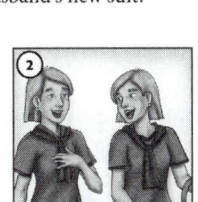

C Write a new question about each picture in Exercise B. Use the words in the box. Write your questions on a piece of paper. *Answers will vary.*

have the same hairstyle	need new jackets	spend a lot on clothes
like cheap clothes	need a new tie	want a new bathing suit

TIME to TALK

ON YOUR OWN. What do you have, need, or want? Make a list of five things. *Answers will vary.*

GROUPS. Now ask your classmates questions. Do they have, need, or want the same things?

Example:
A: I want a new car. Do you want a new car?
B: Yes, I do. I have a car, but it's eight years old.

HAVE	NEED	WANT
		new car

Shopping 119

B Teaching Time: 5–10 min.
- Read the example with the class.
- Have students complete the task.
- Call on students to write questions and answers on the board. Write corrections on the board as needed.
- PAIRS. Have students take turns reading questions and answers.

C Teaching Time: 5–10 min.
- Have students write questions.
- Walk around and help as needed.
- Call on students to say questions and answers. Correct as needed.
- PAIRS. Have students ask and answer each other's questions.

Multilevel Strategy
- **Pre-level, At-level:** Pair pre-level students with at-level students. Have at-level students form the questions and pre-level students form the answers.

Expansion
- Start a discussion on returning and exchanging items. Prompt students with questions such as: *Do you sometimes decide that you don't want something after you buy it? What do you do?*
- **LIFE SKILLS TEST PREP 2** Go to Unit 6, Lesson 5 for more practice in giving reasons for returning or exchanging an item.

---

with third person singular subjects in questions. Listen for and correct errors such as *Does he wants a new car?*

- Students might make a mistake of using *do* and *does* with *be*. Listen for and correct errors such as: *Do you are . . .* and *Do you be . . . ?*

Option
Assign Unit 10 Supplementary Grammar to Communicate 2 Exercises on the Teacher's Resource Disk as homework or on the Student Persistence CD-ROM as self-access practice.

TIME to TALK
Teaching Time: 10–15 min.
- Have two students read the example.
- Have students complete the first part of the task. Each student writes a total of five items.
- Walk around and help as needed.
- GROUPS. Have students ask and answer questions about things they have, need, and want.
- Call on volunteers to say things that people in their group have, need, and want.

Unit 10

Grammar to Communicate 3

Simple Present: Information Questions

Teaching Time: 5–10 min.

- Have students study the chart.
- Say: *To ask information questions in the simple present, use a question word before do / does.* Write a few examples on the board, such as: *What do they want?*
- Have students study the Look Box.
- Add *what kind of* to the question words on the board. Say: *Use what kind of and a noun to ask about specific types of things.* Write a few examples on the board, such as: *What kind of car do you drive? I drive a Toyota.*
- Read the sentences in the chart and have students repeat chorally.
- Ask one student an information question. The student answers and then asks another student a question. Continue until all students have answered and asked questions.

A Teaching Time: 5–10 min.

- Point out that the directory lists the names of the stores in the mall, gives their store hours, and shows their locations. Have students study the directory.
- Read the example with the class.
- Have students complete the task.
- Call on students to say answers. Correct as needed.

B Teaching Time: 10–15 min.

- Read the example with the class.
- Have students complete the task.
- Call on students to write questions on the board. Write corrections on the board as needed.

Multilevel Strategy

- **At-level, Above-level:** When checking answers, call on students to answer the questions. Correct as needed.

Grammar to Communicate 3

SIMPLE PRESENT: INFORMATION QUESTIONS

Wh- word	Do / Does	Subject	Verb	Answers
What	do	I / you / we / they	need?	A cell phone.
How often	does	he	go?	Every day.
What time	does	it	start?	8:00 P.M.

Look
We also use *What kind of* + noun
What kind of car do you want?

A Read the mall directory. Match the questions with the answers.

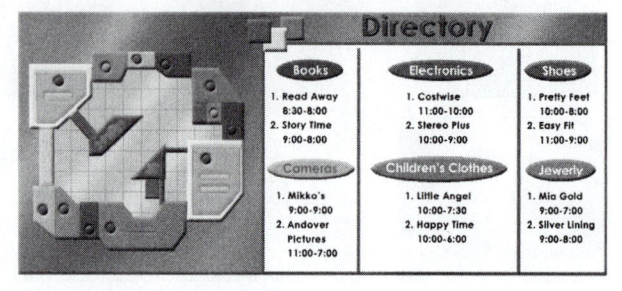

Directory

Books
1. Read Away 8:30-8:00
2. Story Time 9:00-8:00

Electronics
1. Costwise 11:00-10:00
2. Stereo Plus 10:00-9:00

Shoes
1. Pretty Feet 10:00-8:00
2. Easy Fit 11:00-9:00

Cameras
1. Mikko's 9:00-9:00
2. Andover Pictures 11:00-7:00

Children's Clothes
1. Little Angel 10:00-7:30
2. Happy Time 10:00-6:00

Jewelry
1. Mia Gold 9:00-7:00
2. Silver Lining 9:00-8:00

_f_ 1. What does Little Angel sell?   a. 8:00.
_e_ 2. What do people buy at Andover Pictures?   b. 8:30.
_b_ 3. What time does Read Away open?   c. jewelry.
_a_ 4. What time do the bookstores close?   d. electronics.
_d_ 5. What do Stereo Plus and Costwise sell?   e. cameras.
_c_ 6. What does Silver Lining sell?   f. children's clothes.

B Make more questions about the stores in Exercise A.

1. What time do the children's clothes stores open?
   (What time / the children's clothes stores / open)
2. What does Mikkos sell?
   (What / Mikko's / sell)
3. What time do the jewelry stores open?
   (What time / the jewelry stores / open)
4. What do people buy at Story Time?
   (What / people / buy / at Story Time)
5. What time do Pretty Feet and Easy Fit close?
   (What time / Pretty Feet / Easy Fit / close)

Unit 10

Grammar Notes

1. For information questions in the simple present, the question word goes before *do / does.*
2. The phrase *How often* asks about frequency.
3. The phrase *What kind of* asks for a specific type of something.
4. For more information on this grammar topic, see page 256.

C Read the conversations. Write questions. Use *What, What kind, How much,* and *How often* and the verbs in the box. Then listen and check your answers.

~~cost~~	go	have	like	sell

1. **A:** I like the T-shirt in the catalog.
   B: _How much does it cost?_
   A: It's $15.66 including tax.

2. **A:** You have a big car, right?
   B: No, I don't.
   A: _What kind of car do you have?_
   B: I have a very small car.

3. **A:** Julie doesn't like gold earrings.
   B: _What kind of earrings does she like?_
   A: Silver.

4. **A:** Makis and Lit Brothers are good stores.
   B: _What do they sell?_
   A: Clothes, jewelry, umbrellas, handbags—a lot of different things.

5. **A:** My daughter goes to the mall a lot.
   B: _How often does she go?_
   A: Every weekend.

Pia's
1 T-shirt	$15.00
sales tax	.66
	$15.66

TIME to TALK

GROUPS. One student says what he or she wants or needs. The other students ask as many questions as possible. Continue until everyone asks and answers questions. *Answers will vary.*

Example:
A: *I need a new TV.*
B: *What kind of TV do you want?*
A: *I want a 30-inch flat-screen.*
C: *How much do they cost?*
A: *They're on sale for $399 at Great Buy.*

Shopping 121

C Teaching Time: 5–10 min.
- Read the example with the class.
- Have students complete the task.
- 🎧 Play Track 25 while students check their answers. Pause the recording each time an answer is given.
- PAIRS. Have students take turns asking and answering the questions.

Multilevel Strategy

Pre-level: Provide students with the appropriate *wh*-word for each item: (2) *What kind*; (3) *What kind*; (4) *What*; (5) *How often*

Option

Assign Unit 10 Supplementary Grammar to Communicate 3 Exercises on the Teacher's Resource Disk as homework or on the Student Persistence CD-ROM as self-access practice.

TIME to TALK

Teaching Time: 15–20 min.
- Have three students read the example.
- Give students a minute to decide what item to talk about.
- GROUPS. Have students complete the task.
- Walk around and help as needed.
- Ask volunteers to tell the class about something that someone in their group wants or needs.

Multilevel Strategy

- **Pre-level:** Prompt students with questions if necessary (e.g., *What do you need? Do you need a new TV?*).
- **Above-level:** Have students disagree with one another (e.g., *I don't think you need a new TV because . . .*).

Unit 10

Review and Challenge

Grammar

Teaching Time: 5–10 min.

- Read the example with the class.
- Have students complete the task.
- Call on students to write the corrected sentences on the board. Write corrections on the board as needed.

> **Multilevel Strategy**
>
> - **Pre-level:** Tell students what the mistakes are and have them rewrite the sentences.

Dictation

Teaching Time: 5–10 min.

- 🎧 Play Track 26 while students listen and write what they hear.
- 🎧 Play Track 26 again while students check their answers.
- Call on students to write answers on the board.
- 🎧 Play Track 26 again and correct the sentences on the board.

> **Multilevel Strategy**
>
> - **Pre-level:** Give students a worksheet with some of the words from the dictation already provided.

Speaking

Teaching Time: 10–15 min.

- Have students read each situation.
- Have two students read the example.
- PAIRS. Have students complete the task.
- Walk around and help as needed.
- Have pairs take turns performing their conversations for the class.
- **LIFE SKILLS TEST PREP 2** Go to Unit 6, Lesson 4 for more practice in making simple requests about availability of items in a store.

Review and Challenge

Grammar

Find the mistake in each sentence. Circle the letter and correct the mistake.

1. <u>Those</u> stores <u>usually are</u> <u>busy</u>.
      A   Ⓑ   B
   Correct: _Those stores are usually busy._

2. <u>You like</u> <u>these</u> <u>black</u> shoes?
      Ⓐ   B   C
   Correct: _Do you like these black shoes?_

3. How much <u>does</u> the <u>big TV</u> <u>costs</u>?
              A   B   Ⓒ
   Correct: _How much does the big TV cost?_

4. <u>What kind</u> of cell phone <u>John</u> <u>want</u>?
      A   Ⓑ   C
   Correct: _What kind of cell phone does John want?_

5. <u>Do you have</u> <u>always</u> a lot of <u>money</u>?
      A   Ⓑ   C
   Correct: _Do you always have a lot of money?_

Dictation

🎧 **26** Listen. You will hear five sentences. Write them on a piece of paper. _See the audioscript on page 284 for the sentences._

Speaking

PAIRS. Choose one of the situations and write a conversation. _Answers will vary._

> **Situation 1**
> **Customer:** It's your friend's birthday. You want to buy your friend a gift. Ask questions about things in a store.
> **Salesman:** You want to help the customer. Answer questions about things in the store. Ask the customer questions about what his or her friend wants and needs.

> **Situation 2**
> **Parent:** Your son needs a computer for school. You don't know anything about computers.
> **Friend:** You know a lot about computers. Help your friend.

Example: (Situation 1)
A: How much is that jacket?
B: It's $32.40 with tax. What color does your friend like? Does he like green?

Now perform the conversation for the class.

T-122   Center Stage 2

Listening

A 🎧 **27** Listen. Where are the people? Match the conversations with the places.

_c_ Conversation 1
_d_ Conversation 2
_a_ Conversation 3
_b_ Conversation 4

B 🎧 **28** Listen again. Write the questions you hear in each conversation.

Conversation 1: How much _does the flat screen TV cost?_
Conversation 2: What _do you want for your birthday_ ?
Conversation 3: What kind _of bag do you want_ ?
Conversation 4: Where _are the tomatoes_ ?

TIME to TALK

GROUPS. Where do you shop? How often do you shop? What do you buy? How much do things cost? Ask and answer questions. Use the places in the box.
Answers will vary.

buy things from a home shopping network	shop at a convenience store
go to the mall	shop at an outdoor market
order things from a catalog	shop online

Example:
A: How often do you go to the mall?
B: I usually go to the mall every Saturday.
A: What do you buy there?
B: Sometimes I buy clothes or CDs. I often look and don't buy anything. How about you? Do you go to the mall a lot?

Shopping 123

Listening

A Teaching Time: 5–10 min.

- **Warm-Up:** Ask students to look at the pictures and identify the place in each one. Point to individuals in the photos and ask: *What do you think this person is saying?* Encourage students to offer various answers.
- 🎧 Play Track 27 while students listen.
- 🎧 Play Track 27 again while students listen and choose the correct answers.
- Call on students to say answers. Correct as needed.

B Teaching Time: 5–10 min.

- Read the example with the class.
- Ask students to read through the question beginnings before they listen.
- 🎧 Play Track 28 while students listen and complete the task.
- 🎧 Play Track 28 again while students check their questions. Call on students to read the questions. Correct as needed.

Multilevel Strategy

- **At-level, Above-level:** When checking the completed questions, call on students to say answers. Correct as needed.

Option

Assign Unit 10 Supplementary Review and Challenge Exercises on the Teacher's Resource Disk as homework or on the Student Persistence CD-ROM as self-access practice.

TIME to TALK

Teaching Time: 10–15 min.

- Have two students read the example conversation.
- Have students read through the phrases in the box.
- GROUPS. Have students complete the task.
- Walk around and help as needed.
- Ask volunteers to tell the class a sentence about the shopping habits of someone in their group.

Unit 10   T-123

Reading and Writing

Reading

A Teaching Time: 10–15 min.

- Remind students that a newsletter is a short report of news or information for people with certain interests. Have students look at the picture on the newsletter. Ask: *What is the newsletter about? What is a yard sale?*
- Ask students to read through the answer choices before they read the newsletter.
- Have students read the newsletter silently. Then read it aloud. Pause after each few words and have students repeat chorally.
- Have students complete the task.
- Call on students to say the answer. Correct as needed.

B Teaching Time: 5–10 min.

- Read the example with the class.
- Have students complete the task.
- Call on students to write answers on the board. Write corrections on the board as needed.
- PAIRS. Have students take turns reading questions and answers.

Reading and Writing

Reading

A Read the newsletter. Where are yard sales? Check (✓) the correct answer.

☐ in shopping malls ☑ in front of people's houses ☐ in stores

New to the U.S.
A NEWSLETTER FOR NEWCOMERS

Do you have anything in your home that you don't need or want? For example, do you have an old television, or clothes that you don't wear anymore? Do you want some extra money? Have a yard sale!

What is a yard sale? At these sales, people sell their old things. On warm weekend mornings, the sellers put the things for sale on tables in front of their house or apartment. Then they wait for their customers. Where do the customers come from? On weekends, people often drive around and look for yard sales. Yard sales usually start at 8:00 or 9:00 A.M.

What kinds of things do people sell at yard sales? They sell everything! They sell furniture, electronics, clothes, children's toys, CDs, and jewelry. People like yard sales because the prices are usually great—and there's no sales tax! Buyers and sellers talk about the price. If the buyer likes the price, he usually pays the seller in cash. Sellers sometimes take a check, but they never take a credit card.

B Read the newsletter again. Answer the questions. Write complete sentences.

1. What kinds of things do people buy at yard sales?
   They buy electronics, clothes, furniture, children's toys, CDs, and jewelry.
2. Do things at yard sales usually cost a lot of money?
   No, they don't.
3. When do people usually have yard sales?
   People usually have yard sales on weekends.
4. What time do yard sales usually start?
   They usually start at 8:00 or 9:00 A.M.
5. How do buyers pay for the things they want?
   They usually pay for things in cash.

Unit 10

Language Note

- **Exercise A.** Explain that a yard is the area around a house. It's usually covered with grass.
- Tell students that yard sales and tag sales are also often called garage sales when they happen in or near a person's garage.

Option

- Have students reread the last two sentences of the reading.
- Start a discussion on checking accounts. If necessary, explain that when you have a checking account, you put money in the bank and then write checks to pay for things. Ask students why some people use checks instead of cash.

T-124 Center Stage 2

Prewriting

Read the paragraph about outdoor markets.

> In my country, outdoor markets are a popular way of shopping. The market near my home is open every Thursday from 7:00 in the morning until noon. I buy a lot of fruit and vegetables there, but people also buy clothes, shoes, CDs, and many other things there. I like outdoor markets because they always have fresh fruit and vegetables.

Writing

Write a paragraph about shopping in your country. Use the paragraph above as a model.
Answers will vary.

Writing Tip

Use *because* to give a reason for something. *Because* connects the fact and the reason in one sentence.

Example: Outdoor markets are popular **because** they always have fresh fruit and vegetables.
(fact) (reason)

New to _____
A NEWSLETTER FOR NEWCOMERS

Shopping 125

(Possible answers: *Checks are safer in the mail. There is a record of payment.*)

- Start a discussion on ATMs. If necessary, explain that an ATM is a machine outside a bank where you can get money from your account. Ask students where they can use the ATM card and where the money comes from when they use the ATM card.
- **LIFE SKILLS TEST PREP 2** Go to Unit 6, Lesson 1 for more practice in using ATMs and to Unit 6, Lesson 3 for more practice in reading and filling out a check.

Multilevel Strategy

- **Pre-level:** While students are completing their graphic organizers, copy the paragraph from Prewriting on the board. Underline the information that students should substitute in their paragraphs. Have students copy the paragraph and substitute the underlined parts with information they recorded in their graphic organizers.

Prewriting

Teaching Time: 5–10 min.

- Have students read the paragraph.
- Read the paragraph out loud. Pause after each few words and have students repeat chorally.
- Check students' comprehension by asking a few questions, such as: *How long is the outdoor market open? What can you buy there?*

Writing

Teaching Time: 20–25 min.

- Ask students to name some other places to buy things, such as a mall, on the Internet, etc. Record students' answers on the board.
- Draw the following graphic organizer on the board.

  Outdoor markets — Open from 7:00–noon; Sell fruit and vegetables

- Ask students to list some facts about outdoor markets in the paragraph. As students say facts, add them to the graphic organizer.
- Tell students to choose one place from the list on the board.
- Have students make their own graphic organizers with facts about the place they chose.
- Tell students to use the ideas in their graphic organizers to write a paragraph about shopping in their country.
- Have students study the Writing Tip.
- Have students reread the last sentence of the paragraph. Tell them that the paragraph finishes with the person's opinion of the topic and a reason for the opinion.
- Write on the board: *I like ___ [type of store or shopping area] because ___ [reason].* Tell students to complete this sentence with their own words and to make it the last sentence of their paragraph.
- Have students complete the task.
- Walk around and help as needed.
- Call on volunteers to read their paragraphs. Correct as needed. You can also have students write their paragraphs on a separate piece of paper. Collect their work and provide individual feedback.

Unit 10 T-125

Unit 11
Holidays and Special Occasions

Learning Goals
- Learn words to describe holidays and special occasions
- Learn about direct and indirect objects; simple present: information questions; and *who* as subject and object
- Listen to a conversation and a report about special occasions
- Read and write a newsletter
- Talk about special occasions

Learner Persistence

Students are more likely to persist when they feel they are making progress in the class. Have students report on experiences they have using English outside of class. It will help them recognize their accomplishments.

Warm-up

Teaching Time: 5–10 min.

- Write on the board: *Occasions* and *Holidays*.
- Tell students that a holiday is a day when people celebrate something and many people don't have to work. An occasion is a time when something special happens, such as an event or a ceremony.
- Ask students to name some holidays and special occasions (occasions: anniversary, birthday, wedding; holidays: New Year's Day, Independence Day). Record students' responses on the board.

Vocabulary

Teaching Time: 10–15 min.

- Have students look at the pictures. Ask the students what occasion each picture shows.
- 🎧 Play Track 29 while students read and listen.
- Read the words and phrases aloud and have students repeat chorally.
- Have students complete the task.
- Call on students to say answers. Correct as needed.

Unit 11
Holidays and Special Occasions

Grammar
- Direct and Indirect Objects
- Simple present: Information Questions
- *Who* as Subject and Object

Vocabulary

🎧 **29** Read and listen. Then circle the things that people do on special occasions.

1. birthday
2. (have a party)
3. (make a cake)
4. (thank someone)
5. (invite someone to a party)
6. (get flowers)
7. (visit)
8. (give a gift)
9. groom
10. bride
11. relatives
12. wedding
13. (dance)
14. host
15. guest
16. hostess
17. (celebrate)
18. invitation

126 Unit 11

Expansion Have students look again at the ideas from the Warm-up. Ask students what people often do on those occasions and holidays. Prompt students with questions such as: *Do people usually dance at weddings?* Record students' responses on the board.

Language Note

Vocabulary. Tell students that the word *dance* can be a verb and a noun (an occasion). For example: *People dance at parties. There is a dance at school on Friday night.*

T-126 Center Stage 2

Listening

A 🎧 **30** Listen. Petra is talking about her birthday. Circle the things that Petra tells Julie.

1. (She misses her family.)
2. She usually has a small party.
3. (The party is at her house.)
4. (Her friends send cards.)
5. (She gets some gifts.)

B 🎧 **31** Read and listen again. Write the missing words. Use the words in the box.

| do you | ~~How do you~~ | makes | me cards |

Petra: Oh, this weekend is my first birthday alone—my family and friends aren't here. I really miss them.

Julie: Oh, that's hard. So... _How do you_ 1. usually celebrate your birthday?

Petra: Well, my friends send _me cards_ 2., and all of my relatives call me.

Julie: Do you have party?

Petra: Oh, yes. We always have a big party.

Julie: Who _do you_ 3. invite?

Petra: My friends, my parents' friends, my sisters' friends, and my relatives.

Julie: Wow. You need a big place for a party like that. Where do you usually have it?

Petra: Oh, we have a big house.

Julie: And who _makes_ 4. the food for all those people?

Holidays and Special Occasions 127

Listening

A Teaching Time: 10–15 min.

- **Warm-up:** Ask students about different ways to celebrate birthdays. Record students' answers on the board.
- Read the example with the class.
- Ask students to read through the sentences before they listen.
- 🎧 Play Track 30 while students listen.
- 🎧 Play Track 30 again while students listen and complete the task.
- PAIRS. Have students compare answers.
- Call on students to say answers. Correct as needed.

B Teaching Time: 15–20 min.

- Have students read through the answer choices before they listen.
- 🎧 Play Track 31 while students listen and write the words they hear.
- 🎧 Play Track 31 again while students check their answers.
- Call on students to say answers. Correct as needed.
- Read the conversation aloud. Pause after each few words and have students repeat chorally.
- PAIRS. Ask students to role-play the conversation.

Multilevel Strategy

- **Pre-level:** Have students role-play the completed conversation.
- **At-level:** Write the conversation on the board without the answers. Have students recall the answers as they role-play.
- **Above-level:** Have students create a new conversation about how they celebrate their birthday. Call on pairs to role-play in front of the class.

Option

Assign Unit 11 Supplementary Vocabulary Exercise on the Teacher's Resource Disk as homework or on the Student Persistence CD-ROM as self-access practice.

Expansion

- Tell students that it is common to ask a question such as *Do you want to . . . ?* to invite a person to do something. If the person wants to accept the invitation, he or she often says *Sure* or *OK*. If the person doesn't want to accept the invitation, he or she often says *I'm sorry* and gives a reason.
- PAIRS. Have students role-play making and responding to invitations.
- **LIFE SKILLS TEST PREP** 2 Go to Unit 4, Lesson 2 for more practice in making and responding to invitations.

Unit 11

Grammar to Communicate 1

Direct and Indirect Objects with and without Prepositions

Teaching Time: 5–10 min.

- Tell students that the object always follows the verb.
- Say: *A direct object answers the question who? or what?* Write on the board: *We visit our friends.* Ask: *visit who?* (our friends). *Our friends* is the direct object.
- Say: *An indirect object answers the question to whom? or for whom?* Write on the board: *She gives a present to Tanya.* Ask: *gives a present to whom?* (Tanya). *Tanya* is the indirect object.
- Say: *An indirect object can go after or before a direct object. If it goes after the direct object, it needs to take a preposition.* Write on the board: *I give flowers to my sister. I give my sister flowers.*
- Read the sentences in the chart and on the board and have students repeat chorally.

A Teaching Time: 3–5 min.

- Have students complete the task.
- PAIRS. Have students compare answers.
- Call on students to say answers. Correct as needed.

B Teaching Time: 5–10 min.

- Read the example with the class. Remind students that an indirect object does not need a preposition if it goes before a direct object.
- Have students complete the task.
- Call on students to say answers. Correct as needed.
- PAIRS. Have partners take turns asking and answering questions.

C Teaching Time: 5–10 min.

- Have students study the Look Box. Tell students that some verbs use *to* before an indirect object and some use *for*.
- Have students complete the task.
- Call on students to say answers. Correct as needed.

T-128 Center Stage 2

Grammar to Communicate 1

DIRECT AND INDIRECT OBJECTS WITH PREPOSITIONS

Subject	Verb	Direct Object	Preposition	Indirect Object
I	send	a gift / it	to	my friend. / her.

DIRECT AND INDIRECT OBJECTS WITHOUT PREPOSITIONS

Subject	Verb	Indirect Object	Direct Object
I	send	my friend / her	a gift.

A Underline the direct object. Circle the indirect object.

1. Do you give a <u>birthday present</u> to (your father)?
2. Do you send <u>birthday cards</u> to (your friends)?
3. Do you give <u>money</u> to (your parents)?
4. Do you make <u>birthday cakes</u> for (your friends)?
5. Do you get <u>gifts</u> for (your teachers)?
6. Do you buy <u>flowers</u> for (your mother)?

B Rewrite the questions from Exercise A. Write the indirect objects.

1. Do you give __your father__ a birthday present?
2. Do you send __your friends__ birthday cards?
3. Do you give __your parents__ money?
4. Do you make __your friends__ birthday cakes?
5. Do you get __your teachers__ gifts?
6. Do you buy __your mother__ flowers?

PAIRS. Ask and answer the questions above.

C Complete the sentences. Use *to* or *for*.

1. I send cards __to__ 100 people.
2. I buy presents __for__ my husband.
3. I make a special dinner __for__ my wife.
4. I get a present __for__ my mother.
5. I give money __to__ my nieces and nephews.

Look
I **send** a gift **to** her.
I **give** a gift **to** her.
I **buy** a gift **for** her.
I **get** a gift **for** her.

Unit 11

Grammar Notes

1. A direct object receives the action of a verb. It answers the question *who* or *what*. A direct object usually comes after a verb in a sentence.
2. An indirect object answers the question *to whom* or *for whom*. Sentences in English must have a direct object if they have an indirect object.
3. An indirect object can come after a verb and before a direct object. It can also go after a direct object and the preposition *to* or *for*.
4. Direct objects and indirect objects can be nouns or object pronouns.
5. For more information on this grammar topic, see page 257.

D Read the first sentence. Complete the second sentence. Put the words in the correct order.

1. Parents give their children birthday presents.

   Children often _give birthday presents to their parents._
   (their parents / birthday presents / give / to)

2. Men often send women flowers.

   Women don't usually _send them to men._
   (send / to / them / men)

3. Children hardly ever give money to their parents.

   Parents often _give money to their children._
   (give / to / their children / money)

4. Children often make cards for their parents.

   Parents don't usually _make them for their children._
   (them / their / make / for / children)

5. Mothers often make birthday cakes for their children.

   Children don't usually _make birthday cakes for their mothers._
   (birthday cakes / make / for / their mothers)

6. Parents often have birthday parties for their children.

   Children don't usually _have parties for their parents._
   (their parents / have / for / parties)

PAIRS. Which sentences above are true about your country? Talk with a partner.

TIME to TALK

PAIRS. Ask and answer five questions about gifts. Use the words in the box and your own ideas. *Answers will vary.*

boyfriend / girlfriend	father / mother	candy	computer games
brother / sister	friends	CDs	flowers
children / daughter / son	husband / wife	clothes	toys

Example:
A: Do you give your mother a gift on her birthday?
B: Yes, I do.
A: What do you give her?
B: I usually give her flowers.

Holidays and Special Occasions 129

D Teaching Time: 10–15 min.
- Read the example with the class.
- Have students complete the task.
- Call on students to say answers. Correct as needed.
- PAIRS. Have students check the sentences that are true about their country.
- Call on volunteers to tell the class traditions in their country.

Multilevel Strategy
- **Pre-level:** Help students form the correct word order for each sentence.
- **Above-level:** When students talk about traditions in their country, challenge them to correct the sentences that are not true (e.g., *Women often send flowers to men.*).

Expansion
- Have students underline the direct object and circle the indirect object in the sentences in Exercise D.
- Call on students to say answers. Correct as needed.

Language Note

Exercises A–D. Tell students that direct objects and indirect objects can be nouns or object pronouns (*me, you, him, her, us, them*).

Option

Assign Unit 11 Supplementary Grammar to Communicate 1 Exercises on the Teacher's Resource Disk as homework or on the Student Persistence CD-ROM as self-access practice.

TIME to TALK

Teaching Time: 15–20 min.
- Have two students read the example conversation.
- PAIRS. Have students complete the task.
- Walk around and help as needed.
- Have volunteers present their conversations to the class.

Multilevel Strategy
- **Pre-level:** Copy the example on the board. Tell students to use it as a model. Underline the information that students should substitute in their examples with the words from the box.
- **Above-level:** Challenge students with the task by having them use vocabulary not included in the box.

Unit 11

Grammar to Communicate 2

Simple Present: Information Questions

Teaching Time: 5–10 min.

- Review the meaning of each *wh*-word with the students.
- Write on the board: wh-*word* + do / does + *subject* + *verb*. Tell students that this is a way to make information questions. Write a few examples, such as: *Where do you work?*
- Have students study the chart. Read aloud each question and answer in the chart and have students repeat chorally.
- Pair students and have them take turns asking and answering information questions. Walk around and help as needed.

A Teaching Time: 5–10 min.

- Read the example with the class.
- Have students complete the first part of the task.
- Call on students to say answers. Correct as needed.
- Have students complete the second part of the task.
- Call on students to say questions. Correct as needed.
- **LIFE SKILLS TEST PREP 2** Go to Unit 1, Lesson 3 for more practice in asking questions with *when* and *where*.

B Teaching Time: 15–20 min.

- Tell students that each conversation starts with a sentence about Mother's Day. Then the students write a question about Father's Day.
- Have two students read the example conversation.
- Have students complete the task. Walk around and help as needed.
- 🎧 Play Track 32 while students check their answers.
- 🎧 Play Track 32 again. Pause the recording each time an answer is given.

Grammar to Communicate 2

SIMPLE PRESENT: INFORMATION QUESTIONS

Wh- word	Do / Does	Subject	Verb		Answers
How	do	you / we / they	celebrate	Thanksgiving?	We visit our relatives, and we eat special food.
When					On November 23rd.
Where	does	he / she			At his grandparents' home.
Why					She likes to see her family.

A Complete the questions. Use *do* or *does*.

1. When __do__ Americans celebrate Thanksgiving?
2. How __do__ Americans celebrate Thanksgiving?
3. Where __does__ Gina celebrate Thanksgiving?
4. Why __does__ Gina celebrate Thanksgiving in Seattle?

Read the answers. Write matching questions from above.

1. _When do Americans celebrate Thanksgiving?_ On the fourth Thursday in November.
2. _How do Americans celebrate Thanksgiving?_ Families have a special dinner.
3. _Where does Gina celebrate Thanksgiving?_ With her parents in Seattle.
4. _Why does Gina celebrate Thanksgiving in Seattle?_ Her parents live there.

B 🎧 **32** Read the conversations. Complete the questions about Father's Day. Then listen and check your answers.

1. **Ted:** We celebrate Mother's Day to show that we love our mothers.
   Lia: Why __do you celebrate Father's Day?__
   Ted: To show that we love our fathers, of course!

2. **Ted:** We celebrate Mother's Day on the second Sunday in May.
   Lia: When __do you celebrate Father's Day__?
   Ted: On the third Sunday in June.

3. **Ted:** We celebrate Mother's Day in different ways. Most people send cards.
   Lia: How __do you celebrate Father's Day__?
   Ted: We send cards on Father's Day, too.

4. **Ted:** Mothers often get flowers.
   Lia: What __do fathers get__?
   Ted: Fathers often get ties.

Unit 11

Grammar Notes

1. In information questions, a question word goes before *do / does,* then the subject and the base form of the verb.
2. For more information on this grammar topic, see page 257.

Culture Note

Exercise A. Tell students that Thanksgiving is a holiday in the United States and in Canada. On this day families often get together for a large meal to celebrate and be thankful for food, health, families, etc. Turkey is traditionally an important part of the meal. Thanksgiving is the fourth Thursday in November in the United States and the second Monday in October in Canada.

C Write questions about Chinese New Year. Use *when, where, how,* and *why*. Use *why* two times.

Chinese New Year   envelopes

1. __When does the celebration begin?__   It begins on New Year's Eve.
   (the celebration / begin)
2. __How do families celebrate New Year's Eve?__   They have a special dinner.
   (families / celebrate New Year's Eve)
3. __When do people go to bed?__   They don't. They stay up all night.
   (people / go to bed)
4. __Why do children like the New Year?__   Because they get gifts of money.
   (children / like the New Year)
5. __Where do adults put the money?__   They put it in little red envelopes.
   (adults / put the money)
6. __Why do adults use red envelopes?__   Because red is a lucky color in China.
   (adults / use red envelopes)

TIME to TALK

GROUPS. Talk about how you usually celebrate the New Year in your country. Ask and answer five questions. Use the words in the box and your own ideas. Answers will vary.

New Year's resolutions = a promise to yourself to do something next year

| dance | eat special food | make New Year's resolutions | stay up late |

Example:
A: How do you celebrate the New Year holiday in your country?
B: We have a big party, and we go to our relatives' homes.

Holidays and Special Occasions   131

C Teaching Time: 5–10 min.

- Point out or have students find China on a world map.
- Read the example with the class.
- Have students complete the task.
- Call on students to write questions on the board. Write corrections on the board as needed.
- PAIRS. Have partners take turns reading questions and answers.

Multilevel Strategy

- **Pre-level:** Provide students with the appropriate *wh*-word for each item: (2) *How*; (3) *When*; (4) *Why*; (5) *Where*; and (6) *Why*.

Culture Note

Exercise B. Explain that Mother's Day is celebrated on different days in many countries around the world. It is a holiday for people to honor and show appreciation for their mothers. Father's Day is a similar day for fathers.

Option

Assign Unit 11 Supplementary Grammar to Communicate 2 Exercises on the Teacher's Resource Disk as homework or on the Student Persistence CD-ROM as self-access practice.

TIME to TALK

Teaching Time: 10–15 min.

- Have students study the word box. Tell students that a New Year's resolution is a person's decision to start doing something good or to stop doing something bad on January 1.
- Have two students read the example conversation.
- GROUPS. Have one person in each group ask a question. Everyone else in the group answers. Then, another person asks a question, and everyone answers.
- Walk around and help as needed.
- Call on volunteers to say one way that people celebrate the New Year in one of their classmate's countries.

Unit 11   T-131

Grammar to Communicate 3

Who as Subject and Object

Teaching Time: 5–10 min.

- Write on the board: *We visit relatives.* Ask: *What is the subject in this sentence?* (we). *What is the object?* (relatives).
- Remind students that they know how to make questions about objects. Write: *Who do you visit? We visit relatives.*
- Say: *Don't use do / does when you ask questions about a subject.* Write on the board: *Who + verb + –s.* Add an example: *Who visits relatives? We do.*
- Say: *Use the subject and do / does to make short answers to questions about a subject.*
- Have students study the chart and the Look Box.
- Read the questions and answers in the chart and have students repeat chorally.
- Write a few sentences on the board and have students change them into questions with *who* as an object and subject. For example: *Andrea calls her brother. Who does Andrea call? Who calls her brother?*

A Teaching Time: 5–10 min.

- Read the example with the class.
- First have students underline the subject of each sentence.
- Call on students to say answers. Correct as needed.
- Have students complete the task.
- Call on students to say questions. Correct as needed.

B Teaching Time: 5–10 min.

- Read the example with the class. Tell students the questions in this exercise ask about an object, so they need to use *do / does*.
- Have students complete the task.
- Call on students to say answers. Correct as needed.

Grammar to Communicate 3

WHO AS SUBJECT

Subject	Verb	Object	Answers
Who	invites	the guests?	The hostess does.
Who	gives	gifts?	The guests do.

WHO AS OBJECT

Object	Do / Does	Subject	Verb	Answers
Who	does	the hostess	invite?	The guests.
Who	do	the guests	give gifts to?	To the bride.

A Underline the subjects. Then write questions with *Who*.

1. <u>Children</u> visit their neighbors.
   Who visits their neighbors?
2. <u>The neighbors</u> buy candy.
   Who buys candy?
3. <u>The children</u> wear costumes.
   Who wears costumes?
4. <u>The children</u> say "Trick or Treat!"
   Who says "Trick or Treat!"?
5. <u>The neighbors</u> give candy.
   Who gives candy?

Look

When *who* is the subject of a question, always use a singular verb.

Who visits their neighbors? The children.

B Complete the questions with the words in the box and *do* or *does*.

| give | go | have | make | ~~visit~~ |

1. Who _do_ the children _visit_ ?
2. Who _does_ your brother always _go_ to Halloween parties with?
3. Who _do_ the neighbors _give_ candy to?
4. Who _does_ his mother _make_ costumes for?
5. Who _do_ schools sometimes _have_ parties for?

Halloween costume

Unit 11

Grammar Notes

1. To ask *who* questions about an object use *who* before *do / does*, then the subject and the base form of the verb.
2. To ask *who* questions about a subject, use *who* and verb + –s.
3. *Who* questions can be answered with short answers. For *who* questions about an object, the short answer is just the person or people. For *who* questions about a subject, the short answer is the person or people + *do / does*.
4. For more information on this grammar topic, see page 257.

C Read the answers and write the questions. Put the words in the correct order.

1. _Who usually pays for the wedding?_ — The bride's parents do.
   (for the wedding / usually pays / Who)
2. _Who do they invite to the wedding?_ — Relatives and friends.
   (Who / they / invite / do / to the wedding)
3. _Who sees the bride before the wedding?_ — The bride's family and girlfriends do.
   (sees / the bride / before the wedding / Who)
4. _Who wears white clothes at the wedding?_ — The bride does.
   (white clothes / Who / at the wedding / wears)
5. _Who do the bride and groom sit with?_ — With their parents.
   (do / the bride and groom / Who / sit with)

PAIRS. Ask the questions above. Answer with information about weddings in your country. _Answers will vary._

Example:
A: *Who pays for the wedding?*
B: *The bride's parents usually pay.*

TIME to TALK

GROUPS. Ask and answer the questions. _Answers will vary._

Do you go to a lot of parties? Who invites you? How often do you go?	Do you send a lot of cards? Who do you send cards to? What kind of cards do you send?
Do you have a lot of parties? Who do you invite to the parties? When do you have them?	Do you get a lot of gifts? Who do you get gifts from? When do you get gifts?

Example:
A: *Do you go to a lot of parties?*
B: *Yes, I do.*
C: *Who invites you?*
B: *My friends.*
A: *How often do you go to parties?*
B: *Usually every Saturday.*

Holidays and Special Occasions 133

C Teaching Time: 10–15 min.
- Read the example with the class. Tell students to look at the answers to help them decide if the question is about a subject or an object.
- Have students complete the task.
- Call on students to say questions. Correct as needed.
- PAIRS. Have partners take turns asking and answering the questions.
- Walk around and help as needed.

Multilevel Strategy
- **Pre-level:** Tell students that questions 2–4 ask about a subject, and question 5 asks about an object. Help students form the questions if necessary.
- **At-level, Above-level:** After completing the pair activity, call on volunteers to say one thing about weddings in their partner's country.

Culture Note
Exercise B. Halloween is celebrated in the United States and Canada on October 31. On this day children wear costumes and go to their neighbors' houses to ask for candy. Children say "Trick or Treat" at each house, suggesting that they'll play a trick on the people living there if the people don't give them candy (a treat).

Option
Assign Unit 11 Supplementary Grammar to Communicate 3 Exercises on the Teacher's Resource Disk as homework or on the Student Persistence CD-ROM as self-access practice.

TIME to TALK
Teaching Time: 15–20 min.
- Have three students read the example conversation.
- GROUPS. Have students ask and answer questions about each topic.
- Walk around and help as needed.
- Call on students to present some facts they learned about their classmates.

Unit 11   T-133

Review and Challenge

Grammar

Teaching Time: 5–10 min.

- Read the example with the class.
- Have students complete the task.
- Call on students to say the corrected sentences. Correct as needed.

Multilevel Strategy

- **Pre-level:** Tell students what the mistakes are and have them rewrite the sentences.

Dictation

Teaching Time: 5–10 min.

- 🎧 Play Track 33 while students listen and write what they hear.
- 🎧 Play Track 33 again while students check their answers.
- Call on students to write answers on the board.
- 🎧 Play Track 33 again and correct the sentences on the board.

Multilevel Strategy

- **Pre-level:** Give students a worksheet with some of the words from the dictation already provided.

Speaking

Teaching Time: 10–15 min.

- Have two students read the example conversation.
- GROUPS. Have students complete the task.
- Walk around and help as needed.

Multilevel Strategy

- **Above-level:** Challenge students with the task by having them tell the class one similarity or difference in traditions in different countries.

T-134 Center Stage 2

Review and Challenge

Grammar

Find the mistake in each sentence. Write the letter in the blank and correct the mistake.

__B__ 1. How <u>you</u> <u>do</u> <u>celebrate</u> the holiday?   Correct: _How do you celebrate the holiday?_
           A   B   C

__C__ 2. When <u>do</u> <u>you</u> give <u>to your wife flowers</u>?   Correct: _When do you give flowers to your wife?_
              A   B   C

__B__ 3. Who <u>does</u> <u>buy</u> candy <u>for her</u>?   Correct: _Who buys candy for her?_
               A   B   C

__A__ 4. Who <u>do</u> <u>she</u> <u>send</u> cards <u>to</u>?   Correct: _Who does she send cards to?_
              A   B   C

__C__ 5. Why <u>does</u> she <u>likes</u> the holiday?   Correct: _Why does she like the holiday?_
               A   B

__B__ 6. I give <u>to</u> <u>her</u> a lot of gifts.   Correct: _I give her a lot of gifts._
             A   B   C

Dictation

🎧 **Track 33** Listen. You will hear five sentences. Write them on a piece of paper. *See the audioscript on page 285 for the sentences.*

Speaking

GROUPS. How do people in your country celebrate the occasions in the box? Ask and answer questions. *Answers will vary.*

| the birth of a baby |
| a high school graduation |
| a wedding |

Example:
A: How do you celebrate a wedding in India?
B: Well, the day before the wedding, the groom's mother and sisters go to the bride's house. They bring the bride gifts like jewelry and fruit...

134 Unit 11

Option

- Invite students to bring in pictures of a typical celebration or event from their country. They can bring in their own photos or pictures from magazines, books, or online.
- Have students describe some of the traditions of the celebration or event to the class.

Listening

wrap a gift

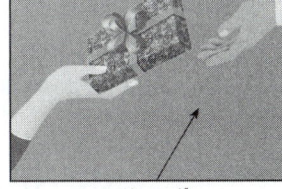

receive a gift

A 🎵 34 Listen. A reporter talks about gift giving in different parts of the world. Check (✓) the places she talks about.

- ☑ Asia
- ☑ China
- ☐ Europe
- ☐ Mexico
- ☐ North America
- ☑ Brazil
- ☑ Egypt
- ☑ Japan
- ☑ The Middle East
- ☑ South America

B 🎵 35 Read the sentences. Listen again to the report. Write the correct places from Exercise A. Then listen again and check your answers.

1. People give gifts with two hands. — _China and Japan_
2. People give gifts with their right hand. — _Egypt and the Middle East_
3. People don't wrap gifts in white paper. — _Asia_
4. People don't wrap gifts in purple paper. — _Brazil_
5. People don't give knives as gifts. — _South America and Asia_

TIME to TALK

GROUPS. Ask and answer the questions about gift giving in your country.
Answers will vary.
1. When do people in your country give gifts?
2. Who do they give gifts to?
3. What kinds of gifts do people give or never give?
4. What color paper do people in your country wrap gifts in?

Example:
A: When do people in your country give gifts?
B: They give gifts on birthdays and at Christmas.

Tell the class about gift giving in your group.

Holidays and Special Occasions 135

Listening

A Teaching Time: 5–10 min.

- **Warm-up:** Have students look at the pictures. Read the captions with the class. Ask students to guess what the listening is about. Then point out or have students find on a world map the countries and regions listed in the exercise.
- Ask students to read through the answer choices before they listen.
- 🎧 Play Track 34 while students listen.
- 🎧 Play Track 34 again while students listen and complete the task.
- Call on students to say answers. Correct as needed.

B Teaching Time: 5–10 min.

- Explain that a custom is a tradition.
- Read the example with the class.
- 🎧 Play Track 35 while students listen and complete the task.
- 🎧 Play Track 35 again while students check their answers. Pause the recording each time an answer is given.

Option

Assign Unit 11 Supplementary Review and Challenge Exercises on the Teacher's Resource Disk as homework or on the Student Persistence CD-ROM as self-access practice.

TIME to TALK

Teaching Time: 10–15 min.

- Have two students read the example.
- GROUPS. Have students take turns reading questions and having others answer.
- Walk around and help as needed.
- Have volunteers report back to the class some of the customs they discussed.

Unit 11   T-135

Reading and Writing

Reading

A   Teaching Time: 10–15 min.

- Remind students that a newsletter is a short report of information for people with certain interests. Ask: *Who is this newsletter for?* (people who are new to the United States). *What is the article about?* (Valentine's Day).
- Have students read the paragraph silently. Then read it aloud. Pause after each few words and have students repeat chorally. Explain any unfamiliar vocabulary.
- Have students answer the question.
- Call on students to say their answers.

B   Teaching Time: 10–15 min.

- Have students study the Look Box. Tell them to put the preposition at the end in questions with *who* as the object.
- Read the example with the class.
- Have students complete the task.
- Call on students to write questions on the board. Write corrections on the board as needed.
- PAIRS. Have students take turns reading questions and answers.

Expansion Start a discussion on Valentine's Day in different countries. Prompt students with questions such as: *Do people give gifts on Valentine's Day in your country? What kind of gifts do people give?*

Reading and Writing

Reading

A   Read the information about Valentine's Day. Do you have a similar holiday in your country? Write the name of the holiday. _Answers will vary._

New to the U.S.
A NEWSLETTER FOR NEWCOMERS
Volume XXXIII

Valentine's Day
In the United States, Valentine's Day is a popular holiday. Valentine's Day is always on February 14. On Valentine's Day people celebrate love and friendship. Husbands and boyfriends often give gifts to their wives or girlfriends. Sometimes women buy presents for men. People usually buy chocolate candy and flowers. Red roses are for true love. Pink roses are for new love. Yellow roses are for friendship. Many people give cards. Small children often buy or make them. Then they take them to school. They give them to their friends.

B   Read the answers to questions about the reading. Then write the questions.

1. _What do Americans celebrate on Valentine's Day?_
   They celebrate love and friendship.
2. _When do Americans celebrate Valentine's Day?_
   Americans celebrate Valentine's Day on February 14.
3. _Who buys presents?_
   Women sometimes buy presents for men.
4. _What are yellow roses for?_
   Yellow roses are for friendship.
5. _Who do children make cards for?_
   They make cards for their friends.

Look
When *who* is the object of a question, the preposition comes at the end.
Who do you buy cards **for**?
Who does she go to parties **with**?

Unit 11

T-136   Center Stage 2

Prewriting

Think of your favorite holiday in your country. Write answers to these questions about the holiday. Write on a piece of paper. Answers will vary.

- When is the holiday?
- How do people celebrate the holiday?
- Who do you celebrate the holiday with?
- Why is this your favorite holiday?

Writing

Write a paragraph about a holiday in your country. Use the paragraph on page 136 as a model. Answers will vary.

New to _____
A NEWSLETTER FOR NEWCOMERS
Volume XXXIII

Writing Tip

The adverbs *sometimes*, *often*, and *usually* can go in the middle or at the beginning of a sentence. When the adverb comes at the beginning of the sentence, a comma (,) follows it.

Example: **Sometimes,** women buy presents for men.

Women **sometimes** buy presents for men.

Holidays and Special Occasions 137

Prewriting
Teaching Time: 5–10 min.

- Have a volunteer read the questions.
- Have students write answers to the questions.
- Walk around and help as needed.

Writing
Teaching Time: 15–20 min.

- Have students use the information from the Prewriting exercise to write their paragraphs. Tell students to use the paragraph on page 136 as a model.
- Walk around and help as needed.
- Call on volunteers to read their paragraphs. Correct as needed. You can also have students write their paragraphs on a separate piece of paper. Collect their work and provide individual feedback.

Multilevel Strategy

- **Pre-level:** While students are completing the prewriting task, write the following on the board:

  My favorite holiday is ___ . This holiday is on ___ . In ___ people usually ___ . I always celebrate it with ___ . It is my favorite holiday because ___ .

  Have students copy the paragraph and fill in the blanks with information from Prewriting. Help students if necessary.

Language Note

Before students write their paragraphs, have them study the Writing Tip. Tell students that some of the frequency adverbs can go at the beginning of a sentence or before the verb.

Unit 11 T-137

Unit 12
At Work

Learning Goals

- Learn work vocabulary
- Learn about simple present and present progressive; stative verbs; and *like / need / want* + infinitive
- Listen to a conversation and a job interview
- Read a personal description and fill in a form
- Talk about work

Learner Persistence

Establish specific learning goals for the class and keep track of students' success in reaching them. Students will feel a sense of accomplishment when they know they have achieved an objective.

Warm-Up

Teaching Time: 3–5 min.

Have students look at the pictures. Point to each one and ask: *What's the place? How do you know? What are the people doing?*

Vocabulary

Teaching Time: 15–20 min.

- Have students look at the pictures. Explain unfamiliar vocabulary. For example, say: *A real estate agent helps people buy and sell their homes.*
- 🎧 Play Track 36 while students read and listen.
- Read the words and phrases aloud and have students repeat chorally.
- Have students complete the task.
- PAIRS. Have students compare answers.
- **LIFE SKILLS TEST PREP 2** Go to Unit 12, Lesson 1 for more practice in reading a simple paycheck stub. Go to Unit 12, Lesson 3 for more practice in reading and talking about a work schedule.

Expansion Have students make sentences about people, places, and activities they often see.

Unit 12
At Work

Grammar
- Simple Present and Present Progressive
- Stative Verbs
- Like / Need / Want + Infinitive

Vocabulary

🎧 **CD 2 TRACK 36 Read and listen.** Then circle the people, places, and activities that you often see.
Answers will vary.

1. be off
2. manager
3. have experience
4. interview
5. day-care center
6. day-care worker
7. take care of children
8. make an appointment
9. co-worker
10. real estate agent
11. make money
12. paycheck

138 Unit 12

Multilevel Strategy

- **Pre-level:** Have students work in groups to make sentences using the words they circled.
- **Above-level:** Have students also circle things they often do. Then have students make sentences about the places they often see and things they do. Challenge students with the task by having them add sentences using vocabulary not listed in the book.

Culture Note

Exercise B. Point out Mr. Yu's question *So, what's up?* Explain that *What's up?* means *What's happening?* or *What's going on?* Tell students that the question is informal and usually used in conversation with people you know well.

T-138 Center Stage 2

Listening

A 🎧 37 **Listen. Check (✓) the true statements.**

☐ 1. Doris is talking to her friend.
☑ 2. Liz usually works on Mondays.
☑ 3. Doris works on Tuesdays.
☐ 4. Doris works on Saturdays.

B 🎧 38 **Read and listen again. Write the missing words. Use the words in the box.**

| doing | ~~don't~~ | has | I'm working | to work | works |

Mr. Yu: Yes, Doris? Please, come in. So, what are you doing here today? You _don't_ (1) usually work on Mondays, do you?

Doris: No, _I'm working_ (2) for Liz today. She's visiting her mom in the hospital.

Mr. Yu: Oh, that's right. How is her mother _doing_ (3)?

Doris: She's doing very well.

Mr. Yu: Oh, that's good. So, what's up?

Doris: Well, my husband _has_ (4) a new job, and he _works_ (5) on Tuesdays now, too. And we don't have day care on Tuesdays.

Mr. Yu: So are you asking me for Tuesdays off?

Doris: Oh no, I need _to work_ (6) 40 hours a week. We need the money . . .

At Work 139

Option

Assign Unit 12 Supplementary Vocabulary Exercise on the Teacher's Resource Disk as homework or on the Student Persistence CD-ROM as self-access practice.

Listening

A Teaching Time: 10–15 min.

- **Warm-up:** Point to the schedule on page 138. Explain that an employee is a worker. Ask questions such as: *Which days does Kim / Shelly work? What time does Kim / Shelly start?*
- Ask students to read through the sentences before they listen.
- 🎧 Play Track 37 while students listen.
- 🎧 Play Track 37 again while students listen and complete the task.
- PAIRS. Have students compare answers.
- Call on students to say answers. Correct as needed.

B Teaching Time: 15–20 min.

- Ask students to read through the answer choices before they listen.
- 🎧 Play Track 38 while students listen and write the words they hear.
- 🎧 Play Track 38 again while students check their answers.
- Call on students to say answers. Correct as needed.
- Read the conversation aloud and have students repeat chorally.
- PAIRS. Ask students to role-play the conversation.

Multilevel Strategy

- **Pre-level:** Have students role-play the completed conversation.
- **At-level, Above-level:** Write the conversation on the board and erase some words. Have students recall the conversation as they role-play.

Unit 12 T-139

Grammar to Communicate 1

Simple Present and Present Progressive

Teaching Time: 10–15 min.

- Draw the following graphic organizer on the board.

Simple present	Present progressive
base form of verb; base form of verb + –s for *he*, *she*, or *it*	form of *be* + verb + –ing
Use it to talk about . . .	**Use it to talk about . . .**
routines	actions that are happening now
schedules	actions that are happening these days
general facts	

- Have students copy the graphic organizer into their notebooks.
- Call on students to say sentences for each example in the graphic organizer. For example: *I read a book everyday* (routine). *I'm working today* (actions that are happening these days).
- Have students study the charts.
- Read the sentences and questions in the charts and have students repeat chorally.
- Ask students questions in the simple present and the present progressive and have them answer with short answers.

A Teaching Time: 5–10 min.

- Read the example with the class.
- Have students study the Look Box. Tell them to use contractions in negative sentences.
- Have students complete the task.
- Call on students to say answers. Correct as needed.

Grammar to Communicate 1

SIMPLE PRESENT

Subject	Verb		Do / Does	Subject	Verb	
I / You / We / They	work	every day.	Do	I / you / we / they	work	every day?
He / She / It	works		Does	he / she / it		

PRESENT PROGRESSIVE

Subject	Be	Verb + -ing		Be	Subject	Verb + -ing	
I	am			Are	you		
You / We / They	are	working	now.	Am	I	working	now?
He / She / It	is			Are	we / they		
				Is	he / she / it		

A Complete the sentences. Use the correct form of the verbs.

1. The boy ___is getting___ a haircut.
      (get)
2. The barber ___is cutting___ the boy's hair.
      (cut)
3. The barber ___is working___.
      (work)
4. The boy ___is sitting___ in a chair.
      (sit)
5. The boy ___is wearing___ a blue smock.
      (wear)

Look
Contractions:
I don't work every day.
He doesn't work every day.
I'm not working today.
She's not working today.
We're not working today.

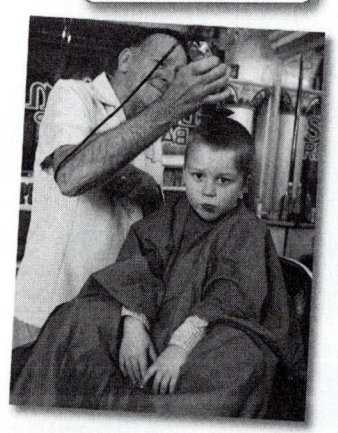

PAIRS. Look at the picture on pages 138-139. Talk about Jack and Teresa. What do they do every day? Where are they right now? What are they doing?
Answers will vary.

140 Unit 12

- PAIRS. Have students make sentences in the simple present and the present progressive about the pictures on pages 138 and 139.
- Walk around and help as needed.
- Call on volunteers to say one of their sentences.

Multilevel Strategy

- **Pre-level:** Have students write one sentence in the simple present and one in the present progressive.

Language Notes

1. Use the simple present to talk about routines, schedules, and general facts.
2. Use the base form of the verb for the simple present. With subjects *he, she,* and *it*, add *–s* to the base form of the verb.
3. To make *yes / no* questions in the simple present, use *do / does*, then the subject and the base form of the verb.
4. Use the present progressive to talk about actions that are happening now or these days.
5. Use a form of *be* + verb + –ing to form the present progressive.
6. To make *yes / no* questions in the present progressive, put a form of *be* before the subject.

T-140 Center Stage 2

B Look at the pictures on pages 138-139. Answer the questions. Use the simple present or the present progressive.

1. What does Jack do? — He's a real estate agent.
2. What does Jack do every day? — He sells houses.
3. What is Jack doing right now? — He's talking on the phone.
4. Where does Teresa work? — She works at a day-care center.
5. What is Teresa doing right now? — She's taking care of a child.
6. What is Kim doing? — She's interviewing a person.

Look
Use the simple present for routines.
Use the present progressive for actions happening now.

I **work** at a bank three time a week.
I'**m working** right now.

C 🎧 39 Complete the sentences. Use the simple present or the present progressive. Use contractions where possible. Then listen and check your answers.

Tim: Hi, Dana. This is Tim. What's up? What ___are you doing___?
1. (you /do)

Dana: I ___'m eating___ lunch.
2. (eat)

Tim: Really? But it's only 11:00. ___Do you have___ lunch this early every day?
3. (you/ have)

Dana: Yeah, usually. I ___start___ work early, at 7:00, so I'm always hungry
4. (start)
at this time. And my boss ___goes___ out around 11:00, so it's
5. (go)
always quiet. What ___are you doing___ right now?
6. (you/do)

Tim: I ___'m driving___. I ___'m going___ to a movie.
7. (drive)   8. (go)

Dana: A movie? But it's Monday! Why aren't you at work?

Tim: I ___have___ the first Monday of every month off.
9. (have)

TIME to TALK
PAIRS. Talk about four people you know. What do they do? Where do they live? What are they probably doing right now? *Answers will vary.*

What do they do? = What is their job?

Example:
A: My father lives in California. He's a real estate agent. He sells houses, but he's not selling houses now. This week he's on vacation. He's probably at the beach.

At Work 141

---

7. For more information on this grammar topic, see page 257.

Option

Assign Unit 12 Supplementary Grammar to Communicate 1 Exercises on the Teacher's Resource Disk as homework or on the Student Persistence CD-ROM as self-access practice.

B Teaching Time: 5–10 min.
- Have students study the Look Box. Explain that the first question and answer are in the simple present because they are about a routine (Jack's job) and not about what is happening now.
- Read the example with the class.
- Have students complete the task.
- Call on pairs of students to read aloud questions and answers. Correct as needed.

C Teaching Time: 5–10 min.
- Read the example with the class. Tell students to look for clues that will help them decide whether the simple present or the present progressive is the correct tense to use.
- Have students complete the task.
- 🎧 Play Track 39 while students check their answers. Pause the recording each time an answer is given.
- PAIRS. Have students role-play the completed conversation.

Expansion
- Bring into class several magazine pictures of people doing a variety of activities. Distribute a picture to each group.
- GROUPS. Have students work together to create a short story about what the people in the pictures are doing right now as well as some general information about the people or their routines. For example: *The woman is playing at the beach with her family. She's laughing. She usually works a lot.*

TIME to TALK
Teaching Time: 15–20 min.
- Read the example with the class.
- Have students choose four people they know and write their names on a piece of paper.
- PAIRS. Have students take turns telling each other about the people on their lists. Walk around and help as needed.

Multilevel Strategy
- **Pre-level, At-level:** During the pair activity, walk around and ask students questions about the people they wrote on their paper (*What does your brother do?*).
- **Above-level:** During the pair activity, walk around and ask students more investigative questions about the people they wrote on their paper (*Why is your father on vacation now?*).

Unit 12 T-141

Grammar to Communicate 2

Stative Verbs

Teaching Time: 5–10 min.

- Remind students that most verbs show action. Give a few examples of action verbs, such as *talk* and *jump*, and ask students to say a few others.
- Then say: *Some verbs don't show action. These verbs are called* stative verbs.
- Have students study the chart.
- Read the sentences and have students repeat chorally.
- Have students study the Look Box. Say: *With stative verbs, use the simple present to talk about actions that are happening now. Do not use the present progressive.* Write on the board examples, such as: *He's in class right now, and he knows the answer.*
- Call on students to say sentences using the stative verbs in the chart.

A Teaching Time: 3–5 min.

- Read the first sentence. Tell students *hear* is a stative verb.
- Read each sentence aloud. Have students call out the stative verbs. Correct as needed.

B Teaching Time: 5–10 min.

- Read the example with the class.
- Have students complete the task.
- PAIRS. Have students compare answers.
- Call on students to say answers. Correct as needed.

Grammar to Communicate 2

STATIVE VERBS

Subject	Verb	
I	hear	my boss.
She	knows	the answers.
He	wants	a new car.
It	needs	gas.
We	see	our friends.
They	understand	the schedule.
You	like	your job.

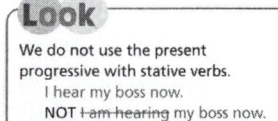

Look
We do not use the present progressive with stative verbs.
I hear my boss now.
NOT I am hearing my boss now.

Bob is a great worker!

I hear my boss. He's talking about me again.

A Circle the stative verb in each sentence.

1. I (hear) the manager. She's talking to my co-workers. She talks to them every Friday.
2. I (see) the mechanic. He's fixing my car. He fixes cars every day.
3. Mia's eating with a co-worker now. They often eat together. Mia (likes) her co-worker.
4. Jackie (wants) lunch. Her secretary is buying it for her. She often buys Jackie's lunch.
5. Jim is working today. He works seven days a week. He (needs) a day off.
6. They (know) their boss's wife. They are talking to her right now. They talk to her a lot.

B Circle the correct form of the verb for each sentence.

1. Take my car. I'm not needing / (I don't need) it right now.
2. Don't get me a sandwich. I'm having / (I have) a sandwich in my bag.
3. Please help me. (I don't understand) / I'm not understanding this.
4. Who are those people? (Do you know) / Are you knowing them?
5. Listen. (Do you hear) / Are you hearing that?
6. Don't buy any coffee for Emily. She's not liking / (She doesn't like) coffee.

Unit 12

Grammar Notes

1. Stative verbs do not show action. They are not used in the present progressive, even to describe actions that are occurring right now or these days.
2. For more information on this grammar topic, see page 257.

Center Stage 2

C Write sentences about yourself. Write negative statements where necessary.

1. <u>I have a good job. OR I don't have a good job.</u>
    (I / have / a good job)
2. <u>My teacher knows my family. OR My teacher doesn't know my family.</u>
    (My teacher / know / my family)
3. <u>My friend has a nice office. OR My friend doesn't have a nice office.</u>
    (My friend / have / a nice office)
4. <u>My family and I need a vacation. OR My family and I don't need a vacation.</u>
    (My family and I / need / a vacation)
5. <u>I need a cup of coffee right now. OR I don't need a cup of coffee right now.</u>
    (I / need / a cup of coffee / right now)

D Look at the picture. Then write sentences. Use the simple present or the present progressive.

1. <u>Ahmed drives a cab 8 hours every day.</u>
    (Ahmed / drive a cab / 8 hours every day)
2. <u>Ahmed isn't driving now.</u>
    (Ahmed / drive / now / not)
3. <u>He doesn't drive at night.</u>
    (He / not / at night / drive)
4. <u>He and his family are eating dinner.</u>
    (He and his family / eat dinner)
5. <u>He has two sons.</u>
    (He / have / two sons)
6. <u>Ahmed likes his job.</u>
    (Ahmed / like / his job)

TIME to TALK

PAIRS. Read the questions. Match the questions with the people in the box. Then ask and answer the questions. Then talk about other things that people ask or say.

1. Do you want paper or plastic?
2. What do you want on your sandwich? waiter
3. Where are you going? cab driver
4. Who knows the answer to number 3? teacher
5. Who's calling, please? receptionist
6. How often do you brush your teeth? dentist

| cab driver | cashier | dentist | receptionist | teacher | waiter |

Example:
A: "Do you want paper or plastic?" I think a cashier asks that.
B: Yes, in a supermarket. She also says, "Do you have a store card?"

At Work 143

Option

Assign Unit 12 Supplementary Grammar to Communicate 2 Exercises on the Teacher's Resource Disk as homework or on the Student Persistence CD-ROM as self-access practice.

C Teaching Time: 5–10 min.
- Have students look at the verbs in the exercise. Ask if they are action verbs or stative verbs.
- Have students complete the task. Walk around and help as needed.
- Call on students to read their sentences. Correct as needed.
- PAIRS. Have students take turns reading their sentences to each other.

D Teaching Time: 5–10 min.
- Read the example with the class.
- Remind students to use the simple present for general facts and stative verbs.
- Have students complete the task.
- Call on students to say answers. Correct as needed.

TIME to TALK

Teaching Time: 10–15 min.
- Have two students read the example.
- PAIRS. Have students complete the task.
- GROUPS. Have pairs of students compare their answers with another pair.

Multilevel Strategy
- **Pre-level:** Provide students with additional things people in each job say. Then assist students with the task.
- **Above-level:** Have students write additional things that people in each job ask or say. Have pairs make short conversations and role-play in front of the class.

Unit 12   T-143

Grammar to Communicate 3

Like / Need / Want + Infinitive

Teaching Time: 5–10 min.

- Have students study the chart and the Look Box.
- Ask students: *What are some things that you like? need? want?* Record students' answers on the board in complete sentences, for example: *Miguel likes video games.*
- Then ask: *What do you like to do? need to do? want to do?* Record students' answers on the board in complete sentences, for example: *Angela needs to go to the store.*
- Point to the first set of sentences and say: *We can use a noun after the words like, need,* and *want.* Point to the second set of sentences and say: *We can also use an infinitive.*
- Read the sentences aloud and have students repeat chorally.
- Pair students and have them take turns asking and answering questions with *like, need,* and *want.*

A Teaching Time: 5–10 min.

- Read the example with the class. Tell students that an infinitive has the word *to* before a verb.
- Have students complete the task.
- Call on students to say answers. Correct as needed.

B Teaching Time: 10–15 min.

- Read the example with the class.
- Have students complete the task.
- Call on volunteers to say answers. Correct as needed.
- PAIRS. Have students compare sentences.
- **LIFE SKILLS TEST PREP 2** Go to Unit 11, Lesson 4 for more practice in learning appropriate job interview behavior.

Grammar to Communicate 3

LIKE / NEED / WANT + INFINITIVE

Subject	Verb	Infinitive	
I	like	to work	hard.
You / We / They	need / want	to get	a job.
She	likes	to work	hard.
He	wants	to get	a good job.
It	needs	to be	

Look
We can use an infinitive or a noun after the verbs *like, need,* and *want.*

I want <u>to make</u> a lot of money.
       infinitive

I want a <u>vacation</u>.
      noun

A Check (✓) the sentences that have infinitives. Then underline the infinitives.

✓ 1. Do you want <u>to get</u> a new job? ☐ 6. You need an appointment.
☐ 2. Do you want a new job? ☐ 7. They want people with experience.
✓ 3. The manager wants <u>to meet</u> you. ✓ 8. Does the manager want <u>to see</u> me?
✓ 4. You need <u>to call</u> in the morning. ☐ 9. He likes his boss.
✓ 5. Do I need <u>to ask</u> questions? ✓ 10. Does he like <u>to interview</u> people?

B Leo has a job interview tomorrow morning. What does he need to do? Make sentences with the words in the box. Write the sentences in the correct columns.

ask questions about the job	find information about the job	go to bed early
be on time	get a haircut	talk about his experience
eat a good breakfast	get up early	wear nice clothes

THE DAY BEFORE THE INTERVIEW	THE MORNING OF THE INTERVIEW	AT THE INTERVIEW
He needs to get a haircut. He needs to find information about the job. He needs to go to bed early.	He needs to get up early. He needs to eat a good breakfast.	He needs to ask questions about the job. He needs to wear nice clothes. He needs to be on time. He needs to talk about his experience.

PAIRS. Compare sentences. Are your sentences in the same columns?

Unit 12

Multilevel Strategy

- **Pre-level:** Have students work in pairs or groups to complete the task. Help students with the task if necessary.
- **Above-level:** Have students add to their charts some additional things that are important to do the day before an interview, on the morning of an interview, and at an interview. For example, students might write: *The day before the interview he needs to get directions to the place.*

Grammar Notes

1. Use *like / need / want* to express likes, needs and desires.
2. *Like / need / want* can be followed by a verb or a noun.
3. If you use a verb after *like / need / want,* use an infinitive form of the verb (e.g., *I need to read this book.*).
4. For more information on this grammar topic, see page 257.

Center Stage 2

C Write sentences about yourself and people you know. Use the words in the box with the correct form of *want* or *need*. Answers will vary. Sentences must have subject-verb agreement.

I	doesn't need	to buy a house
My co-worker	doesn't want	to change jobs
My co-workers	don't need	to get a college degree
My family	don't want	to get married
My friend	need	to move to a different city
My friends	needs	to speak excellent English
	want	to take a vacation
	wants	

1. A friend of mine wants to change jobs.
2. _____
3. _____
4. _____
5. _____
6. _____

TIME to TALK

GROUPS. Talk about three future goals. What do you want to do? What do you need to do? Answers will vary.

Example:
A: I like to fix things. I want to be plumber, but first I need to finish high school.
B: I like cars. I need a car for my job. I want to buy a used car. First I need to save $1,000.

WRAP-UP. Now tell the class about the people in your group.

Example:
C: Nikos likes to fix things. He wants to be plumber. First he needs to finish high school. And Alex likes cars. He needs a car for his job.

I like to fix things.

At Work 145

C Teaching Time: 5–10 min.

- Read the example with the class. Tell students that *a friend of mine* means *my friend*.
- Tell students to use one word or phrase from each column in each sentence.
- Have students complete the task. Walk around and help as needed.
- PAIRS. Have students take turns reading their sentences to each other.

Option

Assign Unit 12 Supplementary Grammar to Communicate 3 Exercises on the Teacher's Resource Disk as homework or on the Student Persistence CD-ROM as self-access practice.

TIME to TALK

Teaching Time: 10–15 min.

- Explain that a goal is something you hope to do in the future. It is usually something that is not easy for you to do.
- Have two students read the example conversation.
- GROUPS. Have students complete the task. Walk around and help as needed.
- Have volunteers report back to the class things they learned about people in their group.

Multilevel Strategy

- **Pre-level:** Write the following on the board: *I like ___ . I want to ___ , but first I need to ___ .* Tell students to fill in the blanks with true information and use the sentences to talk about their goals with other students. Walk around and help as needed.
- **At-level, Above-level:** During the group activity, walk around and ask students questions about their goals (e.g., *When do you want to do that? Why do you need to do that?*).

Unit 12 T-145

Review and Challenge

Grammar

Teaching Time: 5–10 min.

- Read the example with the class.
- Have students complete the task.
- 🎧 Play Track 40 while students check their answers. Pause the recording each time an answer is given.
- PAIRS. Have students role-play the corrected conversation.

Dictation

Teaching Time: 5–10 min.

- 🎧 Play Track 41 while students listen and write what they hear.
- 🎧 Play Track 41 again while students check their answers.
- Call on students to write answers on the board.
- 🎧 Play Track 41 again and correct the sentences on the board.

> **Multilevel Strategy**
>
> - **Pre-level:** Give students a worksheet with some of the words from the dictation already provided.

Speaking

Teaching Time: 10–15 min.

- Have two students read the example aloud.
- PAIRS. Have students write their questions. Ask students to share their ideas and record questions on the board.
- PAIRS. Have students complete the task.
- Walk around and help as needed.
- Call on volunteers to role-play their interviews for the class.
- **LIFE SKILLS TEST PREP 2** Go to Unit 11, Lesson 4 for more practice in responding appropriately to job interview questions and learning appropriate job interview behavior.

T-146 Center Stage 2

Review and Challenge

Grammar

🎧 **40** Find and correct seven mistakes. The first mistake is corrected for you. Then listen and check your answers.

                      Are you waiting
Caroline: ~~Do you wait~~ for me?
                       to
Bill: Yes, I am. I need ∧ talk to you.
                     do
Caroline: Why ∧ you need to talk to me?

Bill: It's about Jake. Is he here today?
                   's cleaning
Caroline: Yes. He ~~cleans~~ up right now. Why?
          wants   *don't need*
Bill: He ~~is wanting~~ more hours, but we ~~aren't needing~~ extra workers right now.

Caroline: So tell him.
                               needs
Bill: But he has a new baby. He ~~is needing~~ the money now.

Caroline: Mason doesn't want to work on Saturdays. Maybe Jake wants to work then.

Bill: That's a good idea.

Dictation

🎧 **41** Listen. You will hear five sentences. Write them on a piece of paper. *See the audioscript on page 286 for the sentences.*

Speaking

PAIRS. Imagine that you are looking for a new job. Follow these steps:
1. Make a list of five questions a job interviewer might ask. Use the simple present or the present progressive.
2. Ask and answer the questions.
3. Change roles. *Answers will vary.*

Example:
A: Do you have a job now?
B: Yes, I do.
A: Where do you work?
B: I work at a shoe store.
A: Why are you looking for a new job?...

146 Unit 12

Option

- Before class, make a copy of the grammar exercise on page 146 as a transparency to use with an overhead projector.
- Ask a volunteer to make corrections to the conversation on the transparency. Correct as needed. Have students check their work with the transparency.

Culture Note

Speaking. In the United States, interviewers are not allowed to ask job candidates certain questions such as religion, age, nationality, marital or family status, physical disabilities, or medical history.

Listening

A 🎧 **42** Listen. Mrs. Pineiro is looking for a job. Who is she talking to? Check (✓) the correct answer.

- ✓ A job interviewer
- ☐ The manager at Little Friends
- ☐ A woman who helps people find jobs
- ☐ Mrs. Anderson

B 🎧 **43** Read the statements about Mrs. Pineiro. Write T (true) or F (false) for each statement. Listen again and check your answers.

__F__ 1. Her children do not go to school.
__F__ 2. She wants to work two hours a week.
__F__ 3. She wants to work in the afternoon.
__T__ 4. She has a high school diploma.
__T__ 5. She doesn't drive.
__T__ 6. She lives near Little Friends.
__F__ 7. She comes from a small family.
__T__ 8. She wants to work at Little Friends.

TIME to TALK

GROUPS. Discuss the questions about your country. Answers will vary.

1. Do a lot of women have jobs outside the home?
2. What kinds of jobs do women usually have?
3. What kinds of jobs do women almost never have?
4. Do you think some jobs are good only for women or for men? Which jobs? Why?

Now tell the class the interesting things that you learned from your discussion.

Example:
A: In Chen's country, a lot of women have jobs outside the home. They work on farms and in factories...

At Work 147

Listening

A Teaching Time: 5–10 min.

- **Warm-up:** Have students look at the picture. Ask: *Where are the people? How do you know? What do you think they're doing?*
- Have students read through the answer choices before they listen.
- 🎧 Play Track 42 while students listen.
- 🎧 Play Track 42 again while students listen and complete the task.
- PAIRS. Have students compare answers.
- Call on a student to say the answer. Correct as needed.

B Teaching Time: 5–10 min.

- Read the example with the class.
- Have students complete the task.
- 🎧 Play Track 43 while students listen and check their answers.
- Call on students to say answers. Correct as needed.

Multilevel Strategy

- **Pre-level:** Tell students there are four false statements.
- **At-level, Above-level:** When checking answers, challenge students to correct the false statements.

Option

Assign Unit 12 Supplementary Review and Challenge Exercises on the Teacher's Resource Disk as homework or on the Student Persistence CD-ROM as self-access practice.

TIME to TALK

Teaching Time: 10–15 min.

- Read the example with the class.
- Tell students that they can say: *Tell me more about that* or *Why do you think that?* if they want to hear more about a topic.
- GROUPS. Have students take turns asking and answering questions.
- Walk around and help as needed.
- Invite volunteers to share with the class things they learned.

Unit 12 T-147

Reading and Writing

Reading

A **Teaching Time: 10–15 min.**

- Have students read through the questions before reading the paragraphs.
- Have students read the paragraphs silently. Then read them aloud. Pause after each few words and have students repeat chorally. Explain any unfamiliar vocabulary.
- Have students complete the task.
- PAIRS. Have students share their answers.
- Call on volunteers to say one way they are similar to and different from Imelda.

B **Teaching Time: 10–15 min.**

- Have students read through the form. Explain unfamiliar vocabulary. For example, say: *Background means things in your past. An institution is a school or organization.*
- Have students reread the paragraphs and complete the form.
- Call on students to say answers. Correct as needed.
- **LIFE SKILLS TEST PREP 2** Go to Unit 11, Lesson 2 for more practice in filling out a simple job application.

Reading and Writing

Reading

A Imelda Aquino has an appointment with a career counselor. Read the paragraphs and answer the questions. *Answers will vary.*

1. How is Imelda like you? _____
2. How is she different from you? _____

> My name is Imelda Aquino. I live in Jersey City. I come from the Philippines. My first language is Tagalog, but I also speak Spanish. I am learning English now.
>
> In the Philippines I was an elementary school teacher at Baluarte Elementary School in Iloilo City for five years. I have a bachelor's degree in education from the University of the Philippines. Right now I am working part-time as a cashier at Lucky's Supermarket.
>
> I am looking for a job as a teacher's aide. I like children and I like to teach. In the future, I want to teach in an elementary school.

B Complete the form with information about Imelda.

COUNSELING & CAREER SERVICES

Today's Date: 3/19/06   Name: Imelda Aquino

List any foreign languages that you speak: Tagalog, Spanish

Educational Background
Check (✓) all that apply. Write the institution's name and location, as well as your major field of study.

	Name and location of institution	Major
✓ Graduated from high school	Pasay City High School, Pasay City	—
☐ Associate's Degree	—	—
✓ Bachelor's Degree	University of Philippines, Manila	education
☐ Master's Degree (or higher)	—	—
☐ Other? Please explain.	—	—

Work Experience

Employer	Job title or position	Years employed
Lucky's Supermarket	Part-time cashier	
Baluarte Elementary School	Elementary school teacher	5

Future Plans
What are your educational and career goals? Right now I'm looking for a job as a teacher's aide. In the future, I want to teach in an elementary school.

Unit 12

Culture Note

Exercise B. Tell students that a career counselor asks questions about a person's interests and likes. Based on this information, a career counselor gives advice about what jobs and professional training might be good for the person.

Option

- Have students reread Imelda's information on page 148 and say what kind of information is in each paragraph. Record their responses on the board as an outline.

Center Stage 2

Prewriting

Fill in the form with information about yourself. Answers will vary.

COUNSELING & CAREER SERVICES

Today's Date: _____ Name: _____

List any foreign languages that you speak: _____

Educational Background
Check (✓) all that apply. Write the institution's name and location, as well as your major field of study.

	Name and location of institution	Major
❏ Graduated from high school	_____	_____
❏ Associate's Degree	_____	_____
❏ Bachelor's Degree	_____	_____
❏ Master's Degree (or higher)	_____	_____
❏ Other? Please explain.	_____	_____

Work Experience

Employer	Job title or position	Years employed
_____	_____	_____
_____	_____	_____
_____	_____	_____

Future Plans
What are your educational and career goals?
_____
_____

Writing

Write about your goals on a piece of paper. Use the paragraphs on page 148 as a model.
Answers will vary.

> **Writing Tip**
> A paragraph has one topic. If you start a new topic, start a new paragraph. Look at the reading on page 148. Each paragraph has a different topic:
> Paragraph 1 = personal information
> Paragraph 2 = education and work
> Paragraph 3 = future plans

At Work 149

Prewriting

Teaching Time: 10–15 min.

- Have students complete the form with their own information.
- Walk around and help as needed.

Writing

Teaching Time: 15–20 min.

- Have students study the Writing Tip. Tell them to use the information on their forms to write three paragraphs about themselves. The topics of the paragraphs should be the same as those in the Writing Tip.
- Have students write their paragraphs.
- Walk around and help as needed.
- Collect students' work and provide individual feedback.
- **LIFE SKILLS TEST PREP 2** Go to Unit 11, Lesson 3 for more practice in putting events in chronological order.

> **Multilevel Strategy**
> - **Pre-level:** While students are completing the prewriting task, copy the paragraphs from page 148 on the board. Underline the information that students should substitute in their paragraphs. Have students copy the paragraphs and substitute the underlined parts with true information.

   I. personal information
      A. name
      B. where she lives
      C. where she's from
      D. languages
   II. education and work
      A. past job
      B. education
      C. job now
   III. future plans
      A. job wanted now
      B. reasons for plans
      C. job wanted in the future

- Tell students that this is an outline and that they can use it as a guide to write information about themselves.

Unit 12   T-149

Game 3
Units 9–12

Answers will vary. Possible answers:

1. **A:** He plays computer games on weekends.
   B: Does he play computer games on weekends?
   C: What does he do on weekends?

2. **A:** The dress doesn't cost $100.
   B: Does the dress cost $100?
   C: How much does the dress cost?

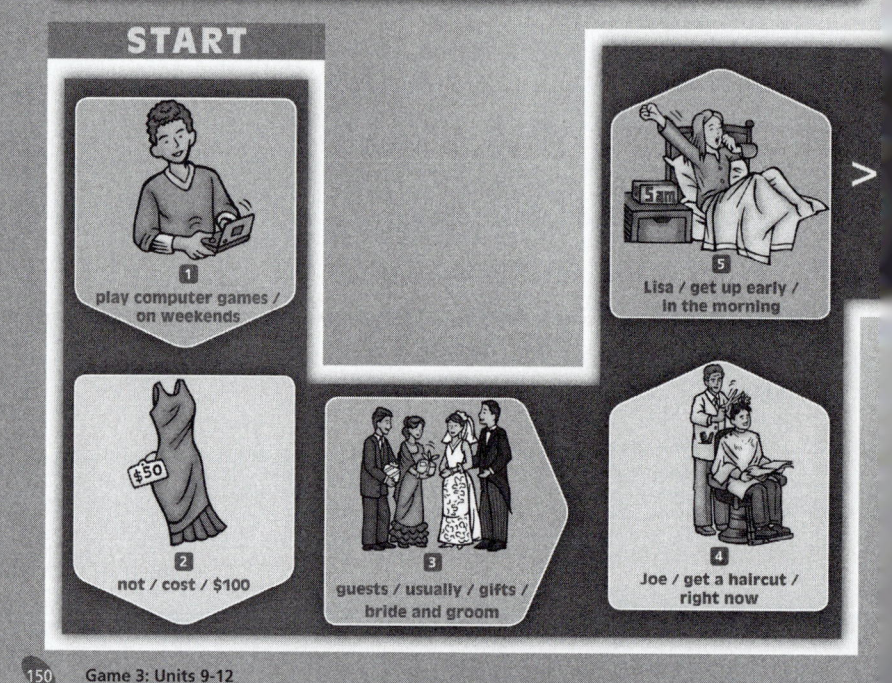

3. **A:** Guests usually give gifts to the bride and groom.
   B: Do guests usually give gifts to the bride and groom?
   C: Who usually gives gifts to the bride and groom? / What do guests usually give to the bride and groom? / Who do guests usually give gifts to?

4. **A:** Joe is getting a haircut right now.
   B: Is Joe getting a haircut right now?
   C: What is Joe doing right now?

5. **A:** Lisa gets up early in the morning.
   B: Does Lisa get up early in the morning?
   C: When does Lisa get up?

T-150　Center Stage 2

6. **A:** Cory brushes his teeth after breakfast.
   B: Does Cory brush his teeth after breakfast?
   C: What does Cory do after breakfast? / When does Cory brush his teeth?

7. **A:** Joe and Val celebrate Thanksgiving.
   B: Do Joe and Val celebrate Thanksgiving?
   C: How do Joe and Val celebrate Thanksgiving?

8. **A:** Alex wants to go on vacation.
   B: Does Alex want to go on vacation?
   C: Where does he want to go?

9. **A:** Margo drinks ten cups of coffee every day.
   B: Does Margo drink ten cups of coffee every day?
   C: How many cups of coffee does Margo drink every day?

10. **A:** The convenience store never closes at 9 P.M.
    B: Does the convenience store close at 9 P.M.?
    C: When does the convenience store close?

11. **A:** Luisa is inviting Mark to her birthday party.
    B: Is Luisa inviting Mark to her birthday party?
    C: Who is Luisa inviting to her birthday party?

12. **A:** Sue has a lot of experience.
    B: Does Sue have a lot of experience?
    C: How much experience does Sue have?

13. **A:** Pam doesn't do housework in the afternoon.
    B: Does Pam do housework in the afternoon?
    C: What does Pam do in the afternoon?

14. **A:** The boys don't like the ties.
    B: Do the boys like the ties?
    C: What don't the boys like?

15. **A:** Louise always gets flowers on her birthday.
    B: Does Louise always get flowers on her birthday?
    C: Who always gives her flowers on her birthday? / What does she always get on her birthday?

16. **A:** Dan is making an appointment right now.
    B: Is Dan making an appointment right now?
    C: What is Dan doing right now?

Game 3 T-151

Unit 13
Feelings and Opinions

Learning Goals

- Learn words to describe feelings and express opinions
- Learn about simple past of *be*: statements, *yes / no* questions, and information questions
- Listen to conversations about feelings and opinions
- Read and write a formal letter
- Talk about feelings and express opinions

Learner Persistence

Frequently praise students for their successes and point out their achievements, even small ones. A sense of continued progress will encourage students to keep coming to class.

Warm-up

Teaching Time: 3–5 min.

- Ask students to list some words to describe a good restaurant and a bad restaurant. Record students' answers on the board.
- Have students look at the pictures on pages 152 and 153. Ask questions such as: *Which restaurant is good? Which restaurant is bad? How do you know?*

Vocabulary

Teaching Time: 15–20 min.

- Explain any unfamiliar vocabulary. For example, say: *When a person is in a bad mood, he or she is unhappy, sad, or angry.*
- 🎧 Play Track 44 while students read and listen.
- Read the words and phrases aloud and have students repeat chorally.
- Have students complete the task.
- Call on students to say answers. Correct as needed.

Expansion

- On the board, write words with a negative meaning from the vocabulary list in one column, such as: *crowded, terrible, angry, rude, dirty*, etc.

T-152 Center Stage 2

Unit 13
Feelings and Opinions

Grammar
- Simple Past of *Be*: Statements
- Simple Past of *Be*: Yes / No Questions
- Simple Past of *Be*: Information Questions

Vocabulary

🎧 **44** Read and listen. Circle the positive words. Underline the negative words.

1. angry
2. rude
3. in a bad mood
4. noisy
5. slow
6. dirty
7. terrible food
8. worried
9. crowded
10. (wonderful) food
11. (good service)
12. (in a good mood)
13. (clean)

The food is wonderful!

152 Unit 13

- Ask students to add opposites to the words. Add these to the second column, writing each word next to its opposite. Tell students to first look for opposites in the vocabulary list on page 152. Then encourage them to use a dictionary to find opposites that they don't know.

Teaching Tip

Expansion. Teaching words with opposite meanings is a good way to increase students' vocabulary. Many words have "natural" opposites, and learning these word pairs together makes sense to students. Understanding a word's opposite helps students complete their comprehension of the word.

Listening

A 🎵 45 Listen. Check (✓) the good things about Angel's vacation last week.

- ✓ 1. the location of his mother-in-law's house
- ☐ 2. the people at the beach
- ✓ 3. the price of the airline tickets
- ✓ 4. the warm water
- ✓ 5. the weather

B 🎵 46 Read and listen again. Write the missing words. Use the words in the box.

| How much | ~~How was~~ | was | Were | weren't | Were they |

David: I love Miami. _How was_ the weather?
1.

Angel: It was wonderful. And my mother-in-law's house is only about ten minutes from the beach. We were there every day from 9:00 to 4:00. The water _was_ really warm.
2.

David: Great . . . _How much_ were the airline tickets? _Were they_ expensive?
3.   4.

Angel: No, they _weren't_. They were only $159 from New York.
5.

David: Wow, that's cheap. _Were_ your kids with you?
6.

Angel: Of course! It was spring vacation so they were off all week.

Feelings and Opinions 153

Listening

A Teaching Time: 10–15 min.

- **Warm-up:** Write on the board: *vacation*. Ask students: *What do you think of when you see the word vacation?* Record students' answers on the board.
- Ask students to read through the answer choices before they listen.
- 🎧 Play Track 45 while students listen.
- 🎧 Play Track 45 again while students listen and complete the task.
- Call on students to say answers. Correct as needed.

B Teaching Time: 15–20 min.

- Ask students to read through the answer choices before they listen.
- 🎧 Play Track 46 while students listen and complete the task.
- 🎧 Play Track 46 again while students check their answers.
- Call on students to say answers. Correct as needed.
- Read the conversation aloud. Pause after each few words and have students repeat chorally.
- PAIRS. Have students role-play the conversation.

Multilevel Strategy

- **Pre-level:** Have students role-play the completed conversation.
- **At-level, Above-level:** Have students write four additional lines to the conversation and role-play the conversation in front of the class.

Culture Note

Exercise B. Many schools in the United States close for a one-week vacation during the late winter or early spring. Families often travel and go on vacation at this time, especially to places with warmer weather.

Option

Assign Unit 13 Supplementary Vocabulary Exercise on the Teacher's Resource Disk as homework or on the Student Persistence CD-ROM as self-access practice.

Unit 13   T-153

Grammar to Communicate 1

Simple Past of *Be*: Statements

Teaching Time: 5–10 min.

- Say: *The past is any time before now. Use the simple past to talk about things that happened before now.*
- Say: *The verb be has two forms in the simple past. Use* was *with I, he, she, and it. Use* were *with you, we, and they.*
- Say: *For negative sentences, add* not *to* was *or* were. *You can also use contractions* wasn't *and* weren't.
- Have students study the charts.
- Read each example and have students repeat chorally.
- Write a few sentences in the simple present. Call on students to come to the board and rewrite the sentences in the simple past.

A Teaching Time: 5–10 min.

- Read the example with the class. Tell students to underline the subject of each sentence to help them decide whether *was* or *were* is the correct word.
- Have students complete the task.
- Call on students to say answers. Correct as needed.

Multilevel Strategy

- **Pre-level:** Have students work in pairs or groups to complete the task. Help students with the task if necessary.
- **At-level:** After students have completed the task, have them write two additional sentences about where they were yesterday at 1:00 P.M.
- **Above-level:** After students have completed the task, have them write two sentences about themselves and two sentences about a family member.

B Teaching Time: 5–10 min.

- Hold up a calendar. Point to today's date and say: *This is today.*
- Point to yesterday's date. Say: *The day before today is called* yesterday.

T-154   Center Stage 2

Grammar to Communicate 1

SIMPLE PAST OF *BE*: STATEMENTS

Subject	Be		Subject	Be	Not	
I			I			
He			He			
She	was		She	was		
It		at home.	It		not	at work.
You			You			
We	were		We	were		
They			They			

Contractions
was + not → wasn't
were + not → weren't

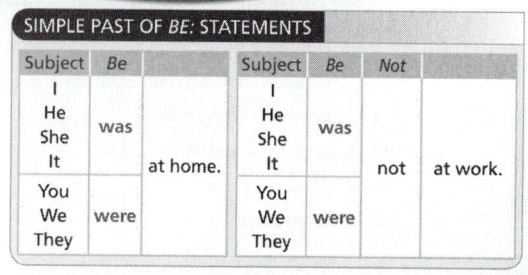

There	Be				There	Be + Not		
There	was	a lot of	food.		There	wasn't	any	food.
	were	three	kids.			weren't		kids.

A Complete the sentences about yesterday at 1:00 P.M. Use *was* or *were*.

1. I __was__ at work. My co-workers and I __were__ busy.
2. My daughter and her friend __were__ at home all day. They __were__ bored.
3. My husband __was__ at a restaurant with a co-worker. They __were__ at lunch.
4. My neighbors __were__ at home. They __were__ sick.
5. My sister __was__ late for lunch. My mother and father __were__ worried.

B Look at the calendar. Match the dates on the left with the time expressions on the right.

__b__ 1. June 7   a. last month
__e__ 2. June 7, 6 P.M. b. yesterday
__h__ 3. June 6   c. yesterday morning
__c__ 4. June 7, 8 A.M. d. yesterday afternoon
__a__ 5. May 8   e. yesterday evening
__f__ 6. June 7, 10 P.M. f. last night
__g__ 7. June 1   g. last week
__d__ 8. June 7, 1 P.M. h. the day before yesterday

JUNE
S M T W T F S
            1 2 3 4 5 6 7
(8) 9 10 11 12 13 14
today

154   Unit 13

- Point to the date two days ago. Say: *This is the day before yesterday.*
- Go over the example with the class. Point to the calendar and say: *June 7 was yesterday, so answer* b *is correct.*
- Have students complete the task.
- Call on students to say answers. Correct as needed.
- **LIFE SKILLS TEST PREP 2** Go to Unit 4, Lesson 1 for more practice in reading calendars.

Grammar Notes

1. Use the simple past to talk about things that happened before now.
2. There are two forms of *be* in the simple past. The past of *am* and *is* = *was*. The past of *are* = *were*.
3. Do not make contractions with affirmative forms of *be* in the simple past.
4. Use contractions or full forms with negative forms of *be*. For example: *I was not late.* = *I wasn't late. We were not there.* = *We weren't there.*
5. For more information on this grammar topic, see page 258.

C Write true sentences about yourself. Use time expressions from Exercise B. *Answers will vary.*

1. I was bored ___last night___.
2. I was late _____.
3. I was sick _____.
4. The homework wasn't easy _____.
5. My lunch wasn't very good _____.

bored

Complete the sentences. Use *was, were, wasn't,* or *weren't.*

6. I <u>was / wasn't</u> in a good mood yesterday evening.
7. The weather <u>was / wasn't</u> wonderful yesterday.
8. My friends <u>were / weren't</u> scared last night.
9. The teacher <u>was / wasn't</u> angry last week.
10. My neighbors <u>were / weren't</u> worried last month.

scared

D Complete the sentences. Circle the correct form of the verbs.

1. There was / (were) some dirty dishes in my bedroom. My mother was angry.
2. There (was) / were a fire in our building yesterday. We were scared.
3. There was / (were) two big tests last week. I was worried.
4. There wasn't / (weren't) any good movies on TV last night. I was bored.
5. There (wasn't) / weren't any homework last week. The students were in a good mood.
6. There wasn't / (weren't) any clean shirts in my father's closet. He was in a bad mood.

TIME to TALK

PAIRS. Tell your classmate about the last time you were at one of these events.
Answers will vary.

| children's birthday party | graduation | large party | wedding |

Example:
A: *I was at a children's birthday party last week. The party was for my son's best friend. There were about ten kids at the party. The weather wasn't great, so the party was inside. The children were in a good mood . . .*

Feelings and Opinions 155

C Teaching Time: 5–10 min.
- Read the example with the class.
- Have students complete the task.
- Walk around and help as needed.
- Call on students to say one sentence in the past about themselves. Correct as needed.

D Teaching Time: 3–5 min.
- Read the example with the class.
- Have students complete the task.
- PAIRS. Have students compare answers.
- Call on students to say answers. Correct as needed.

Watch Out!

Exercise B. In English we say *yesterday morning, yesterday afternoon,* and *yesterday evening,* but we say *last night* (not *yesterday night*). Listen for and correct this error.

Option

Assign Unit 13 Supplementary Grammar to Communicate 1 Exercises on the Teacher's Resource Disk as homework or on the Student Persistence CD-ROM as self-access practice.

TIME to TALK

Teaching Time: 15–20 min.
- Read the example with the class.
- Ask students to list some things to describe the events, such as: *type of event, time, food, decorations,* and so on. Tell them to use these ideas when talking about their event.
- PAIRS. Have students complete the task with a partner.
- Walk around and help as needed.

Multilevel Strategy
- **Pre-level:** Have students write their sentences before they talk with a partner.
- **Above-level:** Challenge students to describe a great event. Then challenge students to describe a terrible event.

Unit 13   T-155

Grammar to Communicate 2

Simple Past of *Be*: Yes / No Questions; *Was there / Were there*: Questions

Teaching Time: 5–10 min.

- Review forming questions with *be* in the present. Write on the board: am / is / are + *subject*. Ask students a few simple present *yes / no* questions and have them answer with short answers.
- Say: *Questions with be in the simple past are very similar.* Write on the board: was / were + *subject*.
- Have students study the chart.
- Read aloud the questions and answers and have students repeat chorally.
- Ask questions in the simple present and have students change them into the simple past. For example: *Are there a lot of trees? Were there a lot of trees?*

A Teaching Time: 5–10 min.

- Read the example with the class. Remind students to use the correct subject pronoun in each short answer.
- Have students complete the task.
- Have a volunteer read aloud each question to a student of his or her choice. Those chosen students read aloud the answers to the question. Correct as needed.

B Teaching Time: 10–15 min.

- Read the example with the class.
- Have students complete the task.
- Call on students to say questions. Correct as needed.
- PAIRS. Have students take turns asking and answering the questions.
- Walk around and help as needed.

Grammar to Communicate 2

SIMPLE PAST OF BE: YES / NO QUESTIONS

Be	Subject			Subject	Be		Subject	Be + Not
Was	I / he / it	busy?	Yes,	I / he / it	was.	No,	I / he / it	wasn't.
Were	you / we / they			you / we / they	were.		you / we / they	weren't.

WAS THERE / WERE THERE: QUESTIONS

| Was / Were | there | a lot of / many | food? / kids? | Yes, there | was. / were. | No, there | wasn't. / weren't. |

A Look at the pictures on pages 152–153. Answer the questions about last night at Del Fino's and Vinnie's restaurants.

	DEL FINO'S	VINNIE'S
1. Was the food good?	No, it wasn't.	Yes, it was.
2. Were the waiters polite?	No, they weren't.	Yes, they were.
3. Were the customers angry?	Yes, they were.	No, they weren't.
4. Was the service fast?	No, it wasn't.	Yes, it was.
5. Were the plates clean?	No, they weren't.	Yes, they were.
6. Was the restaurant noisy?	Yes, it was.	No, it wasn't.
7. Was the cook in a good mood?	No, he wasn't.	Yes, he was.

B Write questions. Put the words in the correct order.

1. __Was the teacher nice?__
   (the / Was / nice / teacher)
2. __Was the classroom crowded?__
   (Was / crowded / classroom / the)
3. __Was the homework difficult?__
   (homework / Was / the / difficult)
4. __Were your classes long?__
   (Were / long / classes / your)
5. __Were your classes at night?__
   (at night / classes / your / Were)
6. __Were the tests easy?__
   (tests / easy / Were / the)

PAIRS. Think of a class you were in. Ask and answer the questions above.

156 Unit 13

Grammar Notes

1. To make a question in the simple past with *be*, use *was / were* + subject or *Was / Were there* + subject.
2. To answer *yes / no* questions with short answers, use subject + *was / were* (+ *not*). Do not use contractions in affirmative short answers. Use full forms or contractions in negative short answers.
3. For more information on this grammar topic, see page 258.

T-156 Center Stage 2

C Complete the questions. Use *Was there* or *Were there*. Then complete the answers.

1. __Were there__ a lot of people? Yes, __there were.__
2. __Was there__ good food? Yes, __there was.__
3. __Was there__ a line? No, __there wasn't.__
4. __Were there__ a lot of different dishes on the menu? Yes, __there were.__
5. __Were there__ a lot of salespeople? No, __there weren't.__
6. __Were there__ a lot of cheap things? Yes, __there were.__

PAIRS. Which questions are about a restaurant? Which questions are about a store? Which questions are about both? Answers will vary. Possible answers:
restaurant: 2, 4; store: 5, 6; both: 1, 3, 6

Example:
A: I think number 1 is about a restaurant or a store.

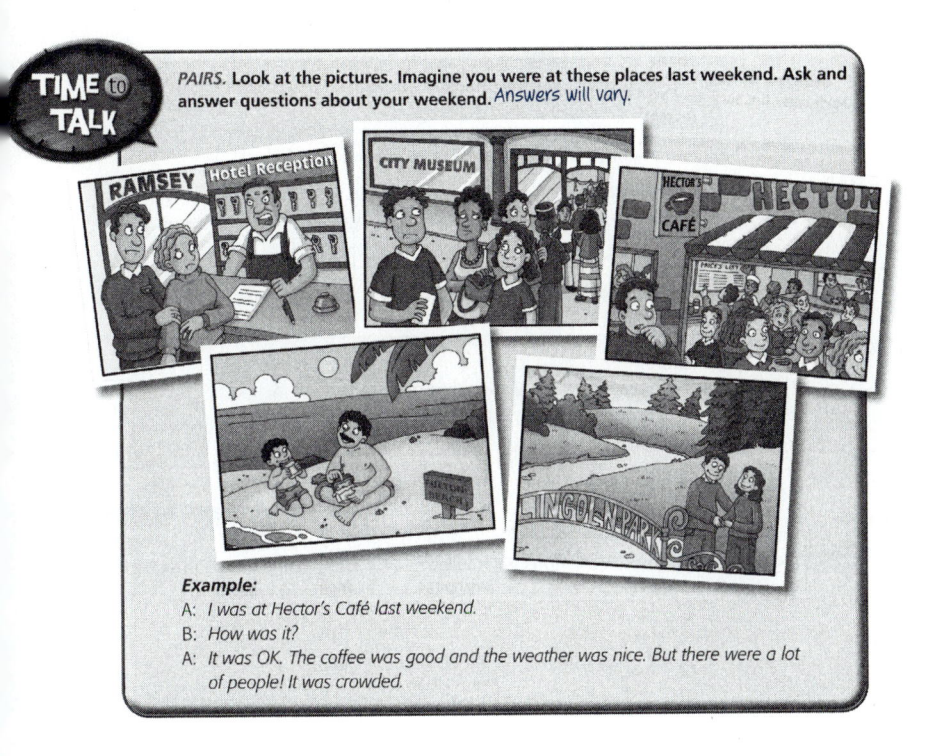

TIME to TALK

PAIRS. Look at the pictures. Imagine you were at these places last weekend. Ask and answer questions about your weekend. Answers will vary.

Example:
A: I was at Hector's Café last weekend.
B: How was it?
A: It was OK. The coffee was good and the weather was nice. But there were a lot of people! It was crowded.

Feelings and Opinions 157

C Teaching Time: 10–15 min.
- Read the example with the class.
- Remind students to use *was* if the noun is singular and *were* if the noun is plural.
- Have students complete the task.
- Call on pairs of students to read aloud questions and answers. Correct as needed.
- Read the example for the second part of the task with the class.
- PAIRS. Have partners reread each question and mark it as *R* for *restaurant*, *S* for *store*, or *B* for *both*. Then have them discuss their choices. Walk around and help as needed.

Multilevel Strategy
- **Pre-level:** Allow students to express basic agreement or disagreement and attempt to explain if possible.
- **At-level:** Encourage students to explain their agreement or disagreement.
- **Above-level:** Have students explain their reasoning and challenge them with more questions.

Option
Assign Unit 13 Supplementary Grammar to Communicate 2 Exercises on the Teacher's Resource Disk as homework or on the Student Persistence CD-ROM as self-access practice.

TIME to TALK
Teaching Time: 10–15 min.
- Have students look at each picture. Ask: *Where are they?* to clarify each place.
- Have two students read the example conversation.
- PAIRS. Have students complete the task. Walk around and help as needed.
- Have volunteers report back to the class about their partner's imaginary weekend.

Expansion
- PAIRS. Have students play Twenty Questions.
- One student thinks of a place he or she was last weekend.
- The other student asks *yes / no* questions to guess where the person was. Students try to guess the correct place by asking as few questions as possible.
- Have students switch roles.

Unit 13 T-157

Grammar to Communicate 3

Simple Past of *Be*: Information Questions

Teaching Time: 5–10 min.

- Review making information questions with *be* in the simple present. Write on the board: *wh-word* + *am / is / are* + *subject*. Ask students a few information questions and have them answer with short answers.
- Say: *Make information questions in the simple past the same way. Just use past forms of* be. Write on the board: *wh-word* + *was / were* + *subject*.
- Have students study the chart.
- Read each question and answer and have students repeat chorally.
- Ask students a few information questions in the simple past and have them answer.

A **Teaching Time: 10–15 min.**

- Read the example with the class.
- Have students complete the task.
- Call on students to read the questions. Correct as needed.
- Have students study the Look Box before the pair activity.
- Have two students read the example.
- PAIRS. Have students complete the task.
- Walk around and help as needed.

Multilevel Strategy

- **Pre-level:** Help students identify the correct word from the box for each question. Then have them complete the task.
- **Above-level:** For the pair activity have students ask one additional question to each statement using the other *wh-* words (e.g., *How was class? What was the topic?*).

B **Teaching Time: 5–10 min.**

- Read the example with the class.
- PAIRS. Have students complete the questions.
- Have students take turns asking and answering questions about their partner's trip.
- Walk around and help as needed.

T-158 Center Stage 2

Grammar to Communicate 3

SIMPLE PAST OF *BE*: INFORMATION QUESTIONS

Wh- word	Be	Subject		Answers
When	was	the party?		On Saturday night.
Why		the party	on Saturday?	Saturday was my birthday.
Where	were	you	last night?	I was at the movies.
How		the children	yesterday?	They were very good.

A Write questions. Use *How* and the words in the box.

| ~~class~~ | school | the party | work | your day |

1. You weren't in class yesterday. You call a classmate and ask:
   A: _How was class?_
2. It's 8:00 P.M. Your mother had a long day. You ask:
   A: _How was your day?_
3. It's 4:00 P.M. Your son is home from school. You ask:
   A: _How was school?_
4. It's Sunday. Your friend was at a party last night. You ask:
   A: _How was the party?_
5. It's 6:00 P.M. Your husband or wife is home from work. You ask:
   A: _How was work?_

PAIRS. Ask and answer the questions above. Use the expressions in the Look Box. Answers will vary.

Example:
A: How was class?
B: Pretty bad. The test was difficult.

Look
really good = very good
pretty good = good
pretty bad = bad
really bad = very bad

B **PAIRS.** Complete the questions with *was* or *were*. Then think about the last time you were in another city or country. Ask and answer the questions.

1. Where _were_ you?
2. When _were_ you there?
3. Who _was_ with you?
4. Why _were_ you there?
5. How _was_ it?
6. How long _were_ you there?

Unit 13

Grammar Notes

1. In simple past information questions, *was* or *were* comes after the *wh-*word.
2. For more information on this grammar topic, see page 258.

C

47 Complete the conversation. Use *Where*, *How*, *Who*, and *Why* and the correct form of *be*. Then listen and check your answers.

Matt: _How was_ your day yesterday?
1.

Bob: It was really good.

Matt: _Where were_ you?
2.

Bob: I was at the beach.

Matt: But it was Thursday. _Why were_ you at the beach on Thursday?
3.

Bob: Thursday's my day off.

Matt: _Who was_ with you?
4.

Bob: My girlfriend and her mother.

Matt: Her mother? _Why was_ her mother with you?
5.

Bob: Her mother likes the beach.

Matt: Oh . . . OK. _How was_ the beach?
6.

Bob: It was very nice. There weren't many people, and it was a beautiful day.

Matt: _How was_ the water?
7.

Bob: It was pretty cold. The water is always cold around here.

TIME to TALK

PAIRS. Student A: Look at the picture on page 270.
Student B: Look at the picture on page 272.
You were both on an airplane last weekend, but your experiences were very different. How were they different? Ask and answer questions. *Answers will vary.*

Example:
A: *How was the weather on the day of your flight?*
B: *It was wonderful. It was a beautiful day. How was your weather?*
A: *It was terrible!*

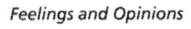

Feelings and Opinions 159

C Teaching Time: 10–15 min.

- Read the example with the class.
- Have students complete the task.
- Play Track 47 while students check their answers.
- Pause the recording each time an answer is given.
- PAIRS. Have partners role-play the completed conversation.

Multilevel Strategy

- **Pre-level:** Help students identify the correct *wh*-word for each question. Ask students to look at each answer and say whether it is about a location, person, or reason. Then have them complete the task.
- **At-level, Above-level:** After students have completed the task, have them ask a partner two questions about what they did yesterday. After checking answers, call on students to say what their partner did yesterday.

Option

Assign Unit 13 Supplementary Grammar to Communicate 3 Exercises on the Teacher's Resource Disk as homework or on the Student Persistence CD-ROM as self-access practice.

TIME to TALK

Teaching Time: 10–15 min.

- Tell students to ask questions in the simple past with *was* and *were*.
- Have two students read the example conversation.
- PAIRS. Have students complete the task.
- Walk around and help as needed.

Unit 13 T-159

Review and Challenge

Grammar

Teaching Time: 5–10 min.

- Read the example with the class.
- Have students complete the task.
- PAIRS. Have students compare answers.
- 🎧 Play Track 48 while students check their answers.

Dictation

Teaching Time: 5–10 min.

- 🎧 Play Track 49 while students listen and write what they hear.
- 🎧 Play Track 49 again while students check their answers.
- Call on students to write answers on the board.
- 🎧 Play Track 49 again and correct the sentences on the board.

> **Multilevel Strategy**
>
> - **Pre-level:** Give students a worksheet with some of the words from the dictation already provided.

Speaking

Teaching Time: 10–15 min.

- Have two students read the example conversation.
- PAIRS. Have students complete the task.
- Walk around and help as needed.
- Have students perform their conversations for the class.

> **Multilevel Strategy**
>
> - **Pre-level:** Pair pre-level students to complete the task. Have them write one conversation and practice it for natural delivery.
> - **At-level, Above-level:** Pair at-level students with above-level students. Tell pairs to try to use the questions in a creative way in their conversations. Prompt students with suggestions if necessary.

T-160 Center Stage 2

Review and Challenge

Grammar

🎧 **48** Complete the conversation. Use the words in the box. Then listen and check your answers. (Be careful! There is one extra answer.)

| How | it | they | ~~was~~ | wasn't | were | weren't | what | Where |

Greg: I miss my old apartment. It __was__ really nice.
                                    1.

Pearl: __Where__ was it?
           2.

Greg: On Cherry Street in Overbrook.

Pearl: Was __it__ big?
              3.

Greg: No, it __wasn't__. There __were__ five
              4.   5.
rooms, but __they__ were small.
            6.

Pearl: Were there a lot of stores in the neighborhood?

Greg: No, there __weren't__. They were all far away.
                    7.

Pearl: So __what__ was nice about the apartment?
              8.

Dictation

🎧 **49** Listen. You will hear five sentences. Write them on a piece of paper. *See the audioscript on page 287 for the sentences.*

Speaking

PAIRS. Write a short conversation for each question. Then perform one of your conversations for the class. *Answers will vary.*

1. Why were you late this morning?
2. It's midnight. Where were you?
3. How was the movie?
4. Why weren't you in class yesterday?

Example:
A: *Why were you late this morning?*
B: *The traffic was terrible...*

160 Unit 13

Listening

A 🎧 50 Listen. What are the people talking about? Match the conversations with the topics. (Be careful! There are two extra topics.)

- _c_ Conversation 1   a. a class
- _d_ Conversation 2   b. a sports event
- _f_ Conversation 3   c. a job interview
- _b_ Conversation 4   d. a movie
-                        e. a new DVD
-                        f. a test

B 🎧 51 Listen again. Complete the sentences about the conversations. Use the words in the box.

| ~~bad~~ | difficult | great | sick |
| bored | easy | rude | worried |

Conversation 1
1. The weather was __bad__.
2. The questions were __difficult__.

Conversation 2
3. She was __bored__.
4. The man behind her was __rude__.

Conversation 3
5. He was __worried__ at first.
6. The test was __easy__.

Conversation 4
7. The man wasn't there because he was __sick__.
8. The game was __great__.

TIME to TALK

GROUPS. Talk about experiences in your past. Choose from the topics in the box or your own ideas. Ask and answer questions. *Answers will vary.*

Example:
A: I was at a movie last night.
B: Was it good?
A: Yes, it was.
B: Who was in it?

a difficult test	a restaurant
a job interview	a sports event
a movie	a trip

Feelings and Opinions   161

Listening

A   **Teaching Time: 5–10 min.**

- **Warm-up:** Have students look at the picture. Ask them: *Where are they? How do you know? How do they feel?*
- Ask students to read through the list of topics before they listen.
- 🎧 Play Track 50 while students listen.
- 🎧 Play Track 50 again while students listen and complete the task.
- Call on students to say answers. Correct as needed.

B   **Teaching Time: 5–10 min.**

- Read the example with the class.
- 🎧 Play Track 51 while students listen and complete the task.
- PAIRS. Have students compare answers.
- 🎧 Play Track 51 again while students check their answers. Pause the recording each time an answer is given.

Option

Assign Unit 13 Supplementary Review and Challenge Exercises on the Teacher's Resource Disk as homework or on the Student Persistence CD-ROM as self-access practice.

TIME to TALK   **Teaching Time: 10–15 min.**

- Have two students read the example conversation.
- GROUPS. Have groups complete the task.
- Walk around and help as needed.
- Call on students to perform their conversations for the class.

Unit 13   T-161

Reading and Writing

Reading

A **Teaching Time: 10–15 min.**

- Ask a few questions about the letter, such as: *Who is the letter to / from? Where does Brenda Reese live?*
- Have students read the letter silently. Then read it aloud. Pause after each few words and have students repeat chorally. Explain any unfamiliar vocabulary.
- Have students check the correct answer.
- Call on a student to say the answer. Correct as needed.
- **LIFE SKILLS TEST PREP 2** Go to Unit 5, Lesson 4 for more practice in reading and comparing basic information in simple advertisements.

B **Teaching Time: 10–15 min.**

- Have students reread the letter and complete the task.
- Call on students to say answers. Correct as needed.

Expansion When checking Exercise B, have students say the paragraph where they found each answer (1. first paragraph, 2. third paragraph, 3. second paragraph, 4. first paragraph, 5. third paragraph).

Reading and Writing

Reading

A Read the letter. Check the word that describes Mrs. Reese's feelings.

- ☑ angry
- ☐ bored
- ☐ scared
- ☐ worried

George Harrison, Manager
Price Wise Electronics
115 West Broadway
Freemont, CA 94538

1329 Market Street
Freemont, CA 94538

June 28, 2006

Dear Mr. Harrison:

In last week's newspaper, there was an ad for a sale on Saturday, June 26th, at your Freemont Store. The ad said Keiko TVs were $299.

I was at your store on Saturday morning. There were a lot of TVs, but there weren't any Keikos. Some TVs were on sale, but there weren't any for $299. The salesman said there was a mistake in the ad.

Was your ad wrong? Why weren't there any Keiko TVs for $299? I would like to buy a Keiko for the price in the ad. Please call me at (111) 917-2525. Thank you.

Sincerely,

Brenda Reese
Brenda Reese

Price Wise Electronics
One-day sale only!
All Keiko TVs
Regular price $480
Sale price $299

B Circle the correct answers.

1. When was Mrs. Reese at Price Wise?
   a. On Friday morning.   **(b.)** On Saturday morning.
2. What did she want to buy?
   (a.) A Keiko TV.   b. A Sony TV.
3. What was the problem?
   (a.) There weren't any Keiko TVs.   b. No TVs were on sale.
4. Where did Mrs. Reese see the ad?
   (a.) In the newspaper.   b. On TV.
5. Why is Mrs. Reese writing a letter?
   (a.) She wants a TV for $299.   b. She doesn't want to pay for a TV.

Unit 13

T-162 Center Stage 2

Writing

Think about a time when you were unhappy with a business. Write a letter to the manager. Use the letter on page 162 as a model. Answers will vary.

Writing Tip

Business letters look different from personal letters. Follow the instructions below.

- Write the recipient's name here.
- Write the business address here.
- Write your address here.
- Write today's date here.

Dear _____:

Write about these questions:
- Why are you unhappy?
- What happened?
- What do you want the recipient of this letter to do?

Sincerely,

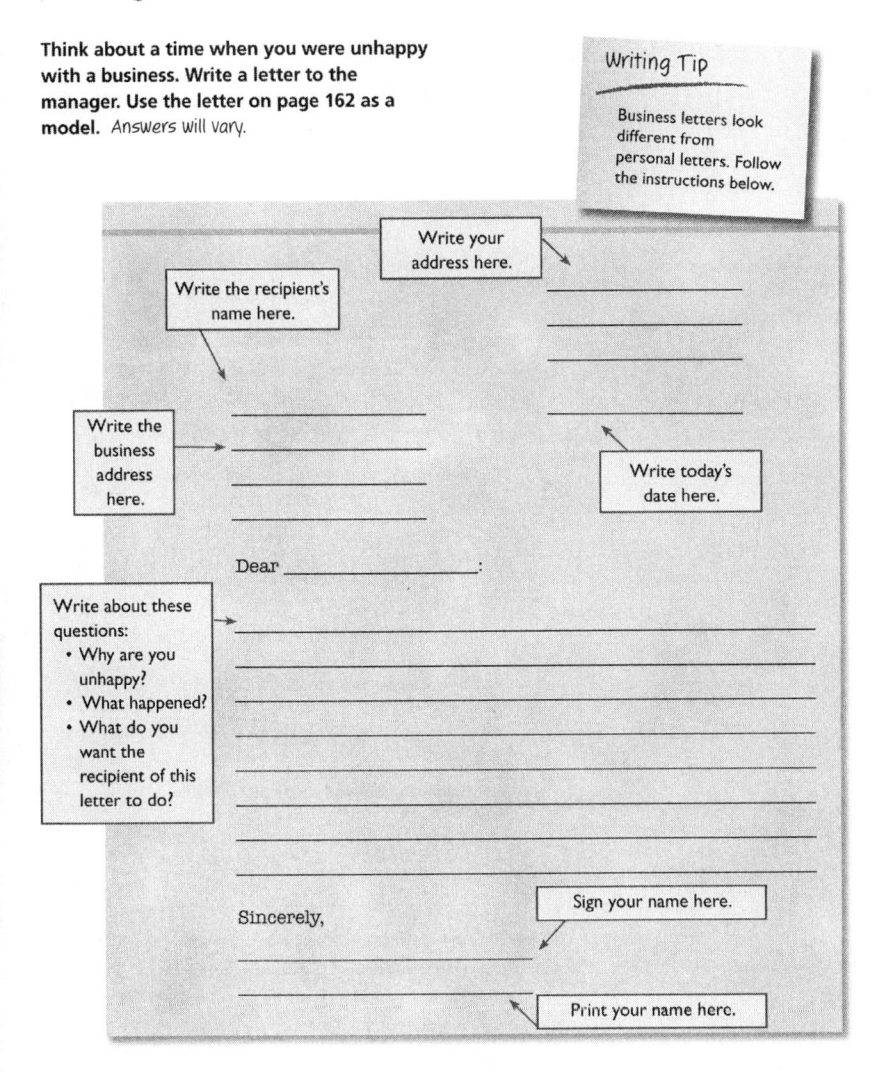

Sign your name here.

Print your name here.

Feelings and Opinions 163

Writing

Teaching Time: 20–30 min.

- Give students a few minutes to think about some situations they could write about. Ask volunteers to share their ideas. Record them on the board.
- Have students study the Writing Tip. Point to and read each instruction on the blank letter. Explain unfamiliar vocabulary as necessary, for example: *The recipient is the person you're writing to.*
- As you point to the instructions for the body of the letter, tell students to write one paragraph for each question. Remind students to indent for each new paragraph.
- Walk around and help as needed.
- Call on volunteers to read their letters to the class. Correct as needed. You can also have students write their letters on a separate piece of paper. Collect their work and provide individual feedback.

Culture Note

Writing. Most companies in the United States are very serious about their customers' satisfaction. A letter of complaint to a company can be an effective way to get what you want.

Unit 13 T-163

Unit 14
Fact or Fiction?

Learning Goals
- Learn words to describe events
- Learn about simple past: regular verbs, irregular verbs, and negative statements
- Listen to a conversation and a radio report about an event
- Read a police report and write about an incident for a police report
- Talk about events

Learner Persistence
Point out to students that things they learn in class are relevant to their lives and help them communicate better with English speakers.

Warm-up
Teaching Time: 3–5 min.

- Have students look at the title of the unit. Tell students that a fact is something that is true and fiction is a story that a person creates. Fiction is not true.
- Ask students to name some newspapers, magazines, television programs, etc., that give facts. Then ask them to name some that are fiction.

Vocabulary
Teaching Time: 15–20 min.

- Have students look at the pictures and read their captions. Explain unfamiliar vocabulary as necessary, for example: *When you chase someone, you follow them quickly. Many dogs like to chase cats.*
- Ask students to read through the headlines before they read and listen.
- 🎧 Play Track 52 while students read and listen.
- Read the words and phrases aloud and have students repeat chorally.
- Call on a student to say the answer. Correct as needed.

Expansion Have students write statements about themselves with the vocabulary words. The statements may be true or false. For example: *I scream at scary movies.* Call on students to read their statements aloud. Have the rest of the class guess whether the statement is fact or fiction.

Unit 14
Fact or Fiction?

Grammar
- Simple Past: Regular Verbs
- Simple Past: Irregular Verbs
- Simple Past: Negative Statements

Vocabulary

🎧 **52** Read and listen. Circle the best newspaper headline for the story.

- Gorilla on Canal Street
- Police visit the city zoo
- New job for zoo worker

1. forget the keys
2. leave the keys
3. get out
5. happen [*what happened?*]
6. lose his keys
8. catch
9. take back

Unit 14

Multilevel Strategy
- **Pre-level:** Have students each write one statement with one of the vocabulary words.
- **At-level, Above-level:** Have students write one true statement and one false statement.

T-164 Center Stage 2

Listening

A 🎧 53 Listen. Steve and Marie are talking about a story in yesterday's newspaper. Check (✓) the places Steve talks about.

- ☑ a bus stop
- ☐ a police station
- ☑ a street
- ☑ a park
- ☐ a small town
- ☑ a zoo

B 🎧 54 Read and listen again. Write the missing words. Use the words in the box.

| didn't | ~~ran~~ | took | walked | watched |

Marie: A gorilla?

Steve: Yeah, you heard me —a gorilla. First he _ran_ into the park. Then he ran across Canal Street. All the people in their cars stopped and _watched_ him. Then he _walked_ to the bus stop, and stood next to it. The people all screamed, but the gorilla _didn't_ move. He just stood there.

Marie: Oh, please!

Steve: Really! Look. It's in the paper. A policeman took a picture of it.

Marie: Wow! That's really strange. Where is he now? Is he back in the zoo?

Steve: Yes, the police caught him and _took_ him back.

Fact or Fiction? 165

4. scream
7. chase
10. change jobs

Language Note

Exercise B. Point out Marie's line: *Oh, please!* Tell students that people say this when they don't believe what a person is telling them.

Option

Assign Unit 14 Supplementary Vocabulary Exercise on the Teacher's Resource Disk as homework or on the Student Persistence CD-ROM as self-access practice.

Listening

A Teaching Time: 10–15 min.

- **Warm-up:** Ask students to read through the answer choices before they listen. Ask a question about each choice. Ask, for example: *What do you do at a bus stop?* (wait for a bus) *Which word is a place for cars to drive?* (street) *Is New York City a small town?* (no)
- 🎧 Play Track 53 while students listen.
- 🎧 Play Track 53 again while students listen and complete the task.
- Call on students to say answers. Correct as needed.

B Teaching Time: 15–20 min.

- Ask students to read through the answer choices before they listen.
- 🎧 Play Track 54 while students listen and write the words they hear.
- 🎧 Play Track 54 again while students check their answers.
- Call on students to say answers. Correct as needed.
- PAIRS. Ask students to role-play the conversation.

Multilevel Strategy

- **Pre-level:** Have students role-play the completed conversation.
- **At-level:** Copy the conversation on the board and erase some words. Have students recall the conversation as they role-play.
- **Above-level:** Have students role-play a new conversation about a real or imaginary event. Tell them to use the conversation in the book as a model. Call on pairs to role-play in front of the class.

Unit 14 T-165

Grammar to Communicate 1

Simple Past: Regular Verbs

Teaching Time: 10–15 min.

- Remind students that the past is any time before now.
- Say: *To make the simple past with regular verbs, add –ed to the base form of the verb.* Write on the board and read a few examples, such as *walk / walked*.
- Draw the following graphic organizer on the board.

If a verb ends in . . .	Do this to make the simple past.	Examples
e	add –d	like / liked
consonant + y	change y to i, and add –ed	try / tried
vowel + consonant	double the consonant and add –ed	shop / shopped

- Tell students that these are spelling rules for making simple past forms.
- Have students study the chart.
- Read the sentences in the chart and have students repeat chorally.
- Say a few sentences in the simple present and have students change them to the simple past.

A Teaching Time: 5–10 min.

- Read the example with the class.
- Have students complete the task.
- Call on students to say answers. Correct as needed.
- PAIRS. Have students write their sentences and then read them to their partner.

B Teaching Time: 5–10 min.

- Have students study the Look Box. Explain to students that the final –ed can be pronounced three different ways.
- Point to the symbol /ɪd/. Explain that –ed is pronounced /ɪd/ when a verb ends in /t/ or /d/. Write examples on the board: *started, ended*.

- Point to the symbol /t/. Explain that the symbol means the sound of the letter t. Write examples on the board: *looked, jumped*.
- Point to the symbol /d/. Tell students that the symbol means the sound of the letter d. Explain that most often –ed is pronounced /d/. Write examples on the board: *hugged, closed*.
- Have students circle the verbs. Call on students to say answers. Correct as needed.
- 🎧 Play Track 55 while students listen and complete the task.
- Call on students to say answers. Correct as needed.

Grammar to Communicate 1

SIMPLE PAST: REGULAR VERBS

Subject	Verb + -ed		Time Expression
I / You / He	worked		last Saturday.
It	closed		last night.
We / They	moved	to Miami	last year.

Look
See page 262 for spelling rules with the Simple Past.

A Complete the sentences. Use the verbs in the box.

changed   ~~lived~~   moved   started   worked

1. In 1995 I __lived__ in **Los Angeles**.
2. In 1998 I __worked__ in **a restaurant**.
3. I __changed__ jobs **in 2003**.
4. I __moved__ to **Chicago in 2004**.
5. I __started__ **English class in 2005**.

move

PAIRS. Change the bold words in the sentences. Write true sentences about yourself on a piece of paper.
Answers will vary.

B 🎧 55 Circle the verb in each sentence. Then listen. What are the sounds of the verb endings? Check (✓) the correct column.

Look
Pronunciation of final -ed
listened   /d/
cooked   /t/
waited   /ɪd/

	/d/	/t/	/ɪd/
1. I (invited) friends home last month.	☐	☐	✓
2. I (exercised) the day before yesterday.	✓	☐	☐
3. I (washed) my hair last night.	☐	✓	☐
4. I (started) dinner at 6:00 last night.	☐	☐	✓
5. I (cooked) yesterday morning.	☐	✓	☐
6. I (called) my friend yesterday.	✓	☐	☐
7. I (watched) TV yesterday afternoon.	☐	✓	☐

Unit 14

Grammar Notes

1. The simple past tells about actions that happened before now. Use it to talk about actions that are finished.
2. Simple past verbs do not change forms (except for *was / were*) with subjects.
3. For most verbs, add *-ed* to the base form to make the simple past.
4. If a verb ends in *e*, then just add *–d*.
5. If a verb ends in a consonant + *y*, change *y* to *i*, and add *–ed*.
6. If a verb ends in a vowel + a consonant, double the consonant and add *–ed*.
7. For more information on this grammar topic, see page 258.

Center Stage 2

C **PAIRS.** Change the time expressions in the sentences in Exercise B. Make the sentences true about yourself. Write them on a piece of paper. Read your sentences to your partner.
Answers will vary.

Example:
                   last Saturday
I invited friends home ~~last month~~.

D Read about Vincent's activities every day. Rewrite the sentences to talk about his day yesterday.

Every day	Yesterday
1. Vincent works every day.	1. He worked yesterday.
2. He fixes computers.	2. He fixed computers yesterday.
3. He walks to the bus stop in the morning.	3. He walked to the bus stop in the morning yesterday.
4. He talks to his wife at lunchtime.	4. He talked to his wife at lunchtime yestereday.
5. He finishes work at 5:30.	5. He finished work at 5:30 yesterday.
6. He plays with his baby son after dinner.	6. He played with his baby son after dinner yesterday.
7. He listens to the radio at night.	7. He listened to the radio at night yesterday.

PAIRS. Now circle the activities above that you did yesterday. Tell your partner.
Answers will vary.

Example:
A: *I worked yesterday. How about you?*
B: *I worked yesterday, too. I also listened to the radio.*

TIME to TALK

PAIRS. When did you last do the things in the box? Tell your partner. If you don't remember, say "I don't remember." Answers will vary.

ask for directions	move
change jobs	play cards
clean your house	stay up late
cook	wash a car
invite someone to your house	watch a good movie
miss a bus	wait for a bus

miss the bus

Example:
A: *I waited for a bus yesterday. How about you?*
B: *Yesterday, I missed the bus, so I was late to school.*

Fact or Fiction? 167

C Teaching Time: 5–10 min.
- Read the example with the class.
- Have students complete the task. Walk around and help as needed.
- PAIRS. Have partners share their sentences.
- Call on students to say one sentence about something their partner did.

D Teaching Time: 5–10 min.
- Read the example with the class.
- Have students complete the task.
- Call on students to write sentences on the board. Write corrections on the board as needed.
- Have students circle what they did yesterday.
- PAIRS. Have partners tell each other their sentences.

Option
Assign Unit 14 Supplementary Grammar to Communicate 1 Exercises on the Teacher's Resource Disk as homework or on the Student Persistence CD-ROM as self-access practice.

TIME to TALK
Teaching Time: 10–15 min.
- Review past time expressions. Ask questions such as: *How do you say the week before this one?* (last week).
- If students don't remember the last time they did something, tell them they can say: *I don't remember when I* + simple past verb.
- PAIRS. Have students complete the task.
- Walk around and help as needed.
- Call on students to say one sentence about something their partner did.

Unit 14 T-167

Grammar to Communicate 2

Simple Past: Irregular Verbs
Teaching Time: 5–10 min.

- Have students study the chart and the Look Box.
- Say: *Some verbs are irregular. Don't add –ed to these verbs to make past forms.*
- Read each sentence in the chart and verb in the Look Box and have students repeat chorally.
- Say a base form of a verb and have a volunteer use it in a sentence in the simple past. For example: *Go; I went to the store last night.* Repeat with other verbs.

A   Teaching Time: 10–15 min.
- Read the example with the class.
- Have students complete the task.
- Call on students to say answers. Correct as needed.

Multilevel Strategy

- **Pre-level, At-level:** Pair pre-level students with at-level students to complete the task. Have pre-level students read the sentences in the right column and at-level students match them with the sentences in the left column.
- **Above-level:** Pair students and have them quiz each other on irregular verbs after they have completed the task.

Expansion Have students say the base form of each verb that is given in the simple past. For example: *get up / got up*, etc.

B   Teaching Time: 3–5 min.
- Read the examples with the class.
- Have students complete the task.
- Call on students to say answers. Correct as needed.

T-168   Center Stage 2

Grammar to Communicate 2

SIMPLE PAST: IRREGULAR VERBS

Subject	Verb		Time Expression
I / You / He	had	dinner	last week.
It	came		last night.
We / They	did	the dishes	yesterday.

Look
The past form for many verbs is irregular. It does not end in *–ed*.
come → came
do → did
go → went
have → had
read → read
run → ran
say → said

I went to the movies yesterday.
NOT I ~~goed~~ to the movies.

A Match the simple present sentences with the simple past sentences.

_d_ 1. Sara's late for work.
_c_ 2. Sara's boyfriend is angry with her.
_g_ 3. Max is looking for a taxi.
_e_ 4. Max doesn't have his cell phone.
_f_ 5. Max's boss is talking to him.
_i_ 6. Sara doesn't have her bag.
_a_ 7. Sara doesn't know the person on the phone.
_b_ 8. Max didn't sleep much last night.
_h_ 9. Max wasn't at work yesterday.

a. She <u>called</u> the wrong phone number.
b. He <u>drank</u> two cups of coffee after dinner.
c. She <u>forgot</u> his birthday.
d. She <u>got up</u> late.
e. He <u>left</u> his cell phone at home.
f. He <u>made</u> a big mistake at work yesterday.
g. He <u>missed</u> the bus.
h. He <u>spent</u> the day with a friend.
i. She <u>took</u> the wrong bag.

B Write the simple past of the verbs. Look at the underlined verbs in Exercise A for help. Then check (✓) the correct column.

	SIMPLE PAST	REGULAR	IRREGULAR
call	called	✓	
drink	drank		✓
forget	forgot		✓
get up	got up		✓
leave	left		✓
make	made		✓
miss	missed	✓	
spend	spent		✓
take	took		✓

spend time with your family

168   Unit 14

Grammar Notes
1. Some verbs have irregular forms in the simple past. Do not add *–ed* to these verbs.
2. For more information on this grammar topic, see page 258.

Option
- Before class, make flashcards with the present of an irregular verb on one side. Hold up cards randomly. Have students say the simple past form of the verb.
- Divide up cards among pairs of students. Have them take turns showing cards and saying the form. Have pairs switch card sets.

C Write true sentences about yourself. Complete the sentences with time expressions.
Answers will vary.
1. I wrote a letter _____.
2. I heard a funny story _____.
3. I woke up early _____.
4. I lost something _____.
5. I knew the answers _____.
6. I went to the bank _____.
7. I saw a friend _____.
8. I ate out _____.

Write the simple past form of these verbs.

write	wrote	wake	woke	know	knew	see	saw
eat	ate	hear	heard	lose	lost	go	went

D Some students did not do their homework. Below are the excuses or reasons they gave. Complete the sentences. Use the simple past form of the verbs.

1. The dog __ate__ my homework. (eat)
2. I __lost__ my book. (lose)
3. I __did__ the wrong page. (do)
4. I __read__ the wrong book. (read)
5. I __left__ my homework at home. (leave)
6. I __forgot__ about it. (forget)

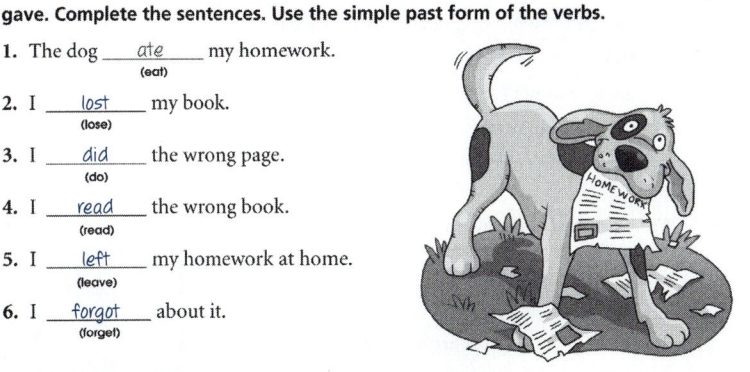

PAIRS. You are teachers. Which excuses do you believe?
Answers will vary.

TIME to TALK

PAIRS. Write short conversations for the questions in the box.
Student A: Ask one of the questions.
Student B: Answer with an excuse. Then change roles. Answers will vary.

Where are your books?	Why aren't you wearing your uniform?
Where is your homework?	Why isn't dinner ready?
Why are you late?	Why weren't you in class yesterday?

Example:
A: *Where are your books?*
B: *I left them on the bus.*

WRAP-UP. Now read one of your conversations for the class. Who has the best excuse?

Fact or Fiction?

C Teaching Time: 5–10 min.
- If necessary, review past time expressions. Ask questions such as: *What's the week before this week?* (last week)
- Have students complete the task.
- Call on students to say answers. Correct as needed.

D Teaching Time: 5–10 min.
- Read the example with the class.
- Have students complete the task.
- Call on students to say answers. Correct as needed.
- PAIRS. Have students decide which excuses they believe. Call on students to tell the class which excuses they believe. Ask other students if they agree.

Multilevel Strategy
- **At-level, Above-level:** When calling on students to share their opinions, challenge at-level and above-level students to give their reasons why they believe or don't believe the excuses.

Expansion Have a student pretend to be the teacher. Have other students stand in a line and say an excuse to the teacher. Have the "teacher" explain why or why not an excuse is believable. Rotate the teacher after three exchanges.

Option
Assign Unit 14 Supplementary Grammar to Communicate 2 Exercises on the Teacher's Resource Disk as homework or on the Student Persistence CD-ROM as self-access practice.

TIME to TALK

Teaching Time: 15–20 min.
- PAIRS. Have students write their conversations and practice reading them.
- Have students perform their conversations for the class.
- Conduct an informal vote. Have students raise their hands to vote for the best excuse.

Unit 14 T-169

Grammar to Communicate 3

Simple Past: Negative Statements

Teaching Time: 5–10 min.

- Review how to make negative sentences in the present. Write a few sample sentences on the board, such as: *I don't have time.*
- Say: *The simple past is very similar. Use* did not *and a verb. You can also use the contraction* didn't.
- Call on volunteers to change the sentence on the board to simple past (*I didn't have time*).
- Have students study the chart and the Look Box. Tell students not to add *-ed* to the verb in negative statements.
- Read each example in the chart and have students repeat chorally.

A Teaching Time: 3–5 min.

- Read the example with the class.
- Have students complete the task.
- Call on students to say answers. Correct as needed.

B Teaching Time: 5–10 min.

- Have students look at the picture. Tell students that the sentences in the exercise have some surprising facts.
- Read the example with the class.
- Have students complete the task.
- Call on students to say answers. Correct as needed.

Expansion Ask students if they know any surprising facts. Have students share them with the class.

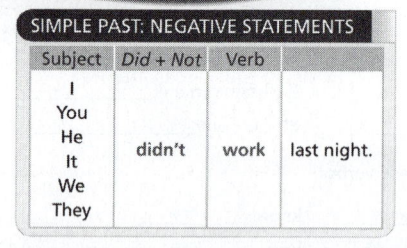

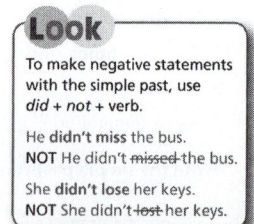

Grammar to Communicate 3

SIMPLE PAST: NEGATIVE STATEMENTS

Subject	Did + Not	Verb	
I / You / He / She / It / We / They	didn't	work	last night.

Look

To make negative statements with the simple past, use *did + not + verb*.

He **didn't miss** the bus.
NOT He didn't ~~missed~~ the bus.

She **didn't lose** her keys.
NOT She didn't ~~lost~~ her keys.

A Make each sentence true about yourself. Circle the affirmative or negative form of the verb. *Answers will vary.*

1. I ate / (**didn't eat**) breakfast at 3 A.M. yesterday.
2. I **stayed up** / **didn't stay up** all night last night.
3. I **got up** / **didn't get up** at 4:00 yesterday afternoon.
4. I **called** / **didn't call** ten people yesterday.
5. I **slept** / **didn't sleep** at work yesterday.

B Write a negative statement. Then write an affirmative statement.

1. Simon Ward ___didn't eat___ two hamburgers.
   (not / eat)
   He ___ate___ twenty hamburgers.
   (eat)

2. Sonya Keller ___didn't sleep___ for twelve hours.
   (not / sleep)
   She ___slept___ for two days.
   (sleep)

3. Bill Lau ___didn't drink___ fifteen glasses of water
   (not / drink)
   in two hours. He ___drank___ them in twenty minutes.
   (drink)

4. Anna Valdez ___didn't have___ seven sons. She ___had___ seventeen sons.
   (not / have)   (have)

5. Sharon Beck ___didn't study___ two languages. She ___studied___ twenty languages.
   (not / study)   (study)

6. Tony DePalma and John Banker ___didn't walk___ for two hours. They ___walked___
   (not / walk)   (walk)
   for two years.

Strange But True

Simon Ward eats 20 hamburgers!

Unit 14

Grammar Notes

1. Use *did not* + verb to make negative statements in the simple past.
2. *Did not* can be contracted as *didn't*.
3. Use *did not* or *didn't* for all subjects. The form doesn't change.
4. For more information on this grammar topic, see page 258.

Watch Out!

Exercise B. Students frequently make the mistake of using *did not* or *didn't* + a simple past verb. Listen for and correct errors such as *I didn't made*.

Center Stage 2

C Complete the story. Use the correct form of the verbs.

In May of 1990 I __spent__ a week on an island in Greece. I
1. (spend)

__went__ with a Greek friend.
2. (go)

The first night we __were__
3. (be)

tired, so we __didn't stay__ late. We __went__ to bed at about 10:00. At about 1 A.M.
4. (not / stay up)   5. (go)

I __heard__ a noise and __woke up__. My friend __didn't hear__ anything and
6. (hear)   7. (wake up)   8. (not / hear)

she __didn't wake up__. I woke her up and I __asked__ her, "What's that noise?" She
9. (not / wake up)   10. (ask)

__answered__, "I don't know. But don't worry. Nothing happens on this island." Then she
11. (answer)

__went__ back to sleep. All night I __listened__ to the noise. I __didn't sleep__.
12. (go)   13. (listen)   14. (not / sleep)

At 5 A.M. my friend __got up__ and __said__, "I know—that noise is a donkey!
15. (get up)   16. (say)

On May 1st, kids here put donkeys on people's roofs. It's a tradition". I __didn't believe__ her at
17. (not / believe)

first, but then we __went__ outside, and there __was__ a donkey on the roof!
18. (go)   19. (be)

TIME to TALK

ON YOUR OWN. Write a story on a piece of paper. Start the story with a sentence from the box. Talk about what happened next. Make as many negative statements as you can. Answers will vary.

I drank two cups of coffee after dinner.	I lost my wallet.
I forgot my keys.	I made a mistake at work.
I forgot my wife's/husband's birthday.	I missed the bus.
I heard a strange noise.	My dog got out of the house and ran away.

PAIRS. Tell your story to your partner.

Example:
A: I drank two cups of coffee after dinner, so I didn't sleep well. I didn't hear my alarm clock in the morning, so I didn't wake up on time. I was late, so I didn't . . .

Fact or Fiction?

C Teaching Time: 10–15 min.

- Read the example with the class. Ask: *When was this story?* (1990). Say: *Nineteen-ninety was before now, so use the simple past.*
- Have students complete the task.
- Call on students to take turns reading the completed story to the class. Correct as needed.

Expansion

- For homework, have students find interesting facts in books or on the Internet.
- During the next class have students read their facts and vote for the one they find most interesting.

Option

Assign Unit 14 Supplementary Grammar to Communicate 3 Exercises on the Teacher's Resource Disk as homework or on the Student Persistence CD-ROM as self-access practice.

TIME to TALK

Teaching Time: 15–20 min.

- Read the example with the class.
- Tell students to talk about their story first and make a list of ideas. Then tell them to decide which ideas to use and write the story.
- PAIRS. Have students complete the task.
- Walk around and help as needed.
- Call on students to read their stories aloud.

Multilevel Strategy

- **Pre-level:** Have students use the sentences found in the box.
- **At-level:** Encourage students to write one original sentence not found in the box.
- **Above-level:** Have students write original sentences not found in the box.

Review and Challenge

Grammar

Teaching Time: 5–10 min.

- Read the example with the class.
- Have students complete the task.
- Call on students to read the corrected sentences.

> **Multilevel Strategy**
>
> - **Pre-level:** Tell students what the mistakes are and have them rewrite the sentences.

Dictation

Teaching Time: 5–10 min.

- 🎧 Play Track 56 while students listen and write what they hear.
- 🎧 Play Track 56 again while students check their answers.
- Call on students to write answers on the board.
- 🎧 Play Track 56 again and correct the sentences on the board.

> **Multilevel Strategy**
>
> - **Pre-level:** Give students a worksheet with some of the words from the dictation already provided.

Speaking

Teaching Time: 10–15 min.

- Read the example with the class.
- Give students a few minutes to decide which story to tell.
- GROUPS. Have students complete the task. Walk around and help as needed.
- Call on students to tell the class the group's best story.

> **Multilevel Strategy**
>
> - **Pre-level:** Have students practice telling the story only on pages 164–165 to a partner and listen to other students' stories.

T-172 Center Stage 2

Review and Challenge

Grammar

Find the mistake in each sentence. Circle the letter. Then correct the mistake.

1. I <u>change</u> jobs <u>last</u> month.
   A (B) C
   Correct: _I changed jobs last month._

2. They <u>goed</u> to a restaurant and <u>ate</u>.
   A (B) C
   Correct: _They went to a restaurant and ate._

3. We <u>not</u> <u>see</u> them <u>last</u> night.
   (A) B C
   Correct: _We didn't see them last night._

4. He didn't <u>stayed</u> here yesterday.
   A B (C)
   Correct: _He didn't stay here yesterday._

5. You <u>didn't</u> <u>did</u> the dishes <u>yesterday</u>.
   A (B) C
   Correct: _You didn't do the dishes yesterday._

6. She <u>didn't</u> <u>works</u> yesterday.
   A (B) C
   Correct: _She didn't work yesterday._

Dictation

🎧 56 Listen. You will hear five sentences. Write them on a piece of paper. *See the audioscript on page 287 for the sentences.*

Speaking

GROUPS. 1. Look at pages 164–165. With a partner, practice telling the story.
2. Now choose an experience from the box. Tell your group a true story.
Answers will vary.

| a funny experience | a scary experience |
| a happy experience | a strange experience |

Example:
A: *I had a funny experience two years ago. It was early in the morning. I got in my car to drive to work. I started the car, but then I heard a funny noise. I stopped the car. I looked in the engine. There was a cat in the engine!*

WRAP-UP. Now choose the best story in the group and tell the class.

172 Unit 14

Listening

A 🎵 57 Listen to the radio report. Check (✓) the news you hear.

☐ international news ☑ funny news ☐ important news

B 🎵 58 Listen again. Read the sentences. For each sentence, write *T* (true) or *F* (false).

Story 1
- _T_ 1. A woman took a day off because she wanted to meet the U.S. president.
- _F_ 2. Her boss wrote a note for her.
- _T_ 3. The president signed her excuse note.

Story 2
- _F_ 1. The little boy didn't want to go to school.
- _F_ 2. The police officer was late for work.
- _T_ 3. The driver of the car was seven years old.

TIME to TALK

PAIRS. Put the pictures in order. Write *1* for the first event that happened, *2* for the second event, and *3* for the last event. Then tell your partner the story. Answers will vary. Possible order:

_2_ a. _3_ b. _1_ c.

GROUPS. Now tell your story to a group. Does everyone have the same story?

Fact or Fiction? 173

Listening

A Teaching Time: 5–10 min.

- **Warm-up:** Ask students where they can find out about news (radio, TV, newspapers, Internet). Tell students they are going to listen to a news story from a radio report.
- Ask students to read through the answer choices before they listen.
- 🎧 Play Track 57 while students listen.
- 🎧 Play Track 57 again while students listen and complete the task.
- Call on a student to say the answer. Correct as needed.

B Teaching Time: 5–10 min.

- Ask students to read through the sentences before they listen.
- 🎧 Play Track 58 while students listen and complete the task.
- Call on students to say answers. Correct as needed.

Multilevel Strategy

- **Pre-level:** Tell students there are three false sentences.
- **At-level, Above-level:** When checking answers, challenge students to correct false statements.

Option

Assign Unit 14 Supplementary Review and Challenge Exercises on the Teacher's Resource Disk as homework or on the Student Persistence CD-ROM as self-access practice.

TIME to TALK

Teaching Time: 10–15 min.

- Have students choose an order for the pictures. Tell them that they can use the pictures in any order they want.
- Walk around and help as needed.
- PAIRS. Have students tell each other their stories.
- Have students take turns telling their stories to the class.

Expansion After students tell their stories to the class, have students vote for the most creative and / or their favorite one.

Unit 14 T-173

Reading and Writing

Reading

A **Teaching Time: 10–15 min.**

- Point to the police report. Explain to students that a police report is a form that a police officer fills out when he or she investigates a crime. It is an official document that tells what happened.
- Have students read the report silently. Then read it aloud. Pause after each few words and have students repeat chorally.
- Have students choose the correct answer.
- Call on a student to say the answer. Correct as needed.

B **Teaching Time: 5–10 min.**

- Ask students to identify any unfamiliar vocabulary on the form. Explain unknown words, for example: *A witness is a person who sees a crime. When police investigate a person to see if he or she committed a crime, the person is called a suspect. An incident is an event, or something that happened.*
- Have students complete the task.
- Call on students to say answers. Correct as needed.

Expansion

- Ask students what number they would call if someone robbed their house (911).
- If necessary, explain that people call 911 when there is an emergency. Ask students to give examples of emergencies. (Possible answers: health emergencies, like a heart attack; a stranger in your house; a fire.)
- Explain that when you call 911, you have to explain what the emergency is and say where you are.
- **LIFE SKILLS TEST PREP 2** Go to Unit 10, Lesson 2 for practice in learning how to report an emergency.

Reading and Writing

Reading

A Read the police report in Exercise B. What happened? Circle the correct answer.

1. Somebody stole things from an office.
2. Somebody stole things from a person on the street.
3. Somebody stole things from an apartment.

steal / stole

B Read the report again. Then complete the missing information.

CITY OF CHANDLER POLICE
Stolen Property Report

Date of incident: May 30, 2006
Witness's name(s): Wendy and Harry Chen
Witness's address: 15 Linwood Ave., #4A, Chandler, TX
Witness's phone number: 111-987-5236

Description of suspect: Include hair color, eye color, race, weight, height, clothing, etc. He was a white man with black hair, about 6 feet tall. He had on jeans and an orange shirt.

Description of incident:
On May 30, 2006, at 9:30 P.M my neighbors, Wendy and Harry Chen, heard a loud noise in my apartment. I was at work, so they called the police. Then they watched my apartment door. They saw a man at the door of my apartment. He was white and had black hair. He was about 6 feet tall. He had on jeans and an orange shirt. He ran away with my TV and a large bag. When I got home at 10:00 P.M., the Chens went with me into my apartment. The kitchen window was broken, and the apartment was a mess. The burglar took my Sovy 14 inch TV, $300 in cash, and two gold rings.

Stolen items: What did the suspect take? If you don't know, write "?"

Description	Make	Model	Serial #	Value
14 inch TV	Sovy	?	?	$200
cash				$300
2 gold rings	?	?		?

Unit 14

Culture Note

- **Exercise B.** Remind students that in the United States people measure height in feet and inches. There are 12 inches in 1 foot. One foot is equal to approximately 30 centimeters.
- **LIFE SKILLS TEST PREP 2** Go to Unit 7, Lesson 2 for more practice in understanding the American system of measuring dimensions.

T-174 Center Stage 2

Prewriting

GROUPS. Talk about crimes. Ask and answer these questions with your group: Answers will vary.

- What crimes have happened to you or people you know?
- What other local crimes have you read or heard about?
- When and where did the crime happen?
- What exactly happened?

Take notes during your discussion. Write on a piece of paper.

Writing Tip

We sometimes use the word *when* to show the time relationship between two ideas in a sentence.

Example:
When I got home at 10 P.M., the Chens heard me.
(I got home at 10 P.M. At that time, the Chens heard me.)

Writing

Complete the police report. You can write about a true crime from your group discussion, or an imaginary one. Use the police report on page 174 as a model. Answers will vary.

CITY OF CHANDLER POLICE
— Stolen Property Report —

Date of incident: _____
Witness's name(s): _____
Witness's address: _____
Witness's phone number: _____
Description of suspect: Include hair color, eye color, race, weight, height, clothing, etc. _____
_____
_____
Description of incident: _____
_____
_____
_____
_____
_____
_____
_____
Stolen items: What did the suspect take? If you don't know, write "?".
Description | Make | Model | Serial # | Value

Fact or Fiction? 175

Option

Before class, find and cut out several descriptions of crimes from the police blotter of the local newspaper. If students have difficulty thinking of an incident to write about, have them use one of these descriptions as a basis for their writing.

Prewriting

Teaching Time: 10–15 min.

- GROUPS. Have students discuss the questions.
- Draw the following graphic organizer on the board.

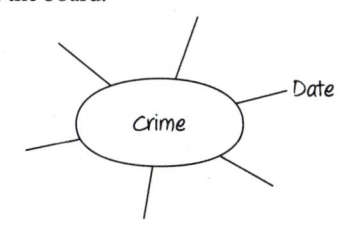

[graphic organizer: "Crime" in center with lines radiating out, one labeled "Date"]

- Have students look again at the description of the incident on page 174. Ask: *What information is in the police report?* Record students' answers on the graphic organizer.
- Have students make graphic organizers with the information from their incidents. Walk around and help as needed.

Writing

Teaching Time: 15–20 min.

- Have students study the Writing Tip. Tell them *when* replaces the words *at the time(s) that*. For example: *When we got to the party, everyone was leaving. We got to the party at the time that everyone was leaving.*
- Tell students to use their graphic organizers to write about the crime.
- Walk around and help as needed.
- PAIRS. Have students compare their forms.

Multilevel Strategy

- **Pre-level:** While students are completing the prewriting task, copy the incident description from page 174 on the board. Underline the information that students should substitute in their descriptions. Have students copy the description and substitute the underlined parts with information from Prewriting.

Unit 14 T-175

Unit 15
Life Stages

Learning Goals
- Learn words to describe life stages
- Learn about simple past: *yes / no* questions; information questions; information questions with *Who* and *What* as subject; and *How long ago / How long*
- Listen to a conversation and an interview about a famous person
- Read and write a short biography
- Talk about life stages

Learner Persistence
Students may find it difficult to reach their educational goal if their other basic needs aren't met first. Provide students with information on basic community resources and services, for example, those that provide food, clothing, medical care, emotional services, etc.

Warm-up
Teaching Time: 3–5 min.

Tell students that a life stage is an important time in a person's life. Ask students to list some important life stages. Record students' answers on the board.

Vocabulary
Teaching Time: 15–20 min.

- 🎧 Play Track 2 while students read and listen.
- Read the words and phrases aloud and have students repeat chorally.
- Have students complete the task.
- Call on students to say a life stage that happens to most people in their country.

Expansion
- PAIRS. Have students discuss and write what some of the life stages shown on the pictures mean and what steps a person needs to follow in order to reach them. For example: *When you become a citizen, you can vote. You need to take a test to become a citizen.*

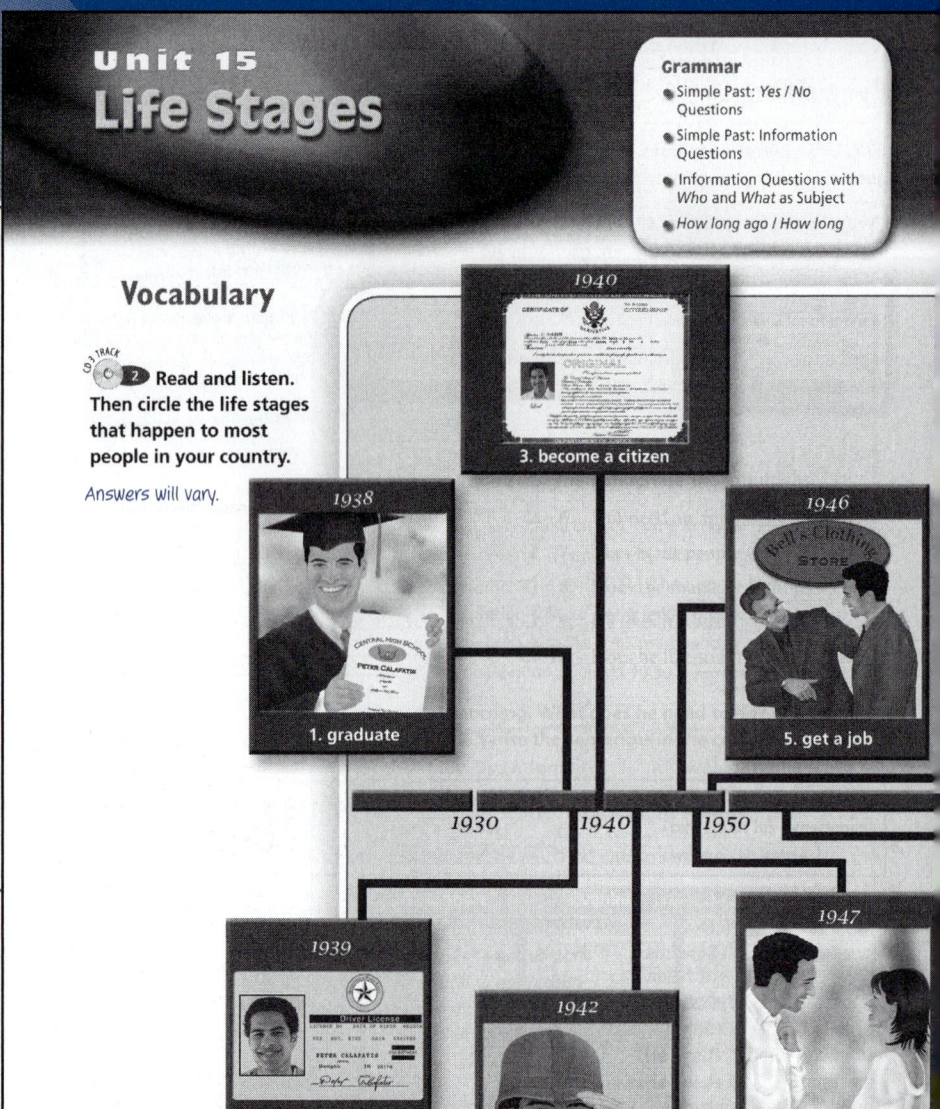

Unit 15
Life Stages

Grammar
- Simple Past: *Yes / No* Questions
- Simple Past: Information Questions
- Information Questions with *Who* and *What* as Subject
- *How long ago / How long*

Vocabulary

🎧 **TRACK 2** Read and listen. Then circle the life stages that happen to most people in your country.

Answers will vary.

1. graduate (1938)
2. get a driver's license (1939)
3. become a citizen (1940)
4. be in the military (1942)
5. get a job (1946)
6. meet (1947)

176 Unit 15

- Walk around and help as needed.
- Call on pairs to present their ideas to the class.

Multilevel Strategy
- **Pre-level:** Have students make a list of words or phrases for two life stages of their choice. Walk around and offer necessary vocabulary if needed.
- **At-level, Above-level:** Have students write two complete sentences for each life stage. Walk around and offer necessary vocabulary if needed.

T-176 Center Stage 2

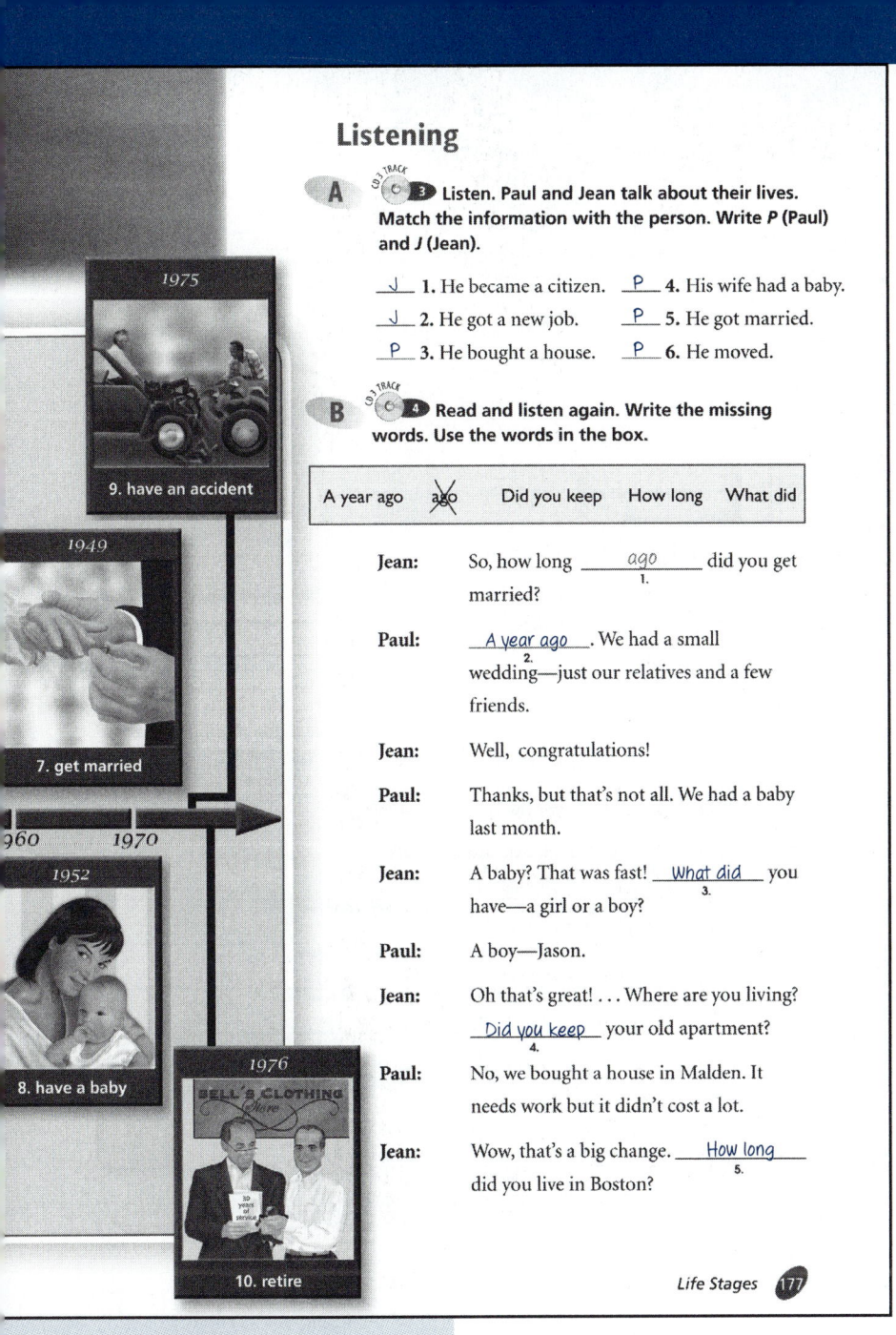

Listening

A Listen. Paul and Jean talk about their lives. Match the information with the person. Write *P* (Paul) and *J* (Jean).

_J_ 1. He became a citizen.   _P_ 4. His wife had a baby.
_J_ 2. He got a new job.   _P_ 5. He got married.
_P_ 3. He bought a house.   _P_ 6. He moved.

B Read and listen again. Write the missing words. Use the words in the box.

| A year ago | ~~ago~~ | Did you keep | How long | What did |

Jean: So, how long ___ago___ did you get married?
                         1.

Paul: _A year ago_. We had a small
              2.
wedding—just our relatives and a few friends.

Jean: Well, congratulations!

Paul: Thanks, but that's not all. We had a baby last month.

Jean: A baby? That was fast! _What did_ you
                                      3.
have—a girl or a boy?

Paul: A boy—Jason.

Jean: Oh that's great! ... Where are you living?
Did you keep your old apartment?
       4.

Paul: No, we bought a house in Malden. It needs work but it didn't cost a lot.

Jean: Wow, that's a big change. _How long_
                                          5.
did you live in Boston?

Life Stages   177

7. get married
8. have a baby
9. have an accident
10. retire

Listening

A Teaching Time: 10–15 min.

- **Warm-up:** Have students study the timeline on pages 176–177. Ask questions about the man's life stages. For example, ask: *When did he get married?*
- Ask students to read through the answer choices before they listen.
- 🎧 Play Track 3 while students listen.
- 🎧 Play Track 3 again while students listen and complete the task.
- 🎧 Play Track 3 again while students check their answers. Pause the recording each time an answer is given.

B Teaching Time: 15–20 min.

- Ask students to read through the answer choices before they listen.
- 🎧 Play Track 4 while students listen and complete the task.
- 🎧 Play Track 4 again while students check their answers.
- Call on students to say answers. Correct as needed.
- Read the conversation aloud. Pause after each few words and have students repeat chorally.
- PAIRS. Ask students to role-play the conversation.
- **LIFE SKILLS TEST PREP 2** Go to Unit 2, Lesson 5 for more practice in giving and receiving sympathy and congratulations.

Multilevel Strategy

- **Pre-level:** Have students role-play the completed conversation.
- **At-level, Above-level:** Have students role-play a new conversation about their own life stages. Tell students to use the conversation in the book as a model. Ask pairs to role-play in front of the class.

Culture Note

Exercise B. Read the second sentence in Paul's second line (*We had a baby last month.*). Tell students that in the United States, both men and women say *We're having* (or *We had*) *a baby.*

Option

Assign Unit 15 Supplementary Vocabulary Exercise on the Teacher's Resource Disk as homework or on the Student Persistence CD-ROM as self-access practice.

Unit 15   T-177

Grammar to Communicate 1

Simple Past: Yes / No Questions

Teaching Time: 5–10 min.

- Review *yes / no* questions in the simple present. Write on the board: *Do I talk a lot?*
- Tell students: *yes / no questions in the simple past are very similar.*
- Point to the question. Say: *Do is simple present. For the simple past, use* Did. Write: *Did I talk a lot yesterday?*
- Say: *Short answers are similar. Use* did *for the simple past.* Write: *Yes, you did.* and *No, you didn't.*
- Have students study the chart.
- Read the questions and answers in the chart and have students repeat chorally.
- Ask students *yes / no* questions and have them answer with short answers.

A Teaching Time: 5–10 min.

- Read the example with the class.
- Have students study the Look Box.
- Say: *Only use* go to *when you talk about traveling to a place. Do not use* to *when you talk about an activity. For example: They went to the lake. They went fishing there.*
- Have students complete the task.
- PAIRS. Have students ask and answer the questions. Walk around and help as needed.

B Teaching Time: 10–15 min.

- Read the examples with the class.
- Have students complete the task.
- Call on students to say answers. Correct as needed.

Multilevel Strategy

- **Pre-level, At-level:** Have at-level students help pre-level students with the task. After checking answers, have pairs take turns asking and answering the questions.
- **Above-level:** After checking answers, pair students and have them ask questions about what their partner did last summer. For example:
  A: *Did you go on vacation last summer?*
  B: *Yes, I did.*

Grammar to Communicate 1

SIMPLE PAST: YES / NO QUESTIONS

Did	Subject	Verb		Short Answers
Did	I / you / he / we / they	live	there a long time?	Yes, I / you / he / we / they did. No, I / you / he / we / they didn't.

Look
Did you **go fishing** a lot? See page 265 for a list of other expressions with *go + verb + -ing*

A Answer the questions with true information. Use short answers.

When you were a child . . .

1. . . . did you live in a big city? <u>Yes, I did. OR No, I didn't.</u>
2. . . . did you walk to school? <u>Yes, I did. OR No, I didn't.</u>
3. . . . did you go swimming a lot? <u>Yes, I did. OR No, I didn't.</u>
4. . . . did your mother have a job? <u>Yes, she did. OR No, she didn't.</u>
5. . . . did your grandparents live with you? <u>Yes, they did. OR No, they didn't.</u>
6. . . . did you and your family go fishing? <u>Yes, we did. OR No, we didn't.</u>

PAIRS. Ask and answer the questions above.

B Complete the conversations. Use *did* or *didn't*.

1. A: <u>Did Lynn read a lot last summer?</u>
   (Lynn / read / a lot last summer)
   B: <u>Yes, she did. She read Harry Potter books.</u>
   (yes / she / read / Harry Potter books)

2. A: <u>Did Robert go fishing with his father last year?</u>
   (Robert / go fishing / with his father last year)
   B: <u>No, he didn't. He went with his uncle.</u>
   (no / he / go / with his uncle)

3. A: <u>Did Karen have a full-time job last year?</u>
   (Karen / have / a full-time job last year)
   B: <u>No, she didn't. She had a part-time job.</u>
   (no / she / have / a part-time job)

4. A: <u>Did Jason go swimming at the beach yesterday?</u>
   (Jason / go swimming / at the beach yesterday)
   B: <u>No, he didn't. He visited his grandparents.</u>
   (no / he / visit / his grandparents)

Unit 15

Grammar Notes

1. Use *did* + subject + base form of a verb to make *yes / no* questions in the simple past. Form questions with regular and irregular verbs this way.
2. Do not make contractions with *did* in short answers with *yes*.
3. Make the contraction *didn't* or use the full form *did not* in short answers with *no*.
4. Use *did* and *didn't* with all subjects.
5. For more information on this grammar topic, see page 259.

Center Stage 2

C Complete the questions. Use *was*, *were*, or *did*.

Look
Do not use *did* in questions with the verb *be*. Use *was* or *were*.
Were you a good student?
Yes, I was. / No, I wasn't.
Did you like school?
Yes, I did. / No, I didn't.

1. **Were** you a happy child?
2. **Did** you spend a lot of time with your cousins?
3. **Were** you tall for your age?
4. **Did** you have a best friend?
5. **Were** you friendly with your neighbors?
6. **Did** you take care of a younger brother or sister?
7. **Did** you do a lot of housework?
8. **Were** you a serious child?

PAIRS. Ask and answer the questions above.

TIME to TALK

GROUPS. Ask and answer five questions about your childhood. Use the words in the boxes or your own ideas. *Answers will vary.*

When you were a child, did you ...?
get up early every day	have lunch at home
go bowling	live on a farm
have a pet	spend a lot of time with relatives

Were you ...?
curious	friendly	lonely	noisy
cute	funny	neat	shy

WRAP-UP. Now tell the class about your partner.

Example:
A: When he was a child, Manuel lived on a farm. He got up early every day. He was a friendly boy ...

Life Stages 179

C Teaching Time: 10–15 min.
- Have students study the Look Box. Review with students how to make simple past yes / no questions with *be* (*Was / Were* + subject). Say: *Do not use* did *in questions or answers with* be.
- Read the examples with the class. Tell students to look at the sentences in the exercise for clues. Say: *If there is a verb other than* be, *use* did.
- Have students complete the task.
- Call on students to say answers. Correct as needed.
- PAIRS. Have students ask and answer the questions.

Watch Out!

Exercise B. Students often make the mistake of using a simple past verb in questions with *did*. Listen for and correct errors such as *Did they went?*

Option

Assign Unit 15 Supplementary Grammar to Communicate 1 Exercises on the Teacher's Resource Disk as homework or on the Student Persistence CD-ROM as self-access practice.

TIME to TALK

Teaching Time: 10–15 min.
- Model a few questions by asking them to individual students. For example, ask: *When you were a child, did you live on a farm?*
- Read the example with the class.
- Have students complete the activity.
- Call on volunteers to tell the class about their partners.

Unit 15   T-179

Grammar to Communicate 2

Simple Past: Information Questions; Information Questions with *What* and *Who* as Subject

Teaching Time: 5–10 min.

- Review the meaning of the *wh*-words with the students.
- Say: *Use a wh-word before* did *to make information questions in the simple past.*
- Have students study the first chart.
- Read the questions and answers in the chart and have students repeat chorally.
- Ask students a few information questions and have them answer.
- Say: *Information questions can also ask about a subject. Use* What *or* Who *and a simple past verb. Don't use* did *in these questions.*
- Have students study the second chart.
- Read the questions and answers in the chart and have students repeat chorally.

A Teaching Time: 5–10 min.

- Read the example with the class. Tell students to use the clues in parentheses to help them choose the correct *wh*-word. Say: *Atlanta* is a place, so the correct *wh*-word is *where*.
- Have students complete the task.
- Call on students to say answers. Correct as needed.
- PAIRS. Have students ask and answer the questions.
- Call on students to say a sentence about their partner's experiences with learning how to drive.

B Teaching Time: 10–15 min.

- Read the example with the class.
- Call on students to come to the board and write the questions. Correct as needed.

Grammar to Communicate 2

SIMPLE PAST: INFORMATION QUESTIONS

Wh- Word	Did	Subject	Verb		Answers
What	did	I	buy?		A car.
Where		you			At Jake's Cars.
When		they	get	the car?	In October.
Why		she			For work.

INFORMATION QUESTIONS WITH *WHAT* AND *WHO* AS SUBJECT

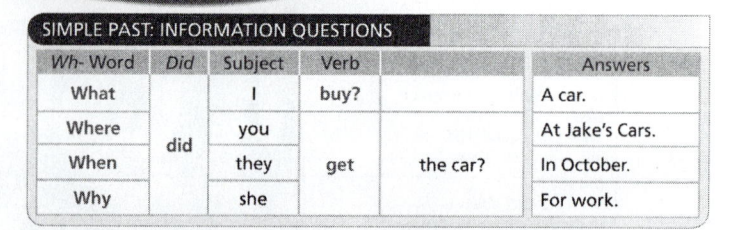

Wh- Word	Verb		Answers
What	happened?		We had an accident.
Who	called	the police?	My friend did.

A Complete the questions. Use *Where, When, Who, How,* or *How old.*

1. __Where__ did you drive the first time? (In Atlanta.)
2. __Who__ taught you to drive? (My father.)
3. __How__ did you feel? (I was scared.)
4. __How old__ were you? (I was 18.)
5. __When__ did you get your license? (In 1999.)

PAIRS. Talk to someone who has a driver's license. Ask the questions above.

B Write questions about your first day at school. Put the words in the correct order.

1. When did you start school for the first time?
   (you / When / start / did / for the first time / school)
2. Who took you to school?
   (school / took / Who / you / to)
3. How did you feel?
   (feel / did / you / How)
4. What was your teacher's name?
   (name / was / What / teacher's / your)
5. Who were your classmates?
   (classmates / were / Who / your)

Unit 15

Multilevel Strategy

- **At-level, Above-level:** Call on only at-level and above-level students to write the questions on the board. After completing the task, call on at-level and above-level students to answer the questions with true information.
- **Pre-level:** Have students copy the questions from the board.

Grammar Notes

1. To make information questions in the simple past, use a *wh*-word before *did*.
2. Use *What* or *Who* and a simple past verb to ask questions about a subject. For example: *What made that noise? Who said that?*
3. For more information on this grammar topic, see page 259.

Center Stage 2

C Read the answers. Then write questions about the underlined words. Use *What, Where, When, Who, Why, How much,* or *How old*.

1. Where did Loretta get her first job?
   Loretta got a job in a café. Her sister worked there, too.
2. When did Loretta get the job?
   Loretta got the job in 1992.
3. What did she do at the café?
   She made coffee and sandwiches at the café.
4. How old was she?
   She was 16.
5. Why did she get a job?
   She got a job because she needed the extra money.
6. Where was the café?
   The café was near her home.
7. Who did she meet at the café?
   She met her boyfriend at the café.
8. When did she leave the café?
   She left the café in 1995.

TIME to TALK

PAIRS. Talk about the first time you did something. Ask and answer questions. Use the ideas in the box or your own ideas. Answers will vary.

| bought your first car | got your first job | moved away from home |
| flew on an airplane | met your husband/wife | spoke English for the first time |

Example:
A: I got my first job in a restaurant when I was 15.
B: What did you do there?

Life Stages 181

C Teaching Time: 5–10 min.

- Read the example with the class. Tell students to read the answers to help them guess what *wh*-words to use.
- Have students complete the task.
- Call on students to write questions on the board. Write corrections on the board as needed.

Multilevel Strategy

- **Pre-level:** Provide students with the appropriate *wh*-word or phrase for each item: (2) *When*; (3) *What*; (4) *How old*; (5) *Why*; (6) *Where*; (7) *Who*; and (8) *When*.

Option
Assign Unit 15 Supplementary Grammar to Communicate 2 Exercises on the Teacher's Resource Disk as homework or on the Student Persistence CD-ROM as self-access practice.

TIME to TALK

Teaching Time: 15–20 min.

- Have two students read the example.
- Brainstorm possible questions for each idea in the box with the students. Write the questions on the board.
- PAIRS. Have students complete the activity.
- Walk around and help as needed.
- Ask students to share with the class some information they learned about their partner.

Unit 15   T-181

Grammar to Communicate 3

How long ago / How long: Information Questions

Teaching Time: 10–15 min.

- Draw the following graphic organizer on the board, filling in the current year for the last date.

Lydia moved to Lima.	Lydia moved to Miami.	Lydia moved to Lisbon.	Lydia moved to Hong Kong.
2000	2003	2006	20___.

- Point to the first sentence and date. Say: *Lydia moved to Lima [X] years before now.* Write on the board: *Lydia moved to Lima [X] years ago.* Tell students that *ago* means *before now*.
- Say: *To find out when something in the past happened, use:* How long ago. Ask: *How long ago did Lydia move to Lisbon?*
- Point to the first two dates. Write on the board: *Lydia lived in Lima for three years.* Tell students: *Use* for *to talk about a period of time*.
- Say: *To ask about a period of time ask:* How long. Ask: *How long did Lydia live in Lisbon?*
- Have students study the chart and the Look Box.
- Say: *Ago means before now.* Write on the board and read: *We left a few minutes ago. = We left a few minutes before now.* Use *ago* with a period of time, not a specific time. For example: *They bought it two years ago.* Not: *They bought it in 2004 ago.*
- Copy the Look Box on the board. Point to *Tuesday* in the Look Box. Say: *Today is Tuesday. Sunday was two days ago.* Say: *It rained on Sunday and Monday. It rained for two days.*
- Read each question and answer in the chart and have students repeat chorally.

A Teaching Time: 5–10 min.

- Read the example with the class.
- Have students complete the task.
- Call on students to say answers. Correct as needed.

B Teaching Time: 10–15 min.

- Read the examples with the class. Remind students to use *for* to talk about a period of time and *ago* to say how much time before now.
- Have students complete the task.
- Call on students to say answers. Correct as needed.
- PAIRS. Have students tell their partners three sentences about important events in their lives.
- Ask volunteers to say a sentence about one event in their partner's life.

Grammar to Communicate 3

HOW LONG AGO / HOW LONG: INFORMATION QUESTIONS

How Long Ago	Did			Time Expression	Ago
How long ago	did	you meet?	We met	ten years / five days / two minutes	ago.

How Long	Did			For	Time Expression
How long	did	they stay?	They stayed	for	ten years. / five days. / two minutes.

A Complete the sentences with *for* or *ago*.

1. Linda was a high school student twenty years __ago__.
2. She was married fifteen years __ago__.
3. Linda studied at a university __for__ four years.
4. Linda took English classes in her country __for__ a year.
5. Linda became a citizen a year __ago__.
6. Linda didn't have a car a few years __ago__.
7. Linda didn't stay at her first job __for__ a long time.

Look
Two days ago   For two days   Now
Sunday   Monday   Tuesday

becoming a citizen

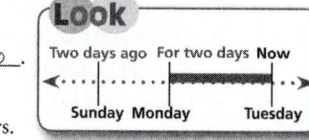

B Change the underlined words in the sentences. Use *for* or *ago*.

1. Tran was born <u>in 1970</u>.   __Tran was born (X) years ago.__
2. He lived in Vietnam <u>from 1970 to 1985</u>.   __He lived in Vietnam for fifteen years.__
3. He graduated from college <u>in 1995</u>.   __He graduated from college (X) years ago.__
4. He worked in an office <u>from 1997 to 1998</u>.   __He worked in an office for one year.__
5. He got married <u>in 1999</u>.   __He got married (X) years ago.__
6. He became a father <u>in 2001</u>.   __He became a father (X) years ago.__

PAIRS. Now talk about three important events in your life. Use *for* or *ago*.
Example: Answers will vary.
A: *I lived in Cuba for ten years.*

Unit 15

Grammar Notes

1. *How long ago* means *how much time before now*.
2. Answer a question that asks *how long ago* with a time expression + *ago*.
3. Use *ago* in short answers. For example: *How long ago did they eat? They ate an hour ago.*
4. Use *how long* to ask about a period of time.
5. Answer a question that asks *how long* with *for* + a time expression.
6. Include *for* in short answers. For example: *How long did you wait? For two hours.*
7. For more information on this grammar topic, see page 259.

Center Stage 2

C Read about Arnold Schwarzenegger's life. Write questions. Then answer the questions.

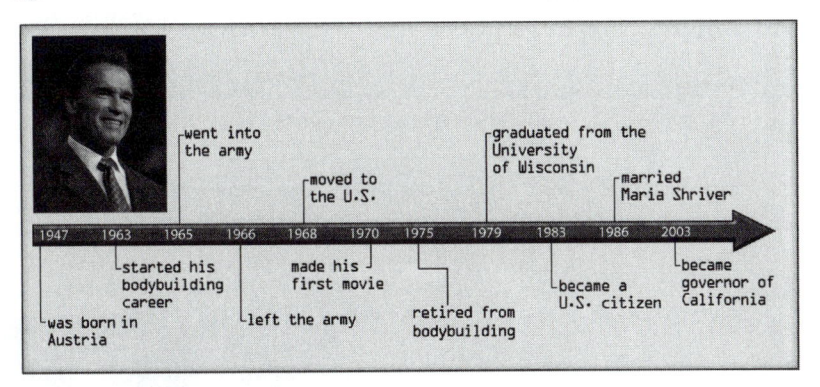

Timeline:
- 1947 — was born in Austria
- 1963 — started his bodybuilding career
- 1965 — went into the army
- 1966 — left the army
- 1968 — made his first movie
- 1970 — moved to the U.S.
- 1975 — retired from bodybuilding
- 1979 — graduated from the University of Wisconsin
- 1983 — became a U.S. citizen
- 1986 — married Maria Shriver
- 2003 — became governor of California

1. How long did Arnold Schwarzenegger live in Austria? — For twenty-one years.
   (How long / Arnold Schwarzenegger / live / in Austria)
2. How long ago did he move to the United States? — (X) years ago.
   (How long ago / he / move / to the United States)
3. How long ago did he graduate from college? — (X) years ago.
   (How long ago / he / graduate from college)
4. How long was he in the army in Austria? — For one year.
   (How long / was / he / in the army in Austria)
5. How long ago did he get married? — (X) years ago.
   (How long ago / he / get married)
6. How long did he work as a bodybuilder? — For twelve years.
   (How long / he / work / as a bodybuilder)
7. How long ago did he become governor of California? — (X) years ago.
   (How long ago / he / become / governor of California)

TIME to TALK

ON YOUR OWN. Draw a timeline for your life. Use the timeline in Exercise C as a model. Use the ideas in the box or your own ideas. *Answers will vary.*

became a U.S. citizen	got a green card	moved to a new place
bought a car	got a job	started English classes
bought a house	got married	was in the military
came to the United States	had a child	went to school

PAIRS. Now exchange timelines with your partner. Ask and answer questions with *How long* and *How long ago*.

Life Stages 183

Option

Assign Unit 15 Supplementary Grammar to Communicate 3 Exercises on the Teacher's Resource Disk as homework or on the Student Persistence CD-ROM as self-access practice.

C Teaching Time: 5–10 min.
- Read the examples with the class.
- Remind students to use *How long ago* to ask when something in the past happened, and *How long* to ask about a period of time.
- Have students complete the task.
- Call on students to say questions and answers. Correct as needed.

Multilevel Strategy
- **Pre-level, At-level:** Pair pre-level students with at-level students to complete the task. Have at-level students form the questions and dictate them to their partner. Have pre-level students form the answers.
- **Above-level:** Have students write three additional questions after they have completed the task. After checking answers, call on students to read their additional questions. Call on other students to say answers. Correct as needed.

TIME to TALK

Teaching Time: 15–20 min.
- Have each student make a list of important events in his or her life.
- Tell students to choose five to seven events to include in their timelines and to put them in order.
- Have students complete the task.
- PAIRS. Have partners exchange their timelines and ask questions with *How long ago* and *How long*.
- Walk around and help as needed.

Unit 15 T-183

Review and Challenge

Grammar

Teaching Time: 5–10 min.

- Read the example with the class.
- Have students complete the task.
- 🎧 Play Track 5 while students check their answers.
- PAIRS. Have students role-play the completed conversation.

Dictation

Teaching Time: 5–10 min.

- 🎧 Play Track 6 while students listen and write what they hear.
- 🎧 Play Track 6 again while students check their answers.
- Call on students to write answers on the board.
- 🎧 Play Track 6 again and correct the sentences on the board.

Multilevel Strategy

Pre-level: Give students a worksheet with some of the words from the dictation already provided.

Speaking

Teaching Time: 10–15 min.

- Have two students read the example.
- PAIRS. Have students complete the task. Walk around and help as needed.
- PAIRS. Have students compare the completed timelines.

T-184 Center Stage 2

Review and Challenge

Grammar

A 🎧 5 Complete the conversation. Use the words in the box. Then listen and check your answers. (Be careful! There are two extra words.)

| ago | for | Did | didn't | H̶o̶w̶ | long | took | was | Were | When |

Meg: ___How___ long ago did you come to the United States?
        1.

Aida: I came here 15 years ago. My first home

        ___was___ in Los Angeles.
        2.

Meg: How ___long___ did you live there?
              3.

Aida: I was there ___for___ two years.
                      4.

Meg: ___Did___ you work there?
        5.

Aida: No, I didn't. I ___took___ classes.
                          6.

Meg: ___When___ did you move here?
          7.

Aida: Three years ___ago___.
                       8.

Los Angeles

Dictation

🎧 6 Listen. You will hear five sentences. Write them on a piece of paper. *See the audioscript on page 288 for the sentences.*

Speaking

PAIRS. **Student A:** Look at the timeline about Bruce Lee's life on page 271.
Student B: Look at the timeline on page 273. Ask and answer questions to complete the timeline. Use *where, when, who, what,* and *how long ago.*
Answers will vary.
Example:
A: Where was Bruce Lee born?
B: He was born in San Francisco. When was he born?

Kung Fu master Bruce Lee in
Enter the Dragon, 1973

184 Unit 15

Culture Notes

- **Speaking.** Bruce Lee (1941–1973) was a Chinese actor born in the United States. He was very famous for his skill at kung fu, an ancient Chinese style of fighting. He made many martial arts movies.
- **Exercise A.** Frida Kahlo (1907–1954) was a famous Mexican painter. She often painted pictures of herself. She had many problems in her personal life, including several health problems, and she showed these in her art. She was the wife of another famous Mexican painter, Diego Rivera.

Listening

A 🎧 **7** Listen. A reporter is interviewing Mariela Lopez. What did Ms. Lopez do? Check the correct answer.

- ☐ She painted.
- ☑ She wrote a book.
- ☐ She got married two times.

Frida and Diego Rivera, 1931, one of Frida Kahlo's paintings

B 🎧 **8** Listen again. Answer the questions. Write complete sentences.

1. Who was Frida Kahlo?
   She was an artist.
2. Where was she from?
   She was from Mexico.
3. What happened to her when she was 18?
   She was in a terrible bus accident.
4. Who did she get married to?
   She got married to another great Mexican painter, Diego Rivera.
5. How long were they married?
   They were married for twenty-four years.
6. When did she die?
   She died in 1954.

TIME to TALK

GROUPS. Talk about the past of someone famous in your country or someone important in your life. Ask and answer questions. Answers will vary.

Example:
A: George Washington was the first president of the United States.
B: When did he become president?
A: I'm not sure about the date, but it was over 200 years ago.

Life Stages 185

Listening

A Teaching Time: 5–10 min.

- **Warm-up:** Have students look at the picture and read the caption. Ask: *What did Frida Kahlo do?* (She was a painter.) Ask students if they know who Frida Kahlo was. Have them tell the class a few facts. If they are not familiar with her, tell students a few things about Frida Kahlo. Tell students they will listen to an interview about Frida Kahlo.
- Ask students to read through the answer choices before they listen.
- 🎧 Play Track 7 while students listen.
- 🎧 Play Track 7 again while students listen and complete the task.
- Call on a student to say the answer. Correct as needed.

B Teaching Time: 5–10 min.

- Read the example with the class.
- Ask students to read through the questions before they listen.
- 🎧 Play Track 8 while students listen and complete the task.
- 🎧 Play Track 8 again while students listen and check their answers.
- Call on students to say answers. Correct as needed.

Option

Assign Unit 15 Supplementary Review and Challenge Exercises on the Teacher's Resource Disk as homework or on the Student Persistence CD-ROM as self-access practice.

TIME to TALK

Teaching Time: 10–15 min.

- Have two students read the example conversation.
- Ask: *What questions can you ask to learn more about the person?* Record students' questions on the board. For example: *Why was the person famous? What did he or she do?*
- PAIRS. Have students complete the task.
- Walk around and help as needed.
- Have students take turns telling facts they learned to the class.

Unit 15   T-185

Reading and Writing

Reading

A   **Teaching Time: 10–15 min.**

- Ask students to read through the answer choices before they read the story.
- Have students read the story silently. Then read it aloud. Pause after each few words and have students repeat chorally. Explain any unfamiliar vocabulary.
- Have students choose the best title.
- Call on a student to say the answer. Correct as needed.

Expansion Ask questions such as the following to check students' comprehension of the story: *How long ago was her grandmother born? Where did her grandparents meet? How long were her grandparents married?*

B   **Teaching Time: 5–10 min.**

- Have students reread the story and complete the task.
- PAIRS. Have students compare answers.
- Call on students to say answers. Correct as needed.

Reading and Writing

Reading

A   A student interviewed her grandmother and wrote about her. Read the story. Check (✓) the best title for the story.

- ☑ A Love Story
- ☐ A Handsome Man
- ☐ Many Children

My grandmother was born on January 17, 1909, in New York City. She had three brothers. She was the only girl in her family. She was tall and pretty, and she liked to dance. She was a very good dancer.

In the summer of 1929, she went on a vacation with some friends. They stayed at a big hotel. At a dance at the hotel, she met a tall, handsome man. He asked her to dance, and seven days later, they got married. It was the beginning of a very long love story.

In 1987, after 58 years of marriage, three sons, and six grandchildren, my grandfather died. He was 82 years old. Today, my grandmother still likes to dance, but she misses her favorite dance partner.

B   Match the topic with the paragraph.

_b_   1. Paragraph 1   **a.** after her grandfather's death

_c_   2. Paragraph 2   **b.** before her grandmother's marriage

_a_   3. Paragraph 3   **c.** her grandmother and grandfather's first meeting

Unit 15

Option

- PAIRS. Have partners think of a famous person they want to teach the class about. The person may be American or from their own country.
- Students write a role-play interview to present to the class. One student is the interviewer, and the other is the famous person of their choice. Students may look up information on the Internet or in books to find the facts.
- Have students practice their interviews for homework.
- Students present their role-play interviews to the class.
- After their presentations, have students write about the life of the famous person.

Center Stage 2

Prewriting

Think of a person who is 60 years old or older. Write ten questions to ask about his or her past. Then interview the person. Write the answers. Answers will vary.

1. Where were you born?
   László was born in Budapest, Hungary, in 1940.
2. _____
3. _____
4. _____
5. _____

Writing

Write about the life of the person you interviewed. Write one paragraph for each important part of the person's life. Use the story on page 186 as a model. Answers will vary.

Writing Tip

We often start a sentence with a time expression. Put a comma (,) between the time expression and the subject.

Example:
In the summer of 1929, she went to the mountains with some friends.

Life Stages 187

Language Note

- **Writing.** Have students study the Writing Tip.
- Model with a few sentences on the board, such as: *On October 28, 1935, John Jenkins was born. John Jenkins was born on October 28, 1935.*
- Tell students that if the time and place expressions are the beginning of a sentence, they need a comma after them.

Prewriting
Teaching Time: 10–15 min.

- Encourage students to think of people they might want to interview. Tell them to choose someone who speaks English.
- Have students write questions they want to ask. Walk around and help as needed.
- Have students conduct their interviews for homework.

Writing
Teaching Time: 15–20 min.

- Have students look again at the story on page 186. Remind them that each paragraph tells about a different life stage. Review the answers to Exercise B on page 186.
- Tell students to organize the information from their interviews and to make one paragraph for each life stage.
- Have students complete the task. Walk around and help as needed.
- Call on volunteers to read their stories to the class. Correct as needed. You can also have students write their stories on a separate piece of paper. Collect their work and provide individual feedback.

Multilevel Strategy

- **Pre-level:** Have students copy the answers from the Prewriting task.
- **Above-level:** Have students add more information about the person they interviewed.

Unit 15 T-187

Unit 16
Looking Ahead

Learning Goals
- Learn words to describe future actions
- Learn about *Be going to*: statements, *yes / no* questions, and information questions
- Listen to a conversation and a weather report
- Read a weekend calendar and write a paragraph about an event
- Talk about the future

Learner Persistence
Research shows that students whose friends and family support their educational efforts are more likely to persist. Involve your students' friends and families in your class.

Warm-up
Teaching Time: 3–5 min.

- Hold up a calendar. Point to today's date. Say: *This is today.* Ask: *What is the word for the day before today?* (yesterday). *What is the word for the day after today?* (tomorrow).
- Write *tomorrow* on the board. Ask: *What are your plans for tomorrow?* Allow students to answer with simple verb forms. For example: *visit friends, clean the house*, etc. Record students' answers on the board.

Vocabulary
Teaching Time: 15–20 min.

- Have students look at the vocabulary list. Explain unfamiliar vocabulary. For example: *When you have people over, you invite them to your house.*
- 🎧 Play Track 9 while students read and listen.
- Read the phrases aloud and have students repeat chorally.
- Have student complete the task.
- PAIRS. Have students share answers with a partner.

Expansion
- Write the following questions on the board: *Where do you buy groceries? When do you usually leave your*

T-188 Center Stage 2

Unit 16
Looking Ahead

Grammar
- *Be going to*: Statements
- *Be going to*: Yes / No Questions
- *Be going to*: Information Questions

Vocabulary

🎧 **9** Read and listen. Then circle the things that you are going to do tomorrow. Answers will vary.

1. leave the house
2. stay at home
3. buy groceries
4. pick up someone
5. take someone somewhere
6. go on a picnic
7. tonight
8. have people over
9. play cards

RON

188 Unit 16

house? When do you have people over? Who do you have over? Do you play cards? What card games do you play?

- PAIRS. Have students practice asking and answering the questions.

Listening

A 🎧 **10** Listen. What does Amir want to do? Check (✓) the correct answer.

☐ 1. He wants to use his mother's car.
☑ 2. He wants to go to a soccer game.
☐ 3. He wants to pick up his uncle.
☐ 4. He wants to go to a birthday party.

B 🎧 **11** Read and listen again. Write the missing words. Use the words in the box.

going to	to do	We're not	~~When are you~~

Mom: Are you going to stay the whole weekend? ___When are you___ going to leave?
  1.
Amir: Sunil's ___going to___ pick me up after
  2.
school on Friday.
Mom: On Friday? When are you going ___to do___
  3.
your homework?
Amir: On Sunday night.
Mom: What time are you going to be home on Sunday?
Amir: Don't worry. ___We're not___ going to be late.
  4.
We're going to leave San Jose in the morning.
Mom: And where are you going to stay?
Amir: With Sunil's uncle. He lives there.
Mom: What's his name? Do I know him?
Amir: Yes, Mom, you met him at Sunil's birthday party.

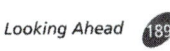

Looking Ahead 189

Option

Assign Unit 16 Supplementary Vocabulary Exercise on the Teacher's Resource Disk as homework or on the Student Persistence CD-ROM as self-access practice.

Listening

A Teaching Time: 10–15 min.

- **Warm-up:** Write on the board the word *permission*. Explain that when you ask permission, you ask if you're allowed or permitted to do something. Ask students to name some things that children ask permission to do.
- Ask students to read through the sentences before they listen.
- 🎧 Play Track 10 while students listen.
- 🎧 Play Track 10 again while students listen and complete the task.
- Call on students to say the answer. Correct as needed.

B Teaching Time: 15–20 min.

- Ask students to read through the answer choices before they listen.
- 🎧 Play Track 11 while students listen and complete the task.
- 🎧 Play Track 11 again while students check their answers.
- Call on students to say answers. Correct as needed.
- Read the conversation aloud. Pause after each few words and have students repeat chorally.
- PAIRS. Ask students to role-play the conversation.

Multilevel Strategy

- **Pre-level:** Have students role-play the completed conversation.
- **At-level, Above-level:** Write the conversation on the board and erase some words. Have students recall the conversation as they role-play.

Unit 16 T-189

Grammar to Communicate 1

Future with *Be going to*: Statements

Teaching Time: 10–15 min.

- Have students study the chart and the Look Box.
- Say: *The future is any time after now. Tomorrow is the day after today. It's in the future.*
- Write on the board: be going to + verb. Say: *Use* be going to *and the base form of a verb to talk about plans for the future.*
- Tell students they can use contractions for negative sentences.
- Read the sentences in the chart and Look Box aloud and have students repeat chorally.
- Tell students that in conversation, *going to* often sounds like one word: *gonna*. It is only used in conversation, not writing.
- Say: *Tell me what you're going to do tomorrow.* Have students say their plans using *be going to*.

A   Teaching Time: 5–10 min.

- Have students look at the weather chart. Read the headings across the top. Point out the key at the bottom.
- Have students look at the picture showing different temperatures. Read the words aloud and have students repeat chorally.
- Read the example with the class. Point out to students that the sentences are about the weather today. Tell them to look at the weather chart and write new sentences about the weather tomorrow.
- Have students complete the task.
- Call on students to write answers on the board. Write corrections on the board as needed.
- **LIFE SKILLS TEST PREP 2** Go to Unit 7, Lesson 1 for more practice in understanding temperatures in Celsius and Fahrenheit.

Grammar to Communicate 1

FUTURE WITH *BE GOING TO*: STATEMENTS

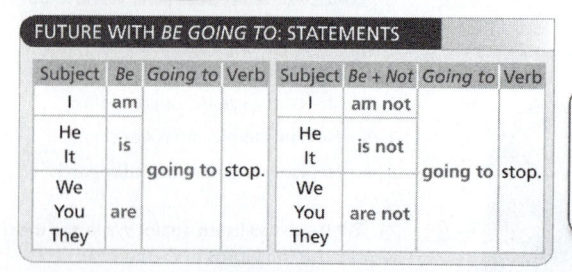

Subject	Be	Going to	Verb	Subject	Be + Not	Going to	Verb
I	am			I	am not		
He / It	is	going to	stop.	He / It	is not	going to	stop.
We / You / They	are			We / You / They	are not		

Look
Contractions:
I'm not going to go.
He isn't going to go.
We're going to go.
We aren't going to go.

A Look at the weather chart for different cities. Write sentences about the weather tomorrow.

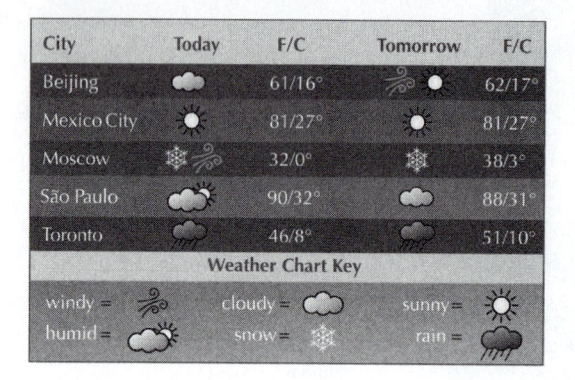

City	Today	F/C	Tomorrow	F/C
Beijing	cloudy	61/16°	windy/sunny	62/17°
Mexico City	sunny	81/27°	sunny	81/27°
Moscow	snow/windy	32/0°	snow	38/3°
São Paulo	humid	90/32°	cloudy	88/31°
Toronto	rain	46/8°	rain	51/10°

Weather Chart Key
windy =   cloudy =   sunny =
humid =   snow =   rain =

1. Xihua lives in Beijing. It's cloudy and cool today.
   It's going to be sunny and windy tomorrow.
2. Flor lives in Mexico City. It's sunny today. It's warm.
   It's going to be sunny and warm tomorrow.
3. Mariya lives in Moscow. It's windy today. It's snowing.
   It's going to snow tomorrow. It's going to be cold.
4. Jarbas lives in São Paulo. It's humid today. It's hot.
   It's going to be cloudy and hot tomorrow.
5. Paulette lives in Toronto. It's raining today. It's cool.
   It's going to rain tomorrow. It's going to be cool.

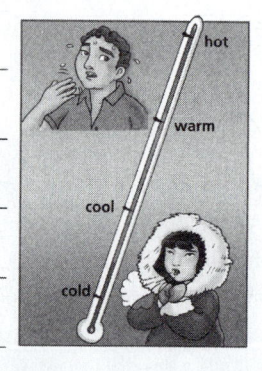

190 Unit 16

Grammar Notes

1. Use *be going to* and the base form of a verb for plans in the future.
2. Use the correct form of *be* for the subject.
3. Use full forms and contractions with subject pronouns and forms of *be*. For example: *He is going to go. He's going to go. He is not going to go. He isn't going to go. He's not going to go.*
4. For more information on this grammar topic, see page 259.

Culture Note

Exercise A. Remind students that in the United States, people measure temperatures in degrees Fahrenheit.

Center Stage 2

B Look at Exercise A. What are the people going to do tomorrow? Complete the sentences. Use *be going to*.

1. Mariya __is going to take__ her children to school.
   (take)
2. Mariya's children __are not going to ride__ their bikes to school.
   (not / ride)
3. Paulette says, "I __'m not going to play__ tennis."
   (not / play)
4. Paulette says, "My children __are going to take__ their umbrellas."
   (take)
5. Flor and her husband __are going to go__ to the park.
   (go)

C Write sentences with *be going to*. Use the words in the box or your own ideas. Answers will vary.

| be late | go outside | play soccer | wear sunglasses |
| drive to work | go to the laundromat | watch a movie at home | wear a T-shirt |

1. It's going to be cloudy and cool tomorrow.
   People __aren't going to wear sunglasses.__
   I __'m going to wear a jacket.__

2. It's going to be sunny and hot tomorrow.
   My family and I _____
   My friend _____

3. It's going to snow tomorrow.
   Children _____
   I _____

4. It's going to rain tomorrow.
   I _____
   The bus _____

laundromat

TIME to TALK

PAIRS. Look at the weather report in your local newspaper. What is the weather going to be like for the next few days? What are you going to do? What are you not going to do? Tell your partner. Answers will vary.

Example:
A: It's going to be hot and humid tomorrow. Are you going to go to the beach?
B: No, I'm not. I'm going to class.

Looking Ahead 191

B Teaching Time: 5–10 min.
- Read the examples with the class. Tell students to use contractions where possible.
- Have students complete the task.
- Call on students to say answers. Correct as needed.

C Teaching Time: 5–10 min.
- Read the examples with the class.
- Have students read through the answer choices before they begin the task.
- Have students complete the task.
- Call on students to say their answers. Correct as needed.

Multilevel Strategy
- **Pre-level:** Help students identify the appropriate phrases from the box for each item.
- **Above-level:** Have students use only their own ideas to complete the task.

(written *F* for short). People in other parts of the world use degrees Celsius (written *C* for short).

Option

Assign Unit 16 Supplementary Grammar to Communicate 1 Exercises on the Teacher's Resource Disk as homework or on the Student Persistence CD-ROM as self-access practice.

TIME to TALK

Teaching Time: 15–20 min.
- Have two students read the example.
- PAIRS. Have students complete the task.
- Walk around and help as needed.

Multilevel Strategy
- **Pre-level:** Have students write three sentences about the weather and their plans for tomorrow and read them to their partner. Help students form correct sentences.
- **At-level, Above-level:** Have students report on their partner's plans to the class.

Unit 16   T-191

Grammar to Communicate 2

Future with *Be going to*: Yes / No Questions

Teaching Time: 5–10 min.

- Say: *To ask a question with* be going to, *put* be *before the subject.*
- Tell students that they can answer with short answers and use contractions for negative short answers.
- Have students study the chart and the Look Box.
- Read the questions and answers and have students repeat chorally.
- Ask one student a question with *be going to*. The student answers and then asks another student a question. Continue until all students have asked and answered questions.

A Teaching Time: 5–10 min.

- Read the example with the class.
- Have students complete the task.
- Call on students to say answers. Correct as needed.
- PAIRS. Have students take turns asking and answering questions.

Multilevel Strategy

- **Pre-level, At-level:** Pair pre-level students with at-level students and have them take turns asking and answering questions.
- **Above-level:** Pair above-level students. Have them ask their partner follow-up questions. For example:
  A: *Are you going to go on a picnic next week?*
  B: *No, I'm not.*
  A: *Are you going to stay home?*
  B: *Yes, I am.*

B Teaching Time: 5–10 min.

- Read the example with the class. Tell students that *soon* and *later* are future time expressions. Explain that they do not mean a specific time. *Soon* means in a short time from now. *Later* means after the present time.

T-192   Center Stage 2

Grammar to Communicate 2

FUTURE WITH *BE GOING TO*: YES / NO QUESTIONS

Be	Subject	Going to	Verb		Short Answers				
Am	I				you	are.		you	aren't.
Is	she / it	going to	stop?	Yes,	she / it	is.	No,	she / it	isn't.
Are	you / we / they				I	am.		I'm	not.
					we / they	are.		we / they	aren't.

A Complete the questions with the missing words.

Look
There are two negative short answers with *is not* and *are not*.
No, it isn't.   No, it's not.
No, they aren't.   No, they're not.

1. __Are__ you going to go on a picnic next week?
2. Is it going __to__ be sunny at 7:00 tomorrow evening?
3. __Are__ your friends going to pick you up this evening?
4. Are you __going__ to go to the laundromat tomorrow?
5. __Is__ your school going to be open tomorrow?
6. Are you going __to__ play cards tonight?
7. Is the weather __going__ to be good tomorrow?
8. __Are__ you going to have people over this weekend?

PAIRS. Ask and answer the questions above.

B Look at the sentences. Write questions.

1. It's not raining now. __Is it going to rain__ soon?
2. The children aren't studying now. __Are they going to study__ later?
3. I'm not doing the dishes now. __Are you going to do the dishes__ later?
4. John isn't using the phone now. __Is he going to use the phone__ soon?
5. We aren't going to the movies now. __Are we going to go to the movies__ later?
6. The bus isn't leaving now. __Is it going to leave__ soon?

Unit 16

- Have students complete the task.
- Call on students to say questions. Correct as needed.

Grammar Notes

1. To change a sentence with *be going to* to a *yes / no* question, switch the order of the subject and form of *be*. For example: *They are going to go. Are they going to go?*
2. For short answers with *yes*, use subject + form of *be*. Do not use contractions.
3. For short answers with *no*, use subject + form of *be + not*. Use full forms or contractions.
4. For more information on this grammar topic, see page 259.

C Write future time expressions. Use *this*, *tomorrow*, and *next* with the words in the box.

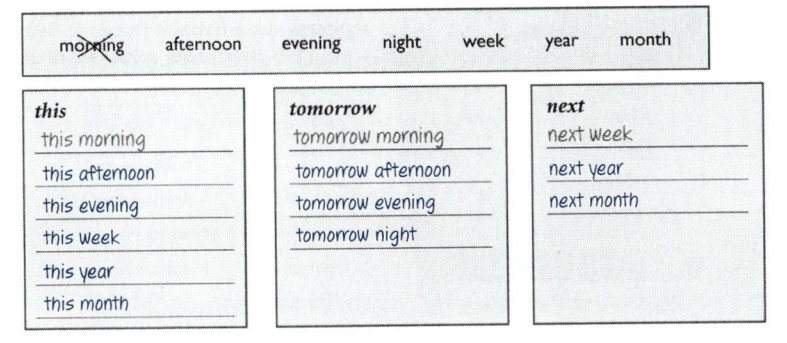

~~morning~~   afternoon   evening   night   week   year   month

this	tomorrow	next
this morning	tomorrow morning	next week
this afternoon	tomorrow afternoon	next year
this evening	tomorrow evening	next month
this week	tomorrow night	
this year		
this month		

D Write questions. Use the correct form of *be going to*. Then answer the questions with true information.

1. Are you going to eat out tomorrow night? — Yes, I am. OR No, I'm not.
   (you / eat out / tomorrow night)
2. Are you going to take an English class next year? — Yes, I am. OR No, I'm not.
   (you / take an English class / next year)
3. Is it going to be hot this month? — Yes, it is. OR No, it's not. OR No, it isn't.
   (it / be / hot / this month)
4. Are you going to go to the laundromat tonight? — Yes, I am. OR No, I'm not.
   (you / go to the laundromat / tonight)
5. Are you going to be busy next week? — Yes, I am. OR No, I'm not.
   (you / be / busy / next week)
6. Is your teacher going to work next month? — Yes, he / she is. OR No, he's / she's not. OR No, he / she isn't.
   (your teacher / work / next month)
7. Is a new shopping mall going to open here this year? — Yes, it is. OR No, it's not. OR No, it isn't.
   (a new shopping mall / open / here / this year)

TIME to TALK

ON YOUR OWN. Think of three plans. How are you going to prepare for them? Make a list of sentences. *Answers will vary.*

PAIRS. Read your sentences to your partner. Can your partner guess what you are going to do? Then changes roles.

Example:
A: Next month, I'm going to order a cake.
B: Hmm—I need more information.
A: OK. I'm going to buy a white dress.
B: Oh! Are you going to get married?
A: Yes, I am. I'm going to get married in April.

Looking Ahead 193

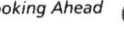

Grammar to Communicate 3

Be going to: Information Questions; What / Who as Subjects

Teaching Time: 5–10 min.

- Say: *To ask an information question with be going to, use a wh-word before the form of be.*
- Have students study the charts.
- Read the questions and answers in the charts and have students repeat chorally.
- Ask students a few information questions and have them answer.

A Teaching Time: 5–10 min.

- Read the example with the class.
- Have students complete the task.
- Call on students to say answers. Correct as needed.
- PAIRS. Have students discuss which questions aren't polite in American culture as well as those that aren't polite in their own culture.
- Call on students to say which questions aren't polite in certain cultures.

B Teaching Time: 5–10 min.

- Have students study the Look Box. Give a few examples such as: *In ten minutes* means *ten minutes later than now.*
- Read the example with the class. Tell students *In two years* is the more logical answer in this sentence.
- Have students complete the task.
- Call on students to say answers. Correct as needed.

Grammar to Communicate 3

BE GOING TO: INFORMATION QUESTIONS

Wh- word	Be	Subject	Going to	Verb	Answers
Where	are	we	going to	sleep?	At my house.
What	are	you	going to	do?	I'm going to buy food.
When	is	he	going to	go?	In two hours.
How long	is	it	going to	work?	For a week.
How much	is	it	going to	cost?	$25.00.

WHAT / WHO AS SUBJECT

What / Who	Be	Going to	Verb	Answers
What	is	going to	happen?	He's going to drive us.
Who	is	going to	drive?	Paul is going to drive.

A Complete the questions. Use *How much, When,* or *Who*.

1. __Who__ is going to get married?   Martha and Ed.
2. __When__ are they going to get married?   Next August.
3. __How much__ is the wedding going to cost?   A lot of money.
4. __Who__ is going to pay?   Martha's parents.
5. __When__ are they going to have a baby?   In one year.

PAIRS. Which questions are not polite to ask in American culture? In your culture? *Answers will vary.*

B Read and circle the correct answers.

1. **Lucy:** Your daughter is 20, right? When is she going to graduate from college?
   Fran: In twenty years. / (In two years.)
2. **Lucy:** So your wife is pregnant! When is she going to have the baby?
   Brad: (In one month.) / In one year.
3. **Lucy:** Your husband is 65 now, right? When is he going to retire?
   Rita: In three minutes. / (In three years.)
4. **Lucy:** When is your son going to get married?
   Tony: (In six months.) / In sixty years.

Look

Use *in* with a period of time.
I'm going to get a haircut in three days.

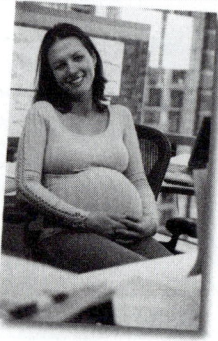

pregnant

Unit 16

Grammar Notes

1. Use *wh*-word + *be* + subject + *going to* + verb to ask information questions about the future.
2. The form of *be* changes with the subject.
3. *Who* and *What* can be the subject of a question. Use: *Who / What + is going to* + verb to ask about a subject.
4. For more information on this grammar topic, see page 259.

Language Note

Exercises A and B. Say: *In conversation, people often make contractions with wh-words and is. For example: Who's going to do that? When's Derrick going to pick us up?*

Center Stage 2

C Answer the questions with true information. Use *in* and time expressions. Answers will vary.

1. When are you going to have a day off? _In a month._
2. When are you going to retire? _____
3. When are you going to celebrate your birthday? _____
4. When are you going to get a haircut? _____
5. When are you going to go to the dentist? _____

D Write questions. Use the correct form of *be going to*.

1. _What is Michael going to study at college?_
   (What / Michael / study)
2. _Where is he going to live?_
   (Where / he / live)
3. _How much is it going to cost?_
   (How much / it / cost)
4. _When is he going to graduate?_
   (When / he / graduate)
5. _When is Sandra going to start her new job?_
   (When / Sandra / start / her new job)
6. _How much is she going to make?_
   (How much / she / make)
7. _What is she going to do?_
   (What / she / do)
8. _Who is going to take care of her daughter?_
   (Who / take care of her daughter)

PAIRS. Ask and answer the questions. Which are polite? Which are not polite? Answers will vary.

TIME to TALK

ON YOUR OWN. What are you going to do in the future? Write your short-term and long-term goals. Answers will vary.

SHORT-TERM GOALS	LONG-TERM GOALS
This month: _____	Next year: _get a new job_
Next month: _____	In two years: _____
This year: _improve my English_	In five years: _____

GROUPS. Ask and answer questions about your goals.

Example:
A: What are you going to do in five years?
B: I'm going to move to Florida.
C: Why are you going to move to Florida?
B: Because Minnesota is too cold.

Looking Ahead 195

C Teaching Time: 5–10 min.
- Read the example with the class.
- Have students complete the task. Walk around and help as needed.
- Call on students to say answers. Correct as needed.

D Teaching Time: 10–15 min.
- Read the example with the class.
- Have students complete the task.
- Call on students to say answers. Correct as needed.
- PAIRS. Have students discuss which questions are polite and which are impolite.

Multilevel Strategy
- **Pre-level, Above-level:** Have above-level students help pre-level students form the questions. For the pair activity, have pre-level students read the questions and above-level students answer.

Expansion
Start a discussion on conversation topics in different countries. For example, you might ask: *Which topics are not polite in the United States? Is that the same in your country? Can you talk about some topics with some people, for example, your family or someone you know very well?*

Teaching Tip

Time to Talk. Before asking and answering questions, have students write an estimated date for each answer. That way they can focus more on the grammar during the activity and less on the content of their answers.

Option

Assign Unit 16 Supplementary Grammar to Communicate 3 Exercises on the Teacher's Resource Disk as homework or on the Student Persistence CD-ROM as self-access practice.

TIME to TALK Teaching Time: 10–15 min.
- Tell students to first write their goals in the chart.
- Have three students read the example conversation.
- GROUPS. Have students complete the task.
- Walk around and help as needed.
- Have students tell about the goals of people in their group.

Unit 16 T-195

Review and Challenge

Grammar

Teaching Time: 5–10 min.

- Read the example with the class.
- Have students complete the task.
- 🎧 Play Track 12 while students check their answers.
- Have two students read the completed conversation to check the answers. Correct as needed.

Dictation

Teaching Time: 5–10 min.

- 🎧 Play Track 13 while students listen and write what they hear.
- 🎧 Play Track 13 again while students check their answers.
- Call on students to write answers on the board.
- 🎧 Play Track 13 again and correct sentences on the board.

Multilevel Strategy

- **Pre-level:** Give students a worksheet with some of the words from the dictation already provided.

Speaking

Teaching Time: 10–15 min.

- Give students a few minutes to think about some details of their trips, such as where they're going to go, why, what they're going to do there, etc.
- Have two students read the example.
- GROUPS. Have students complete the task.
- Walk around and help as needed.
- Call on students to tell the class about the travel plans of another person in the group. Have them point out the locations on a world map.

T-196 Center Stage 2

Review and Challenge

Grammar

🎧 **12** Complete the conversation. Use the words in the box. Then listen and check your answers. (Be careful! There are four extra words.)

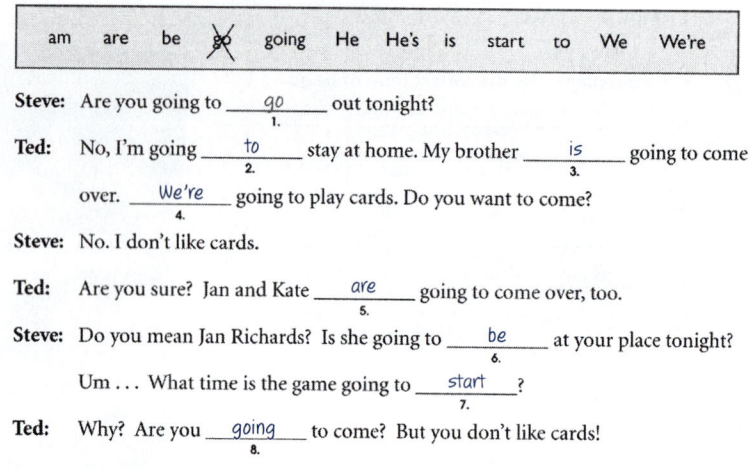

| am | are | be | ~~go~~ | going | He | He's | is | start | to | We | We're |

Steve: Are you going to __go__ out tonight?
 1.

Ted: No, I'm going __to__ stay at home. My brother __is__ going to come
 2. 3.
over. __We're__ going to play cards. Do you want to come?
 4.

Steve: No. I don't like cards.

Ted: Are you sure? Jan and Kate __are__ going to come over, too.
 5.

Steve: Do you mean Jan Richards? Is she going to __be__ at your place tonight?
 6.
Um . . . What time is the game going to __start__?
 7.

Ted: Why? Are you __going__ to come? But you don't like cards!
 8.

Dictation

🎧 **13** Listen. You will hear five sentences. Write them on a piece of paper. *See the audioscript on page 289 for the sentences.*

Speaking

GROUPS. Imagine you have one year to travel around the world. Where are you going to go? Ask and answer questions. Use the words in the box and your own ideas. *Answers will vary.*

| Where . . . (go) | Who . . . (go with) | How long . . . (stay) |
| When . . . (go) | What . . . (do) | What . . . (see) |

Example:
A: *Where are you going to go?*
B: *First, I'm going to go to Egypt.*

Sphinx and pyramid in Egypt

196 Unit 16

Listening

A 🎧 **14** Listen to the weather report. What day is it? Check (✓) the correct answer.

- ✓ Wednesday
- ☐ Thursday
- ☐ Friday
- ☐ Saturday
- ☐ Sunday

B 🎧 **15** Listen again. What is the weather going to be like? Complete the chart.

	WEDNESDAY	THURSDAY	FRIDAY	SATURDAY	SUNDAY
sunny	✓			✓	
cloudy		✓			
windy		✓			
rainy		✓	✓		✓
cold					
cool		✓			✓
warm	✓				
hot				✓	
humid				✓	

TIME to TALK

ON YOUR OWN. Think of a city you know well or that you have information about. Imagine you are going to visit the city.

GROUPS. Talk to your group about your trip. What does the city look like? What are you going to do there? What are you going to wear? How are you going to travel there? Can your group guess the city? *Answers will vary.*

Example:
A: It's a beautiful warm city with beaches.
B: Are you going to go to Miami?
A: No, I'm not.
C: How are you going to get there? Are you going to drive?
A: No, I'm going to fly.
C: Are your go to travel to San Juan?...

Looking Ahead 197

Listening

A Teaching Time: 5–10 min.

- **Warm-up:** Have students look at the map. Point to different locations with weather symbols and ask questions such as: *What's the weather going to be here? Is it going to be cool here?*
- 🎧 Play Track 14 while students listen.
- 🎧 Play Track 14 again while students listen and complete the task.
- Call on a student to say the answer. Correct as needed.

B Teaching Time: 5–10 min.

- Ask students to read through the answer choices on the chart before they listen.
- 🎧 Play Track 15 while students listen and complete the task.
- 🎧 Play Track 15 again while students listen and check their answers.
- Say the day and have students call out the answers.

Option

Assign Unit 16 Supplementary Review and Challenge Exercises on the Teacher's Resource Disk as homework or on the Student Persistence CD-ROM as self-access practice.

TIME to TALK

Teaching Time: 10–15 min.

- Give students a few minutes to choose their city and think about what they're going to take and do.
- Brainstorm with the class possible questions to ask. Write students' questions on the board.
- GROUPS. Have students complete the task.
- Walk around and help as needed.

Expansion

- PAIRS. Have students play Twenty Questions.
- Each student chooses a city that he or she is going to visit.
- The other student asks *yes / no* questions to guess the city. Students try to guess the correct city by asking as few questions as possible.

Unit 16

Reading and Writing

Reading

A Teaching Time: 5–10 min.

- Have students look at the pictures on the community calendar and say what they see.
- Ask students to read through the answer choices before they read. Explain unfamiliar vocabulary if necessary. For example, say: *Artists show the things they make at an art exhibit.*
- Have students complete the task.
- Call on students to say answers. Correct as needed.
- **LIFE SKILLS TEST PREP 2** Go to Unit 4, Lesson 1 for more practice in reading calendars.

B Teaching Time: 10–15 min.

- Read the example with the class.
- Have students complete the task.
- Call on students to say answers. Correct as needed.

Reading and Writing

Reading

A Read the weekend calendar. Check (✓) the things that are going to happen on Saturday.

☐ an art exhibit ☑ a dance ☐ a movie ☑ a picnic

COMMUNITY CALENDAR: FRIDAY, MAY 6–SUNDAY, MAY 8

Friday, May 6	Saturday, May 7	Sunday, May 8
Art exhibit *Picasso's Life and Work* 5–9 P.M., City Museum $5	NYC Firefighters Annual Picnic 12–2 P.M. Prospect Park Free—bring a dish to share	Cinco de Mayo Celebrate this Mexican holiday 9 P.M., Flushing Meadows Park, Free Music
Outdoor movie *Beauty and the Beast* 7 P.M., Central Park Free		NYC Police Department Ball Dinner and Dance 8 P.M.–midnight Sheraton Ballroom
		Special event for Mother's Day Read to your mom! 3–5 P.M., Public Library— Children's Room Free

B Read about the people. Then look at the calendar and answer the questions.

1. Seth is 6 years old. He loves to read. What is he going to do on Mother's Day?
   He is probably going to go to the library with his mother.

2. Mrs. Fremont is married to a NYC firefighter. Where is she going to have lunch on Saturday?
   She is probably going to have lunch at the NYC Firefighters Annual Picnic in Prospect Park.

3. Mr. and Mrs. Sangha are going to go to the art exhibit. How much are they going to pay?
   They are going to pay $10.

4. Ms. Chen is a police officer. Where are she and her boyfriend going to be on Saturday night?
   They are probably going to be at the NYC Police Department Ball Dinner and Dance.

5. Lisa Gutierrez is from Mexico. She loves music. What is she going to do on Saturday?
   She is probably going to go to the Cinco de Mayo Celebration in Flushing Meadows Park.

6. Mr. Amadou works on Saturday and Sunday, but he has Friday night off. Where is he going to take his 5-year-old son on Friday evening?
   He is probably going to take his son to see Beauty and the Beast in Central Park.

198 Unit 16

Language Note
- **Exercise B.** Tell students to use the word *probably* when they think something is going to happen, but they are not completely sure.
- The word *probably* goes between the form of *be* and *going to*.

Option
Have students organize an event outside of class or plan to go to an already organized event. Encourage students to bring their family and friends so other students can get to know them.

Center Stage 2

Prewriting

Read the note. Then find a calendar of events from your local newspaper. Read about the events, and plan a nice weekend.

Answers will vary.

Puerto Rican Day Parade

Hi Barbara,
How are you doing? Do you have any plans for the weekend? Are you and Hank going to go to the Puerto Rican Day Parade? There's going to be a band with live music in the city on Saturday. Dan's going to be in the parade, so I'm going to take the kids. My mother's going to come over and take care of the baby. The weather report says it's going to be beautiful. Call me and we can make plans.
Liz

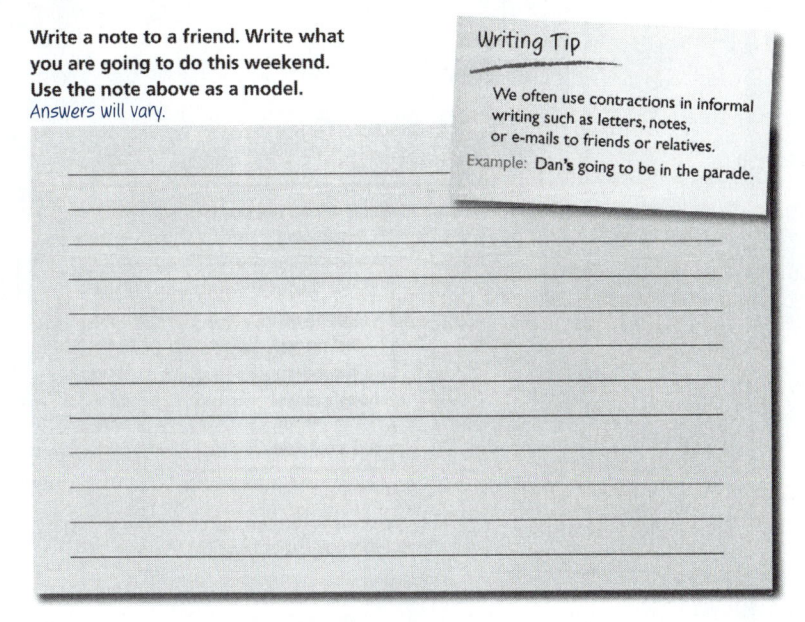

Writing

Write a note to a friend. Write what you are going to do this weekend. Use the note above as a model.
Answers will vary.

Writing Tip
We often use contractions in informal writing such as letters, notes, or e-mails to friends or relatives.
Example: Dan's going to be in the parade.

Looking Ahead 199

Option

- Have students each create an advertisement for a local event they think other students in the class might enjoy.
- Tell them to create poster-like ads with all the information that someone needs to attend, such as time, date, place, price, etc.
- Remind them to also include details about why the event is going to be interesting. For example: *There's going to be live music.*
- Have students present their posters to the class and display them in the classroom.

Prewriting

Teaching Time: 10–15 min.

- Ask students to bring in information about upcoming local events a few days before you assign this task. Suggest students look in the arts and metro sections of local newspapers.
- Have students read the note silently. Then read it aloud. Pause after each few words and have students repeat chorally.
- PAIRS. Have students share their plans for the weekend.

Writing

Teaching Time: 15–20 min.

- Have students study the Writing Tip. Then ask: *Are you going to write something formal or informal?* (informal). Have students reread the directions if necessary. Tell students that it is all right to use contractions in this assignment.
- Tell students to organize their ideas before they write. First, they need to make a list of what they are going to do. Then they need to decide who they are going to write to. Tell students to include details about the events and activities they are going to write about.
- Have students complete the task.
- Walk around and help as needed.
- Call on volunteers to read their notes. Correct as needed. You can also have students write their notes on a separate piece of paper. Collect their work and provide individual feedback.

Multilevel Strategy

- **Pre-level:** While students are completing the prewriting task, copy the note on the board. Underline the information students should substitute in their notes. Have students copy the note and substitute the underlined parts with information about an event they have chosen.

Unit 16　T-199

Game 4
Units 13–16

Answers will vary. Possible answers:

1. **A:** There were a lot of cars.
   B: It was hot.

2. **A:** The waves were too big.
   B: The water was cold.

3. **A:** They went home.
   B: They were in a bad mood.

4. **A:** They relaxed.
   B: They had a barbecue.

5. **A:** He was born in Poza Rica, Veracruz.
   B: He was born in México.

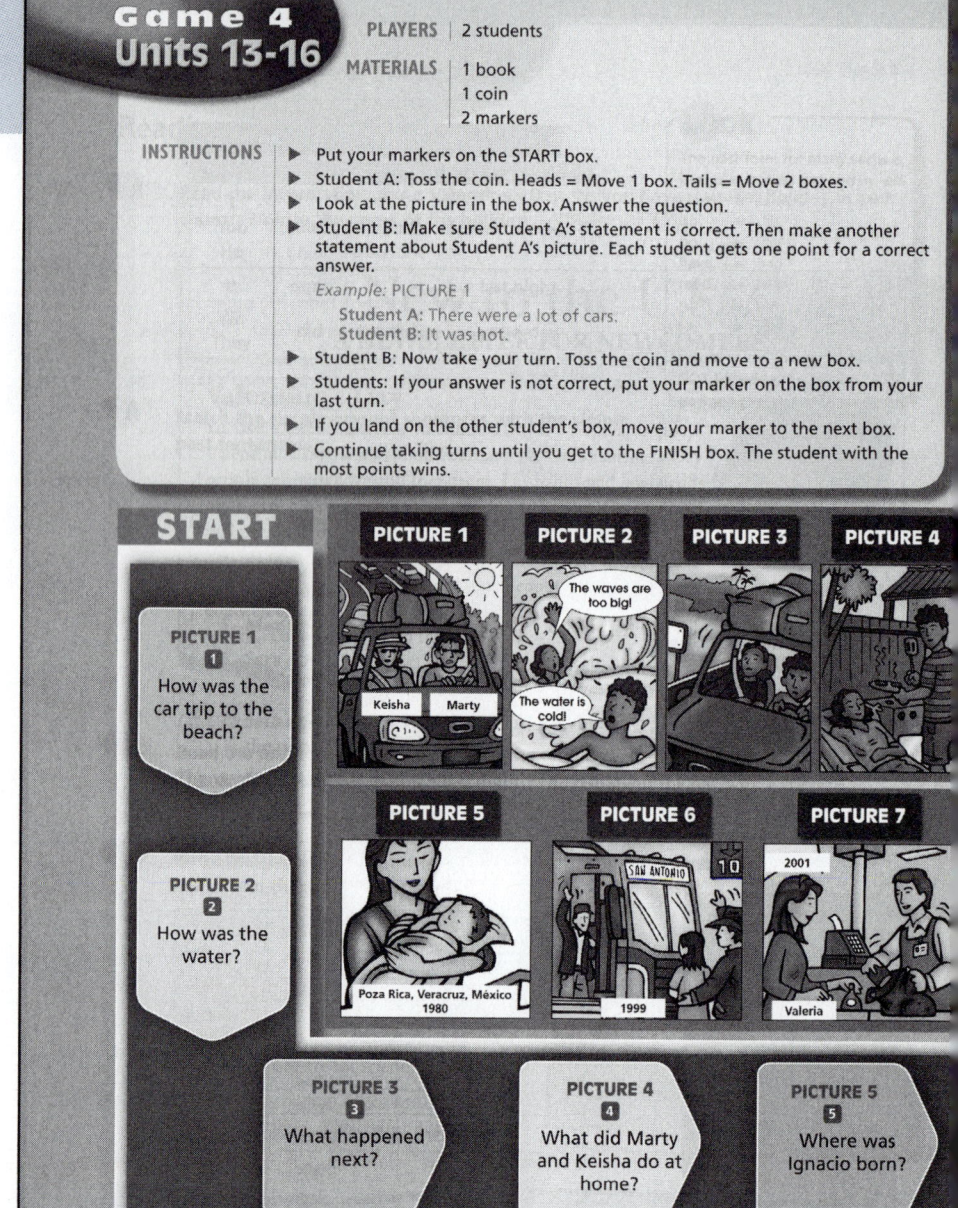

T-200 Center Stage 2

6. **A:** He went to San Antonio.
   B: He left México.

7. **A:** He met her at a supermarket.
   B: He met her at work.

8. **A:** They got married.
   B: They had a wedding.

9. **A:** Ignacio and Valeria had a baby.
   B: They had a baby girl. Her name is Inez.

10. **A:** He graduated from college.
    B: He finished business school.

11. **A:** He is going to get a new job.
    B: He is going to work in an office.

12. **A:** He is going to learn how to drive.
    B: He is going to get a driver's license.

13. **A:** He is going to buy a house.
    B: He and his family are going to move.

14. **A:** Ignacio is going to become a U.S. citizen.
    B: Ignacio is going to be very happy.

Game 4: Units 13-16 201

Game 4   T-201

Unit 17
Health

Learning Goals
- Learn health vocabulary
- Learn about *should*: affirmative and negative statements, *yes / no* questions, and information questions
- Listen to a conversation and a report about health
- Read medicine labels and write an e-mail
- Talk about health

Learner Persistence

Have students do group projects over extended period of time to motivate them to attend class. When students know that others are counting on them to attend class so the group can work together, they are more likely to persist.

Warm-up

Teaching Time: 3–5 min.

Have students look at the picture. Ask questions about it, such as: *Where are the people? Who works at a clinic? When do you go to a clinic? What do you get at a pharmacy?*

Vocabulary

Teaching Time: 15–20 min.

- Have students look at the pictures. Explain unfamiliar vocabulary. For example, say: *Sometimes when you go to the doctor, he or she writes on a piece of paper medicine that you need to buy. That's a prescription.*
- 🎧 Play Track 16 while students read and listen.
- Read the words and phrases aloud and have students repeat chorally.
- Have students complete the activity.
- PAIRS. Have students share their answers.

Expansion Have volunteers act out the conditions or actions on the list or other ones they know. Have the rest of the class guess the words being acted out.

Unit 17
Health

Grammar
- *Should*: Affirmative and Negative Statements
- *Should*: Yes / No Questions
- *Should*: Information Questions

Vocabulary

🎧 **16** Read and listen. Then circle the health problems you have today.
Answers will vary.

1. prescription
2. get a prescription
3. see a doctor
4. take someone's temperature
5. pharmacist
6. have the flu
7. hurt
8. have a pain
9. sneeze
10. have allergies
11. put on a Band-Aid
12. have a cut
13. have a cough

202 Unit 17

Multilevel Strategy

- **All-levels:** Have pre-level students take turns acting out the words. Have at-level and above-level students guess the words being acted out by the pre-level students.

Language Note

Exercise B. Point out the word *kid* in the conversation. Tell students that *kid* is an informal way to say *child*. Explain that Glenda thinks the doctor is inexperienced because he is young. Ask students if, in their opinion, Dr. Mendez is a kid.

T-202 Center Stage 2

Listening

A 🎧 **17** Listen. Abby is talking to her mother-in-law, Glenda. Check (✓) the statements that are true.

- ✓ 1. Abby had a baby a month ago.
- ☐ 2. Abby's baby is sick.
- ☐ 3. It is cold outside.
- ☐ 4. Glenda likes Dr. Mendez a lot.
- ✓ 5. Glenda is worried about her grandson.
- ✓ 6. Abby wants to go out to lunch.

B 🎧 **18** Read and listen again. Write the missing words. Use the words in the box.

should	~~should we~~	shouldn't	shouldn't be

Abby: So, where ___should we___ go for lunch?

Glenda: Go? Oh, I don't think we ___should___ go out for lunch.

Abby: Why not?

Glenda: Well, the baby ___shouldn't be___ around a lot of people. What if someone has a cold and coughs on him?

Abby: But that's crazy!

Glenda: Really? I don't agree. Should we call the doctor and ask?

Abby: No, we ___shouldn't___! He told me it was OK.

Glenda: Who told you? Dr. Mendez? Why should we believe him? He's just a kid!

Health 203

Listening

A Teaching Time: 10–15 min.

- **Warm-up:** Start a discussion on caring for babies. Prompt students with questions such as: *How old does a baby need to be before he or she goes out in public? Can cold weather make babies sick? How can you protect babies from getting sick?*
- Ask students to read through the sentences before they listen.
- 🎧 Play Track 17 while students listen.
- 🎧 Play Track 17 again while students listen and complete the task.
- Call on students to say answers. Correct as needed.

B Teaching Time: 15–20 min.

- Have students read through the answer choices before they listen.
- 🎧 Play Track 18 while students listen and complete the task.
- 🎧 Play Track 18 again while students check their answers.
- Call on students to say answers. Correct as needed.
- Read the conversation aloud. Pause after each few words and have students repeat chorally.
- PAIRS. Ask students to role-play the conversation.

Multilevel Strategy

- **Pre-level:** Have students role-play the completed conversation.
- **At-level, Above-level:** Write the conversation on the board and erase some words. Have students recall the conversation as role-play.

Option

Assign Unit 17 Supplementary Vocabulary Exercise on the Teacher's Resource Disk as homework or on the Student Persistence CD-ROM as self-access practice.

Grammar to Communicate 1

Should: Affirmative and Negative Statements

Teaching Time: 5–10 min.

- Write on the board *advice*. If necessary, tell students that when you give a person advice, you tell the person it is a good idea to do something or it's not a good idea to do something.
- Say: *This class starts at [time].* Write on the board: *You should arrive before [time]. You shouldn't arrive after [time].*
- Underline the words *should* and *shouldn't*. Tell students to use these words to give advice.
- Have students study the chart.
- Read the sentences in the chart and have students repeat chorally.

A Teaching Time: 5–10 min.

- Ask students to read through the sentences in the box before they begin the task.
- Read the example with the class.
- Have students complete the task.
- Call on students to say answers. Correct as needed.
- **LIFE SKILLS TEST PREP 2** Go to Unit 9, Lesson 3 for more practice in identifying common symptoms.
- **LIFE SKILLS TEST PREP 2** Go to Unit 9, Lesson 5 for more practice in identifying common diseases and conditions.

Multilevel Strategy

- **Pre-level:** Have students work in pairs or groups to complete the task. Help students with the task if necessary.
- **Above-level:** After students have completed the task, have them write one additional recommendation for each condition.

Grammar to Communicate 1

SHOULD: AFFIRMATIVE AND NEGATIVE STATEMENTS

Subject	Should	Verb	Subject	Should + Not	Verb
I / You / She / We / They	should	go out.	I / You / She / We / They	shouldn't	go out.

A Write a sentence from the box under each picture. If you need more room, write on a piece of paper. There can be more than one correct answer. *Answers will vary. Possible answers:*

He shouldn't go out in the hot sun.	He should put ice on his back.
She should take some aspirin.	She shouldn't go to work.
He should take some medicine.	She shouldn't eat anything.
She should see a doctor.	He should take some aspirin.

1. Rose has a headache.
   She should take some aspirin.
2. Luz is nauseous. 
   She shouldn't go to work.
3. Amit has a fever. 
   He shouldn't go out in the hot sun.
4. Arthur has heartburn. 
   He should take some medicine.
5. Ramon has a backache. 
   He should put ice on his back.
6. Cecile has a stomachache. 
   She shouldn't eat anything.

Unit 17

Grammar Notes

1. Use *should* and the base form of a verb to give advice.
2. *Should* never changes forms. Use *should* with all subjects.
3. Use *should not* or *shouldn't* and the base form of a verb to make negative sentences.
4. Use *should* to give advice for the present and the future.
5. For more information on this grammar topic, see page 260.

T-204 Center Stage 2

B Complete the sentences with *should* or *shouldn't*.

1. Alicia took her son's temperature. It is 102°F (38.8°C).

   a. _She should take her son to the doctor._
   (take her son to the doctor)

   b. _He shouldn't go to school._
   (go to school)

2. Mike's son had a bike accident. His arm hurts a lot.

   a. _He shouldn't call the pharmacist._
   (call the pharmacist)

   b. _He should go to the hospital._
   (go to the hospital)

3. Betty's daughter has a small cut on her finger.

   a. _She should put a Band-Aid on it._
   (put a Band-Aid on it)

   b. _She shouldn't call the doctor._
   (call the doctor)

C PAIRS. Give advice. Write sentences with *should* or *shouldn't*. Answers will vary.
Possible answers:

1. I have a backache.   _You should do exercises._
2. I have an earache.   _You should see a doctor._
3. I have the flu.   _You shouldn't go to work._
4. I'm tired all the time. _You should take vitamins._
5. My feet hurt.   _You should sit down._
6. I have heartburn.   _You should take some medicine._

TIME to TALK

GROUPS. Find out the meanings of the words in the chart. Then talk about what you should and shouldn't do for each problem and complete the chart. Answers will vary.

IF YOU HAVE...	YOU SHOULD...	YOU SHOULDN'T...
a sore throat	gargle	
bad breath		
insomnia		
a sunburn		

gargle

Health

Option

Assign Unit 17 Supplementary Grammar to Communicate 1 Exercises on the Teacher's Resource Disk as homework or on the Student Persistence CD-ROM as self-access practice.

B Teaching Time: 5–10 min.

- Read the example with the class. Tell students to make logical sentences with *should* and *shouldn't*.
- Have students complete the task.
- Call on students to say answers. Correct as needed.
- **LIFE SKILLS TEST PREP 2** Go to Unit 9, Lesson 1 for more practice in identifying parts of the body and face.

C Teaching Time: 10–15 min.

- Read the example with the class.
- PAIRS. Have students complete the task. Walk around and help as needed.
- Call on pairs to read their sentences to the class. Correct as needed.
- **LIFE SKILLS TEST PREP 2** Go to Unit 9, Lesson 2 for more practice in learning words to talk about injuries.

Multilevel Strategy

- **Pre-level:** Group all pre-level students. Work with them and brainstorm possible responses. After checking answers, have pairs take turns reading the sentences.
- **At-level, Above-level:** Have at-level students think of two additional conditions and act them out while above-level students make recommendations. For example, the at-level student grabs his or her stomach and says: *My stomach hurts.* The above-level student responds: *You shouldn't eat anything! You should stay home.*

TIME to TALK

Teaching Time: 15–20 min.

- GROUPS. Have students use dictionaries or ask one another to find the meanings of the words in the chart.
- Have students complete the chart.
- Walk around and help as needed.
- Call on students to say some of their group's sentences.

Multilevel Strategy

- **All-levels:** Place students in mixed-level groups. Have at-level and above-level students brainstorm ideas for each problem. Assign pre-level students as recorders and have them write the ideas in the chart. Then have them present their group's ideas to the class.

Unit 17

Grammar to Communicate 2

Should: Yes / No Questions

Teaching Time: 5–10 min.

- Say: *To ask yes / no questions with should, put should before the subject.*
- Write on the board a few sentences such as: *We should exercise more.*
- Have volunteers change each sentence into a question.
- Have students study the grammar chart.
- Read each question and short answer in the chart and have students repeat chorally.

A Teaching Time: 3–5 min.

- Read the example with the class.
- Have students complete the task.
- PAIRS. Have students compare answers.
- Call on students to say answers. Correct as needed.

B Teaching Time: 10–15 min.

- Read the example with the class.
- Have students complete the task.
- Call on students to write questions on the board. Write corrections on the board as needed.
- PAIRS. Have students take turns asking and answering the questions.

Grammar to Communicate 2

SHOULD: YES / NO QUESTIONS

Should	Subject	Verb		Short Answers
Should	I / you / she / we / they	call	the doctor?	Yes, I / you / she / we / they should. No, I / you / she / we / they shouldn't.

A Answer the questions. Write short answers. *Answers will vary. Possible answers:*

1. Should people smoke? — No, they shouldn't.
2. Should people drink water every day? — Yes, they should.
3. Should people eat a lot of red meat? — No, they shouldn't.
4. Should people eat a lot of fruit and vegetables? — Yes, they should.
5. Should people drink a lot of alcohol? — No, they shouldn't.

PAIRS. Compare your answers.

B Read the sentences. Write questions. Use *should*.

1. Mr. Smith has the flu.
   Should he go to work?
   (he / go / to work)
2. Mrs. Jones is 80 years old and healthy.
   Should she exercise?
   (she / exercise)
3. Tran is 20 and healthy.
   Should he see a doctor every month?
   (he / see / a doctor every month)
4. Ana is a 6-week-old baby.
   Should her parents take her to the beach?
   (her parents / take her / to the beach)
5. Mona and Jason just ate a big lunch.
   Should they go swimming?
   (they / go swimming)
6. Marcus is six. His temperature is 99° (37.2°C).
   Should he go to school today?
   (he / go / to school today)

It's just a cold, right, Doc?

PAIRS. Ask and answer the questions above. Use short answers. Do you and your partner agree? *Answers will vary.*

Unit 17

Grammar Notes

1. To make *yes / no* questions with *should*, change the order of *should* and the subject.
2. Use full forms or contractions in negative short answers.
3. For more information on this grammar topic, see page 260.

Language Note

- **Exercise B.** Point out the speech bubble in the picture. Tell students that people use the word *right* and a question mark at the end of a sentence to check that the sentence is true.
- Tell students that *right?* can be used with affirmative and negative sentences.

Center Stage 2

C Complete the questions. Use *should* and the verbs in the box.

brush	eat	have	see
drink	exercise	keep	~~sleep~~

1. _Should_ babies _sleep_ on their stomachs or on their backs?
2. _Should_ you _exercise_ once a week for two hours or every day for 30 minutes?
3. _Should_ children _drink_ a lot of milk or a lot of fruit juice?
4. _Should_ children _eat_ a lot of French fries or a lot of salad?
5. _Should_ you _have_ a large meal for lunch or for dinner?
6. _Should_ you _see_ a doctor or a dentist for a toothache?
7. _Should_ people with allergies _keep_ cats at home?
8. _Should_ you _brush_ your teeth before you eat or after you eat?

PAIRS. Ask and answer the questions above. Do you agree?

> **Look**
> Use *or* in questions with two possible answers.
> A: I need a prescription. Should I see the doctor or the nurse?
> B: You should see the doctor.

TIME to TALK

PAIRS. Write two questions with *should* about each situation. Then discuss the answers to the questions. Answers will vary.

SITUATIONS	QUESTIONS
1. A teenager is heavy.	Should he exercise?
2. A woman is pregnant.	
3. A couple had a baby a few weeks ago.	
4. A little boy is afraid of the dark.	

WRAP-UP. Now change partners and ask your questions. Do you and your new partner have the same answers?

Example: A: Should the teenager exercise?
B: Yes, he should. He will feel better.

Health 207

C Teaching Time: 10–15 min.

- Have students study the Look box.
- Write on the board: *call the doctor now* and *call the doctor later*. Tell students that they can make questions about choices with *should*. Use *or* between the choices. Write on the board and read: *Should I call the doctor now or later?*
- Read the example with the class.
- Have students complete the task.
- Call on students to read the questions aloud. Correct as needed.
- PAIRS. Have students take turns asking and answering the questions.
- Call on volunteers to tell the class their opinions on each topic. Ask them to explain their opinions.

Option
Assign Unit 17 Supplementary Grammar to Communicate 2 Exercises on the Teacher's Resource Disk as homework or on the Student Persistence CD-ROM as self-access practice.

TIME to TALK

Teaching Time: 15–20 min.

- Read the example with the class.
- PAIRS. Have students write questions.
- Walk around and help as needed.
- PAIRS. Have students change partners and complete the Wrap-up task.
- Call on pairs to read their questions and answers to the class.

Expansion
- Have each student choose a health topic from the unit or one of his or her own.
- Have students use the Internet or other information sources to find medical advice on the topic.
- Have students make posters to teach the class about things they should or shouldn't do related to the health topic and present their posters to the class.
- If possible, display students' posters around the classroom.

Unit 17

Grammar to Communicate 3

Should: Information Questions

Teaching Time: 5–10 min.

- Review *yes / no* questions by having students change a few *should* statements into questions.
- Say: *To ask information questions, use a wh-word before should.* Give a few examples, such as: *Where should she go?*
- Have students look at the picture. Say: *Use which and a noun to ask questions about choice.* For example: *Which medicine should he take? There are four different kinds.*
- Write on the board: *how long* and *how often*. Tell students to use *how long* to ask about a period of time or a length of time. Tell them to use *how often* to ask about the frequency of something.
- Have students study the chart.
- Read the questions and answers in the chart and have students repeat chorally.

A Teaching Time: 5–10 min.

- Read the example with the class.
- Have students complete the task.
- Call on students to say answers. Correct as needed.
- **LIFE SKILLS TEST PREP 2** Go to Unit 9, Lesson 6 for more practice in identifying common prescription and nonprescription medicines.

Grammar to Communicate 3

SHOULD: INFORMATION QUESTIONS

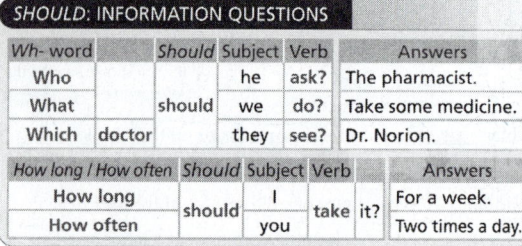

Wh- word		Should	Subject	Verb	Answers
Who			he	ask?	The pharmacist.
What		should	we	do?	Take some medicine.
Which	doctor		they	see?	Dr. Norion.

How long / How often	Should	Subject	Verb		Answers
How long	should	I	take	it?	For a week.
How often		you			Two times a day.

A Complete the questions with *should* and *take*. Then match the questions with the answers.

_b_ 1. Mr. Lang has a cough.
   Which medicine _should he take?_

_d_ 2. Lynn and Robert have heartburn.
   Which medicine _should they take_?

_e_ 3. Ruth and Steve have allergies.
   Which medicine _should they take_?

_c_ 4. Alison's eight-year-old son has a cough.
   Which medicine _should he take_?

_a_ 5. Ms. Bryant has a headache.
   Which medicine _should she take_?

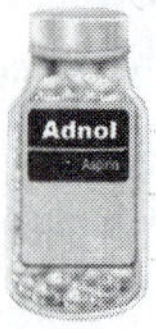

a. Adnol Aspirin
b. Bronchusin Cough Syrup 
c. Bell's Children's Cough Syrup 
d. Tumex Antacid for Heartburn Relief 
e. Viva Allergy Relief 

208 Unit 17

Grammar Notes

1. To make information questions with *should*, use the same word order as *yes / no* questions, and put a *wh-* word at the beginning. For example: *Should I take something? What should I take?*
2. Use *which* and a noun to ask questions about choices.
3. For more information on this grammar topic, see page 260.

T-208 Center Stage 2

B Complete the questions. Use *How often, Where, What, Who,* and *Should.*

1. _How often should_ people take aspirin? Every four to six hours.
2. _Who should_ a patient ask for medical advice? A doctor.
3. _Where should_ parents put medicine? In a safe place, away from children.
4. A baby has a cold. _What should_ his mother give him? Baby cough syrup.
5. _How often should_ healthy people see the doctor? Twice a year.

C Read the sentences. Look at the answers. Write questions with *should.* Use *How many, What, When,* and *Who.*

1. The doctor should give Al a prescription for the pain.
   Who should the doctor give a prescription to? To Al.
   What should the doctor give to Al? A prescription.

2. You should ask the nurse about the medicine tomorrow.
   What should you ask the nurse about tomorrow? The medicine.
   Who should you ask about the medicine tomorrow? The nurse.

3. The children should take two pills every 12 hours.
   How often should the children take two pills? Every 12 hours.
   How many pills should the children take every 12 hours? Two.

TIME to TALK

CLASS. Play this Doctor and Patient game. Half of the class will be patients. The other half will be doctors. Answers will vary.

Patients: Look at the vocabulary on pages 202–203 and choose two problems. Then go sit with a doctor. Explain one problem to the doctor. Ask questions about what you should do. Then go to a new doctor. Explain the second problem and ask questions.

Doctors: Sit with a patient and give advice. Answer his or her questions.

Example:
A: Doctor, I have a backache. Should I go to the gym?
B: No, you shouldn't. You should rest at home.

Health 209

B Teaching Time: 5–10 min.
- Read the example with the class.
- Have students complete the task.
- Call on pairs of students to read the questions and answers. Correct as needed.

C Teaching Time: 5–10 min.
- Read the examples with the class.
- Call on volunteers to come to the board and write the questions. Correct as needed.

Multilevel Strategy
- **At-level, Above-level:** Call on only at-level and above-level students to write the questions on the board.
- **Pre-level:** Have students copy the questions from the board.

Option
Assign Unit 17 Supplementary Grammar to Communicate 3 Exercises on the Teacher's Resource Disk as homework or on the Student Persistence CD-ROM as self-access practice.

TIME to TALK
Teaching Time: 15–20 min.
- Have two students read the example.
- Have students complete the task.
- Walk around and help as needed.
- **LIFE SKILLS TEST PREP 2** Go to Unit 9, Lesson 4 for more practice in making an appointment with the doctor.

Multilevel Strategy
- **Pre-level:** Help students write two questions to ask the "doctor" about the problems they have chosen. Help the "doctors" give advice to the "patients."
- **Above-level:** Challenge the students with the task by having them disagree with the "doctor's" recommendation in order to add complexity to the conversation.

Unit 17 T-209

Review and Challenge

Grammar

Teaching Time: 5–10 min.

- Read the example with the class.
- Have students complete the task.
- PAIRS. Have students compare answers.
- Play Track 19 and have students check their answers.
- PAIRS. Have students role-play the corrected conversation.

Expansion Call on students to suggest other things that Teri should or shouldn't do. For example: *She should take the baby to the emergency room.*

Dictation

Teaching Time: 5–10 min.

- Play Track 20 while students listen and write what they hear.
- Play Track 20 again while students check their answers.
- Call on students to write answers on the board.
- Play Track 20 again and correct the sentences on the board.

Multilevel Strategy

- **Pre-level:** Give students a worksheet with some of the words from the dictation already provided.

Speaking

Teaching Time: 10–15 min.

- Have two students read the example conversation.
- Work with the students to explain the medical conditions in the box. Ask a few students to look them up in a dictionary and read their definitions to the class.
- GROUPS. Have students complete the task.
- Walk around and help as needed.
- Call on students from each group to say some of their group's advice. If students in other groups disagree with the advice, encourage students to explain their ideas. For example: *People with asthma shouldn't smoke because smoking makes it harder to breathe.*

Option

Before class, make a copy of the grammar exercise on page 210 as a transparency to use with an overhead projector. Ask a volunteer to make corrections to the conversation on the transparency. Correct as needed. Have students check their work with the transparency.

Option

- Have students think about how much of each food group they usually eat and how much they *should* eat.
- Ask students to each write three sentences about changes they should make in their diets. For example: *I should eat more green vegetables. I shouldn't eat a lot of bread.*

Review and Challenge

Grammar

19 Correct the conversation. There are six mistakes. The first mistake is corrected for you. Then listen and check your answers.

Teri: The baby is sick. What ~~I should~~ *should I* do?

Jon: You should ~~to~~ call the doctor.

Teri: But it's 9 P.M. The doctor's not in his office.

Jon: What's wrong with the baby?

Teri: He feels hot.

Jon: Did you take his temperature?

Teri: No, I didn't. ~~We should~~ *Should we* take him to the hospital?

Jon: No, we ~~don't~~ *shouldn't*. You should ~~do~~ take his temperature.

Teri: I'm worried.

Jon: You ~~should no~~ *shouldn't* worry. He's fine.

Dictation

20 Listen. You will hear five sentences. Write them on a piece of paper. *See the audioscript on page 290 for the sentences.*

Speaking

GROUPS. Find out the meanings of the medical conditions in the box. Ask a classmate or look in the dictionary. What should people with the conditions do? What shouldn't they do? *Answers will vary.*

| asthma | diabetes | high blood pressure | high cholesterol |

Example:
A: People with asthma should not have cats.
B: And they shouldn't smoke . . .

WRAP-UP. Share your ideas with the class. Do you have the same answers?

Unit 17

Listening

A 🔊 21 Look at the different kinds of food in the picture. What do you think the listening will be about? Check (✓) the correct answer. Then listen. Was your answer correct?

❏ grocery shopping ☑ eating healthy food ❏ cooking for special occasions

B 🔊 22 Listen again. How much of each food group should people eat a day? Write the correct amounts.

Look
1 ounce = 31.103 grams
8 ounces = 1 cup

1. grains
   6 ounces
2. vegetables
   2 1/2 cups
3. fruit
   2 cups
4. low-fat milk products
   3 cups
5. meat group
   5 1/2 ounces

(food pyramid image with labels: oil, fats, & sweets; milk group; meat & protein group; vegetable group; fruit group; grains)

TIME to TALK

GROUPS. Discuss the questions. _Answers will vary._

1. What are some things that you should *not* eat a lot of?
2. How much exercise should the people in these age groups get every day? What kind of exercise?
   a. children   b. teenagers   c. middle-aged people   d. seniors (over 65)
3. Doctors agree that stress (worrying) is bad for your health. What should people do to have less stress? What do you do to have less stress in your life?
4. What other things should people do to stay healthy?

WRAP-UP. Compare your answers with another group. Do you agree?

Health

Listening

A Teaching Time: 5–10 min.

- **Warm-up:** Have students look at the illustration. Ask them to identify foods they know. Point out the name of each food group. Explain unfamiliar vocabulary. For example, say: *Your body needs protein to be strong. Meat, fish, eggs, and beans have protein.* Call on volunteers to give a few more examples of foods in each group.
- Have students predict what the listening will be about.
- 🎧 Play Track 21 while students listen.
- 🎧 Play Track 21 again while students listen and complete the task.
- Call on a student to say the answer. Correct as needed.
- LIFE SKILLS TEST PREP 2 Go to Unit 5, Lesson 1 for more practice in identifying common foods and their containers.

B Teaching Time: 5–10 min.

- Have students study the Look Box.
- 🎧 Play Track 22 while students listen and complete the task.
- 🎧 Play Track 22 again while students listen and check their answers.
- LIFE SKILLS TEST PREP 2 Go to Unit 5, Lesson 2 for more practice in identifying and asking for common quantities of food.
- LIFE SKILLS TEST PREP 2 Go to Unit 5, Lesson 3 for more practice in reading basic information on food packaging and labels.

Option

Assign Unit 17 Supplementary Review and Challenge Exercises on the Teacher's Resource Disk as homework or on the Student Persistence CD-ROM as self-access practice.

TIME to TALK

Teaching Time: 10–15 min.

- GROUPS. Have students complete the task.
- Walk around and help as needed.
- Call on volunteers to tell the class some of their answers.

Multilevel Strategy

- **All-levels:** Place students in mixed-level groups. Have at-level and above-level students brainstorm ideas for each question. Assign pre-level students as recorders and have them write the ideas on a piece of paper.

Unit 17

Reading and Writing

Reading

A Teaching Time: 10–15 min.

- Point out the pictures and captions *tablet*, *capsule*, and *tablespoon*. Tell students that these are measurements of medicine. If necessary, explain that a label is a piece of paper on food, medicine, etc., that gives information about it.
- Have students read the labels silently. Then read them aloud. Pause after each few words and have students repeat chorally.
- Have students choose the correct answer.
- Call on a student to say the answer. Correct as needed.
- **LIFE SKILLS TEST PREP 2** Go to Unit 9, Lesson 7 for more practice in reading medicine labels, including dosages.

B Teaching Time: 5–10 min.

- Have students complete the task.
- PAIRS. Have students compare answers.
- Call on students to say answers. Correct as needed.

Expansion

- Have students copy the chart from page 212 into their notebooks.
- Assign the following task for homework: Have students find three medicines in their home or in a store. Have them write the names of the medicines at the top of each column and complete the chart with the information about each medicine.

Reading and Writing

Reading

A Read the medicine labels. Which medicine should you *not* give to an 8-year-old child? __Medicine A__

Medicine A

DIRECTIONS
- **Adults:** take 1 tablet every 4 to 6 hours
- If pain or fever does not respond to 1 tablet, 2 tablets may be used, but do not take more than 6 tablets in 24 hours, unless directed by a doctor.
- **Children:** do not give to children under 12

tablet

Medicine B

DIRECTIONS
Adults and children 6 years and over:
1 capsule daily, not more than 1 capsule in 24 hours
Children under 6 years:
Ask a doctor.

capsule

Medicine C

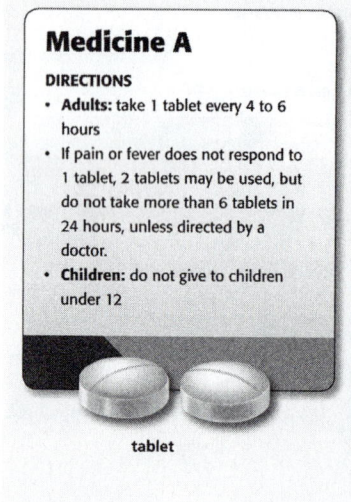

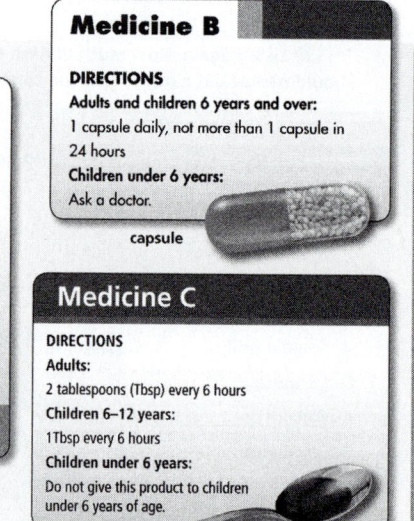

DIRECTIONS
Adults:
2 tablespoons (Tbsp) every 6 hours
Children 6–12 years:
1 Tbsp every 6 hours
Children under 6 years:
Do not give this product to children under 6 years of age.

tablespoon

B Read the medicine labels again. Answer the questions. Complete the chart.

	MEDICINE A	MEDICINE B	MEDICINE C
1. How often should a person take it?	every 4–6 hours	daily	every 6 hours
2. How much should an adult take each time?	1 or 2 tablets	1 capsule	2 tablespoons
3. How much should an 11-year-old child take each time?	do not take	1 capsule	1 tablespoon
4. How much should a 6-year-old child take each time?	do not take	ask a doctor	do not take

Writing

Read the e-mail. Then write an e-mail to a doctor with some questions about a medical problem. The problem can be real or imaginary. Use Mrs. Lang's e-mail as a model. *Answers will vary.*

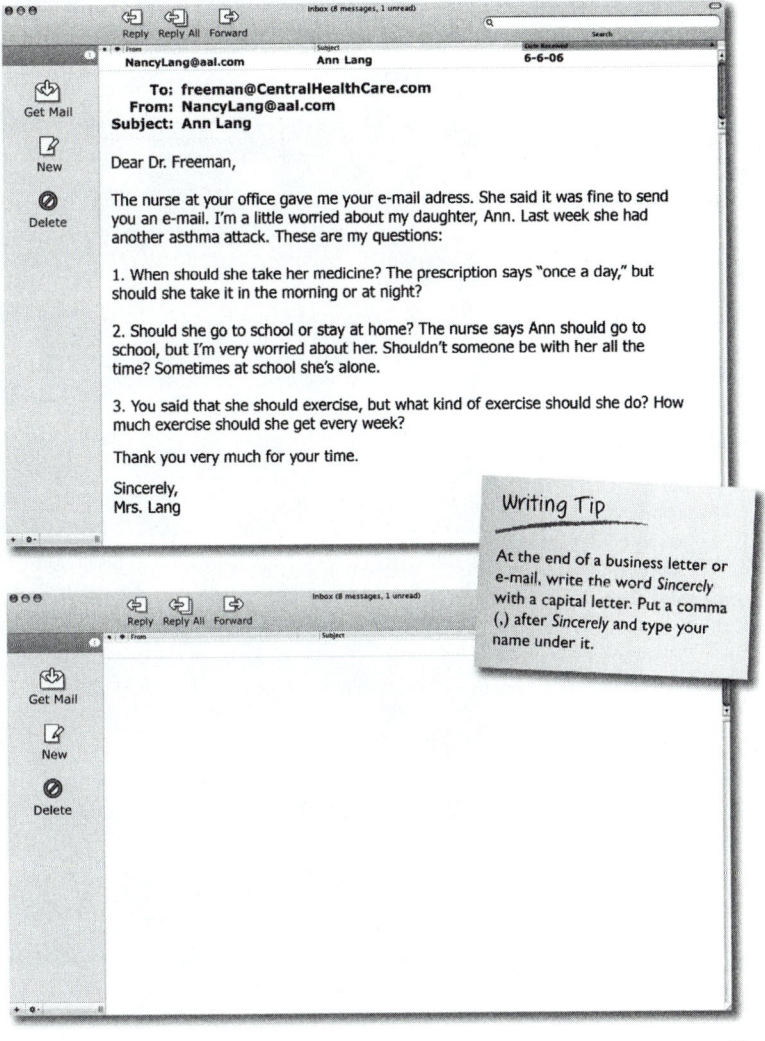

From: NancyLang@aal.com
Subject: Ann Lang
Date Received: 6-6-06

To: freeman@CentralHealthCare.com
From: NancyLang@aal.com
Subject: Ann Lang

Dear Dr. Freeman,

The nurse at your office gave me your e-mail adress. She said it was fine to send you an e-mail. I'm a little worried about my daughter, Ann. Last week she had another asthma attack. These are my questions:

1. When should she take her medicine? The prescription says "once a day," but should she take it in the morning or at night?

2. Should she go to school or stay at home? The nurse says Ann should go to school, but I'm very worried about her. Shouldn't someone be with her all the time? Sometimes at school she's alone.

3. You said that she should exercise, but what kind of exercise should she do? How much exercise should she get every week?

Thank you very much for your time.

Sincerely,
Mrs. Lang

Writing Tip

At the end of a business letter or e-mail, write the word *Sincerely* with a capital letter. Put a comma (,) after *Sincerely* and type your name under it.

Health 213

Writing

Teaching Time: 30–35 min.

- Ask students to say some questions that patients typically ask a doctor. Record the questions on the board.
- Have students read the e-mail silently. Ask them a few questions about the e-mail, such as: *Who is the e-mail to? Who is it from? Who has the health problem?*
- Have each student write down three medical problems that they could ask questions about. Then have each student choose one problem to write about.
- Ask students to study the Writing Tip. Tell them that it is polite to use *Sincerely* in letters and e-mails.
- Have students complete the task.
- Walk around and help as needed.
- **LIFE SKILLS TEST PREP 2** Go to Unit 1, Lesson 6 for practice in writing an absence note.
- Call on volunteers to read their e-mails to the class. Correct as needed. You can also have students write their e-mails on a piece of paper. Collect their work and provide individual feedback.

Language Note

Writing. Tell students that people also sometimes use *Sincerely* when they write letters or e-mails to friends, but they don't use it with people they know very well.

Unit 17 T-213

Unit 18
A Place to Live

Learning Goals
- Learn words to describe places to live
- Learn about comparative and superlative of adjectives
- Listen to a conversation and a radio report about places to live
- Read a real estate web site and write an e-mail
- Talk about places to live

Learner Persistence

Encourage students to reflect on how much they are learning in a journal. Students can express any difficulties they may be having in class, as well as what they'd like to review and learn more about. The more you know about your students' needs, the better you can meet them. Students are more likely to persist when their needs are being met.

Warm-up
Teaching Time: 3–5 min.

Have students look at the pictures. Ask them to point to places to live and name them.

Vocabulary
Teaching Time: 15–20 min.

- Have students look at the pictures and explain unfamiliar vocabulary. For example, say: *Buses, trains, and taxis are kinds of public transportation. Something that is modern has a new style.*
- 🎧 Play Track 23 while students read and listen.
- Read the words and phrases aloud and have students repeat chorally.
- Have students complete the task.
- Call on students to tell the class their answers.

Multilevel Strategy

- **Pre-level:** Have pairs practice pronouncing the words in the list to one another.
- **At-level, Above-level:** Have students make sentences about their neighborhoods using the words they circled and their own vocabulary. Call on students to read their sentences.

Unit 18
A Place to Live

Grammar
- Comparative of Adjectives
- Superlative of Adjectives
- Comparative and Superlative

Vocabulary

🎧 **TRACK 23** Read and listen. Then circle the words that describe your home and your neighborhood.
Answers will vary.

1. low rent
2. close to public transportation
3. public transportation
4. convenient
5. dangerous street
6. ugly
7. pretty view
8. high rent
9. modern
10. safe
11. far from public transportation
12. in the country

Expansion
- Write the following words on the board in one column: *low, close, public, ugly, dangerous, convenient, modern.*
- Have students find in the vocabulary list or a dictionary the opposites of the words on the board and write them down.

T-214 Center Stage 2

Listening

A 🎧 **24** Listen. Doug is looking for an apartment. Which apartment is he going to visit? Check (✓) the correct answer.

- ☐ The apartment on Mercer Street
- ☐ The apartment in Brighton Park
- ☐ The apartment in the West End
- ☑ The apartment on Trenton Street

B 🎧 **25** Read and listen again. Write the missing words. Use the words in the box.

| ~~best~~ | cheaper | cheapest | more | than | the most |

Miranda: The __best__ apartment is on Mercer Street near the new theater. It's $1,300 a month.

Doug: Wow. That's expensive. How about the other two apartments? Are they __cheaper__ than that?

Miranda: Yes, they are, but the Mercer Street apartment is in __the most__ convenient location.

Doug: But I don't want to spend that much money. How much is the __cheapest__ apartment?

Miranda: It's $400 a month, but it's also the smallest. And it's the farthest from downtown. It's out in Brighton Park.

Doug: Oh, that is far. How about the last apartment?

Miranda: It's in a better location __than__ the Brighton Park apartment. It's also larger and sunnier, and it's in a __more__ modern building.

A Place to Live 215

Language Note

Exercise B. Point out the word *downtown* in the conversation. Explain that *downtown* is the center or main business area of a city or town.

Option

Assign Unit 18 Supplementary Vocabulary Exercise on the Teacher's Resource Disk as homework or on the Student Persistence CD-ROM as self-access practice.

Listening

A Teaching Time: 10–15 min.

- **Warm-up:** Ask students how people find places to live (for example: *newspaper ads, signs in public places such as grocery stores and libraries, real estate agents*).
- Ask students to read through the answer choices before they listen.
- 🎧 Play Track 24 while students listen.
- 🎧 Play Track 24 again while students listen and complete the task.
- Call on a student to say the answer. Correct as needed.

B Teaching Time: 15–20 min.

- Have students read through the answer choices before they listen.
- 🎧 Play Track 25 while students listen and complete the task.
- 🎧 Play Track 25 again while students listen and check their answers.
- Call on students to say answers. Correct as needed.
- Read the conversation aloud. Pause after each few words and have students repeat chorally.
- PAIRS. Ask students to role-play the conversation.
- **LIFE SKILLS TEST PREP 2** Go to Unit 8, Lesson 2 for more practice in describing and asking about an apartment for rent.

Multilevel Strategy

- **Pre-level:** Have students role-play the completed conversation.
- **At-level, Above-level:** Have students role-play a new conversation and talk about places where they live. Tell them to use the conversation in the book as a model. Call on pairs to role-play in front of the class.

Unit 18 T-215

Grammar to Communicate 1

Comparative of Adjectives

Teaching Time: 5–10 min.

- Before class, find magazine pictures to demonstrate comparative adjectives, such as people of different ages to show *younger* and *older*.
- Say: *We use comparative forms of adjectives to say how two things are different.* Point to each person or object from the magazine pictures and make sentences with *than*. For example: *The man is older than the boy.*
- Have students study the chart, the picture, and the Look Box.
- Say: *Add -er to an adjective to make the comparative form. If an adjective ends in -e, only add -r. If it ends in -y, change -y to -i and add -er. Don't add -er to adjectives that have two or three syllables. Use* more *with these adjectives. Some adjectives are irregular. Don't add -er to them.*
- Read the adjectives and have students repeat chorally.
- Write a few adjectives on the board and call on students to say the comparative forms.

A Teaching Time: 5–10 min.

- Read the example with the class.
- Have students complete the task.
- Call on students to say answers. Correct as needed.
- **LIFE SKILLS TEST PREP 2** Go to Unit 7, Lesson 3 for more practice in understanding the American system of measuring distance.

B Teaching Time: 5–10 min.

- Read the examples with the class. Say: *Expensive has three syllables. That's why we add* more *to make the comparative.*
- Have students complete the task.
- Call on students to say answers. Correct as needed.

Grammar to Communicate 1

COMPARATIVE OF ADJECTIVES

Adjective	Comparative	Rules to Form Comparatives
small	smaller	With one syllable: Add -er
nice	nicer	With one syllable ending in -e: Add -r
pretty	prettier	With two syllables ending in -y: Change the -y to -i, and add -er
modern	more modern	With two or three syllables: Add *more* + adjective

Irregular Adjectives

Adjective	Comparative
good	better
bad	worse
far	farther

small   smaller

Look
We often use *than* with comparatives.
His house **is smaller than** her house.
This house **is more modern than** that one.

A Read the chart. Complete the sentences. Write *Home A* and *Home B*.

	SIZE	YEAR BUILT	RENT	DISTANCE TO SUBWAY	LOCATION	NUMBER OF WINDOWS
home A	8 rooms	1960	$1,000	1 mile	on quiet street, near lake and park	15
home B	5 rooms	2000	$900	1/2 mile	on city street, next to stores	5

1. __Home B__ is smaller than __Home A__.
2. __Home B__ is more modern than __Home A__.
3. The rent for __Home A__ is higher.
4. __Home B__ is closer to the subway than __Home A__.
5. __Home A__ is sunnier than __Home B__.
6. __Home A__ is closer to the park than __Home B__.

B Write the comparative form of the adjectives.

1. old — older
2. expensive — more expensive
3. low — lower
4. noisy — noisier
5. close — closer
6. convenient — more convenient
7. far — farther
8. dark — darker
9. sunny — sunnier
10. bad — worse
11. safe — safer
12. good — better

216 Unit 18

Grammar Notes

1. Comparative adjectives compare two nouns.
2. Add *–er* to one-syllable adjectives to make the comparative form.
3. When a two-syllable adjective ends in *y*, change *y* to *i* and add *–er* to make the comparative form.
4. Add *more* before most adjectives with two or more syllables to make the comparative form.
5. *Good*, *bad*, and *far* have irregular comparative forms (*better*, *worse*, and *farther*).
6. For more information on this grammar topic, see page 260.

T-216 Center Stage 2

C Write sentences about Home A and Home B in Exercise A. Use comparatives.

1. Home A is larger than Home B.
   (large)
2. Home A is older than Home B.
   (old)
3. Home A is in a prettier area than Home B.
   (in a pretty area)
4. Home B is farther from the lake than Home A.
   (far from the lake)
5. Home B is closer to stores than Home A.
   (close to stores)
6. Home A is more expensive than Home B.
   (expensive)
7. Home B is noisier than Home A.
   (noisy)
8. Home B is more convenient than Home A.
   (convenient)

D PAIRS. Look at the pictures on pages 214–215. Talk about Kathy's place and Estelle's place. Use the comparative form of the words in the box. Answers will vary. Possible answers:

| big | convenient | modern | noisy | pretty | quiet | small |

Look
River Street is quieter than Mercer Street.
NOT River Street is more quiet than Mercer Street.

Example:
A: Estelle's place is quieter than Kathy's place.
Estelle's place is prettier than Kathy's place.
Estelle's place is bigger than Kathy's place.
Kathy's place is more convenient than Estelle's place.
Kathy's place is more modern than Estelle's place. Kathy's place is smaller than Estelle's place.

TIME to TALK

PAIRS. Talk about five differences between where you live now and your old home. Talk about the apartments or houses, the neighborhoods, and the neighbors. Use the comparative forms of the words in the box. Answers will vary.

cheap / expensive	convenient / inconvenient	large / small	quiet / noisy
clean / dirty	friendly / unfriendly	modern / old	safe / dangerous
close / far	good / bad	pretty / ugly	sunny / dark

Example:
A: My new apartment is more modern than my old apartment. And my new neighborhood is safer than my old neighborhood.
B: That's good.
A: But my new neighbors are noisier than my old neighbors.

A Place to Live 217

C Teaching Time: 5–10 min.
- Read the example with the class.
- Have students complete the task.
- Call on students to write sentences on the board. Write corrections on the board as needed.

Multilevel Strategy
- **Pre-level, Above-level:** Have above-level students help pre-level students complete the task. Have above-level students explain to pre-level students how and where they found the answers.

D Teaching Time: 5–10 min.
- Have students study the Look Box. Tell students that some adjectives don't follow the rules of forming comparatives.
- Have students look at the pictures on pages 214–215.
- Read the example with the class.
- PAIRS. Have students complete the task. Walk around and help as needed.
- Call on students to say one of their sentences.
- **LIFE SKILLS TEST PREP 2** Go to Unit 8, Lesson 3 for more practice in describing common problems in an apartment.

Language Note

Exercises C and D. If an adjective ends with consonant-vowel-consonant pattern, double the consonant and add *–er* to form the comparative. For example: big / bigger, hot / hotter, fat / fatter, thin / thinner, sad / sadder.

Option

Assign Unit 18 Supplementary Grammar to Communicate 1 Exercises on the Teacher's Resource Disk as homework or on the Student Persistence CD-ROM as self-access practice.

TIME to TALK

Teaching Time: 10–15 min.
- Have two students read the example conversation.
- PAIRS. Have students complete the task.
- Walk around and help as needed.

Unit 18 T-217

Grammar to Communicate 2

Superlative of Adjectives

Teaching Time: 5–10 min.

- Before class, find magazine pictures to show superlative adjectives, such as three people of different ages to show *the youngest* and *the oldest*.
- Say: *The superlative forms of adjectives show how more than two things are different.* Point to each person or object and say the corresponding superlative adjective.
- Have students study the chart, the pictures, and the Look Box.
- Say: *Add -est to an adjective to make the superlative form. If an adjective ends in -e, only add -st. If it ends in -y, change -y to -i and add -est. Don't add -est to adjectives that have two or three syllables. Use* the most *with these adjectives. Some adjectives are irregular. Don't add -est to them.* Remind students that they need to say *the* with superlative forms.
- Read the adjectives and their superlatives and have students repeat chorally.
- Write a few adjectives on the board and call on students to say the superlative forms.

A Teaching Time: 3–5 min.

- Have students complete the sentences.
- Call on students to say answers. Correct as needed.
- PAIRS. Have students tell each other about rooms in their own house or apartment.

B Teaching Time: 5–10 min.

- Read the examples with the class. Remind students to use *the* before the superlative forms of adjectives.
- Have students complete the task.
- Call on students to say answers. Correct as needed.

Grammar to Communicate 2

SUPERLATIVE OF ADJECTIVES

Adjective	Superlative	Rules to Form Superlatives
small	the smallest	With one syllable: Add -est
nice	the nicest	With one syllable ending in -e: Add -st
pretty	the prettiest	With two syllables ending in -y: Change the -y to -i, and add -est
modern	the most modern	With two or three syllables: Add *most* + adjective

Irregular Adjectives

Adjective	Superlative
good	the best
bad	the worst
far	the farthest

small smaller smallest

A Write about the rooms in your house. Answers will vary.

1. The biggest room is _____.
2. The smallest room is _____.
3. The sunniest room is _____.
4. The most crowded room is _____.
5. The most comfortable room is _____.

Look

We use *the* with superlatives.
Our house is **the most modern**.
That room is **the sunniest**.
Her room is **the biggest**.

B Write the superlative form of the words.

1. big — the biggest
2. comfortable — the most comfortable
3. sunny — the sunniest
4. quiet — the quietest
5. crowded — the most crowded
6. good — the best
7. dark — the darkest
8. noisy — the noisiest
9. bad — the worst
10. old — the oldest
11. ugly — the ugliest
12. modern — the most modern
13. safe — the safest
14. expensive — the most expensive

Unit 18

Grammar Notes

1. Superlative adjectives compare three or more nouns.
2. Add *–est* to one-syllable adjectives to make the superlative form. When a two-syllable adjective ends in *y*, change *y* to *i* and add *–est* to make the superlative form.
3. Add *most* before most adjectives with two or more syllables to make the superlative form.
4. Use *the* before superlative adjectives.
5. *Good, bad,* and *far* have irregular superlative forms (*best, worst,* and *farthest*).
6. For more information on this grammar topic, see page 260.

Center Stage 2

C Complete the sentences. Use superlatives.

1. _The smallest_ room is the bathroom.
   (small)
2. _The noisiest_ room is the living room.
   (noisy)
3. _The ugliest_ room is the dining room.
   (ugly)
4. _The coldest_ room is my bedroom.
   (cold)
5. _The nicest_ room is the kitchen.
   (nice)
6. _The most expensive_ things are in the living room.
   (expensive)
7. _The most uncomfortable_ chairs are in the kitchen.
   (uncomfortable)

PAIRS. Which sentences above are true about your home? Tell your partner. *Answers will vary.*

D Write sentences. Use the superlative form of the adjectives. Then circle the sentences you agree with.

1. _Orange is the worst color for a living room._
   (orange / bad / color for a living room)
2. _Rugs are the dirtiest things in a home._
   (rugs / dirty / things in a home)
3. _A closet is the most important thing in a bedroom._
   (a closet / important / thing in a bedroom)
4. _The kitchen is the most comfortable room in a house._
   (the kitchen / comfortable / room in a house)
5. _Yellow is the best color for a kitchen._
   (yellow / good / color for a kitchen)

PAIRS. Read the sentences you circled. Do you and your partner agree?

TIME to TALK

PAIRS. Look at the ads on page 274. Compare the furniture stores. Use the words in the box and your own ideas. *Answers will vary.*

| cheap | comfortable | expensive | good | interesting |
| modern | nice | pretty | stylish | traditional |

Example:
A: *Best for Less* has the best prices.
B: Yes, but the furniture in *Designs for Today* is the most interesting.

In your opinion, which furniture store is the best of the three? Why?

A Place to Live 219

C Teaching Time: 5–10 min.
- Read the example with the class. Remind students to use *the* with superlatives.
- Have students complete the sentences.
- Call on students to say answers. Correct as needed.
- PAIRS. Have students read each other sentences that are true about their own homes.

D Teaching Time: 5–10 min.
- Read the example with the class.
- Have students complete the task.
- Call on students to say answers. Correct as needed.
- PAIRS. Have students compare the sentences they circled.

Multilevel Strategy
- **Pre-level:** Pair pre-level students for the partner activity. Have them take turns reading the sentences they circled.
- **At-level, Above-level:** Pair at-level students with above-level students for the partner activity. Have students change the sentences they don't agree with while reading their sentences to a partner (e.g., *Orange isn't the worst color for a living room. Black is the worst color for a living room.*).

Option
Assign Unit 18 Supplementary Grammar to Communicate 2 Exercises on the Teacher's Resource Disk as homework or on the Student Persistence CD-ROM as self-access practice.

TIME to TALK
Teaching Time: 10–15 min.
- Have two students read the example.
- PAIRS. Have students complete the task.
- Walk around and help as needed.
- Call on volunteers to say which furniture store they think is the best and explain why.

Unit 18 T-219

Grammar to Communicate 3

Comparative and Superlative

Teaching Time: 5–10 min.

- Remind students to use comparative forms to compare two nouns and to use superlative forms to compare three or more nouns.
- Remind students to use *–er* and *–est* to make comparative and superlative forms with one-syllable adjectives and two-syllable adjectives that end in *y*.
- Remind students to add *more* and *the most* before adjectives that have two or more syllables to make comparative and superlative forms.
- Have students study the chart.
- Read the words in the chart and have students repeat chorally.

A Teaching Time: 5–10 min.

- Read the examples with the class.
- Have students complete the task.
- Call on students to read questions. Correct as needed.
- Call on volunteers to answer each question.

B Teaching Time: 5–10 min.

- While students are completing Exercise A, copy the chart on the board.
- Read the examples with the class.
- Call on volunteers to come to the board and fill in the information in the chart. Correct as needed.

Grammar to Communicate 3

COMPARATIVE AND SUPERLATIVE

Adjective	Comparative	Superlative
small	smaller	the smallest
nice	nicer	the nicest
pretty	prettier	the prettiest
famous	more famous	the most famous

Irregular Adjectives

Adjective	Comparative	Superlative
good	better	the best
bad	worse	the worst
far	farther	the farthest

Rio de Janeiro

A Complete the questions. Use the comparative or the superlative.

1. (better, the best)
   a. Which city has ___better___ weather—Rio de Janeiro or Chicago?
   b. Which city has ___the best___ weather—Toronto, Tokyo, or Honolulu?
2. (smaller, the smallest)
   a. Which country is ___the smallest___—Haiti, Vietnam, Canada, or Russia?
   b. Which country is ___smaller___—Venezuela or China?
3. (more famous, the most famous)
   a. Which city has ___the most famous___ buildings—Seoul, San Juan, or Paris?
   b. Which city has ___more famous___ buildings—Dallas or London?
4. (closer, the closest)
   a. Which country is ___closer___ to your country—Canada or France?
   b. Which country is ___the closest___ to your country—China, Italy, or the U.S.?

B Complete the chart.

ADJECTIVE	COMPARATIVE	SUPERLATIVE
1. bad	worse	the worst
2. big	bigger	the biggest
3. cheap	cheaper	the cheapest
4. dangerous	more dangerous	the most dangerous
5. expensive	more expensive	the most expensive

ADJECTIVE	COMPARATIVE	SUPERLATIVE
6. good	better	the best
7. high	higher	the highest
8. hot	hotter	the hottest
9. nice	nicer	the nicest
10. pretty	prettier	the prettiest

Unit 18

Grammar Notes

1. Use comparative forms to compare two nouns. Use superlative forms to compare three or more nouns.
2. For more information on this grammar topic, see page 260.

Option

- Before class make a set of flashcards with an adjective written on each one.
- Hold up each card and have students say the comparative and superlative form of the adjective.
- Students can make their own sets of flashcards and practice saying comparative and superlative forms individually or with a partner.

Center Stage 2

C Compare the places. Write sentences with comparatives and superlatives. Write on a piece of paper if you need more room.

Look
Russia, Canada, and China are countries.
Russia is the biggest of the three.

1. A town is bigger than a village. A city is the biggest of the three.
   a city / a village / a town / (BIG)
2. The Atlantic Ocean is larger than the Mediterranean Sea. The Pacific Ocean is the largest of the three.
   the Pacific Ocean / the Atlantic Ocean / the Mediterranean Sea / (LARGE)
3. A house is smaller than an apartment building. A room is the smallest of the three.
   a room / an apartment building / a house / (SMALL)
4. San Diego is hotter than Toronto. Rio de Janeiro is the hottest of the three.
   Toronto / Rio de Janeiro / San Diego / (HOT)

D Complete the questions. Use the comparative or superlative form. Add *than* where necessary.

1. Is a home in the city __better than__ a home in the country? (good)
2. What is __the best__ thing about a big city? (good)
3. What is __the worst__ thing about a big city? (bad)
4. Is it __worse__ to live in a dangerous or an ugly neighborhood? (bad)
5. Which neighborhood in your city has __the cheapest__ apartments? (cheap)
6. Which is __more important__ to you, a neighborhood with cheap homes or a neighborhood with good schools? (important)

GROUPS. Discuss the questions.

TIME to TALK
GROUPS. Compare the city you live in now with other cities you know well. Talk about five differences. Use the topics in the box and your own ideas. Answers will vary.

| buses | parks | universities |
| museums | sports teams | weather |

Example:
A: Chicago has better sports teams than Atlanta.
B: Yes, but the weather is nicer in Atlanta.
C: Yeah, but Miami's weather is the best, and its sports teams are good, too.

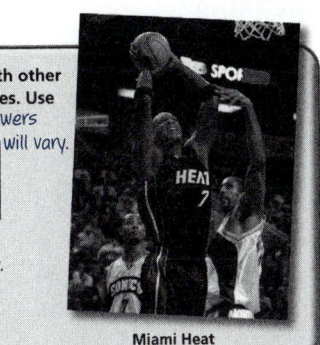

Miami Heat

A Place to Live 221

C Teaching Time: 5–10 min.
- Have students study the Look Box.
- Read the example with the class.
- Call on students to come to the board and write the sentences. Correct as needed.

Multilevel Strategy
- **At-level, Above-level:** Call on only at-level and above-level students to write sentences on the board.
- **Pre-level:** Have students copy the sentences from the board.

D Teaching Time: 5–10 min.
- Read the example with the class.
- Have students complete the task.
- Call on students to say answers. Correct as needed.
- GROUPS. Have students read each question and talk about the answers.
- Call on volunteers to give their groups' opinions. Encourage them to explain the reasons for their opinions.

Option
Assign Unit 18 Supplementary Grammar to Communicate 3 Exercises on the Teacher's Resource Disk as homework or on the Student Persistence CD-ROM as self-access practice.

TIME to TALK
Teaching Time: 10–15 min.
- Have three students read the example conversation.
- Give students a few minutes to write the names of some cities they know well.
- On the board, write a list of adjectives and other vocabulary from the unit in addition to the vocabulary listed in the box.
- GROUPS. Have students complete the task.
- Walk around and help as needed.

Unit 18 T-221

Review and Challenge

Grammar

Teaching Time: 5–10 min.

- Read the example with the class.
- Have students complete the task.
- Call on students to write corrected sentences on the board. Write corrections on the board as needed.

Multilevel Strategy

- **Pre-level:** Tell students what the mistakes are and have them rewrite the sentences.

Dictation

Teaching Time: 5–10 min.

- 🎧 Play Track 26 while students listen and write what they hear.
- 🎧 Play Track 26 again while students check their answers.
- Call on students to write answers on the board.
- 🎧 Play Track 26 again and correct sentences on the board.

Multilevel Strategy

Pre-level: Give students a worksheet with some of the words from the dictation already provided.

Speaking

Teaching Time: 5–10 min.

- Have students look at the pictures.
- PAIRS. Have students complete the task. Walk around and help as needed.
- Have partners compare their answers with those of another pair.
- Call on students to say their choices for each person or family.
- **LIFE SKILLS TEST PREP 2** Go to Unit 8, Lesson 1 for more practice in reading signs and ads for apartments.

Review and Challenge

Grammar

Find the mistake in each sentence. Circle the letter and correct the mistake.

1. Chinatown is <u>more</u> <u>famouser</u> <u>than</u> Diamond Hill.
                A   (B)   C
   Chinatown is more famous than Diamond Hill.

2. <u>Which</u> neighborhood has the <u>worstest</u> <u>schools</u>?
    A   (B)   C
   Which neighborhood has the worst schools?

3. <u>Is</u> Dolores Street <u>nicer</u> <u>to</u> Mission Street?
    A   B   (C)
   Is Dolores Street nicer than Mission Street?

4. This is <u>the</u> <u>most</u> <u>prettiest</u> neighborhood.
           A   (B)   C
   This is the prettiest neighborhood.

5. This house is <u>more</u> <u>moderner</u> <u>than</u> that house.
                       A   (B)   C
   This house is more modern than that house.

Chinatown, San Francisco

Dictation

🎧 **26** Listen. You will hear five sentences. Write them on a piece of paper. _See the audioscript on page 291 for the sentences._

Diamond Hill, San Francisco

Speaking

PAIRS. Wayne, Jerry, and Hiro and Satoko are looking for apartments. Look at the pictures. Then read the apartment ads on page 273. Which apartment is the best for Wayne? For Jerry? For Hiro and Satoko? _Answers will vary._

Wayne    Jerry and his kids    Hiro, Satoko, and their grandson

Unit 18

Option

- Bring in several pages of real estate ads from the local newspaper.
- Have students look at the ads and find one house or apartment that might be good for them.
- If necessary, explain abbreviations such as _BR_ and _bdrm_ (bedroom), _B_ and _bth_ (bathroom), _Gar_ and _grg_ (garage), _W / D_ (washer / dryer), and _mo_ (month).
- Call on volunteers to tell about the house or apartment they chose.

T-222   Center Stage 2

Listening

A 🎧 **27** Listen to a radio report about the best cities to live in. Check (✓) the topics the reporter talks about.

- ✓ clean air and water
- ☐ number of jobs
- ✓ cost of living
- ✓ public transportation
- ☐ friendly people
- ✓ restaurants and nightlife
- ☐ noise and traffic
- ✓ safety and crime
- ☐ number of doctors
- ✓ weather

Hong Kong

B 🎧 **28** Listen again. Check (✓) the correct information about the cities.

CITY NAME	CLEAN	EXCITING	EXCELLENT PUBLIC TRANSPORTATION	GOOD WEATHER	SAFE
Hong Kong		✓			
Tokyo			✓		✓
Vancouver	✓		✓	✓	✓
Vienna	✓		✓	✓	✓
Zurich	✓		✓	✓	✓

TIME to TALK

In your opinion, what is important in a neighborhood or home? What is not important? Look at the list below. Write *1* for the most important, *2* for important, and *3* for less important. *Answers will vary.*

- ___ a lot of children in the neighborhood
- ___ a lot of parks
- ___ close to family
- ___ close to supermarkets and other stores
- ___ the cost of living
- ___ friendly people
- ___ good jobs
- ___ good public schools
- ___ good public transportation
- ___ safety
- ___ the weather
- ___ other? _____

GROUPS. Explain your answers to your classmates.

Example:
A: The most important things for me are good schools and safety because I have children.
B: Good schools aren't important to me. The most important thing for me is good public transportation because I don't have a car.

A Place to Live 223

Listening

A Teaching Time: 5–10 min.

- **Warm-up:** Ask students to list the best cities to live in and the reasons why they are the best. Record students' ideas on the board.
- Ask students to read through the answer choices before they listen.
- 🎧 Play Track 27 while students listen.
- 🎧 Play Track 27 again while students listen and complete the task.
- Call on students to say answers. Correct as needed.

B Teaching Time: 5–10 min.

- Have students look at the categories in the chart.
- 🎧 Play Track 28 while students listen and complete the task.
- 🎧 Play Track 28 again while students listen and check their answers. Pause the recording each time an answer is given.

Option

Assign Unit 18 Supplementary Review and Challenge Exercises on the Teacher's Resource Disk as homework or on the Student Persistence CD-ROM as self-access practice.

TIME to TALK

Teaching Time: 10–15 min.

- Have students rate the importance of each factor.
- Have two students read the example conversation.
- GROUPS. Have students discuss their answers.
- Call on volunteers to say a sentence about what's important to one of the people in their group.

Unit 18 T-223

Reading and Writing

Reading

A Teaching Time: 10–15 min.

- Ask students to look at the company's name on the web page. If necessary, explain that real estate is land, houses, or apartments that a person owns.
- Have students study the Look Box. Tell students that buying a house is an example of an investment.
- Have students read the web page silently. Then read it aloud. Pause after each few words and have students repeat chorally.
- Have students complete the task.
- Call on a student to say the answer. Correct as needed.
- **LIFE SKILLS TEST PREP 2** Go to Unit 12, Lesson 4 for practice in identifying the parts of a computer.

B Teaching Time: 5–10 min.

- Ask students to read through the sentences before they read the web page.
- Have students complete the task.
- PAIRS. Have students compare answers.
- Call on students to say answers. Correct as needed.
- **LIFE SKILLS TEST PREP 2** Go to Unit 5, Lesson 4 for more practice in reading and comparing basic information in simple advertisements.

Reading and Writing

Reading

A Read the web page. What is the best title for the page? Check (✓) the correct answer.

- ☐ Houses for Sale
- ☑ Buying a Home
- ☐ Renting a Home

Look
investment = something that you buy because it will be more valuable or useful later

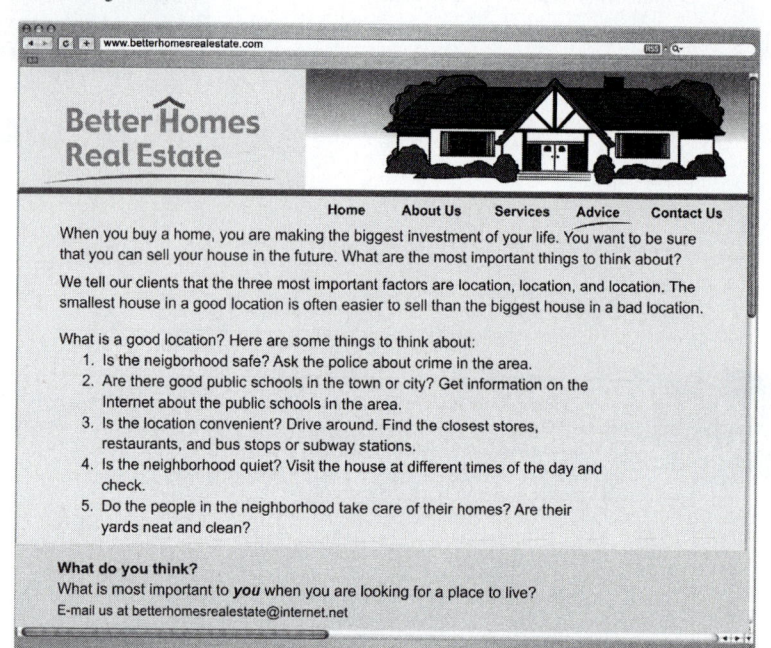

Better Homes Real Estate

Home | About Us | Services | Advice | Contact Us

When you buy a home, you are making the biggest investment of your life. You want to be sure that you can sell your house in the future. What are the most important things to think about?

We tell our clients that the three most important factors are location, location, and location. The smallest house in a good location is often easier to sell than the biggest house in a bad location.

What is a good location? Here are some things to think about:
1. Is the neighborhood safe? Ask the police about crime in the area.
2. Are there good public schools in the town or city? Get information on the Internet about the public schools in the area.
3. Is the location convenient? Drive around. Find the closest stores, restaurants, and bus stops or subway stations.
4. Is the neighborhood quiet? Visit the house at different times of the day and check.
5. Do the people in the neighborhood take care of their homes? Are their yards neat and clean?

What do you think?
What is most important to *you* when you are looking for a place to live?
E-mail us at betterhomesrealestate@internet.net

B Read the web page again. For each statement, write *T* (true) or *F* (false).

_T_ 1. Houses in good locations are easier to sell than houses in bad locations.
_T_ 2. The Internet has information about the best public schools in an area.
_T_ 3. It's harder to sell a house in a bad neighborhood than in a safe neighborhood.
_F_ 4. A big house is always better than a small house.
_F_ 5. Convenience is the most important thing.

Unit 18

Center Stage 2

Prewriting

Read Cara's e-mail. For Cara, what is most important about a place to live? *Safety and convenience.*

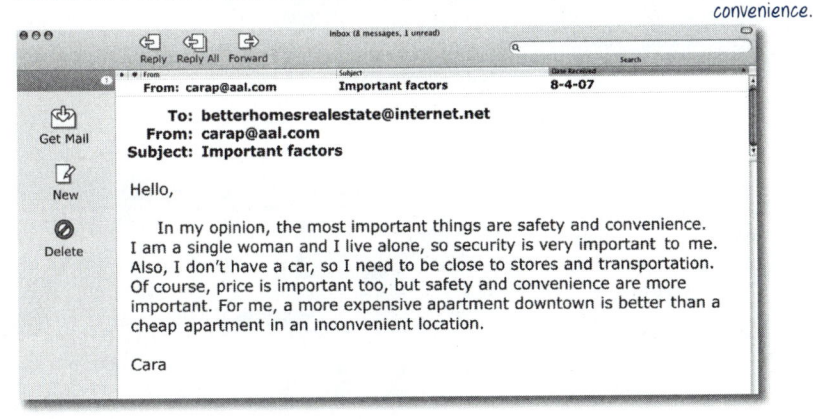

```
Inbox (8 messages, 1 unread)
                                                    Search
From                    Subject              Date Received
From: carap@aal.com     Important factors    8-4-07

To: betterhomesrealestate@internet.net
From: carap@aal.com
Subject: Important factors

Hello,

   In my opinion, the most important things are safety and convenience.
I am a single woman and I live alone, so security is very important to me.
Also, I don't have a car, so I need to be close to stores and transportation.
Of course, price is important too, but safety and convenience are more
important. For me, a more expensive apartment downtown is better than a
cheap apartment in an inconvenient location.

Cara
```

Writing

Write your own e-mail. Write about what is most important to you in a place to live. Use Cara's e-mail as a model. *Answers will vary.*

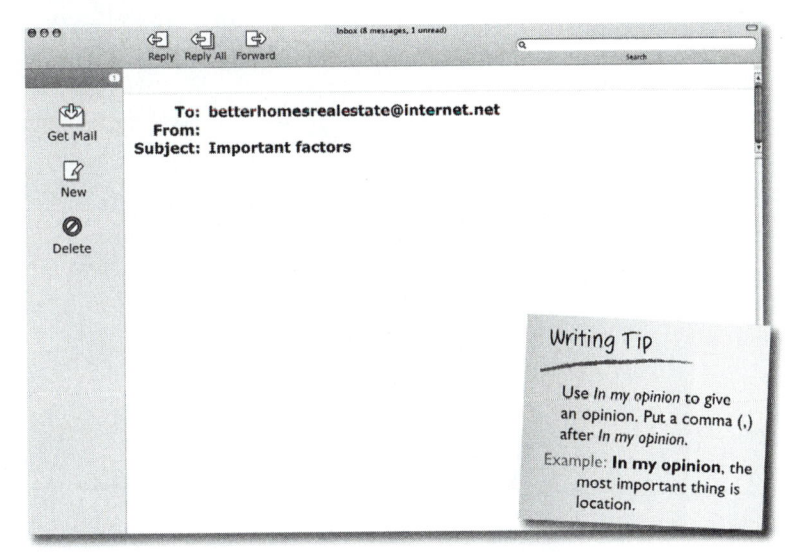

```
To: betterhomesrealestate@internet.net
From:
Subject: Important factors
```

Writing Tip

Use *In my opinion* to give an opinion. Put a comma (,) after *In my opinion*.
Example: **In my opinion**, the most important thing is location.

A Place to Live 225

Prewriting

Teaching Time: 5–10 min.

- Have students read the example e-mail. Explain unfamiliar vocabulary.
- Have students write two things that are important to Cara.
- Call on students to say answers. Correct as needed.

Writing

Teaching Time: 20–25 min.

- Draw the following graphic organizer on the board.

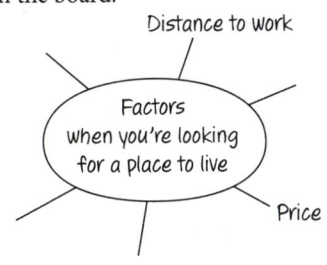

  Distance to work — Factors when you're looking for a place to live — Price

- Ask students to name factors that people consider when they're looking for a place to live. Add their answers to the graphic organizer.
- Have students study the Writing Tip. Write on the board: *In my opinion, the most important thing is ___ .* Have students complete the sentence in their own way and use it in their e-mail.
- Have students decide and write down on an extra piece of paper which things are most important to them when looking for a place to live. Encourage them to use ideas from the graphic organizer and their own ideas.
- Ask students to write a few words about why each thing is important to them.
- Have students complete the task.
- Walk around and help as needed.
- Call on volunteers to read their e-mails. Correct as needed. You can also have students write their e-mails on a separate piece of paper. Collect their work and provide individual feedback.

Multilevel Strategy

- **Pre-level:** While students are completing the prewriting task, write the following on the board: *In my opinion, the most important thing is ___ because ___ . Another important thing is ___ because ___ .* Group pre-level students and work with them to brainstorm possible answers. Then have them complete the sentences.
- **Above-level:** Challenge students to write additional reasons for their opinions.

Unit 18 T-225

Unit 19
Future Changes

Learning Goals
- Learn words to describe future events
- Learn about *will*: affirmative and negative statements, *yes / no* questions, and information questions
- Listen to a conversation and a radio report about future events
- Read and write about New Year resolutions
- Talk about the future

Learner Persistence
At the end of class, briefly review the lesson points and remind students what they've learned. Use this strategy to show students that each class is valuable.

Warm-up
Teaching Time: 3–5 min.

- Write on the board *prediction*. Explain that prediction is when a person says what he or she thinks will happen in the future. For example, when a weather forecaster gives the weather for tomorrow, he or she makes a prediction about the weather.
- Ask students to list some other things people make predictions about.

Vocabulary
Teaching Time: 15–20 min.

- Have students look at the pictures. Explain unfamiliar vocabulary. For example, say: Get in touch *means to communicate with someone, often by phone or mail. When you have a good time, you enjoy what you're doing.*
- 🎧 Play Track 29 while students read and listen.
- Read the words and phrases aloud and have students repeat chorally.
- Have students complete the task.
- PAIRS. Have students compare answers.

Expansion Have students make sentences about the pictures using the words and phrases in the list.

Unit 19
Future Changes

Grammar
- *Will*: Affirmative and Negative Statements
- *Will*: Yes / No Questions
- *Will*: Information Questions

Vocabulary

🎧 **29** Read and listen. Which changes do you think are in your future? Tell your partner. *Answers will vary.*

1. get a raise
2. get in touch with someone
3. make plans
4. start a business
5. get bad news
6. succeed
7. have a good time

Unit 19

Multilevel Strategy

- **Pre-level:** Have students work in pairs to make one sentence about each picture. Assist students with the task.
- **At-level:** Encourage students to use words and phrases not included on the list.
- **Above-level:** Have students write a short story about each picture.

Center Stage 2

Listening

A 🔊 **30** Listen. Betty is visiting a fortune teller. What does the fortune teller see in Betty's future? Check (✓) the correct answer.

❏ good things ☑ bad things ❏ good and bad things

B 🔊 **31** Read and listen again. Write the missing words. Use the words in the box.

| ~~will~~ | will it be | won't | won't be | You'll |

Betty: So, tell me! What do you see? Will there be any changes in my life?

Fortune teller: Yes, there ___will___ . I see a handsome, dark man. He will get in touch with you soon.
                                 1.

Betty: That sounds interesting. Will he be tall?

Fortune teller: No, he ___won't___ .
                          2.

Betty: Oh... Well, why will he get in touch with me?

Fortune teller: He will have some news for you.

Betty: What kind of news ___will it be___ ? Will it be good or bad?
                              3.

Fortune teller: I'm sorry, but it ___won't be___ good... I also see money.
                                      4.

Betty: Oh, good!

Fortune teller: Hmmmm...

Betty: What's the matter?

Fortune teller: Well, you won't *get* money. ___You'll___ lose it.
                                                  5.

Future Changes 227

Language Notes

- **Exercise B.** Say that people often make the sound *hmmmm* when they're thinking about what to say.
- Explain that *What's the matter?* means *What's wrong?* or *What's the problem?*

Option

Assign Unit 19 Supplementary Vocabulary Exercise on the Teacher's Resource Disk as homework or on the Student Persistence CD-ROM as self-access practice.

Listening

A **Teaching Time: 10–15 min.**

- **Warm-up:** Write on the board *fortune teller*. Explain that a fortune teller is a person who tells you about your future. Ask students their opinions of fortune tellers. Prompt students with questions such as: *Do you believe that some people are really able to see the future?*
- Ask students to read through the answer choices before they listen.
- 🎧 Play Track 30 while students listen.
- 🎧 Play Track 30 again while students complete the task.
- Call on a student to say the answer. Correct as needed.

B **Teaching Time: 15–20 min.**

- Have students read through the answer choices before they listen.
- 🎧 Play Track 31 while students listen and complete the task.
- 🎧 Play Track 31 again while students listen and check their answers.
- Call on students to say answers. Correct as needed.
- Read the conversation aloud. Pause after each few words and have students repeat chorally.
- PAIRS. Ask students to role-play the conversation.

Multilevel Strategy

- **Pre-level:** Have students role-play the completed conversation.
- **At-level, Above-level:** Have students continue the conversation while they role-play. Prompt them with suggestions (e.g., *Ask about a job.*). Ask pairs to role-play in front of the class.

Unit 19 T-227

Grammar to Communicate 1

Will: Affirmative and Negative Statements

Teaching Time: 5–10 min.

- Remind students that future is the time after now. Tell them that they already know one way to talk about the future (*be going to*).
- Write on the board a few phrases such as: *drive flying cars, recycle more*. Ask students: *Do you think these things are part of the future?* Invite students to add some ideas of their own.
- Write on the board *will*. Say: *Use* will *to make predictions about the future*. Make sentences with *will* and the phrases on the board, such as: *In the future, people will drive flying cars.*
- Have students study the chart.
- Tell students they can use contractions with *will*.
- Read the sentences and phrases in the chart and have students repeat chorally.

A Teaching Time: 5–10 min.

- Ask students to name some other future time expressions such as: *in [number] days, tomorrow*. Record expressions on the board.
- Have students complete the task.
- PAIRS. Have students tell each other their sentences.
- Call on volunteers to say one prediction about their partner's future.

B Teaching Time: 5–10 min.

- Read the example with the class.
- Have students complete the task.
- Call on students to say answers. Correct as needed.

Grammar to Communicate 1

WILL: AFFIRMATIVE AND NEGATIVE STATEMENTS

Subject	Will	Verb		Subject	Will + Not	Verb		Contractions
I / You / He / She / It / We / They	will	make	him happy.	I / You / He / She / It / We / They	will not	make	him happy.	I + will → I'll you + will → you'll he + will → he'll she + will → she'll it + will → it'll we + will → we'll they + will → they'll
There	will	be	good news.	There	will not	be	good news.	will + not → won't

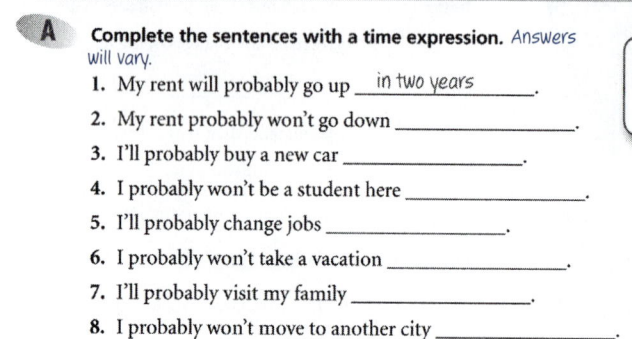

A Complete the sentences with a time expression. *Answers will vary.*

1. My rent will probably go up __in two years__.
2. My rent probably won't go down _____.
3. I'll probably buy a new car _____.
4. I probably won't be a student here _____.
5. I'll probably change jobs _____.
6. I probably won't take a vacation _____.
7. I'll probably visit my family _____.
8. I probably won't move to another city _____.

Look
go up = ↑
go down = ↓

PAIRS. Tell each other your sentences.

B Rewrite the sentences about Mr. and Mrs. Smith's future. Use *won't* and the words in the box. Do not change the meaning of the sentences.

| bad | ~~difficult~~ | girl | short | smaller | ugly |

1. They'll have an easy life. — *They won't have a difficult life.*
2. She'll be a good mother. — *She won't be a bad mother.*
3. He'll buy her pretty things. — *He won't buy her ugly things.*
4. They'll have a boy. — *They won't have a girl.*
5. Their son will be tall. — *Their son won't be short.*
6. They'll move to a bigger apartment. — *They won't move to a smaller apartment.*

Unit 19

Multilevel Strategy

- **Pre-level:** Help students identify the correct word from the box for each sentence. Then have them complete the task.
- **At-level, Above-level:** Have students make one prediction about two classmates after they have completed the task. Call on students to read their predictions to the class.

Grammar Notes

1. Use *will* and the base form of a verb to make predictions.
2. To make contractions with subject pronouns and *will*, add *'ll* to any subject pronoun.
3. To make negative statements, use *will not* or *won't*.
4. Use *will, will not,* and *won't* for all subjects.
5. Use *will probably* and *probably won't* for predictions that are likely to happen, but that you aren't 100 percent sure about.
6. For more information on this grammar topic, see page 261.

T-228 Center Stage 2

C Sara is an optimist. She thinks the future will be good. Keith is a pessimist. He thinks the future will be bad. Complete their statements with *will* or *won't*.

Sara

1. I __will get__ a good job in two years.
   (get)
2. My boss __will give__ me a raise.
   (give)
3. It __won't rain__ at the beach this weekend.
   (not rain)
4. My new business __won't succeed__.
   (not succeed)
5. I __will have__ a lot of problems in my
   (have)
   classes next year.
6. My friends and I __won't have fun__ this summer.
   (not have fun)

Keith

D Write five predictions about events in a few years. Write your predictions on a piece of paper. Use *probably* and *will* or *won't* with the words in the box. Answers will vary.

I	my friends	become a U.S. citizen	move to a bigger home
my boss	my husband and I	change jobs	move to a different city
my daughter	my mother	get a raise	retire
my father	my son	get married	start a business
my friend	my wife and I	have a baby	succeed in business

PAIRS. Tell your partner your sentences.

Example:
A: *My husband will probably change jobs in a few years. How about you?*
B: *My girlfriend and I probably won't change jobs. But we'll probably get married in a few years.*

TIME to TALK

PAIRS. Look at the photos on page 97. Make predictions about the people in the pictures. Talk about what will and won't happen. Make at least five predictions.
Answers will vary.

Example: (page 97, picture a)
A: *The girl and her mother will stop fighting. She will listen to her mother.*
B: *Her mother will not stay angry with her. They will be nice to each other.*

Future Changes 229

C Teaching Time: 3–5 min.
- Explain that an optimist usually thinks that good things will happen, and a pessimist usually thinks that bad things will happen.
- Read the example with the class.
- Have students complete the task.
- Call on students to say answers. Correct as needed.

D Teaching Time: 10–15 min.
- Have students write their predictions. Walk around and help as needed.
- Have two students read the example.
- PAIRS. Have students complete the task. Walk around and help as needed.

Language Note

Exercises A and B. Remind students to use *will* to make predictions. Say: *Don't use* will *to talk about future plans.* Remind students that they can use the present progressive to talk about plans for the future.

Option

Assign Unit 19 Supplementary Grammar to Communicate 1 Exercises on the Teacher's Resource Disk as homework or on the Student Persistence CD-ROM as self-access practice.

TIME to TALK

Teaching Time: 10–15 min.
- Have two students read the example conversation.
- Have students complete the task.
- Walk around and help as needed.
- Call on pairs to tell the class one of their predictions.

Unit 19 T-229

Grammar to Communicate 2

Will: Yes / No Questions

Teaching Time: 5–10 min.

- Say: *To ask yes / no questions about future predictions, put will before the subject.*
- Write on the board a few sentences such as: *I will move.* Have volunteers change each sentence into a question.
- Have students study the chart.
- Read each question and short answer and have students repeat chorally.
- Ask students a few questions and have them answer with short answers.

A Teaching Time: 5–10 min.

- Read the example with the class.
- Have students complete the task.
- PAIRS. Have students compare answers.
- Call on students to say answers. Correct as needed.

Multilevel Strategy

- **Pre-level:** Have students work in pairs to complete the task. After checking answers, have them take turns asking and answering the questions.
- **At-level, Above-level:** After checking answers, have students take turns asking and answering the questions. Have students explain their opinions.

B Teaching Time: 10–15 min.

- Read the example with the class.
- Have students complete the first part of the task.
- Call on students to say the questions. Correct as needed.
- PAIRS. Have students take turns asking and answering the questions.
- Walk around and help as needed.

Grammar to Communicate 2

WILL: YES / NO QUESTIONS

Will	Subject	Verb			Short Answers					
Will	I / you / he / she / it / we / they	change	a lot in the next ten years?	Yes,	I / you / he / she / it / we / they	will.	No,	I / you / he / she / it / we / they	won't.

Will	There	Be			Short Answers				
Will	there	be	problems in the next ten years?	Yes,	there	will.	No,	there	won't.

A What do you think life will be like in 2050? Write short answers.

1. Will people work five days a week? _Yes, they will._ OR _No, they won't._
2. Will men and women have the same jobs? _Yes, they will._ OR _No, they won't._
3. Will most people live to 100? _Yes, they will._ OR _No, they won't._
4. Will children go to school 12 months a year? _Yes, they will._ OR _No, they won't._
5. Will there be better public transportation? _Yes, there will._ OR _No, there won't._
6. Will most people get married? _Yes, they will._ OR _No, they won't._

PAIRS. Compare your answers.

B Will things be the same in ten years? Write questions.

1. My boss drives to work every day. _Will he drive to work every day in ten years?_
2. My friend eats a lot of fast food. _Will he / she eat a lot of fast food in ten years?_
3. There aren't a lot of good jobs. _Will there be a lot of good jobs in ten years?_
4. There's a lot of traffic. _Will there be a lot of traffic in ten years?_
5. College costs a lot of money. _Will college cost a lot of money in ten years?_
6. My friends pay for everything in cash. _Will they pay for everything in cash in ten years?_

PAIRS. Ask and answer the questions above. Use *probably* or *probably not* in your answers. _Answers will vary._

Example:
A: My boss drives to work every day.
B: Will your boss drive to work every day in ten years?
A: Yes, he probably will. He lives far from the office.

Unit 19

Grammar Notes

1. To make *yes / no* questions with *will*, change the order of *will* and the subject.
2. Do not use contractions in affirmative short answers. Use full forms or contractions in negative short answers.
3. For more information on this grammar topic, see page 261.

T-230 Center Stage 2

C

Complete the sentences about life in the year 2050. Use *will* or *won't*.

1. People __will read OR won't read__ newspapers.
   (read)
2. People __will use OR won't use__ cash in stores.
   (use)
3. People __will buy OR won't buy__ food on the Internet.
   (buy)
4. The price of water __will go up OR won't go up__.
   (go up)
5. The price of computers __will go down OR won't go down__.
   (go down)
6. There __will be OR won't be__ computers in every home.
   (be)

PAIRS. Change the statements above to questions. Ask the questions. Answer with *will* or *won't*.
Answers will vary.

Example:
A: *Will people read newspapers in 2050?*
B: *No, they won't.*

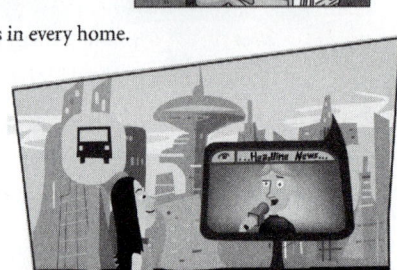

TIME to TALK

PAIRS. *Someday* means "at some time in the future." Look at the ideas in the box. Will these things happen someday? Ask and answer questions. Answers will vary.

- commute to Earth from the moon
- find intelligent life on other planets
- fly to work
- live on the moon
- make friends with computers
- take vacations on the moon

Example:
A: *Will we find intelligent life on other planets someday?*
B: *Yes, I think we will.*

WRAP-UP. What other things will probably happen in the future? Ask and answer questions with *will*.

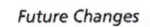

Future Changes 231

C Teaching Time: 10–15 min.

- Read the example with the class.
- Have students complete the first part of the task.
- Call on students to say answers. Correct as needed.
- Have two students read the example.
- PAIRS. Have students change the statements to questions and answer them.
- Walk around and help as needed.

Multilevel Strategy

- **Pre-level, At-level:** Pair pre-level and at-level students. Have pre-level students ask *why* and at-level students explain their opinions. For example:
  A: *Will people read newspapers in 2050?*
  B: *No, they won't.*
  A: *Why?*
  B: *Because they will read the news on the Internet.*
- **Above-level:** Have pairs talk about other things in the future in addition to the ones in Exercise C.

Option

Assign Unit 19 Supplementary Grammar to Communicate 2 Exercises on the Teacher's Resource Disk as homework or on the Student Persistence CD-ROM as self-access practice.

TIME to TALK

Teaching Time: 10–15 min.

- Have students look at the picture, and ask a few questions, such as: *Where are they? Are the creatures friendly?*
- Have two students read the example.
- Present two ways for students to indicate that their predictions are their opinions. Tell them that they can say *in my opinion* or *I think* before a sentence with *will / won't*.
- PAIRS. Have students complete the task.
- Call on volunteers to state their opinions about an event that will or won't happen. For example: *I think people will fly to work. Roads will get too busy, so some people will start to fly.*
- Ask students to name other things that might happen in the future.

Unit 19 T-231

Grammar to Communicate 3

Will: Information Questions

Teaching Time: 5–10 min.

- Say: *To ask information questions, use a question word before* will. Write on the board and read a few examples, such as: *What will you get at the store?*
- Say: *It's possible to use* who *and* what *as the subjects of questions with* will. Write on the board and read a few examples, such as: *What will happen? Who will go with you?*
- Have students study the charts.
- Read the questions and answers in the charts and have students repeat chorally.
- Write a few statements on the board and have volunteers change them into questions. For example: *Miguel will buy a car. Who will buy a car?*

A Teaching Time: 5–10 min.

- Have each student tell the class what sign he or she is.
- Have volunteers read each horoscope aloud to the class. Explain unfamiliar vocabulary.
- Have students complete the task.
- Call on students to say answers. Correct as needed.

Expansion PAIRS. Have students tell their partners what their horoscope says and their opinion of the prediction.

Grammar to Communicate 3

WILL: INFORMATION QUESTIONS

Wh- word	Will	Subject	Verb	Answers
What	will	I	do?	You'll find a new job.
Who		you	call?	The boss.
How much		he	pay you?	A lot.
When		they	see you?	From 9 to 5 tomorrow.

WILL: QUESTIONS WITH WHAT / WHO AS SUBJECT

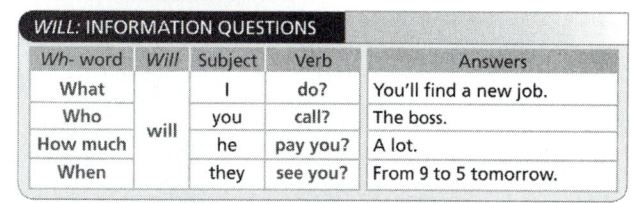

Wh- word	Will	Verb		Answers
What	will	happen	to me in the future?	You'll get married.
Who		make	a lot of money?	You will.

A Read the horoscopes and the questions below. Which horoscopes are the questions about? Circle the correct answers.

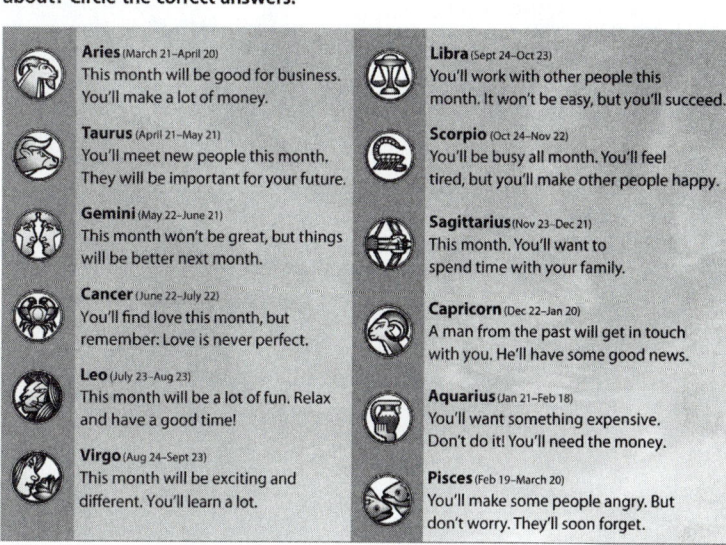

Aries (March 21–April 20)
This month will be good for business. You'll make a lot of money.

Taurus (April 21–May 21)
You'll meet new people this month. They will be important for your future.

Gemini (May 22–June 21)
This month won't be great, but things will be better next month.

Cancer (June 22–July 22)
You'll find love this month, but remember: Love is never perfect.

Leo (July 23–Aug 23)
This month will be a lot of fun. Relax and have a good time!

Virgo (Aug 24–Sept 23)
This month will be exciting and different. You'll learn a lot.

Libra (Sept 24–Oct 23)
You'll work with other people this month. It won't be easy, but you'll succeed.

Scorpio (Oct 24–Nov 22)
You'll be busy all month. You'll feel tired, but you'll make other people happy.

Sagittarius (Nov 23–Dec 21)
This month. You'll want to spend time with your family.

Capricorn (Dec 22–Jan 20)
A man from the past will get in touch with you. He'll have some good news.

Aquarius (Jan 21–Feb 18)
You'll want something expensive. Don't do it! You'll need the money.

Pisces (Feb 19–March 20)
You'll make some people angry. But don't worry. They'll soon forget.

1. What will be better next month?
   a. Aquarius   **b. Gemini**

2. How much money will he make?
   a. Pisces   **b. Aries**

3. Where will she meet them?
   a. Taurus   b. Libra

4. Why will it be fun?
   a. Leo   b. Cancer

Unit 19 — 232

Grammar Notes

- To make information questions with *will*, use the same word order as *yes / no* questions, and put a question word at the beginning.
- *Who* and *what* can be subjects of questions with *will*.
- For more information on this grammar topic, see page 261.

Culture Note

- **Exercise A.** Explain that horoscopes tell what will happen to people based on when they were born. Horoscopes often appear in magazines and newspapers.
- Invite students to briefly tell their opinions on or experiences with horoscopes.

T-232 Center Stage 2

B Imagine you have these horoscopes. Write questions about the horoscopes. Use *will*.

1. Capricorn — Who will get in touch with me?
   (Who / get in touch with me)
2. Pisces — Who will I make angry?
   (Who / I / make angry)
3. Gemini — When will things get better?
   (When / things / get better)
4. Libra — Who will I need to work with?
   (Who / I / need to work with)
5. Scorpio — Why will I feel tired?
   (Why / I / feel tired)

C 🎵 32 Complete the questions with *What, What kind of, When, Where,* or *Who*. Use *will*. Then listen and check your answers.

Carol: Your horoscope says, "You will find the love of your life."
Seth: When will I meet her?
         (1. meet)
Carol: This month.
Seth: What will her name be?
         (2. be)
Carol: Her name? Horoscopes don't give names!
Seth: Where will I find her?
         (3. find)
Carol: It doesn't say the place. It also says you will get some news late in the month.
Seth: What kind of news will it be?
         (4. be)
Carol: It will be good news.
Seth: Who will give me the good news?
         (5. give)
Carol: Your new girlfriend, of course!

TIME to TALK

ON YOUR OWN. What would you like to know about your future? Write a list of questions. *Answers will vary.*
GROUPS. Student A: You are the fortune teller. Answer the questions of the people in your group. Tell them about their future.
Students B, C, D: Ask the fortune teller your questions. Do you like the fortune teller's answers?
Example:
B: When will I get a raise?
A: You won't get a raise this year. You'll probably get a raise next year.
C: How many children will I have?
A: You'll have three children.

Future Changes 233

B Teaching Time: 5–10 min.
- Read the example with the class.
- Have students complete the task.
- Call on students to write questions on the board. Write corrections on the board as needed.

Multilevel Strategy

- **Pre-level:** Help students form the correct word order for each question. After checking answers, have students take turns reading the questions to a partner.
- **At-level:** After checking answers, have students take turns asking the questions and answering them based on the information on page 232.
- **Above-level:** After checking answers, have students take turns reading the questions and answering them in their own way.

C Teaching Time: 5–10 min.
- Read the example with the class.
- Have students complete the task.
- 🎧 Play Track 32 and have students check their answers.
- Call on students to say answers. Correct as needed.
- PAIRS. Ask students to role-play the completed conversation.

Option
Assign Unit 19 Supplementary Grammar to Communicate 3 Exercises on the Teacher's Resource Disk as homework or on the Student Persistence CD-ROM as self-access practice.

TIME to TALK

Teaching Time: 15–20 min.
- Have students write down several questions they have about their future.
- Have three students read the example conversation.
- GROUPS. Have students complete the task. Have each student ask the "fortune teller" one question. Then have students switch roles. Tell students to continue to take turns asking questions and playing the role of fortune teller.
- Walk around and help as needed.

Unit 19   T-233

Review and Challenge

Grammar

Teaching Time: 5–10 min.

- Read the example with the class.
- Have students complete the task.
- 🎧 Play Track 33 while students check their answers.
- Ask two students to role-play the conversation to check the answers. Correct as needed.

Dictation

Teaching Time: 5–10 min.

- 🎧 Play Track 34 while students listen and write what they hear.
- 🎧 Play Track 34 again while students check their answers.
- Call on students to write answers on the board.
- 🎧 Play Track 34 again and correct sentences on the board.

Multilevel Strategy

- **Pre-level:** Give students a worksheet with some of the words from the dictation already provided.

Speaking

Teaching Time: 10–15 min.

- Have two students read the example.
- PAIRS. Have students complete the task.
- Walk around and help as needed.
- Call on volunteers to tell the class one of their partner's predictions.
- **LIFE SKILLS TEST PREP 2** Go to Unit 2, Lesson 5 for more practice in giving and receiving sympathy and congratulations.

Review and Challenge

Grammar

🎧 **33** Find and correct the mistakes in the conversation. There are seven mistakes. The first mistake is corrected for you. Then listen and check your answers.

Paul: Mom, I want to move closer to my job.
Mom: But where ~~you will~~ *will you* live?
Paul: I'll ~~to~~ find an apartment. It won't ~~is~~ *be* hard.
Mom: But who will cook for you?
Paul: I ~~cook~~ *'ll cook*.
Mom: Will ∧*you* visit me often?
Paul: Yes, ~~I'll~~ *I will*. Every weekend.
Mom: Good. Then I'll make you food for the week, and you ~~will no~~ *won't* need to cook.

Dictation

🎧 **34** Listen. You will hear five sentences. Write them on a piece of paper. *See the audioscript on page 292 for the sentences.*

Speaking

PAIRS. Write a list of six predictions about classmates. Give reasons for your predictions. Use the ideas in the box and your own ideas. *Answers will vary.*

buy a house	graduate from college	move to another city
find a good job	have a lot of children	retire at a young age
get a big raise	make a lot of money	start a business someday

Example:
A: *Luz is smart and hardworking. She will probably find a good job.*
B: *I think so, too. And she'll make a lot of money someday.*

Unit 19

Option

Before class, make a copy of the grammar exercise on page 234 as a transparency to use with an overhead projector. Ask a volunteer to make corrections to the conversation on the transparency. Correct as needed. Have students check their work with the transparency.

T-234 Center Stage 2

Listening

A 🎧 **35** Listen to the radio report. Two reporters are talking about a new way of paying for things. According to Rob Willis, how will people pay for things in the future?

☐ with credit cards   ☐ with phone cards   ☐ with tickets   ☑ with cell phones

B 🎧 **36** Listen again. Why doesn't Carlos Icaza think the new technology will succeed? Check (✓) his reasons.

☐ 1. It will be a big computer.
☐ 2. The price will go down.
☑ 3. It will be too expensive.
☑ 4. People will lose it.
☑ 5. It won't work in a lot of places.

TIME to TALK

GROUPS. Talk about how technology will probably change people's lives in the next 100 years. Write at least one change for each category. *Answers will vary.*

MEDICINE	EDUCATION
find a cure for cancer	get more education from TVs and computers
TRANSPORTATION	**ENTERTAINMENT**

WRAP-UP. Now share your ideas with the class.

Example:
GROUP A: We think that medicine will change a lot in 100 years. For example, scientists will probably find a cure for cancer.
GROUP B: We think that children won't go to school. They'll get education from TVs and computers.

Future Changes 235

Option

Assign Unit 19 Supplementary Review and Challenge Exercises on the Teacher's Resource Disk as homework or on the Student Persistence CD-ROM as self-access practice.

Listening

A Teaching Time: 5–10 min.

- **Warm-up:** Ask students to name some ways that people pay for things (cash, checks, credit cards, debit cards, etc.). Ask students if they think that people will pay for things differently in the future.
- Ask students to read through the answer choices before they listen.
- 🎧 Play Track 35 while students listen.
- 🎧 Play Track 35 again while students complete the task.
- Call on a student to say the answer. Correct as needed.
- Ask students comprehension questions about the report. Modify the questions to the level of the students.

Multilevel Strategy

- **Pre-level:** Ask students *yes / no* questions (e.g., *Do the new cell phones have a small computer in them?*).
- **At-level:** Ask students information questions (e.g., *What is convenient about the new cell phones?*).
- **Above-level:** Ask students open-ended or critical thinking questions (e.g., *Do you think it's a good idea to use cell phones to pay for things? Why?*).

B Teaching Time: 5–10 min.

- Ask students to read through the answer choices before they listen.
- 🎧 Play Track 36. Have students listen and complete the task.
- 🎧 Play Track 36 again while students listen and check their answers.
- Call on students to say answers. Correct as needed.

TIME to TALK
Teaching Time: 10–15 min.

- **GROUPS.** Have students complete the first part of the task.
- Walk around and help as needed.
- Have two students read the example conversation.
- Call on volunteers to tell the class some of their group's predictions.

Multilevel Strategy

- **All-levels:** Place students in mixed-level groups. Have at-level and above-level students brainstorm ideas for each category. Assign pre-level students as recorders and have them write the ideas in the chart.

Unit 19   T-235

Reading and Writing

Reading

A   **Teaching Time: 10–15 min.**

- If necessary, explain New Year resolutions. For example, say that people often decide that they will change some things in their life at the beginning of a new year.
- Ask students to read through the answer choices before they read the paragraph.
- Have students read the paragraphs silently. Then read them aloud. Pause after each few words and have students repeat chorally.
- Have students complete the task.
- Call on students to say answers. Correct as needed.

B   **Teaching Time: 5–10 min.**

- Ask students to read through the answers before they reread the paragraph.
- Have students complete the task.
- Call on students to say answers. Correct as needed.

Reading and Writing

Reading

A Every year on New Year's Day, many Americans make New Year resolutions. Read Mary's New Year resolutions. Write the number of the paragraph next to the topic. (Be careful. There is one extra topic.)

_2_ family   _3_ health   _1_ work   ___ love life

My New Year Resolutions

1. I won't be late to work, and I won't take any time off. If the kids get sick, my husband will stay home with them. At the end of the year, I will ask my boss for a raise, and he'll give it to me. I won't take "no" for an answer.

2. At home, my husband will help me more with the kids and the housework. We'll try to eat dinner together every night. We won't watch as much TV. Instead, we'll read or play games. We'll also go to bed early. That way, we'll all get enough sleep and we won't get sick.

3. Finally, I will lose 20 pounds this year. I'll eat healthy food and exercise every day. I won't eat fast food or sweets. By summertime, I'll look great in a bathing suit.

B Read Mary's resolutions again. Then read the sentences. Write *T* (true) or *F* (false).

_T_ 1. Mary was probably late to work a lot last year.
_F_ 2. Mary probably got a raise last year.
_T_ 3. Mary's husband does not help very much with the children.
_T_ 4. Mary and her family probably got sick a lot last year.
_F_ 5. Mary probably doesn't like fast food and sweets.

Unit 19

Option

- Draw the following graphic organizer on the board.

  Exercise more   Stop smoking

  New Year resolutions

- Ask students to name some New Year resolutions. If necessary, prompt them by having them name resolutions they or people they know have made in the past.

Prewriting

What things in your life would you like to change this year? Write a list.
Answers will vary.
_____
_____
_____

Writing

Write a paragraph about the things in your life that you would like to change in the next year. Use the reading on page 236 as a model.
Answers will vary.

My New Year Resolutions
_____
_____
_____
_____
_____
_____
_____
_____
_____
_____
_____

Writing Tip

We use the word *instead* to show different ideas in two sentences.
We won't watch as much TV. We'll read or play games **instead**.
(= In the past, we watched TV. Now we will watch less TV.)

Future Changes 237

Language Note

Writing. Have students look again at Mary's New Year resolutions. Point out that each topic starts a new paragraph. Remind students to start a new paragraph each time they write about a new topic.

Prewriting
Teaching Time: 10–15 min.

- Have students look again at Mary's New Year resolutions. Remind them that Mary made several resolutions about her work, her family, and her health.
- Write the topics on the board. Invite students to say some other topics that people make resolutions about, for example, love life, money, school, and home. Add those to the board. Or have students look again at the New Year resolutions in the graphic organizer they made in the Option.
- Have students write some areas in their lives where they want to make changes.

Writing
Teaching Time: 15–20 min.

- Have students study the Writing Tip. Explain that *instead* means *in place of*. *Instead* shows a different option.
- Have students complete the task.
- Walk around and help as needed.
- Call on volunteers to read their paragraphs to the class. Correct as needed. You can also have students write their paragraphs on a piece of paper. Collect their work and provide individual feedback.

Multilevel Strategy

- **Pre-level:** While students are completing the prewriting task, write the following on the board: *I won't ___ . I will ___ instead. I will ___ . I will also ___ . Finally, I will ___ .*
Have students copy the paragraph and fill in the blanks with their ideas from Prewriting.

Unit 19   T-237

Unit 20
Transportation

Learning Goals
- Learn transportation vocabulary
- Learn about *have to; would like;* and *can / could / would*
- Listen to conversations about travel and transportation
- Read and write a complaint letter
- Talk about transportation and travel

Learner Persistence
At the end of each class, tell students what they'll be doing in the next class. Be sure to include something that students will enjoy and can look forward to.

Warm-up
Teaching Time: 3–5 min.

Tell students that transportation is a way of getting from one place to another. Ask students to name some types of transportation. Record their answers on the board (for example, *car, bicycle, bus, train*).

Vocabulary
Teaching Time: 15–20 min.

- Have students look at the pictures. Explain unfamiliar vocabulary. For example, say: *You buy a round-trip ticket to travel somewhere and then to travel back to where you started. You buy a one-way ticket to travel to a place, but not for the trip back.*
- 🎧 Play Track 37 while students read and listen.
- Read the words and phrases aloud and have students repeat chorally.
- Have students complete the activity.
- PAIRS. Have students compare their answers.
- Call on students to say their answers.

Expansion Ask students to name some advantages and disadvantages of different types of transportation. For example: *Buses are usually inexpensive, but sometimes they are slow.* Record students' ideas on the board.

Unit 20
Transportation

Grammar
- Have to
- Would like
- Can / Could / Would

Vocabulary

🎧 **37** Read and listen. What do the words describe? A plane, train, taxi, bus, or subway? Tell your partner.

1. seat belt
2. passenger
3. flight attendant
4. airplane
5. pilot
6. show your ticket
7. one-way ticket
8. get off
9. subway
10. get on
11. reserve
12. reserve in advance
13. train station
14. schedule
15. sold out
16. round trip ticket

Answers will vary. Possible answers:
Plane: 1, 2, 3, 4, 5, 6, 7, 8, 10, 11, 12, 14, 15, 16
Train: 2, 6, 7, 8, 10, 11, 12, 13, 14, 15, 16
Taxi: 1, 2
Bus: 2, 6, 7, 8, 10, 11, 12, 14, 15, 16
Subway: 2, 6, 8, 9, 10, 14

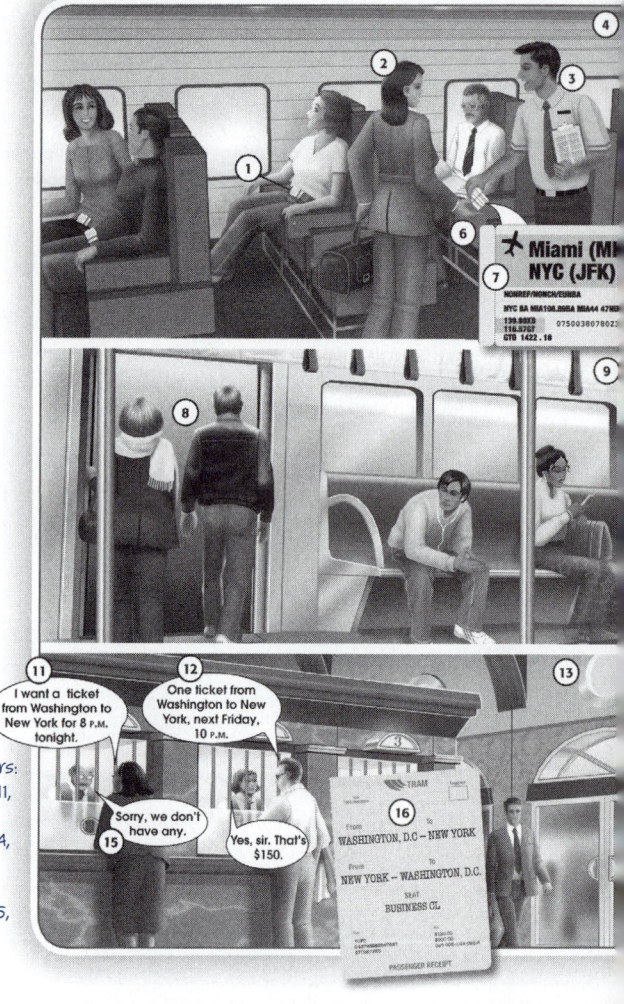

T-238 Center Stage 2

Listening

A 🎧 38 Listen. Mrs. Jones is talking to a ticket agent. Complete the sentences. Circle the correct answers.

> **Look**
> reserve a ticket in advance = buy a ticket early

1. Mrs. Jones **did** / **didn't** reserve seats on the 2:55 train.
2. There **are** / **aren't** any seats on the 2:55 train.
3. The 5:30 train **is** / **isn't** full.
4. Mrs. Jones **is** / **isn't** traveling alone.
5. Mrs. Jones **is** / **isn't** going to wait for the later train.

B 🎧 39 Read and listen again. Write the missing words. Use the words in the box.

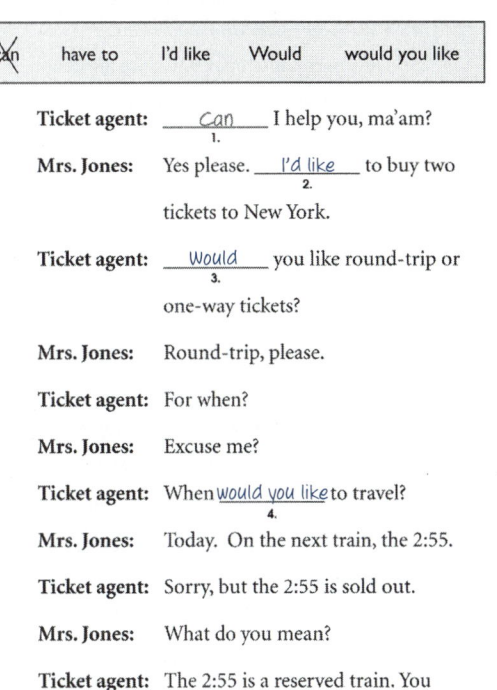

~~can~~	have to	I'd like	Would	would you like

Ticket agent: __Can__ I help you, ma'am?
                  1.

Mrs. Jones: Yes please. __I'd like__ to buy two
                              2.
tickets to New York.

Ticket agent: __Would__ you like round-trip or
                  3.
one-way tickets?

Mrs. Jones: Round-trip, please.

Ticket agent: For when?

Mrs. Jones: Excuse me?

Ticket agent: When __would you like__ to travel?
                         4.

Mrs. Jones: Today. On the next train, the 2:55.

Ticket agent: Sorry, but the 2:55 is sold out.

Mrs. Jones: What do you mean?

Ticket agent: The 2:55 is a reserved train. You
__have to__ reserve tickets in advance.
   5.

Transportation 239

Listening

A Teaching Time: 10–15 min.

- **Warm-up:** Ask students if they have ever traveled by train. Ask where they buy train tickets. Ask if they usually buy their tickets before the day they travel.
- Have students read the Look Box. If necessary, explain that a ticket agent is a person at a train station who sells tickets.
- Ask students to read through the sentences before they listen.
- 🎧 Play Track 38 while students listen.
- 🎧 Play Track 38 again while students complete the task.
- Call on students to say answers. Correct as needed.

B Teaching Time: 15–20 min.

- Have students read through the answer choices before they listen.
- 🎧 Play Track 39 while students listen and complete the task.
- 🎧 Play Track 39 again while students listen and check their answers.
- Call on students to say answers. Correct as needed.
- Read the conversation aloud. Pause after each few words and have students repeat chorally.
- PAIRS. Have students role-play the conversation.

> **Multilevel Strategy**
>
> - **Pre-level:** Have students role-play the completed conversation.
> - **At-level, Above-level:** Copy the conversation on the board and erase some words. Have students recall the conversation as they role-play.

Language Note

Exercise B. Point out the word *ma'am* in the conversation. Tell students that it is a polite way to address a woman.

Option

Assign Unit 20 Supplementary Vocabulary Exercise on the Teacher's Resource Disk as homework or on the Student Persistence CD-ROM as self-access practice.

Unit 20 T-239

Grammar to Communicate 1

Have to

Teaching Time: 5–10 min.

- Ask students: *What are some things you need to do today?* Record students' answers on the board, such as: *pick up kids*.
- Write on the board: *have to* and *has to*. Say: *Use* have to *and* has to *to talk about things you need to do*.
- Make sentences with *have to* and the phrases on the board. For example, say: *I have to pick up my kids*.
- Have students study the chart and the first Look Box.
- Read the sentences in the chart and have students repeat chorally.

A Teaching Time: 3–5 min.

- Read the example with the class.
- Have students complete the task.
- Call on students to say answers. Correct as needed.

B Teaching Time: 10–15 min.

- Have students study the second Look Box. Explain that *must* is usually for signs and instructions and that *have to* is usually for conversations.
- Read the example with the class.
- Have students complete the first part of the task.
- Call on students to say answers. Correct as needed.
- Have students complete the second part of the task.
- PAIRS. Have students compare sentences.
- Call on students to say answers. Correct as needed.

Expansion Have students make sentences with *have to* and *has to* about things people need to do when traveling by other forms of transportation.

Grammar to Communicate 1

HAVE TO

Subject	Have to		Subject	Has to	
I			He		leave.
You	have to	leave.	She	has to	
We			It		stop here.
They					

Look
We use *have to* when we need to do something.

A Which kinds of transportation do the sentences describe? Check (✓) the correct answers.

Answers will vary. Possible answers:

	Bus	Subway	Plane	Taxi
1. Passengers have to wait on the street.	✓	☐	☐	✓
2. The passenger has to talk to the driver.	✓	☐	☐	✓
3. Passengers have to wait in the station.	✓	✓	☐	☐
4. The driver has to stop at every stop.	✓	✓	☐	☐
5. The driver has to open and close the doors.	✓	✓	☐	☐
6. You have to reserve your seat in advance.	☐	☐	✓	☐

B Rewrite the sentences with *have to* or *has to*.

1. Passengers must wear seat belts.
   Passengers have to wear seat belts.
2. Passengers must pay for their tickets on the plane.
   Passengers have to pay for their tickets on the plane.
3. The pilot must wear a uniform.
   The pilot has to wear a uniform.
4. Flight attendants must take care of the passengers' children. Flight attendants have to take care of the passengers' children.
5. That man must turn off his cell phone now.
   That man has to turn off his cell phone now.
6. You must pay to watch the movie.
   You have to pay to watch the movie.

Look
Have to and *must* are similar in meaning. *Have to* is more common in conversation.
You **have to** wait at the bus stop.
You **must** wait at the bus stop.

PAIRS. Circle the statements above that are true about traveling by plane. Then compare sentences with your partner. Did you circle the same statements?
Answers will vary.

Unit 20

Grammar Notes

1. Use *have to* / *has to* or *must* with the base form of a verb to express a need to do something.
2. *Have to* is more common in conversation than *must*.
3. Use *have to* with *I*, *you*, *we*, and *they*. Use *has to* with *he*, *she*, and *it*. Use *must* with all subjects.
4. For more information on this grammar topic, see page 261.

Watch Out!

Exercises A and B. Students often add *-s* to the base form of the verb with third person singular subjects. Listen for and correct errors such as *he have to goes* and *he has to goes*.

T-240 Center Stage 2

C 🎧 40 Complete the conversations with *has to* or *have to*. Then listen and check your answers.

1. **A:** Excuse me? Where does the bus usually stop?
   B: You _have to_ wait next to that sign.
2. **A:** I need to get off. Is the driver going to stop here?
   B: Yes. The driver _has to_ stop at every bus stop.
3. **A:** Are you ready?
   B: No, I _have to_ get some money for the bus.
4. **A:** Excuse me, this woman _has to_ sit down. She's sick.
   B: Oh, sure. Here—I'll help you.
5. **A:** Sorry, but I _have to_ run. My bus is coming.
   B: OK, I'll talk to you later.

D Complete the sentences. Circle the correct answers.

1. The driver **has** / **(has to)** have a special license.
2. The driver **has** / **(has to)** wear a uniform.
3. The driver always **(has)** / **has to** some money with him.
4. The passengers **have** / **(have to)** sit in the back seat.
5. The passengers **have** / **(have to)** pay in cash.
6. The driver **(has)** / **has to** a good job.

PAIRS. Which sentences above are about taxicabs? Which sentences are about the subway? Which are about both? Answers will vary.

Look
Use *have to* when something is necessary.
You **have to** buy a ticket.
Use *have* + noun for possessions.
You **have** a ticket.

TIME to TALK
PAIRS. Imagine that you are going to travel to another country next month. Talk about five things you have to do before you leave. Answers will vary.
Example:
A: *I have to buy a plane ticket.*
B: *I have to ask my boss for time off.*

Transportation 241

C Teaching Time: 5–10 min.
- Have two students read the example.
- Have students complete the task.
- 🎧 Play Track 40 while students check their answers. Pause the recording each time an answer is given.
- PAIRS. Have students read the completed conversations with a partner.

D Teaching Time: 5–10 min.
- Have students study the Look Box. Tell them to use *have to* with a verb and *have* with a noun.
- Read the example with the class.
- Have students complete the first part of the task.
- Call on students to say answers. Correct as needed.
- PAIRS. Have students complete the second part of the task.
- Call on volunteers to say answers. Correct as needed.

Expansion
- PAIRS. Have students tell each other one thing that they have to do and one thing that they have. For example: *I have a dog. I have to feed him two times a day.*
- Call on volunteers to say one thing that their partner has to do and one thing that their partner has.

Option
Assign Unit 20 Supplementary Grammar to Communicate 1 Exercises on the Teacher's Resource Disk as homework or on the Student Persistence CD-ROM as self-access practice.

TIME to TALK
Teaching Time: 10–15 min.
- Have two students read the example.
- PAIRS. Have students complete the task.
- Walk around and help as needed.
- Call on volunteers to say one thing their partner has to do.

Unit 20 T-241

Grammar to Communicate 2

Would like

Teaching Time: 5–10 min.

- Bring stores' newspaper advertisements and distribute them to groups of students.
- Write on the board: *What do you want? What do you want to buy?* Record students' answers on the board. For example: *I want a DVD player. Calvin wants to buy a phone.*
- Write on the board: *would like.* Say: *Would like* means *want*, *but it is more polite.*
- Call on volunteers to change *want* in each question and sentence on the board to *would like.*
- Say: *The contraction of* would like *is* 'd like. Call on volunteers to change *would like* to *'d like* in sentences with subject pronouns. For example: *I would like a DVD player. I'd like a DVD player.*
- Have students study the chart.
- Read the sentences, questions, and answers in the chart and have students repeat chorally.

A Teaching Time: 5–10 min.

- Read the example with the class.
- Have students complete the activity.
- Call on students to say answers. Correct as needed.
- **LIFE SKILLS TEST PREP 2** Go to Unit 4, Lesson 3 for practice in asking for and giving simple directions.

Multilevel Strategy

- **At-level, Above-level:** Assign roles (e.g., flight attendant) to students and have them develop one item into a short role-play that they perform for the class.
- **Pre-level:** Ask students questions about the role plays (e.g., *What happened?*).

Grammar to Communicate 2

WOULD LIKE

Subject	Would like		Noun	Contractions		
I / He / We / You / They	would like	to buy	one ticket.	I'd / He'd / We'd / You'd / They'd	like	one ticket, please.
			a ticket, please.			to buy a ticket, please.

Would	Subject	Like		Noun	Answers
Would	you	like	to buy	a one-way ticket?	Yes, please.
				a ticket?	No, thank you.

A Read the sentences. Who are the passengers talking to? Write *passenger*, *flight attendant*, or *bus driver*.

1. I'd like a window seat, please.   *flight attendant*
2. I'd like to get off at the next stop.   *bus driver*
3. We'd like to change our seats.   *flight attendant*
4. Would you like my seat?   *passenger*
5. Would you like to read my newspaper?   *passenger*

window seat

B Rewrite the sentences. Use *to* + verb.

1. I'd like a glass of water, please. — *I'd like to drink a glass of water, please.* (drink)
2. I'd like a magazine, please. — *I'd like to read a magazine, please.* (read)
3. I'd like a sandwich, please. — *I'd like to have a sandwich, please.* (have)
4. Would you like some music? — *Would you like to listen to some music?* (listen to)
5. Would you like my cell phone? — *Would you like to use my cell phone?* (use)

Now rewrite the sentences. Do not use *to* + verb.

6. I'd like to drink a cup of coffee, please. — *I'd like a cup of coffee, please.*
7. I'd like to have a newspaper, please. — *I'd like a newspaper, please.*
8. I'd like to buy three tickets, please. — *I'd like three tickets, please.*
9. Would you like to eat some fruit? — *Would you like some fruit?*
10. Would you like to have a cup of tea? — *Would you like a cup of tea?*

242   Unit 20

B Teaching Time: 10–15 min.

- Read the examples with the class.
- Call on students to come to the board and write the sentences. Correct as needed.

Multilevel Strategy

- **At-level, Above-level:** Call on only at-level and above-level students to write sentences on the board.
- **Pre-level:** Have students copy the sentences from the board.

Grammar Notes

1. *Would like* means *want*, but *would like* is more polite.
2. Use *would like* with the base form of the verb or a noun.
3. To make contractions with subject pronouns and *would*, add *'d* to any subject pronoun.
4. Use *would you like* to ask polite questions about what people want.
5. For more information on this grammar topic, see page 261.

Watch Out!

Exercise C. Students may mistakenly add *–s* to *would like* with third person singular subjects. Listen for and correct errors such as *he would likes.*

T-242   Center Stage 2

C Serge is a flight attendant. Read the list of things passengers on the plane want. Write sentences with *would like*.

Ms. Amar (31A)—some coffee	1. Ms. Amar would like some coffee.
Mr. Fong (11B)—something to eat	2. Mr. Fong would like something to eat.
Mr. and Mrs. Lin (9G-H)—magazines	3. Mr. and Mrs. Lin would like magazines.
Mr. Quinn (15B)—watch a movie	4. Mr. Quinn would like to watch a movie.
Ms. Gomez (22J)—change seats	5. Ms. Gomez would like to change seats.

PAIRS. What are some things you would like right now in class?

D Sue and Bob are on a train. Bob is in a bad mood. Sue wants to help him. Write Sue's questions. Use *Would you like* and the words in the box.

| an aspirin   my jacket   some water   something to eat   something to read   to sit here |

1. **Bob:** I have a headache.
   Sue: Would you like an aspirin?
2. **Bob:** I'm bored.
   Sue: Would you like something to read?
3. **Bob:** I'm thirsty.
   Sue: Would you like some water?
4. **Bob:** I'm hungry.
   Sue: Would you like something to eat?
5. **Bob:** I'm cold.
   Sue: Would you like my jacket?
6. **Bob:** I don't like my seat.
   Sue: Would you like to sit here?

TIME to TALK

PAIRS. Look at the picture. What are the people saying? Write short conversations. Answers will vary.

Example:
A: Would you like to sit down?
B: Thank you very much, young man.

Transportation

C Teaching Time: 5–10 min.
- Read the example with the class.
- Have students complete the activity.
- Call on students to say answers. Correct as needed.
- PAIRS. Have students tell each other sentences about three things they would like.
- Walk around and help as needed.

D Teaching Time: 5–10 min.
- Explain that when a person is in a bad mood, he or she is not happy.
- Read the example with the class.
- Have students complete the activity.
- Call on students to say the questions. Correct as needed.
- PAIRS. Have students practice the completed conversations with a partner.

Option
Assign Unit 20 Supplementary Grammar to Communicate 2 Exercises on the Teacher's Resource Disk as homework or on the Student Persistence CD-ROM as self-access practice.

TIME to TALK

Teaching Time: 10–15 min.
- Have two students read the example.
- Call on volunteers to say what is happening in the picture.
- Have students complete the activity.
- Ask partners to act out one conversation for the rest of the class.

Expansion
- GROUPS. Have students act out a scene in a restaurant. One student is the waiter or waitress and asks questions about what the customers would like. The other students are the customers and say what they would like to order.
- **LIFE SKILLS TEST PREP 2** Go to Unit 5, Lesson 5 for more practice in using *would like* while ordering from a menu.

Unit 20 T-243

Grammar to Communicate 3

Can / Could / Would

Teaching Time: 5–10 min.

- Say: *Use* can I *or* could I *to politely ask for something you want.* Write on the board: *Can I have a glass of water? Could I have a tissue?*
- Say: *Also use* can I *or* could I *to politely ask for permission to do something.* Write on the board: *Can I open the window? Could I talk to you for a minute?*
- Write on the board: *Can you . . . ?, Could you . . . ?,* and *Would you . . . ?* Say: *Use* Can you, Could you, *and* Would you *to politely ask someone to do something.* Write on the board: *Can you tell me the time? Could you pass me the salt? Would you say that again?*
- Have students study the chart and the Look Box. Tell students to use *please* to make polite requests.
- Read the questions and answers in the chart and have students repeat chorally.

A Teaching Time: 5–10 min.

- Read the example with the class.
- Have students complete the activity.
- Call on students to say answers. Correct as needed.
- **LIFE SKILLS TEST PREP 2** Go to Unit 1, Lesson 7 for more practice using *could I* and *could you* to make requests and ask for permission.

Multilevel Strategy

- **Pre-level, Above-level:** Pair pre-level students with above-level students to complete the task. Have pre-level students read the statements in the left column and above-level students match them with the correct request in the right column.

Grammar to Communicate 3

CAN / COULD / WOULD

Can / Could / Would	Subject	Verb		Answers
Can Could	I	have	a one-way ticket, please?	Sure. Sorry, that train is sold out.
Can Could Would	you	give	me a one-way ticket, please?	Of course. I'm sorry. We're sold out.

Look
To make requests, use *would, could,* or *can.* We often use *please* with polite requests.

A Match the situations with the requests.

_e_ 1. Myra wants to look at a schedule.   a. "Could I have a ticket, please?"
_f_ 2. Anna's bag is heavy.   b. "Can I ask you a question?"
_g_ 3. Alan's in a taxi. He's cold.   c. "Would you show me your tickets, please?"
_a_ 4. Rick doesn't have a ticket for the bus.   d. "Can I change my seat?"
_b_ 5. Chris wants some information.   e. "Could I have a schedule, please?"
_d_ 6. Louisa doesn't like her seat.   f. "Would you help me with my bag, please?"
_c_ 7. The flight attendant thinks two passengers are in the wrong seats.   g. "Can you close the window, please?"

B Change the sentences to requests. Use *please*.

1. Give me two tickets.   Can you give me two tickets, please? (can)
2. Open the window.   Would you open the window, please? (would)
3. Sit down.   Could you sit down, please? (could)
4. Wait.   Would you wait, please? (would)
5. Help me.   Can you help me, please? (can)
6. Take me to the airport.   Could you take me to the airport, please? (could)

PAIRS. Think of a situation for each request above. Answers will vary.

Example:
A: *In number 1, the speaker is in a train station and wants to take a train.*

244 Unit 20

B Teaching Time: 5–10 min.

- Read the example with the class.
- Have students complete the activity.
- Call on students to say answers. Correct as needed.
- PAIRS. Have students think of a situation for each request.
- Call on volunteers to say their answers.

Grammar Notes

1. To ask permission to do something or to ask for something, use *can I* or *could I* and the base form of a verb.
2. To ask a person to do something for you, use *can you, could you,* or *would you* and the base form of a verb.
3. To answer affirmatively, people often say *sure* or *of course.*
4. To answer negatively, people often say *sorry* or *I'm sorry* and give a reason why the answer is no.
5. For more information on this grammar topic, see page 261.

T-244 Center Stage 2

C 🎧 **41** Write requests. Use *Can*, *Could*, or *Would* and *Please*. Then listen and compare your requests.

1. You're in a cab and you're hot. The windows aren't open. You are talking to the cab driver.
   A: _Can you open the windows, please?_
   B: It's windy today. I'll turn on the air conditioner.

2. You want to get a round-trip ticket to Chicago. You are talking to a ticket agent.
   A: _Could I have a round-trip ticket to Chicago, please?_
   B: Sure. That'll be $35.

3. You want to get off at the next stop. You ask the bus driver.
   A: _Can I get off at the next stop, please?_
   B: No problem.

4. You need some coffee. You are talking to a flight attendant.
   A: _Could I have some coffee, please?_
   B: Sure. Here you are.

5. You want to stop at the next street. You are talking to the cab driver.
   A: _Would you stop at the next street, please?_
   B: Okay.

6. You're a flight attendant. A passenger should go back to his seat. You are talking to him.
   A: _Would you go back to your seat, please?_
   B: All right.

7. You're getting in a cab. Your friend is coming. Ask the cab driver to wait.
   A: _Could you wait a minute, please?_
   B: OK.

TIME to TALK

GROUPS. What requests do people often make in the places in the box? Make a list of three requests for each place. *Answers will vary.*

| at a train station | at a travel agency | at airport customs | at airport security |

WRAP-UP. Tell another group your requests. Can they guess the place?

Example:
A: Here is my request: Could I reserve a seat on the 9:55 to Philadelphia, please?
B: Are you at airport customs?
A: No.
B: I know. You're at a train station.

Transportation 245

C Teaching Time: 10–15 min.
- Read the example with the class.
- Have students complete the activity.
- 🎧 Play Track 41 while students check their answers.
- Ask pairs to role-play the completed conversations for the class to check answers. Correct as needed.

Multilevel Strategy
- **Pre-level:** Help students write the requests. After checking answers, have students take turns reading the completed conversations.
- **At-level, Above-level:** Give each pair a situation, such as a ticket agent and a customer, two passengers on a plane, a teacher and a student, etc. Have students make a short conversation with at least one question with *can, could,* or *would*. Have students act out their situations for the class.

Language Note

Exercise C. Tell students that *no problem, OK,* and *all right* are all ways to say *yes* to a request.

Option

Assign Unit 20 Supplementary Grammar to Communicate 3 Exercises on the Teacher's Resource Disk as homework or on the Student Persistence CD-ROM as self-access practice.

TIME to TALK

Teaching Time: 10–15 min.
- Have two students read the example conversation.
- GROUPS. Have students complete the task.
- Have groups take turns telling another group their requests and guessing where their conversation is happening.

Multilevel Strategy
- **Pre-level:** Tell students that they can use the requests from Exercises A, B and C. Have students choose one place from the box and write three requests.

Unit 20 T-245

Review and Challenge

Grammar

Teaching Time: 5–10 min.

- Read the example with the class.
- Have students complete the task.
- Call on students to write answers on the board. Write corrections on the board as needed.

> **Multilevel Strategy**
>
> - **Pre-level:** Tell students what the mistakes are and have them rewrite the sentences.

Dictation

Teaching Time: 5–10 min.

- 🎧 Play Track 42 while students listen and write what they hear.
- 🎧 Play Track 42 again while students check their answers.
- Call on students to write answers on the board.
- 🎧 Play Track 42 again and correct sentences on the board.

> **Multilevel Strategy**
>
> **Pre-level:** Give students a worksheet with some of the words from the dictation already provided.

Speaking

Teaching Time: 10–15 min.

- Have two students read the example.
- PAIRS. Have students prepare their conversation. Walk around and help as needed.
- Have students perform their conversations for the class.
- **LIFE SKILLS TEST PREP 2** Go to Unit 4, Lesson 2 for practice in making and responding to invitations.

Review and Challenge

Grammar

Find the mistake in each sentence. Circle the letter and correct the mistake.

1. Would you please to sit down? Correct: _Would you please sit down?_
   A   B   Ⓒ
2. We like to have some water, please. Correct: _We'd like to have some water, please._
   Ⓐ B   C
3. The child have to have a ticket. Correct: _The child has to have a ticket._
             Ⓐ   B   C
4. Do you like a one-way ticket? Correct: _Would you like a one-way ticket?_
   Ⓐ   B   C
5. She would likes a different seat. Correct: _She would like a different seat._
   A   Ⓑ   C
6. I can use your pen, please? Correct: _Can I use your pen, please?_
   Ⓐ B   C

Dictation

🎧 **42** Listen. You will hear five sentences. Write them on a piece of paper. See the audioscript on page 293 for the sentences.

Speaking

PAIRS. Choose one of the situations and write a conversation. Then perform your conversation for the class. *Answers will vary.*

> **Situation 1**
> *Student A:* You live in Los Angeles. You have to travel to Las Vegas because your mother is sick. You don't have a lot of money, but you really want to get there quickly. You go to a travel agency.
> *Student B:* You are a travel agent. A customer walks into your office.
>
> **Situation 2**
> *Student A:* You are at the train station. You have to travel from New York to Washington, D.C. today. This is the first time you are traveling by train.
> *Student B:* You are a ticket agent at Union Station in Washington, D.C. It is a very busy weekend, and many of the reserved trains are sold out. A customer comes up to your window.

Example: (Situation 1)
A: Hello. I'd like to buy a ticket from Los Angeles to Las Vegas.
B: OK. What kind of ticket would you like? . . .

Watch Out!

- **Grammar.** Students may confuse *would like* and *like*. Point out that *would like* means *want* and *like* means *enjoy*.
- Students might use *do* or *does* in questions with *would like*. Listen for and correct errors such as *Do you would like a ticket?*

Listening

A 🎧 **43** Listen to the conversation. Where are the people? Check (✓) the correct answer.

- ☐ on a flight from New York to Las Vegas
- ☐ on a flight from Los Angeles to Las Vegas
- ☑ on a flight from Las Vegas to New York
- ☐ on a flight from Los Angeles to New York

B 🎧 **44** Listen again. Match the start of each sentence with the correct endings.

_b_ 1. The woman would like   a. basketball.
_c_ 2. The man would like   b. a newspaper.
_d_ 3. The woman has to   c. some water.
_e_ 4. The woman liked   d. go to the restroom.
_g_ 5. The man has   e. Las Vegas.
_a_ 6. The woman loves   f. see the woman at the basketball game.
_f_ 7. The man would like to   g. two tickets to a basketball game.

TIME to TALK

GROUPS. Imagine that you are on an airplane. Students A, B: You are passengers. Student C: You are a flight attendant. Write a conversation about one of the situations. Answers will vary.

Situation 1: The flight is very rough. Some of the passengers are scared.

Situation 2: The passengers are complaining about everything. The flight attendant is polite, but she is losing her patience.

Situation 3: A young couple is traveling with their two sons. The children are behaving very badly. They won't listen to their parents. The other passengers are angry.

WRAP-UP. Now perform your conversation for the class.

Example: (Situation 1)
A: *Mommy! I'm scared, and I have to go to the bathroom!*
B: *Oh, Timmy, can you wait? We have to stay in our seats right now.*

Transportation 247

Listening

A Teaching Time: 5–10 min.

- **Warm-up:** Have students look at the picture. Ask where the people are (on an airplane). Ask students to point out clues in the picture that tell them the people are on an airplane (overhead luggage compartments, attendant's uniform, drink cart in the aisle).
- Ask students to read through the answer choices before they listen.
- 🎧 Play Track 43 while students listen.
- 🎧 Play Track 43 again while students complete the task.
- Call on a student to say the answer. Correct as needed.

B Teaching Time: 5–10 min.

- Ask students to read through the sentence parts before they listen.
- 🎧 Play Track 44 while students listen and complete the task.
- 🎧 Play Track 44 again while students listen and check their answers.
- Call on students to say answers. Correct as needed.

Option

Assign Unit 20 Supplementary Review and Challenge Exercises on the Teacher's Resource Disk as homework or on the Student Persistence CD-ROM as self-access practice.

TIME to TALK

Teaching Time: 10–15 min.

- Have two students read the example.
- GROUPS. Have students prepare their conversations.
- Walk around and help as needed.
- Have students perform their conversations for the class.

Unit 20 T-247

# Reading and Writing

Reading

A Teaching Time: 10–15 min.

- Ask students a few questions about the letter, such as: *Who is the letter to? Who is the letter from? Where does Emily O'Toole work? What state is Roxbury in?*
- Ask students to read through the answer choices before they read the letter.
- Have students read the letter silently. Then read it aloud. Pause after each few words and have students repeat chorally.
- Have students check the correct answer.
- Call on a student to say the answer. Correct as needed.

B Teaching Time: 5–10 min.

- Ask students to read through the questions before they reread the letter.
- Have students complete the task.
- Call on students to say answers. Correct as needed.

Reading and Writing

Reading

A Read the letter. What is the problem? Check (✓) the correct answer.

- ❏ The number 12 bus driver does not stop after 11:00 P.M.
- ❏ Mr. and Mrs. Thomas have to take the number 12 bus every day.
- ✓ The number 12 bus does not come at the times on the schedule.

Emily O'Toole
Public Transportation Commissioner
City of Boston
20 Harrison Ave.
Roxbury, MA 02119

5 Washington St., Apt. 2A
Roxbury, MA 02119
May 28, 2006

Dear Ms. O'Toole:

I am writing because I would like to report a problem on the Roxbury bus line. My husband and I do not have a car, so we have to take the number 12 bus every day. My husband has to be at work by 7:00 A.M. I have to take the bus home after work at 11:00 P.M. The number 12 bus schedule says that on weekdays the buses run every 20 minutes from 6:00 A.M. until midnight. However, my husband often has to wait 30 minutes for a bus in the morning. I have the same problem at night.

We would like your help. A few months ago, we called the transportation hotline to complain, but they didn't do anything. Could you please someone to contact us? Thank you for your attention.

Sincerely,

Frances Thomas
Frances Thomas

B Read the letter again. Answer the questions. Write in complete sentences.

1. Why do Mr. and Mrs. Thomas have to take the bus?
   They have to take the bus because they don't have a car.
2. What time does Mrs. Thomas get off work?
   She gets off work at 11:00 P.M.
3. How long do Mr. and Mrs. Thomas usually have to wait for the bus?
   They usually have to wait thirty minutes.
4. What did Mrs. Thomas do a few months ago?
   A few months ago she called the transportation hotline to complain.

Unit 20

Language Note

Exercise B. Explain that *get off work* means *finish working*.

Prewriting

GROUPS. Are there problems with the transportation in your city or town? Make a list of things that you would like the city to fix. *Answers will vary.*

1. The city does not take care of the roads.

Writing

Choose a problem from the list your group wrote. Write a letter of complaint to the appropriate city official. Find the name and address in the local phone book. Use the letter on page 248 as a model. *Answers will vary.*

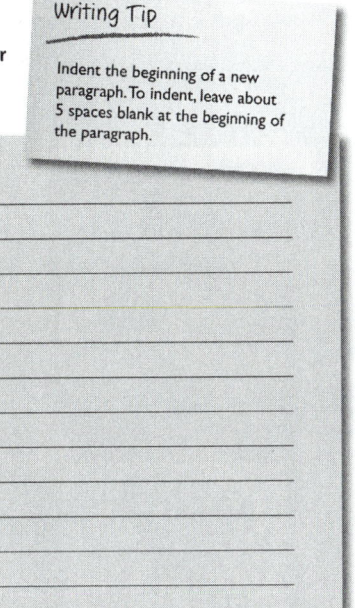

Writing Tip

Indent the beginning of a new paragraph. To indent, leave about 5 spaces blank at the beginning of the paragraph.

Transportation 249

Prewriting
Teaching Time: 10–15 min.

- Read the example with the class.
- GROUPS. Have students complete the activity.
- Walk around and help as needed.
- Call on students to tell the class the problems they listed. Record students' answers on the board.

Writing
Teaching Time: 15–20 min.

- After students have chosen their problems, have them work together to determine the appropriate city officials to direct their letters to. Walk around and help as needed.
- Have students study the Writing Tip.
- Ask students to look at the letter on page 248. Ask them to identify the topic of each paragraph (first paragraph: description of the problem, second paragraph: what the writer of the letter wants).
- Tell students to use the same organization for their letters and to indent each paragraph.
- Have students complete the activity.
- Walk around and help as needed.
- Call on volunteers to read their letters. Correct as needed. You can also have students write their letters on a piece of paper. Collect their work and provide individual feedback.

Option

- Tell students that the blue pages in a phone book list government offices and services.
- Have students use the Internet to determine to whom their letters should be addressed and to find the correct addresses.
- **LIFE SKILLS TEST PREP 2** Go to Unit 3, Lesson 4 for more practice in understanding and using the white pages of a phone directory.
- **LIFE SKILLS TEST PREP 2** Go to Unit 3, Lesson 5 for more practice in understanding and using yellow, blue, and white pages of a phone directory.

Unit 20 T-249

Game 5
Units 17–20

Answers will vary. Possible answers:

1. **A:** What should Bill do?
   B: He should take an aspirin.
   C: How many should he take?

2. **A:** Is Brutus bigger than Chico?
   B: Yes, he is.
   C: Who is smaller?

3. **A:** Will her rent probably go up in six months?
   B: Yes, it will probably go up in six months.
   C: How much will her rent go up in six months?

4. **A:** Does he have to wear a uniform?
   B: Yes, he has to wear a uniform.
   C: Where does he have to wear a uniform?

5. **A:** Should Tommy go to school today?
   B: No, he shouldn't go to school today.
   C: What should he do today?

Game 5 Units 17-20

PLAYERS: 3 students
MATERIALS: 1 book, 1 coin, 3 markers

INSTRUCTIONS
- Put your markers on the START box.
- Student A: Toss the coin. Heads = Move 1 box. Tails = Move 2 boxes.
- Make a question about the picture in the box.
- Students B, C: Make sure Student's A question is correct. Then Student B answers Students A's question. Student C makes a new question about Student A's picture. Give 1 point for a correct answer or question:

Example: PICTURE 1
Student A: What should Bill do?
Student B: He should take an aspirin.
Student C: How many should he take?

- Student B: Now take your turn.
- Students: If your answer is not correct, put your marker on the box from your last turn. If you land on another student's box, move your marker to the next box.
- Continue taking turns until you get to the FINISH box. The student with the most points wins.

T-250 Center Stage 2

6. **A:** Is Betty thinner than Luz?
   B: No, Betty isn't thinner than Luz.
   C: Who is thinner, Luz or Betty?

7. **A:** Will Frank and Tania start a business next year?
   B: Yes, they will start a business next year.
   C: Who will Tania start a business with next year?

8. **A:** What would you like to drink?
   B: I would like a soda.
   C: What kind of soda would you like?

9. **A:** What should Larry do?
   B: He should take an allergy medicine.
   C: Should he stay inside?

10. **A:** Is Cathy's coffee worse than Paul's coffee?
    B: Yes, Cathy's coffee is worse than Paul's coffee.
    C: Is Ida's coffee the worst?

11. **A:** Will they have a good time on New Year's Eve in 2010?
    B: Yes, they will have a good time on New Year's Eve in 2010.
    C: What will they do on New Year's Eve in 2010?

12. **A:** Would you close the window please?
    B: Sure.
    C: Could you close the window please?

13. **A:** What should Alice do?
    B: She should put on a Band-Aid.
    C: Should she see a doctor?

14. **A:** Is the black chair more comfortable than the white chair?
    B: No, the black chair isn't more comfortable than the white chair.
    C: Is the red chair the most comfortable of the three?

15. **A:** Will Antonio probably get a raise next month?
    B: Yes, he will probably get a raise next month.
    C: What will Antonio probably get next month?

16. **A:** Would she like to buy a ticket to Los Angeles?
    B: No, she would like to buy a ticket to Chicago.
    C: Where would she like to go?

Game 5 T-251

Grammar Summaries

Unit 1 People

Be: Affirmative and Negative Statements
1. Use the verb *be* to make an affirmative statement:
   He **is** quiet.
2. Use the verb *be* and *not* to make a negative statement:
   He **is not** quiet.
3. *You* is singular (one person) or plural (two or more people).
   Bill, you're quiet.
   Dan and Alice, you're quiet.
4. There are two forms—the full form (*I am*) and the contracted form (*I'm*). The contracted form is more common in conversation.
5. There are two forms of negative contractions. They have the same meaning.
   You're not quiet. = **You aren't** quiet.
6. There is only one negative contraction for *I*:
   I'm not

Be: Yes / No Questions and Short Answers
1. For *yes / no* questions with the verb *be*, change the word order of the subject (*he, she, they*, etc.) and the verb (*am, is, are*).
   They are late.   **Are they** late?
2. There are two negative short answers. They have the same meaning.
   No, it**'s not**.   No, it **isn't**.
3. There is only one negative short answer for *I*:
   No, I'm not.

Regular Count Nouns and Irregular Nouns
1. Add *–s* to change regular singular nouns to plural nouns.
   student ⟶ student**s**
2. Add *–es* to regular nouns that end in *–s*.
   boss ⟶ boss**es**
3. Some plural nouns are irregular. They do not end in *–s* or *–es*.
   child   children
4. Look at page 263 for spelling rules for plural nouns. Look at page 264 for pronunciation rules for plural nouns.

Unit 2 Families

Possessive Adjectives
1. Possessive adjectives come before nouns.
   My name is Sylvia.
2. Possessive adjectives do not change forms. Use the same form with singular and plural nouns.
   Her brother is here.
   Her brothers are here.
3. *Your* is singular (one person) or plural (two or more people).
   Your mother is tall, **Lucy**.
   Your mother is tall, **Ken and Lucy**.
4. Be careful! Do not confuse *Its* with *It's*.
   The dog's ears aren't white. **Its** nose is white.
   (**Its**=possessive adjective)
   Don't worry. **It's** friendly.
   (**It's**=It is)

Possessive Nouns
1. Add *'s* after singular nouns.
   My sister**'s** name is Anna.
2. Add *'* after the *–s* ending of regular plural nouns.
   My sister**s'** names are Michele and Janine.
3. Add *'s* after irregular plural nouns.
   The women**'s** names are Meg and Gina.
4. When there are two nouns, add *'s* to the last noun.
   Dan and Sue**'s** last name is Riley.
5. Be careful! The possessive *'s* is different from the contraction *'s* for *is*.
   Dan**'s** last name is Riley. (possessive)
   Dan**'s** late for work today. (contraction)
6. Look at page 264 for pronunciation rules for possessive nouns.

Be: Information Questions
1. In information questions, *is* or *are* comes after the *wh-* word (*who, what*, etc.)
   How old is he?
   Where are your sisters?
2. In conversation, use the contracted form of *is* (*'s*) after the *wh-* word.
   What**'s** your name?   (=What is your name?)
   Who**'s** in the picture?   (=Who is in the picture?)
3. Use *how* + adjective to ask questions.
   How old are you?

Grammar Summaries

UNIT 3 Jobs

A and *An* with Singular Count Nouns
1. Use *a* before singular nouns that begin with a consonant (*b, c, d, f, g, h, j, k, l, m, n, p, q, r, s, t, v, w, x, y, z*)
   My brother is **a m**echanic.
2. Use *an* before singular nouns that begin with a vowel (*a, e, i, o, u*).
   My sister is **an a**ccountant.
3. Do not use *a* or *an* before plural nouns.
   My brother and sister are engineers.
   NOT My brother and sister an engineers.
4. Use *a* before *u* if the *u* sounds like *you*.
   Paul is **a university** worker.
   [pronounced **you•**niversity]
5. Use *an* before *h* if the *h* is silent.
   Sheila is **an honest** waitress.
   [the *h* is NOT pronounced.]
   Sheila is **a hard-working** waitress.
   [the *h* is pronounced.]

Adjective and Noun Word Order
1. Adjectives describe people and things. Use adjectives after the verb *be* or before a noun.
   The job is **interesting**.
   She's an **excellent** hairdresser.
2. Adjectives do not change form with plural nouns.
   The **waiter** is **careful**. The waiters are careful.
   NOT The waiters are carefuls.
3. Use *a* before an adjective that begins with a consonant + a singular noun.
   It is a **good job**.
4. Use *an* before an adjective that begins with a vowel + a singular noun.
   It is **an interesting job**.
5. Do not use *a* or *an* before an adjective alone.
   It **is interesting.** NOT It is an interesting.

A / An / Ø and *The*
1. Use *the* before singular and plural nouns.
   The **worker** is neat.
   The **workers** are neat.
2. Use *the* when the noun is the only one in that situation.
   Jerry is **the** mechanic at A-1 Garage (=Jerry is the only mechanic at A-1 Garage.)
3. Also use *the* for the second time you talk about something.
   I work at a garage. **The** garage is big.
4. Use *a/an* when the singular noun is one of many. The noun is NOT the only one.
   Jerry is **a** mechanic. (=Jerry is not the only mechanic.)
5. Do NOT use an article when the plural noun is two (or more) of many.
   Jerry and Tom are mechanics. (=Jerry and Tom are not the only mechanics.)

UNIT 4 Places

There is / There are: Statements
1. Make sentences with *There is* and singular nouns:
   There is a restaurant near my home.
2. Make sentences with *There are* and plural nouns:
   There are restaurants near my home.
3. There are two forms—the full form (*There is*) and the contracted form (*There's*). *There are* does not have a contracted form.
4. The subject comes after *There is* or *There are*. *There* is NOT the subject.

Some / A lot of / Any
1. Use *some* with plural nouns in affirmative statements. Use *any* with plural nouns in negative statements.
   There **are some** restaurants.
   There **aren't any** stores.
2. Use *a lot of* with plural nouns in affirmative and negative statements.
   There are a **lot of** good restaurants.
   There aren't a lot of cheap stores.
3. Use *a lot of* for large numbers.
   Use *some* for small numbers.
   Use *any* for zero in negative statements.
   There are **a lot of** people here. (50 people)
   There are **some** people here. (5 people)
   There aren't **any** people here. (0 people)
4. We can use plural nouns without *some* or *any*.
   There are expensive stores on 5th Avenue in New York.
5. We can use *no* instead of *not any*.
   There are **no** restaurants near here.
6. Be careful! The pronunciation of *there, their*, and *they're* is the same. The meaning is different.
   There is a good restaurant near here.
   They're in the restaurant. (they are)
   Their table is ready. (His and her table)
   The restaurant isn't here. It's over **there**. (a specific place)

Is there / Are there
1. In questions with *Is there*, use *a* or *an*.
   Is there a bank near here?
   Is there an office building near here?
2. In questions with *Are there*, use *any* or *a lot of*.
   Are there any banks near here?
   Are there a lot of stores here?
3. Use *there is* or *there are* to talk about something the first time. Use *it* or *they* the second time.
   A: Is there a big store near here?
   B: Yes, **there is. It** is expensive.
   A: Are there restaurants near here?
   B: Yes, **there** are. **They**'re on Main Street.

Grammar Summaries T-253

Unit 5 Food and Drink

Count and Noncount Nouns
1. Count nouns are singular (1 apple) or plural (2 apples.) We can count them.
2. Use *a* or *an* with singular count nouns in affirmative and negative statements.
   There is **a** banana in the bag.
   There isn't **an** orange in the bag.
3. We can not count noncount nouns. They do not have plural forms. Do not add *–s* or *–es*.
   The **fruit** is good.
   NOT ~~The fruits are good~~.
4. Use the singular form of the verb (*is*, for example) with noncount nouns.
   There is some meat on the table.
   NOT ~~There are some meat on the table~~.
5. Use *How much* to ask about the price of both count and noncount nouns.
   How much is the fruit?   Three **dollars**.

Quantifiers: *Some / A little / A lot of / A few / Any*
1. We can use full forms (*there is not /there are not*), but we usually use contractions in conversation.
   There **aren't** any oranges.
2. Use *some* with noncount nouns and plural nouns in affirmative statements.
   There **is some** milk.   There **are some** eggs.
3. Use *any* with noncount nouns and plural nouns in negative statements.
   There **isn't any** milk.   There **aren't any** eggs.
4. Use *a little* with noncount nouns. Use *a few* with plural count nouns.
   There is **a little** sugar.   There are **a few** cookies.
5. Use *a lot of* in affirmative and negative statements, with both noncount nouns and plural count nouns.
   There **is a lot** of rice.   There aren't **a lot of** oranges.
6. We can use noncount and plural nouns alone.
   There **is sugar** in the cookies.
7. We can use *no* instead of *not any*.
   There **is no** salt in the soup.
   There **isn't any** salt in the soup.
8. When we talk about a specific amount of food, we use words for containers or weight.
   There are **two bottles** of soda.

Count and Noncount Nouns: *Yes / No* Questions
1. Use *Is there a / an* with singular count nouns in *yes / no* questions.
   Is there **a** banana in the bag?
2. Use *Are there any* with noncount nouns and plural nouns in *yes / no* questions.
   Are there any eggs?
3. Use *How much* with noncount nouns. Use *How many* with plural count nouns.
   How much milk is there?
   How many bottles of milk are there?

Unit 6 Physical Exercise

Present Progressive: Statements
1. For the present progressive, use the simple present of the verb *be* and a verb + *-ing*.
   I **am** tal**king**.
   Linda **is** tal**king**.
   Mike and Lee **are** tal**king**.
2. Use the present progressive to talk about activities happening now.
   The children are in bed. They **are sleeping**.
3. With the present progressive, we understand that the time is now or right now. We can say *now* or *right now*, but it is not necessary.
   I'm **writing right now**. OR I'm **writing**.
4. There are two forms—the full form and the contracted form. The contracted form is more common in conversation.
   I **am eating.**   (Full form)
   I'**m eating.**   (Contracted form)
5. There are two forms of negative contractions. The meaning is the same.
   You're **not** sleeping.   =   You **aren't** sleeping.
   He's **not** sleeping.   =   He **isn't** sleeping.
   They're **not** sleeping.   =   They **aren't** sleeping.
6. There is only one negative contraction for *I*.
   I'm **not** running.
7. Look at page 262 for spelling rules for the present progressive.

Present Progressive: *Yes / No* Questions
1. To make a *yes / no* question, change the word order of the subject and the verb.
   They are eating.   **Are they** eating?
2. There are two negative short answers. They have the same meaning.
   Are they eating?   No, they'**re not**. OR
                      No, they **aren't**.
3. There is only one negative short answer for *I*.
   Are you running?   **No, I'm not.**

Present Progressive: Information Questions
1. In information questions, *is* or *are* comes after the *wh-* word (*what*, *where*, etc.).
   What is Chris doing?
2. In conversation, the contracted form is common after the *wh-* word.
   What's she eating? (=What is she eating?)
3. Look at the difference in these questions.
   Who's Mary talking to?
   (Conversation and informal writing)
   To whom is Mary talking?
   (Formal English)

Grammar Summaries

Unit 7 Do's and Don'ts

Imperatives
1. To make an affirmative imperative, use the base form of the verb. To make a negative imperative, use *don't* + the base form of the verb.
    - Wait for me. (Affirmative)
    - Don't wait for me. (Negative)
2. *You* is the subject of imperative, but we do not usually say *you* in the sentence.
    - Please close the door.
    - NOT ~~Please you~~ close the door.
3. Use *please* to be polite. Put *please* at the beginning or end of the sentence.
    - Please don't talk.
    - Don't talk, please.

Prepositions
1. Many sentences have prepositions. A preposition always has an object. The object is a noun or pronoun.
    - Listen **to** your **mother**.
    -        preposition   noun (object)
2. Some prepositions give location.
    - Put the wastebasket **in** the room.
    - **behind** the door.
    - **under** the desk.
3. Some prepositions come after verbs or adjectives.
    - **Look at** these sentences. (Verb + preposition)
    - Be **nice to** your sister. (Adjective + preposition)

Object Pronouns
1. Use an object pronoun in place of a noun after a verb or preposition.
    - Wait for **him**. (Object pronoun)
    - the bus. (Noun)
    - Mr. Chiu. (Noun)
2. *You* is an object pronoun and a subject pronoun.
    - I'm listening to **you**.
    - **You** aren't listening to me.

Unit 8 Possessions

This / That / These / Those
1. Use *this* and *that* for singular nouns. Use *these* and *those* for plural nouns.
2. Use *this* and *these* for things near you. Use *that* and *those* for things not near you.
3. Use *this / that / these / those* before a noun.
    - **This** camera is nice.
    - (This + noun + verb)
4. You can use *this / that / these / those* as a pronoun.
    - **This** is my camera.
    - (This + verb)

Possessive Adjectives and Pronouns
1. Use a possessive adjective before a noun. Do not use a possessive pronoun before a noun.
    - **My shoes** are clean.
    - NOT ~~Mine~~ shoes are clean.
2. Possessive pronouns do not change forms. Use the same form to refer to singular and plural nouns.
    - The pen is **mine**.
    - The pens are **mine**.
    - NOT ~~The pens are mines~~.
3. *His* is both a possessive adjective and a possessive pronoun.
    - **His** hair is black.
    - (possessive adjective, describes hair)
    - **His** is blond.
    - (possessive pronoun, replaces *his hair*.)

Simple Present: *Have*
1. Use *have* or *has* to talk about possessions.
    - I **have** a car. (The car is my possession.)
2. Use *have* with *I, you, we*, and *they*.
    - I **have** a new car.
    - My wife and I **have** a new car.
    - You **have** a new laptop.
    - They **have** a new computer.
3. Use *has* with the third person singular (*he, she, it*).
    - Mr. Robinson **has** a new computer.
    - She **has** a new cell phone.

Grammar Summaries

Unit 9 Routines

Simple Present: Affirmative Statements
1. Use the simple present to talk about everyday activities and things that happen again and again.
   > My brother **works** on Tuesday.
   > (=This is his routine.)
   > I **eat** ice cream after dinner.
   > (=This is my habit.)
2. *You* is singular (one person) or plural (two or more people).
   > **Bill, you** sleep a lot.
   > **Dan and Alice, you** sleep a lot.
3. The third person singular (*he, she, it*) of *have* is *has*.
   > I **have** a cup of coffee.
   > He **has** a cup of coffee.
4. Look at page 264 for information about the pronunciation of the third person singular *-s-* or *-es* (*he, she, it*).

Simple Present: Spelling Rules
1. For the third person singular (*he, she, it*) of the simple present, add *–s* or *–es* to the base form of the verb. Look at page 263 for more spelling rules.
   > He cook**s** every day.
   > She wash**es** her hair in the morning.

Simple Present: Negative Statements
1. With *I, you, we,* and *they,* use *do not* + the base form of the verb in negative statements.
   > **We do not stay up** late on weekends.

   With *he, she,* and *it,* use *does not* + the base form of the verb in negative statements.
   > **She does not stay up** late on weekends.
2. Use *don't* + verb or *doesn't* + verb for negative statements in conversation.
   > I **don't** sleep a lot.
   > He **doesn't** sleep a lot.
3. When you have one subject and two negative verbs in the simple present, you can connect the verbs with *or*. Do not repeat *don't* or *doesn't* after *or*.
   > They **don't cook** or **wash** the dishes in the evening.
   > NOT ~~They don't cook or don't wash the dishes in the evening.~~

Unit 10 Shopping

Frequency Adverbs with the Simple Present
1. Use frequency adverbs to say how often people do things or how often something happens.
   > I **never** pay for things with a credit card.
   > (=0% of the time)
   > The store **always** opens at 9 o'clock.
   > (=100% of the time)
2. Use frequency adverbs *before* the base form of the verb.
   > I **often buy** things at the mall.
   > I **don't often buy** things at the mall.
   > **Do you often buy** things at the mall?
3. Use frequency adverbs *after* the verb *be*.
   > The store **is usually** busy on the weekend.
4. We also put *sometimes* at the beginning or end of sentences.
   > We **sometimes** go to that store.
   > **Sometimes** we go to that store.
   > We go to that store **sometimes**.

Simple Present: Yes / No Questions
1. To make a *yes / no* question, add *do* or *does* before the subject and the base form of the verb.
   > **They spend** a lot of money.
   > **Do they spend** a lot of money?
   > **He spends** a lot of money.
   > **Does he spend** a lot of money?
2. When you use *does* in a *yes / no* question, do not use *–s* or *–es* at the end of the base form of the verb.
   > **Does** it **close** at 6 o'clock?
   > No, it closes at 6:30.
   > NOT ~~Does it closes at 6 o'clock?~~
3. Use *do* or *does* in short answers.
   > Do you have a new car?
   > Yes, we **do**. OR No, we **don't**.
   > Does she have a new car?
   > Yes, she **does**. OR No, she **doesn't**.
4. Remember: For questions with the verb *be*, use *is, am,* or *are* in short answers.
   > Is the store big?
   > Yes, it **is**. OR No, it **isn't**.

Simple Present: Information Questions
1. In information questions, *does* or *do* comes after the *wh-* word (*what, how much,* etc.)
   > **What does** the store **sell**?
   > **How much do** the shoes **cost**?
2. When you use *does* in an information question, do not use *–s* or *–es* at the end of the base form of the verb.
   > How much does it cost?
   > NOT How much does it ~~costs?~~
3. We can also use *do / does* with the expression *What kind of* + noun.
   > What kind of car **do** you want?

Unit 11 Holidays and Special Occasions

Direct and Indirect Objects
1. Some verbs have direct and indirect objects. The verbs *buy, get, give, make,* and *send* have both direct and indirect objects.
2. When a sentence has a direct and indirect object, the objects can come in either order.

    I send **cards to many people**.

    (direct object + preposition + indirect object)

    I send **many people cards**.

    (indirect object + direct object).

3. When the indirect object is a pronoun (*me, him, her, them,* etc.) put the direct object after the pronoun.

    I send **them cards.**

    (indirect object pronoun) (direct object)

Simple Present: Information Questions
1. In information questions, *does* or *do* comes after the wh- word (*how, why,* etc.)

    How do you **celebrate** your birthday?
    Why does she **give** him candy?

2. When you use *does* in an information question, do not use –s or –es at the end of the base form of the verb.

    When **does** the party **start**?
    NOT When does the party starts?

Who as Subject and Object
1. When *who* is the subject of the question, use verb + -s after *who*.

    Who   cooks the food?
    (subject) (verb)

2. When *who* is the object of the question, add *do* or *does* before the subject.

    Who do you **invite**? My friends.
    (object) (subject)

3. In formal English, use *whom* for a question about an object. Use *who* for informal questions.

    Whom do people invite to a wedding? (formal)
    Who do people invite to a wedding? (informal)

4. When a verb has a preposition, put the preposition at the end of the question in conversation.

    Who do you **give** flowers **to**?
    I **give** flowers **to** my girlfriend.
    Who does he **buy** gifts **for**?
    He **buys** gifts **for many** people.

5. In formal English, do not use prepositions at the end of questions. Put the preposition before *whom*.

    To whom do people give gifts? (formal)
    Who do people give gifts **to**? (informal)

Unit 12 At Work

Simple Present and Present Progressive
1. Use the simple present to talk about routines, schedules, and general facts.

    My brother **works** everyday. (routine)
    The store **closes** at 9:00. (schedule)
    A lot of women in the U.S. **work**. (general fact)

2. Use the present progressive to talk about activities happening now or these days:

    I **am reading** right **now**.
    We **are studying** English **these days**.

Stative Verbs
1. Stative verbs do not describe actions. Some common stative verbs are: *be, have, know, like, need, understand, want, hear, see.* (See page 265 for a list of more stative verbs.)
2. Use the simple present with stative verbs. Do not use the present progressive.

    This book **costs** a lot.
    NOT This book is costing a lot.

3. Some stative verbs can also be used as action verbs, but with different meanings. When they are used as action verbs, they can be used in the present progressive or simple present.

    have=stative verb meaning possession
    I **have** a car now. (possession)
    NOT I'm having a car now.

    have=action verb meaning eat
    I'm **having** dinner now. (action)
    I **have** dinner at 6:00 every night. (habit)

Like / Need / Want + Infinitive
1. If you use a verb after *need, want,* or *like,* use the infinitive form of the verb.
    (Infinitive=*to* + the base form of the verb)

    I need **to get** a job.
    He doesn't want **to work** part-time.
    She likes **to work** in the morning.

2. Don't forget! You can also use a noun or pronoun after *need, want* and *like*.

    I need a **job**. I need **it** now.
    She wants two **eggs**. She wants **them** now.
    He likes his **boss**. He likes **her** a lot.

Grammar Summaries

Unit 13 Feelings and Opinions

Simple Past of *Be*: Statements
1. *Was* is the past of *am* and *is*. *Were* is the past of *are*.
   I **was** here yesterday.   I **am** here today.
   You **were** late yesterday. You **are** late today.
2. *There was* is the past of *there is*. *There were* is the past of *there are*.
   There **was** a line yesterday.
   There **were** a lot of cars yesterday.
3. *Was not* is the past of *am not* and *is not*. *Were not* is the past of *are not*.
   The weather **was not** bad yesterday.
   The weather **is not** bad today.
   We **were not** busy yesterday.
   We **are not** busy today.
4. There are two negative forms—the full form (*I was*) and the contracted form (*I wasn't*). The contracted form is more common in conversations. There are no contracted forms for the affirmative (*was, were*).
5. *There wasn't* is the past of *there isn't*. *There weren't* is the past of *there aren't*.
   There wasn't a lot of food. There weren't any lines.
6. Past time expressions can go at the beginning or at the end of a sentence.
   Last night I was at home.
   I was at home **last night**.

Simple Past of *Be*: Yes / No Questions
1. To make a *yes / no* question with the past of *be*, change the word order of the subject (*he, she, they*, etc.) and the verb (*was / were*).
   They were on vacation last week.
   Were they on vacation last week?
2. To make a *yes / no* question with the past of *there was* or *there were*, change the word order of the two words.
   There was a test in class yesterday.
   Was there a test in class yesterday?
3. Look at the different short answers.
   Was the food good?
   Yes, **it** was. OR No, **it** wasn't.
   Was there a lot of food?
   Yes, **there** was. OR No, **there** wasn't.

Simple Past of *Be*: Information Questions
1. In information questions, *was* or *were* come after the *wh-* word (*how, where,* etc.).
   How was the party?
   Where were the children?
2. Be careful! Questions with *who* have two forms.
   Who was at the party?
   My friends were at the party.
   Who were you with at the party?
   I was with my friends.

Unit 14 Fact or Fiction

Simple Past: Regular Verbs
1. For the simple past, add *–ed* to the base form of the verb.
   I cook**ed** yesterday evening.
   I cook every evening.
2. If the verb ends in *–e*, add *–d*.
   The stores **close** at 6:00 P.M. every day.
   The stores **closed** at 6:00 P.M. yesterday.
3. If the verb ends in a consonant + *-y*, change the *–y* to *–i*. Then add *–ed*.
   They study every day.
   They stud**ied** yesterday.
4. If the verb ends in consonant + vowel + consonant, double the consonant. Then add *–ed*.
   We stop at 5 P.M. every day.
   We sto**pped** at 5 P.M. yesterday.
5. Look at page 262 for more spelling rules. Look at page 264 for pronunciation rules for the *–ed* ending of regular past tense verbs.

Simple Past: Irregular Verbs
1. Many verbs are irregular. The simple past of these verbs do not have *–ed* at the end. Here are some common irregular past tense verbs.
   do → did   eat → ate
   go → went   have → had
2. Look at page 265 for a list of irregular past forms of verbs.

Simple Past: Negative Statements
1. For the negative past form of verbs, use *did not* + the base form of the verb.
   I **did not watch** TV last Sunday.
   I **watched** TV last Monday.
   I **did not eat** dinner at 6 o'clock.
   I **ate** dinner at 8 o'clock.
2. Use *didn't* + the base form of the verb for negative statements in conversation.
   I **didn't watch** TV last Sunday.
   I **didn't eat** dinner at 6 o'clock.
3. Do not use the *–ed* ending or the irregular past form in negative sentences.
   He **didn't work** yesterday.
   NOT He didn't worked yesterday.
   I **didn't take** the bus yesterday.
   NOT I didn't took the bus yesterday.
4. The affirmative and negative forms of the past are the same for all persons (*I, you, he, she, it, we, they*).
   She walk**ed** to the office yesterday.
   She walks to the office every day.
   They **didn't have** breakfast yesterday.
   They don't have breakfast every day.
5. Be careful! The past of *be* is *was / wasn't* and *were / weren't*. Do not use *didn't* with the past of *be*.
   I **wasn't** at home last night.
   NOT I didn't be at home last night.

Grammar Summaries

UNIT 15 Life Stages

Simple Past: Yes / No Questions
1. To make a *yes / no* question, add *did* before the subject and use the base form of the verb.
   They got married in 1998.
   Did they get married in 1998?
   She retired in 2004.
   Did she retire in 2004?
2. When you use *did* in a *yes / no* question, do not use *–ed* at the end of the base form of the verb.
   Did it close last year?
   NOT Did it ~~closed~~ last year?
3. Use *did* in short answers.
   Did you meet a long time ago?
   Yes, we **did**. OR No, we **didn't**.
4. For questions with the verb *be*, do not use *did*. Use *was* or *were*.
   Was he married for a long time?
   Yes, he **was**. OR No, he **wasn't**.

Simple Past: Information Questions
1. In information questions, *did* comes after the *wh-* word (*what, how much,* etc.)
   Where did you **live**?
   Why did he **live** in Miami?
2. When you use *did* in an information question, do not use *–ed* at the end of the base form of the verb.
   When **did** they **move**?
   NOT ~~When did they moved?~~
3. When *who* or *what* is the subject of a question, do not use *did* in the question. Use the past form of the verb.
   Who   got   married?
   (Subject) (Verb)
   What   happened?
   (Subject) (Verb)

How long ago / How long
1. Use *ago* after an expression of time—for example, *two months ago* or *five days ago*. *Ago* tells us "when before now."
   She graduated **two months ago.**
   (=two months before now)
   They visited us **five days ago.**
   (=five days before now)
2. Use *for* before an expression of time—for example, *for two months* or *for five days*.
   He lived there **for two months.**
   (=from October 10th to December 10th)
   They stayed here **for five days**.
   (=from Friday to Wednesday.)
3. Use *how long ago* to ask when an event happened.
   How long ago did you get married?
   (=when before now)
   Five years ago.
4. Use *how long* to ask about the period of time.
   How long were they married?
   (=how many years)
   For five years.

UNIT 16 Looking Ahead

Future with *Be going to*: Statements
1. Use *be going to* + verb to talk about the future. Use *am, is,* or *are* before *going to*.
   I **am going to leave** at 8 tomorrow.
   Linda **is going to meet** me tomorrow afternoon.
   Mike and Lee **are going to play** cards with us tomorrow night.
2. Always use the base form of the verb after *be going to*.
   The store **is going to close.**
   NOT ~~The store is going to closing~~.
3. Here are some common future time expressions:

later	this week
soon	this month
today	this year
this morning	next week
this afternoon	next month
this evening	next year
tomorrow	in one week
tomorrow morning	in two months

4. Sometimes people use *this morning* and *this afternoon* to talk about the past. For example, at 7 o'clock in the evening, someone says:
   I went to the store this morning.
   I went to the library this afternoon.
5. People often say *gonna* for *going to*. We do not write *gonna*.

Future with *Be going to*: Yes / No Questions
1. To make a *yes / no* question, change the word order of the subject and the verb *be*.
   They are going to stay home.
   Are they going to stay home?
2. There are two negative short answers. They have the same meaning.
   Are they going to eat out?
   No, they'**re not**. OR No, they **aren't**.

Be going to: Information Questions
1. In information questions, *am, is,* or *are* comes after the *wh-* word (*what, where,* etc.)
   What is Chris going to do?
   Where are you going to wait?
2. In conversation, the contracted form is common after the *wh-* word.
   What's she going to wear?
   (=What is she going to wear?)
   Where's he going to work?
   (=Where is he going to work?)
3. When *who* or *what* is the subject of the question, do not use *he, she, it,* etc., in the question.
   Who is going to come?
   (Subject)

Grammar Summaries

Unit 17 Health

Should: Affirmative and Negative Statements
1. Use *should* and *should not* to give advice and express opinions.
2. Use the base form of the verb after *should* or *should not*.
   > You **should take** the medicine right now.
   > You **should not forget**.
3. Use *shouldn't* + the base form of the verb for negative statements in conversation.
   > You **shouldn't go** to work.
   > The baby **shouldn't go** out in the sun.
4. The affirmative and negative forms are the same for all persons (*I, you, he, she, it, we, they*).
   > I **should call** the doctor.
   > She **should call** the doctor.
   > We **shouldn't eat** cake.
   > They **shouldn't eat** cake.
5. Use *should* to talk about the present and the future.
   > You should put a band-aid on the cut **right now**.
   > You should stay in bed all day **tomorrow**.

Should: Yes / No Questions
1. To make a *yes / no* question, put *should* before the subject and use the base form of the verb.
   > **We should eat** more fish.
   > **Should we eat** more fish?
   > **She should exercise** every day.
   > **Should she exercise** every day?
2. Use *should* in short answers.
   > Should I ask the pharmacist?
   > Yes, you **should**. OR No, you **shouldn't**.
3. Use *or* in questions with two possible answers.
   > Should I take two **or** three pills?
   > You should take two pills.
   > Should I stay home **or** go to work?
   > You should stay home.

Should: Information Questions
1. In information questions, *should* comes after the *wh-* word (*what, how much,* etc.)
   > **Where should I go?**
   > **How often should** he **take** the medicine?
2. Use *which* to ask questions about a choice. There is usually a noun after *which*.
   > **Which cough syrup** should I buy?
   > (There are five kinds of cough syrup.)
   > **Which hospital** should we go to?
   > (There are 10 hospitals in the city.)
3. Be careful! Questions with *who* have two forms.
   > **Who should take** the medicine?
   > (subject)
   > **Who should I call?**
   > (object)

Unit 18 A Place to Live

Comparative of Adjectives
1. Use the comparative to compare two people, places, or things.
   > Tim's car is **cheaper than** Jan's car.
   > Houses are **more expensive than** apartments.
2. Use *-er* with adjectives that have one syllable.
   > small → small**er**   cheap → cheap**er**
3. Use *-er* with two-syllable adjectives that end in *-y*. (Change the *–y* to *–i*.)
   > prett**ier** [pret·ty]   dirt**ier** [dir·ty]
   >   1   2   1   2   1   2   1   2
4. We usually use *more* with two-syllable adjectives and adjectives with three or more syllables.
   > **more modern**   [mod·ern]
   >   1   2
   > **more beautiful** [beau·ti·ful]
   >   1   2   3
5. The comparative forms of *good, bad,* and *far* are irregular.
   > good → **better**   bad → **worse**
   > far → **farther**

Superlative of Adjectives
1. Use the superlative to compare three or more people, places, or things.
   > We looked at five cars. The Honda Civic was **the cheapest**.
   > There are three apartments for rent. The one on 1st Street is the **most expensive**.
2. Use *the + -est* with adjectives that have one syllable.
   > small → **the** small**est** / cheap → **the** cheap**est**
3. Use *the + -est* with two-syllable adjectives that end in *-y*. (Change the *–y* to *–i*.)
   > **the** prett**iest** [pret·ty]   **the** dirt**iest** [dir·ty]
4. We usually use *the most* with two-syllable adjectives and adjectives that have three or more syllables.
   > **the most modern**   [mod·ern]
   > **the most beautiful**   [beau·ti·ful]
5. The superlative forms of *good, bad,* and *far* are irregular.
   > good → **the best**   bad → **the worst**
   > far → **the farthest**

Comparative and Superlative
1. Use the comparative to compare two people, places, or things. Use the superlative to compare three or more people, places, or things.
   > Tim's car is **nicer than** Jan's car.
   > We looked at five apartments.
   > The apartment on Park Avenue was **the nicest**.
2. There are a few exceptions to the rules for forming the comparative and superlative. Here are some examples:
   > more bored   the most bored
   > quieter   the quietest
   > simpler   the simplest
3. Look at page 263 for spelling rules with comparative and superlative forms.

Grammar Summaries

Unit 19 Future Changes

Will: Affirmative and Negative Statements

1. Use *will* + verb to make predictions about the future. (You think something will happen, but you aren't sure.)
    Things **will be** more expensive next year.
2. Use the base form of the verb after *will*. For the negative of *will*, use *will not* and the base form of the verb.
    Tony and Rosa **will get** married.
    They **will not have** children.
3. Use the contraction *'ll* or *won't* + base form of the verb in conversation.
    You'll get a raise.
    You **won't lose** your job.
4. The affirmative and negative forms are the same for all persons (*I, you, he, she, it, we, they*).
    She **will meet** new people.
    They **won't be** from here.
5. We often use *probably* when we make predictions. Be careful! The word order is different with *will* and *won't*.
    He **will probably go** to the game.
    He **probably won't go** to the game.
6. We can also use *be going to* to make predictions about the future.
    He **is going to find** a good job.
7. Do not use *will* for plans about the future. Use *be going to* for future plans.
    We **are going to buy** a new car next year.

Will: Yes / No Questions

1. To make a *yes / no* question, put *will* before the subject and use the base form of the verb.
    They will need money.
    Will they need money?
2. We use *will* or *won't* in short answers.
    Will she get a raise?
    Yes, she **will**. OR No, she **won't**.

Will: Information Questions

1. In information questions, *will* comes after the *wh-* word (*what, where*, etc.)
    What will Chris buy?
    Where will you go?
2. When *who* or *what* is the subject of the question, do not use *he, she, it*, etc., in the question.
    Who will go to the bank? Jane will.
    (Subject)

Unit 20 Transportation

Have to

1. Use *have to* or *has to* + infinitive form of the verb to talk about necessity.
    I **have to leave.** (=It is necessary for me to leave.)
2. Use *have to* with *I, you, we,* and *they*.
    I **have to** go.
    They **have to** buy round-trip tickets.
3. Use *has to* with the third person singular (*he, she, it*).
    He **has to** wait for the next train.
    The bus **has to** stop.
4. We also use *must* to talk about necessity, but *have to* is more common in conversation.
    You **must sit** in seat 4B.

Would like

1. *Would like* is a polite way of saying *want*.
    We would like some coffee, please.
2. Use the contraction *'d* + verb in conversation.
    I'd like a seat near the window.
3. *Would like* is the same for all persons (*I, you, he, she, it, we, they*).
    They**'d like** some tea.
    She**'d like** a different seat.
4. Use a noun or an infinitive after *would like*.
    I'd like **a sandwich.**
    I'd like **to have** a sandwich.
5. *Would you like . . .* is a polite way of asking people if they want something.
    A: **Would you like** to sit down?
    B: No, thank you. I'm fine.
6. Be careful! Don't confuse *would like* and *like*. *Would like* means *want*. *Like* means *enjoy*.
    Would you like (=Do you want) some tea?
    Do you like (=Do you enjoy) tea?

Can / Could / Would

1. There are several ways to make polite requests:
    Can you close the window, please?
    Can/Could I have two tickets, please?
    Could you close the window, please?
    Would you close the window, please?
2. *Can, could,* and *would* in polite requests are similar in meaning, but *could* and *would* are a little more polite.
3. Use *please* to be more polite. Put *please* at the end of the question or before the verb.
    Would you show me your ticket, **please**?
    Would you **please** show me your ticket?
4. There are many different answers to polite requests. *Sure* and *Of course* are common answers for *yes*. For *no*, we often say *Sorry* (or *I'm sorry*) and give a reason.
    A: Could you move your bag, please?
    B: Sure.
    A: Can you give me a dollar for the bus?
    B: I'm sorry, but I don't have any money.

Grammar Summaries T-261

Charts

Spelling Rules: Present Progressive

1. Add –*ing* to the base form of the verb. rain → rain**ing**

2. If a verb ends in –*e*, drop –*e* and add –*ing*. smoke → smok**ing**

3. If a verb ends in –*ie*, change –*ie* to –*y* and add –*ing*. die → dy**ing**

4. If a verb is one syllable and ends in consonant + vowel + consonant (CVC), double the final consonant and add –*ing*. stop → stopp**ing**

5. Do not double the consonant if it is *w, x,* or *y*. Simply add –*ing*. snow → snow**ing**
   fix → fix**ing**
   play → play**ing**

6. If the word has two or more syllables and ends in consonant + vowel + consonant (CVC), double the final consonant only if it is stressed. permit → permitt**ing**
   visit → visit**ing**

Spelling Rules: Simple Past of Regular Verbs

1. Add –*ed* to the base form of the verb. rain → rain**ed**

2. If a verb ends in –*e*, add –*d*. smoke → smok**ed**

3. If a verb ends in –*ie*, add –*d*. die → di**ed**

4. If the verb is one syllable and ends in consonant + vowel + consonant (CVC), double the final consonant and add –*ed*. stop → stopp**ed**

5. Do not double the consonant if it is *w, x,* or *y*. Simply add –*ed*. snow → snow**ed**
   fix → fix**ed**
   play → play**ed**

6. If the word has two or more syllables and ends in consonant + vowel + consonant (CVC), double the final consonant only if it is stressed. Then add –*ed*. permit → permitt**ed**
   visit → visit**ed**

Spelling Rules for Plural Nouns

1. Add –es to words that end in –ch, –s, –sh, –ss, –x, or –z.	watch → watch**es** bus → bus**es** dish → dish**es** pass → pass**es** box → box**es**
2. Add –es to words that end in –o.	potato → potato**es**
3. If the word ends in consonant + –y, change –y to –i and add –es.	country → countr**ies**
4. Add –s to words that end in vowel + –y.	day → day**s**

Simple Present: Third Person Singular Spelling Rules

1. Add –es to words that end in –ch, –s, –sh, –ss, –x, or –z.	teach → teach**es** wash → wash**es** miss → miss**es** fix → fix**es** fizz → fizz**es**
2. Add –es to words that ends in –o.	do → do**es**
3. If the word ends in consonant +–y, change –y to –i and add –es.	cry → cr**ies**
4. Add –s to words that end in vowel + –y.	play → play**s**

Comparative Form of Adjectives

1. If the word ends in 1 vowel + 1 consonant, double the consonant and add –er.	thin → thinn**er**
2. If the word ends in –y, change –y to –i and add –er.	pretty → pretti**er**
3. If the word ends in –e, add –r.	nice → nic**er**

Superlative Form of Adjectives

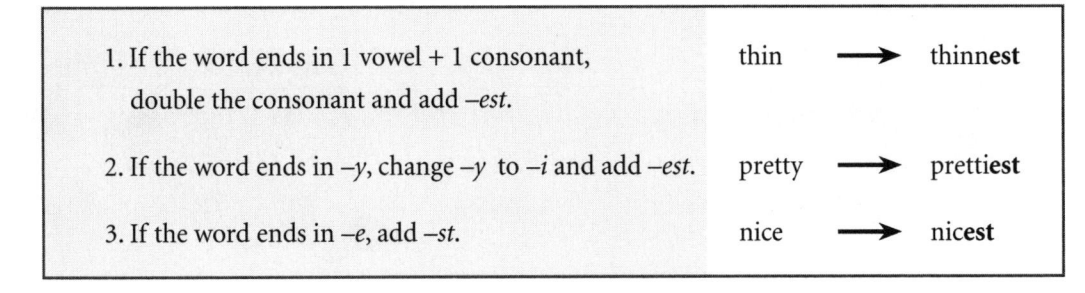

1. If the word ends in 1 vowel + 1 consonant, double the consonant and add –est.	thin → thinn**est**
2. If the word ends in –y, change –y to –i and add –est.	pretty → pretti**est**
3. If the word ends in –e, add –st.	nice → nic**est**

Pronunciation Rules

1. If the word ends in a vowel sound or /b/, /d/, /g/, /l/, /m/, /n/, /ŋ/, /ɹ/, /θ/, /v/ or /w/,

    it is pronounced /z/.
    gives   onions   Tom's

2. If the word ends in /f/, /h/, /k/, /p/, /t/ or /ð/,

    it is pronounced /s/.
    walks   maps   Matt's

3. If the word ends in /tʃ/, /dʒ/, /s/, /ʃ/, /z/ or /ʒ/,

    it is pronounced /ɪz/.
    sneezes   watches   Nash's

4. If the base form ends in a vowel sound or /b/, /dʒ/, /g/ /l/, /m/, /ŋ/, /ɹ/, /θ/, /v/, /w/, /z/, or /ʒ/,

    it is pronounced /d/.
    snowed   mailed

5. If the base forms ends in /tʃ/, /f/, /h/, /k/, /p/ or /s/,

    it is pronounced /t/, /ʃ/, or /ð/
    stopped   laughed

6. If the base form ends in /d/ or /t/,

    it is pronounced /ɪd/.
    needed   wanted

Telling Time

It's 5:10.
It's ten past five.
It's ten after five.

It's 6:30.
It's half past six.

It's 10:15.
It's a quarter past ten.

It's 9:50.
It's ten to ten.

It's 8:45.
It's a quarter to nine.

It's 11:00 in the morning.
It's 11 A.M.

It's 12:00 during the day.
It's 12 P.M. It's noon.

It's 11:00 at night.
It's 11 P.M.

It's 12:00 at night.
It's 12 A.M. It's midnight.

Charts

GO + VERB + –ING

go bowling	go hiking	go sailing
go camping	go horseback riding	go shopping
go dancing	go hunting	go skating
go fishing	go jogging	go skiing
go golfing	go running	go swimming

IRREGULAR VERBS

Base form	Simple Past	Base form	Simple Past
be	was	make	made
become	became	meet	met
buy	bought	pay	paid
catch	caught	put	put
come	came	read	read
cost	cost	ride	rode
cry	cried	ring	rang
cut	cut	run	ran
do	did	say	said
drink	drank	see	saw
drive	drove	sell	sold
eat	ate	send	sent
feel	felt	shine	shone
find	found	sit	sat
fly	flew	sleep	slept
forget	forgot	speak	spoke
get	got	spend	spent
give	gave	stand	stood
go	went	steal	stole
have	had	swim	swam
hear	heard	take	took
hit	hit	teach	taught
hold	held	think	thought
hurt	hurt	try	tried
know	knew	wake	woke
leave	left	wear	wore
lose	lost	win	won
		write	wrote

COMMON STATIVE VERBS

Senses	Possession	Likes	Needs	Mental States	Measurement	Description
feel	belong	hate	need	agree	cost	be
hear	have	like	want	believe	weigh	look
see	own	love		forget		seem
smell				know		
sound				remember		
taste				think		
				understand		

Partner Activities

From Time to Talk, PAGE 33

1. waiter
2. hairdresser 
3. engineer 
4. accountant 
5. Mónica 
6. Lynn 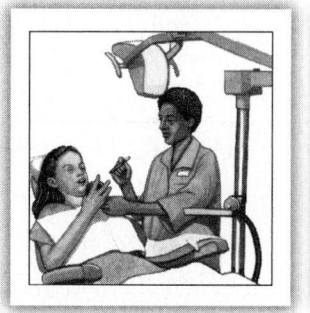
7. Julio 
8. Michael 
9. Pete 
10. Lili 
11. Ali 
12. Nicole 

She says, "I don't understand."

Tôi Không muon.

Partner Activities

From Review and Challenge, Speaking, PAGE 34

Mechanic's helper wanted
- light maintenance
- oil changes
- general duties

FT - 1 yr. exp. necessary
Call Rob 111-539-7777

AUTO MECHANICS NEEDED
5+ yrs. exp.
FT & PT positions avail.
Great money!
Call Nick
111-222-3333

MECHANIC
Busy auto repair shop
PT, Saturdays only
1 yr. exp.
$20/hr.
Call 111-444-5555

Mechanic
EXP. WITH TRUCKS NECESSARY
Exp. with pump trucks vacuum trucks, and vactors a big plus. +
Call Al 111-567-2222

avail. = available
exp. = experience
FT = full time
a plus (+) = wanted
PT = part-time
hr = hour
yr = year
yrs = years

From Time to Talk, PAGE 55

ACE Supermarket
SUPER SAVINGS ON FRUIT AND VEGETABLES!

- Apples **$1.75 lb.**
- Bananas **$2.50 lb.**
- Potatoes **59¢ lb.**
- Spinach **$3.00 lb.**
- Lettuce **$2.00 lb.**

From Review and Challenge, Speaking, PAGE 46

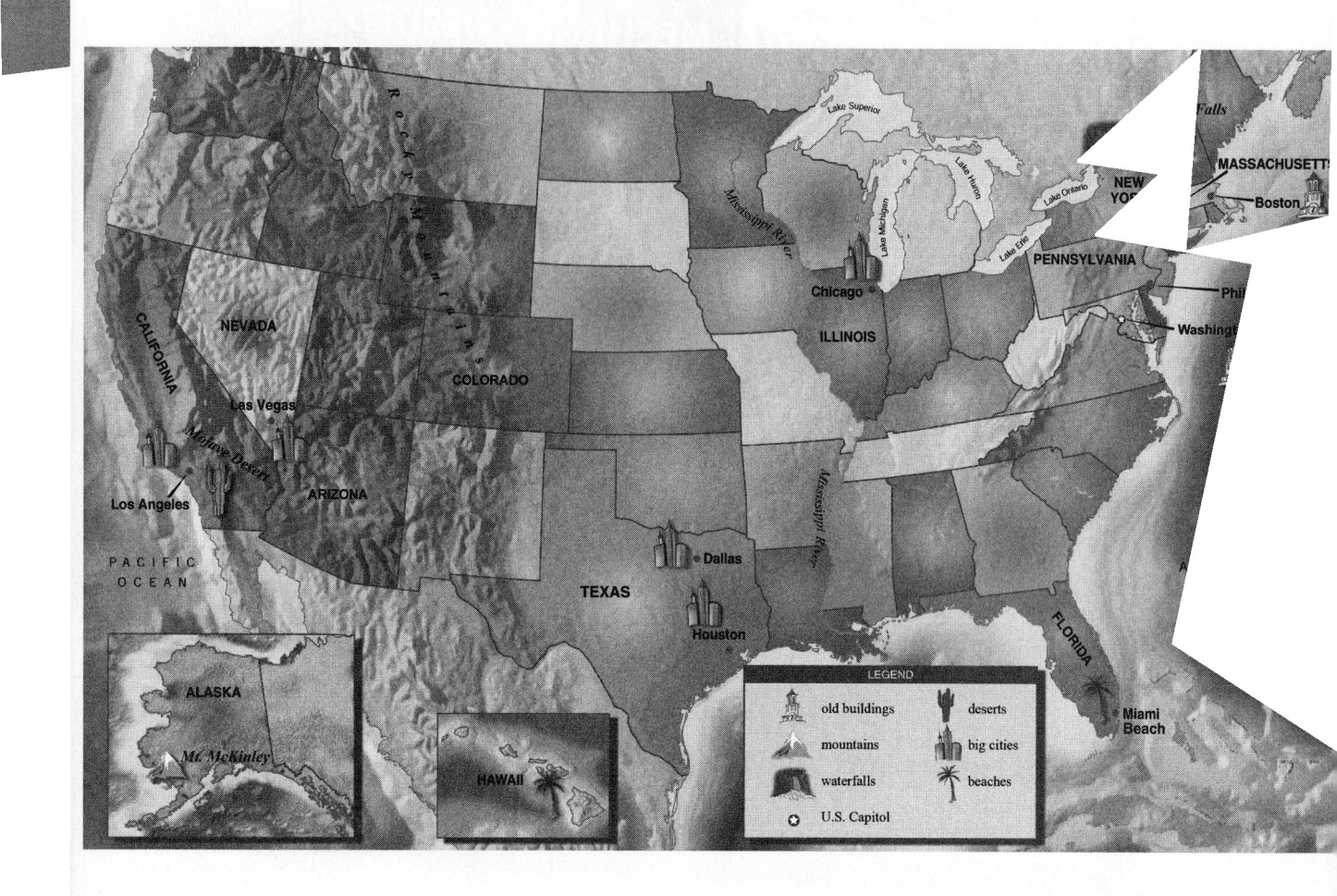

From Time to Talk, PAGE 55

Deluxe supermarket
GREAT PRICES ON FRUIT AND VEGETABLES

fruit and vegetables

potatoes 69¢ lb.
bananas $2.50 lb.
apples $1.85 lb.
spinach $3.50 lb.
lettuce $2.50 lb.

From Speaking, PAGE 60

Lou's Food to Go

Menu

Chicken Soup............$3.00
Cheese Sandwich.......$3.00
Fried eggs on toast....$5.50

Hamburger............$5.00
Cheeseburger.........$5.50
Pizza....................$3.50/slice

Coffee............$1.00
Tea................$1.00
Soda.............$1.50

From Time to Talk, PAGE 71

Partner Activities

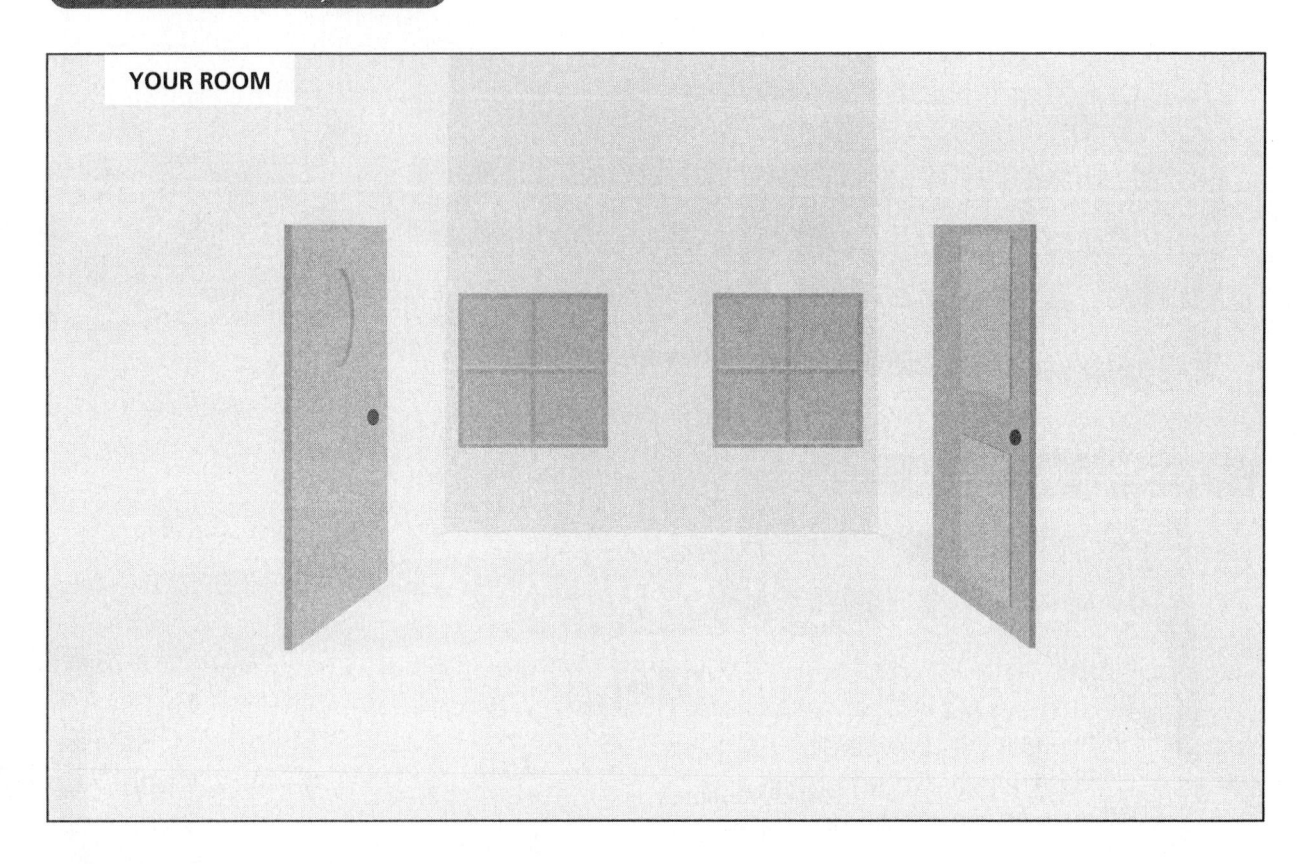

From Time to Talk, PAGE 81

YOUR ROOM

From Time to Talk, PAGE 159

Partner Activities

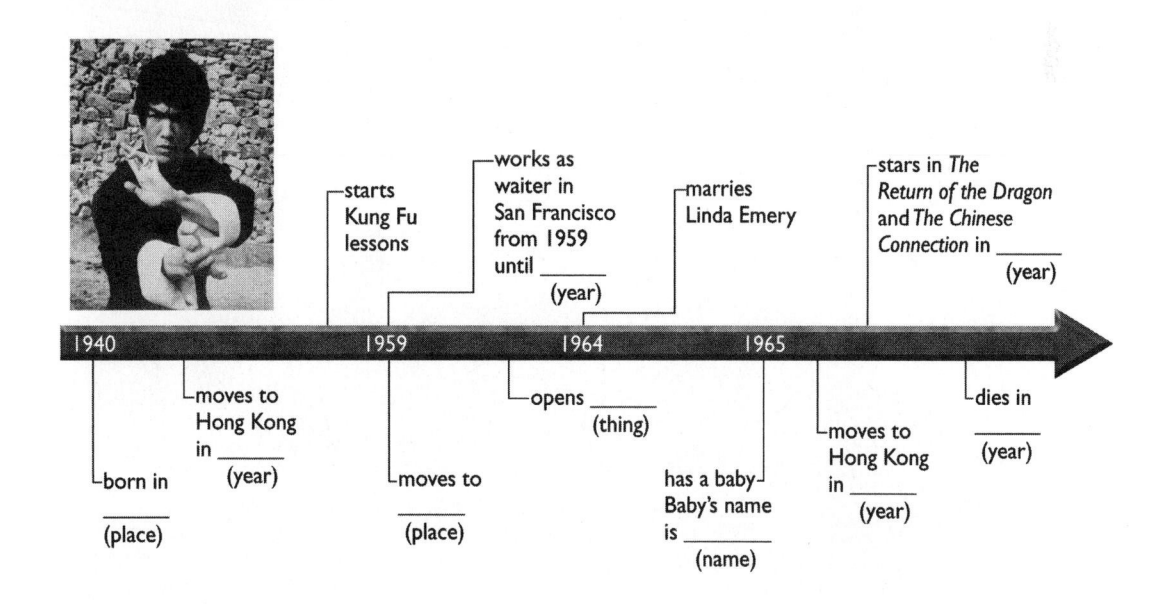

From Time to Talk, PAGE 71

From Time to Talk, PAGE 184

- born in _____ (place)
- moves to Hong Kong in _____ (year)
- 1940
- starts Kung Fu lessons
- 1959
- moves to _____ (place)
- works as waiter in San Francisco from 1959 until _____ (year)
- 1964
- opens _____ (thing)
- marries Linda Emery
- 1965
- has a baby. Baby's name is _____ (name)
- moves to Hong Kong in _____ (year)
- stars in *The Return of the Dragon* and *The Chinese Connection* in _____ (year)
- dies in _____ (year)

Partner Activities T-271

From Time to Talk, PAGE 81

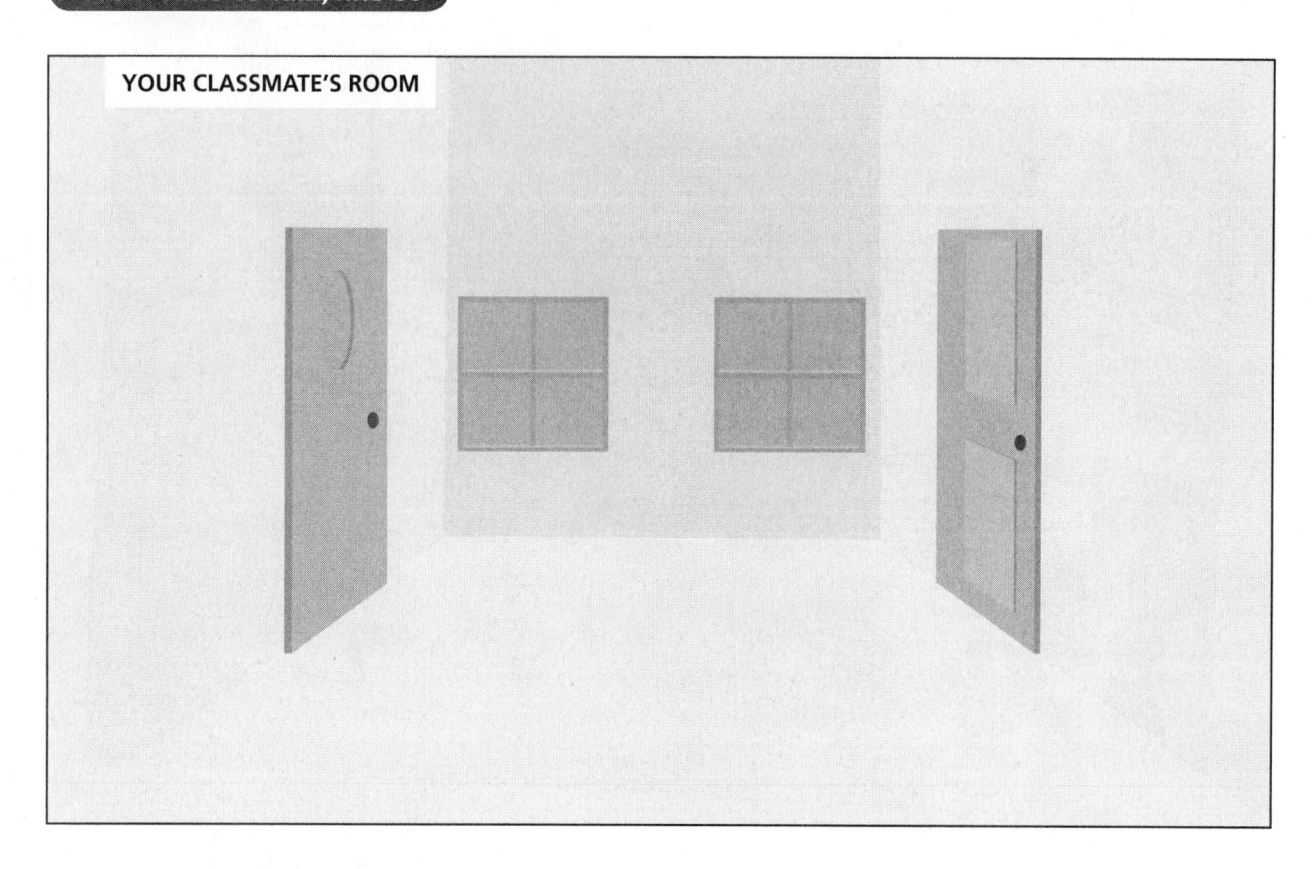

YOUR CLASSMATE'S ROOM

From Speaking, PAGE 159

Partner Activities

From Time to Talk, PAGE 184

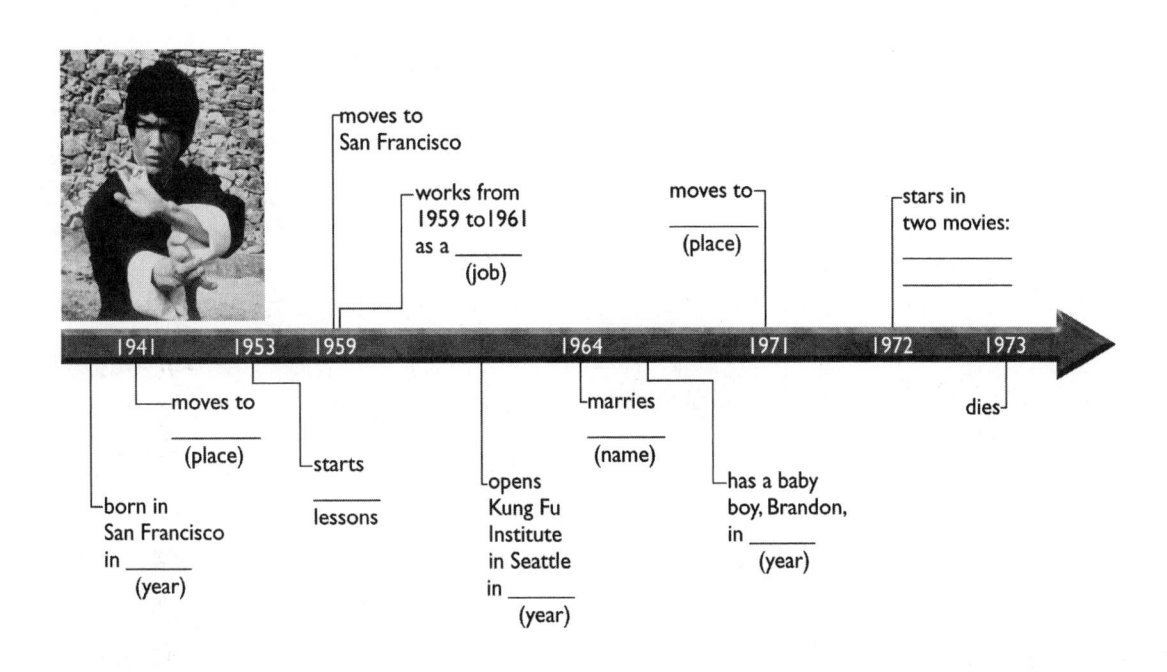

- moves to San Francisco
- works from 1959 to 1961 as a _____ (job)
- moves to _____ (place)
- stars in two movies: _____ / _____

1941 — 1953 — 1959 — 1964 — 1971 — 1972 — 1973

- born in San Francisco in _____ (year)
- moves to _____ (place)
- starts _____ lessons
- opens Kung Fu Institute in Seattle in _____ (year)
- marries _____ (name)
- has a baby boy, Brandon, in _____ (year)
- dies

From Speaking, PAGE 222

Apartments

2 BR. Great loc. near pub. trans., supermarket, & park.

No pets or smoking. $800 incl. util.

Studio in new bldg. Best loc. downtown, near shops, restaurants, clubs.

$750. Pking extra $150. pets OK.

Cute 3 BR house in quiet, friendly neighborhood 15 miles from city. Lrg. yard and 2-car garage.

$800, all util. incl. Pets OK.

Lrg. 3 BR. Great bldg., central loc. near hospitals and universities.

$1000 incl. 1 pking space.

bldg. = building
lrg. = large
pub. trans. = public transportation
BR = bedroom
loc. = location
util. = utilities (heat, hot water, electricity)
incl. = including or included
pking = parking

From Time to Talk, PAGE 219

DESIGNS FOR TODAY
ALL OF THE MOST EXCITING NEW DESIGNS

$1,500
$3,000
$5,000

American Homes
Come home to the best

$900
$175
$350

BEST FOR LESS
More for your money

$400
$55
$75

	Designs for Today	American Homes	Best for Less
Sofa	$3,000	$900	$400
Lamp	$1,500	$175	$55
Rug	$5,000	$350	$75

From Speaking, PAGE 60

Sheila's
soups, salads, and sandwiches

Soups
Tomato soup	$5.00
Chicken soup	$5.00
Fish soup	$5.50

Salads
Egg salad	$5.50
Chicken salad	$6.00
Potato salad	$5.50
Mixed salad	$5.00
Fruit salad	$5.50

Sandwiches
Cheese sandwich	$6.00
Egg salad sandwich	$6.50
Chicken salad sandwich	$6.50
Hamburger	$7.00
Cheeseburger	$8.00

Partner Activities

From Time to Talk, PAGE 33

1. Martin
2. Meg 
3. Marina  
4. John

5. nurse
6. dentist 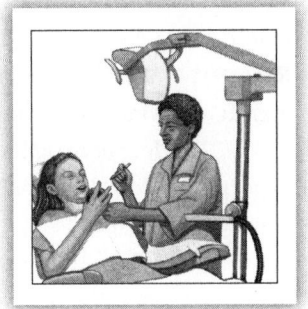
7. mechanic 
8. electrician 

9. Pete
10. Lili 
11. Ali 
12. Nicole 

She says, "I don't understand."

Tôi Không muon.

Partner Activities T-275

Audioscript

Unit 1: People

Listening, A and B, page 3

Ava: Patty isn't here. Where is she?
Mia: She's with her new boyfriend.
Ava: Her new boyfriend?
Mia: Yeah. His name's Álvaro.
Ava: Álvaro? Is he American?
Mia: No, he's not. He's Mexican.
Ava: Is he good-looking?
Mia: He's OK. He's tall. He isn't thin, but he isn't heavy. He's average weight.
Ava: Are he and Patty students in the same class?
Mia: No, they're not. They're neighbors. And he's a doctor, not a student.
Ava: A doctor? Is he old?
Mia: No, he's not old. He's about 35.
Ava: 35? But Patty's only 22.
Mia: So? 35 isn't old!

Grammar to Communicate 2, C, page 7

Lara: Are you a student in this class?
Bob: No, I'm the teacher.
Lara: Oh, are you Professor Michaelson?
Bob: Yes, I am. Are you in English 101?
Lara: Yes, I am.
Bob: Then you're in my class. Welcome.

Grammar to Communicate 3, B, page 8

1. Are your classmates noisy?
2. Are most actors rich?
3. Are most actresses beautiful?
4. Are your parents young?
5. Are your friends smart?
6. Are the classes small at your school?

Review and Challenge

Grammar, page 10

Juan: Hello. I'm Juan Montero.
Nicole: Hi. My name is Nicole Summers.
Juan: Are you from Miami?
Nicole: Yes, I am. My boyfriend is from here, too.
Juan: My girlfriend and I are not from here. We're from Caracas, Venezuela.
Nicole: Is Caracas nice?
Juan: Very nice. The people are friendly.

Dictation, page 10

1. I'm late.
2. Are they here now?
3. Are they men or women?
4. She isn't short.
5. He's tall and handsome.

Listening, A and B, page 11

Reporter: Good Morning. This is Amy Warren reporting for WKBC. Today's topic is happiness. What are the secrets of happy people? A new study says that one secret is marriage. 38 percent of married women and 42 percent of married men say they are very happy. But only 22 percent of single people are happy. A second secret is age. 65 percent of people who are 50 say they are happy, but only 52 percent of 20-year-olds are happy. Isn't that interesting? So, what is the secret to a happy life? Let's ask some people on the street. Hello, sir? I'm a reporter for WKBC News. May I ask you a question?
Man 1: Okay . . .
Reporter: What is the secret to a happy life?
Man 1: Hmmm . . . Oh, I know—good health and the love of a good woman.
Reporter: How about you? Are you happy?
Man 2: Yes, I am.
Reporter: What's your secret?
Man 2: Well, I'm an easygoing guy. Life is short, so I try to have fun.
Reporter: Excuse me, ma'am?
Woman: I don't have time! I'm late for work!
Reporter: Oh well, she's probably not a good person to ask! For WKBC, this is Amy Warren . . .

Unit 2: Families

Listening, A and B, page 15

Mark: Is this your family?
Elena: Yes, it is.
Mark: Wow, your family is big! Is she your mother?
Elena: Yeah. She's my mom.
Mark: She's beautiful—like you!
Elena: Thank you!
Mark: Who are they? Are they your brothers?
Elena: No, they're my father's brothers—my uncles.
Mark: Really? How old are they?
Elena: Eduardo is 10, and Felipe is 12.
Mark: Wow . . . Your uncles are children!
Elena: That's right!

Grammar to Communicate 1, C, page 17

Stan: Hi. I'm your new neighbor. My name is Stan Sims.
Betty: It's nice to meet you, Stan. I'm Betty.
Stan: Nice to meet you, too. Um … are you Josh's mother?
Betty: No, Ann and Jim Parr are his parents. Their apartment is next door.
Stan: Oh. Well, he's very noisy! His music is always so loud.
Betty: Um … that's our daughter's music. Is it loud? Sorry!
Stan: Oh! Um .. that's OK … It is nice music. Is she a music student?
Betty: Yes, she is! We're very proud of her.

Grammar to Communicate 3, C, page 21

1. **A:** Where are your parents from?
   B: My parents are from South Korea.
2. **A:** How is your family?
   B: My family's fine, thanks.
3. **A:** How old are you?
   B: I'm 19.
4. **A:** Who's Nina?
   B: Nina is my aunt—my mother's sister.
5. **A:** Where are the children?
   B: The children are at my mother's house.
6. **A:** How tall is your brother?
   B: My brother is six feet tall.
7. **A:** What are your uncles' names?
   B: My uncles' names are Greg and Norman.

Review and Challenge
Grammar, page 22

Andrea: This is a nice picture. Who's in it?
Leona: Oh, that's my son, Paul. And here's a picture of his children—my two grandsons and my granddaughter.
Andrea: What are their names?
Leona: The boys' names are Bill and Tommy. Their sister's name is Alicia.
Andrea: They're cute! How old is Alicia?
Leona: Oh, she's 7 years old. And here she is in a picture with her mother.
Andrea: Oh, so that's your daughter-in-law. She's pretty.
Leona: Yes, she is.

Dictation, page 22

1. Is she your mother?
2. No, she's my mother-in-law.
3. How old are they?
4. Who is he?
5. They're my mother's brothers.

Listening, A and B, page 23

Reporter: Good afternoon. This is Carla Espinoza for World Beat. This week, our topic is family life around the world. Today, let's look at two families, from two very different parts of the world: Italy and Saudi Arabia. Silvia Bertolino is from an Italian family. She is 10 years old. Her father is 42 and her mother is 37. Silvia's family is like many Italian families today. In Italy, the age of marriage for most women is about 27. For men, it's a little older—about 30. Like many Italian children these days, Silvia is an only child—she has no brothers or sisters. Silvia is close to both her parents. Saleh Al-Ahmed is from Saudi Arabia. He is one of ten children. In Saudi Arabia, many family members live together in one large house. In Saleh's house, for example, there are 14 people: Saleh, his parents, his father's parents, three of Saleh's seven sisters, his two married brothers, his brothers' wives, and their two children. Saleh's four married sisters live in their own houses with their husbands, children, and in-laws. In Saudi Arabia, married women usually live with their in-laws. That's all for today. Tomorrow, we'll talk about Brazil and Mexico.

Unit 3: Jobs
Listening, A and B, page 27

Bill: Hey, Nick, what's up? How are you?
Nick: I'm great. I have a new job.
Bill: Really?
Nick: Yeah, I'm a cook at Rico's on First Street.
Bill: Oh, my friend Andy is a cook there too.
Nick: Oh yeah, Andy…he's the breakfast cook. I'm the lunch cook.
Bill: So, how is it?
Nick: Well, it isn't an easy job, but it's interesting. The restaurant is always busy.
Bill: Is the pay good?
Nick: It's not bad. And the boss is a nice guy. How about you? Are you still in school?
Bill: No, I'm an electrician now.
Nick: An electrician! Good for you!
Bill: Yeah, it's great. Anyway, I have to get going— I'm late for work! I'll see you later—Oh, and say hi to Andy for me!
Nick: I will. Take it easy!
Bill: You too.

Review and Challenge
Dictation, page 34

1. She's a good dentist.
2. Are you the doctor?
3. The mechanics are fast.
4. It isn't an interesting job.
5. They're messy cooks.

Audioscript

Listening, A and B, page 35

Man:	Good morning, Stage Restaurant.
Gabriella:	Hello. I'm calling about the job in Sunday's Newspaper . . . for a waitress?
Man:	Just a minute, please. I'll get the manager.
Tommy:	Hello? This is Tommy. So . . . are you an experienced waitress?
Gabriella:	Yes, I am.
Tommy:	How much experience?
Gabriella:	One year at McDonald's and one year as the morning waitress at Bob's Diner in Brooklyn.
Tommy:	Oh, Bob's Diner. It's a very busy place . . . lots of customers. Are you fast?
Gabriella:	Yes, I think so. And I'm very organized.
Tommy:	Good. Are you available on weekends?
Gabriella:	I'm available on Saturdays, but not on Sundays.
Tommy:	Are you available in the morning?
Gabriella:	Yes, I am.
Tommy:	Okay, I need a waitress Wednesdays to Saturdays, from 5:00 to 11:00 A.M. Are you interested?
Gabriella:	Yes, I am.
Tommy:	Can you come in today for an interview?
Gabriella:	What time?
Tommy:	3:00. Ask for me—Tom Jackson.
Gabriella:	Tom Jackson. Great! Thank you very much.
Tommy:	Oh, wait a minute. What's your name?
Gabriella:	Oh, I'm sorry. I'm Gabriella Campozano.
Tommy:	Okay, Gabriella, so we'll see you at 3:00.
Gabriella:	Okay, thanks a lot. Goodbye.
Tommy:	'Bye.

Unit 4: Places

Listening, A and B, page 39

Pedro:	Hi, Natasha! How are you? How's your new apartment?
Natasha:	It's great! And it's in a wonderful neighborhood.
Pedro:	Really?
Natasha:	There are some nice stores and cafés, and there's a new movie theater on the next street.
Pedro:	It sounds nice. Are there any good restaurants?
Natasha:	Yes. There's a good restaurant near my apartment building. It's expensive, but the food is excellent. There are also some cheap restaurants in the neighborhood.
Pedro:	Is there a supermarket near your apartment?
Natasha:	No, there isn't a supermarket, but there's a big outdoor market.
Pedro:	And is there a nice park?
Natasha:	There aren't any parks, but there's a beautiful beach.
Pedro:	Wow. You're lucky! My apartment is nice, but there aren't any restaurants in my neighborhood, and there isn't a beach! Hey—are there any apartments for rent in your building?
Natasha:	I'm not sure, but I'll ask.
Pedro:	Thanks.

Review and Challenge

Grammar, page 46

A: I'm from Pittsburgh. It's a great city. There are a lot of stores and beautiful houses.
B: Are there any good restaurants?
A: Oh, yes. There are some Italian and Chinese restaurants in my neighborhood. And they're cheap, too.
B: Is there an art museum in Pittsburgh?
A: Yes. There are three.
B: Is there a new airport?
A: No, there isn't. But our airport is nice.
B: So Pittsburgh is a small city.
A: Yes, it is. But it's really nice.

Dictation, page 46

1. Is there a movie theater near your apartment?
2. There are some expensive stores in the mall.
3. Are there any cheap restaurants?
4. There aren't any supermarkets.
5. There's an apartment building near my house.

Listening, A and B, page 47

Woman 1:	Shopping for food is so different here in the United States!
Woman 2:	Really? How?
Woman 1:	Well, in the United States, there are big supermarkets, but in Colombia, there are a lot of small food stores. For example, in my neighborhood, there's a bakery with delicious bread. There is also an outdoor market with wonderful fruit and vegetables.
Woman 2:	Are there any big supermarkets in Colombia?
Woman 1:	Yes, of course there are some big supermarkets. But small stores and outdoor food markets are more popular than supermarkets.
Woman 2:	But what about price? In the United States, the food in small stores is usually expensive.
Woman 1:	Really? That's interesting. In Colombia, big supermarkets are expensive. The food in small stores and outdoor markets is cheap.

Audioscript

Unit 5: Food and Drink

Listening, A and B, page 53

René: Look at these oranges-- $1.89 a pound! That's crazy! Fruit in the United States is so expensive! In Haiti, the fruit is delicious, and it's very cheap.
Lynn: How much are oranges in Haiti?
René: Oh, an orange is just a few cents—maybe 25 cents a pound.
Lynn: That is cheap! Is everything there so cheap?
René: Well, some food is. Vegetables are really cheap…and rice is too, but meat is expensive. And fruit is really cheap. Hmm…There aren't any tomatoes.
Worker: There are a few tomatoes over there, next to the bananas.
René: Oh, great. Thanks. Hmm, is there any spinach?
Worker: It's right here. How much do you need?
René: Just a little. One package is fine.
Lynn: Wow, these tomatoes are expensive—$5.00 a pound!
René: $5.00 a pound? How many are there in a pound?
Worker: A few—about 3 or 4.
René: Forget it!! At that price, I don't need any . . .

Grammar to Communicate 1, D, page 55

1. **Man:** How much are the bananas?
   Woman: They're $1.79.
2. **Man:** How much is the milk?
   Woman: It's $1.89.
3. **Man:** How much is the juice?
   Woman: It's $3.06.
4. **Man:** How much is the rice?
   Woman: It's $2.89.
5. **Woman:** How much are the potatoes?
   Man: They're $1.99.
6. **Woman:** How much are the eggs?
   Man: They're $1.79.
7. **Woman:** How much is the candy?
   Man: It's $2.50.
8. **Woman:** How much is the coffee?
   Man: It's $3.49.
9. **Woman:** How much are the oranges?
   Man: They're $2.00.

Grammar to Communicate 3, A, page 58

1. **Woman 1:** Is there any coffee?
   Woman 2: Yes, there is.
2. **Woman 1:** Are there any eggs?
   Woman 2: No, there aren't.
3. **Woman 1:** Is there any tea?
   Woman 2: Yes, there is.
4. **Woman 1:** Are there any cookies?
   Woman 2: Yes, there are.
5. **Man 1:** Are there any nuts?
   Man 2: No, there aren't.
6. **Man 1:** Is there any sugar?
   Man 2: Yes, there is.
7. **Man 1:** Is there any candy?
   Man 2: No, there isn't.
8. **Man 1:** Is there any juice?
   Man 2: No, there isn't.

Review and Challenge

Grammar, page 60

A: How many potatoes are there?
B: There aren't any potatoes, but there are a few tomatoes.
A: Is there any fruit?
B: There's a little.
A: Is there any beef?
B: No, there isn't any beef.
A: Okay. And how much soda is there?

Dictation, page 60

1. There's an onion in the bag.
2. Is there any meat?
3. There's a little ice cream.
4. How many apples are there?
5. There isn't any candy here.

Listening, A and B, page 61

Sarah: Alice, is that you?
Alice: Yes? Oh, hi, Sarah! How are you?
Sarah: Fine . . . I'm fine. I'm surprised to see you here. Don't you usually shop at Joe's?
Alice: Yes, but I'm not happy with Joe's.
Sarah: Really? Why?
Alice: Well, it isn't very clean. There are never any shopping carts, there are long lines, and the workers aren't helpful.
Sarah: Well, the workers are very nice at Sam's. And it's very clean. But it's expensive. The prices are good at Joe's, right?
Alice: Yes, but they're still too expensive.
Sarah: But Sam's isn't very convenient for you. Your new apartment isn't near here, is it?
Alice: You're right. That is a problem. I'm still not sure what to do . . .

Unit 6: Physical Exercise

Listening, A and B, page 65

Maria: Hello, Jenny? It's Maria! How are you doing?
Jenny: Oh hi, Maria! I'm great. How are you? How's college?
Maria: Oh, it's okay. Is Mom there?
Jenny: No, she isn't. She's at the health club.
Maria: At the health club? What's she doing there?
Jenny: She's swimming.
Maria: What? Mom's swimming!
Jenny: Yeah.
Maria: Well, is Dad at home?
Jenny: No, he isn't. He's out too.
Maria: What's he doing?
Jenny: He's out riding his bike.
Maria: What??? Dad is riding a bike!
Jenny: Yup.
Maria: Amazing…Well, is Bob at home?
Jenny: Nope.
Maria: Wait, let me think … he's running.
Jenny: No, he's playing tennis.
Maria: Bob? Playing tennis? Are you kidding? It's Sunday afternoon, and he and Dad aren't watching a soccer game on TV?
Jenny: It's true!!!! Everyone's out exercising.
Maria: What's going on there? Are you all going exercise crazy?
Jenny: Everybody except me.
Maria: Why? What are you doing?
Jenny: I'm talking to you!

Grammar to Communicate 3, C, page 71

Alice: Hi? Jean? This is Alice. Is Rita there?
Jean: No, she's not.
Alice: What's she doing?
Jean: She's playing tennis with Sue.
Alice: How about Tom? Is he at home?
Jean: No, he's not.
Alice: What's he doing?
Jean: He's playing soccer.
Alice: Who's he playing with?
Jean: With Phil and some other friends.
Alice: Where are they playing?
Jean: At Sandy Field.
Alice: Sandy Field? Why are they playing at Sandy Field?
Jean: Because another team is playing at Bradley Field today.
Alice: What are you eating?
Jean: Me? I'm eating an apple…And why are you asking so many questions today?

Review and Challenge

Grammar, page 72

Mike: Hi, Tina. It's me, Mike. What are you doing?
Tina: I'm reading a book.
Mike: Where are you?
Tina: At the health club.
Mike: Why are you reading a book at the health club?
Tina: I'm sitting in the café. I'm waiting for Sara.
Mike: Is she exercising?
Tina: No, she's not. She's taking a shower. Oh, she's coming now.
Sara: Hi, Tina!…Who are you talking to?
Tina: I'm talking to Mike.

Dictation, page 72

1. What are they doing?
2. They're playing soccer.
3. Are they playing in a park?
4. No, they're not.
5. She's not watching a game.

Listening, A and B, page 73

Billy: Good morning. This is Billy Jackson, here at the Summer Olympics. First, let's see how the marathoners are doing. Hello, Fatima?
Fatima: Good morning, Billy! Well, no surprises here today. We're 30 minutes into the race, and so far the Brazilian, Roberto Moto, is winning. But two brothers from Kenya, Kamau Ngugi and Yoni Ngugi, are running close behind him.
Billy: Thank you, Fatima. Now, down to the tennis courts … Hello, Pam? Is anything happening there today?
Pam: Hi, Billy. There aren't any matches today, but the Canadian player Christie Daniels is practicing on center court—in the rain.
Billy: That's why she's a winner! Thanks, Pam … Now, let's see how things are going at the swimming pool … Jerry? What's happening there?
Jerry: Well, the women's 100-meter race is tomorrow, so the swimmers are practicing for that. A group of women are swimming in the pool right now.
Billy: Who's looking good?
Jerry: Well, Yuko Kamata from Japan is swimming really well.
Billy: Thanks, Jerry … Now, back to the marathon …

T-280 Audioscript

Unit 7: Do's and Don'ts

Listening, A and B, page 77

Mother:	Matthew, what are you doing?
Matthew:	I'm doing my homework.
Mother:	Really? Then why is the TV on? You aren't doing your homework! You're watching TV! Turn it off right now!
Matthew:	But I am doing my homework...
Mother:	So where is it?
Matthew:	Here.
Mother:	OK, now listen to me. First, finish your homework. Do it right now, and don't be careless. Then, clean your room. Make your bed and put your clothes in the closet. Don't put them under your bed, like last time.
Matthew:	Yes, Mom.
Mother:	Oh, and one more thing. Don't touch the telephone!
Matthew:	But Sylvia is waiting for me to call!
Mother:	Well, too bad. Call her tomorrow. And don't eat potato chips! We're having dinner in an hour!

Grammar to Communicate 3, C, page 83

Ana:	What exercises are you doing?
Tomás:	B and C.
Ana:	Are they difficult?
Tomás:	I'm not sure. I'm starting them now. Sit down and help me.
Ana:	Okay. Hmm. They are difficult.
Tomás:	David's a good student. Ask him for help.
Ana:	He's not in class today.
Tomás:	Then ask her.
Ana:	Who?
Tomás:	Safira. She's your friend, right?
Ana:	Yes, she is. Hey, Safira! Help us with Exercises B and C.
Safira:	I'm busy!

Review and Challenge

Dictation, page 84

1. Don't put your shoes in the closet.
2. Listen to them.
3. Wait for me.
4. Please put the bike behind the door.
5. Please don't turn on the TV.

Listening, A and B, page 85

CONVERSATION 1

Man:	Stop! Put your hands on your head. Stay where you are. Don't move.

CONVERSATION 2

Woman:	Open your mouth and say ahhhhhhh.
Man:	Ahhhhhhhh.
Woman:	Good. Now, look at the light. Don't close your eyes.

CONVERSATION 3

Man:	Okay, go ahead and rinse.
Man:	Okay?
Woman:	Mmm-hmm.
Man:	Okay, so sit back and open your mouth. Not so wide—close it a little, please. Perfect! You're doing great! We're almost finished.

CONVERSATION 4

Man:	Watch out! There's a car coming.
Woman:	Oh, thank you.

CONVERSATION 5

Woman:	We are approaching Dulles International Airport. Please put your bags under your seat.

CONVERSATION 6

Announcer:	Flight #243 is now boarding at Gate 27.
Man:	Have a great trip!
Woman:	Write to me!
Man:	You too! And call me when you get there.

Unit 8: Possessions

Listening, A and B, page 89

Sammi:	What's that in your hand?
Bob:	This is a camera.
Sammi:	Really? But it's the size of a credit card!
Bob:	I know. Isn't it cool? My brother has one, and it takes great pictures.
Sammi:	Amazing...Excuse me, ma'am, what are those, over there, on the wall?
Saleswoman:	Oh, those are speakers.
Sammi:	They're so small!
Saleswoman:	Yes, but the sound is excellent. Listen to this...
Bob:	Wow! Those are great!
Sammi:	Hey. What's this?
Saleswoman:	That's mine. It's not for sale.
Bob:	But what is it?
Saleswoman:	It's a radio. We have other radios over there.
Sammi:	Amazing...it's so thin—like a piece of paper! Is this yours too?
Saleswoman:	No, it isn't. Phil, is this cell phone yours?
Phil:	No, it's not mine.
Bob:	Hey, that cell phone is mine. And those keys are mine too.
Sammi:	These? Here you are. And are these your sunglasses?

Audioscript T-281

Grammar to Communicate 1, C, page 91

1. **A:** What's this?
   B: It's a wallet.
2. **A:** What are these?
   B: They're rings.
3. **A:** What's that?
   B: It's a backpack.
4. **A:** What are those?
   B: They're sunglasses.
5. **A:** What are these?
   B: They're earrings.
6. **A:** What's that?
   B: It's a radio.

Grammar to Communicate 1, D, page 91

1. That is a nice ring.
2. Those are beautiful earrings.
3. That is a nice watch.
4. Those are beautiful sunglasses.

Grammar to Communicate 2, C, page 93

1. **A:** Are these glasses yours?
   B: Yes, they are.
2. **A:** Are these Nicole's glasses?
   B: No. Hers are different.
3. **A:** Hello. I'm Ming Lee and this is my wife, Chiao-lun.
   B: It's nice to meet you.
4. **A:** My name is Ed. What's yours?
   B: Hi, Ed. I'm Stella.
5. **A:** Is that the children's dog?
   B: No. Theirs is black.
6. **A:** Is that a picture of you and Chris?
   B: Yes. And that's our home.
7. **A:** Who's the woman with Ari?
   B: That's his wife.
8. **A:** Is Ari's home in Boston?
   B: No. His is in Cambridge. His brother's is in Boston.

Grammar to Communicate 2, D, page 93

1. **A:** Here's your book.
   B: That's not mine.
2. **A:** Bill and Sue, your dogs are nice.
   B: Those dogs aren't ours.
3. **A:** Are those our records?
   B: No, these are yours.
4. **A:** Is Anna's cell phone black?
   B: No, hers is blue.
5. **A:** They can't find their keys.
   B: Are those keys on the table theirs?
6. **A:** Is that his car in front of the house?
   B: No, his is at home.

Review and Challenge

Grammar, page 96

Carrie: Are these your earrings?
Nadia: Yes, they are. And these are my rings.
Carrie: They're nice. And is that your cell phone over there on the table?
Nadia: No, this is my cell phone.
Carrie: Maybe it's Ann's phone. She has a red phone.
Nadia: No, it's not hers. Her phone is in her bag.

Dictation, page 96

1. This is a camera.
2. Is this radio yours?
3. We have a new computer.
4. My sister has a great stereo.
5. Those are mine.

Listening, A and B, page 97

CONVERSATION 1
Man: Here you go.
Woman: Wait a minute. This is hers, not mine. I ordered fish.
Man: Oh, sorry about that. Here you go. Can I get you anything else right now?

CONVERSATION 2
Man 1: Excuse me, I'm with airport security. Is that your briefcase over there?
Man 2: Where? No, it's not. This is mine, right here.
Man 1: Excuse me, miss, is this yours?
Woman: That? No, sorry, it isn't.
Man 3: Excuse me, sir, is there a problem?
Man 1: Is this yours?
Man 3: That's my briefcase, yes. What's the problem?

CONVERSATION 3
Woman: Are these yours?
Man: No, they're Jamie's.
Woman: Jamie!!
Jamie: Yeah? What's wrong?
Woman: What are your sneakers doing in the middle of the living room?
Jamie: Those aren't mine.
Woman: Well then whose are they? And why are they in the middle of the living room?

CONVERSATION 4
Policeman: Is this your car?
Woman: Yes. Why?
Policeman: It's in a no parking zone.
Woman: No, it isn't. Look at that sign. It says no parking except on Sundays.
Policeman: Today's Saturday.

Audioscript

Woman: Oh…well look at all those cars over there. Are you going to give them tickets too?

Policeman: No, theirs are on the right side of the street. Yours is the only car on the left side.

Unit 9: Routines

Listening, A and B, page 103

Taka: Hey, Monique, you come from France, right?

Monique: Yes, why?

Taka: It says here that in France, most workers have a two-hour break for lunch. Is that true?

Monique: Well, it depends on the job, but in general, it's true. Many people in France have lunch at home. My mother, my sister, and I eat lunch together every day. But my father works in another city, so he doesn't eat with us.

Taka: Really? That's interesting. In Japan, we only have an hour for lunch, so we don't have time to go home. I think I like the French way!

Monique: I do too, but there is one problem. We start work at 8:30, but because we have a break for lunch from 12-2:00, we work until 6:00. In Japan, you only work until 5:00 right?

Taka: No, we don't! Many people go to work at 8:00 in the morning and finish at 6:00 or even later. My father has his own business. He works 12 hours a day or more. On weekdays, he leaves the house at 7:00, and gets home at 10:00 at night, so he doesn't eat lunch or dinner with us.

Monique: Business owners in France work long days too. But most of the French work five days a week. They have weekends off, except people who work in banks and shops. They work on Saturday, so they don't work on Sunday or Monday.

Grammar to Communicate 2, B, page 106

1. My daughter brushes her hair all the time.
2. My mother reads the newspaper.
3. My friend Sam drinks coffee.
4. My sister takes the bus to work.
5. My uncle washes his car once a week.

Review and Challenge

Grammar, page 110

Woman: My roommates and I don't have the same routines. Julia gets up late, at around 10:00 A.M. Katie and I get up early. Katie has class at 8:00 A.M., and I start work at 9:00 A.M. Julia doesn't work. She just takes two classes in the afternoon. She's lucky because she finishes early. Then she goes out with friends. She doesn't study very much, and she doesn't cook. Katie and I study and go to work every day. Julia's life is pretty good!

Dictation, page 110

1. I don't eat with my family.
2. My mother works from 9 to 4.
3. My brother has lunch at home.
4. My father doesn't finish late.
5. My children leave the house early.

Listening, A and B, page 111

Reporter: Good morning. This is Claire Goodwin reporting. Today we are looking at the way that people around the world spend—and don't spend—their time. The information in this report comes from a study by the Roper Center for Public Opinion Research. Let's start with sleep, work and food. First, sleep—something that we all need. On average, the typical adult sleeps 7.4 hours a day. People from Japan don't sleep much—only 6.7 hours a day. People from South Africa sleep the most—7.9 hours. How about work? The average adult works 9.6 hours a day, but workers in Argentina and Turkey work 9.8 hours a day on average. And what about housework? It depends on whether you are a man or a woman. Worldwide, only 15% of men do housework every day, but in South Africa the percentage is 29%. In Turkey and Egypt, the number of men who do housework every day or most days is low, only 6% in Turkey and 4% in Egypt. Finally, let's discuss food and eating. 79% of people around the world eat at home with their family every day or almost every day. And who cooks? Mostly women—only 21% of men worldwide cook every day. In Egypt, the typical man doesn't cook much. Only 2% of Egyptian men say that they cook every day or most days.

Unit 10: Shopping

Listening, A and B, page 115

Martin: Honey? Do you have your credit card?

Veronica: Yes, I do. But where's yours?

Martin: At home.

Veronica: You never have your credit card with you!

Martin: That's why I don't spend a lot of money.

Veronica: You don't, but I do! So, what do you want this time?

Martin: Great Buy has DVD players on sale. They're 25% off.

Veronica: Do we need a DVD player?

Martin: Well, movies are all on DVD these days.

Veronica: But we never watch movies.

Audioscript T-283

Martin: That's because we don't have a DVD player.
Veronica: Okay, so what kind is it?
Martin: It's a Sovy.
Veronica: And how much does it cost?
Martin: $199.
Veronica: Forget it! That's a lot of money.
Martin: You always say that.
Veronica: And you always want to spend a lot of money!

Grammar to Communicate 1, C, page 117

1. I am always friendly.
2. The store sometimes has sales.
3. I am never late for work.
4. The store always opens at 9:00.
5. The customers are usually nice.
6. I love my job. It is never boring.
7. The customers often ask me questions.

Grammar to Communicate 3, C, page 121

1. **A:** I like the T-shirt in the catalog.
   B: How much does it cost?
   A: It's $15.66 including tax.
2. **A:** You have a big car, right?
   B: No, I don't.
   A: What kind of car do you have?
   B: I have a very small car.
3. **A:** Julie doesn't like gold earrings.
   B: What kind of earrings does she like?
   A: Silver.
4. **A:** Marks and Lit Brothers are good stores.
   B: What do they sell?
   A: Clothes, jewelry, umbrellas, handbags—a lot of different things.
5. **A:** My daughter goes to the mall a lot.
   B: How often does she go?
   A: Every weekend.

Review and Challenge
Dictation, page 122

1. She never shops at that store.
2. What kind of camera do you want?
3. How much does this DVD cost?
4. Does the customer want the jacket?
5. Do you and your friend often go to the mall?

Listening, A and B, page 123
CONVERSATION 1
Man: What kind of TV are you looking for—a regular or a flat screen?
Woman: How much does the flat screen TV cost?
Man: It's usually $499, but it's on sale this week for only $299. And the price includes the sales tax.
Woman: Wow! That's a great price for a flat screen, but it's still too expensive for me.

CONVERSATION 2
Man: What do you want for your birthday? Do you like any of the rings?
Woman: I like all of them, but they're so expensive.
Man: Don't worry about that. It's your birthday!
Woman: Oh, honey. You're so sweet, but we don't have enough money to buy things like this. Anyway, I don't need a new ring.

CONVERSATION 3
Woman: Paper or plastic?
Man: Excuse me?
Woman: What kind of bag do you want?
Man: I'm sorry?
Woman: Do you want a paper bag or a plastic one?
Man: Oh, paper please.

CONVERSATION 4
Man: Where are the tomatoes?
Woman: I'm sorry, we don't have any today.
Man: But you always have tomatoes!

Unit 11: Holidays and Special Occasions
Listening, A and B, page 127

Julie: Hey, Petra. What's wrong? You don't look very happy.
Petra: Oh, this weekend is my first birthday alone—my family and friends aren't here. I really miss them.
Julie: Oh, that's hard. So . . . how do you usually celebrate your birthday?
Petra: Well, my friends send me cards, and all of my relatives call me.
Julie: Do you have a party?
Petra: Oh, yes. We always have a big party.
Julie: Who do you invite?
Petra: My friends, my parents' friends, my sisters' friends, and my relatives.
Julie: Wow. You need a big place for a party like that. Where do you usually have it?
Petra: Oh, we have a big house.
Julie: And who makes the food for all those people?
Petra: My mother, my sisters, and I make almost everything. My grandmother makes the birthday cake.
Julie: Do all of the people at the party give you gifts?
Petra: I get some gifts and a lot of flowers and chocolates.
Julie: And what do you want this year?
Petra: I want to celebrate my birthday with my family and friends!

Audioscript

Grammar to Communicate 2, B, page 130

1. **Ted:** We celebrate Mother's Day to show that we love our mothers.
   Lia: Why do you celebrate Father's Day?
   Ted: To show that we love our fathers, of course!
2. **Ted:** We celebrate Mother's Day on the second Sunday in May.
   Lia: When do you celebrate Father's Day?
   Ted: On the third Sunday in June.
3. **Ted:** We celebrate Mother's Day in different ways. Most people send cards.
   Lia: How do you celebrate Father's Day?
   Ted: We send cards on Father's Day, too.
4. **Ted:** Mothers often get flowers.
   Lia: What do fathers get?
   Ted: Fathers often get ties.

Review and Challenge
Dictation, page 134

1. I send my friends cards.
2. When do you give presents?
3. Who pays for the party?
4. Who does your family visit on the holiday?
5. Children give flowers to their teachers.

Listening, A and B, page 135

Reporter: Good afternoon. This is Carla Espinoza for World Beat. This week, our topic is gift-giving around the world. In every country, people give gifts on special occasions. But gift-giving customs are different in different countries. Before you give someone from another country a gift, you need to learn about that country's customs. Here are some questions to ask: What kinds of gifts do people usually give in that country? What kinds of gifts do they never give? When do they give gifts? Why do they give them? Who do they give them to? What do you do when someone gives you a gift? Here are some interesting facts. People in China and Japan always use two hands when they give or receive a gift. But in Egypt and most Middle Eastern countries, you give and receive gifts only with your right hand. In most countries, people wrap gifts in paper. However, the color of the paper is very important. In many parts of Asia, white is not a good color for gift wrapping, because people there wear white when someone dies. In Brazil, the color purple has the same meaning, so Brazilians hardly ever wrap gifts in purple paper. And in both South America and Asia, people never give knives to their friends because a knife means the end of the friendship. That's all for today. Tomorrow, we'll talk about the gifts people give and get on New Year's Day.

Unit 12: At work

Listening, A and B, page 139

Doris: Excuse me, Mr. Yu?
Mr. Yu: Yes, Doris? Please, come in. So, what are you doing here today? You don't usually work on Mondays, do you?
Doris: No, I'm working for Liz today. She's visiting her mom in the hospital.
Mr. Yu: Oh, that's right. How is her mother doing?
Doris: She's doing very well.
Mr. Yu: Oh, that's good. So, what's up?
Doris: Well, my husband has a new job, and he works on Tuesdays now, too. And we don't have day care on Tuesdays.
Mr. Yu: So… are you asking me for Tuesdays off?
Doris: Oh no, I need to work 40 hours a week. We need the money. If possible, I want to work Saturdays.
Mr. Yu: Hmmm…I don't know right now. It's quiet then.

Grammar to Communicate 1, C, page 141

Tim: Hi, Dana. This is Tim. What's up? What are you doing?
Dana: I'm eating lunch.
Tim: Really? But it's only 11:00. Do you have lunch this early every day?
Dana: Yeah, usually. I start work early, at 7:00, so I'm always hungry at this time. And my boss goes out around 11:00, so it's always quiet. What are you doing right now?
Tim: I'm driving. I'm going to a movie.
Dana: A movie? But it's Monday! Why aren't you at work?
Tim: I have the first Monday of every month off.

Review and Challenge
Grammar, page 146

Caroline: Are you waiting for me?
Bill: Yes, I am. I need to talk to you.
Caroline: Why do you need to talk to me?
Bill: It's about Jake. Is he here today?
Caroline: Yes. He's cleaning up right now. Why?
Bill: He wants more hours, but we don't need extra workers right now.
Caroline: So tell him.
Bill: But he has a new baby. He needs the money now.
Caroline: Mason doesn't want to work on Saturdays. Maybe Jake wants to work then.
Bill: That's a good idea.

Audioscript T-285

Dictation, page 146

1. Why are you wearing a suit?
2. I'm going to an interview.
3. Do you want to get a new job?
4. I do housework every day.
5. My co-worker needs a day off.

Listening, A and B, page 147

Man: Hello, Mrs. Pineiro? Please, come in and sit down.
Mrs. Pineiro: Thank you.
Man: So, you need a job.
Mrs. Pineiro: Yes, that's right.
Man: Are you looking for a part-time job or a full-time job?
Mrs. Pineiro: A part-time job. I need to be home by 2:00 in the afternoon, when my kids come home from school.
Man: I understand. Do you have any work experience?
Mrs. Pineiro: Well, not really. I'm a homemaker. Sometimes I take care of my neighbor's children.
Man: Hmmm…Do you have a high school diploma?
Mrs. Pineiro: Yes, I do.
Man: Great. And do you have a driver's license?
Mrs. Pineiro: No, I don't. Is that a problem?
Man: Well, for some jobs, you need to know how to drive.
Mrs. Pineiro: Oh.
Man: I'm looking at a list of available jobs, and I don't see anything…oh, wait a minute. Little Friends is looking for a daycare worker—and the hours are perfect—Monday to Friday from 8:00 to 12:00.
Mrs. Pineiro: Oh, Little Friends is in my neighborhood.
Man: Let's see—they want someone with a high school diploma—that's no problem. And it says you need to love children—I don't think that's a problem, right?
Mrs. Pineiro: No, of course not! I love kids.
Man: Hmmm…
Mrs. Pineiro: What's wrong?
Man: Well, they want someone with experience.
Mrs. Pineiro: But I have a lot of experience with children! I have my own kids, and I come from a big family.
Man: Okay, okay. You're right. That is experience. I'm writing all of the information on this form . . . OK, take this to office 255, and speak with Mrs. Anderson. She'll schedule an interview for you.
Mrs. Pineiro: Thank you so much!
Man: You're welcome—and good luck.
Mrs. Pineiro: Thank you!

Unit 13: Feelings and Opinions

Listening, A and B, page 153

Man: So, Angel, where were you last week?
Angel: I was in Miami for my mother-in-law's 80th birthday.
Man: Oh, so your wife has relatives in Miami.
Angel: Yeah, her whole family is there, but we never have the time or the money to visit them. This was our first visit.
Man: I love Miami. How was the weather?
Angel: It was wonderful. And my mother-in-law's house is only about ten minutes from the beach. We were there every day from 9:00 to 4:00. The water was really warm.
Man: Great. How much were the airline tickets? Were they expensive?
Angel: No, they weren't. They were only $159 from New York.
Man: Wow, that's cheap! Were your kids with you?
Angel: Of course! It was spring vacation, so they were off all week.
Man: Oh, that's right. And how were the beaches? Were they crowded?
Angel: Yes, they were. There were people everywhere.
Man: Yeah, Miami is always crowded on school vacation weeks.

Grammar to Communicate 3, C, page 159

Matt: How was your day yesterday?
Bob: It was really good.
Matt: Where were you?
Bob: I was at the beach.
Matt: But it was Thursday. Why were you at the beach on Thursday?
Bob: Thursday's my day off.
Matt: Who was with you?
Bob: My girlfriend and her mother.
Matt: Her mother? Why was her mother with you?
Bob: Her mother likes the beach.
Matt: Oh…OK. How was the beach?

Audioscript

Bob: It was very nice. There weren't many people, and it was a beautiful day.
Matt: How was the water?
Bob: It was pretty cold. The water is always cold around here.

Review and Challenge
Grammar, page 160
Greg: I miss my old apartment. It was really nice.
Pearl: Where was it?
Greg: On Cherry Street in Overbrook.
Pearl: Was it big?
Greg: No, it wasn't. There were five rooms, but they were small.
Pearl: Were there a lot of stores in the neighborhood?
Greg: No, there weren't. They were all far away.
Pearl: So what was nice about the apartment?

Dictation, page 160
1. Were there a lot of people at the party?
2. I was in a bad mood yesterday.
3. My family and I weren't at home last Sunday.
4. Was the restaurant clean?
5. How was your day off?

Listening, A and B, page 161
CONVERSATION 1
Woman: So, how was it?
Man: It was terrible. I was late because of the bad weather. The manager was really angry with me. And her questions were pretty difficult.
Woman: Oh, no. That's really too bad.
Man: Yeah…

CONVERSATION 2
Man: So, how was it?
Woman: It was pretty bad. It was really long and boring. And there were a lot of people in the theater and they were very noisy. A man behind me was on his cell phone the whole time!
Man: Wow, that's rude!
Woman: It sure is!

CONVERSATION 3
Woman: How was it?
Man: It was okay. I was really worried about it at first, but it was pretty easy.
Woman: Was it long?
Man: Not really. It was only two pages.
Woman: How many questions were there?
Man: About 25.

CONVERSATION 4
Man: I'm sorry I wasn't there last night. I was sick.
Woman: I'm sorry you weren't there, too. It was a really great game.
Man: How was your son?
Woman: He was wonderful! I think he was scared at first, but he was fine after about ten minutes. I was really happy for him.
Man: How was the other team? Were they good?
Woman: Yes, they were, but our team was better!

Unit 14: Fact or Fiction?
Listening, A and B, page 165
Steve: You'll never believe what happened yesterday on Canal Street.
Marie: Oh, Steve. Is this one of your strange but true stories?
Steve: But this really happened. I promise!
Marie: OK, go ahead. I'm listening.
Steve: Well, the police don't know how, but a gorilla got out of the city zoo.
Marie: A gorilla?
Steve: Yeah, you heard me —a gorilla. First he ran into the park. Then he ran across Canal Street. All the people in their cars stopped and watched him. Then he walked to the bus stop and stood next to it. The people all screamed, but the gorilla didn't move. He just stood there.
Marie: Oh, please!
Steve: Really! Look. It's in the paper. A policeman took a picture of it.
Marie: Wow! That's really strange. Where is he now? Is he back in the zoo?
Steve: Yes, the police caught him and took him back.

Grammar to Communicate 1, B, page 166
1. I invited friends home last month.
2. I exercised the day before yesterday.
3. I washed my hair last night.
4. I started dinner at 6:00 last night.
5. I cooked yesterday morning.
6. I called my friend yesterday.
7. I watched TV yesterday afternoon.

Review and Challenge
Dictation, page 172
1. I heard an interesting story yesterday.
2. I didn't watch TV last night.
3. They didn't go to class last week.
4. We arrived late and missed the bus.
5. She didn't do her homework.

Listening, A and B, page 173

Reporter: Good morning, this is Peter Williams, with this week's strange but true news stories. First, from California and Florida, we have two great excuse stories. Do you need a day off from work? Well, here's an idea: The President of the United States visited a town in California. A woman from the town didn't go to work that day because she wanted to meet the President. But she didn't want to have a problem with her boss, so she wrote an excuse note. Then she asked the President to sign it. "He did, but he laughed first," she said. Hmmm... What do you think—Did her boss laugh when he read the note? And here's one for our young listeners: In Florida, a police officer stopped a car because there was something strange about the driver—he was only 7 years old! The boy's excuse? He didn't want to be late for school, so he took the family car. I'm Peter Williams, for this week's strange but true ...

Unit 15: Life Stages

Listening, A and B, page 177

Jean: Hey, Paul! How are you? So what's new?
Paul: Umm ... Where do I start? Well, first...I got married last year.
Jean: Really?
Paul: Yeah. I finally did it.
Jean: That's wonderful! Who's the lucky woman? Do I know her?
Paul: Yes, you do. You met her at Doug's wedding two summers ago. Her name's Patricia Cooper.
Jean: Oh yeah ... Patricia. I remember her! So how long ago did you get married?
Paul: A year ago. We had a small wedding—just our relatives and a few friends.
Jean: Well, congratulations!
Paul: Thanks, but that's not all. We had a baby last month.
Jean: A baby? That was fast! What did you have—a girl or a boy?
Paul: A boy—Jason.
Jean: Oh that's great! ... Where are you living? Did you keep your old apartment?
Paul: No, we bought a house in Malden. It needs work, but it didn't cost a lot.
Jean: Wow, that's a big change. How long did you live in Boston?
Paul: For 15 years. I miss the city, but life is really different with a wife and a baby. That's enough about me. What's up with you?
Jean: Well, I have some news too. I became a citizen in March.
Paul: Oh, that's great! And fast, too. How long ago did you come here?
Jean: I came to the United States 8 years ago.
Paul: And are you still at the same job?
Jean: No, I left that job three months ago. I got a new job at International Hotels. The money's great, and I'm a manager now.
Paul: Good for you.

Review and Challenge

Grammar, page 184

Meg: How long ago did you come to the United States?
Aida: I came here 15 years ago. My first home was in Los Angeles.
Meg: How long did you live there?
Aida: I was there for two years.
Meg: Did you work there?
Aida: No, I didn't. I took classes.
Meg: When did you move here?
Aida: Three years ago.

Dictation, page 184

1. How long ago did you get the car?
2. How long did your grandmother live?
3. We didn't visit my parents two weeks ago.
4. We waited for five hours.
5. Did you know your grandparents?

Listening, Exercise A and B, page 185

Reporter: Good afternoon, and welcome to this week's program. I'm here today with Mariela Lopez. Her new book is about the life of artist Frida Kahlo. Welcome, Ms. Lopez.
Mariela: Thank you.
Reporter: So, tell us about Frida Kahlo. Who was she, and why did you write a book about her?
Mariela: Frida Kahlo was a great Mexican painter. She was married to another great Mexican painter, Diego Rivera. I wrote about Ms. Kahlo because I love her paintings. I wanted to know more about her life.
Reporter: And what did you learn?
Mariela: Well, like many famous artists, Frida Kahlo had an interesting but very difficult life.
Reporter: Why do you say "difficult"? What happened to her?
Mariela: When Frida was 18 years old, she was in a terrible bus accident. The experience changed her life. She started to paint at that time.
Reporter: What kind of paintings did she do?
Mariela: It isn't easy to describe her paintings. They're very different from other artists' paintings. A lot of them are about the accident and her feelings about it.

T-288 Audioscript

Reporter: And how did she meet Diego Rivera?
Mariela: They met when Rivera did a painting at her high school.
Reporter: When did they get married?
Mariela: When Frida was 20.
Reporter: And how long were they married?
Mariela: Well, they were married twice.
Reporter: Twice? How did that happen?
Mariela: They got married for the first time in 1929. Then in 1939, they got divorced. They remarried in 1940. Frida died in 1954, so they were married for 24 years.
Reporter: We need to take a short break, but we'll be right back with more about the life and art of Frida Kahlo.

Unit 16: Looking Ahead

Listening, A and B, page 189

Amir: Mom, Sunil invited me to go to a soccer game with him in San Jose this weekend. Can I go?
Mom: San Jose? That's pretty far away. Are you going to take the bus?
Amir: No, Sunil's going to drive.
Mom: Sunil? Does he have his driver's license?
Amir: Of course!
Mom: But he doesn't have a car. Whose car is he going to use?
Amir: His mother's going to give him her car for the weekend.
Mom: The weekend? Are you going to stay the whole weekend? When are you going to leave?
Amir: Sunil's going to pick me up after school on Friday.
Mom: On Friday? When are you going to do your homework?
Amir: On Sunday night.
Mom: What time are you going to be home on Sunday?
Amir: Don't worry. We're not going to be late. We're going to leave San Jose in the morning.
Mom: And where are you going to stay?
Amir: With Sunil's uncle. He lives there.
Mom: What's his name? Do I know him?
Amir: Yes, Mom, you met him at Sunil's birthday party. His name is Rupesh.
Mom: Oh, Rupesh. All right, I guess it's okay. But I want Rupesh's telephone number, please. And make sure you call me when you get there.
Amir: Of course. Thanks, Mom. You're the best. Oh, and just one more thing…
Mom: Don't even ask! I'm not going to give you any money.
Amir: Ah, Mom, come on…

Review and Challenge

Grammar, page 196

Steve: Are you going to go out tonight?
Ted: No, I'm going to stay at home. My brother is going to come over. We're going to play cards. Do you want to come?
Steve: No. I don't like cards.
Ted: Are you sure? Jan and Kate are going to come over too.
Steve: Do you mean Jan Richards? Is she going to be at your place tonight? Um…What time is the game going to start?
Ted: Why? Are you going to come? But you don't like cards!

Dictation, page 196

1. What are you going to do this Saturday?
2. Is it going to rain tomorrow?
3. I'm not going to stay home.
4. We're going to have people over next week.
5. When is he going to come?

Listening, A and B, page 197

Natalie: And here's Chet Kraft with the 5-day forecast. Good morning, Chet.
Chet: Good morning, Natalie.
Natalie: So, Chet, what do you think?? Is this beautiful weather going to stay around for the weekend?
Chet: Well, Natalie, I'm going to give you the good news first. Today is going to be a beautiful day. There's going to be a lot of sunshine and it's going to be warm. And for the rest of your week? Not so great. Tomorrow morning it's going to be cloudy, windy, and cool. In the afternoon it's going to rain. And I'm afraid it's going to rain again on Friday.
Natalie: Oh, Chet! Please give us some good news for the weekend!
Chet: Well, Natalie, I think you and our listeners are going to be happy—On Saturday, it's going to be perfect beach weather sunny, no clouds, and in the 80s. It's going to be a little humid, but the water temperature is going to be perfect for swimming—about 75 degrees.
Natalie: And what about Sunday? Are we going to have good picnic weather?
Chet: Well, it's a little early to say, but it looks like some cool, rainy weather is going to come in from Canada late Saturday evening. So, this is my advice. If you are going to go to a picnic on Sunday, wear a sweater, and take your umbrella.

Audioscript T-289

Natalie: Thanks, Chet. That was Chet Kraft, with the morning weather update. Tune in at 10:00 for more on the weekend weather.

Unit 17: Health

Listening, A and B, page 203

Glenda: Abby, yoo hooo! Where is my perfect grandson and his beautiful mother?
Abby: We're out here!
Glenda: What are you doing outside? The baby shouldn't be out! He's only a month old!
Abby: The doctor said the fresh air is good for him. And it's warm out.
Glenda: Don't get angry, Abby. I'm just thinking about my grandson's health.
Abby: I know, I'm sorry . . . So, where should we go for lunch?
Glenda: Go? Oh, I don't think we should go out for lunch.
Abby: Why not?
Glenda: Well, the baby shouldn't be around a lot of people. What if someone has a cold and coughs on him?
Abby: But that's crazy!
Glenda: Really? I don't agree. Should we call the doctor and ask?
Abby: No, we shouldn't! He told me it was OK.
Glenda: Who told you? Dr. Mendez? Why should we believe him? He's just a kid!
Abby: Dr. Mendez is 30 years old, and he's a great doctor. Now, what about lunch? Should we go to the Museum Café or Jake's Barbecue?

Review and Challenge

Grammar, page 210

Teri: The baby is sick. What should I do?
Jon: You should call the doctor.
Teri: But it's 9 P.M. The doctor's not in his office.
Jon: What's wrong with the baby?
Teri: He feels hot.
Jon: Did you take his temperature?
Teri: No, I didn't. Should we take him to the hospital?
Jon: No, we shouldn't. You should take his temperature.
Teri: I'm worried.
Jon: You shouldn't worry. He's fine.

Dictation, page 210

1. Should I go to the hospital?
2. You shouldn't take that medicine.
3. Which doctor should I call?
4. You should stay in bed.
5. What should I ask the pharmacist?

Listening, A and B, page 211

Reporter: This is Leslie Lu with the weekly health report. Of course, everyone wants to be healthy. But how? What should you eat? What shouldn't you eat? Here is some advice from the U.S. government. There are 5 important food groups. You should eat different things from each group every day. What are the groups? Grains, for example bread, cereal, rice, or pasta; vegetables; fruit; and milk products, for example, milk, cheese and yogurt. The last group is the meat group, but the name is confusing because it includes not just meat, but chicken, fish, nuts and beans too. How much should you eat every day? Well, first, let's talk about grains. Most adults should eat six ounces of whole grains, which is about 6 slices of bread, or 3 cups of rice. And think brown, not white: brown rice, not white rice, and so on. And vegetables? You should eat about 2 and ½ cups a day. That's, say, three carrots, a few leaves of spinach, and a little broccoli. Choose vegetables in dark, bright colors—for example, dark green vegetables such as spinach and orange vegetables such as carrots. And fruit? You should eat about 2 cups of fruit every day. That's two apples, for example. Try to eat fruit of many different colors—for example, a green apple, some blueberries, and an orange. What about milk? You should have about 3 cups of low-fat or fat-free milk products every day. You shouldn't drink whole milk or eat a lot of cheese because it has a lot of fat. Finally, you should eat about 5 and 1/2 ounces a day from the meat group, including meat, chicken, beans, fish, or nuts. For example, you can eat a piece of chicken, some beans, and about ten nuts. But be careful—you shouldn't eat a lot of red meat. Of course, every person is different. For more information about your age and weight group, call or write to the U.S. Department of Agriculture at . . .

Unit 18: A Place to Live

Listening, A and B, page 215

Miranda: Hello, Morgan Realty. This is Miranda.
Doug: Hi. I'm looking for a one-bedroom apartment, and I saw your ad in Sunday's paper.
Miranda: Which neighborhoods are you interested in?
Doug: Well, I don't have a car, so I need to be close to public transportation.
Miranda: Hmmm . . . Let me see. OK, I have three apartments near public transportation. The best apartment is on Mercer Street near the new theater. It's $1,300 a month.
Doug: Wow. That's expensive. How about the other two apartments? Are they cheaper than that?

Audioscript

Miranda: Yes, they are, but the Mercer Street apartment is in the most convenient location.

Doug: But I don't want to spend that much money. How much is the cheapest apartment?

Miranda: It's $400 a month, but it's also the smallest. And it's the farthest from downtown. It's out in Brighton Park.

Doug: Oh, that is far. How about the last apartment?

Miranda: It's in a better location than the Brighton Park apartment. It's also larger and sunnier, and it's in a more modern building.

Doug: How much is it?

Miranda: It's $500 a month—oh, but wait a minute. That's with utilities, so it's really cheaper than the Brighton Park apartment.

Doug: And where is it?

Miranda: It's on Trenton Street, next to the post office.

Doug: That sounds perfect. When can I see it?

Miranda: Well, first you need to come to the office and fill out a rental application form . . .

Review and Challenge
Dictation, page 222
1. Which house is the cheapest?
2. The most comfortable chair is in the living room.
3. The bedroom is larger than the kitchen.
4. This apartment is more convenient than my apartment.
5. Is your home closer to the mall than my home?

Listening, A and B, page 223

Reporter: Good afternoon, this is Dolores Oakes reporting for World Beat. Today we are going to talk about the best cities in the world to live in. But first, what do we mean by "the best"? Of course, different people are looking for different things. In fact it is not possible to say that one city is better than another, or that one city is the best of all. Remember that as we look at what some famous magazines, newspapers, and websites are saying. Three cities are on many 10-best lists: Vienna, Austria; Zurich, Switzerland; and Vancouver, Canada. What makes these cities special? Well, they are generally safe cities. They are safer than other cities with the same number of people. They are also cleaner, and they have better public transportation than many other cities of the same size. They are also "healthy" cities—they have excellent doctors and hospitals, and clean air and water. Finally, their weather is rarely very hot or very cold. In Asia, Tokyo and Hong Kong are often on the 10 best lists. Why? Well, Tokyo has better public transportation than almost any other city in the world. In addition, it is perhaps the safest large city in the world, with a lower crime rate than other large cities. As for Hong Kong, many people think it is the most exciting city in Asia, with the best restaurants and nightlife. Many people say that Hong Kong has the best of both East and West. But before you pack your suitcase and buy your tickets to one of these cities, you should know one thing: They are all very expensive to live in. So for many of us, they are not the best, or even a good choice. Next week, we'll look at which cities are on the list of the 10 worst places to live, and why.

Unit 19: Future Changes
Listening, A and B, page 227

Betty: So, tell me! What do you see? Will there be any changes in my life?

Woman: Yes, there will. I see a handsome, dark man. He will get in touch with you soon.

Betty: That sounds interesting. Will he be tall?

Woman: No, he won't.

Betty: Oh… Well, why will he get in touch with me?

Woman: He will have some news for you.

Betty: What kind of news will it be? Will it be good or bad?

Woman: I'm sorry, but it won't be good …I also see money.

Betty: Oh, good!

Woman: Hmmmm…

Betty: What's the matter?

Woman: Well, you won't get money. You'll lose it.

Betty: Really? How much will I lose? How will I lose it?

Woman: I'm not sure, but it will be a lot of money.

Betty: Oh no! I'm starting a new business, and I need every penny. Can you see anything about that? Will I succeed?

Woman: Let me see…Uh oh…

Betty: What? What do you see?

Woman: I'm sorry, but it looks like there will be some problems. Wait a minute! Where are you going?

Betty: I'm going to find a different fortune teller—one who can see some good news!

Grammar to Communicate 3, C, page 233

Carol: Your horoscope says, "You will find the love of your life."

Seth: When will I meet her?

Carol: This month.

Seth: What will her name be?

Carol: Her name? Horoscopes don't give names!

Seth: Where will I find her?

Carol: It doesn't say the place. It also says you will get some news late in the month.

Seth: What kind of news will it be?
Carol: It will be good news.
Seth: Who will give me the good news?
Carol: Your new girlfriend, of course!

Review and Challenge
Grammar, page 234

Paul: Mom, I want to move closer to my job.
Mom: But where will you live?
Paul: I'll find an apartment. It won't be hard.
Mom: But who will cook for you?
Paul: I'll cook.
Mom: Will you visit me often?
Paul: Yes, I will. Every weekend.
Mom: Good. Then I'll make you food for the week, and you won't need to cook.

Dictation, page 234
1. You'll have a good time.
2. They'll get in touch with you next month.
3. She won't live alone.
4. Will prices go down?
5. When will I get a raise?

Listening, A and B, page 235

Carlos: Good afternoon. This is Carlos Icaza with today's technology update. Reporter Rob Willis is at the Technology Fair in Tokyo, Japan. So, Rob, what new products will we see in the stores next year?
Rob: Well, cell phones are really hot this year.
Carlos: Cell phones? But they're old news!
Rob: Not these cell phones. I think that very soon these cell phones will replace credit cards, bank cards, and even cash.
Carlos: Really? How will that happen?
Rob: Well, these cell phones are not just phones. They're also very small computers.
Carlos: So?
Rob: When you're in a store or restaurant, you will just hold your cell phone up to a special machine. The machine will get in touch with your bank or credit card company. If you have the money or credit in your account, you'll be able to buy anything that you want.
Carlos: But what will happen if you lose your cell phone, or if someone steals it?
Rob: You'll call the bank or credit card company and cancel it. You won't lose more than $50.
Carlos: But wait a minute. You'll only be able to buy things with your cell phone in stores and restaurants with those special machines. That won't be very convenient.
Rob: That's true right now, but the machines will be everywhere in a year or two.
Carlos: And how much will a cell phone like that cost?
Rob: They won't be cheap at first—maybe $500 or so—but the prices will go down.
Carlos: What? At $500, nobody will buy them! I don't think this idea will ever succeed.
Rob: Well, talk to me in a year or so, and we'll see who was right.

Unit 20: Transportation
Listening, A and B, page 239

Ticket Agent: Can I help you, Ma'am?
Mrs. Jones: Yes, please. I'd like to buy two tickets to New York.
Ticket Agent: Would you like round-trip or one-way tickets?
Mrs. Jones: Round-trip, please.
Ticket Agent: For when?
Mrs. Jones: Excuse me?
Ticket Agent: When would you like to travel?
Mrs. Jones: Today. On the next train, the 2:55.
Ticket Agent: Sorry, but the 2:55 is sold out.
Mrs. Jones: What do you mean?
Ticket Agent: The 2:55 is a reserved train. You have to reserve tickets in advance.
Mrs. Jones: But we have to be in New York tonight! My son has to go to an important job interview. Could you please look again?
Ticket Agent: Sorry, Ma'am. There are no seats on the 2:55. But there is a train at 5:30. It gets into New York at 9:30.
Mrs. Jones: But that's three hours from now. What are we going to do here in the train station for three hours?
Man: Lady, can you hurry up? I'm going to miss my train!
Ticket Agent: Ma'am, do you want tickets for the 5:30 or not?
Mrs. Jones: All right, give me two.
Ticket Agent: That'll be one hundred and twenty dollars.

Grammar to Communicate 1, C, page 241
1. **A:** Excuse me? Where does the bus usually stop?
   B: You have to wait next to that sign.
2. **A:** I need to get off. Is the driver going to stop here?
   B: Yes. The driver has to stop at every bus stop.
3. **A:** Are you ready?
   B: No, I have to get some money for the bus.
4. **A:** Excuse me, this woman has to sit down. She's sick.

B: Oh, sure. Here—I'll help you.
5. A: Sorry, but I have to run. My bus is coming.
B: OK, I'll talk to you later.

Grammar to Communicate 3, C, page 245

1. A: Can you open the windows, please?
   B: It's windy today. I'll turn on the air conditioner.
2. A: Could I have a round-trip ticket to Chicago, please?
   B: Sure. That'll be $35.
3. A: Can I get off at the next stop, please?
   B: No problem.
4. A: Could I have some coffee, please?
   B: Sure. Here you are.
5. A: Would you stop at the next street, please?
   B: Okay.
6. A: Would you go back to your seat, please?
   B: All right.
7. A: Could you wait a minute, please?
   B: OK.

Review and Challenge
Dictation, page 246

1. Could you open the window, please?
2. Would you like to sit here?
3. He has to get off now.
4. You have to turn off your cell phone.
5. I'd like a seat near the door, please.

Listening, A and B, page 247

Airline attendant: Would you like a newspaper or magazine?
Veronica: Could you give me a newspaper, please?
Airline attendant: Here you go . . . And for you, sir?
Tom: No, thank you . . . but I would like a bottle of water, if you don't mind.
Airline attendant: Of course, but can you wait a few minutes? We have to finish with the magazines first. Some passengers don't have any magazines yet.
Tom: Oh, that's fine. Thanks.
Veronica: Excuse me. I'm sorry to bother you, but I have to go to the restroom.
Tom: No problem.
Airline attendant: Here's your water, sir.
Tom: That was fast! Thank you very much.
Airline attendant: You're welcome.
Veronica: Excuse me again...Sorry!
Tom: Don't worry about it. Would you like a piece of gum?
Veronica: Sure, thanks.
Tom: So, are you from Las Vegas?
Veronica: Oh, no. I'm from New York. I was on vacation.
Tom: Was this your first visit to Las Vegas?
Veronica: Yes, it was.
Tom: And how did you like it?
Veronica: I loved it. Are you from Las Vegas?
Tom: No, I'm not. I'm from Los Angeles, but I'm in Las Vegas a lot. I'm Tom Lewis, by the way.
Veronica: Nice to meet you, Tom. I'm Veronica Lane. Are you going to New York on business?
Tom: Yes, I am. I have to meet a client there. I'll just be in town for a few days.
Veronica: Oh.
Tom: But I travel to New York often. My best friend lives there. In fact, I have two tickets to a basketball game tomorrow night, and we're going to go.
Veronica: Really? I love basketball! Which game?
Tom: The Knicks game at Madison Square Garden.
Veronica: I'm going to that game too! With my sister. Maybe we'll see you there!
Tom: Great!! I'd really like that . . .

Index

ACADEMIC SKILLS

Grammar
a / an / Ø 28, 31, 32, 253
adjectives
    comparative, 216–217, 220–221, 260
    how +, 20, 252
    irregular, 216, 218, 260
    noun word order and, 30, 31, 253
    plural forms, lack of, 30, 253
    possessive, 16–17, 92, 93, 252, 254
    superlative, 218–221, 260
    that / those, 90, 91, 255
    this / these, 90, 91, 255
    with *be* 4–9
adverbs, 116–117, 137, 256
affirmative statements, 66, 78, 104, 109, 118, 154–155, 204–205, 228–229, 252, 256, 258, 260, 261
and, 75, 87
be, 4–6, 20, 154–159, 179, 252
be going to, 190–196, 259
can / could / would, 244–245, 261
contractions, 4, 5, 16, 18, 92, 93, 140, 199, 252, 254, 256, 258, 260, 261
count nouns, 54–59, 252, 254
direct objects, 128–129, 257
either, 109
go + verb + *–ing* for leisure activities, 178
have, 94–95, 255
have to, 240–241, 261
how long ago / how long, 182–183, 259
how much / how many, 59–60, 254
imperatives, 78–79, 255
indirect objects, 128–129, 257
infinitives, 144–146, 257
information questions, 20–21, 70–71, 120–121, 130–131, 158–159, 180–181, 194–195, 208–209, 232–233, 252, 256, 257, 258, 259, 260, 261
Is there / Are there, 44–45, 253
like / need / want + infinitive, 144–145, 257
must, 240, 261
negative statements, 66, 108, 109, 118, 170–171, 204–205, 252, 256, 258, 260
noncount nouns, 54–59, 254
nouns
    count, 8, 28, 54–58, 252, 254
    irregular, 8, 252
    noncount, 54–56, 58, 252, 254
    plural, 8, 9, 28, 252
    possessive, 18, 252
or, 113

prepositions, 80–81, 128, 129, 194, 255
pronouns
    object, 82, 255
    possessive, 92–93, 255
    subject 82, 99, 255
quantifiers, 56–57, 254
should, 204–209, 260
some / a lot of / any, 42, 253, see also quantifiers
some / a little / a lot of / a few / any, 56, 254 see also quantifiers
subject, 132, 133, 194, 232, 257, 259, 261
the, 32, 253
there is/there are, 40–43, 45, 253
these / those, 90–91, 255
this / that, 90–91, 255
too, 109
verb tense
    future, 190–195, 228–233, 259, 261
    present progressive, 66–68, 70, 72, 140–141, 254
        compared with simple present, 140–142, 257
    simple past, 154–159, 166–171, 178–181, 258
    simple present, 94–95, 104–106, 108, 116–121, 130–131, 140–141, 168, 255, 256
        compared with present progressive, 140–142, 257
verbs
    -ing form, 66, 67, 254
    endings, 106, 256
    irregular, 168, 258
    regular, 166, 258
    stative, 142–143, 257
what / who as subject, 194, 232, 259
what kind of, 120
who as subject and object, 132–133, 257
will, 228–233, 261
word order, 30, 31, 34, 253
would like, 242–243, 261
yes / no questions, 6–7, 68–69, 118–119, 156–157, 178–179, 192–193, 206–207, 230–231, 252, 254, 256, 258, 259, 260, 261

Listening
activities, 65
apartments, 215
biography of famous artist, 185
celebrations, 127
changes in technology, 235
conversations, 15, 22, 35, 39, 61, 65, 85, 89, 99, 103, 118, 127, 152–153, 161, 189, 227, 247
cross-cultural comparisons, 23, 61, 103, 111, 135
descriptions of people, 3, 11
descriptions of past events/experiences, 153, 161, 165, 173, 177, 185

families, 15, 23
food, 53, 211
giving gifts, 135
health, 203, 211
instructions and warnings, 77, 85, 97
interviews, 35, 147
jobs, 27, 35
numbers and percentages, 11, 111
ordering food, 97
personal information, 11, 27
places, 39, 135
plans, 189
predictions, 227, 235
quality of life, 11, 223
reports, 11, 23, 73, 111, 173, 185, 197, 223, 235
routines, 103, 111
travel reservations, 239
shopping, 47, 53, 61, 89, 115, 123
sports events, 73
weather report, 197
work schedules, 139

Reading
accident reports, 8
ads, 162, 267, 269, 274
apartment listings, 273
application forms 148
biography, 186
business cards, 33
calendars, 198
common signs, 79, 86
comprehension, 2, 3
daily planner, 112
e-mail, 213, 225
evaluation forms, 36–37
home insurance form, 98
horoscopes, 232–233
instructions, 86
interviews, 186
letters, 162, 248
mall directory, 120
maps, 40, 268
medicine labels, 208, 212
menus, 269, 274
newsletters, 62, 124, 136
personal information forms, 24
personal notes, 199
police reports, 174
postcards, 48–49
receipts, 55
recipes, 57

registration forms, 12
resolutions, 236
resumes, 34
safety and emergency procedures, 86
schedules, 107, 111, 112
shopping, 124
sports reports, 74
survey, 112
timelines, 183
travel guide, 87
web pages, 224

Speaking
activities, 67, 69, 71, 72
comparisons, 61, 221
compliments, 91
families, 17, 19, 21, 23
food, 57, 59
foreign languages, 96
games, 50–51, 100–101, 150–151, 200–201, 250–251
instructions/orders/warnings, 79, 81, 83–85
interviewing classmates, 5
jobs, 29, 31, 33–35
places, 43, 45, 46, 217
possessions, 91, 93, 95–97
prices, 55, 60
sports, 73
stories, 172

Writing
address letters, 163
answers, short and long, 178, 185, 195, 198, 230
because, 125
biography, 187
capitalization, 13
commands, 82
compliments, 91
contractions, 199
conversations, 71, 72, 83, 84, 93, 100–101, 121, 122, 130, 159, 160, 169, 178, 184, 196, 210, 241, 246–247
counseling and career services forms, 148–149
daily planner, 113
daily routines, 113
Dear + name + comma, 49
diaries, 113
e-mails, 213, 225
evaluation forms, 37
events in progress, 75
family trees, 19

Index T-295

food, 63
for example, 63
full forms vs. contractions, 25
holidays, 137
indents, 249
in my opinion, 225
instead, 237
interviews, 187
letters, 163, 249
newsletters, 63, 125, 137
opinions, 225
paragraphs, 13, 25, 87, 99, 104, 149
personal information forms, 25
plans, 199
police reports, 175
postcards, 49
predictions, 229, 231, 234
questions, 6, 7, 20–21, 24, 25, 31, 45, 69, 70, 119–121, 123, 130–134, 157, 158, 178–180, 183, 194, 206–209, 220, 221, 243
registration forms, 13
reports, 75
requests, 244–246
resolutions, 237
sentences, 29, 145, 190, 218, 219, 228, 229, 240, 242, 247
shopping, 116, 117, 125
sincerely, 213
statements, 4–5, 41, 154, 170, 204, 205
stories, 171
summaries, 37
time expressions, 154, 155, 169, 187, 193, 228
timelines, 183
travel guide, 87
when, 175

LIFESKILLS

Business and Employment
ads, 162, 267, 269, 274
business cards, 33
counseling and career forms, 148–149
employee evaluations, 36–37
receipts, 55
registration forms, 12–13
resumes, 34
work-related activities, 138–149
work schedules, 103, 107

Consumer Education
ads, 162, 267, 269, 274
business letters, 162, 163
home purchases, 224

insurance application forms, 98–99
shopping, 114–125

Environment and World
calendars, 154, 198
daily activities, 111–113
facts, 164–175
holidays and special occasions, 126–137, 155
maps/directories, 40, 46
news, 173
places, 40–42, 47, 157, 223
signs, 58, 79
technological advances, 235
travel guides, 87
travel plans, 196
weather charts, 190, 197
weather reports, 197

Government and Community
dwellings, 215, 217, 221–224
police reports, 174–175
registration forms, 12–13
rules, 83
transportation, 238–249
vehicle operator's licenses, 241

Health and Nutrition
exercise, 64–75
food, 52–63, 211
medical conditions, 210
medical treatment, 208–210, 212, 213
recipes, 57
symptoms, 204–207

Interpersonal Communication
advice, 205
asking questions, 25
compliments, 91
criticism, 79
descriptions, 2–3
excuses, 169
interviews, 146, 186–187
newsletters, 62–63, 124–125, 136–137
postcards, 48–49
requests, 244–245

People
actions, 76–82
activities, 108–113, 166, 167
ages, 5

Index

athletes, 73
descriptions, 2–6, 9, 32, 33
experiences, 153, 161, 165, 173, 177, 185
family relationships, 14–21
famous, 22
feelings and opinions, 152–163
fortune tellers, 233
goals, 145, 195
horoscopes, 232–233
jobs, 26–35
life stages, 176–187
looking ahead, 188–199
plans, 193
questions about, 7
resolutions, 236–237
statements about, 104, 105
women's jobs, 147

Resources
possessions, 88–99
public places, 39, 42, 46, 61

Safety and Security
instructions, 86
police reports, 174–175

Time and Money
time expressions, 104, 154, 155, 193, 228
timelines, 183, 184

UNIT 1   TEST

Name: _____   Date: _____

A **Listen. Read each question. Circle the letter of the correct answer.**

1. Is Ahmed Danielle's friend?   a. Yes, he is.   b. No, he isn't.
2. Are Ahmed and Danielle neighbors? a. Yes, they are.   b. No, they aren't.
3. Is Danielle a teacher?   a. Yes, she is.   b. No, she isn't.
4. Is Ahmed a student?   a. Yes, he is.   b. No, he isn't.
5. Is Ahmed tall?   a. Yes, he is.   b. No, he isn't.
6. Is Ahmed heavy?   a. Yes, he is.   b. No, he isn't.
7. Is Danielle 25?   a. Yes, she is.   b. No, she isn't.
8. Is Ahmed 25?   a. Yes, he is.   b. No, he isn't.

B **Complete each conversation. Circle the correct answer.**

1. **A:** Is your child **tall / young**?
   B: Yes, he's 6.

2. **A:** Are your neighbors **heavy / middle-aged**?
   B: No, they're average weight.

3. **A:** Is Cecilia **old / beautiful**?
   B: Yes, she is. She's good-looking.

4. **A:** Is the girl **quiet / married**?
   B: No, she's talkative.

5. **A:** Are they short?
   B: No, they're **thin / average height**.

6. **A:** Is your teacher serious?
   B: No, she isn't. She's **heavy / funny**.

C **Look at the picture. Match the beginnings with the endings of the sentences. Write the correct letters.**

____ 1. Diego and Patrick aren't   a. heavy.
____ 2. Anna isn't   b. young.
____ 3. The children are   c. thin.

Diego   Anna   Patrick

T-298   Unit 1 Test

UNIT 3 TEST

Name: _____   Date: _____

E Read the evaluation form. Then complete each sentence. Circle the letter of the correct answer.

EMPLOYEE EVALUATION

Name: Katie Hanson   Position: Hairdresser
Date of Hire: 7 / 14 / 06   Date of Review: 10 / 14 / 06

Please evaluate the employee. Circle one number for each item.

Rating System: 1 = poor 2 = fair 3 = good

Relationship with kitchen staff	1	2	③
Relationship with customers	1	2	③
Organization	①	2	3

Summary

Katie is a good hairdresser. She is hardworking, nice, and patient. But she isn't organized. Her work area isn't neat. But the customers are happy with her work. They say she is experienced and honest. She is friendly with the staff.

Manager (please sign): _Tom Jacobs_

1. Katie is _____.
   a. a customer   b. an employee

2. Katie is _____.
   a. a manager   b. a hairdresser

3. Tom is _____.
   a. a customer   b. a boss

4. Katie _____ nice to the staff.
   a. is   b. isn't

5. Katie's relationship with customers is _____.
   a. good   b. poor

6. Katie's organization is _____.
   a. poor   b. fair

7. Katie is _____.
   a. patient   b. quiet

8. Katie is _____.
   a. neat   b. messy

9. Katie _____ honest.
   a. is   b. isn't

T-306   Unit 3 Test

UNIT 1 TEST

Name: _____ Date: _____

F Read the paragraph and the registration form. Then read the questions. Write *Y* for *Yes* or *N* for *No*.

> My name is Antonia Vera Petrova. I'm from St. Petersburg, Russia. I am Russian. I'm married. My husband, Marius, isn't Russian. He's from Romania. He's Romanian. My birthday is in October. I am 33. Marius is 35.

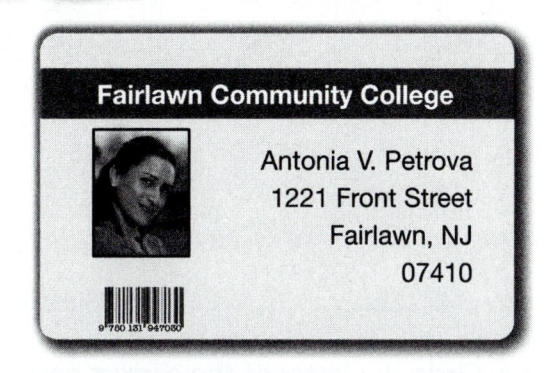

Fairlawn Community College

Antonia V. Petrova
1221 Front Street
Fairlawn, NJ
07410

FAIRLAWN COMMUNITY COLLEGE REGISTRATION FORM

PLEASE PRINT.   DATE July 7, 2007

NAME Petrova   Antonia   V.
      LAST   FIRST   MIDDLE INITIAL

ADDRESS 1221 Front Street   Fairlawn   NJ   07410
         STREET   CITY   STATE ZIP CODE

TELEPHONE NUMBER (973) 555-1256

SEX   MALE   (FEMALE)   DATE OF BIRTH October 27, 1973

NATIONALITY Russian

1. Is Antonia's last name Petrova? _____
2. Is Antonia Romanian? _____
3. Are Antonia and Marius American? _____
4. Is Marius married? _____
5. Is Antonia 33? _____
6. Is Antonia a female? _____
7. Is Antonia's zip code NJ? _____
8. Is Antonia's telephone number 07410? _____

UNIT 2   TEST

Name: _____   Date: _____

A Listen. Complete each sentence. Circle the letter of the correct answer.

1. The house in the picture is in _____.
   a. Florida   b. California

2. The boy in the picture is _____.
   a. Amy's nephew   b. Amy's son

3. The boy's name is _____.
   a. Terry   b. Ben

4. The boy is _____.
   a. 5 years old   b. 7 years old

5. The girl is _____.
   a. the boy's sister   b. the boy's cousin

6. The girl's father is _____.
   a. Amy's brother   b. Amy's father

7. The girl is _____.
   a. 5 years old   b. 7 years old

8. The girl is _____.
   a. short   b. tall

B Look at Nina's family tree. Then complete the sentences. Use family words.

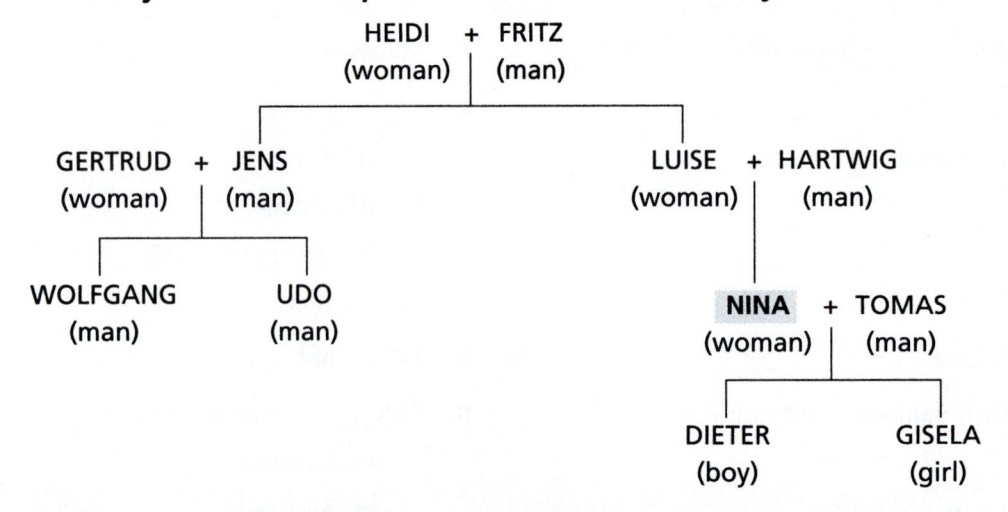

```
                    HEIDI  +  FRITZ
                   (woman)   (man)
          ┌───────────┴───────────┐
   GERTRUD + JENS           LUISE + HARTWIG
   (woman)  (man)          (woman)  (man)
    ┌────┴────┐                  │
 WOLFGANG   UDO              NINA  +  TOMAS
  (man)    (man)            (woman)   (man)
                             ┌────┴────┐
                          DIETER     GISELA
                          (boy)      (girl)
```

1. Tomas is Nina's _____.   5. Gertrud is Nina's _____.
2. Dieter is Nina's _____.   6. Fritz is Nina's _____.
3. Gisela is Dieter's _____.   7. Hartwig is Tomas's _____.
4. Udo is Nina's _____.   8. Jens is Hartwig's _____.

Unit 2 Test   T-301

UNIT 2   TEST

Name: _____ Date: _____

C Complete each conversation. Circle the letter of the correct answer.

1. **A:** Is he _____ cousin?
    B: Yes, he is.
    a. your
    b. you
    c. Jacks
    d. she

2. **A:** Are the boys your sons?
    B: Yes, _____ are.
    a. you
    b. your
    c. they
    d. their

3. **A:** Hello. _____ name is Ana.
    B: Hi, Ana. It's nice to meet you.
    a. I
    b. Your
    c. My
    d. Her

4. **A:** Your _____ dog is big.
    B: Yes, he is!
    a. parents
    b. parents'
    c. parent
    d. their

5. **A:** What are your _____?
    B: Their names are Ted and Max.
    a. uncles names
    b. uncles' names
    c. uncle's names
    d. uncle's name's

6. **A:** _____ are you?
    B: I'm 6 feet, 3 inches.
    a. How tall
    b. How old
    c. How
    d. Who

7. **A:** Is Brent your uncle?
    B: Yes. He's _____ brother.
    a. my father
    b. my fathers
    c. my father's
    d. my fathers'

8. **A:** _____ is your class?
    B: At 10:00 A.M.
    a. Where
    b. Who
    c. What
    d. When

9. **A:** Where is she?
    B: _____.
    a. In New York
    b. At 6:00 P.M.
    c. Pictures of my family
    d. My mother

10. **A:** Who is he?
    B: He's _____ father.
    a. my husband
    b. my husbands'
    c. my husbands
    d. my husband's

Unit 2 Test

UNIT 2 TEST

Name: _____   Date: _____

D Read the form. Then complete the paragraph.

Section I—Contact Information

| NAME | LAST: Parker | FIRST: Gary | MIDDLE: Roy |

ADDRESS STREET: 400 Flower St.   APT. NO.: 14C
CITY: Daytona Beach   STATE: FL   ZIP CODE: 30001

TELEPHONE DAYTIME: 315-555-2222   EVENING: 315-555-3045
CELL PHONE: 927-555-9021

Section II—Employment Information

EMPLOYMENT STATUS ☑ Full-time   ☐ Part-time   ☐ Unemployed

EMPLOYER	EMPLOYER'S ADDRESS	JOB TITLE / POSITION
Central Adult School	7666 Center St. Daytona Beach, FL 30002	Teacher

Section III—Household Information

NAME	RELATIONSHIP TO YOU	DATE OF BIRTH (MM/DD/YY)	SEX
Gary Parker	Self	04 / 05 / 70	M
Della Parker	Wife	06 / 13 / 72	F
Emily Parker	Daughter	12 / 02 / 03	F

SIGNATURE _A. Guerrero_   TODAY'S DATE 09/09/2006

Gary's middle name is _____. His last name is _____. His
                            1.   2.
address is _____ Street, Apt. 14C, Daytona Beach, Florida. His cell phone number is
                 3.

_____. He is a _____ at the Central Adult School. He is married. His
       4.   5.

wife's name is _____, and his daughter's name is _____. His daughter's
                     6.   7.

date of birth is _____.
                        8.

UNIT 3   TEST

Name: _____   Date: _____

A 🔊 4   Listen. Complete each sentence. Write *T* for *Terry*, *J* for *Joanne*, or *C* for *Carolina*.

1. _____ is an engineer.
2. _____ is an accountant.
3. _____ is smart.
4. _____'s job is interesting.
5. _____ is a nurse.
6. _____ is late for work.

B 🔊 5   Listen to each conversation. Then complete the sentences. Use the words in the box.

an attorney	a fast worker	a mechanic	a waitress

Conversation 1:   1. Janice is _____.
Conversation 2:   2. Pamela is _____.
Conversation 3:   3. Denise is _____.
Conversation 4:   4. Pete is _____.

C   Match each picture with a word. Write the correct letter.

a.   b.   c.   d.

e.   f.   g.   h.

____ 1. attorney   ____ 3. interpreter   ____ 5. nurse   ____ 7. hairdresser
____ 2. mechanic   ____ 4. waiter   ____ 6. plumber   ____ 8. cook

T-304   Unit 3 Test

UNIT 3 TEST

Name: _____ Date: _____

D Look at the picture. Complete the paragraph about the people in the picture. Use *a*, *an*, *Ø*, or *the*.

Look at the picture of my friends. My friend Leslie is the woman with long hair, and _____ tall guy is her
                                                                                      1.
husband, Ken. They have _____ son, Brett. He's _____ child in the picture. He's _____ nice boy. Leslie is
                         2.   3.   4.
_____ homemaker, and Ken is _____ cook. The woman with black hair is my friend Rachel. Rachel is _____
   5.   6.   7.
electrician. The short man is Dave, and the heavy man is Don. Dave and Don are _____ plumbers. They are
                                                                                8.
_____ good workers. Their job is _____ difficult.
   9.   10.

Unit 3 Test   T-305

UNIT 1   TEST

Name: _____   Date: _____

D Complete each sentence. Circle the letter of the correct answer.

1. The _____ are beautiful.
   a. childs
   b. children
   c. child

2. They _____ funny.
   a. am
   b. is
   c. are

3. Two _____ in my class are 50.
   a. woman
   b. womans
   c. women

4. The _____ are hardworking.
   a. student
   b. students
   c. studentes

5. Mr. Roberts _____ married.
   a. not be
   b. are not
   c. is not

6. _____ my neighbor.
   a. She's
   b. She
   c. She's is

E Complete each conversation. Circle the letter of the correct answer.

1. **A:** _____ tall?
   B: No. He is short.
   a. Is he
   b. He's
   c. He is

2. **A:** Are Pam and Heather smart?
   B: Yes, _____.
   a. she is
   b. they are
   c. they're

3. **A:** The dog is quiet.
   B: _____ friendly?
   a. It's
   b. It is
   c. Is it

4. **A:** Is Bob your friend?
   B: No, _____.
   a. he isn't
   b. he not
   c. isn't

UNIT 4   TEST

Name: _____   Date: _____

A 🎧 6 Listen. Complete each sentence. Circle the correct answer.

1. There **are / aren't** restaurants in Lynn's neighborhood.
2. There **are / aren't** cheap stores in Lynn's neighborhood.
3. There **are / aren't** outdoor markets in Lynn's neighborhood.
4. There **are / aren't** parks near Lynn's apartment.
5. There **are / aren't** restaurants in Ryan's neighborhood.
6. There **are / aren't** apartments for rent in Lynn's building.

B 🎧 7 Listen. You will hear four sentences. Circle the letter of each sentence you hear.

1. a. There are a lot of good-looking people.
   b. There aren't a lot of good-looking people.
2. a. There's a hotel near the airport.
   b. There isn't a hotel near the airport.
3. a. There aren't any apartment buildings.
   b. Are there any apartment buildings?
4. a. There are good supermarkets.
   b. There's a good supermarket.

C Look at the map. For each sentence, write *T* for *True* or *F* for *False*.

1. There isn't an airport in the picture. _____
2. There aren't any stores in the picture. _____
3. There isn't a store on Center Street. _____
4. There are two supermarkets in the picture. _____
5. There's an outdoor market on River Street. _____
6. There aren't any hospitals in the picture. _____
7. There are some buildings on Elm Street. _____
8. There's a university on River Street. _____
9. There are a lot of cafés in the picture. _____

Unit 4 Test   T-307

UNIT 4   TEST

Name: _____   Date: _____

D Complete each conversation. Use the words in the box.

| a | are some | Is there | there are | there isn't |
| a lot of | Are there | It's | there is | there's |

1. **A:** _____ a university in this city?
   B: Yes, there is. It's a good school.

2. **A:** Are there mountains on the island?
   B: Yes, _____.

3. **A:** Is your neighborhood nice?
   B: Yes. There are _____ good restaurants near my apartment building. There are six restaurants on my street!

4. **A:** _____ any new stores in your neighborhood?
   B: Yes, there are.

5. **A:** There's _____ museum on Water Street.
   B: Yes, it's near the park.

6. **A:** Is there a desert in her country?
   B: No, _____.

7. **A:** There _____ interesting museums in this city.
   B: Yes, and one is in my neighborhood.

8. **A:** _____ a big outdoor market between the hospital and the park.
   B: Yes. It's near my office. It's very good.

9. **A:** Is there a waterfall in these mountains?
   B: Yes, _____.

10. **A:** Is there a beautiful waterfall in your country?
    B: Yes, there is. _____ in Niagara Falls.

T-308   Unit 4 Test

UNIT 4 TEST

Name: _____ Date: _____

E Read the postcard. Then answer the questions.

Dear Pei Ling,

I'm at my cousin's apartment in Chicago. The neighborhood is great. The people in the apartment building are nice. There's a big lake with a beach, and there are a lot of people there every day. The supermarket is small, but it's near the apartment. There are a lot of stores with beautiful things. And the restaurants are excellent! There's only one problem. Everything is very expensive!

See you soon,
Juan

Pei Ling Tran
2470 Joy Street
Sacramento, CA 94204

1. Is Pei Ling in Chicago?
   _____

2. Is Juan at Pei Ling's apartment?
   _____

3. Are there nice people in the apartment building?
   _____

4. Where are a lot of people every day?
   _____

5. Is there a supermarket near the apartment?
   _____

6. What are in a lot of stores?
   _____

7. How are the restaurants in Chicago?
   _____

8. Are there a lot of cheap things in Chicago?
   _____

Unit 4 Test   T-309

UNIT 5   TEST

Name: _____   Date: _____

A 🔊 8   Listen. Complete each sentence. Circle the letter of the correct answer.

1. Vegetables at Good Food Market are _____.
   a. cheap
   b. expensive
   c. delicious

2. Peppers at Shop-A-Lot are _____.
   a. 50 cents a pound
   b. expensive
   c. $2.21 a pound

3. _____ is cheap at Shop-A-Lot.
   a. Fruit
   b. Cheese
   c. Lettuce

4. There is _____ lettuce next to the spinach.
   a. a little
   b. some
   c. a lot of

5. There _____ potatoes in the recipe.
   a. aren't any
   b. are a few
   c. are a lot of

6. The potatoes are _____ a pound.
   a. $10.00
   b. $3.50
   c. $2.00 or $3.00

B 🔊 9   Listen to each conversation. For each sentence, write *T* for *True* or *F* for *False*.

Conversation 1:   1. There aren't any vegetables.   _____
Conversation 2:   2. The tea is in a box.   _____
Conversation 3:   3. There isn't any mayonnaise.   _____
Conversation 4:   4. There are a lot of cookies.   _____

C Write the words in the box in the correct columns.

| apples | beef | chicken | milk | onions |
| bananas | carrots | juice | mushrooms | oranges |

FRUIT	VEGETABLES	MEAT	DRINKS

Unit 5 Test

UNIT 5   TEST

Name: _____   Date: _____

D   Complete each sentence. Use the words in the box.

a	any	Is	much
any	Are	many	some

1. _____ there any mayonnaise at home?
2. How _____ bags of spinach are there?
3. There aren't _____ onions in the food.
4. There are _____ peppers in the soup.
5. There isn't _____ cheese at home.
6. _____ there eggs on the counter?
7. How _____ tea is there?
8. There's _____ bag of candy on the table.

E   Look at the pictures. Complete each sentence. Circle the correct answer.

1. There is **a few / a lot of** fruit.
2. There are **some / any** vegetables.
3. There are **a few / a little** carrots and tomatoes.
4. There are **a few / any** apples and bananas.
5. There is **some / a few** spinach.

Unit 5 Test   T-311

UNIT 5 TEST

Name: _____   Date: _____

F Read the paragraph. Then match the questions with the answers. Write the correct letters.

New to the U.S.
A NEWSLETTER FOR NEWCOMERS
Volume XXXIII

Cajun Food. One kind of American food is Cajun, and it's popular in the state of Louisiana. There are usually three parts to Cajun meals: meat or fish, a vegetable, and rice, bread, or another grain. In Cajun food, there are a lot of ingredients from the area. Onions, peppers, and celery are popular because there's a lot of flavor in these vegetables. Different kinds of peppers are also common ingredients, and sometimes Cajun food is spicy. Boudin (a kind of sausage), gumbo (a kind of soup), and jambalaya (a dish with rice and spices) are three typical Cajun dishes.

_____ 1. Where is Cajun food popular?   a. a vegetable
_____ 2. What is celery?   b. jambalaya
_____ 3. What is gumbo?   c. a kind of soup
_____ 4. What is a typical Cajun dish?   d. in Louisiana

G Read the paragraph again. For each sentence, write *T* for *True* or *F* for *False*.

1. There isn't any rice in Cajun food. _____
2. Onions are an ingredient in Cajun food. _____
3. There isn't a lot of flavor in onions, peppers, and celery. _____
4. Cajun food isn't spicy. _____
5. Boudin is one kind of Cajun food. _____

T-312 Unit 5 Test

UNIT 6   TEST

Name: _____   Date: _____

A 🎧 10 **Listen. Complete each sentence. Circle the letter of the correct answer.**

1. Mom is _____.
   a. watching TV   b. sitting   c. swimming

2. Dad is _____.
   a. at the park   b. playing tennis   c. sitting down with Uncle Dan

3. Joey is _____.
   a. going home   b. not at the park   c. playing soccer

4. Alan is _____.
   a. Jessica's brother b. practicing tennis c. not at home

5. Grandma is _____.
   a. at her apartment   b. with Joey and Alan c. talking to Elena and Jessica

B 🎧 10 **Listen again. For each sentence, write *T* for *True* or *F* for *False*.**

1. Elena is talking on the phone.   _____
2. Mom is with Aunt Karen.   _____
3. Uncle Dan is practicing soccer.   _____
4. Jessica is Elena's sister.   _____
5. Grandma is sitting outside.   _____

C Match the pictures with the words. Write the correct letter.

a.   b.   c.   d.

_____ 1. practicing tennis   _____ 3. sitting
_____ 2. taking a shower   _____ 4. going for a walk

D Complete the sentences. Circle the correct answers.

1. I'm doing exercises. I'm **running / watching a soccer game.**
2. She's going home. She's **walking / taking a shower.**
3. We're sitting down. We're **watching a tennis match / practicing tennis.**
4. He's in the water. He's **riding a bike / swimming.**

Unit 6 Test   T-313

UNIT 6 TEST

Name: _____   Date: _____

E Complete each conversation. Use the words in the box.

are	are you	Is	not going home	Where
are eating	he	'm going for a walk	She's	Who is

1. **A:** What _____ doing?
   B: Right now I'm reading.

2. **A:** _____ not watching TV.
   B: Really? What is she doing?

3. **A:** Is Matthew wearing jeans?
   B: No. _____ is wearing shorts.

4. **A:** Where are the women?
   B: They're in the kitchen. They _____.

5. **A:** I _____.
   B: Good idea. Where are you going?

6. **A:** Are Kim and Jessica going home now?
   B: No. They're _____. They're going to the park.

7. **A:** _____ your brother playing soccer?
   B: Yes, he is.

8. **A:** Why _____ we working today?
   B: Because it's Monday.

9. **A:** _____ are they going?
   B: To the shopping mall.

10. **A:** _____ she talking to?
    B: Her brother, Jerry.

UNIT 6 TEST

Name: _____ Date: _____

F Read the paragraph. Then look at the underlined words in each sentence. Circle the letter of the sentence that has a similar meaning.

> A HOCKEY GAME
>
> Twelve people are playing. There are six people on each team. The players on our team are wearing white jerseys and black pants. The other team is wearing red jerseys and blue pants. All the players are wearing skates on their feet and helmets on their heads. Every player is holding a stick. There is one puck.
>
> There are some good players on our team. Right now Justin Mahoney is hitting the puck with his stick. He's passing it to . . . Victor Petrov! Now Petrov is hitting the puck. The other team is trying to get the puck, too, but it's difficult for them.
>
> A lot of spectators are here tonight, and they're very noisy. They're standing and cheering for the players! This is a great game!

1. Our team is wearing white jerseys.
    a. They are wearing white shirts.
    b. They are wearing white shorts.

2. All the players are wearing skates on their feet.
    a. The players are wearing sneakers.
    b. The players aren't wearing sneakers.

3. Victor Petrov is hitting the puck.
    a. Petrov is wearing a puck.
    b. Petrov is playing with the puck.

4. There are a lot of spectators.
    a. Spectators are playing the game.
    b. Spectators are watching the game.

G Read the paragraph again. For each sentence, write *T* for *True* or *F* for *False*.

1. Two teams are playing. _____
2. Justin Mahoney is playing in the game. _____
3. The players are hitting people with their sticks. _____
4. The puck isn't moving. _____

Unit 6 Test

UNIT 7   TEST

Name: _____   Date: _____

A 🔊 **11** **Listen. Then read the sentences. Check (✓) the box if Dad says the sentence. Cross (X) the box if he doesn't.**

- ❏ 1. Go to a soccer game.
- ❏ 2. Come inside.
- ❏ 3. Don't wear track suits and sneakers.
- ❏ 4. Clean your rooms.
- ❏ 5. Eat dinner.

B 🔊 **12** **Listen. You will hear five sentences. Circle the letter of each sentence you hear.**

1. a. Please touch the food.
   b. Please don't touch the food.

2. a. Talk to them.
   b. Talk to him.

3. a. Ask for some tea.
   b. Ask her for some tea.

4. a. Put the things on the bed.
   b. Put the things under the bed.

5. a. Take the food to the party, please.
   b. Please take the food to the party.

C Complete each sentence. Circle the correct answer.

1. **Put / Turn off / Ask** the food on the table.
2. The soccer game is starting now. Please **put / turn on / take** the TV.
3. **Turn on / Finish / Put** your homework before you play.
4. Why is the wastebasket on the table? Please **touch / move / finish** it.
5. It's noisy. Please **take / put / turn off** the music.
6. **Put / Move / Take** some cookies to your grandmother's house.
7. The restaurant is hot. **Ask / Take / Start** the waiter for some cold water.
8. It isn't your food. Don't **touch / start / put** it, please.

T-316   Unit 7 Test

UNIT 7 TEST

Name: _____   Date: _____

D Look at the picture. Complete each sentence. Use the words in the box. (Be careful! There are two extra words.)

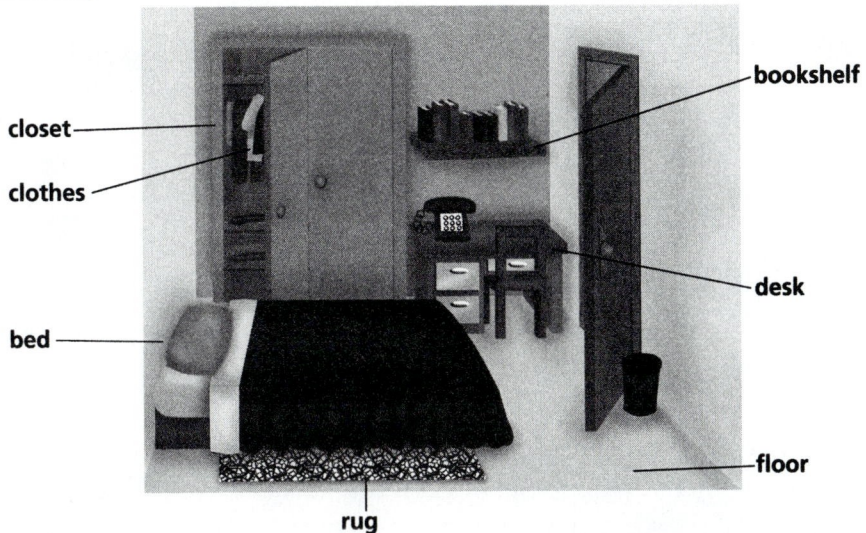

| above | behind | in | in front of | on | under |

1. The bookshelf is _____ the desk.
2. The bed is _____ the closet.
3. The clothes are _____ the closet.
4. The rug is _____ the floor.

E Complete each sentence. Circle the correct answer.

1. It's time for dinner. _____ the food on the table.
   a. Please put   b. Not put please   c. Don't put please

2. _____ your book now. Read it later.
   a. Not start   b. Start   c. Don't start

3. Their daughter is beautiful. Look at _____.
   a. him   b. she   c. her

4. There's a lot of food. _____ something.
   a. Eat please   b. Please eat   c. Please don't eat

5. Our neighbor is very friendly. Talk to _____.
   a. he   b. his   c. him

6. They're going to the restaurant with us. Wait for _____.
   a. them   b. they   c. their

Unit 7 Test   T-317

UNIT 7   TEST

Name: _____ Date: _____

F Read the instructions. Who are they for? Match the instructions with the pictures. Write the correct letters.

a.

b.

c.

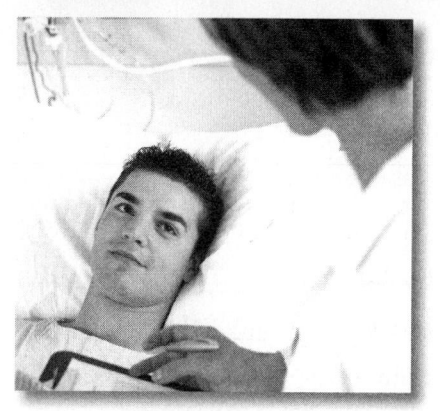

d.

_____ 1. Stay in bed and sleep a lot. Watch TV or read, but don't walk and don't do exercises. Take your medicine.

_____ 2. Start work at 8:00. Don't sit down, and wear comfortable shoes. Be nice to customers and smile. Tell customers about the food. Work hard.

_____ 3. There's school tomorrow, and it's late. Go to bed. Don't read or watch TV. Turn off the light and go to sleep.

_____ 4. There isn't any juice at home. Please buy some apple juice and orange juice. There are a lot of vegetables, so don't buy any tomatoes, carrots, or lettuce. Get some ice cream and some cookies.

G Read the instructions again. Who is saying them? Match the speakers with the instructions. Use the words in the box.

| a boss | a doctor | a husband | a parent |

1. Instruction #1: _____
2. Instruction #2: _____
3. Instruction #3: _____
4. Instruction #4: _____

T-318   Unit 7 Test

UNIT 8   TEST

Name: _____   Date: _____

A 🎵 **13** **Listen. For each sentence, write *T* for *True* or *F* for *False*.**

1. There aren't any pictures in Josh's apartment. _____
2. Josh has a TV in his apartment. _____
3. Josh has a digital camera. _____
4. Kim has a camera. _____
5. The cell phone isn't Josh's. _____

B 🎵 **14** **Listen. You will hear five sentences. Circle the letter of each sentence you hear.**

1. a. That's a small camera.   b. This is a small camera.
2. a. Those keys are mine.   b. These keys are mine.
3. a. Their DVDs are there.   b. The DVDs are theirs.
4. a. Are these CDs yours?   b. Are these your CDs?

C **Complete each sentence. Circle the letter of the correct answer.**

1. Shelly is talking to her friend. She's using her _____.
    a. credit card   b. cell phone

2. We have a _____ now, so we're watching a lot of movies.
    a. DVD player   b. CD player

3. Brian is listening to music. He has _____.
    a. CDs   b. a calendar

4. Tina is reading a book. She's using her _____.
    a. glasses   b. keys

5. Turn off the _____. It's noisy!
    a. alarm clock   b. camera

6. Denise is playing records on her _____.
    a. radio   b. record player

7. Noemi and Hector are doing homework on their _____.
    a. computers   b. contact lenses

8. That _____ is Matt's. His money is inside it.
    a. record   b. wallet

Unit 8 Test   T-319

UNIT 8 TEST

Name: _____   Date: _____

D Complete each conversation. Use the words in the box. (Be careful! There are three extra words.)

has	hers	that	those
have	mine	these	your
her	our	this	yours

(After class)

Janelle: Bye. See you later!

Heather: Wait. Are _____ your keys over there on the desk?
                          1.

Janelle: Oh, yes, they are. Thanks.

Heather: Sure. And is the red backpack _____, too?
                                            2.

Janelle: No, it's not _____. I _____ my backpack here. Maybe it's Sarah's.
                          3.   4.

Heather: No, Sarah _____ a blue backpack. Maybe it's Sandra's.
                       5.

Janelle: Who's Sandra?

Heather: She's the girl from Korea. She sits there in the front.

Janelle: Oh yeah. You're right. It's _____.
                                         6.

(At the store)

Ken: Wow. Look at the TV!

Sophia: Where? Oh . . . _____ TV here?
                            7.

Ken: No, I'm looking at _____ big TV over there in the store window, the silver TV.
                            8.

Sophia: Oh, yeah, it is really big. But we have a TV.

Ken: Yeah, but _____ TV is small.
                   9.

Sophia: It's *not* small. And we're *not* buying a new TV!

T-320   Unit 8 Test

UNIT 8 TEST

Name: _____   Date: _____

E Read the insurance form. Then complete the paragraph.

STANDARD HOME INSURANCE APPLICATION FORM

Property Description

Please include the serial number and value. If you are not sure, write "?".

Quantity	Description	Make	Model	Serial Number	Value
1	computer	Kell	520	2039481726	$1,000
1	computer	Trac	680	2983102933	$750
1	TV	Fishell	900X	8739283	$400
1	stereo	Nikel	?	?	$150

We have two computers in our home. My _____1._____ is a Kell 520, and my husband has a _____2._____ 680. The serial number of mine is _____3._____, and the serial number of his is 2983102933. Mine is worth $1,000, and his is worth _____4._____. We have a new _____5._____ 900X TV, serial number _____6._____. We have a _____7._____ stereo, but it's old. I don't have the _____8._____ or the serial number. It's worth about _____9._____.

Unit 8 Test   T-321

UNIT 9   TEST

Name: _____ Date: _____

A 🎧 15 **Listen to Raul and Ceci's conversation. Read each sentence. Write *R* if the sentence is about Raul. Write *C* if it is about Ceci.**

_____ 1. This person usually eats lunch in restaurants.

_____ 2. This person likes to eat out in restaurants, but doesn't have time.

_____ 3. This person usually eats lunch at work.

_____ 4. This person has a thirty-minute break for lunch.

_____ 5. This person has three breaks at work.

_____ 6. This person is not from Colombia.

_____ 7. This person likes the Colombian way.

_____ 8. This person works until 5:00.

B   Complete each sentence. Circle the letter of the correct answer.

1. I'm at my job in my office. I'm _____.
   a. reading a magazine   b. working

2. Every day she _____ because she starts work at 6:00 in the morning.
   a. has lunch   b. gets up early

3. The dentist says, "_____."
   a. Brush your teeth   b. Stay up late

4. The kitchen is messy. Please _____.
   a. take the bus   b. wash the dishes

5. I don't want to cook dinner, so we're _____.
   a. eating out   b. having lunch

6. Children usually _____ for about eight hours every night.
   a. sleep   b. get up

7. We're _____ because our clothes are dirty.
   a. doing the laundry   b. brushing our teeth

8. When Tricia takes a break at work, she often _____.
   a. stays up late   b. drinks coffee

9. Mark doesn't have a car. He _____ to work.
   a. eats out   b. takes the bus

T-322   Unit 9 Test

UNIT 9 TEST

Name: _____ Date: _____

C Look at the chart. Complete each sentence with the correct form of the word in parentheses. (Be careful! Some sentences are negative.)

	Nella	Preston	Ayako	Mohammed
go to school	7:45 A.M.	8:00 A.M.	7:00 P.M.	10:00 A.M.
come home from school	3:00 P.M.	11:00 A.M.	9:00 P.M.	2:00 P.M.
study	4:00–8:00 P.M.	8:00–9:00 P.M.	5:30–6:30 P.M.	7:00–9:00 A.M.
start work		11:30 A.M.	9:00 A.M.	5:00 P.M.
finish work		7:30 P.M.	5:00 P.M.	12:00 A.M.
watch tv	9:00–10:00 P.M.	9:30–10:00 P.M.	9:30–11:30 P.M.	12:30–1:00 A.M.

1. Nella and Preston _____ (go) to school in the morning.

2. Ayako _____ (come) home from school at 9:00 P.M.

3. Mohammed _____ (start) work at 5:00 A.M.

4. Preston _____ (study) from 8:00 to 9:00 P.M.

5. Ayako _____ (finish) work at 5:00 P.M.

6. Nella and Ayako _____ (watch) TV in the morning.

7. Ayako _____ (go) to school in the evening.

8. Mohammed _____ (watch) TV from 12:30 to 1:00 A.M.

9. Preston _____ (start) work in the morning.

10. Nella and Preston _____ (come) home from school at night.

Unit 9 Test T-323

UNIT 9   TEST

Name: _____ Date: _____

D Read about Jessica's activities. Then complete the paragraph.

Morning	Afternoon	Night
6:00 get up make breakfast 6:30 eat breakfast 6:45–7:45 help kids get ready for school take them to the bus stop 8:00–12:00 clean the house do laundry go to the supermarket	12:00–2:00 make dinner 2:00 get ready for work 2:30 go to work 3:00–11:00 work	11:30 get home from work talk with Dan go to bed

   I work in a restaurant. My hours are from 3:00 P.M. to _____ P.M. Monday
                                                              1.
to Friday. On weekdays I get up at _____. I make breakfast for my husband,
                                        2.
Dan, and our son and daughter. We _____ at 6:30, and then my husband goes
                                           3.
to work. I help the children get ready for school. Then I _____ and wait for the
                                                                   4.
bus to come. Then I go home and I clean the house. Sometimes I _____ or go to
                                                                         5.
the supermarket. Then I _____, but I don't eat it. I put it in the refrigerator. It's
                                6.
for my family to eat later. After that, I get ready for work. My mom comes to our house at 2:30, and
I _____. My kids get home from school at 3:30, and they stay with my mom.
       7.
My husband gets home from work around 6:00, and my mom leaves. My husband and kids eat the
dinner in the refrigerator. My kids do their homework, play or watch TV, and go to bed. I get home at
_____. My husband and I _____, and then we go to bed.
       8.   9.

T-324   Unit 9 Test

UNIT 10 TEST

Name: _____ Date: _____

A 🎧 16 Listen. For each sentence, write *Lisa* or *Ted*.

1. _____ has cash.
2. _____ wants to buy some sneakers.
3. _____ doesn't usually wear sneakers.
4. _____ doesn't have good sneakers.
5. _____ thinks the sneakers are expensive.
6. _____ always wants to spend a lot of money.

B 🎧 17 Listen to each conversation. For each question, circle the letter of the correct answer.

Conversation 1:   1. Does the man pay for something in cash?
        a. Yes, he does.   b. No, he doesn't.

Conversation 2:   2. Are things in the store on sale?
        a. Yes, they are.   b. No, they aren't.

Conversation 3:   3. How often does the woman buy things from catalogs?
        a. Always.   b. Never.

Conversation 4:   4. Where are the men going?
        a. To a convenience store.   b. To a department store.

C Read the sentences. For each sentence, write *T* for *True* or *F* for *False*.

1. There is food at a convenience store.   _____
2. If a watch is 25 percent off, it's on sale.   _____
3. You need a receipt to buy something at a store.   _____
4. Stores usually close in the morning and open at night.   _____
5. Department stores have clothes.   _____
6. When you sell something, you spend money on it.   _____
7. Some people pay for things at a store with cash.   _____
8. Things at department stores are never on sale.   _____

UNIT 10   TEST

Name: _____   Date: _____

D   Write sentences. Put the words in the correct order.

1. _____
   (things / pay / I / with / for / credit cards / usually)

2. _____
   (often / sale / are / things / on)

3. _____
   (prices / that / good / has / store / always)

E   Write questions. Put the words in the correct order.

1. _____
   (the / have / does / receipt / Thierry)

2. _____
   (they / sell / what / do)

3. _____
   (cash / you / have / do)

4. _____
   (you / of / want / what / do / kind / DVD player)

F   Read each question. Circle the letter of the correct answer.

1. Do you buy things at convenience stores?
   a. Yes, I do.
   b. Because it's convenient.
   c. No, I never buy things at supermarkets.

2. Do we need cash?
   a. Yes, I have cash.
   b. Because I don't have the receipt.
   c. No, we don't.

3. How often do they go to the mall?
   a. They hardly ever go.
   b. Yes, they do.
   c. They spend money at the mall.

UNIT 10   TEST

Name: _____   Date: _____

G Read the newsletter. Then answer the questions. Circle *Yes* or *No*.

New to the U.S.
A NEWSLETTER FOR NEWCOMERS

Do you want to sell things you make? Do you have things you don't use or want? Do you want to have some extra money? Start to sell your things! Try an online auction!

In an online auction, sellers use a Web site to show pictures of things they want to sell. Shoppers look at the Web site and offer money for the things they want.

What's for sale at online auctions? Almost anything! People sell houses, cars, trips, furniture, clothing, and more on auction Web sites. They're a good way for shoppers to find things they want, and many times shoppers pay low prices. Prices are usually great!

Online auctions are open twenty-four hours a day, seven days a week. You only need a computer, and it's possible to shop anywhere, anytime. Most sellers take credit cards. Some take checks, but they usually don't take cash. When a seller accepts a buyer's offer, the buyer sends a payment. Then the seller sends the product.

1. Do people sell things in online auctions?   Yes   No
2. Do people buy things in online auctions?   Yes   No
3. Do people sell clothing in online auctions?   Yes   No
4. Are things at online auctions usually expensive?   Yes   No
5. Does a person go to a store to buy something from an online auction?   Yes   No
6. Are online auctions open when stores are closed?   Yes   No
7. Do people usually pay for things with cash at online auctions?   Yes   No

H Read the newsletter again. Then answer each question. Circle the letter of the correct answer.

1. Do shoppers buy things or sell things?
   a. They buy things.   b. They sell things.

2. What do you need to shop in an online auction?
   a. a computer   b. cash

3. How does a buyer get a product in online auctions?
   a. The buyer goes to the store.   b. The seller sends it.

Unit 10 Test   T-327

UNIT 11   TEST

Name: _____   Date: _____

A 🎧 18 Listen. Match the beginnings and endings of the sentences. Write the correct letters.

____ 1. Mia misses   a. a party on the weekend.
____ 2. Mia's friends send her   b. a birthday cake.
____ 3. Mia always has   c. flowers on her birthday.
____ 4. Mia's grandmother and aunts make   d. the food for the party.
____ 5. Mia's mother makes   e. birthday cards.
____ 6. Mia usually gets   f. a celebration with her friends.
____ 7. Mia doesn't get   g. a lot of gifts.
____ 8. This year Mia wants to have   h. her family and friends.

B Complete each sentence. Check (✓) the correct columns.

	a woman	a man	a man or a woman
1. A bride is _____.			
2. A guest is _____.			
3. A hostess is _____.			
4. A relative is _____.			
5. A groom is _____.			

C Read the conversation. Then complete each sentence. Circle the letter of the correct answer.

Aunt Tasha: You're a beautiful bride! Here—this is for you. Open it later.

Kristen: Thank you! I'm happy you're here, Aunt Tasha.

1. The women are at a _____.
   a. wedding   b. birthday party   c. dance

2. Kristen is Tasha's _____.
   a. hostess   b. relative   c. bride

3. Kristen is _____.
   a. having a party for Tasha   b. giving Tasha a gift   c. thanking Tasha

4. Tasha is _____.
   a. the groom   b. a guest   c. the host

T-328   Unit 11 Test

UNIT 11 TEST

Name: _____ Date: _____

D Complete each sentence. Put the words in the correct order.

1. People often _____ on their birthdays.
   (gifts / to / children / give)

2. In our family, we _____ for holidays and birthdays.
   (send / cards / relatives)

3. My father always _____ on Mother's Day.
   (my / gets / a / mom / present / for)

4. My grandmother _____ when I visit her.
   (me / cake / makes / a)

E Complete each question. Put the words in the correct order.

1. _____ the new year in your country?
   (they / celebrate / do / when)

2. _____ at a birthday party?
   (says / who / "Happy birthday")

3. _____ parties—at their house or at a restaurant?
   (do / have / they / where)

4. _____ to parties?
   (people / do / invite / who)

5. _____ at weddings?
   (presents / people / why / give / do)

6. _____ in your office?
   (flowers / gets / who)

UNIT 11   TEST

Name: _____   Date: _____

F   Read the newsletter. For each sentence, write *T* for *True* or *F* for *False*.

New to the U.S.
A NEWSLETTER FOR NEWCOMERS
Volume XXXIII

Labor Day

Labor Day is a big holiday in the United States. Labor Day is always the first Monday of September. Many workers relax and take a break from work that day. Many offices are closed. For some people, Labor Day is the end of summer. Students usually start school the day after Labor Day. A lot of people like to go to the beach or a park and be outside. Many people cook food outside. They eat food like hot dogs and hamburgers. It's a day for many families and friends to be together. People don't send cards or give presents for Labor Day.

1. People don't celebrate Labor Day in the United States.   _____
2. Labor Day is always in September in the United States.   _____
3. Labor Day is never on a Sunday in the United States.   _____
4. Summer starts on Labor Day in the United States.   _____
5. Many people work on Labor Day.   _____
6. Students usually go to school on Labor Day.   _____
7. A lot of people are outside on Labor Day.   _____
8. Friends don't visit on Labor Day.   _____
9. People don't receive cards or gifts for Labor Day.   _____

UNIT 12   TEST

Name: _____   Date: _____

A 🔊 **19** **Listen. Then complete each sentence. Circle the correct answer.**

1. Today Iris is working **in the morning / in the afternoon / at night**.
2. **Mr. Ho / Danielle / Iris's day care worker** isn't working today.
3. **Danielle / Iris's husband / Iris** has a new job.
4. **The day care worker / Danielle / Iris's husband** works on Saturdays.
5. **Mr. Ho / A day care worker / Danielle** takes care of Iris's children when she and her husband are at work.
6. Iris wants to work **on Saturdays / thirty hours a week / on Sundays**.
7. Iris's husband doesn't work on **Sundays / weekends / Mondays**.
8. Iris needs **a new job / to make money / a vacation**.
9. Mr. Ho is Iris's **boss / co-worker / day care worker**.

B **Complete each sentence. Use the words in the box.**

be off   have experience   make an appointment   make money   take care of

1. I need to see the dentist. I'm calling his office to _____.
2. I'm looking for a job because I need to _____.
3. I like to _____ children. I want to be a day care worker.
4. I like to _____ on Saturdays. I don't want to work that day.
5. I help my aunt with my young cousins every day. I _____ with children.

C **Match the beginnings with the endings of the sentences. Write the correct letters.**

_____ 1. A real estate agent is   a. money you get for work.
_____ 2. A day care worker is   b. a person you work with.
_____ 3. A paycheck is   c. a person who helps you buy a house or an apartment.
_____ 4. A co-worker is   d. a person who takes care of children.

UNIT 12   TEST

Name: _____   Date: _____

D Complete the phone conversation. Write the correct forms of the words in parentheses. Use the simple present and the present progressive.

Kelly: Hello?

Stan: Hey, it's Stan. What _____ right now?
　　　　　　　　　　　　　　　　1. (you / do)

Kelly: I _____. Why?
　　　　　　　2. (work)

Stan: Do you want _____ lunch with me?
　　　　　　　　　　　　　　3. (have)

Kelly: I'm not sure. Where _____?
　　　　　　　　　　　　　　　　　4. (go)

Stan: Charlie's. It's a new restaurant near my office. Some of my co-workers _____ there
　　　5. (eat)
every day, and they _____ it a lot.
　　　　　　　　　　　　6. (like)

Kelly: I don't know. I need _____ something important for my boss.
　　　　　　　　　　　　　　　　　　7. (finish)

Stan: You always say that! You _____ a break!
　　　　　　　　　　　　　　　　　　　　8. (need)

Kelly: Wait a second. My phone _____ . . . Oh no. It's my boss. I'm sure she's looking for
　　　　　　　　　　　　　　　　　　　　　　　9. (ring)
that report. . . .

Stan: That's OK. I _____. You're busy. Maybe next time.
　　　　　　　　　　　　　10. (understand)

Kelly: Yeah. Call me later.

Stan: OK. Bye.

UNIT 12 TEST

Name: _____   Date: _____

E Read the paragraph and the form. Complete each sentence. Circle the correct answer.

My name is Wei Zhang. I live in San Francisco. I come from Beijing, China. My first language is Chinese. I also speak Japanese, and I'm studying English now.

In China I was an engineer at Omni Group in Beijing for three years. I have a bachelor's degree in engineering from Tsinghua University in Beijing. Right now I'm working full-time as a cook at a restaurant downtown called The Keystone.

Right now I'm not looking for a job. I want to be a student again! I'm hardworking, and I like to learn. I want to get a master's degree in engineering.

PERSONAL INFORMATION

Today's Date: _8/25/07_   Name: _Wei Zhang_

List any languages that you speak: _Chinese, Japanese, English_

Educational Background

Check (✓) all that apply. Write the institution's name and location, as well as your major field of study.

	Name and location of institution	Major
✓ Graduated from high school	International School of Beijing, Beijing	–
❑ Associate's Degree	–	–
✓ Bachelor's Degree	Tsinghua University, Beijing	engineering
❑ Master's Degree (or higher)	–	–
❑ Other? Please explain.	–	–

Work Experience

Employer	Job title or position	Date employed
Omni Group	engineer	Jan. 2003–Jan. 2006
The Keystone	cook	Sept. 1, 2006–present

Future Plans

What are your educational and career goals?
I want to get a master's degree in engineering.

---

1. Chinese, Japanese, and English are **places / languages**.
2. Wei **doesn't have any / has some** experience as an engineer.
3. Wei's university is in **Japan / Beijing**.
4. Wei has **a master's degree / a job**.
5. Wei's job title now is **student / cook**.
6. Wei's employer now is **The Keystone / Tsinghua University**.
7. Wei likes to **learn / cook**.
8. Wei's goal is to **get a master's degree / get a full-time job**.

UNIT 13   TEST

Name: _____   Date: _____

A 🎧 20 Listen. Complete each sentence. Use the words in the box.

| cheap | great | nice | warm |
| crowded | near | slow | wonderful |

1. The people in Cancun were _____.
2. The weather was _____.
3. The apartment is _____ the beach.
4. The water was _____.
5. The beaches were _____.
6. The service at the restaurant was _____.
7. The airline tickets were _____.
8. Yoko's vacation was _____.

B Match the beginnings with the endings of the sentences. Write the correct letters.

____ 1. There are a lot of people here. It's really   a. wonderful.
____ 2. It's not quiet here. This place is   b. worried.
____ 3. This is very bad. It's   c. terrible.
____ 4. The table isn't dirty. It's   d. slow.
____ 5. I'm so happy. I'm   e. crowded.
____ 6. She's thinking about a problem, and she's   f. noisy.
____ 7. This is so good! It's   g. clean.
____ 8. This car isn't fast. It's   h. in a good mood.

T-334   Unit 13 Test

UNIT 13   TEST

Name: _____   Date: _____

C Complete each sentence. Use *was*, *were*, *wasn't*, or *weren't*.

1. Yesterday was a very bad day for me. I _____ in a good mood.

2. There was a party last night, but Zach and Kristi _____ there. Zach was at work, and Kristi was sick.

3. The service at the restaurant _____ excellent. The waiter was nice, and he was very helpful.

4. There _____ a lot of people at the new museum every day last week. It was very crowded.

D Complete each question. Put the words in the correct order.

1. **A:** You're late. _____?
      (you / where / were)
   B: At work. There was a big meeting this afternoon.

2. **A:** _____?
      (the / was / movie / how)
   B: Really great. You need to see it.

3. **A:** _____ at the party?
      (food / was / there / good)
   B: Yes. Everything was delicious.

4. **A:** _____ at the shopping mall on Saturday?
      (people / lot / were / of / there / a)
   B: Yes. It's always crowded on the weekends.

5. **A:** _____?
      (why / sale / things / were / on)
   B: Because the store manager wants to sell everything fast.

6. **A:** _____?
      (wedding / night / was / at / their)
   B: Yes. It started at 8:00.

Unit 13 Test   T-335

UNIT 13 TEST

Name: _____ Date: _____

E Read the letter. Then answer each question. Circle the letter of the correct answer.

> Richard Starr, Manager
> Candy Foot Shoes
> 218 K Street, NW
> Washington, DC 20006
>
> 410 9th Street, NE
> Washington, DC 20002
>
> September 20, 2007
>
> Dear Mr. Starr:
>
> Last week there was a sign for a sale on Wednesday, September 19, at your Candy Foot store in Georgetown. The sign said women's Comfort Step shoes were on sale for $40.
>
> I was at your store on Wednesday morning. There were a lot of shoes, but there weren't any Comfort Steps. Some shoes were on sale, but there weren't any for $40.
>
> Was your sign wrong? Why weren't there any Comfort Step shoes for $40? I would like to buy a pair of Comfort Steps for the price on the sign. Please e-mail me at gingergreen@hartagency.com. Thank you.
>
> Sincerely,
> *Ginger Green*
> Ginger Green

1. Who is the letter from?
   - a. Richard Starr
   - b. Ginger Green
   - c. Comfort Step

2. Who is Richard Starr?
   - a. a store manager
   - b. an unhappy customer
   - c. a salesperson

3. How does Ms. Green feel?
   - a. angry
   - b. worried
   - c. patient

4. Where was the sign?
   - a. at the store
   - b. in the newspaper
   - c. at the Hart Agency

5. When was Ms. Green at the store?
   - a. this morning
   - b. Wednesday
   - c. September 20

6. What was at the store?
   - a. shoes for $40
   - b. shoes on sale
   - c. Comfort Steps

7. What was the problem?
   - a. There weren't a lot of shoes.
   - b. The shoes were the wrong size.
   - c. There weren't any Comfort Steps.

8. What does Ms. Green want?
   - a. $40
   - b. a new sign
   - c. Comfort Step shoes for $40

UNIT 14   TEST

Name: _____   Date: _____

A 🎧 **21** Listen. Then answer each question. Circle the letter of the correct answer.

1. _____ is telling a strange but true story.
   a. Kerri   b. Russ

2. A zoo worker lost _____.
   a. a key   b. an ostrich

3. The story about the ostrich was _____.
   a. in the paper   b. on the news

4. The park is _____ the zoo.
   a. across from   b. next to

5. A lot of people _____ when they saw the ostrich.
   a. screamed   b. ran

6. _____ chased the ostrich.
   a. Some kids   b. The zoo workers

7. The ostrich ran into _____.
   a. a supermarket   b. the street

8. Now the ostrich is _____.
   a. with the police b. at the zoo

B Complete each sentence. Circle the correct answer.

1. Ada always **forgets** / **catches** her mother's birthday.
2. My dog often **gets out of** / **loses** the yard and runs to the neighbor's house.
3. What's that noise? What's **happening** / **catching** out there?
4. The bird is flying away! Quick, **leave** / **catch** him!
5. Don't forget to **lose** / **take back** that book to the library.
6. People usually **scream** / **chase** when they see a gorilla on the street.
7. The police **are leaving** / **are chasing** a burglar.
8. She's very unhappy. She needs to **change jobs** / **take back jobs**.
9. Martin sometimes **gets out** / **loses** his wallet, and then he buys a new one.
10. Don't **leave** / **change** your cell phone in the taxi cab!

UNIT 14 TEST

Name: _____ Date: _____

C Complete each conversation. Use the simple past forms of the words in parentheses.

A: Hey, how was your weekend? You went to a wedding, right?

B: Yeah. It was nice, thanks. And it was big! The bride and groom _____ 400 people!
   1. (invite)

A: Wow, that *is* big.

B: And the celebration was great. Everyone _____ until late at night. We _____ to leave!
   2. (dance)   3. (not want)

C: Hi, how are you?

D: Well, I'm not having a very good day. It _____ this morning, when I got up late. I _____ time to exercise.
   4. (start)   5. (not have)

C: Oh, sorry to hear it.

D: Thanks. And I usually have coffee in the morning, but there wasn't any coffee in the house. So I _____ tea. And I _____ a taxi to work because I missed the bus.
   6. (drink)   7. (take)

E: How was dinner at the new restaurant last night?

F: It was great. But James _____. He _____ he had a lot of work to do.
   8. (not go)   9. (say)

E: Yeah, I think he _____ dinner at his office.
   10. (eat)

UNIT 14 TEST

Name: _____   Date: _____

D Read the police report. For each sentence, write *T* for *True* or *F* for *False*.

PLEASANT VALLEY POLICE
Stolen Property Report

Date of incident: July 2, 2007
Witness's name(s): Cindy and Javier Garcia
Witness's address: 2012 Bell Road, Pleasant Valley, IA
Witness's phone number: 563-555-4092

Description of suspect: Include hair color, eye color, race, weight, height, clothing, etc.
black pants and a black shirt.

Description of incident:
On July 2, 2007 at 2:30 in the afternoon, my neighbors Cindy and Javier Garcia heard a noise in my house. I wasn't at home, so they called the police. Then they watched the door of my house. A woman came out. She was white and had red hair. She was short, about five feet tall, and thin. She had on black pants and a black shirt. She drove away in a white car. She took my computer, my DVD player, and a big bag. When I got home at 3:30, Cindy and Javier went with me into my house. The door was broken, and my house was very messy. The burglar took my new Ledd 660 computer, my Troy DVD player, and a gold watch.

Stolen items: What did the suspect take? If you don't know, write "?"

Description	Make	Model	Serial #	Value
computer	Ledd	660	100998323	$750
DVD	Troy	?	283949494	$250
gold watch	?	?	?	$200

---

1. Someone took things from Cindy and Javier Garcia.   _____
2. Cindy and Javier Garcia called the police.   _____
3. The suspect was a woman.   _____
4. The suspect had on red and white clothes.   _____
5. Cindy and Javier Garcia saw the burglar.   _____
6. Cindy and Javier Garcia took the computer.   _____
7. The burglar was in the house when the other people went in.   _____
8. The house was neat when the people went in.   _____
9. The value of the DVD player is $250.   _____
10. Cindy and Javier Garcia wrote the police report.   _____

Unit 14 Test   T-339

UNIT 15   TEST

Name: _____   Date: _____

A 🎧 22 Listen to the conversation. Then check (✓) the things each person did.

	had a baby	became a citizen	got a new house or apartment	got a new job	graduated
Cara					
Sa'id					

B 🎧 22 Listen to the conversation again. Then complete each sentence. Use the words in the box. (Be careful! There are two extra phrases.)

| four months ago | six months ago | ten months ago |
| four years ago | six years ago | ten years ago |

1. Sa'id came to the United States _____.
2. Sa'id left his job at the hotel _____.
3. Cara got married _____.
4. Cara met Henry _____.

C Match the sentences with the sentences that have a similar meaning. Write the correct letters.

_____ 1. They graduated.   a. They talked for the first time.
_____ 2. They got married.   b. They had a wedding.
_____ 3. They retired.   c. They learned to drive.
_____ 4. They met.   d. They became parents.
_____ 5. They got jobs.   e. They hit something with the car.
_____ 6. They had a baby.   f. They stopped working when they got older.
_____ 7. They got driver's licenses. g. They finished school.
_____ 8. They had an accident.   h. They started to work.

UNIT 15 TEST

Name: _____ Date: _____

D Read the answers. Write *Yes / No* questions. Use *Was / Were* or *Did*.

1. _____
   Yes, I did. I graduated in 1995.

2. _____
   Yes, she was. My daughter was in the military for five years.

3. _____
   No, they didn't go to the mall. They went to the movies.

E Read the answers. Write questions about the underlined words. Use *What, Where, When, Who, Why, How much,* or *How old*.

1. _____
   Greg changed jobs <u>because he didn't like the long hours</u>.

2. _____
   Lulu and Anthony had their first baby <u>in 2006</u>.

3. _____
   We got married <u>in the Bahamas</u>.

4. _____
   They were <u>25</u>.

F Read the answers. Write questions about the underlined words. Use *How long* or *How long ago*?

1. _____
   He got his driver's license <u>two years ago</u>.

2. _____
   Nancy and Brett stayed at the party <u>for a few hours</u>.

3. _____
   My brother moved to Houston <u>seven months ago</u>.

Unit 15 Test   T-341

UNIT 15 TEST

Name: _____   Date: _____

G Read the story. Then complete each sentence. Circle the letter of the correct answer.

> My name is Victoria McKenna. My grandfather, Victor McKenna, was born on July 15, 1920 in the city of Philadelphia. He had one sister named Margaret. When he was young, Victor was tall and good-looking. He was very nice. He liked to talk to people. He was very friendly and curious.
>
> One night in the winter of 1942, he went to a party with Margaret and some friends. He talked to a lot of people. Then he saw a beautiful woman. He was usually very talkative, but with this woman, my grandfather was shy. He finally asked her to dance. They started to talk, and he learned her name was Bette. A week later, she became his girlfriend, and a month later, they got married. It was the beginning of a long love story.
>
> My grandparents had four children and eight grandchildren. In 2002, after sixty years of marriage, my grandmother died. She was 82 years old. Today my grandfather still likes to talk, but he misses my grandmother.

1. This story is about _____.
   a. Victor
   b. Victoria
   c. Bette

2. Victor's _____ is Victoria.
   a. wife
   b. child
   c. grandchild

3. Victor usually liked to _____ a lot.
   a. dance
   b. learn
   c. talk

4. Victor met Bette _____.
   a. at a dance
   b. at his friend's house
   c. at a party

5. Victor was usually _____.
   a. shy
   b. friendly
   c. a good dancer

6. Victor met Bette _____.
   a. in 1920
   b. in 1942
   c. in 2002

7. Victor and Bette were married _____.
   a. sixty years ago
   b. for sixty years
   c. in 1960

8. Victor misses _____.
   a. Bette
   b. Margaret
   c. Victoria

9. This story is about _____.
   a. friendship
   b. love
   c. neighbors

T-342   Unit 15 Test

UNIT 16   TEST

Name: _____   Date: _____

A **Listen. Then complete each sentence. Circle the correct answer.**

1. Min-hee is going to **get married / go to a wedding**.
2. Min-hee's **mother / brother** is going to drive.
3. Min-hee's **mother / brother** has a car.
4. Min-hee is going to pick up Penny on **Friday / Saturday**.
5. Penny is going to do her homework on **Friday / Sunday**.
6. The girls are going to be home on Sunday **morning / afternoon**.
7. **Min-hee / Min-hee's cousin** lives in New Hope.
8. They are going to stay **in a hotel / at Jin's house**.
9. Penny **is / isn't** going to get a new dress for the wedding.
10. Penny's dad **is / isn't** going to go to the wedding.

B **Complete each sentence. Use the words in the box.**

| buy groceries | have people over | pick up someone | take someone somewhere |
| go on a picnic | leave the house | stay at home | tonight |

1. I want to _____. I'm going to go to the park and eat outside.
2. I'm going to go out _____. I'm going to do something at 9:00 P.M.
3. I need to _____. I'm going to go to the store and get some fruit and vegetables.
4. I'm at home, but I want to go somewhere. I'm going to _____.
5. I'm going to _____. Beth and I are leaving work at 5:00. She's going with me to the mall in my car.
6. I'm going to _____. I'm going to Erin's house to get her.
7. I want to _____. I'm going to invite some friends to my house.
8. I'm in my house, and I'm happy. I'm going to _____.

Unit 16 Test   T-343

UNIT 16 TEST

Name: _____ Date: _____

C Find the mistake in each conversation. Circle the letter and correct the mistake.

1. **A:** It's not going to rain tomorrow.
        A   B

   B: No, it's going be sunny and warm.   Correct: _____
                   C

2. **A:** You are going to meet us at the restaurant?
           A   B

   B: No, I'm going to have dinner with my family.   Correct: _____
                  C

3. **A:** How long are you play cards?
           A   B

   B: A long time. We're going to play all night.   Correct: _____
                        C

4. **A:** Are they going to go on a picnic?
           A

   B: Yes, they're. They're going to leave soon.   Correct: _____
              B   C

5. **A:** When is your daughter going graduate?
              A   B

   B: June 8th. We're going to have a party that day.   Correct: _____
                          C

6. **A:** Her parents are going to be 68 in August.
                     A   B

   B: Yes, but they're no going to retire.   Correct: _____
                          C

7. **A:** What are the children going to do after dinner?
                                    A

   B: They're going to finishing their homework.   Correct: _____
                    B   C

8. **A:** What you are going to do tonight?
           A   B

   B: I'm going to go to the movies.   Correct: _____
              C

9. **A:** The weather is nice right now.
                    A

   B: It is going to be nice tomorrow, too?   Correct: _____
           B   C

10. **A:** Is Mom going to go to the grocery store?
            A

    B: Yes, but she isn't go to buy any cookies.   Correct: _____
                   B   C

T-344 Unit 16 Test

UNIT 16   TEST

Name: _____   Date: _____

D Read the weekend calendar. Answer the questions.

COMMUNITY CALENDAR: FRIDAY, JULY 6–SUNDAY, JULY 8

Friday, July 6	Saturday, July 7	Sunday, July 8
Meet children's book writer Sid Garvey and hear a story Ages 3–5 12:00 noon, Public Library	Outdoor Market First Ave. and Branch St. Starts at 7:00 A.M. Buy fresh fruit and vegetables!	5K Run / Walk to Support General Hospital Starts at 1200 Oak Street 8:00 A.M. $25
Flower Scouts Annual Picnic 5:00 P.M.–7:00 P.M. Grove Park, Shelter 1 $3 for dinner Free ice cream	Community Soccer Championship Game 10:00 A.M. Free Admission Soda and Water $1	Tennis Lessons Open to children and adults Kennedy Courts $10 per person Wear sneakers
Grupo Uno Concert of Traditional Music from Bolivia 7:30 P.M. Lobby of the Grand Hotel $5 per person	Concert in the Park River City Orchestra at Palmer Park Classical Music 7:00 P.M.–9:00 P.M. Free	Movie in the Park Outdoors at Koor's Park 9:00 P.M. *Burglars!* Children ages 12 and up Free

1. What time is the outdoor market going to start?
   _____

2. What is going to happen at 8:00 on Sunday morning?
   _____

3. Which place is going to have good activities for 4-year-old children?
   _____

4. Which activity is going to have ice cream?
   _____

5. What is going to start at 10:00 on Saturday morning?
   _____

6. Is the concert in the park going to be free?
   _____

7. How much is it going to cost to take a tennis lesson?
   _____

8. When is the Flower Scouts Annual Picnic going to finish?
   _____

9. Patsy loves music. What is she going to do on Friday?
   _____

10. Is the movie in the park going to finish at 9:00 P.M.?
    _____

Unit 16 Test   T-345

UNIT 17   TEST

Name: _____   Date: _____

A 🎧 **24** Listen to Rita's conversation with her mom. Then read each sentence. Check (✓) the box if Rita's mom agrees with the statement. Cross (X) the box if she doesn't.

1. The baby shouldn't eat meat. ❏
2. The baby likes chicken. ❏
3. Rita and her mom should watch TV. ❏
4. TV isn't good for babies. ❏
5. Rita should call the doctor. ❏
6. Rita and her brother are fine. ❏
7. Rita shouldn't worry. ❏
8. Rita should drink some tea. ❏

B Answer each question. Circle the letter of the correct answer.

1. What do you get from a doctor?
   a. a temperature
   b. a prescription
2. What do you do when you have a small cut?
   a. have the flu
   b. put on a Band-Aid
3. When do people usually see a doctor?
   a. when they have health problems
   b. when they don't have allergies
4. Who gives people medicine?
   a. a prescription
   b. a pharmacist

C Read the sentences. For each sentence, write *T* for *True* or *F* for *False*.

1. When you have a stomachache, your stomach doesn't hurt. _____
2. When people have allergies, they sometimes sneeze. _____
3. When someone gets a cut, they usually have a cough. _____
4. When you have a backache, you have a pain in your back. _____

Unit 17 Test

Audioscript for Exercise A:

Rita: Hi, Mom, I'm home. Where are you?
Mom: I'm out here with the baby.
Rita: What are you doing? Mom, thanks for your help, but the baby shouldn't eat meat!
Mom: Why?
Rita: She's only 2 months old!
Mom: So? It's chicken—it's good for her. And she likes it! She should eat meat if she likes it. I have experience with babies, you know.
Rita: I know you have experience, Mom. I'm just worried about the baby's health.
Mom: I know, I know. . . . So, it's still early. We should watch TV for a little while. What do you say?
Rita: Watch TV? With the baby? I don't think we should do that.
Mom: Why not?
Rita: Well, we never watch TV with her. TV isn't good for babies. It's noisy.
Mom: That's crazy! Maybe when children are older it's not good for them, but she's just a baby!
Rita: Really? I don't agree. Maybe I should call the doctor and ask. . . .
Mom: No, you shouldn't! You should listen to me! I took care of you and your brother, and you're both fine. You really shouldn't worry so much.
Rita: Well, you *did* do a good job with Mike and me. Do you really think I should stop worrying?
Mom: Yes! Now, go sit down in the living room, and let's watch something good. I'm going to make you some tea, and you're going to drink it and relax.

Unit 18

A

Pompton Park apartment: check (✓) lines 1–4;
Orange Street apartment: check (✓) lines 5–6;
New Street apartment: check (✓) lines 7–10

B

1. convenient
2. close to
3. modern
4. dangerous
5. public transportation
6. pretty
7. in the country
8. low rent
9. far from

C

1. the cheapest
2. more modern than
3. noisier than
4. older than
5. the most convenient
6. higher than
7. The smallest
8. The most expensive
9. worse than
10. the best

D

1. T
2. F
3. F
4. F
5. T
6. T
7. T
8. T

Audioscript for Exercise A:

Doug: Hello, H & H Realty. This is Doug.
Luz: Hi. My name is Luz Ramirez. I saw your ad in Sunday's paper. I'm looking for a one-bedroom apartment close to public transportation.
Doug: Hmmm. . . . Let me see. OK, I have three apartments near public transportation. The biggest apartment is out in Pompton Park. The rent for that apartment is only $750 a month, but it's the farthest from downtown.
Luz: Oh, Pompton Park *is* far. How about the other apartments? Are they closer than that?
Doug: Yes, they are, but the Pompton Park apartment is the nicest.
Luz: But I don't want to be so far away from the city. Which apartment is the closest apartment to downtown?
Doug: Let's see. . . . The apartment with the best location is on Orange Street. It's next to the Bentley Hotel.
Luz: Wow, that's a *great* location. How much is it?
Doug: It's $900 a month.
Luz: Hmmm. OK. And how about the last apartment?
Doug: Well, that's on New Street. So it's also in a better location than the Pompton Park apartment. And it's more modern and prettier. It's in the newest building of the three.
Luz: How much is it?
Doug: It's $1,000 a month—oh, but wait a minute. That's with utilities, so really it's cheaper than the Orange Street apartment.
Luz: And that's on New Street?
Doug: Yes, next to the big movie theater.
Luz: That sounds perfect. When can I see it?
Doug: Well, first you need to come to the office and fill out a rental application form. . . .

Unit 19

A

1. Yes
2. No
3. Yes
4. Yes
5. No
6. Yes
7. Yes
8. Yes
9. No

B

1. S
2. S
3. D
4. D
5. S
6. D
7. S

C

1. I'll be / I will be
2. I'll look / I will look
3. Will you live
4. I'll look for / I will look for
5. it won't be / it will not be
6. where will you find
7. How much will your rent be
8. Will she buy
9. she won't / she will not
10. We won't need / We will not need
11. What will you do
12. I'll come / I will come
13. you'll go / you will go

Sa'id: Wow! You got married! You waited a long time! How long ago did you meet him?
Cara: Umm... six years ago.
Sa'id: Wow.
Cara: Yeah. I wanted to do a lot of things before I got married.
Sa'id: Really? Like what?
Cara: Well, I went to college, and now I'm an accountant. After I graduated I got a job at Phillips-Bueller. I started there about 5 months ago.
Sa'id: Cool. And do you and Henry live in your old apartment?
Cara: No, we bought an apartment downtown. You know, you and Kate and the baby need to come visit....

Unit 16

A
1. go to a wedding
2. brother
3. mother
4. Saturday
5. Sunday
6. afternoon
7. Min-hee's cousin
8. at Jin's house
9. isn't
10. isn't

B
1. go on a picnic
2. tonight
3. buy groceries
4. leave the house
5. take someone somewhere
6. pick up someone
7. have people over
8. stay at home

C
1. C, going to be
2. A, Are you
3. B, you going to play
4. B, they are
5. B, going to graduate
6. C, not going
7. C, finish
8. A, What are you
9. B, Is it
10. C, going to buy

D
1. The outdoor market is going to start at 7:00 A.M.
2. The 5K Run/Walk (to Support General Hospital) is going to happen at 8:00 on Sunday morning.
3. The public library is going to have good activities for 4-year-old children.
4. The Flower Scouts Annual Picnic is going to have ice cream.
5. The Community Soccer Championship Game is going to start at 10:00 on Saturday morning.
6. Yes, it is. OR Yes, the concert in the park is going to be free.
7. It is going to cost $10 to take a tennis lesson.
8. The Flower Scouts Annual Picnic is going to finish at 7:00 P.M.
9. She is going to go to the Grupo Uno Concert (of Traditional Music from Bolivia) / to the lobby of the Grand Hotel.
10. No, it isn't. OR No, the movie in the park isn't going to finish at 9:00 P.M.

Audioscript for Exercise A:

Penny: Dad, Min-hee invited me to go with her to a wedding in New Hope this weekend. Can I go?
Dad: New Hope? That's pretty far away. How are you going to get there?
Penny: Min-hee's brother is going to drive.
Dad: Min-hee's brother? Does he have his driver's license?
Penny: Of course! He got it two years ago.
Dad: Does he have a car? Whose car is he going to use?
Penny: Their mother is going to give him the car for the weekend.
Dad: The weekend? Are you going to stay the whole weekend?
Penny: No, we're not going to stay the whole weekend—just Saturday night. Min-hee and her brother are going to pick me up on Saturday afternoon.
Dad: OK. But when are you going to do your homework? Remember that we're going to your sister's soccer game on Friday night.
Penny: I know, Dad. I'm going to do it on Sunday.
Dad: What time are you going to be home on Sunday?
Penny: In the afternoon. We're going to leave New Hope in the morning.
Dad: And where are you going to stay?
Penny: With Min-hee's cousin. She lives in New Hope.
Dad: What's her name? Do I know her?
Penny: Yes, Dad, you met her at Min-hee's birthday party. Her name is Jin.
Dad: Oh, Jin. All right, I guess it's okay. But I want Jin's telephone number, please. And call me when you get there.
Penny: Of course. Thanks, Dad. You're great. Oh, and just one more thing....
Dad: I'm not going to buy you a new dress for the wedding.
Penny: Ah, Dad, come on....

Unit 17

A
1. X
2. ✓
3. ✓
4. X
5. X
6. ✓
7. ✓
8. ✓

B
1. b
2. b
3. a
4. b

C
1. F
2. T
3. F
4. T

D
1. Should I call
2. you shouldn't / you should not
3. You should take
4. Should she exercise
5. she should
6. her brothers should exercise

E
1. How often should I give the baby the medicine?
2. Who should patients tell about their allergies?
3. How many pills should an adult take?
4. What should Drew buy?

F
1. b
2. b
3. a

G
1. every 2–4 hours
2. Medicine B
3. 1 tablet
4. talk to a doctor or pharmacist
5. Medicine A

Mark: Great. Were your husband's brothers and sisters there, too?
Yoko: Yes, the whole family was there, including our nieces and nephews. It was spring vacation, so they were off all week.
Mark: Oh, that's right. And how were the beaches? Were they crowded?
Yoko: Yes, they were. Actually, there were people everywhere. One night we were at a restaurant, and the service was *so* slow! It was because there were so many people.
Mark: Yeah, Cancun is always crowded on school vacation weeks. How much were the airline tickets? Were they expensive?
Yoko: No, they weren't. They were only $220 from Atlanta.
Mark: Wow, that's cheap!
Yoko: Yeah. It was a wonderful vacation.

Unit 14

A
1. b 3. a 5. a 7. b
2. b 4. a 6. a 8. b

B
1. forgets
2. gets out of
3. happening
4. catch
5. take back
6. scream
7. are chasing
8. change jobs
9. loses
10. leave

C
1. invited
2. danced
3. didn't want / did not want
4. started
5. didn't have / did not have
6. drank
7. took
8. didn't go / did not go
9. said
10. ate

D
1. F 4. F 7. F 9. T
2. T 5. T 8. F 10. F
3. T 6. F

Audioscript for Exercise A:

Russ: Hey, Kerri! You'll never believe what happened yesterday on Cherry Street.
Kerri: Oh, Russ. Is this one of your strange but true stories?
Russ: Well, it *is* strange, but it really happened. I promise!
Kerri: OK, go ahead. I'm listening.
Russ: Well, a worker at the city zoo lost an ostrich!
Kerri: An ostrich? But ostriches are *really big* birds—more than two hundred pounds! How is it possible to lose one?
Russ: Well, the worker forgot to close the door to its cage, and it got out.
Kerri: Oh, please!
Russ: Really! Look. It's in the paper. Someone took a picture of it.
Kerri: Oh, my gosh!
Russ: I know! So, the ostrich walked out of the zoo. And you know there's a park across from the zoo?
Kerri: Yeah. . . .
Russ: Well, it went to the park. A lot of people screamed when they saw it. But there were some kids, and they weren't scared. The kids chased it. It ran into the street, but all the cars stopped.

Kerri: Wow! That's really strange. Where is the ostrich now? Is it back in the zoo?
Russ: Yes, the police caught him and took him back.

Unit 15

A
Cara: got a new house or apartment, got a new job, graduated
Sa'id: had a baby, became a citizen, got a new job

B
1. ten years ago
2. six months ago
3. four months ago
4. six years ago

C
1. g 3. f 5. h 7. c
2. b 4. a 6. d 8. e

D
1. Did you graduate (in 1995)?
2. Was your daughter in the military?
3. Did they go to the mall?

E
1. Why did Greg change jobs?
2. When did Lulu and Anthony have their first baby?
3. Where did you get married?
4. How old were they?

F
1. How long ago did he get his driver's license?
2. How long did Nancy and Brett stay at the party?
3. How long ago did your brother move to Houston?

G
1. a 4. c 7. b
2. c 5. b 8. a
3. c 6. b 9. b

Audioscript for Exercise A:

Cara: Hey, Sa'id! How are you? What's new?
Sa'id: Hi, Cara! Umm. . . . Where do I start? Well, first, Kate and I had a baby in September.
Cara: Oh that's wonderful! . . . What did you have—a girl or a boy?
Sa'id: A girl. Her name is Nicole.
Cara: Well, congratulations!
Sa'id: Thanks. But that's not all . . . I became a citizen last year.
Cara: That's great. Hey—how long ago did you come here?
Sa'id: I came to the United States ten years ago.
Cara: That's right. . . . And where are you living now? Did you keep your house?
Sa'id: Yes, we still live in the old neighborhood.
Cara: And are you still working at the hotel?
Sa'id: No, I left that job six months ago, and I got a new job at D & E. The money's great, and the job is really interesting.
Cara: Wow, that's a big change. But it sounds good.
Sa'id: It is. But that's enough about me. What's up with you?
Cara: Well, I have some news too. Henry and I got married four months ago.
Sa'id: Henry—your boyfriend from a few years ago?
Cara: That's right.

Center Stage 2

F

1. F   4. F   7. T
2. T   5. F   8. F
3. T   6. F   9. T

Audioscript for Exercise A:

Gus: Hey, Mia. You don't look very happy. What's wrong?
Mia: Oh, my birthday is on Wednesday, and it's my first birthday without my family and friends—they aren't here. I miss them.
Gus: Oh, that's hard. So . . . how do you usually celebrate your birthday?
Mia: Well, my friends send me cards, and all of my relatives call me. Then on the weekend I always have a party.
Gus: Who do you invite?
Mia: We always have so many guests! We invite my friends, my parents' friends, and my relatives.
Gus: Where do you usually have the party?
Mia: We have it at my parents' house. It's a pretty big house.
Gus: And who makes the food for all those people?
Mia: My grandmother and my aunts make everything. They're great cooks. Oh, and my mother always makes a birthday cake.
Gus: Do the people at the party give you gifts?
Mia: No, they usually don't. I get some flowers and chocolates, but I don't get a lot of gifts. Gifts are usually for children in our family.
Gus: And how do you want to celebrate this year?
Mia: I want to have a celebration with my friends. I want to eat out in a restaurant, I think. I want my friends to go and celebrate with me there.
Gus: Sounds good. Tell me the time and place, and I'll be there!

Unit 12

A

1. in the morning   4. Iris's husband   7. Sundays
2. Danielle   5. A day care worker   8. to make money
3. Iris's husband   6. on Sundays   9. boss

B

1. make an appointment   4. be off
2. make money   5. have experience
3. take care of

C

1. c   2. d   3. a   4. b

D

1. are you doing   6. like
2. am working / 'm working   7. to finish
3. to have   8. need
4. are you going   9. is ringing
5. eat   10. understand

E

1. languages   4. a job   7. learn
2. has some   5. cook   8. get a master's degree
3. Beijing   6. The Keystone

Audioscript for Exercise A:

Iris: Excuse me, Mr. Ho?
Mr. Ho: Yes? Oh, hi, Iris. Please, come in. So, what are you doing here? You don't usually work in the mornings, do you?
Iris: No, I'm working for Danielle this morning. She's taking her son to school. Today is his first day.
Mr. Ho: Oh, that's right. So, what's up?
Iris: Well, my husband has a new job. . . . He's a manager now.
Mr. Ho: Great. Congratulations!
Iris: Thanks. But there's one problem: he works on Saturdays now, too. Our children usually go to day care when we work, but our day care worker doesn't work on Saturdays.
Mr. Ho: So . . . are you asking me for Saturdays off?
Iris: Well, yes. But I want to change my schedule. If possible, I want to work on Sundays. My husband doesn't work then, so he can take care of the children.
Mr. Ho: Hmmm . . . I don't know right now. It's not very busy on Sundays.
Iris: Well, I want to work forty hours a week. We need the money.
Mr. Ho: OK. I need to look at the schedule. Ask me again tomorrow.
Iris: Sure. Thanks.

Unit 13

A

1. nice   3. near   5. crowded   7. cheap
2. great   4. warm   6. slow   8. wonderful

B

1. e   3. c   5. h   7. a
2. f   4. g   6. b   8. d

C

1. wasn't   2. weren't   3. was   4. were

D

1. Where were you   4. Were there a lot of people
2. How was the movie   5. Why were things on sale
3. Was there good food   6. Was their wedding at night

E

1. b   3. a   5. b   7. c
2. a   4. a   6. b   8. c

Audioscript for Exercise A:

Mark: So, Yoko, where were you last week?
Yoko: I was in Cancun for my father-in-law's 70th birthday.
Mark: Cancun? Cool. So, your husband has relatives there?
Yoko: Yeah, his whole family lives there, but we hardly ever have the time or the money to visit them. This was our second visit.
Mark: I love Cancun.
Yoko: Now I do, too! The people there were really nice.
Mark: How was the weather?
Yoko: It was great. And my father-in-law's apartment is near the beach—only about five minutes away. We were there every day from 11:00 to 6:00. The water was really warm.

Unit Test Answer Key and Audioscript   T-363

Audioscript for Exercise A:

Raul: Hey, Ceci, do you want to have lunch with me on Wednesday?
Ceci: I don't know. I don't usually eat out for lunch.
Raul: Really? I eat out almost every day.
Ceci: Well, I *like* to eat out in restaurants, but I don't have time to eat out or go home for lunch when I'm working. I eat at work.
Raul: How long is your lunch break?
Ceci: I have thirty minutes for lunch.
Raul: Only thirty minutes? What's your work schedule?
Ceci: Well, I start at 8:00. I have a fifteen-minute break in the morning, usually around 10:00. Then my lunch break is at 12:30. It's thirty minutes. I have one more break in the afternoon. That's usually around 3:00.
Raul: Wait a minute . . . you're from Colombia, right?
Ceci: Yes. Why?
Raul: Well, I heard that in Colombia most workers have a two-hour break for lunch. Is that true?
Ceci: It depends on the job, but in general it's true. A lot of families have lunch at home together.
Raul: Wow! So it's a big change for you to have only thirty minutes for lunch now. I think I like the Colombian way.
Ceci: Well, there *is* one problem. People in Colombia start work at 8:30, but because they have a break for lunch from 2:00 to 4:00, they work until about 7:00 or 8:00. Here I only work until 5:00. So, I like the American way!

Unit 10

A
1. Ted 3. Lisa 5. Ted
2. Lisa 4. Lisa 6. Lisa

B
1. a 2. a 3. b 4. a

C
1. T 3. F 5. T 7. T
2. T 4. F 6. F 8. F

D
1. I usually pay for things with credit cards.
2. Things are often on sale.
3. That store always has good prices.

E
1. Does Thierry have the receipt?
2. What do they sell?
3. Do you have cash?
4. What kind of DVD player do you want?

F
1. a 2. c 3. a

G
1. Yes 4. No 6. Yes
2. Yes 5. No 7. No
3. Yes

H
1. a 2. a 3. b

Audioscript for Exercise A:

Lisa: Ted, do you have any cash?
Ted: Yes, I do. Why?
Lisa: I want to buy some sneakers in that store.
Ted: OK. Use your credit card.
Lisa: They don't take credit cards there. They only take cash.
Ted: Do you need sneakers?
Lisa: Well, everyone is wearing them these days.
Ted: But *you* don't wear sneakers.
Lisa: That's because I don't have any good ones!
Ted: OK. How much do they cost?
Lisa: Well, the regular price is $100. But today they're on sale for 25 percent off.
Ted: They're $75?! Forget it! That's a lot of money!
Lisa: You always say that!
Ted: And you always want to spend a lot of money!

Audioscript for Exercise B:

Conversation 1:
Enid: Your total is $45.34.
Max: Here's $50.
Enid: OK. . . . And $4.66 is your change.

Conversation 2:
Barbie: Hi. Welcome to Barbie's Boutique. Everything in the store is 25 percent off today.
Peichi: Oh, great!

Conversation 3:
Fred: Do you buy things from catalogs?
Mona: No. I always shop in stores.

Conversation 4:
Al: I want to go in this store.
Hugo: OK. What do you want to buy?
Al: A bottle of water or soda.

Unit 11

A
1. h 3. a 5. b 7. g
2. e 4. d 6. c 8. f

B
1. a woman 4. a man or a woman
2. a man or a woman 5. a man
3. a woman

C
1. a 2. b 3. c 4. b

D
1. give gifts to children 3. gets a present for my mom
2. send relatives cards 4. makes me a cake

E
1. When do they celebrate 4. Who do people invite
2. Who says "Happy birthday" 5. Why do people give presents
3. Where do they have 6. Who gets flowers

T-362 Center Stage 2

E
1. a 3. c 5. c
2. c 4. b 6. a

F
1. d 2. b 3. a 4. c

G
1. a doctor 2. a boss 3. a parent 4. a husband

Audioscript for Exercise A:

Dad: Ella! Eric! Where are you?
Ella: We're outside, Dad.
Eric: We're playing soccer.
Dad: Well, finish your game.
Ella: Why? What's happening?
Dad: Aunt Betty and Uncle Don are coming for dinner.
Eric: Really?
Ella: Tonight?
Dad: Yes. Come inside. Take showers and put on nice clothes. Don't wear track suits and sneakers.
Eric: Aw, Dad!
Dad: And Mom is busy in the kitchen, so help her with the house. Clean your rooms.
Ella: OK.
Dad: And put your clothes in the closet. Don't put them under the bed.
Ella: Fine.
Dad: And don't eat any cookies or candy. Mom is making a big dinner.
Eric: But Dad . . . !
Dad: And don't complain.
Ella: OK.
Eric: All right.

Audioscript for Exercise B:

1. Please don't touch the food.
2. Talk to them.
3. Ask her for some tea.
4. Put the things on the bed.
5. Please take the food to the party.

Unit 8

A
1. F 3. T 5. T
2. T 4. T

B
1. a 2. a 3. b 4. a

C
1. b 3. a 5. a 7. a
2. a 4. a 6. b 8. b

D
1. those 4. have 7. this
2. yours 5. has 8. that
3. mine 6. hers 9. our

E
1. computer 4. $750 7. Nikel
2. Trac 5. Fishell 8. model
3. 2039481726 6. 8739283 9. $150

Audioscript for Exercise A:

Josh: Kim? Liz? Is that you?
Kim: Yeah. It's us.
Josh: Hi! Come in.
Kim: Thanks. Wow, Josh! Your apartment is great. . . .
Liz: Yeah. What's that on the wall?
Josh: It's a picture of my family.
Liz: Oh, sorry. Not the picture . . . that.
Josh: Oh, that's my television.
Kim: But it's flat. It looks like a picture.
Josh: Yeah, it's a flat screen TV. It's new.
Kim: Cool.
Liz: Yeah. Oh, and the picture of your family is nice, too.
Josh: Thanks. I have a digital camera. It's pretty good.
Kim: I'm looking for a new camera. Mine is really old.
Josh: Here's my camera. If you're looking for a new one, this model isn't too expensive. . . .
Kim: It's nice. . . . Oh, Josh, is this cell phone yours?
Josh: No, it's not mine.
Liz: Hey, that's mine. And those keys are mine, too.
Kim: These? Here. Take them. And are these your sunglasses?
Liz: Oops. Yes.

Audioscript for Exercise B:

1. That's a small camera.
2. Those keys are mine.
3. The DVDs are theirs.
4. Are these CDs yours?

Unit 9

A
1. R 3. C 5. C 7. R
2. C 4. C 6. R 8. C

B
1. b 4. b 7. a
2. b 5. a 8. b
3. a 6. a 9. b

C
1. go 6. don't watch / do not watch
2. comes 7. goes
3. doesn't start / does not start 8. watches
4. studies 9. starts
5. finishes 10. don't come / do not come

D
1. 11:00 6. make dinner
2. 6:00 7. go to work
3. eat breakfast 8. 11:30
4. take them to the bus stop 9. talk
5. do laundry

Unit Test Answer Key and Audioscript T-361

Audioscript for Exercise A:

(A. = Announcer)

A.: Welcome to Good Food Market.
Cal: Look at these peppers—$2.21 a pound! That's crazy! Vegetables here are so expensive!
Dana: Yeah. The food at Good Food Market is fresh, but it's expensive.
Cal: At Shop-A-Lot, the food is fresh, too, but it's cheap.
Dana: What's Shop-A-Lot?
Cal: It's a supermarket near my apartment building.
Dana: Oh. How much are peppers at Shop-A-Lot?
Cal: Not a lot—maybe 50 cents a pound.
Dana: That is cheap! Is everything there so cheap?
Cal: Not everything, but a lot of food is. Fruit is really cheap . . . and meat is too. . . . Hmm. . . . There isn't any lettuce here.
Dana: Yes, there is. There's some lettuce over there, next to the spinach.
Cal: Oh, great. Thanks. Hey, are there any potatoes?
Dana: Yes. They're right here. How many do you need?
Cal: I need a lot—there are ten in the recipe. . . . Wow, the potatoes are expensive here, too—$3.50 a pound!
Dana: $3.50 a pound? How many potatoes are there in a pound?
Cal: About two or three. These potatoes are big. Hmmm. Are there any small potatoes?
Dana: Oh, yeah. There are some over there. . . .

Audioscript for Exercise B:

Conversation 1:
A: Are there a lot of vegetables?
B: No. There are a few vegetables.

Conversation 2:
A: Is there any tea?
B: Yes. There's a box of tea in the kitchen.

Conversation 3:
A: Is there a lot of mayonnaise?
B: Yes, there is.

Conversation 4:
A: Are there any cookies?
B: Yes, there are a lot of cookies.

Unit 6

A
1. b
2. b
3. c
4. c
5. c

B
1. T
2. T
3. F
4. F
5. T

C
1. d
2. b
3. a
4. c

D
1. running
2. walking
3. watching a tennis match
4. swimming

E
1. are you
2. She's
3. He
4. are eating
5. 'm going for a walk
6. not going home
7. Is
8. are
9. Where
10. Who is

F
1. a
2. b
3. b
4. b

G
1. T
2. T
3. F
4. F

Audioscript for Exercise A:

Elena: Hello?
Mom: Hi, Elena. It's Mom!
Elena: Hi, Mom! How's your vacation with Aunt Karen?
Mom: It's nice. We're having fun. We're sitting by the pool and watching people right now. Is Dad there?
Elena: No, he isn't. He's with Uncle Dan.
Mom: With Uncle Dan? What are they doing?
Elena: They're playing tennis.
Mom: Really?
Elena: Yeah.
Mom: Well, what about your brothers? Is Joey there?
Elena: No, he isn't. He's out, too.
Mom: What's he doing?
Elena: He's at the park. He's playing soccer.
Mom: Then let me talk to Alan.
Elena: He's not here either. He's riding his bike.
Mom: Your father and your brothers are out, and you're home all alone?
Elena: No, I'm not alone. My friend Jessica is here. And Grandma is here with us.
Mom: Oh. What are you doing?
Elena: We're sitting outside and we're talking. Grandma is telling us stories.
Mom: Well, that's really nice.
Elena: I know. Listen, we're busy right now. Grandma is telling a really good story.
Mom: OK. Tell Dad to call me later.
Elena: OK. Bye, Mom.
Mom: Bye, Sweetheart.

Unit 7

A
1. X
2. ✓
3. ✓
4. ✓
5. X

B
1. b
2. a
3. b
4. a
5. b

C
1. Put
2. turn on
3. Finish
4. move
5. turn off
6. Take
7. Ask
8. touch

D
1. above
2. in front of
3. in
4. on

T-360 Center Stage 2

Joanne: No, I'm a nurse now at Mercy Hospital.
Terry: A nurse! Good for you!
Joanne: Yeah, it's great. Anyway, I have to get going—I'm late for work! I'll see you later—Oh, and say hi to Carolina for me!
Terry: I will. Take care!
Joanne: You, too.

Audioscript for Exercise B:

Conversation 1:
Polly: So, Janice, you work in a restaurant now? What do you do?
Janice: I'm a waitress. And it's a difficult job!

Conversation 2:
Trish: Pamela is an interpreter.
Bob: She's so hardworking!
Trish: Yes, she's a fast worker, too.

Conversation 3:
Obi: Denise has a new job.
Sonia: Really? Is she a dentist?
Obi: No, her husband is a dentist. She's a mechanic.

Conversation 4:
Raj: Pete, is your job easy?
Pete: No, but sometimes it's boring.
Raj: What do you do?
Pete: I'm an attorney.

Unit 4

A
1. are
2. are
3. aren't
4. are
5. aren't
6. are

B
1. a
2. b
3. a
4. b

C
1. T
2. F
3. T
4. T
5. F
6. F
7. T
8. F
9. F

D
1. Is there
2. there are
3. a lot of
4. Are there
5. a
6. there isn't
7. are some
8. There's
9. there is
10. It's

E
1. No, she's not.
2. No, he's not.
3. Yes, there are.
4. A lot of people are at the beach every day.
5. Yes, there is.
6. Beautiful things are in a lot of stores.
7. The restaurants are excellent.
8. No, there aren't.

Audioscript for Exercise A:

Ryan: Hi, Lynn! How are you? How's your new apartment?
Lynn: Oh, hey, Ryan. It's great, thanks!
Ryan: How's the neighborhood?
Lynn: Nice. There are some quiet cafés, and there are some excellent restaurants on the next street.
Ryan: It sounds perfect. Are there any good stores?
Lynn: Yes. There's a good store near my apartment building. It's expensive, but the things are beautiful. There are also some cheap stores in the neighborhood.
Ryan: Are there any outdoor markets near your apartment?
Lynn: No, there aren't, but there's a big supermarket.
Ryan: And is the beach close to you?
Lynn: There isn't a beach, but there are some beautiful parks.
Ryan: Wow. You're lucky! My apartment is nice, but there aren't any restaurants in my neighborhood, and there isn't a park!
Lynn: Well, there are some apartments for rent in my building.
Ryan: Really?
Lynn: Yeah. . . . Here's the office number. Call to get more details.
Ryan: Great.

Audioscript for Exercise B:

1. There are a lot of good-looking people.
2. There isn't a hotel near the airport.
3. There aren't any apartment buildings.
4. There's a good supermarket.

Unit 5

A
1. b
2. a
3. a
4. b
5. c
6. b

B
1. F
2. T
3. F
4. T

C

FRUIT	VEGETABLES	MEAT	DRINKS
oranges	carrots	beef	milk
bananas	onions	chicken	juice
apples	mushrooms		

D
1. Is
2. many
3. any
4. some
5. any
6. Are
7. much
8. a

E
1. a lot of
2. some
3. a few
4. a few
5. some

F
1. d
2. a
3. c
4. b

G
1. F
2. T
3. F
4. F
5. T

Unit Test Answer Key and Audioscript T-359

Unit Test Answer Key and Audioscript

Unit 1

A
1. b
2. b
3. a
4. b
5. a
6. b
7. b
8. a

B
1. young
2. heavy
3. beautiful
4. quiet
5. average height
6. funny

C
1. c
2. a
3. b

D
1. b
2. c
3. c
4. b
5. c
6. a

E
1. a
2. b
3. c
4. a

F
1. Y
2. N
3. N
4. Y
5. Y
6. Y
7. N
8. N

Audioscript for Exercise A:

Lee: Danielle isn't here. Where is she?
Mia: She's with Ahmed.
Lee: Ahmed? Is he Danielle's friend?
Mia: No, he's not. He's her boyfriend.
Lee: Really? Are he and Danielle neighbors?
Mia: No, they're not. They're teachers at the same school.
Lee: Interesting. . . . Is he good-looking?
Mia: Sure, he's OK. He's pretty tall. And he isn't thin, but he isn't heavy. He's average weight. He's twenty-five years old.
Lee: Twenty-five? He's young!
Mia: No, twenty-five isn't young.
Lee: Twenty-five? But Danielle is thirty-five!
Mia: So? Thirty-five isn't old, and twenty-five isn't young!

Unit 2

A
1. b
2. a
3. b
4. b
5. b
6. a
7. a
8. b

B
1. husband
2. son
3. sister
4. cousin
5. aunt
6. grandfather
7. father-in-law
8. brother-in-law

C
1. a
2. c
3. c
4. b
5. b
6. a
7. c
8. d
9. a
10. d

D
1. Roy
2. Parker
3. 400 Flower
4. 927-555-9021
5. teacher
6. Della
7. Emily
8. 12/02/03

Audioscript for Exercise A:

Kirk: Wow, Amy, this is a good picture. Where is this house? Is it in California?
Amy: No. It's in Florida.
Kirk: And who are the children?
Amy: The boy is my nephew, and the girl is my niece.
Kirk: Are they your sister's children?
Amy: Well, the boy is my sister's son. His name is Ben.
Kirk: He's cute. How old is he?
Amy: He's seven years old.
Kirk: And is the girl his sister?
Amy: No. She's his cousin—my brother's daughter.
Kirk: What's her name?
Amy: Terry.
Kirk: Is she seven years old, too?
Amy: No. She's five years old.
Kirk: Wow! She's tall!

Unit 3

A
1. T
2. C
3. C
4. T
5. J
6. J

B
1. a waitress
2. a fast worker
3. a mechanic
4. an attorney

C
1. d
2. b
3. e
4. a
5. c
6. h
7. g
8. f

D
1. the
2. a
3. the
4. a
5. a
6. a
7. an
8. Ø
9. Ø
10. Ø

E
1. b
2. b
3. b
4. a
5. a
6. a
7. a
8. b
9. a

Audioscript for Exercise A:

Joanne: Hey, Terry, what's up? How are you?
Terry: Oh hi, Joanne. I'm great. I have a new job.
Joanne: Really?
Terry: Yeah, I'm an engineer at Florida Science.
Joanne: Great! My friend Carolina is a worker there, too. She's an accountant.
Terry: Oh yeah . . . Carolina. She's smart.
Joanne: So, how is the job?
Terry: Well, it isn't an easy job, but it's interesting. I'm always busy.
Joanne: Are the people nice?
Terry: Yes. And my boss is patient. How about you? Are you still in school?

T-358 Center Stage 2

UNIT 20 TEST

Name: _____   Date: _____

H Read the letter. Then answer each question.

> Alisha Epstein   12 Fifth Ave., Apt. B
> Public Transportation Commissioner   Portland, OR 97204
> City of Portland   February 2, 2007
> 1800 Wilmington St.
> Portland, OR 97204
>
> Dear Ms. Epstein:
>
>   I am writing because I would like to report a problem on the Portland train line. I don't have a car, so I take the train every day. I take train number 88 to work every morning, and I take it home every evening. I have to be at work at 9:00 A.M., and I often take the train home after work at 8:00 or later. The number 88 train schedule says that on weekdays the trains run every eight minutes from 7:00 A.M. until 10:00 P.M. However, I often have to wait fifteen or twenty minutes for a train in the morning, and I have the same problem at night.
>
>   I would like your help. A few months ago, I called the transportation hotline to complain, but they didn't do anything. Could you please ask someone to contact me? Thank you for your attention.
>
> Sincerely,
>
> *Camilla Clark*
> Camilla Clark

1. Who is this letter from?   _____
2. Who is the Public Transportation Commissioner?   _____
3. What street does Camilla live on?   _____
4. Is this the first time Camilla is telling someone about the problem?   _____

I Read the letter again. Complete each sentence. Circle the letter of the correct answer.

1. Camilla _____ the train to work.
   a. takes   b. is going to start taking   c. doesn't take

2. Camilla has problems with the train _____.
   a. in the morning   b. at night   c. in the morning and at night

3. Camilla's problem is that the train _____.
   a. doesn't come after 10:00 P.M.   b. is often late   c. makes a lot of stops

4. Camilla would like _____.
   a. a schedule for train 88   b. to talk to Ms. Epstein   c. someone to contact her

UNIT 20 TEST

Name: _____ Date: _____

E Complete each sentence. Use *have to* or *has to*.

1. Workers at that company _____ wear uniforms.
2. This is our stop. We _____ get off the bus here.
3. She _____ go now because her train is leaving soon.

F Complete the sentences and questions. Put the words in the correct order.

1. **A:** _____ to drink?
   (you / something / would / like)
   B: Yes, please. I'll have soda.

2. **A:** _____ their seats.
   (passengers / like / change / to / would / these)
   B: OK. There are some seats in the back of the bus.

3. **A:** _____ next to the window.
   (sit / would / she / to / like)
   B: Sure. No problem.

4. **A:** _____ the movie?
   (your / to / would / like / son / watch)
   B: Maybe later. He's reading now.

G Complete each question. Use *Can I*, *Could I*, *Can you*, *Could you*, or *Would you*.

1. **A:** _____ show me your ticket, please?
   B: Sure. Here it is.

2. **A:** _____ give us directions to the train station?
   B: Sure. Turn left onto Bird Road and then go straight.

3. **A:** _____ use your car? I need to go to the supermarket.
   B: No problem. The keys are on the table.

UNIT 20 TEST

Name: _____ Date: _____

A 🔊 27 **Listen. Then complete each sentence. Circle the letter of the correct answer.**

1. Sara wants a _____ ticket.   a. round-trip   b. one-way
2. Sara wants to travel _____.   a. today   b. tomorrow
3. The _____ flight isn't sold out.   a. 8:45   b. 11:30
4. Sara has an appointment _____.   a. tonight   b. tomorrow
5. Sara will arrive in Boston at _____. a. 11:30   b. 1:00

B 🔊 28 **Listen. You will hear five sentences. Circle the letter of each sentence you hear.**

1. a. The passengers have to sit down now.   b. The passenger has to sit down now.
2. a. Excuse me. Could you help me, please?   b. Excuse me. Would you help me, please?
3. a. We have to get off at the next stop.   b. He has to get off at the next stop.
4. a. I'd like to have a window seat.   b. He'd like to have a window seat.
5. a. Could I help you with something?   b. Can I help you with something?

C Match the beginnings with the endings of the sentences. Write the correct letters.

_____ 1. A schedule   a. is a place where people get on and get off of trains.
_____ 2. A subway   b. shows the times that trains or buses leave and arrive.
_____ 3. A passenger   c. controls an airplane.
_____ 4. A flight attendant   d. is a train that goes under the ground.
_____ 5. A pilot   e. keeps a person in his or her seat on a train, plane, or car.
_____ 6. A train station   f. travels on a bus, train, or plane.
_____ 7. A seatbelt   g. serves food and drinks to people on a plane.

D Complete each sentence. Circle the correct answer.

1. Show your ticket before you **get on** / **get off** the plane.
2. She has a **one-way** / **round-trip** ticket. She's taking the train from here to Los Angeles, and tomorrow she's taking the train back again.
3. A lot of people take that train, so you should **reserve** / **get on** a ticket in advance.

UNIT 19 TEST

Name: _____ Date: _____

D Read Eva's New Year Resolutions. For each sentence, write *T* for *True* or *F* for *False*.

> ## My New Year Resolutions
>
> 1. I won't stay at my job at the office. I hate that job. I'll look for a new job. I'll get a job in a store at the mall. I will be hardworking, but I won't work every day. At the end of the year, I will ask my new boss for a raise, and she will give it to me. I won't take "no" for an answer.
> 2. I spend a lot of money at restaurants. So, I will cook dinner at home a lot more. I will shop at the supermarket and buy fresh food. I'll look at magazines, and I'll find new recipes. That way I won't spend a lot of money, and I'll eat better food.
> 3. Finally, I'll take care of my body. I'll go to bed early, and I'll sleep for eight hours. I'll eat breakfast in the morning. I'll drink eight glasses of water each day, and I won't drink a lot of coffee and soda. I'll exercise three or four times a week. I'll go for walks in the neighborhood, or I'll play tennis with a friend.

1. Eva works at the mall now. _____
2. Eva liked her job last year. _____
3. Eva wants to work this year. _____
4. Eva spent a lot of money at restaurants last year. _____
5. Eva often cooked dinner at home last year. _____
6. Eva will buy food at the supermarket this year. _____
7. Last year, Eva usually went to bed early. _____
8. Last year, Eva drank a lot of soda and coffee. _____
9. Eva will exercise a lot this year. _____

T-354   Unit 19 Test

UNIT 19 TEST

Name: _____ Date: _____

C Complete the conversation. Use *will* or *won't* and the words in parentheses. Put the words in the correct order.

Faith: You know, Dad, next month _____ 25. I want to make a change in my life. I want to
1. (I / be)

live in the city.

Dad: The city? Why?

Faith: There are always things happening there. It's interesting.

Dad: OK. Tell me more about your plan.

Faith: Well, first _____ for an apartment.
2. (I / look)

Dad: Apartments aren't cheap, you know. _____ alone?
3. (you / live)

Faith: No. _____ for a roommate. That way _____ very expensive.
4. (I / look)   5. (it / not / be)

Dad: That's a good idea. But _____ a roommate?
6. (where / you / find)

Faith: Well, my friend Jennifer wants to move to the city, too.

Dad: OK. So _____?
7. (how much / your rent / be)

Faith: Probably about $500 each.

Dad: Hmmm. You don't have a car. Does Jennifer have one?

Faith: No.

Dad: _____ a car?
8. (she / buy)

Faith: No, _____. There are buses in the city, Dad. _____ a car.
9. (she / not)   10. (we / not / need)

Dad: Well, what about coming home to visit? _____ if you want to come home?
11. (what / you / do)

Faith: Don't worry! There are buses from the city to your house every hour. _____ home
12. (I / come)

to see you a lot, and _____ into the city to visit me, too.
13. (you / go)

Unit 19 Test   T-353

UNIT 19   TEST

Name: _____   Date: _____

A 🎧 **26** Listen. Answer each question. Write *Yes* or *No*.

1. Will someone get in touch with Grace? _____
2. Will Grace have news for someone? _____
3. Is there love in Grace's future? _____
4. Does Grace have a boyfriend? _____
5. Will Grace get married? _____
6. Does the fortune teller give Grace some bad news? _____
7. Is Grace starting a new job? _____
8. Does the fortune teller tell Grace about work? _____
9. Is Grace happy with the fortune teller? _____

B Read each pair of sentences. Write *S* if they have similar meanings. Write *D* if they have different meanings.

_____ 1. Mario is going to get a raise.
         Mario is going to make more money.

_____ 2. She wants to get in touch with him.
         She wants to talk to him.

_____ 3. Hope wants to start a business.
         Hope wants to close her business.

_____ 4. Jeff is making plans.
         Jeff isn't thinking about the future.

_____ 5. They are succeeding with their business.
         Their business is good.

_____ 6. The guests are having a good time.
         The guests want to go home.

_____ 7. He doesn't want to get bad news.
         He doesn't want to hear something bad.

Unit 19 Test

D Read the Web page. For each sentence, write *T* for *True* or *F* for *False*.

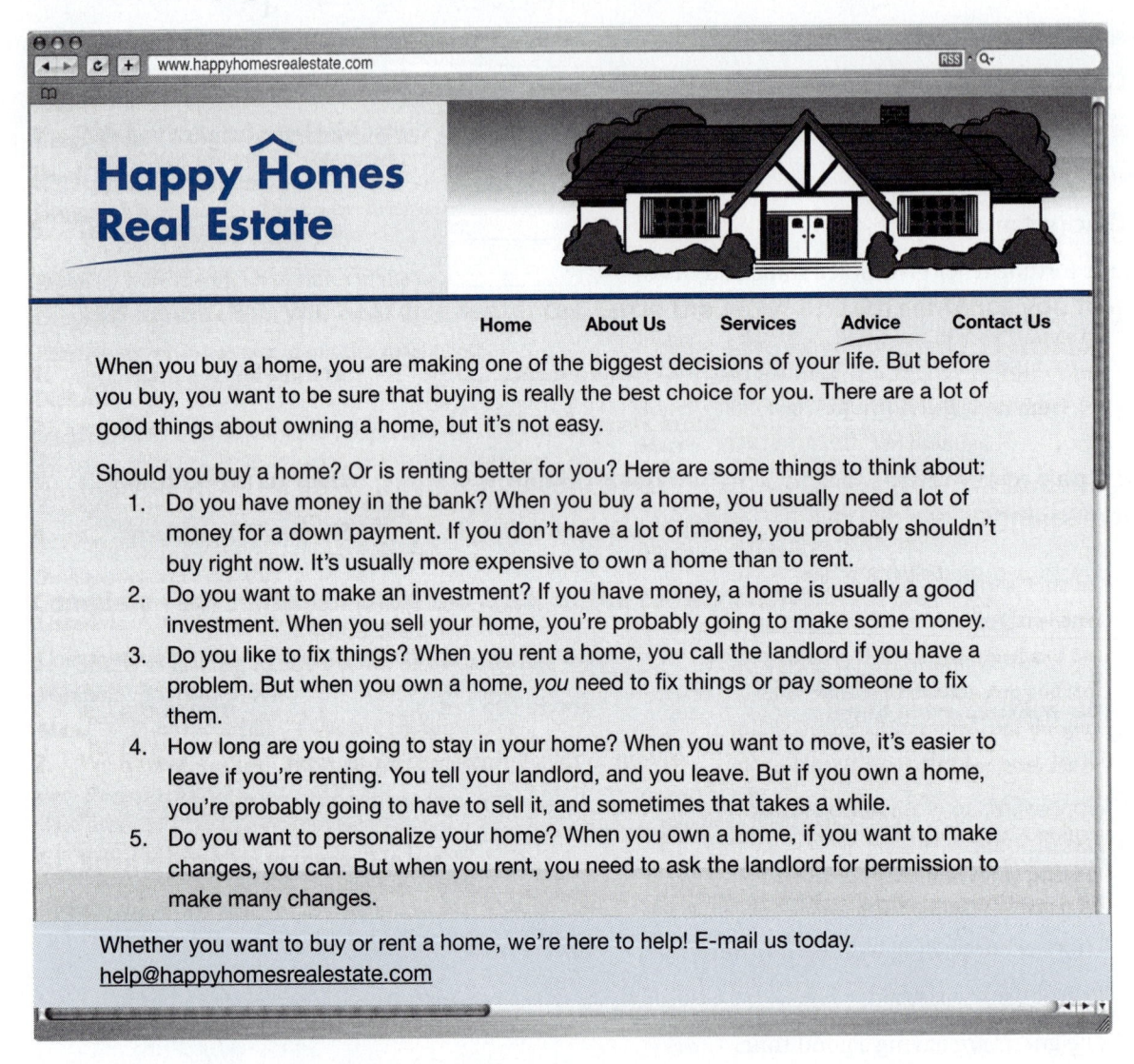

Happy Homes Real Estate

Home **About Us** **Services** **Advice** **Contact Us**

When you buy a home, you are making one of the biggest decisions of your life. But before you buy, you want to be sure that buying is really the best choice for you. There are a lot of good things about owning a home, but it's not easy.

Should you buy a home? Or is renting better for you? Here are some things to think about:

1. Do you have money in the bank? When you buy a home, you usually need a lot of money for a down payment. If you don't have a lot of money, you probably shouldn't buy right now. It's usually more expensive to own a home than to rent.
2. Do you want to make an investment? If you have money, a home is usually a good investment. When you sell your home, you're probably going to make some money.
3. Do you like to fix things? When you rent a home, you call the landlord if you have a problem. But when you own a home, *you* need to fix things or pay someone to fix them.
4. How long are you going to stay in your home? When you want to move, it's easier to leave if you're renting. You tell your landlord, and you leave. But if you own a home, you're probably going to have to sell it, and sometimes that takes a while.
5. Do you want to personalize your home? When you own a home, if you want to make changes, you can. But when you rent, you need to ask the landlord for permission to make many changes.

Whether you want to buy or rent a home, we're here to help! E-mail us today.
help@happyhomesrealestate.com

1. Buying a home is a big decision. _____
2. Buying a home is always better than renting a home. _____
3. You shouldn't buy a home if you have a lot of money. _____
4. When people sell their homes, they always make money. _____
5. It is usually easier to rent a home than to own a home. _____
6. It's easy to move when you rent a home. _____
7. When you own a home, you don't need to ask the landlord about changes. _____
8. Happy Homes Real Estate helps people buy and rent homes. _____

UNIT 18 TEST

Name: _____ Date: _____

C Look at the chart. Complete each sentence. Use the comparative or superlative forms of the adjectives in parentheses. Add *than* when necessary.

	Size	Year built	Rent	Distance to Bus Stop	Location
HOME A	8 rooms	1940	$1,200	1 mile	near the beach and a park
HOME B	12 rooms	2004	$1,800	5 miles	in the country
HOME C	6 rooms	1985	$1,000	¼ mile	on a city street, near stores

1. Home C has _____ rent of the three homes.
   (cheap)
2. Home B is _____ Home A.
   (modern)
3. Home C is _____ Home B.
   (noisy)
4. Home A is _____ Home B.
   (old)
5. Home C has _____ location of the three.
   (convenient)
6. The rent for Home B is _____ the rent for Home A.
   (high)
7. _____ home is Home C.
   (small)
8. _____ home is Home B.
   (expensive)
9. Nick likes to shop and go to restaurants a lot. For him, Home B is _____ Home C.
   (bad)
10. Sheila loves to go to the beach. For her, Home A is _____ house of the three.
    (good)

T-350 Unit 18 Test

UNIT 18   TEST

Name: _____   Date: _____

A Listen. Read each sentence. Then put a check (✓) under the correct apartment.

	Pompton Park Apartment	Orange Street Apartment	New Street Apartment
1. It is the biggest apartment.			
2. Rent is $750 a month.			
3. It is the farthest from downtown.			
4. It is the nicest apartment.			
5. It has the best location.			
6. Rent is $900 a month.			
7. It is in the newest building.			
8. Rent is $1,000 a month.			
9. The price is with utilities.			
10. It is next to the big movie theater.			

B Complete each sentence. Use the words in the box. (Be careful! There are three extra words.)

close to	far from	low rent	public transportation
convenient	high rent	modern	safe
dangerous	in the country	pretty	ugly

1. Their house is very _____. It's near their kids' school and their offices.
2. Her apartment is _____ a supermarket—the supermarket is just across the street.
3. The style of the house is very _____. Everything about it is new.
4. This neighborhood isn't safe. It's a _____ place to live.
5. Joe takes _____ to work every day. He doesn't need a car.
6. My parents think this building is ugly, but I don't agree. I think it's _____.
7. There aren't a lot of cars or people _____, so it's usually quiet there.
8. We don't make a lot of money, so we need an apartment with _____.
9. My husband's office is _____ our home. He drives an hour to get to work.

Unit 18 Test   T-349

D
1. F   4. T   7. F
2. F   5. F   8. T
3. T   6. T   9. T

Audioscript for Exercise A:

(F.T. = Fortune Teller)

Grace: So, tell me! What do you see? Will there be any changes in my life?
F.T.: Yes, there will. I see a tall, beautiful woman. She will get in touch with you soon.
Grace: Interesting. Why will she get in touch with me?
F.T.: She'll have some news for you.
Grace: News for me? What kind of news will it be? Will it be good or bad?
F.T.: It will be good. . . . I also see love.
Grace: Oh, good! I have a boyfriend. . . . Will we get married?
F.T.: Hmmmm. . . .
Grace: What's the matter?
F.T.: Well, you won't get married. You'll find a new boyfriend.
Grace: What?! That's terrible! When is it going to happen? Why will I find a new boyfriend?
F.T.: I'm not sure, but there will be a lot of problems.
Grace: Oh no! Well, I need some good news now. I'm starting a new job soon. Can you see anything about that? Will I succeed?
F.T.: Let me see. . . . Uh oh. . . .
Grace: What? What do you see?
F.T.: I'm sorry, but it looks like there will be some problems at work. . . . Wait a minute! Where are you going?
Grace: I'm going to find a different fortune teller—one who can see some *good* news!

Unit 20

A
1. b   3. b   5. b
2. a   4. b

B
1. a   3. a   5. a
2. b   4. b

C
1. b   4. g   6. a
2. d   5. c   7. e
3. f

D
1. get on   2. round-trip   3. reserve

E
1. have to   2. have to   3. has to

F
1. Would you like something
2. These passengers would like to change
3. She would like to sit
4. Would your son like to watch

G
Answers may vary:
1. Can you / Could you / Would you
2. Can you / Could you / Would you
3. Can I / Could I

H
1. Camilla Clark   2. Alisha Epstein   3. Fifth Ave.   4. No

I
1. a   2. c   3. b   4. c

Audioscript for Exercise A:

(T.A. = Ticket Agent; A.P. = another passenger)

T.A.: Can I help you, Ma'am?
Sara: Yes, please. I need a ticket to Boston.
T.A.: Would you like a round-trip or one-way ticket?
Sara: One-way, please.
T.A.: For when?
Sara: Excuse me?
T.A.: When would you like to travel?
Sara: Today. On the next plane, the 8:45.
T.A.: Sorry, but the 8:45 is sold out.
Sara: What do you mean?
T.A.: There aren't any more tickets for the 8:45 flight. You didn't reserve your ticket in advance.
Sara: But I have to get to Boston tonight! I have an appointment early tomorrow morning. Could you please look again?
T.A.: I'm sorry, Ma'am. There are no seats on the 8:45. But there is a flight at 11:30, and there are still seats available. It gets into Boston at 1:00 in the morning.
Sara: It leaves at 11:30? That's five hours from now. What am I going to do here in the airport for five hours?
A.P.: Lady, can you hurry up? I'm going to miss my plane!
T.A.: Ma'am, do you want a ticket for the 11:30 or not?
Sara: All right. Yes, please.
T.A.: That'll be $152.

Audioscript for Exercise B:

1. The passengers have to sit down now.
2. Excuse me. Would you help me, please?
3. We have to get off at the next stop.
4. He'd like to have a window seat.
5. Could I help you with something?

Unit Test Answer Key and Audioscript   T-367

Multilevel FAQs

Do I need to design additional materials or develop my own lessons?

No. *Center Stage* is designed to maximize your efficiency inside and outside the classroom. Any additional materials needed to maximize multilevel classroom instruction are included in the *Center Stage* components, such as the grammar worksheets found on the Teacher's Resource Disk.

Can I use *Center Stage 2* to teach a multilevel class?

Yes. Each unit of the Teacher's Edition includes multilevel instruction strategies for many of the Student Book activities. These strategies will help you administer the activities to students based on their proficiency level, whether they be pre-level, at-level, or above-level. This way, all students can do something that is meaningful and level-appropriate, while meeting the goal(s) and objective(s) of the lesson.

Is it true that each lesson will meet the needs of the different levels of students in my class?

Yes. The only difference is the task expectations for each level. The multilevel strategies contain tasks that will comfortably fit the abilities of students at any given level. Pre-level students get the extra support and reinforcement they need, and above-level students are challenged to go a bit beyond the original task.

Will my at-level students get lost in the shuffle?

No. While the strategies target mostly pre-level and above-level students, they also offer additional instructions for at-level students. At-level students are often encouraged to join either the pre-level groups as assistants or the above-level groups as partners. Both experiences provide valuable learning opportunities for the at-level students. When they work with the pre-level students, they enhance their own learning by assisting others. While working with above-level students, they are challenged to excel, which will increase their motivation and persistence.

Won't multilevel strategies introduce confusion and disorder into the classroom?

On the contrary, the multilevel strategies are designed to enhance the productivity of your classroom. The strategies target different abilities, which will help you reach more of your students on a daily basis. Furthermore, students learn some transferable skills in the process, such as working on a team and problem-solving strategies.

Will students feel left out if I spend too much time with one group?

No, because we have incorporated a lot of variety with the multilevel strategies so that your time will be balanced among all your students. We should emphasize that the level designations into pre-level, at-level, and above-level do not strictly apply to particular student at all times. In other words, the student who is pre-level for one activity may actually be above-level for another. Therefore, groups are not static; they are always evolving as current students improve their abilities and new students enter your class. In addition, to avoid feelings of resentment among students, you can offer variations of the same task to all your students and have them choose which one they want to do. Students will welcome tasks that are appropriate for their abilities and feel a sense of validation and accomplishment once the tasks are completed.

Will I be able to manage the different groups without feeling overwhelmed?

The strategies are designed so that students can often work independently, with a partner or in a small group. This way, students become responsible for themselves and to one another. In many cases, your role will be to facilitate the different groups, monitor their progress, and be available if needed while students complete their tasks.